JEAN-PHILIPPE RAMEAU

JEAN-PHILIPPE RAMEAU
from Dagoty's *Galerie française* (1770)

Jean-Philippe RAMEAU

His Life and Work

BY

Cuthbert Girdlestone

*With frontispiece
and 5 pages of half-tone
illustrations*

DOVER PUBLICATIONS, INC.
NEW YORK

This Dover edition, first published in 1969, is a newly
revised and corrected edition of the work originally published in 1957 by Cassell and Company Ltd. This
Dover edition is published by special arrangement with the
original publisher.

Standard Book Number: 486-21416-8
Library of Congress Catalog Card Number: 74-78058

Manufactured in the United States of America
Dover Publications, Inc.
180 Varick Street
New York, N.Y. 10014

Preface to the Dover Edition

SEVERAL substantial changes and additions have been made in this edition. The corrected dating by Theodore Besterman of a letter of Voltaire has altered our knowledge of this writer's relations with Rameau concerning *Samson* and has necessitated the rewriting of part of Chapter 1 and the addition of several pages to Chapter 5. The passage on *La Princesse de Navarre* at the beginning of Chapter 12 is new. The revival of *Les Paladins* at Lyons in 1967 has led me to speak at greater length and with more appreciation of this work in Chapter 12.

Some new information on Rameau's correspondent Ducharger has been added in Chapter 13, which also now includes an account of the composer's attempts to get himself accepted in the world of mathematicians and a summary of his intercourse with Padre Martini. The latter discussions draw heavily on Erwin Jacobi's researches in this field. I gratefully acknowledge the frankness with which Dr. Jacobi has always kept me informed of his discoveries, which are still proceeding.

In addition to these lengthier revisions, a number of minor mistakes and omissions throughout the book have been made good, and the bibliography has been considerably augmented.

Performances of Rameau's stage works have become less uncommon since 1958. Among those given in Britain, France, the Netherlands, Belgium, Germany and Switzerland, I would mention those of *Platée* and *Les Paladins*, with which is associated the name of the distinguished Swiss musicologist Renée Viollier, thanks to whose scholarly editorship they have taken place. Mlle Viollier is preparing a performing version of the 1744 *Dardanus* to be given at Lyons in 1969.

Since 1958 Erwin Jacobi has given us the first reliable edition of Rameau's chamber music and is responsible for the complete edition of his writings which is appearing under the auspices of the American Institute of Musicology.

I have also derived much pleasure and benefit from my work with Dr. Philip Gossett, whose expert English translation of Rameau's *Traité de l'harmonie* is being published by Dover Publications, Inc.

In the text, figures within parentheses refer to works listed in the bibliography.

CUTHBERT GIRDLESTONE

September 1968

Preface to the First Edition

MY purpose in writing this book has been to draw the attention of music-lovers to the work and person of Rameau, so that they may acquaint themselves with that work, play it to themselves, if possible have it performed, enjoy it and lead others to enjoy it. His music enfolds a great wealth of beauty of the highest order which is almost unknown and certainly unexploited. The many quotations which I have given will, I trust, whet the reader's curiosity and send him to at least the vocal scores of what has been published in that form. For this is not an antiquarian study of some mediæval poly-phonist, but a signal to call people to a composer who needs only to be played to become alive and who, although he shows his full stature only with orchestra, singers and stage, comes as readily alive on a keyboard, even without a voice, as Bach or Handel or Gluck, the majority of whose choral and dramatic works are most familiar in that medium.

Rameau's life has been, piecemeal, the subject of several studies, all of them earlier than 1918. To the articles by Michel Brenet and Lionel de la Laurencie, behind which stand the earlier researches of Henri Quittard, and to the masterly introductions by Charles Mal-herbe in Volumes I to XVI of the *Œuvres complètes*, this book is greatly indebted. His life and music, as a whole, have been surveyed in two small monographs, both published in 1908, by Louis Laloy and La Laurencie. More recently Jacques Gardien has produced an even slimmer book on the same subject. It is time that something on a larger scale was attempted.

In 1930 Paul-Marie Masson published his great volume on Rameau's operas. This basic study of the greater part of Rameau's output is a treasure to the musicologist and the well-informed Rameau enthusiast, but its plan and almost total lack of examples make it difficult for the music-lover who is neither. Yet its conclusion makes up the finest essay on Rameau's art and musical personality, judged as a whole, that has been written, and deserves separate publication. To anyone who wishes to live intelligently with Rameau's music, Masson must be a constant companion. His work is like gold bars lying in the vaults of the Bank of England; mine must be considered as a little of the small change in which they are eventually coined.

In addition to these, among the works included in Section C of my bibliography I should like to single out the following:

(137), by K. Dale, is an excellent introduction to the study of Rameau's harpsichord music.

(170), by P. Lalo, is an illuminating account of the "discovery" of Rameau, some fifty years ago, by a musician brought up in a tradition which took no account of him.

(176), by P. Lasserre, contains pages on his art with an insight not equalled elsewhere outside the work of Masson.

Finally, I wish to inscribe grateful tributes to the librarians of the libraries where I have studied Rameau's scores or whence I have been allowed to borrow them; to those friends with whom I have discussed him, especially Norman Suckling, whom I have plagued so often and with so much profit to myself; to the patient listeners to whom, "dans la plus stricte intimité", I have "interpreted" him: to Claire Demartinécourt, his *arrière-petite-nièce à la mode de* . . . *Bourgogne*, from whom I have learnt of his ancestors; and above all to my wife, whose inspired practising of his keyboard pieces has embroidered and lightened the *bourdon* of my typewriter and in whose company I have explored many a nook and cranny of his enchanted world.

C. M. G.

Contents

Illustrations

1. *Life: The First Fifty Years*

WHEN we study the lives of the older composers, we find again and again that they sprang from parents who were themselves musicians. Jean-Philippe Rameau is no exception to this apparent rule. At the time of his birth, his father, Jean Rameau, was organist at two churches in Dijon. This city, once the seat of the Dukes of Burgundy, had been since 1477 the capital of the Gouvernement of that province, the meeting-place of its Estates and its Parlement. In 1731 it was to become a bishopric. It boasted a college, founded in 1584 and belonging to the Jesuits.

For two generations Rameaus had been churchwardens of the parish of St. Médard, a post held by Jean's father Antoine and his brother Andoche. Jean is said[1] to have been introduced to the keyboard by a canon organist of the Sainte-Chapelle, the most venerable church in the city. Originally the ducal chapel, founded in the twelfth century and rebuilt in the fifteenth, it enjoyed the honour of being a *peculiar* and dependent only on the Pope. The Order of the Golden Fleece had its seat there; High Mass was sung in it every day, and it possessed a choir of precentors and boys. Stripped of the treasures with which the Valois dukes had enriched it, the Sainte-Chapelle survived the Revolution only to be pulled down in 1821 and replaced by a theatre.

At twenty-four, Jean Rameau became organist of the collegiate church of St. Étienne, the future cathedral.[2] He held this post for twenty-seven years, combining it for a time with one at the abbey of St. Bénigne (the present cathedral), and leaving it in 1689 to occupy the organ-loft at Notre-Dame the next year. His alleged tenure of the organ at St. Michel is more than doubtful. For forty-two years he gave his services in one church or another of his native town. Rameaus were numerous in Dijon; we hear of them living in various districts, occupied with wool-shearing, clothing and employment in church or government administration. Jean seems to have been the first musician in the family.

He had married a wife from Gemeaux, a village some thirteen miles to the north-east. Her name was Claudine Demartinécourt;

---

[1] (85). [2] Now the Chamber of Commerce.

she was the daughter of a notary and belonged to the lesser nobility. Her family house, with its rounded angle, still stands at a street corner of the village, with a little eighteenth-century moulded wooden door. The name was spelt indifferently in one or two words. There exist two genealogical tables of her family—one of 1754, the other of 1630; it claimed to "go back to the Crusades". Actually, the first Demartinécourt in history was a certain Claude who accompanied John the Fearless, then Count of Nevers, in the luckless expedition which went to help King Sigismund of Hungary against the Turks and was almost wiped out at Nicopolis in 1396. On his return he was made bailiff of Aumont by Philip the Bold, and in 1444 was knighted by Philip the Good. His son Antoine fought beside Charles the Rash at Morat in 1476.

Claudine bore her husband eleven children in twenty years. The first four were daughters, the fifth a son, the sixth another daughter. Jean-Philippe was the seventh. After him came four more sons, the last but one being Claude, the organist. Maret speaks of Demoiselle Catherine Rameau,

> his daughter, who died in 1762, a good harpsichord player; for a long while she had taught music in Dijon but for several years before her death her infirmities had made her unable to work and her brother . . . made her an allowance which he always paid punctually.

Who was this Catherine? None of Jean's daughters bears this name. If Maret's information is correct—and there seems to be no reason to doubt it—Catherine may have been an unofficial name which had replaced her baptismal one in ordinary use.

Jean-Philippe was christened on September 25, 1683, at four o'clock in the afternoon, in the church of St. Étienne where the parishioners of St. Médard used an aisle while their own church was being rebuilt.[1] His parents' house still stands in the Rue Vaillant, Nos. 5 and 7; it was then called Cour St. Vincent, Rue St. Michel. He was two years older than Bach, Handel and Domenico Scarlatti, and one year older than Watteau, all of whom he was to outlive.

No infant-prodigy stories are laid to his account; the utmost claimed for him is that he knew his notes before he could read. It is his brother Claude, not he, who is alleged, like Daquin, to have given organ recitals when he was ten. For his schooling, Jean-Philippe was sent to the Jesuit Collège des Godrans, to-day the city library. A schoolfellow of his, the Carmelite Père Gauthier, told Dr. Maret that, though he was unusually quick, he spent his time in form singing or writing music. His performance in school was, in fact, so deplorable that the fathers asked Jean Rameau to take him away. Thus were dashed his parents' hopes of seeing him enter the magistracy.

---

[1] The plans were later changed, and it was pulled down in 1705.

Maret says that, his many occupations and journeyings having prevented him from "chastening his language", his use of French was not of the purest, and that a woman whom he loved having criticized him, he at once set about studying his tongue "par principes" and succeeded in a short while in speaking and writing it grammatically. Another version of this story, not told by Maret, is that he fell in love at seventeen with a young widow, who laughed at the spelling mistakes in his letters to her. But he was always a prolix and unclear writer, surprisingly so, in this eighteenth century when French prose reached its perfection and every letter writer handled his language with limpid elegance.

In later life he was not talkative and seldom spoke of himself. Chabanon, inditing his eulogy a few months after his death, says that the first half of his life is absolutely unknown, and that he never imparted any detail of it to his friends or even to his wife. When, in the year after his death, Dr. Maret, secretary to the Academy of Dijon, collected material for an *Éloge*, he had great difficulty in filling the gaps in the first forty years. Indeed, we know to-day more of Jean-Philippe's existence between 1683 and 1723 than did any of his contemporaries.

By the age of eighteen he had made up his mind that he wanted to be a musician. His father sent him to Italy, the land which still enjoyed pre-eminence in music. He obeyed, but got no farther than Milan. To what he did there and what he heard we have no clue. A few months later he was back in France. In his old age he owned to Chabanon that he regretted not having stayed longer in the country "where he might have perfected his taste". For the next twenty years his presence can be traced in various parts of France, but we cannot form a connected picture of his life. We do not even know whether he returned home on recrossing the Alps. He is said to have joined "as first fiddle" a troupe of travelling Milanese artists. At some stage he was in Montpellier, where a certain Lacroix taught him the "octave rule" for realizing figured bass.[1] According to Maret, he never had a teacher of composition, though it seems unlikely that he did not receive some tuition from his father.

In January 1702, at nineteen, he was engaged as temporary organist at Avignon cathedral pending the arrival of the appointee, Gilles. His contemporary and future rival, Jean-Joseph Mouret, was still living in his native city, but we do not know whether the two met. In May of the same year he is found in Clermont, where he signs a six-year agreement to serve the cathedral chapter as organist.

All we know of this first stay in the capital of Auvergne is that the full term of the contract was not reached, since he was in Paris by 1706

---

[1] See Chapter 13, p. 485.

at the latest, and that he must have left the town in good odour with the chapter since he was reappointed some years later. The earliest evidence of his presence in Paris is on the front page of his first book of harpsichord pieces, which gives his address and calls him organist to the Jesuit Fathers in the Rue St. Jacques and to the Fathers of Mercy, or Mercedarians; the latter's church was in the Rue du Chaume.[1]

The only frequentation of which we can be reasonably sure is that of Louis Marchand, the most distinguished French organist of his day, who then held the post at the Cordeliers', or Franciscans', on the left bank. According to his obituary notice in the *Mercure de France*, he lived opposite the priory in order to hear the more easily the great man perform; "we know this from his own lips". He derived much benefit from this intercourse, according to the writer, but Maret says that he was disappointed to find that Marchand was incorrect in the fugues which he played. He also says that the organist became jealous of his young visitor once he had seen some of Rameau's organ compositions, and refused to have anything more to do with him. Of all these statements, I feel inclined to retain only the facts given by Rameau himself about his abode and interest in Marchand's playing. The title-page of Marchand's harpsichord pieces, dated 1703, calls him organist to the Jesuits of the Rue St. Jacques as well as to St. Benoît and the Cordeliers. I suspect that Rameau's succession to the organ of the first of these churches was due to Marchand's friendship.

In September 1706 he competed for the organ of La Madeleine en Cité and obtained it, but never took up the post, probably because he would have had to give up his two other organs. The issue for July 1708 of Ballard's *Airs sérieux et à boire* includes his harpsichord pieces in a list of publications and calls him organist of the Jesuits and the Mercedarians, so that he may still have been in Paris at that time.

However, the next date in his life of which we can be sure is March 27, 1709, when he signs an agreement with the council of Notre-Dame at Dijon. He was succeeding his father, who had been there since 1690. As at Clermont, the agreement was for six years. The post was shared with one Lorin who was to play on ordinary occasions while Rameau's services were required only on "vigils and holy days and at functions". Once again he did not honour his agreement to the end, and four years later he was succeeded by the same Lorin. This inability to stay long in one place is a nomadic trait found also in his brother Claude and still more in Claude's two sons.

By July 2, 1713, Jean-Philippe was no longer at Dijon. This time there is no hiatus in our knowledge of his movements, thanks to Léon Vallas, whose plotting of his stay in Lyons is the most important single contribution made to his biography since the eighteenth century. Before Vallas's researches it was apparent, from an allusion in an

----

[1] See Appendix A.

article in the *Mercure*,[1] that he had been in that city, but neither date nor length of stay was known.

In July 1713 the city of Lyons was preparing to celebrate the Peace of Utrecht. The festivities included music, and this was placed in the charge of one Rameau, "maître organiste", who turns out to be our Jean-Philippe. Rameau's plans were not carried out, for the city fathers decided to replace the concert by a distribution of alms, an expression of social sense which strikes us, perhaps unjustly, as exceptional at this period. In 1714 he is found employed by the Jacobins, or Dominicans, whose organ had just been restored; presumably he was organist there already in July of the previous year. Receipts signed by him exist; the last is dated December 13, 1714. This was a few days after his father had died, an event which caused a hasty visit to Dijon. He stayed on for his brother Claude's wedding in January, and was back in Lyons before March 17, when he signed another receipt for a payment; now he is styled merely "maître de musique", and he must have resigned from the Jacobins on his father's death. His brother Claude had accompanied him to Lyons, and an agreement between them, settling their father's affairs on their behalf and on that of their brothers and sisters, was signed there on March 24.

In April 1715 he is back in Clermont where he again signs a contract as cathedral organist, this time for twenty-nine years.[2] His stipend of fifty livres a month is twice the amount of that stipulated by his earlier contract and his work includes teaching a chorister "or some other person" to play the organ, and keeping the instrument in order. The bishop at the time was Massillon.

These eight years in Clermont are the darkest in the mystery of his life between twenty and forty. It seems that his motets and cantatas were composed there or in Lyons and it was certainly in Auvergne that he carried on the studies which bore fruit in his first book, *Traité de l'harmonie*, published by Ballard in 1722, on the title-page of which he is described as "organiste de la cathédrale de Clermont". According to a statement made many years later,[3] he had pursued these studies from earliest youth. The following story proves that already in Lyons his mind was working on the fundamental bass.

> In the pit of the Lyons opera house [a man] began to sing audibly and fairly loud the fundamental bass of an air whose words had struck him . . . I learnt that he was a workman whose occupation was hard and rough; his condition and work had long forbidden him opportunities of hearing music and he had been frequenting the opera only since fortune had smiled on him.[4]

---

[1] (15), 91.
[2] See L. Welter, *Quelques précisions sur le second séjour de Rameau à Clermont en qualité d'organiste*: in *Bulletin historique et scientifique de l'Auvergne*, LXXI (1951), 62–64.   [3] (12), 110.   [4] (15), 91.

Hitherto the records of the city and of the Puy de Dôme have revealed nothing about him, and we know no more about his stay there than what Maret tells us. There exist, however, some pupil's harmony exercises corrected by him, dating from 1717.[1] When Maret was preparing his eulogy he consulted a M. de Féligonde, secretary to the Academy of Clermont, and from him he learnt the following anecdote which he inserted in his notes. As it is the only story of any substance about the early Rameau, I give it in full in Maret's words.

Rameau had signed an agreement as organist with the cathedral chapter of Clermont in Auvergne, but he was not long in finding life narrow in this city. The consciousness of his ability made him want to return to Paris. His intention to have his *Traité de l'Harmonie* printed was the motive he thought he could allege to induce the canons to cancel his contract. But whereas the noble ambition to appear on a wider stage incited Rameau to demand his freedom the excellence of his talents made the chapter insensitive to his requests; its resistance compelled him to have recourse to an extraordinary device, blameworthy indeed, but which had the effect he desired.

On the Saturday in the octave of Corpus Christi, at the morning service, having ascended to the loft, he merely put his hand to the keyboard for the first and second couplets, then withdrew, banging the doors; it was thought that the organ-blower was absent and no surprise was felt. But at the evening service it was no longer possible to be deceived and it was clear that he had resolved to show his displeasure through the displeasure he was about to cause in others.

He pulled out all the most unpleasing stops and added to this all possible discords. In vain was he given the sign to stop playing; a choirboy had to be sent up to him; as soon as he appeared Rameau left the keyboard and went out of church. He had put so much art into the mixtures of his stops and the assemblage of the most rending discords that connoisseurs confessed that only Rameau could play so unpleasingly.

The chapter had him reproved, but his answer was that he would never play otherwise as long as his freedom was refused him. It was realized that he could not be turned from his resolve; the chapter gave in; the agreement was cancelled, and on the next few days he showed his satisfaction and gratitude by giving admirable pieces on the organ. He surpassed himself on the Thursday, octave of Corpus Christi, after the return of the procession; this was the day he was playing for the last time. He put so much sweetness into his execution, so much delicacy, brilliance, force and harmony, that he aroused in the souls of the congregation all the sentiments he wished, thereby sharpening the regret with which all felt the loss they were about to sustain.

M. de Féligonde added the vague statement: "He never failed to render service to musicians who sought his protection and he readily served the chapter of our cathedral by the choice of the persons he needed to have under him."[2]

[1] See (229A), 9.   [2] (85), notes 31 and 47.

Maret's account makes it clear that this escapade must have taken place at the end of his second stay. Gardien says it had happened earlier, but it is unlikely that the chapter, once bitten, would appoint him a second time. The truth of the story has also been doubted. It is suspicious that a tale, very like this one, is told of his brother Claude and is substantiated by documents. This time it is a parish church which is the scene of the misbehaviour, Notre-Dame in Dijon, and the body offended is the merchant guild of St. Maurus. This guild had engaged Claude, as parish organist, to play for it on its saint's day, January 15, 1736. He was not pleased with the payment he received and alleged breach of contract. A lawsuit was begun and lasted many months. In spite of this, the merchants asked him to play again the next year, and he agreed. He now took his revenge. At vespers he was silent for much of the time when he should have been playing, and when he did play it was with the worst discords he could concoct. In this case, too, although the parish was not directly involved, a change of venue ensued, and in May he transferred to the cathedral of St. Étienne.[1]

It has been suggested that this story has been fathered on to his elder brother by a natural confusion between them. There is no reason to suppose this. M. de Féligonde seems to suggest that the memory of the event had become traditional in Clermont; it is more likely that Claude deliberately copied his brother when he had decided to be offensive to his defaulting patrons.

Jean-Philippe arrived in Paris in the course of 1722 or early in 1723, in his fortieth year. A certain fame was not long in coming to him. The *Traité de l'Harmonie*, which he had written in Auvergne, and the *Nouveau Système de musique théorique*, which completed it in 1726, earned him the reputation of a learned theoretician before he was recognized as a great dramatic composer. From 1723 on his life is progressively better known. Yet of his first two years in Paris we can say but little. We do not know where he lived. The *Pièces de Clavecin*, published in 1724, bear no address. Of his occupations all we know is that he collaborated with his fellow-townsman Piron, who had come to Paris three years earlier, in providing music for the sketches which Piron wrote for the Fair theatres. The first date we possess of his second stay in the capital is February 8, 1723, when *L'Endriague* was given with a "morceau mis en haute musique" for the benefit of a young singer whom it was desired to help on, a Mlle Petitpas. "Rameau, then very little known, composed for my sake *(pour l'amour de moi)* the music of this piece."[2]

---

[1] (123).

[2] Piron, in (119). The same Piron was later to protest when Maret called Rameau his (Piron's) friend; see Chapter 13, p. 514.

In 1725 there was a display of two Louisiana Indians at one of the Fair theatres, and this was the inspiration of the well-known *Sauvages*. The next year he was again collaborating with Piron in *L'Enrôlement d'Arlequin* and *La Robe de Dissension*, and the partnership did not cease once he had mounted the stage of the Opéra, since in 1734 he wrote music for *Les Courses de Tempé* and in 1744 for *Les Jardins de l'Hymen ou la Rose*, both by Piron. It was at the Fairs that he met Fuzelier, the future librettist of *Les Indes galantes*. Though the precise effect of this apprenticeship cannot be determined, since most of this music is lost or, if re-used, cannot be identified, it must have been considerable. All that we possess is the vocal line of the airs in the *divertissement* that concludes *Les Courses de Tempé*.

On February 25, 1726, at the age of forty-two, he married a girl of nineteen, Marie-Louise Mangot; at this time he was living in the parish of St. Eustache, in that heart of Paris where, with many removals within minute distances, he was to spend the rest of his life.

The Mangots were a family of Lyonnais musicians. The father, Jacques, had come to Paris some time before 1707, the date of his daughter's birth. In her baptism certificate he is called "musicien" and in her marriage settlement "symphoniste du roi". (A woman dancer of the name had performed in Lulli's *Alceste* in 1706; her name is again mentioned in 1709 and 1711, and in this latter year it is associated with that of a Rameau—no doubt Pierre Rameau, the author of *Le Maître à danser*, about whose possible relationship with our Dijonnais nothing is known. She is mentioned again in 1720.) The Mangots lived in the Rue Bailleul, a portion of whose ancient houses still stands, wedged in between the Rues de Rivoli and St. Honoré.

Rameau was married in St. Germain l'Auxerrois, his wife's parish. Marie-Louise is described by Maret as having distinguished manners, a good upbringing, a gift for music, a very pleasing voice and "un bon goût pour le chant". Though not a professional, she sang in several Court performances of her husband's operas, in *Hippolyte et Aricie* in 1734, *Castor et Pollux* in 1738 and *Les Fêtes d'Hébé* (*Les Talents lyriques*) in 1740. She brought him no dowry and in the marriage settlement Rameau gave her two hundred livres "pré-fixes". His supposed avarice—much exaggerated and based partly on his nephew's slanders and partly on reports relating to his old age—did not prevent him from following the inclination of his heart. In spite of the difference in age and his difficult temper, the union seems to have been happy. She bore him four children, two of each sex. One son and one daughter survived him; both of these had children, and the daughter's descendants have been traced by Lionel de la Laurencie.[1] During these years he had continued his studies, and in 1726 Ballard brought out a *Nouveau Système de Musique théorique, pour servir d'introduction au Traité de l'Harmonie*, describing him as "cydevant organiste de la cathédrale de Clermont". He still held no fixed appointment. In 1727 he competed for the organ of the important church of St. Paul, together with Vaudry, Couperin (probably François II's cousin Nicolas, who succeeded him at St. Gervais) and Daquin, but was beaten by Daquin. Marchand, whom Rameau, according to Fétis, blamed for his failure, was not on the jury, which comprised the musicians Lalouette, organist of Notre-Dame, and Foliot, the choirmaster of St. Paul, and a number of clergy and laymen; the minute of the appointment has been preserved.

He must already have been thinking of himself as an opera composer. At Clermont, in his organ-loft, his thoughts had turned to dramatic writing, and in his *Traité* he had laid down the duties of a "musicien dramatique" as if he were one himself.[2] In 1727 he made serious attempts to compose an opera, and wrote a long letter to Houdar de la Motte, hinting that this distinguished writer should provide him with a libretto. La Motte, a man of fifty-five with a full life behind him, failed to acknowledge the letter, but he kept it in his papers, where it was found after his death; it was published in the *Mercure* in 1765, when Rameau had been dead a year. It has often been reprinted, yet I feel justified in giving it once more, both for its interest and because so few of Rameau's letters have come down to us.

October 25: 1727

Whatever reasons you may have, Sir, not to expect from my dramatic music as favourable a success as from that of a composer apparently more experienced in this kind of music[3], allow me to counter them, and at the same time to justify my bias in my own favour, without claiming to draw from my learning any other advantages than those which you will agree with me in feeling to be legitimate.

When one says: a learned musician, one generally means a man whom nothing escapes in the different combinations of notes; but one believes him to be so absorbed in these combinations that he sacrifices everything to them, common sense, wit and feeling. Such a one is but a school musician, of a school where it is a question of notes and nothing more; so that one is right in preferring to him a musician who boasts less science than taste. Yet this latter, whose taste has formed only comparisons within reach of his senses, can at best excel in only a few

---

[1] (168).   [2] (1), 143.

[3] This suggests that Rameau had already approached La Motte and been rebuffed.

kinds of music, I mean, kinds suited to his temperament. If he is naturally tender, he expresses tenderness. If his character is quick, playful, witty, etc., his music corresponds. Take him away from these characters which are natural to him and you will not recognize him. Moreover, as he draws everything from his imagination, without any help from art with relation to his expressions, in the end he runs dry. In the first flush all was brilliant; but this fire is consumed as he tries to rekindle it, and all one finds in him is repetitions or commonplaces.

It is therefore desirable that there should be found for the stage a musician who has studied nature before painting her and who, through his learning, knows how to choose the colours and shades which his mind and his taste make him feel to be related with the required expressions.

I cannot deny that I am a musician; but at least I have more than others the knowledge of colours and shades of which they have but a confused feeling and which they use in due proportion only by chance. They have taste and imagination, but confined in the store of their sensations where the different things cluster in a little patch of colours beyond which they perceive nothing. Nature has not entirely deprived me of these gifts and I have not given myself to combining notes to the extent of forgetting their intimate connexion with that natural beauty which alone is enough to please but which one does not find easily in a ground lacking in seeds and which, especially, has already gone its full length.

Make inquiry of the opinion people have of the two cantatas of mine accepted some twelve years ago, the manuscript copies of which have become so widespread that I have not thought it worth while to have them engraved unless I could add a few others, which I cannot for lack of words. One is called *L'Enlèvement d'Orithie*: it has recitative and well-defined airs; the other is *Thétis*, where you will notice the degree of anger which I give to Neptune and Jupiter according as it is seemly to give more self-possession or more passion to one or the other and as it is suitable that the orders of one or the other should be carried out. You have only to come and hear how I have characterized the song and the dance of the savages who appeared at the Théâtre Italien two years ago and how I have rendered the titles: *Les Soupirs*, *Les Tendres Plaintes*, *Les Cyclopes*, *Les Tourbillons* (that is to say the swirls of dust raised by high winds), *L'Entretien des Muses*, a *Musette*, a *Tambourin*, etc. You will then see that I am not a novice in the art and that it is not obvious that I make a great display of learning in my compositions, where I seek to hide art by very art; for I consider only people of taste and not at all the learned, since there are many of the former and hardly any of the latter. I could make you hear motets of mine with full choir and you would see whether I feel what I seek to express. But this is enough to give you food for thought.

The birth of his first child, Claude, had preceded this letter by two and a half months; he was christened at St. Germain l'Auxerrois on August 8. His second child, Marie-Louise, was christened on November 15, 1732, in the same church, but though the parish was the same the dwelling was not. Rameau had moved in the meantime to the Rue du Chantre, on the site of the present Magasins du Louvre. In September of this year we have the first indication that he is organist at Ste. Croix de la Bretonnerie, his first fixed post since his return to Paris. He kept this post till at least 1738; the date of his retirement from it is not known. In 1736 he was also organist at the church of the Jesuit Novitiate, but had left it by 1738.

Long before this Rameau had met the man who, more than anyone else, was to help him to realize his great desire. This was Le Riche de la Pouplinière, a *fermier-général*, one of the wealthiest men in France and one of the most influential patrons of music and the arts. The son of a *fermier-général*, he had entered the Compagnie of tax farmers in 1721. In 1727 he had been posted to distant Provence by Cardinal Fleury, at the request of the Prince de Carignan, whose successful rival he had been for the favours of the singer Marie Antier, the future Phèdre of Rameau's first opera. Four and a half years later he was back in Paris, living in the Rue Neuve des Petits-Champs, and soon the centre of a society in which writers and musicians played a large and profitable part.

Rameau must have been introduced to this circle before the financier's banishment. The link was probably Piron, who had been the secretary of one Pierre Durey d'Harnoncourt, another Burgundian, when he was *receveur des finances* in Dijon, and had renewed the acquaintance of his former master when he came to seek fortune in Paris in 1719. Durey d'Harnoncourt was a friend and boon companion of La Pouplinière; he no doubt introduced Piron to the hospitable household and Piron introduced Rameau. No dates can be given, but the introduction must date from before 1727 when the *fermier-général* left Paris for Marseilles.

It was at La Pouplinière's that Rameau met his first librettist, Abbé Pellegrin, whose Biblical opera, *Jephté*, set by Montéclair, had been given in 1732. He was a protégé of Durey d'Harnoncourt, through whom he had won a footing in the tax-farmer's hospitable household. Born in Marseilles in 1663 of a family of magistrates, he had been educated by the Jesuits and entered the order of Servites whose novitiate was at Moustiers Sainte-Marie. He left them after ordination in a somewhat irregular way and became chaplain on board one of the King's galleys, making a couple of trips to the Levant. He drifted to Paris in 1704 and entered the literary arena with an *Epistle* on the King's victories which was crowned by the Academy. Mme de Maintenon befriended him and obtained his transfer from the Servites to the congregation of Cluny, the practical effect of which was to release him from monastic obligations. This set him right with the law but did not provide him with a living. Encouraged by his first success, he made himself a purveyor of verse. He traded on the wave of piety that had returned with the declining reign and to which Jean-Baptiste Rousseau owed the fame of his *Odes sacrées*, and he published successively five volumes of religious verse, amounting to more than half a million lines. This task was not undertaken, it seems, in an exclusively commercial spirit; he was a devout priest and a good-living man; on this all his contemporaries are agreed in spite of the slanderous couplet that runs:

> Le matin catholique et le soir idolâtre,
> Il soupait de la messe et dînait du théâtre.

He was not *idolâtre* and derived no sustenance from his clerkship in Holy Orders.

He wrote several tragedies, the best known of which is *Pénélope*, and finally, in 1711, his lack of resources compelled him to stoop to writing for the Fair theatres. His first farce for this stage, *Arlequin à la guinguette*, was also the first play to make use of *écriteaux*, two years before the *Arlequin roi de Sérendib* of Lesage and d'Orneval. Later productions were *Le pied de nez* and *Arlequin, rival de Bacchus*. In 1714 he wrote the text of an opera, *Arion*, set by Matho, and between that year and 1732, the year of *Jephté*, he wrote the texts of nine operas or ballet operas. In due course his archbishop, Cardinal de Noailles, took umbrage at these secular occupations and suspended him *a divinis*, which debarred him from saying mass, though not from receiving the sacraments. *Jephté* was taken off the stage after several performances but was put back later, and on the strength of his takings the Abbé bought himself a new wig which he christened gratefully "ma Jephté". His down-at-the-heels appearance was proverbial and he figures in a skit by Legrand, *La Nouveauté*, as La Rimaille, in an amusing scene in which he and a musician, La Cascade, discuss the possibility of writing, the one an opera without words and the other an opera without music. He lived to be over eighty, dying in 1745 in rather easier circumstances than he had known during most of his picturesque life; he was even able to help his necessitous nephews and nieces. But, to his sorrow, he was never able to have removed the suspension *a divinis*.[1]

Such was the experienced versifier whom Rameau approached for a text. A story, first recorded in 1763, says that Pellegrin consented on condition of a large instalment, in case the opera failed. After hearing the first act at La Pouplinière's he was so impressed that he withdrew this demand. The first contact must have taken place before

---

[1] See (124).

the end of 1732. In March or April 1733, the opera was given privately with La Pouplinière's orchestra and singers at his house in Rue Neuve des Petits-Champs. By July it was being rehearsed at the Opéra, and the first performance was given on October 1. A few days earlier Rameau had celebrated his fiftieth birthday.

2. Chamber Music

BESIDE the impressive mass of more than ninety acts of dramatic music, as well as motets and cantatas, Rameau's fifty-odd pieces for harpsichord and sixteen for trio are a slender legacy. Yet it is only through them that he communicates to-day with the ordinary music-lover. This numerically insignificant part of his work, written before he acquired fame as an operatic composer, represents him in the eyes of the world even more completely than his piano sonatas, up to half a century ago, represented Mozart.

They are by no means unworthy representatives. Though they give but few hints of his dramatic power—hints perceptible only if we know this power at first hand in the operas—they reflect unmistakably his greatness. In size they are trifles, but many of them are strong in conception and execution, and even if we knew nothing else about their creator we could well imagine him capable of working on a broader scale. Since he was fated to survive by such a small fraction of his output, no better choice could have been made. This is not always the lot of great artists, some of whom have been known over long periods only by their weakest work.

It is customary to couple him with Couperin as one couples Mozart with Haydn or Ravel with Debussy. Yet they are not contemporaries. Rameau was fifteen years the younger, and Couperin had published, or was publishing, his most mature work when Rameau's second and third books were printed, in 1724 and 1727–1730. Rameau represents a later stage than Couperin in the growth of French keyboard music. "Growth" in such a context never means "linear development", and Rameau does not "descend from" Couperin any more than Beethoven "descends from" Haydn, as the pestilential analogy with biological evolution may lead simple minds to imagine. Though Couperin and Rameau are sole survivors of their ship, many other keyboard composers, before, during and after the elder musician's lifetime, did not appear in their own generation so markedly inferior. Chambonnières, Louis Couperin, Nicolas Le Bègue, d'Anglebert in the generations before him, Clérambault, Louis Marchand, Gaspard Le Roux, the elder Dandrieu, Elisabeth de la Guerre and Dieupart in his own, Jean-François Dandrieu and Siret just after, are among them. In the early years of the eighteenth century there were in France, broadly speaking, two kinds of composition for the harpsichord: the pieces derived from dances, with no aim other than to evoke, in addition to their musical entertainment, a kind of vicarious pleasure of the dance, and what may be called *genre* pieces, whose extra-musical appeal consisted in calling to mind some external object: person, thing, situation, event. The division was not hard and fast; some dances had evocative names, and many *genre* pieces, even when not called dances, were cast in obvious dance rhythms.

The ancestry of the dance type is clear: it comes from ballet music. The ancestry of the *genre* piece with a name has been traced back to the English virginalists, whence it spread to lute and keyboard music in the seventeenth century. But it is even older. A manuscript collection of Burgundian *basses danses* of the first third or middle of the fifteenth century contains some sixty pieces, all of which bear names such as *Beaulté, La Belle, Engoulesme, La Rochelle, Filles à marier, Le petit Rouen, Le doulx Espoir, L'Espérance de Bourbon.*[1] There is a large minority of descriptive names in *La Rhétorique des Dieux*, that imposing selection of lute music by Denis Gaultier, made for Anne de Chambré, an amateur lute player, in the mid-seventeenth century and published some twenty years ago. There is a minority of them, too, in Chambonnières. A manuscript collection of keyboard pieces in the Bibliothèque Nationale, dated 1675 and assembled for "Instruction und Unterricht", has a number with women's names, *La Sera Diana, L'Albertina, L'Eliana, La Josephina, La Brocardina, La Theodorina*, all called *canzona*.

On the other hand, very few of Louis Couperin's pieces bear titles. There are none in Nicolas Le Bègue, d'Anglebert, Dieupart or Louis Marchand, nor in the elder Dandrieu; none in Rameau's first work. Rameau's book, published in 1706, comes in this respect at the end of a series; in those of Elisabeth de la Guerre and Gaspard Le Roux, which are contemporary, a few pieces have titles, most have not; in the three by the younger Dandrieu every piece has one, and nearly all in Rameau's two later books also bear names.

The older suite of prelude and dance forms was more austere, more purely musical; the writing tended to polyphony or at least to a full harmony[2]; the later *recueils*, divided or not into suites, made an extra-musical appeal which was an unbending from the purer standards of the non-evocative pieces. The difference between titles and no titles

---

[1] (143).

[2] This was the French suite *par excellence*, the outward form of which Bach adopted in his so-called *Little* or *French Suites*, though there is scarcely one piece in the whole forty which could have been written by a *claveciniste*, even the apparently French gavotte in E major. The least un-French are the *Allemande* and *Courante* in D minor with which the *recueil* opens.

is not just one of words; their presence corresponds to a less professional and more intimate attitude to music.   In the dance suite the
typical prelude was a *toccata*, without bar divisions, in free time.   It
was of lutenist ancestry.   Louis Couperin, d'Anglebert, Le Bègue,
Marchand (in one of his two suites), Clérambault, Le Roux and even
Siret, in his second book published in 1719, write in this form, the
older composers sometimes at great length, Clérambault and Le Roux
more briefly.   Very moving when the progressions are coherent, as
in a few of Louis Couperin's and in Clérambault's, they lose urgency
as the harmony wanders and "egrène ses molles arabesques",[1] and are
sometimes not above the level of rambling garrulity.

Rameau's first book was known to Maret and Decroix but not to
Chabanon, and in the nineteenth century it was declared mythical by
Farrenc, among others, who maintained firmly that he had composed
only two *recueils*.   It was rediscovered and republished in the first
volume of the *Œuvres complètes* in 1895.   It comes at the very end of
the reign of the suite in France, looking backward in the form of its
pieces, though harmonically several of them look forward to his later
work.   With all its indebtedness to a dying fashion, it is remarkable
how Ramellian are some of its movements published before the composer was twenty-three.   None is more so than the *Prélude*.   It is in two
parts: the first without bar lines, the second a 12/8 movement "like
a piece of Italian violin music".[2]   In his book of harpsichord pieces,
of about the same date as Rameau's, Dandrieu the elder[3] also opens
with a double prelude though he heads the two parts separately; the
first, *toccata*-like, is in ₵; the second, in 12/8 like Rameau's, wanders,
comfortably and rather mechanically, borne on a single overlapping
figure, found also in Rameau,[4] through various keys and over various
parts of the keyboard, with an unconcern for concluding worthy of
the bar-less preludes.

In both parts of his prelude Rameau shows a grip uncharacteristic
of this form.   He begins well grounded in a tonic bass, with seventh,
ninth and eleventh rising above it, then breaks in a downward scale
rush and relaxes for a few seconds to resume his station on the dominant, with a fresh superstructure of seventh, ninth and eleventh.
Another free passage leads to a spaced-out cadence, and a slowly
established chord ends this section.   Such is Rameau's sole tribute to
a form much honoured by his forerunners.   With its alternation of
tension and release, so weakly marked, as a rule, in this kind of movement, it reveals the dramatic temperament and constructive instinct of

---

[1] Dufourcq's expression.   [2] Pirro.
[3] No doubt the priest-organist of St. Barthélemy, who died in October
1733; he was Jean-François's uncle.
[4] Bars 4–5.

its composer. Its sense of urgency allows no loss of time; as one point is made we pass on to the next. In its form it is indeed a relic of the past, the last glow of a splendid epoch; in its content it ushers in a life full of a new music. Its last bars seem to hold in reserve all the treasures of his work to come; as the chord breaks and the triplet arpeggios ripple downward the music suggests an overbrimming beaker pouring out its precious flow (ex. 1).[1]

The leisurely sequences, which have their counterparts in many a *ritornello* of his operas, are strictly controlled and never lose their direction like Dandrieu's. Under the ceaseless flow of the triplets the harmony is established with the same firmness as in the bar-less part. Bars 3–4 and 8–9 will be echoed in the *Gigue* in the same suite. There is here a gracious ease which is distinctly Italian, and is found again, in Rameau's harpsichord works, only in the two *Gigues* of 1724.

Ex. 1

This first book[2] consists in one suite of nine movements. It is customary to dismiss it as an early attempt of no significance. But indeed the mark of Rameau is already clear on most of its pieces. The first *Allemande* and the *Courante*[3] are slender adumbrations of the powerful movements in the same key in the third book. The *Courante*, in fact, is better built and more original than the corresponding dance in the second book; it comes at times quite close to that of the third and reads like a sketch for its great successor. Compare bars 15–16 with 15–18 and 37–40 of the later dance, where the progression is similar; the jumping bass is full of excitement, and these bars so simply built on a chord of the seventh have an unquestionable grandeur. The characteristic tartness of Rameau is already here. The *Gigue*,

---

[1] The first *double* of the later gavotte with variations steals in very similarly.

[2] I call "second book" the *Pièces de Clavecin* of 1724 and "third book" the *Nouvelles Suites de pièces de Clavecin ou deuxième livre* of 1727–1730.

[3] The *Courante* is in the style called *luthé*. Gaspard Le Roux's first suite, in D minor, has a *Courante luthée*, the writing of which resembles Rameau's.

large-limbed in spite of its spidery gait, ranges far and wide over the keyboard.   It is rather like a model waiting to be clothed, but the last ten bars, with an echo of the *Prélude*, have a lyrical touch.   The *Gavotte* is a first cast of *La Livri*.   The *Vénitienne* is Ramellian only in its second episode, which is also the most personal part of the *Gavotte*.

> It modulates to F sharp minor and to return to A major chooses an easy way out which recalls Beethoven.   It raises the bass quite simply stepwise from F sharp to A (bars 61–65), with a rawness and spareness that makes the modulation quite striking and even somewhat irrelevant in so unpretentious a piece.[1]

I have discussed its title in Appendix B.   I think it was intended as a kind of gondolier's song, a *barcarolle*, in fact, and it should not be hurried; if taken *moderato* the lilt becomes obvious; were it written 6/8 there would be no doubt about it.   The movement gains in character and dignity by this treatment.[2]   The mature Rameau is shadowed forth more faintly by the *Sarabandes* and *Menuet*; this latter, as well as that which opens the second book, sounds like the *double* of an unheard *simple* in crotchets.[3]

It is the custom to say, or rather to repeat the last person to have said it, that this first book shows the influence of Louis Marchand.   As little of this composer's work is available in modern editions, I will dilate a little upon this assertion.

Louis Marchand (1670–1732), one of many musicians of this name, had a great reputation as organist; the story of his refusal to measure himself publicly with Bach is well known.   He was afflicted with dissipated habits, and was little concerned with publishing or even writing down what he composed.   During his life two slim volumes of harpsichord pieces were published by Ballard in 1699 and 1703. At his death he left a chest full of manuscript organ music in the hands of his daughter, who was a religious; from it a small selection was made and published in 1732, and again by Guilmant in *Les Archives des Maîtres de l'Orgue*.   Of his harpsichord music only the gavotte from the second book is included in modern anthologies.

Each book consists in a prelude and dances—six in the first book, eight in the second.   The presence of a prelude without bars and of a chaconne shows the backward-looking character of the music, which stands, speaking loosely, half-way between Louis Couperin and Jean-

---

[1] From an unpublished study by Cecilia Campbell.

[2] The quaver was sometimes used as the unit in slow tempo.   In a MS. collection of pieces of this period for the German flute in the Bibliothèque Nationale is a *La Vénitienne* by a "Mr. Marchand" (probably Joseph, the violinist) in 6/8, marked "lentement et gracieusement".

[3] Compare with those in Bach's B flat *partita* and C major flute sonata.

Philippe. Two texts mention Rameau's acquaintance with the organist. One is the anonymous article which appeared in the *Mercure* a month after his death, from which are drawn the facts given in the previous chapter. The writer adds: "Il avouait . . . qu'il devait à cette liaison beaucoup de lumières tant sur la composition de la musique que sur la pratique savante de l'instrument dont il touchait."[1]

The other is the carefully documented *Éloge* of Dr. Maret which was pronounced before the Academy of Dijon and published in 1765. Here the same facts are repeated, but the important detail is added: "Il reconnut par ses fugues que cet artiste n'était pas bon musicien."

These statements are not contradictory. Rameau may well have been at first carried away by the excellence of Marchand's playing and impressed by the vigour and imagination of his extemporizing, and yet have recognized, on further acquaintance, that there were flaws in his musicianship. The second statement, therefore, does not rule out the possibility of an "influence" or an "affinity" between one and the other. That Rameau's first book shows this influence is repeated by everyone who writes on him, but no one, not even Pirro, has stated by what signs it is to be recognized.

There is perhaps somewhat wider spacing in some of Marchand's pieces than is usual in François Couperin and Clérambault; this is a point of contact with Rameau but doubtful as a sign of influence. In the refrain of the *Gavotte en rondeau* in the first-book we have a flowing bass that resembles some of Rameau's, but it is the only harpsichord piece that shows this trait. Marchand's two gigues flow evenly, whereas Rameau's is both jumpier and more contrapuntal. The melodious bass of Rameau's sarabands and their broken harmony are in nowise like Marchand's, neither is there any marked likeness between their allemandes and courantes. We notice, however, likenesses amounting at times almost to identity of both upper line and harmony between Rameau's gavotte and Marchand's second one, in G minor—that included in anthologies—and though Rameau's is longer and more resourceful the word "influence" might be used here.

If we turn to the *Trio* and the *Duo* in D minor in Marchand's organ pieces and compare them with this same gavotte of Rameau's, the allegation of influence becomes strengthened. The spirit is different but the writing is similar and does to some extent justify the statement in the *Mercure* (ex. 2).

It is when we look at the prelude of Marchand's second book that the momentary discipleship of the younger man becomes indubitable.[2] Here are the same rises by seventh, ninth and eleventh (bars 4–5) as

---

[1] (26), 185.
[2] Appendix C. The first two bar lines are in the original; I have inserted the others for purposes of reference.

in Rameau; the same treble climbing by seconds on a bass that falls by the same intervals (bar 6); the same broken harmony resolving downwards on a ninth (bar 3); the same scale rushes and (bars 2–3) the same progression (Rameau, bottom of p. 1).   There is also a certain likeness of contour and harmony (Marchand, bar 8; Rameau, end of stave 3 and beginning of stave 4).   All this within a very short space amounts to more than coincidence.   The main differences are in the temperaments of the composers.   Marchand is more gracious than the rocky Burgundian; his ascent seventh–ninth–eleventh is not made with Rameau's grim look and set teeth; he rests awhile between his discords on the consonant tenth, and his writing is in three parts,

Ex.2

while Rameau's, save for chords, is in two; gentle Bach-like imitations robe his harmonic skeleton with decency; Rameau's prelude seems uncompromisingly crude and stark beside Marchand's.   But the Dijonnais has it for drive and purpose; he knows where he is going; he rises to a climax (bottom of p. 1), whereas Marchand uses up his finest effect in the third bar, and his end tapers off amiably but weakly.

Marchand's imprint is unmistakable in these two pieces but nowhere else in the volume, and it is transitory; Rameau never returned to the outmoded bar-less prelude,[1] and he needed no one's example to write free-flowing basses.

Marchand's sixteen pieces are all agreeable, and some, like the two preludes, have a personal flavour.   The most stirring is the D minor saraband in the first book, a forceful piece with close-knit harmony and well-marked rhythm, worthy of Louis Couperin at his best; it ought to be included in anthologies.

In Rameau's first *recueil*:

his resourcefulness proves that he is in full command of his harmony. Though his basses remain simple, he varies his treatment of chords. Often, when he comes upon a felicitous discord he develops in a series

---

[1] The 12/8 part of the prelude, moreover, is like Dandrieu's, not Marchand's.

of suspensions but these sequences are not mechanical for he varies them with simple means.[1]

The twenty-one pieces that make up his second book appeared in 1724, one year after the composer's return to Paris. He had by that time written several motets and secular cantatas as well as the *Traité de l'Harmonie*, but nine years were still to elapse before his first opera. The suite form has by now been given up, though the pieces are still grouped by keys, ten in E, ten in D. The majority are *genre* pieces with descriptive titles; eight are dances; a ninth, *Le Lardon*, belongs to both categories. The forms are binary and rondeau, the latter slightly outnumbering the former.

Those in binary form contain a few which are conservative in both structure and writing; the *Allemande* and *Courante* in E minor, for example, are hardly more modern than the similar dances in the first book. *L'Entretien des Muses*, though not deserving the epithet in any other respect, is also conservative in structure; the two halves are of nearly equal length and the second reproduces the first fairly literally. But this is not so with *Le Rappel des Oiseaux* and *Les Soupirs* which, though both shot through with the same motif or type of motif, show no symmetry between the two halves. "The rhythmical figure of *Le Rappel des Oiseaux* is most significant at the end, when the increased insistence of the augmented fourth on the strong beats becomes poignant."[1]

All but the very shortest have the usual arrival on the dominant or relative major at the double bar; after the repeat they begin at once in a new key: the relative major or its dominant if the piece is in the minor; sometimes the relative minor. There is generally a good deal of modulating in the second part, and sometimes the return to the tonic occurs only right at the end. The *Rigaudons* and *Le Lardon* are all in one key. No binary piece shows any approximation to sonata form.

The rondeaux are more varied. Except for the *Musette* and the second *Gigue* they have no more than two couplets, and the *Musette* itself was reduced to two when Rameau re-used it in *Les Fêtes d'Hébé*. The insignificant minuet which opens the book has only one. Practically every rondeau shows thematic kinship between two of its three parts, sometimes between all three. The first two couplets of the *Musette*, all three of the second *Gigue*, the refrain and first couplet of *La Villageoise*, the refrain and second couplet of *Les Tourbillons* all begin alike; the two couplets of *La Joyeuse*—one in the major, the other in the relative minor—are almost identical; so are the refrain and couplets of *Les Niais de Sologne*. In the first couplet of *La Follette* the refrain is recalled. There is general similarity throughout both

---

[1] C. Campbell, *op. cit.*

couplets of the first *Gigue* and all through *La Villageoise* and *La Follette*; the *Tambourin* is through-composed and practically mono-thematic; it also boasts a long coda which, however, might be considered as a third couplet, followed by the return of a much modified refrain.   All this indicates a strong sense of unity which was not as a rule present in Couperin's rondeaux.

Les Cyclopes is on its own.   It opens with a long passage of some fifty bars which can be subdivided thematically into several sections but does not modulate.   The first bar, which has the importance of a refrain, is recalled several times in the latter part.   Then without a break there follow thirty-three bars that modulate and contain recalls of part of the first section—an arpeggio passage divided between the two hands; then the first four bars of the refrain and a development of seven bars.   The second episode, twenty-seven bars long, consists largely of a virtuoso passage resembling one already heard; it opens in the tonic and moves to the dominant.   The rest of the piece recapitulates the first fifty bars.   It is therefore, if one will, a rondeau in two episodes, in which the first return of the refrain is much cut down. But a rondeau in which the refrain is of such length and so complex is so unusual that it is best not to classify the piece though Rameau heads it *rondeau*.   Its recapitulation of the first section at the end relates it to *da capo* movements like the preludes of some of the English suites; its absence of modulation in what looks at first like an exposition prevents us from seeing in it an ancestor of sonata form, though much of the spirit of that form, especially the development principle in all three divisions, is obvious.   But it does adumbrate Mozart's sonata-rondos.

There is an imaginative appreciation of this book and the next in Laloy's *Rameau*, and Kathleen Dale has said as much as can be said on them within the compass of an article.[1]   Her study is full of valuable points; it accompanies its statements with references, and is sensitive to the essence of the music without losing itself in impressionism.   I cannot hope to better it; I only wish it were longer.

Perhaps Rameau's chief originality among harpsichord composers lies in his attempt to use his keyboard as a sustaining instrument.   It is this that makes almost all his pieces sound as effective on the piano as on the harpsichord; indeed, in fear and trembling of purists and archaizers, I venture to say that many sound better on the modern instrument.[2]   Though actual transfers from orchestral writing, like bars 75–85 in the second *Gigue*, are not common, the *Musette* and *Les Cyclopes* have a euphonic fullness which presupposes an orchestral imagination.   The tone differences between the three parts in *L'En-*

---

[1] (137).

[2] Guilmant considered that many of his pieces would go well on the organ.

tretien des Muses also suggest a difference in timbre; indeed, Rameau himself orchestrated the first half of this piece in *Les Fêtes d'Hébé*, II. 5, for flute, violins and bass. The "swirling quavers"[1] and smears of semiquaver arpeggios in *Les Tourbillons*,[2] the prolonging of chords for purposes of colour in *Le Rappel des Oiseaux*,[3] *La Villageoise* (beginning of second couplet) and *Les Cyclopes* (the arpeggios divided between both hands) all point to a desire to utilize resources beyond the reach of the harpsichord, requiring an instrument of greater sustaining power and variety of colour.

Les Niais de Sologne suggests a *vielle* tune with a plodding string bass. The *Rigaudons* and *Tambourin* are ready for orchestration; indeed, the latter, like the *Musette*,[4] was incorporated in *Les Fêtes d'Hébé*.

It is natural that the keyboard writing should look both backward and forward. There is some that is almost *luthé*, in which hardly a chord is heard and all the harmony is in arpeggios; this is so not only in conservative pieces like the E minor *Courante* but in advanced ones like *Le Rappel des Oiseaux* and *Les Soupirs*. The latter is particularly moving in its combination of a style of writing recalling the lute with harmonic boldness; see, for instance, the bars with a slowly rising or falling bass, one step at a time, under an upper pedal; the pedal note is emphasized not by sustaining but by repetition (bars 10–12, 14–16, 34–39). *Le Rappel des Oiseaux* has an effective *luthé* passage (in the second half); the writing recalls Couperin's *La Mystérieuse* and still more a passage in the gigue of Bach's B flat *partita* (bars 9–15 after the double bar in Rameau; 16–24 in Bach). The close linear writing of the older generation is still found in the E minor *Allemande*, in spite of an upper line much adorned with arpeggios which give the piece a three-part fullness though it is written in two. There is linear writing of a more modern kind in the parallel scales of *La Joyeuse* which proceed from Couperin's *Les petits Moulins à vent*. But, as Mellers says rightly,[5] most of his writing is "based more on arpeggio formation than on scale-wise motion". Both *Gigues*, which it is interesting to compare with the older *Gigue* in the 1706 book, make great use of arpeggio triplets in accompaniment and tune. The second, with its melody embodied in gentle showers of descending triplets over a tonic pedal, recalls the 12/8 section of the A minor prelude. The newest and most stirring use of arpeggios is in *Les Cyclopes*, in all three sec-

---

[1] K. Dale's expression.

[2] See Rameau's reference to this piece in his letter to La Motte.

[3] And the "organ-like sonority, reminiscent of the *Prélude*, in the last five bars of the first half" (C. Campbell, *op. cit.*).

[4] Rameau says that it may be transposed to C and played on the viol.

[5] (194).

tions, when what Mellers calls "a non-melodic Alberti bass" advances with gigantic skips amounting sometimes to a thirteenth and demanding a consummate reversed-hand technique.

Wide-spaced, large-limbed writing for the left hand is prominent in *Les Niais*, especially in its second *double*. Here the hand covers in swift semiquavers as much as two and a half octaves, like its long-legged creator striding up and down the Tuileries gardens. The *Cyclopes* figure occurs here as well. These great sweeps give a spaciousness to Rameau's harpsichord music hitherto not found in its literature and occurring even with Bach only in exceptional pieces like the C minor Fantasia. The dramatic expansiveness which it betokens is also new and contrasts with the descriptive qualities of Couperin, which are to Rameau's what those of the essayist are to the playwright's. The word "theatrical", used by Mellers, has a pejorative meaning which makes me hesitate to apply it to Rameau, in whose chamber music there is no touch of Italian rhetoric, but "more brilliant and more immediately emotional than Couperin's" it certainly is.

But this is not all Rameau. There is a reflective side on which Kathleen Dale rightly dwells; in fact, whereas Mellers sees in the qualities just enumerated the staple features of his writing, Mrs. Dale finds it before all restrained, delicate and meditative. If there are the wide-spaced, flourishing pieces, there are also those where the two hands keep close together, shadowing each other, as if for safety, creating a climate of calm.

In most of *L'Entretien des Muses* "a piece of contemplative polyphony, . . . a flow of purling quavers is maintained by the upper, lower and middle parts in turn, the whole sounding like a quiet but earnest conversation floating on the air from a great distance". The hands are seldom far apart, though each one retains its freedom of action; this is most marked at the end of each section when "a long right-hand trill above a rising phrase played by the left in the most expressive register of the instrument" brings to a climax the emotion hitherto diffused rather than expressed. In *Les Tendres Plaintes* a kindred inspiration is linked with the use of wide spacing and a moving bass.

There is in *Les Cyclopes* a *trait* which Rameau considered he had invented and of which he was proud. He draws attention to it in the *Mécanique des Doigts* which accompanies the *recueil*. It is a *batterie* where the left hand passes over the right. "I believe that these *batteries* are peculiar to me; at any rate, none similar have yet appeared; I may say, in their favour, that the eye shares in the pleasure which the ear receives in it."

Like Luc Marchand,[1] he might have called his piece *Le Spectacle*

---

[1] See p. 40.

des Mains. He did not know that Domenico Scarlatti had invented the same figure independently.

Another repeated-note figure in the same piece is one of alternating quavers, in which the left hand "shadows" or overleaps the right. Yet another consists in arpeggios of single notes divided between two hands, the left with *legato* crotchets, the right with *staccato* quavers, the latter falling on the off beats and "giving the effect of harmonics". In fact, *Les Cyclopes*, like *La Forqueray* in the *Pièces en Concert*, is an arsenal of Ramellian virtuosity.

In the little *Lardon* one form of these *batteries* is used with humorous intent. The intruding left-hand notes are cheekily *interlarded*, like bacon strips (*lardons*), between the chords of the right hand; the *staccato* taps are then succeeded by a *sostenuto* phrase that sings with mock solemnity. In the second half of this minute, non-modulating piece, the impudence is suddenly heightened by the flattened leading note, like a rude joke on the part of the intruding left hand. The piece sounds like a parody of Exaudet's well-known minuet to which ridiculous words were to be set a little later.

> Cet étang
> Qui s'étend
> Sur la plai – – ne . . .

Kathleen Dale considers that the mood of these pieces and of the third book is generally restrained; Mellers, that the writing is "virtuoso and theatrical in treatment", at any rate, more so than in Couperin. The few pieces which reflect "a sombre gravity", like the *Allemande* of the third book, he considers less representative than "the audacious descriptive *Rappel des Oiseaux*, a grand Handelian piece like the *Gavotte* with variations, or an expansive virtuoso piece such as *Les Cyclopes*".

This latter piece is not only virtuosity, it is also choreography. There were Cyclops in Lulli's *Persée*, and Rameau's vision is already that of a ballet composer. A piece like this, as well as *La Triomphante*, *Fanfarinette* and *Les Sauvages* in the third book, calls for choreographic rendering as much as the ballet *symphonies* in the operas.

The judgments I have quoted seem contradictory. The truth is that there is great variety of writing, as well as of sentiment, throughout Rameau's fifty harpsichord pieces, and even among the score that make up the 1724 book. This variety is evident to anyone who plays them through and through, and nothing would be gained by enumerating the different moods reflected. The Ramellian acerbity noticeable already in the first book is present here but less sharp than in 1706; less sharp, too, than a few years later in the third book. The most genial of his pieces come from this *recueil* of his fortieth year: the E major and minor group of jigs, rigadoon, musette and tambourin,

La Follette, *La Joyeuse*, *Le Lardon*; these have a *bonhomie* which is exceptional. There is more exuberance, too, than in the first and third books, and a youthful freshness found again in the hunting scene of *Hippolyte et Aricie* and parts of *Dardanus* and *Les Fêtes d'Hébé*. That unearthly sentiment for which I know no name but into which there enters more than a twinge of longing and which is one of Rameau's most exclusive possessions, pervades at least one piece, the lovely *Entretien*, and makes it one of the quickest short-cuts into his private world.

This book was accompanied by a *Méthode de la mécanique des doigts ou l'on enseigne les moyens de se procurer une parfaite exécution sur cet instrument*,[1] a summary which Rameau expanded later into the *Dissertation sur les différentes méthodes d'accompagner pour le clavecin ou l'orgue* (1732). The executant, he says, when he first seats himself, should have his elbows higher than the keyboard, and his hands should drop on to it by the mere natural movement of the wrist joints. Provided the thumb and fifth finger can touch the edges of the keys, the elbows can never be too high. Once the thumb and fifth finger are on the keys, his elbows must drop easily against his sides in their natural position and should normally remain there. The wrist should always remain supple; the fingers should fall on the keys, not strike them, and their motion should flow from one to the other. The weight of the hand should never rest on the fingers; the passage of the thumb under the fingers is prescribed—"cette manière est excellente". As one acquires assurance the height of the seat should be lowered till the elbows are a little below the level of the keyboard; thus will the hands remain as it were glued to the keyboard and acquire a desirable *legato*.

Rameau's third book, *Nouvelles Suites de Pièces de Clavecin*, is not dated. It bears the author's address: Aux Trois Rois, Rue des Deux Boules. Rameau moved to this address some time between his wedding in February 1726 and the birth of his first child in August 1727. The second edition of the 1724 *Pièces de Clavecin*, which is dated 1731, bears the address: Rue de Richelieu, près l'Hôtel de la Paix. Moreover, the engraver, Mlle Roussel, whose name is on the title-page, became Mme Leclair in 1730. It seems likely therefore that this third book came out between 1727 and 1730. It was accompanied by a *Méthode de la mécanique des doigts*, in which he warned executants that:

> The tempo of these pieces is on the fast side rather than the slow, except for the *Allemande*, the *Sarabande*, the *simple* [theme] of the *Gavotte*, *Les Triolets* and *L'Enharmonique*. But remember that it is generally better to sin from excess of slowness than from excess of speed.

---

[1] It is from this that come the comments copied into the Fitzwilliam Museum copy of Duphly's works reproduced on pp. 345–346 of Mellers' *Couperin*, where they are erroneously attributed to Duphly.

Once one has mastered a piece one grasps its sense unconsciously and soon one feels its right tempo.

He boasted of a simplification in the use of clefs—"wherever the hands may turn the clefs never change". A great deal of space was given up to *L'Enharmonique* and enharmonic modulation, and the last paragraph confessed disarmingly:

> I have inserted two consecutive octaves in some of these last pieces on purpose to undeceive those who might have been warned against the effect of these two octaves, and I am convinced that if one consulted only one's ear their absence would be deplored.

This third and last book for solo harpsichord is less homogeneous and more ambitious than the first two. It contains some of his grandest pieces; there is nothing in the earlier books like the sweep of the *Allemande* and the *Courante* with which it opens. There is the same majesty in the *Sarabande* and the same wiry vigour in *La Triomphante* and *Les Sauvages*. There is contemplative lyricism, of a different cast from that of *L'Entretien*, in the *Allemande*, some of the *doubles* in the *Gavotte*, *L'Indifférente*, the *Menuets* and *L'Enharmonique*.

There is, moreover, a dramatic passion new in his keyboard work, in *La Poule*, *Les Sauvages* and *L'Égyptienne*.[1] The spirit of *Fanfarinette* recalls the lighter pieces in the second book. Besides these pieces, all of undoubted charm, there are others which have no earlier counterparts and which are somewhat desiccated. *Les Tricotets* is a rather ungenial joke; it is Couperin's banter[2] but without his smile and twinkle. *Les Trois Mains* and *Les Triolets* sound experimental and lack spontaneity.

It would be interesting to know the dates of composition of these pieces. Unfortunately, almost the only one that is dated is *Les Sauvages*, which is referred to in the composer's letter to La Motte in 1727. Some pieces in the second book, like the *Rigaudons*, *Musette* and *Tambourin*, may come from music written for the Fair theatres, so that the orchestral version of the two latter in *Les Fêtes d'Hébé* may be nearer the original than the harpsichord one. The nature of several 1706 pieces shows that Rameau possessed early some of his most personal characteristics; it would therefore be unwise to refuse others an early date on the grounds of their maturity. Thus, the *Sarabande* and first *Menuet*, which were used in *Zoroastre* and *Castor et Pollux*, *La Triomphante*, the second *Menuet* and *L'Indifférente* may well be based on orchestral originals arising from the early *divertissements*. *L'Enharmonique*, however, was composed for this *recueil* as well as

---

[1] Pirro speaks of "le lyrisme furieux" of *L'Égyptienne*.
[2] And also Bach's; the skittish minuet in the G major *Partita* is very like it.

those pieces where the consecutive octaves occur. The first sketches for *La Poule* may go back to his early years in Paris, when he first met Père Castel. The Jesuit stated later that they had discussed together "the bird songs noted in Kircher, the cry of the hen calling her chickens, the song of the nightingale modulating through all the inflexions of which her throat is capable", and recalled "all the efforts I made, with the help of this great writer [Kircher] to excite his spirits and give him the idea of pieces that imitate the voice of Nature."[1]   It would therefore be wrong to think that all the pieces in each book represent the precise stage of growth reached by Rameau at the time it was published.

With one exception all the numbers in the third *recueil* are, like their predecessors, in either binary or rondeau form. But the differences between the two books in respect of form are very great. Here the great majority—eleven out of fifteen—are binaries; there are only three rondeaux. Moreover, these latter are all in fixed, even rigid, four-square frames. All three sections of *Les Sauvages*—refrain and two couplets—have sixteen bars each; those of *Les Tricotets* have sixteen or twenty-four; *La Triomphante* appears to divide up into sections of twelve bars, but here a slight subtlety breaks imperceptibly the stiffness: the first couplet has eleven bars, the second thirteen, while the refrain has twelve. It is, then, not in the rondeau that problems of architecture interest Rameau. After announcing the Mozartian rondo in *Les Cyclopes*, he returns to the most elementary type of the form.

The rondeaux are enlivened in other ways. In two of them he has given illustrations of those enharmonics to which the French public was so averse and which, following Italian example, he sought to introduce, first into his keyboard music and later into opera. The second couplets of *La Triomphante* and *Les Sauvages*, which modulate rapidly round the keys of F sharp minor and D minor, both contain some of the richest progressions in eighteenth-century music. In *Les Sauvages* the writing is more linear and the impact less startling. In these two rondeaux the audacity of the harmony makes up for the tameness of the construction.

Architecturally the twelve binaries are more adventurous. *L'Indifférente* and the minuets are in the usual dance pattern in which the second half begins with the same strain as the first but is afterwards different. The *Allemande* and *Courante* are in the through-composed style of suite movements with little articulation, and each half is independent, except for the closing bars, though the *Courante* breaks up on analysis into separate themes. *Les Trois Mains* is also different in its two halves except for the final sections, but these are much longer

---

[1] (50), 2007.

than in the *Allemande* and *Courante*; the last twenty-five bars of the
first half are repeated, slightly modified, in the last twenty bars of the
second. *Fanfarinette* and the *Sarabande* are alike in that their two
sections are quite independent of each other except for the very last
bars, and that the second parts are much longer than the first and sound
like *developments*. All these movements, on the whole, look backward, at least in this respect, to the suite.

La Poule might come into this category, for the impression it
makes is monothematic; but actually it is composed, like some of
Mozart's rondos, of a number of short themes, all very similar and
containing the clucking motif in various forms. Some of these are
found in one half only, some are common to both, but only the last
eight bars are identical in each half.

The remaining three pieces, *Les Triolets*, *L'Enharmonique* and
L'Égyptienne, are more modern, more articulated, and look forward
to the mosaic construction of rococo, though the general character is
still one of monothematism. In *Les Triolets* and *L'Égyptienne* the
second half repeats the first with the usual transpositions, except that
a section of five or six bars in the first half is replaced by a new one,
a little longer, in the second. They are like sonatas in which the
development occurs after the beginning of the recapitulation instead of
before. A vestige of this form survives in some of Mozart's two-part
rondos, where the second part recapitulates the first (after the return
of the refrain) but is prefaced by a short new passage.[1] Mozart's
fondness for inserting such a passage just after the *reprise* in his sonatas[2]
may be another relic of this practice.

L'Enharmonique is similar but more complex. Here not once but
twice the second half, which had begun like the first, breaks away from
its path and inserts new material; the first of these new passages is a
veritable *development* and contains the enharmonic change over which
Rameau made heavy weather in his preface.

The broad codas of several of these pieces[3] is another approximation to sonata form.

The *Gavotte* with six *doubles* is, with *Les Niais de Sologne*, the only
set of variations in his work. The theme suggests the lute; in fact, it
resembles a lute piece reproduced by Prunières.[4] The most poetic
doubles are the first and third, in which the theme is not merely pro-

---

[1] E.g. the string quintets in C and G minor; the piano concerto in D,
K. 537.

[2] E.g. the Prague symphony (finale) and Jupiter symphony (first
movement).

[3] E.g. the *Allemande*, *Les Trois Mains*, *L'Enharmonique*, *L'Égyptienne*;
also *Le Rappel des Oiseaux* in the second book.

[4] (211), 222–223.

vided with a new accompaniment or broken up into *divisions* according
to a fixed pattern, but is enriched with a commentary that transforms
it.   In the first *double* the counterpoint steals in from aloft with the
same mysterious tread as the 12/8 section of the *Prélude* in the 1706
book.   The slow-footed theme travels over its path unaltered, and
we have ears only for the counterpoint that wreathes and muses above
it in a spirit redolent of the cadenza in the fifth Brandenburg.   The
counterpoint in the third *double*, which is merely the first with the
parts transposed, breathes the same mood but unfolds it in the area of
Brahms' "tenor thumb", with the expressiveness of a viola.   The
writing here is that of *L'Entretien des Muses*.   The other variations,
though always musical, disguise less subtly their technical interest, and
the piece ends just as we begin to feel that practice is threatening to
overwhelm enjoyment.   This was not the impression of a contemporary who, in recopying it, added nine more *doubles*, each one of
which selects a figure in smaller and smaller notes and sedulously works
with it through the theme whose sombre poetry is dispelled long before
the end.   The same *division*-lover added three variations of the same
kind to *Les Tricotets* and substituted one of his own for Rameau's in
Les Niais de Sologne.   The copy in which they are preserved in the
Bibliothèque Nationale comes from the Decroix gift and is of Rameau's
period, but there is no reason to attribute to him the authorship of
these tiresome additions.

Most of what has been said of the second book holds good of the
keyboard style in this one.   The progress towards breadth of sweep
and fullness of harmony is carried further.   Many pieces range widely
and rapidly up and down the keys, especially the *Courante* and *La
Triomphante*.   Fullness is achieved by consistent working together of
both hands; this is noticeable in the first piece of the book, the A
minor *Allemande*, where the writing is at times in four parts.

Close parallel writing is present also in the minuets, in *L'Indifférente*, *Les Triolets*, *L'Enharmonique* and *La Poule*.   It was present in
La Joyeuse, *Les Tourbillons*, *Les Cyclopes* and the *Rigaudons* of the
second book; I suspect that in the *Rigaudons* and the *Menuets* it may
be due to a transfer to the keyboard of orchestral pieces composed for
the Fairs.   Chording is more consistently present than in 1724, where
its use, as in the *Musette*, was colouristic; here it also serves to reinforce the harmonic structure; see the A major *Sarabande*, *Fanfarinette*
and *La Triomphante*.   In the *Sarabande* the chords are written out
in the original as rapid arpeggios.   Like much in Rameau this piece
looks to past and future; it might have been conceived for some
gigantic lute; still more does it resemble an amplifying of *luthé*
writing for the yet unborn pianoforte—a Bach-Busonizing of Denis
Gaultier or Mézangeau.

In *La Poule*, repeated chords, with slow harmonic rhythm, are

"L'Indifférent" by Antoine Watteau

used with dynamic effect; orchestral influence is clear and the writing is modern; all counterpoint has gone, and the music falls largely into theme and accompaniment.

The quick arpeggios and closing broken chords of *L'Égyptienne* are also new; their effect is more massive than in earlier arpeggios of Rameau's and belongs to the new concerto style; they recur in *La Rameau* and *La Cupis* of 1741 and in *La Dauphine* of 1747. Linear writing of the older type survives, of course; it is present in the first three *doubles* of the *Gavotte*. It is used with greater complexity (*Courante*, *Allemande*, *Fanfarinette*), however, and twice over it is turned to trick effect in order to suggest one part more than is actually written—two parts for one in *Les Tricotets*, three for two in *Les Trois Mains*.

Scale passages in the new concerto style, that decorate but do not help on the harmony, are first found in *doubles* one to three of the *Gavotte*; they will be prominent in *Le Vézinet* in the *Pièces en concert*, and in *La Dauphine*. They are among the most modern features of Rameau's keyboard style. Downward scale rushes just before a close appear in *Les Trois Mains*, *La Poule* and *L'Enharmonique*; they had been hinted at in *Le Rappel des Oiseaux* and *Les Cyclopes* but become identical with their orchestral prototypes only in this book. Hand-crossing proper, of a novel kind, is found only in *Les Trois Mains*, but Rameau uses for the first time now a typically rococo figure in which the hands pursue and imitate each other Scarlatti-wise up and down the keyboard. It occurs in the *Allemande*, as a piece of homophonic and virtuoso frivolity after the contrapuntal gravity of the rest; in the *Gavotte* (fourth *double*) and *La Poule*, with descriptive intent; and later in *Le Vézinet*, *La Forqueray* and *La Dauphine*.

Let us try to summarize the respective characters of these two last books. There is more freshness and exuberance in the second, a more instinctive breaking of new paths; more breadth and more concentrated fullness in the third, a more intellectual approach to his art, a more conscious search for novelty; the "theatricality" (in Mellers' not unfavourable sense) of the second book is absent; there is drama (in *La Poule*, for instance), but except for *Les Sauvages*, less choreography. Of course, exceptions to these sweeping statements can be found in both books, but, speaking generally, the difference is in the direction I suggest. It can best be sensed by putting side by side two pieces of the same mood, chosen one from each *recueil*: *L'Entretien des Muses* and *L'Enharmonique*; the two *Allemandes* and *Courantes*; *Les Cyclopes* and *Les Sauvages*; *Les Tourbillons* and *La Poule*, both of which essay to render sounds or sights in Nature; *La Follette* and *Fanfarinette*; *Les Niais de Sologne* and the *Gavotte*; *Les Tricotets* and *Le Lardon*. This is not to say there is general gain or loss from one book to the other,

but just a ripening of the composer's genius which was to give its full
measure in the next decade of his life.

I feel, nevertheless, that the third *recueil* contains more pieces which
one is tempted to call great—great both in their conception and in
the embodiment of it.   It is difficult to avoid giving this overworked
epithet to the first three, the *Allemande, Courante* and *Sarabande*, to
L'Enharmonique and even—yes, even to *La Poule*.   This latter
suffers from risible associations.   Yet Rameau was deadly earnest in
his attempt to transcribe a sound of Nature, and nothing in the piece
suggests a humorous design, as do, for instance, *Le Lardon* and *Les
Tricotets,* or the bird *charivari* in *Platée*.   Let us forget the unfortunate "Co co co co daï" written under the first bars; let us banish
barnyard imagery and hear or play the piece as the pure music which
it is, the "developing", in Beethoven's not Bach's sense, of an unpromising initial cell.   It soon becomes apparent that the piece is a
drama.   It has the intensity and singlemindedness of a Racine tragedy,
with alternations of hope and despair.   After the G minor opening
the relative major intrudes with brutal vigour, and reigns for a time
before it is displaced by minor keys.   There is a similar bright stretch
in the second half.   Tension and relaxation alternate also in the
thématique.   The clucking theme, whether in G minor or B flat, is
Ramellian in the way it completes its harmony by successive pushes,
after the manner of the A minor prelude; these moments of strain are
followed by easier bars of almost light-hearted twitterings with a
figure found also in the prelude of Bach's A minor English suite or by
others with the pursuing-hands motif, after which the repeated notes
start afresh, in treble or bass, and generally marked *fort*.   If we will
but surrender ourselves to the music, the inexorable hammering of

Ex.3

the main theme will work its full effect.   Were we in any doubt
about the seriousness of the piece the last *fort*, thirteen bars from the
end, should bring us to our senses.   A terrific climax is attained here,
or rather breaks out, if climaxes can be said so to act, with tragic
impatience, as if to close the drama in blood and shrieks[1] (ex. 3).

---

[1] "A passage, harping on the chord of the dominant seventh, which has
in miniature the structure and harmonic effect of the cadenza in the Mozartian concerto" (194).   The climax begins with the descent of mighty
chords four bars earlier.   The dominant seventh bars exhibit to the full
Rameau's love for building up stepwise.

Greatness less dramatic and more majestic is found in the A minor
Courante.   This piece is almost unknown; it is not included in any
anthology and no writer ever mentions it; even Kathleen Dale omits
any reference to it.[1]   Yet it is one of the summits of Rameau's art.
No movement of his combines in such measure emotional force and
cunning artistry.   Its broad sweeps up and down the keyboard, its
striding arpeggios, its contrasted rhythms, its pathetic progressions,
its sequences, strike at the hearer's feelings, whilst its unfailing
coherence satisfies his intelligence with a vision of grandiose oneness.
At first, we are most impressed by its flowing unity, yet analysis shows
it to consist in a number of short motifs, some closed (ex. 4 (a)), some

Ex.4

open (d), combined, dissociated and recombined in many fashions,
like a piece of marquetry.   A mere analysis would lead one to believe
it was a piece of cerebral note-spinning; yet with all its calculated
construction it is emotional, obsessive, almost nerve-racking music.
   It is written almost throughout in three parts.   The predominant
motif is (a), dynamic in its rhythm, expressive in its dissonant harmony, and it is heard in roughly two bars out of three.   It is always
contrasted or combined with one of the various open themes: long

Ex.5

scale sections with or without wrinkles (b) and long-legged arpeggios
that cover two octaves in half a bar (c).   Some of these themes are
exquisitely lyrical, as haunting as Dido's lament, and this union of
rhythmical and harmonic roughness with expressive song is one of
the secrets of this piece's charm.   The hovering between duple and
triple time characteristic of the courante, which generally takes the

---

[1] But it has been recently recorded on the harpsichord by Fernando
Valenti.

form of alternation, is here simultaneous, since (a) is in 6/4 and the
other motifs in dotted 2/2.   The first half is mainly in the minor;
the second passes almost at once into the relative major and remains
there for a spell; this is the most splendid reach of its course (ex. 5).
When it returns to A minor, (c) is reversed and the second half closes
with the torturing sequences already heard at the end of the first
(ex. 6).   Bars 15–18 and 37–40 look back a quarter of a century to
the first A minor *Courante* of 1706.[1]

This haughty though emotional piece does not admit one easily
into its intimacy.   Perhaps the chief obstacle lies in its rhythms.   (a)
must be incisive and ever present; the scales must flow, or swing with
the slow regularity of a pendulum; the arpeggios must stride; the
dotted minims must sustain; all of which is obvious but not easy to

Ex.6

carry off.   Grace notes are less common than elsewhere; those on
(a) are for emphasis and are the equivalents of *sforzandos* on the piano.[2]
More than this it is not useful to say.   The door has to be knocked
on more than once before it will open, but of the riches within there
is no doubt and the effort is worth while.

Rameau devoted a long section of his preface to *L'Enharmonique*,
about which he clearly felt both pride and nervousness:

> The effect one experiences in the twelfth bar of the *reprise* [second
> half] will perhaps at first not be to everyone's taste; yet one becomes
> accustomed provided one lends oneself to it; in fact its beauty is felt once
> one has overcome the first repulsion which unfamiliarity may occasion
> in this case.
>
> The harmony which causes this effect is not cast at random; it is
> grounded in reason and authorized by Nature herself; that is what is

---

[1] See p. 17.

[2] The arpeggiated chords that open each part are in the nature of pre-
luding chords and should not be pedalled.   The movement proper begins
in the second half of the bar.

most piquant[1] for connoisseurs; but the execution must second the author's intention by softening the touch and holding back more and more the *coulés* [*legato* notes] as one draws near to the striking feature on which one should dwell awhile, as is shown by the sign ⌒.[2]

To read this without knowing the music is enough to make one think the piece was just an experiment in harmony.   It is, however, as pure a lyric as *L'Entretien des Muses*, with more poignancy; not for an instant does the inspiration flag; not once do we scent the midnight oil.   The climax comes, not with the precious twelfth bar of the *reprise*, but with the unexpressed pedal point twenty-four bars from the end—a strain at once repeated with the pedal sounded.

Nearly twenty years after the appearance of this book Rameau was impelled to extemporize a little piece for harpsichord which remained unpublished till 1895.   This is *La Dauphine*, the autograph of which was collected by Decroix and given by his heirs to the Bibliothèque Nationale.   The occasion for it was the marriage of the Dauphin with his second wife, Maria-Josepha of Saxony.   It was probably written for a friend and not as a public homage to the princess.   It is the only piece of Rameau's in which the (very slender) inspiration is insufficient to carry him through to the end without tricks or padding.   It contains several clavieristic figures found in the third book and the *Pièces en concert*; the overlapping hands mark time for bars on end and scales pursue each other to no purpose for several more, after which more time is spun out by broken chords and arpeggios, with scale rushes to round it off.   The true Rameau is present in the quasi-*development* section after the double bar and in the unprepared dissonance five bars from the end.

After 1760 his harpsichord music, like his operas, began to be forgotten.   When Chabanon wrote his *Éloge* in 1765 few still played it.   Chabanon, modernist though he was, remained a warm devotee of the great man, and deplored the neglect of these works in which, he said, two merits seldom combined were found, "chant" and "exécution"; that is, they sang and were also pieces for the virtuoso. This insistence on their *cantabilità* is timely.   Of Rameau's harmonic coherence—a quality he himself prized highly—which gives his music, says Bukofzer, "a consistency of structure hitherto unknown",[3] there can be no doubt; but that his music has also its moments of lyricism and is capable of song needs reaffirming.

---

[1] I am tempted to translate this word by "cute".

[2] Thus was fulfilled by a Frenchman the dreadful prophecy which Le Cerf de la Viéville had made thirty years earlier of the Italians: "Les Italiens ont inventé l'abus de la chromatique et je prévois qu'un de ces jours ils en viendront, s'ils peuvent, à l'enharmonique" ((83), II, 95).

[3] (125), Chapter 7.

I have tried to give an objective account of these works sufficiently complete to send readers to explore them or renew acquaintance with them. I have also stated my preference for this or that piece, not to deliver judgments upon them but to introduce the life of personal opinion into a rather dry enumeration of merits. I have implied that the first prelude, that *L'Entretien des Muses*, *Le Rappel des Oiseaux*, *Les Soupirs*, the *Musette* and *Tambourin*, *Les Cyclopes* in the first and second books, the *Allemande*, *Courante* and *Sarabande*, *La Poule* and *L'Enharmonique* in the third, are among the most precious things in all music. Others will make other choices.

The presence of that quality we call "greatness" is indisputable in the second and third books and in much of the *Pièces en concert*, in whichever piece or pieces our own taste elects to find it. Far from me to deny the merit of size and to say that

> La miette de Cellini
> Vaut le bloc de Michel-Ange.

There is greatness in sustaining power that cannot show itself except in terms of size and duration. On this score no eighteenth-century composer equals Bach. But within the compass of his fifty to eighty bars and comparing like with like, allemande with allemande, saraband with saraband, Rameau, so different from Bach in temperament, more nervous, more constantly on pins, perhaps more consciously intellectual, is not his inferior. The full measure of his genius he gave elsewhere; yet, in these restricted forms with which he indulged himself before he reached the stage, the quality of his greatness is unmistakable.

Like other classics he has suffered from bad editions. There exists in particular one execrable travesty of his keyboard music which is widespread enough for a warning against it to be necessary. It is the work of one Hans Huber. It contains eighteen authentic pieces and two spurious ones, *Air* and *Pièce*. The originals are almost unrecognizable under the heavy cloak of editorial accretions. Many coats of chromatic daub have to be peeled off before we come to the genuine Rameau underneath them. The suppression of a few ornaments, the addition of a great many more in the style of the late nineteenth century, the substitution of Brahmsian harmonies for Rameau's, the inflating of chords by trebling the number of their notes, the superposition of chords on a single note in the bass are among the atrocities perpetrated in almost every bar of a protesting text.

There exist two versions of the *Œuvres complètes*, Volume I. The first took such liberties with the original in the matter of ornaments that it had to be withdrawn and replaced by a better one. This is the version from which the current Durand edition is taken. The only reliable edition is the scholarly one by Erwin Jacobi.

I have already said how wholeheartedly I agree with Mrs. Dale and others who say that Rameau's harpsichord music gains by being transferred to the piano. There is no need to imagine that, prophet-wise, he looked longingly ahead to the days of bigger and better instruments. But he must have heard his music less exclusively with the timbre of the harpsichord in his ear; though he always heard it as keyboard music he heard it more abstractly than Couperin did his. Its effects are, of course, all possible on the older instrument, but they are effects of kinds which, common to both harpsichord and piano, are more dynamic on the latter, whereas Couperin's effects are often of a kind which the piano has lost the power of rendering. Let us, therefore, beware of archaizing and of sentimentalizing our Jean-Philippe; let us cease considering him as a composer of boudoir music for a miniature instrument.

*　　　*　　　*　　　*　　　*

Except for *La Dauphine* all Rameau's pieces for harpsichord alone were composed before he began writing for the stage. Once he had come before the footlights it seemed that no form of non-dramatic music could interest him any more. However, eight years after his first opera he published a little volume of suites, his only work of chamber music in the ordinary sense. These, the *Pièces de clavecin en concert*, consist in short movements for harpsichord, violin or flute, and tenor viol, comparable in size and structure with his keyboard solos; an alternative combination allows of a second violin instead of a viol. Formally, their interest lies in the relation between the three instruments. They are not trios in the nineteenth-century sense, neither are they sonatas for two instruments and bass. They are, as the title says, *concerted* movements, the only representatives now remembered, or resuscitated, of a vanished species.

The Italian sonata for two violins and a thoroughbass realized on viol and keyboard was first imitated in France by François Couperin. His contemporary, the priest Sébastien de Brossard, best known for his *Dictionnaire de musique*, composed sonatas for the same combination towards 1695 and also two for violin solo and thoroughbass which must be the oldest duet sonatas written by a Frenchman.[1]

---

[1] "Tous les compositeurs de Paris", says Brossard, "et surtout les organistes avaient en ce temps-là pour ainsi dire la fureur de composer des sonates à la manière italienne" (in (163), I, 143), a fury not confined to France for "les Anglais", wrote Le Cerf with horror, "ont fait des sonates plus *sonates*, plus difficiles et plus bizarres que celles du cinquième opus de Corelli" ((83), II, 101).

About the same time Jean-Ferry Rebel, father of the opera composer who collaborated with Francœur, also wrote sonatas in two or three parts "with bass for the harpsichord". François Duval, a violinist, composed between 1704 and 1720 six books of sonatas for one violin and bass and one book for two violins and bass. By 1720 the *genre* had taken root.

Séré de Rieux, a moderate pro-Italian, admits that French imitators carried Italian "bizarreries" to excess. He also bears witness to the abundant production of imitation Italian music.

> Si la France a cent fois retenti des cantates
> Quel bruit n'excita point la fureur des sonates?
> Essais impétueux des artistes naissants,
> On en vit à foison éclore tous les ans.[1]

In all these works the harpsichord was content to play the thorough-bass and enjoyed no independence. But early in the century solo pieces were written for it in which the composer added a violin part. In these works, as in the many piano sonatas with violin accompaniment of the second half of the century, the violin part could be added or omitted *ad libitum*. Such are the *Pièces de clavecin qui peuvent se jouer sur le violon* (1707) by Elisabeth Jacquet de la Guerre; they are written on two staves and, if a violinist is at hand, may be performed *à deux*, when the keyboard player surrenders the treble and realizes the figured bass as he would in a violin sonata. Some of these pieces have been republished by the *Oiseau Lyre* but without the composer's remarks on the possibility of adding a violin.[2]

Dieupart, a Frenchman who lived most of his life in London, composed, about 1700, six harpsichord suites, also republished by the *Oiseau Lyre*, written on two staves and allowing for an optional violin. Bach, whose own sonatas for harpsichord and violin date from about 1720, knew and transcribed two of these suites.

In 1729, Couperin's daughter, says the *Mercure*, played before the Queen accompanied by the violinist Besson, "who has made a special study of playing with perfection these kinds of pieces by toning down his violin very much".[3] The custom of accompanying with the violin was by this time widespread.

Why had the harpsichord, the humble purveyor of figured basses,

---

[1] (110), IV, 118–119.

[2] She was Elisabeth Jacquet, wife of Marin de la Guerre, organist of the Sainte Chapelle, St. Sèverin and the Grands Jésuites (Rue St. Antoine). Her rare talents were said to be a gift rather of nature than of study. She lived in the Rue Regrattière in the Ile St. Louis where she gave from time to time concerts of her music ((40), II, 166–167; also P. Brunold in *OL* edition of her harpsichord pieces).

[3] (201), 22.

become so overweening as to subdue the queen of the orchestra? It has been suggested[1] that its crisp tone, which had been sufficient for dances and short pieces with well-marked rhythm, showed itself incapable of satisfying the growing desire for the lyrical and the pathetic. To ensure a greater continuity of sound and a more singing character it took into partnership the violin, but as an assistant, not as a mistress. The taste for orchestral writing in keyboard music, already visible in Louis Couperin,[2] sought readily another opportunity for bringing the violin into the home. One should add that the number of amateur musicians was much greater than a generation or so earlier and they aspired to accompany. Le Cerf de la Viéville mocked at this ambition:

> To-day [that is, towards 1700] most young people who learn to play the harpsichord, bass viol or theorbo scorn to learn Pieces. And what do they learn, forsooth? Why, to accompany. Formerly people of quality left to born musicians [i.e. professionals] the trade of accompanying. To-day they take supreme pride in it. To play Pieces, to divert oneself agreeably or to divert one's mistress or one's friend, is beneath them. But to nail oneself for three or four years to a keyboard in order to attain in the end to the glory of being one of a "concert", to be seated between two violins and a bass viol from the Opéra, and to hammer out, by hook or by crook, a few accompaniments which no one will hear: such is their lofty ambition. . . . This infatuation for accompanying is a consequence of the Italian taste.[3]

In Italy nothing is sung without accompaniment.

The art of playing figured bass correctly was not one for the many, and the result of this change of taste was that there was an increase in the number of performers unable to cope with it. For them, music where the keyboard part was written out and enjoyed a measure of independence satisfied a need.

The event to which these manifestations were, so to speak, the prelude was the appearance, about 1734, of the Opus III of Cassanéa de Mondonville. Thirty to forty years ago this work was unknown and I had the good fortune to pick up Walsh's edition of it upon a Cambridge bookstall for a few pence. Now it is comparatively well known and exists in a modern edition; in fact one of its sonatas has been twice published.[4]

Mondonville's six sonatas are written for harpsichord and violin. They are not violin sonatas, either in Bach's or in the nineteenth-century sense, for each instrument has its own part and each plays, on

---

[1] (163), III, 149.

[2] *Oiseau Lyre* edition, pp. 96, 97, 101.

[3] (83), II, 104–106.

[4] Once by Marc Pincherle (*Revue Française de Musicologie*) and once by Ed. Reeser in the supplement to (215).

the whole, continuously; but they are not polyphonic and their idiom is thoroughly modern, announcing at times the *galant* period. They are in the Italian mould of three movements; the first sonata, which opens with a Lullian overture, is the only one which resembles the French suite. The sixth is an imitation concerto, in which *tutti* passages for both instruments alternate with *soli* where one instrument acts as *ripieno* and the other as solo. Musically, these two sonatas are the most interesting; the value of the middle four is mainly historical.

> For the first time, the two associated instruments express themselves with equal interest in two different tongues. The violin tempers the boldness it showed in sonatas accompanied by the mere thoroughbass; the harpsichord raises itself to the plane of the sonata without giving up the volubility, the light and brilliant shine of its solo pieces.[1]

Mondonville showed himself conscious of the novelty of his work and was apparently pleased with the reception it got, since the preface of his Opus V spoke of the "favourable welcome with which the public honoured my first book of harpsichord pieces with violin accompaniment".

Opus V comprises harpsichord pieces "with a part that can be sung by a soprano voice or played on a violin. I considered this plan would interest particularly those who combine the talent of the clavecinist with that of the singer, since they would be able to perform this kind of music". La Laurencie likens them to little solo motets.

After 1734 harpsichord pieces with accompaniment became almost common. About the same time as Rameau's "trios" there appeared Michel Corrette's *Sonates pour le clavecin avec accompagnement de violon*, in which he warned fiddlers that "il faut que le violon joue à demi jeu".[2] This indication is enough to show that the balance established by Mondonville was already broken. In 1745 Guillemain published his Opus XIII, a volume of harpsichord sonatas to which he added a violin accompaniment "to conform to present-day taste"; this was not his original intention, he says, as he had "often noticed that the violin covered [the harpsichord] a little too much, which prevents one from hearing the true subject".

A little-known composer, Luc Marchand,[3] organist in ordinary to His Majesty, published in 1748 a volume of *Pièces de clavecin avec accompagnement de violon, hautbois, violoncelle ou viole, divisées en six suites dont les deux dernières sont pour le clavecin seul, dédiées à Mgr. le Duc de Luynes, pair de France, . . . Œuvre Ier.* The dedication

---

[1] (201).

[2] *A demi jeu* or *à demi* is the equivalent of *mezzo piano*.

[3] Not mentioned by Fétis, Eitner, La Laurencie, Grove, Pincherle or Reeser. Eitner attributes his Opus I to Louis Marchand, the organist, and Écorcheville's catalogue follows him. Riemann has a short entry on him.

emphasizes that it is the composer's first venture. The works are suites, not sonatas, varying from three long movements to eleven short ones. The first begins with a Lullian overture. The accompaniment in the first is for violin; in the second, a Hunt, for hautboy ("because this rustic instrument is suitable for a hunt") or violin; in the third and fourth for 'cello. In the first suite, especially in the fugal part of the overture and *La Mystérieuse*, the violin part is indispensable; in *Le Carillon du Parnasse* it is required for the sonority though not for the harmony. The hautboy in *La Chasse* is nearly as irreplaceable. A note says that the two 'cello suites can be played without accompaniment but the musette, which is in canon between 'cello and harpsichord, would be sadly diminished by the omission.

Although the sixth suite is marked "sans accompagnement", its final movement, a series of variations on *Les Folies françaises*, with the surprising instruction *douloureusement*, has a 'cello part which confines itself to keeping the theme going through the seven variations. In the last one the hands cross alternately in arpeggios of sixteenths and thirty-seconds against held notes on the accompanying instrument; the composer obviously considered that the visual splendour of the performance outweighed its auditory appeal since he called this variation *Le Spectacle des Mains*. Many of the shorter pieces have charm. Two of them show the influence of Rameau: the musette in E major, 3/4, already mentioned, and *Les Titans*, in D minor, 2/4, reflections of the *Musette* and *Les Cyclopes* in the same keys and time-signatures; the latter has the same kind of hand crossings and overstrung Alberti basses, extending to tenths and elevenths, as Rameau's piece.

We have overstepped the year in which Rameau's "trios" appeared, but it was worth while showing that they are members of a once fairly large family. The pieces are grouped in suites; four out of five have three movements, all in the major or minor mode of the same key. Contrast of tempo is not marked with any regularity and there is no reason, except that of key, why a piece should be in one suite rather than another. Only in the fifth does one feel some emotional coherence between the movements.

Rameau wrote a preface in which he explained that the success of recent sonatas which had appeared as harpsichord pieces with a violin had encouraged him to publish similar pieces. He uses the terms "concert" and "concertant", and his remark that he has published his music in score "so that the three instruments may blend and the 'concertants' hear each other, and especially that violin and viol may adapt themselves to the clavecin, distinguishing what is accompaniment from what is part of the subject, in order to play more softly in the former case" does not suggest that he considered the stringed instruments as accessories. He gives detailed instructions concerning held notes in the strings, adding: "Curtailed notes should be articulated clearly but very gently; legato ones should be smooth," and ends up, as so often in his writings, with an appeal to taste: "by grasping the spirit of each piece all will be played as it should be".

But the next paragraph destroys this impression with the tell-tale remark: "These pieces when played on the clavecin alone leave nothing to be desired; indeed, one would never suspect that they were capable of any other adornment" (that is, addition).   Yet one fact proves beyond dispute the interdependence of harpsichord and strings; it is that, when Rameau selected five of these pieces and arranged them for keyboard solo, he considerably altered two of them, *La Livri* and *L'Indiscrète*, by substitution or omission.

The fiddler, flautist and 'cellist who is set to sight-read these "accompaniments" may well feel surprise at such a description being given of the part before him.   The term is as good as any other, but in reality no single word other than *concerts* suits the relation between them and the keyboard.

The manner of combination is not the same in all sixteen movements.   In some the relation between the two groups results in a situation that may be called symphonic.   In the first minuet, for instance, and most of the second, keyboard and strings share the harmonies, the strings in long notes, the harpsichord in slow arpeggios that climb up from the bass with each bar or fill in the middle parts. In *La Boucon*, the first few bars of the keyboard part, when played as a solo, sound complete and it seems impossible that additional parts could do more than enrich the sonority.   Yet Rameau has added to this already substantial music an expressive treble voice for the violin (ex. 7) which turns out to be the middle voice of the keyboard part

Ex.7

transposed an octave higher.   There is here an analogy with the skill with which, in the operas, the vocal part appears to hover and settle on an already self-sufficient orchestral score; if I had to say what his harpsichord music had learnt from his dramatic experience, I would point to such a passage as an answer.

In the episodes of *La Livri* and *La Timide*, particularly in the

F sharp minor episode in the second rondeau, there is a more subtle mode of combination, made up of short contrasted wisps and broad orchestral masses.[1] This is found also in the episodes of *L'Indiscrète* and in the haunting opening of the second minuet, but here the antiphonal character is more strongly marked.

The least satisfactory form of this kind of union is when the strings double the harpsichord part, but they never do so for long.

There is also a good deal of straightforward accompanying in which one is subordinated to the other. The strings have a subordinate role, for instance, in *Le Vézinet*, which is a self-contained harpsichord piece where they punctuate with a rhythmical figure or sustain with minims, after the manner of solo passages in concertos. Much of *La Forqueray* is in the same style. In the refrains of *La Livri*, *L'Indiscrète* and the first rondeau of *La Timide*, the tables are turned and it is the harpsichord that accompanies. But what accompaniment! Rameau considered it as such, since in the two arrangements which he made of *La Livri*, one for harpsichord solo, the other for orchestra in *Zoroastre*,[2] he discarded it, keeping only the viol part as the bass. Yet if the pianist plays his part alone, it leaps into significance and one scarcely feels that it calls for a melodic comment, so rich is its harmony and stirring its cross rhythms (ex. 8).

Ex. 8

In the refrain of *L'Indiscrète* broken chords of five semiquavers to the beat in the harpsichord accompany the strings as they curl in thirds and sixths; the string parts are all that Rameau retained in his solo arrangement. In *La Timide* the keyboard part is weirdly evocative, but when severed from the strings it resembles a beautiful torso without a head; in the solo version Rameau uses only the string parts. Finally, in *La Cupis*, the harpsichord part, although of great beauty and apparently self-supporting, does not once touch the melodic material which passes to and fro between violin and viol.

In quite half the pieces we find passages of true concerted writing. In movements like *La Laborde*, *L'Agaçante* and *La Rameau* there are themes of short, melodic phrases, capable of imitative treatment and of

---

[1] But in *La Timide*, even in the episodes, there persists in both rondeaux the impression of the violin crowning the clavier part that is so strong in the refrains.

[2] As a gavotte in III, 7.

variation. In such passages there is exchange of figures, as between solo and orchestra in a concerto, rapid succession of union and interplay, and, in the *Tambourins*, canonic entries that engage all three protagonists. *La La Poplinière*, musically a somewhat uninteresting piece, is fascinating for the study of variety in combination; there is a little doubling, some piano runs in thirty-seconds with punctuating semiquavers or *tenuti* in the strings, and imitation of short motifs. Nothing lasts long in this whimsical movement, and one kind of writing ousts the other almost as soon as it has been employed as one affection expelled another in the financier's flighty heart.

Finally, there are a few stretches that resemble solo concertos, though obviously, in such small movements, they do not last long. I have mentioned *Le Vézinet*, which is almost entirely in this style.

Ex. 9

In *La Forqueray* we have the nearest approach to the *tutti* and solo alternation of the real concerto, which Mondonville had reproduced in his Opus III, 6. There are two solo sections, separated by a brief *tutti* close. The solo passage work in them has for its background a variety of accompaniments: punctuating quavers and crotchets on the beat or in syncopation, figures derived from the first or second half of the opening theme (exs. 9 and 10). (These quotations are paralleled by passages in the concertos of Philip-Emmanuel Bach.) We have here a glimpse of what Rameau's many-sided genius might have produced in an environment favourable to keyboard concerto writing.

The actual keyboard style, while reminiscent of the solo *recueils*, shows features that are new. Broad registration, already so marked, is present in several "trios": in *La Laborde* where the hands play far apart, and *L'Agaçante*, where they carry themselves in harness from one part of the keyboard to the other. This is taken to the extreme in

Ex.10

the second *La Timide* where three and a half octaves are covered within one bar.

The runs in triplets of *Les Tourbillons* are present in *La Laborde*.

The uneven arpeggios of *La Forqueray* show a breaking down of the more regular figuration of the earlier *recueils*. The importance of scale passages in *Le Vézinet* is a modern feature, Italian and of vocal origin, that looks forward to the *galant* age. The only earlier instance in Rameau was in the *Gavotte* with variations.

Hand crossing of various sorts is frequent: in *La Coulicam* and *Le Vézinet* (where it recalls *Les Trois Mains*), and in *La Rameau*, where it resembles *L'Égyptienne*. A new form of crossing, of the hand-over-hand variety, not found in the solos, appears in the second *La Timide*, where the movement is downward (ex. 11) and *La For-queray*, where diversity of keyboard figuration is greatest.

There occurs, much more often than in the solo pieces, a form of *batterie* by no means peculiar to Rameau but best known to-day through him. More easily illustrated than described, it is used in the *Allemande* and *Gavotte* (fourth *double*) of the third book and in

Ex. 11

L'Égyptienne. Here, Rameau has introduced it into *La Coulicam, Le Vézinet, La La Poplinière* and *La Forqueray*; it is in this last piece that it is used most generously (ex. 12).

In the "Alberti treble" figuration in *Le Vézinet,* unparalleled in the solos, combined with crossings, we may see a reflection of the harpsichord concerto.

Ex.12

The "trios" show an increase in orchestral writing. The short passages in sixths, divided between both hands, in *L'Enharmonique,* were representatives of violin writing frequent in opera; they occur here in *L'Agaçante* and *La Boucon;* in the latter piece they are dotted and remind one of many an elegiac solo in the operas.[1] The passages in thirds in *La Timide* also enter into this category. Orchestral, too, is the occasional use of heavy chords, as in *La Boucon* and *La Pantomime,* before or at the return of the opening, and in the remarkable dissonances in *La Timide* (ex. 11). Previous instances were either descriptive, as in the *Musette* and *Tambourin* of the 1724 *recueil,* or expressive, as in the climax of *La Poule;* in the former, too, the effect is orchestral.

In *Les Cyclopes* and in three pieces of the third *recueil* there appeared another orchestral feature: namely, scale rushes in small notes just before a close. This is common in the *Pièces en concert.*

---

[1] E.g. *Castor et Pollux,* IV, 1.

At least half a dozen show them in either harpsichord or instruments, generally in both.

The majority of the trios are in binary form. *La Laborde* introduces new material after the double bar, in the fashion of a *development* section, and *La Rameau*, like a classical sonata, repeats three-quarters of the first part in the second. At first sight, one would place *La Pantomime* in this category, but on closer examination this turns out to be a genuine sonata-form movement, with a thematic *development* of seventeen bars and a recapitulation in which the "first subject", originally given out with one finger, returns apparently *forte*, with full chording. There is even a recognizable "second subject". It is not surprising that the almost contemporary overture of *Dardanus* should show clearly the element of contrasted themes, so important in later sonata form.

There are two *da capo* movements, both dances, and four rondeaux. Each of these last has two episodes; formally, the most interesting is *L'Indiscrète* where the second episode, in G minor, is a free reproduction of the first which, like the rest of the movement, is in B flat.

La Forqueray is structurally the most impressive piece in the *recueil*. It is through-composed, a fact denoted by the title *fugue*; a fugue in the Bachian sense it certainly is not.[1] It has indeed a subject, given out in D minor by each instrument in turn; when this is done, the harpsichord takes charge and there opens a solo of twelve bars, some of it passage work, some of it sequences of the first two bars, and leading to the relative major. Here, all three instruments join in a short cadence like a *tutti*. The following thirty-seven bars are a second solo passage, consisting in the uneven arpeggios mentioned, in further sequences of the opening bars, hand-over-hand effects and broadly spread arpeggios. With some modulation this brings us back to D minor and leads to an imposing pedal, with violin diminutions in which the harpsichord joins.[2] In the *tutti* coda arise further imitations of the theme and sustaining minims. Although the movement is so homogeneous it allows of a repeat and it gains by being played twice, since there is disparity between the breadth of its conception and its short duration.

Although some of these pieces are among the rarest things that Rameau wrote, the general level of this last volume of instrumental works is perhaps not quite as high as that of the *recueils* of 1724 and 1727–1730. *La Laborde*, *La La Poplinière*, *La Rameau* and *L'Agaçante* are all interesting for technical reasons, but the first two are nevertheless prosaic. *La Rameau* makes great play with the common

---

[1] For Rameau's definition of this word, cf. Chapter 3, p. 77.

[2] When the flute is used it should play an octave higher and attack *ff* the high A and the arpeggios that follow.

chord in arpeggios; pianistically and also structurally it is akin to
L'Égyptienne, with the arpeggios the other way about.   But the key
of B flat and its chord are too heavily emphasized.   The key successions are massive and regular; everything is inexorably and mechanically derived from the opening bar.[1]   It is like a frozen replica of the
earlier piece, with none of the "lyrisme furieux".   *L'Agaçante* shows
plenty of interesting interplay between the instruments and there are
extended endings which give it a certain spaciousness; there is also
opposition of registers; yet one feels that it deserves only too well its
title, in a sense that Rameau never intended.   The composer thought
well enough of it to use it again in *Zoroastre* (II, 4).   *La Coulicam*,
one of the driest of these pieces, has a certain humour, and its beginning with the first and second inversions of the common chord gives
it an air of its own; it reflects a mock bellicosity with drum-taps and
fanfares in keeping with its title.[2]   *Le Vézinet* has a self-conscious,
rather mechanical regularity which makes it pleasanter to play than
to hear.   *L'Indiscrète* is in the mood of many a Couperin *genre* piece.
A truer Rameau note is heard in the loure, *La Pantomime*, very close
to the loures in the operas.   The *Tambourins* belong to the rhythmical
and percussive category of that family of dances; they are less genial
than many of Rameau's but he found place for the first in *Castor et
Pollux* (prologue) and for both in the 1744 version of *Dardanus* (III,
5).   *La Marais* is a straightforward, melodious D major piece that
runs like clockwork without a break from beginning to end.   In fact,
the impression of mechanism is present in more than one of these
movements.

The remaining six are the masterpieces.   *La Forqueray* is Rameau's
most sustained instrumental work.   It was written as an epithalamium
for his friend, the viol composer and player Jean-Baptiste Forqueray,[2]
who had married in March of 1741, the year in which the *Pièces en
concert* appeared.   The swinging octaves and downward scale are
surely meant to symbolize the wedding peal, and the bell-like effects of
much of the keyboard writing must have the same significance.   It
sounds like a later expression of *Les Cyclopes*; stiffer but still vigorous
and large-limbed; less diverse, less warm-hearted, more concentrated.
The difference between them is that between the ages at which they
were composed: forty and nearly sixty.   Each piece is characterized
by its opening.   The bare octave of *La Forqueray* carries its striding
gait through almost every bar, in solo or accompaniment.   The piece
has discarded the episodes which enriched *Les Cyclopes* like a man
advancing in years who throws off unessentials.

La Boucon resembles in spirit some of Rameau's sarabands and

---

[1] This may be intentional.   Cf. Appendix B: *Titles*.
[2] See Appendix B: *Titles*.

still more the pathetic monologues with which so many of his acts open. It is elegiac, with a touch of passion, and each half works up to a gentle climax. Here, as in a few other of the pieces that bear people's names, it is permissible to see a portrait; the original was an amiable and distinguished harpsichord player who became Mme de Mondonville.[1]

La Livri, with its heavy accompaniment, is duskier and near to tragedy. It is, indeed, a *tombeau*; the Comte de Livri, whom it commemorates,[2] had died in July of the same year. Its funereal character is obvious, and the cross-rhythmed accompaniment seems to represent the tolling of deep bells. Each couplet brings a degree of relief which is each time dispelled by relapse into the darkness of the refrain. It is like a rewriting of the early A minor *Gavotte* in the first book. The melodic lines of the two refrains are very similar, and also the contour of the first couplets; the likeness is close again in the progressions in the last bars of the second couplets. It is unlikely that Rameau still remembered the piece he had written thirty-five years earlier; rather have we an instance of an artist's mind travelling unconsciously over a field covered once before and affording thereby an illustration of his growth. The personality is unmistakably the same, but it is slenderer in the earlier piece, stronger and more manifold in the later.

Rameau's minuets are of many kinds. Those of the *Pièces en concert* are dreamers, with sustained harmonies, held notes and slow tempo. The first is more tranquil; the second more poignant; Rameau used it again in *Les Fêtes de Polymnie* (I, 4). The touching figure

Ex.13

(ex. 13) occurs more than once in his music.[3] These movements sound best with the flute, which brings out their orchestral quality.

La Cupis is also a dreaming piece[4] which was to fit perfectly into a pastoral *divertissement* in the prologue of *Le Temple de la Gloire*. Its most poignant moment comes in the bars, laden with swinging thirds, just before the close of each part; they recall the end of *L'Égyptienne* and announce Castor's air in the fourth act of his opera.

---

[1] Cf. Appendix B: *Titles*. [2] Cf. also Chapter 13, p. 477.
[3] E.g., in the saraband in III, 5, of *La Princesse de Navarre*.
[4] Perhaps a *berceuse*. Cf. Appendix B: *Titles*.

La Timide is perhaps the most haunting of this group.   It belongs to a large family of A minor pieces in French music of this period, to which also Bach's English suite in this key is spiritually related.[1] Terms of comparison are not hard to find.   There is one in Michel Blavet's *Les Tendres Badinages* in his *La Bouget* flute sonata.   There is another in Destouches's *Les Élements*, in the solo and chorus "Vole à nos voix" (1st Entrée), which has the same wavy runs in thirds and sixths.   Familiarity with these and other similar pieces enables one to assess what is common property in *La Timide* and what is Rameau's own.   The A major rondeau has a remarkable second couplet with harmonic clashes not found elsewhere in his keyboard music (ex. 11). In both rondeaux the flute is preferable to the violin.

Rameau allows for a violin or a flute.[2]   He also allows for a second violin instead of a viol, but this combination is a *pis aller* and should be avoided as it entails gaps in the harmony and makes the treble top-heavy.   A choice of instruments limited to two is less generous than in many contemporary works, yet it still seems too broad.   Neither *La Coulicam* nor *La Rameau* is really playable on the flute, and Rameau's fine sense of orchestral colour appears for once to have abandoned him.   But we must remember that the eighteenth century was, even more than ours, the age of transcriptions and arrangements.   On one hand, treatises laid down the character that belonged to each instrument, that the musette was guileless and rustic, the German flute tender and sad, the hautboy merry and suitable to rustic revels, with a tender yet martial tone.   These judgments date from 1668.[3]   A hundred and twenty years later the flute is still tender, the hautboy still merry, the trumpet warlike and the horn sonorous and majestic.[4]   For Grétry, the bassoon is lugubrious, to be used in the pathetic; it is meaningless to use it for merriment; the clarinet suits the expression of sorrow, the hautboy is rustic and merry, the flute tender and amorous.[5]   On the other hand, instruments and voices are substituted for each other without compunction.   Gouy

---

[1] The keyboard writing in Bach's prelude is unmistakably French. There is a passage (bars 36–39) close to some in *La Poule* (bars 13–14 and later) and closer still to one in the second *double* of Dandrieu's *L'Hymen* (bars 17–20; cf. Durand, *Les clavecinistes français*, II, 25).

[2] "Flûte", at this date, need it be said, always means "flûte traversière" or German flute.   These *Pièces* are *not* recorder music.

[3] Abbé Michel de Pure: *Idée des spectacles anciens et nouveaux*, 1668.

[4] Marchand, 1783.

[5] Grétry on the clarinet is worth quoting: "It is less pathetic than the bassoon.   When it plays *airs gais* it mingles with them a shade of sadness. If one danced in prison I would like it to be done to the sound of the clarinet."

(1650) replaces voices by viols. Morin says that in his *Chasse au Cerf* hautboys and violins may replace horns and trumpets. Couperin's *Pièces croisées pour clavecin à deux claviers* are "propres à deux flûtes ou hautbois, deux violons, deux violes, et autres instruments à l'unisson". In a *bruit de guerre* by Freillon-Poncin we read: "On peut exécuter le commencement avec toutes sortes d'instruments."

Corelli's sonatas are arranged for the flute. Roland Marais introduces his viol pieces with the announcement that he has endeavoured "à rendre ces pièces propres à être exécutées sur toutes sortes d'instruments comme l'orgue, le théorbe, le luth, le violon, la flûte traversière et surtout le clavecin". Mondonville prefaces his Opus V with the statement that "les personnes qui jouent du clavecin et n'ont point de voix peuvent faire exécuter la partie du chant par un violon". Geminiani arranges his concerti grossi for harpsichord, Blainville does the same with Tartini's sonatas; Locatelli treats his own in the same way. Chabanon was of the opinion that

> there does not exist a truly beautiful instrumental piece that cannot be suited to the voice by adding words. Duets, trios, harpsichord pieces, everything can be arranged with words provided the music has character. . . . Thus we consider that the beginning of the *Stabat* [presumably Pergolese's], sung in chorus and *pianissimo* beside Castor's tomb, would be most suitable.

The breach between theory and practice in this respect is complete and no one seems to mind![1]

The following pieces from Rameau's harpsichord solos and trios were used in his operas:

In *Les Indes galantes*: Act IV, Sc. 6: *Les Sauvages*.

In *Castor et Pollux*: prologue, Sc. 2: 1st minuet (third book): 1st tambourin (*Pièces en concert*).

In *Les Fêtes d'Hébé*: Act II, Sc. 5: *L'Entretien des Muses* (1st half).
    Act III, Sc. 7: *Musette*; *Tambourin* (2nd book).

---

[1] (118).—Vol. III of the *O.C.* contains an arrangement of the *Pièces en concert* for string sextet, to which is added a sixth suite made up of a few harpsichord pieces. This arrangement is preserved in a manuscript from the Decroix collection and is contemporary with Rameau, but it is impossible to believe that the composer had a hand in it. The arrangement is done crudely and with little sensibility for the new medium. When Rameau arranged his harpsichord solos or trios for orchestra he proceeded very differently. The *pièces* which fare least badly are those, like *La Boucon*, which are most like string writing in their original form. These so-called sextets have been recorded by the Hewitt Chamber Orchestra for the Discophiles Français.

In *Dardanus* (1739): Act III, Sc. 3: *Les Niais de Sologne*.

    (1744): Act III, Sc. 5: *Tambourins* (*Pièces en concert*).

In *Les Fêtes de Polymnie*: Act I, Sc. 4: 2nd minuet (*Pièces en concert*).

In *Le Temple de la Gloire*: prologue, Sc. 2: *La Cupis*.

In *Zoroastre*: Act I, Sc. 3: *Les Tendres Plaintes*.

    Act II, Sc. 4: *L'Agaçante*.

    Act III, Sc. 7: Saraband (third book); *La Livri* (as a gavotte).

3. Cantatas and Motets

CANTATAS

THE most far-reaching occurrence in the musical history of the seventeenth and eighteenth centuries is the invasion of all European lands by Italian art. Germany was conquered first, towards 1650; Spain and England succumbed soon after 1700; in France the operation was completed in the years following the Bouffons' performance of *La Serva padrona* in 1752. But, though France gave in last, for more than a century Italian music had been known, admired, attacked and imitated there. No water-tight compartment between the art of the two countries had ever existed, and the music of the peninsula was crossing the Alps all through the seventeenth century. Between 1645 and 1662 several Italian operas were performed in Paris. Frenchmen travelling in Italy acquired a liking, sometimes an enthusiasm, for its music.

One of the most influential of these travellers was M. de Nyert, a nobleman in the suite of the ambassador Créquy, who went to Rome in 1635 and was enraptured by performances of the Barberini opera. His sentiments are given us by Maugars, according to whom he considered Italian singing more expressive, more supple and *nuancé* than French, and he determined to "fit the Italian method with the French".[1] Seconded by the King, he trained two musicians, Bénigne de Bacilly and Michel Lambert, Lulli's future father-in-law, who in their turn trained many more singers. Nyert's attempt to reconcile and combine the two styles is one of many such, the total effect of which was to bring French music closer and closer to Italian.[2]

When Cavalli's *Le Nozze di Peleo e di Teti* was given in Paris in 1654 French artists took subordinate parts, whereas there seem to have been none able to do so in Rossi's *Orfeo* seven years earlier. Italian airs figure largely in Lulli's ballets between 1654 and 1659, although only few Italians sang in them; many French artists were therefore familiar with Italian music at this time. Some had been trained by Nyert or his pupils.[3]

---

[1] (214), xliv–xlv.
[2] It was to him that La Fontaine addressed his *Épître* on opera (1677).
[3] (214), 181.

There is plenty of evidence of enthusiasm for Italian music, or for French music based on Italian models, in the earlier years of Louis XIV's reign. Correspondence between Canon René Ouvrard, choir-master of the Sainte-Chapelle in Paris, and Abbé Nicaise of Dijon, discloses the existence of an interesting circle of Italian devotees. Nicaise corresponded with several Italian composers and went to call on them.[1] Ouvrard had come back from Rome all aflame for Carissimi's music. He was at work from 1663 to 1667 on a "guerre en musique", taken from the story of the Maccabees, in the manner of Carissimi's *Istorie sacre*. He kept in touch with what went on in Rome. He was dismayed when in 1666 the king, at Lulli's instigation, disbanded his little troupe of Italian singers. He possessed a large collection of Italian works which used to pass round his circle. Two other members of it were Dijonnais and one, Maleteste, a councillor of the Parlement of Burgundy, was later to hold weekly concerts of Italian music in his house.[2]

Marc-Antoine Charpentier, who had gone to Rome a painter and returned a musician, was composing cantatas in the Italian style from 1680 onwards for the private concerts of the Princesse de Guise, using up to a dozen singers, with a small band of viols, recorders and flutes.[3] He was a follower of Carissimi, whose music he made known in France. Towards 1680, also, Italian influence, at any rate in church music, was strengthened by the presence in Paris of Paolo Lorenzani and a few Italian singers whom he brought with him into the royal choir.

Another private centre of Italian fervour was the house of Abbé Mathieu, curé of St. André-des-Arts.

> D'un pieux amateur le zèle curieux
> Dans la France attira des motets précieux,
> Qui traçant à nos chants une route nouvelle
> A nos auteurs naissants serviront de modèle.
> D'ouvrages renommés il forma son concert,
> De tous les connaisseurs il fut l'asile ouvert.[4]

M. Mathieu, for several years in the last half-century, had given weekly concerts in his house where was sung only Latin music composed in Italy by the great masters who have shone there since 1650 such as Luigi Rossi, Cavalli, Cassati, Carissimi in Rome, Legrenzi at Venice,

---

[1] Abbé Nicaise was a tuft-hunter by correspondence and a collector of letters from persons distinguished by scholarship or standing. Lombard (179) calls him "the unpaid correspondent of the Europe of learning and the go-between of seekers and enquirers". His epitaph by La Monnoye dubs him "le facteur du Parnasse". The authors of *Ménagiana* say that "it is through him that we learn all that is new in the Republic of Letters, and not only in that realm but at Rome, Florence and elsewhere in Italy as well" (1st edit., 234; in (179), 9).

[2] (214), 313–314.   [3] (133).   [4] (109) 30.

Colonna at Bologna, Alessandro Melani in Rome, Stradella at Genoa and Bassani at Ferrara; he had had more than thirty works printed.[1]

From 1703 on, the collections of *Airs sérieux et à boire* which Ballard published monthly began to include tunes by Carissimi, Bassani, Alessandro Scarlatti and Buononcini.

Jean-Baptiste Rousseau was the first French poet to write librettos for cantatas. Charpentier's works were not printed and the earliest French cantatas to be published were those of J. B. Morin,[2] produced by Ballard in 1706 and 1707, and of Battistin, in 1706.[3] Many more followed: Bernier, who had also lived in Rome,[4] Clérambault,[5] Campra,[6] Elisabeth de la Guerre, Moreau, Destouches, Montéclair, Courbois, and others less well-known. The fashion lasted till about 1740.

"A great deal of France likes and admires the music of the Italians," Le Cerf wrote regretfully in 1705. "There are not only professional musicians but persons of quality and prelates who sing and have performed in their houses nothing but Italian pieces and sonatas."[7]

An anonymous writer in 1713 said:

> Cantatas and sonatas spring up here beneath one's feet; no musician turns up without one in his pocket; none but wishes to be engraved and claims to attack the Italians and spike their guns; poets can hardly keep up with them; . . . in a word, we are smothered with cantatas.[8]

The degree of imitation in all these works varies considerably. Charpentier was by nature an Italianate composer; others were merely copyists. Morin's *L'Aurore*, with its dancing 12/8 rhythm, is thoroughly Italian; several of Campra's sound "Handelian", that is, Buononcinian; but Clérambault's approximate to French opera: his *Médée*, *Orphée* and *Polyphème* might be excerpts from dramatic works. His *Léandre et Héro* and *Alphée et Aréthuse*, though less operatic, are also quite French.

The keenest supporters of Italian music in Louis Quatorzian

---

[1] (110), 112, note.

[2] Il osa le premier exposer la Cantate;
A ce nouvel aspect tout Paris révolté
Sembla frémir d'abord de sa témérité ((109), 34).

[3] Giambattista Stuck, a Florentine of German parentage settled in France.

[4] Rome révère en lui l'ornement de la France,
La France admire en lui l'italique science;
Sous sa main ces deux goûts semblent se réunir
Et par lui la querelle est prête de finir ((109), 34).

[5] Par de lugubres sons Clérambault aux lieux sombres
Attendrit savamment le souverain des ombres ((109), 34).

[6] Born in Aix of a Piedmontese father and a Provençal mother.

[7] (83), I, 44.　　　　　[8] (82).

France were the musicians themselves, professionals and cultured amateurs, except of course the Italian Lulli, whose reasons for excluding his countrymen did not arise from æsthetic principles. Thus, Maugars, violist and translator of Bacon,[1] approved of Italian liberty when it was not excessive and blamed the obstinacy of French composers, who ought "to free themselves from their pedantic rules and journey abroad to observe foreign forms of music".

The opposition came from the conservative, moderately musical general public that "knew what it liked" and was not disposed to admit what had not been familiar in its youth. A certain amount of national pride also entered into this attitude, but this must have been secondary, otherwise it would surely have weighed also with the professionals.

Discussions about the characters and merits of French and Italian music, singers and accompanists, provide a literature that lasts for over a century. The earliest comparison *en règle* is perhaps in Maugars, but polemics do not break out till 1659. Perrin's letter in that year to the archbishop of Turin has an offensive-defensive tone which is significant. He claims for France the right to a purely French music. He enumerates the defects of Italian operas, criticizes their "styles de musique moitié chantants, moitié récitants, qu'ils ont appelés représentatifs, racontatifs, récitatifs", which are like those "plainsong and cloister ditties, . . . so ridiculous and boring that they have deserved the curses which have been showered upon them".[2]

Perrin dislikes Italian music's

> fine sallies which fall so easily into extravagance, its affected and too frequent thunderings, and the licences with which it is laden which, according to their ardent and passionate temperament, express passions admirably, but to our colder and less excitable one sounds like a music of the housetops (*une musique de gouttières*; that is, caterwauling).

Cats and plainsong! No terms of abuse were too strong for such music.

We have seen that Lulli inserted many Italian airs in his early ballets. In one of these, *Le Ballet de la Raillerie* (1659), there occurs an amusing dialogue between French and Italian music in which each disputant sings in his language and to his own style of music.[3]

By the time that the quarrel of the Ancients and the Moderns broke

---

[1] (87).

[2] In (189).—It is curious to find levelled against Italian music by a Frenchman the terrible accusation: "like plainsong", which the pro-Italian Grimm was to bring against French music a century later: "*Atys*, tragedy by the immortal Quinault, set to music, or rather to plainsong, by Lulli" ((71), December 1753).

[3] (189); (214), app.

out Lulli had become one of the glories of Louis le Grand's reign and as such was inevitably approved of by the Moderns. Perrault's *Siècle de Louis le Grand* registers this approval. But at the same time those who were opposed to what was Italian and novel took on the appearance of opponents of the Moderns, and by degrees we find an equivalence establishing itself between Modern and pro-Italian on the one hand and Ancient and Lullist on the other. François de Callières[1] stages a dialogue in the underworld between Orpheus and an Italian musician which is a full-dress criticism of French opera, compared to Italian, and contains several remarks which were to be repeated later. The identification is complete in the title of a *Duo sur la musique ancienne et moderne*[2] where "ancienne" means French *brunettes* and operas, and "modern" Italian cantatas and sonatas.

> Rengaînez vos brunettes,
> Vieux renards à lunettes,
> Amateurs d'opéras,
> N'en êtes-vous point las?
>
> Ecoutez nos cantates
> Ainsi que nos sonates . . .
> Si cela n'est pas beau
> Au moins c'est du nouveau.

The opposition came to a head at the turn of the century and produced a work that ought to rank as a literary classic. In 1697 a Norman priest, François Raguenet, went to Rome in the company of a prelate and spent a year there. He had published an *Histoire de l'Ancien Testament*, an "histoire persane", *Syroës et Mirame*, and biographies of Cromwell[3] and Turenne, the latter of which was to enjoy over forty editions between the year of its appearance and 1883. He was also an archæologist, and his stay in Rome inspired several volumes on that city's monuments and works of art. And it fired him with much more inflammatory designs.

While in the Eternal City he attended the opera and as a result was filled with enthusiasm for the form as he found it in Italy. He expressed his feelings in glowing terms in a small book which he published soon after his return in 1702, *Parallèle des Italiens et des Français en ce qui regarde la musique et les opéras*.[4] The work is somewhat breathless and is not well written; though fault-finding, it is not critical. But the writer's fervour carries the reader along. He did not praise everything in Roman opera and he sought to disarm his opponents by beginning with a list of features in which he considered Lullian opera superior, but the merits of the Italian were more

---

[1] (45), (1689).　　　　[2] (27), 194–195; quoted by (183), 347.

[3] In which, said James II, there were only two true statements, that he was born and that he died. See (83), I, 5.

[4] An English translation was published in 1709. See (95).

numerous than those of the French. It should be remembered that when he was writing, Parisian opera was in a trough; Lulli had died some ten years before and the generation of Campra and Destouches was only just appearing; it seemed that the great founder was to have no descendants.

Raguenet's book acted as a spark which set fire to the anti-Italian musical feeling latent in the land, and two years later a fellow-Norman answered with a much bigger work, the *Comparaison de la musique italienne et de la musique française.* The author, Jean-Laurent Le Cerf de la Viéville, was a young Rouen magistrate born in 1674, and his work is the result of discussions that must have gone on for a long time in musical circles in his province and elsewhere. A second volume appeared in 1705 and that same year Raguenet answered with a *Défense du Parallèle.* A third volume was brought out in 1706, but the author's death in 1707 prevented the writing of a promised fourth part.[1]

Raguenet's book is more than a pamphlet but belongs solely to the field of the dispute with which it is associated. Le Cerf's work is a much vaster undertaking. Both works have suffered from being represented, over and over again, by a small number of quotations, always the same, which give the reader of histories of music the impression that he knows all about their contents without ever having read them. This impression is not so misleading for Raguenet's, which is nevertheless worth running through, but to Le Cerf's it is profoundly unjust.

The *Comparaison* is made up of a number of parts, some of which are in conversation form while others are essays. The style is clearly that of one personality and, though Le Cerf's name appears on no volume nor in any of the editions of 1721, 1725 and 1726, and though in 1743 they were republished, for the last time, together with an *Histoire de la musique depuis son origine jusqu'à présent,* under the name of Bourdelot (who had died in 1685), his authorship was never questioned in the eighteenth century and has been proved again recently by Robert Wangermée.[2] Raguenet, in his reply, calls the author a Norman nobleman, and the *Journal de Trévoux* for November 1704 gives his name: "Mr. de la Vieuville de Fréneuse, garde du sceau de la chancellerie de Normandie." It was partly plagiarized in 1732 by Nicolas Grandval who, in his *Essai sur le bon goût en musique,* abridged Le Cerf's dialogues and put them into letter form.

The speakers are three: one conservative, one rather violently pro-Italian, and the third, a woman, supposed to be impartial and to represent refined, non-technical common sense, but really in alliance with the first. The preface raises the work above the level of controversy and of a mere retort to Raguenet; it regrets that, though there

---

[1] See (155E).   [2] (239).

are plenty of "traités de mécanique et d'artisan" on music, there is no treatise on the beauties of the art—in other terms, no æsthetics of the subject.

This is not the place to present and sum up this long work. I want mainly to draw attention to its riches. It belongs in its dialogue parts to the genre of the *galant* conversation on specialized topics which Fontenelle is thought to have inaugurated with the *Entretiens sur la Pluralité des Mondes*, but, though *enjoué* and non-technical, there is much less of the *galant* about it than in Fontenelle's book. Le Cerf knew that his theme interested many *honnêtes gens* and he had no need to gild his pill and render it palatable with the ingratiating titivations which make Fontenelle's *Entretiens* so irritating.

Le Cerf gives us his observations and criticisms on private music-making, singing, instrumental performance, compositions and com-posers, the importance of staging and machinery; on the popularity of operatic tunes with the common people.[1] The setting of the first conversations, during an interval between two acts of Campra's *Tan-crède*, provides a glimpse of the opera house[2]; another conversation, which takes place during a walk by the Seine, is preceded by a remark-able description of the city and surroundings of Rouen.[3] There are deeper moments when the speakers attempt to go to the root of musical experience and to relate it to life in general and to the need all creatures feel for love.[4] He defines the purpose of sacred music and examines to what extent such music in France and Italy fulfils this purpose; he speaks of the organization of French choirs, of church singers, and of the reforms he deems desirable; of the prevalence of Scripture reading in France and its value for sacred music[5]; and of much else of cultural

---

[1] "The tunes of our operas" have come down among the lower orders; they were first heard from gentlefolk, then sung for a long time and univer-sally, then "learnt from those who frequent them, who have taught them to others, whence in the long run they have reached shop lads and barmaids. ... When I heard the air from *Amadis*: 'Amour, que veux-tu de moi?' sung by every cook in France I had the right to think that this air was already sure of the approval of everyone in France from the princess to the cook, that it delighted equally ignorant and learned; I concluded that it must be very beautiful, quite in keeping with nature, very full of true expression, to have moved so many different hearts and flattered so many different ears" ((83), II, 328).

[2] Thus we learn that patrons took candles with them in order to follow the libretto.

[3] (83), II, 146–148.

[4] (83), II, 157–159.—Écorcheville first drew attention to this in his splen-did and, alas! unobtainable *De Lulli à Rameau* (142), 131.

[5] "Scripture is more venerable and more familiar with us" than with the Italians "and I think we are obliged for this to the Huguenots. ... The prolonged intercourse and frequent disputes we have had with them have

and social interest.   It is a work that overflows the bounds of a merely historico-musical appeal and presents the views on many matters of a representative man and of his circle.   It is written in an urbane, witty and varied style and is emphatically worthy of a place in "literature".[1] Le Cerf was indeed conscious of his command of the language and more than once found fault with Raguenet for his violation of French grammar and usage, putting him right, for instance, when he wrote "Grande-Bretagne" and reminding him that this is one of the cases in which "grand" remains invariable.   He should be available in a modern edition, for his value transcends the limits of that branch of scholarship to which knowledge of it is at present confined.

Le Cerf de la Viéville is himself on the side of the Ancients and conservatives.   He finds fault with Perrault on various grounds, mostly non-musical; he also has a grudge against Fontenelle, because as censor appointed to examine Raguenet's book he had commended it in too flattering terms.   But though his opinions are decided he writes without bitterness or bigotry and is always *de bonne compagnie*.

He keeps most of his severity for pro-Italian Frenchmen.

> What success have those of our masters had who were the zealous admirers and ardent imitators of the Italian manner of composing? Where has it led them?   To write pieces which the public and time have declared pitiable.   What has the learned Charpentier left to keep his memory green?   *Médée, Saul et Jonathas*.   It would have been better to have left nothing at all.[2]

Elsewhere he calls this musician, whom we are coming to look upon, with Lalande, as the greatest French composer of the century, "dur, sec et guindé".[3]

Charpentier was the particular bugbear of the Lullists.   Séré de Rieux makes his Damis complain that he

> Répandit dans *Médée* avec trop d'abondance
> Les charmes déplacés d'une haute science.[4]

Campra, Brossard and Bernier are viewed with disfavour; they "copy" the Italians.

---

brought about that France is, of all Catholic countries, that where the taste for Scripture is most widespread.   It is loved, it is known; its simplicity penetrates us. . . .   Our musicians have followed this praiseworthy taste. They usually work on psalms, on passages chosen from the Bible, on hymns of the Church.   Such is the method of Dumont, Campra, Bernier, etc." ((83), III, 122–123).

[1] Some of his comparisons are amusing.   A *brunette* by Lambert is a bouquet of violets; an air of Lulli's a bouquet of jessamine; an Italian air is a large (*gros*) bouquet of tuberoses ((83), II, 304–305).

[2] (83), II, 347.   [3] (83), III, 138.   [4] (109), 18.

"Bernier's duets and trios are unpleasantly marked with the stamp of Italy"[1]

(he is speaking of his sacred music). Students of Couperin know how earnestly this affable master preached conciliation by word and by note. Le Cerf will have none of such eirenianism. Lochon announces some *Nouveaux Motets dans le goût français-italien*; Le Cerf dubs this title "a sign of ill-omen".

An appeal to authority had been made by Raguenet in his *Défense*. The authority was musico-aristocratic since it was none other than the Duke of Orléans, the future Regent, a pupil of Charpentier, an enthusiastic Italophil and a composer, to boot, whose opera *Penthée*, with words by his friend La Fare, had been performed privately in his apartments at the Palais Royal. Le Cerf was able to counter proudly: "Le Roi est pour nous." Louis XIV, who had flirted with Italian music in his youth but had been weaned from this vicious taste by Lulli, was by then too old to change and remained faithful to the loves of his middle age and to his old favourite.[2]

Animadversions on Italian singing by Frenchmen, and on French singing by Italians, were of long standing. Père Castel was echoing an ancient opinion when he wrote in 1735: "The French find Italian music too vivacious, too quick, too full of licence and caprice, confused and ill-articulated."[3]

Séré de Rieux's Damis complains of "Ces éclats bondissants, ces hoquets, ces passages".[4] This author, like Lochon and Couperin, was a peacemaker and asked his readers not to cultivate exclusive tastes. "All that is essentially good in music must appear such to all sensible nations."[5] He reminded them that Italian music was not generally heard in France to its full advantage. He regretted that the French

> . . . Sur un rebut d'airs dans Paris mal chantés
> Jugent impunément de toutes ses beautés.
> Mais est-ce par des airs que dans Rome on abhorre
> Qu'on doit se prévenir sur un goût qu'on ignore?[6]

He defends those whom Damis and Le Cerf attack: Charpentier, "Neuvièmes et tritons brillèrent sous sa main", he says approvingly; Brossard, "De sons diminués Brossard formant ses basses . . ."; Lalande, who had learnt orchestral brilliance from the Italians without being stigmatized as an imitator:

> Ses violons brillants enchâssés dans ses airs
> Font éclore à propos mille dessins légers;

---

[1] (83), III, 163.　　　　[2] (83), II, 348–351.
[3] (49), (1622).　　　[4] (109), 19.　　　[5] (110), 300.
[6] (109), 26.—Président de Brosses says that one never hears the real Italian vocal music in France.

Campra and Bernier.[1] He takes the offensive in his turn, repeating oft-made criticisms.   French opera music is monotonous.

> Entre les mouvements la ressemblance est grande:
> Tout air est menuet, gavotte ou sarabande.[2]

Michel Lambert's tunes, once so popular, now seem dull.

> Et malgré son recueil que Ballard vendit cher
> Phoebus a décidé qu'il n'avait fait qu'un air.[3]

As we look back on these interminable wrangles, we realize that it is not the musicians but the half-musical who are so violently one thing or the other.   The same will be true in 1734 and again in 1752. It was not merely that Italian music was unfamiliar or capricious, unruly, unpredictable; that its singers hiccuped and its violins ran the tight-rope.   It was also that it *meant* nothing.   These semi-musical diehard partisans of Lulli were the reverse of pure musicians; the music they liked could be, nay, had to be, referred to something outside itself; it expressed a definite sentiment, it painted a situation, phenomenon, object.   The vagaries of pure music were held in check by Lulli, and in the opera he created there was little room for it since every note was referable to a word or a gesture.   It was the intrusion of unfettered, un-*riservata* music, with the unloosing of the dark powers of imagination and enthusiasm which it connoted, that alarmed the Le Cerfs and the Damises and provoked them to that best form of defence, attack.

The alleged complexity and learnedness of Italian music was another source of objection.   The accusation can be understood only if we remember our dates.   It is Lulli and Cavalli who are being opposed, Dumont and Carissimi, Michel Lambert and Alessandro Scarlatti (to take absurd extremes).   In their time simplicity and popularness were indeed on the side of France.   Le Cerf's cooks could all sing: "Amour, que veux-tu de moi?"[4]: they could not have hummed: "Son tutta duolo" or "Se Florindo è fedele".   But with time the two kinds of music exchanged places and qualities.   French music under Italian schooling became more complex and more learned. No one was more responsible for the change than Rameau, as his contemporaries recognized, to blame or to approve.

---

[1] And Handel: "Sa composition infiniment sage et gracieuse semble s'approcher de notre goût plus qu'aucune autre" ((110), 300).

[2] (109), 30.

[3] (110), 66.   Also Raguenet: "The Italians find that our music rocks them and sends them to sleep; even that it is to their taste most flat and insipid."

[4] They could also be edified to it.   Abbé Pellegrin set new words to it: "*Contre le péché en général*, sur l'air d'*Amadis*: 'Amour, que veux-tu de moi?'"

It is to M. Rameau that we owe this mongrel kind which passes
to-day in France for Italian music; a veritable flickering; no agreement
of the tune with the words nor of the airs with the situations of the
characters. . . . Am I fated to hear nothing but this foreign, hateful,
baroque, inhuman music?[1]

M. Rameau is impugned for what deserves our admiration. . . . His
music is neither purely French nor purely Italian. It has the graces and
gentleness of the one without its monotony; the depth and genius of
the other without reeking of learning.[2]

And as French music grew in a sense more aristocratic (for Lulli's
cook-simplicity is a plebeian trait), more remote from the common
people, so Italian music became simpler. Yet in France the old
reproach survived long after it had ceased to be relevant. "Les
Italiens prétendent que notre mélodie est plate et sans aucun chant;
. . . de notre côté nous accusons la leur d'être bizarre et baroque."[3]
Then, suddenly, the simplest and least learned of its masterpieces,
Pergolese's *La Serva padrona*, bursts upon the semi-musical plain man
of the Parisian *grand public*. Its triumph with him is absolute.
Henceforth he is an Ultramontane.

A consideration of Rameau's non-operatic vocal music should
begin with the mention of a bucolic duet or *duo paysan* which was
included in the number for February 1707 of the collection of *Airs
sérieux et à boire* brought out by Ballard month by month from 1695
to 1724. It belongs to a well-defined genre and sets verse in dialect
in which two peasants threaten a certain Lucas whose amorous attempts trespass upon the ground of one of the singers.[4] It is perhaps
fanciful to seek clear signs of Rameau's hand in so conventional a
piece; nevertheless a robustness, a sense of gesture, a racy humour
which make the little piece lively are qualities unmistakably, though
not exclusively, his own. The thoroughbass follows the bass voice
till it comes to the words:

> Pour nous gausser de ly
> Tapons sur sa bedaine,

when it assumes independence to illustrate in repeated notes, and
finally in bars of falling scales, the action of the stick on Lucas'
corporation.

The issue for November 1719 contains the canon *Avec du vin* which
was printed in the *Traité de l'Harmonie* three years later.[5] But by
that time Rameau had probably composed his earliest cantatas and
motets.

The third volume of the *Œuvres complètes* contains eight cantatas.

---

[1] (34a), V, 166.   [2] (69), II (1749), 246–247.
[3] (102) (1754).   [4] (184).   [5] (1), 362.

One of these, *Diane et Actéon*, is by Bodin de Boismortier.   Of the remaining seven, two—*Le Berger fidèle* and *Aquilon et Orithie*—were published between 1731 and 1736; the second of these[1] and a third, *Thétis*, are mentioned in Rameau's letter to La Motte of October 25, 1727, as proofs of his competence to write an opera.   Three others, *Les Amants trahis*, *L'Impatience* and *Orphée*, are almost certainly authentic; Maret mentions the second as having been composed at Clermont, and all three survive in copies from the Decroix gift with Rameau's name; the date of 1721 appears on the first and third.   Maret speaks of two others, *Médée* and *L'Absence*, which dated from Clermont; Decroix was unable to trace them when he made his collection and they are lost.   Finally *La Musette*, also included in the Decroix gift, bears neither name nor date and is more than doubtful.

If we expect to find in Rameau's cantatas those very personal characteristics that make his mature work so unique we shall be disappointed.   They are emphatically first-period works.   The composer shows himself fully master of his art; there is no fumbling, no awkwardness; the skill is fully possessed but the personality is absent. If we could come to them without knowing his greater compositions —and this holds good to some extent for his sacred music—we should find them more attractive than we generally do, for they contain sturdy, well-knit stuff, more absolute and less emotionally interpretative of its text than the operas and ballets.   Considered as pure music they are satisfying.   Their qualities are formal: strength, vigour, balance, directness and clarity.   They give the same kind and degree of enjoyment as Vivaldi's concertos with which they are contemporary.   Their chief drawback is that they tell us nothing of Rameau and little of French music.   Indeed, they are remarkably Italian, far more so than his dramatic music.   This is, of course, understandable since the genre inherited no French tradition; yet it seems strange that Rameau, whose work is rightly looked upon as the highest embodiment of the French classical style, with marked Italian intrusions, should have begun his career as a vocal composer of so Italian a character.

The earliest are probably *Aquilon et Orithie* and *Thétis*, of which Rameau says to La Motte that he wrote them "a dozen years ago". They must, on this count, have been composed in Lyons or in the first months of his stay in Clermont.   Of *L'Impatience*, Maret says that it was composed in Clermont, together with the lost *Médée* and *L'Absence*. They might thus be dated between 1702 and 1706, the approximate years of his first appointment there, but it seems more likely that the latter stay is meant; this would give about 1720 as the year of their composition.   *Orphée* and *Les Amants trahis* bear the date 1721 on the

---

[1] Called *L'Enlèvement d'Orithie* in his letter.

copies that have preserved them for us, so that they cannot be later than that year; how much earlier they may be we do not know, since the date is that of the copy, not necessarily of the original. The cantata whose date is best authenticated is *Le Berger fidèle*, which was performed at a concert in the autumn of 1728 when the *Mercure* of November 22 described it as a "cantate nouvelle".

It would be fanciful to see a progressive development from one work to the other. The least distinguished is perhaps *L'Impatience*, which might be a reason for assigning it to the earlier Clermont period, whereas *Le Berger fidèle* is not only the most interesting and the most French but also the only one in which we perceive an unmistakably Ramellian note.

Except for *Les Amants trahis*, which is for bass and counter-tenor, they are all solo works, with the accompaniment of harpsichord and tenor viol, and sometimes of one or two violins. In three of them the viol part is independent and in *L'Impatience* it plays *obbligato* in *concertante* style. Concerto-like writing for the viol occurs also in *Les Amants trahis* and *Orphée*; this latter is the most fully instrumented and the only one with independent parts for both violin and viol in the same air. *Le Berger fidèle* is the only one to use two violins. They all retain the character of the chamber cantata.

In two of Damon's airs in *Les Amants trahis* and in two of the three airs of *L'Impatience* the viol is treated in a concerto style familiar to us mainly through certain solos of Bach's cantatas and Passions. Though the Italianate *ariettes* inserted in his operas contain many instances of the *obbligato* use of violin and flute, nowhere else does Rameau treat thus the viol or the 'cello. The two airs in *L'Impatience*, particularly, are for him unusual examples of absolute writing; the interest in them is mainly musical and the setting bears little relationship to the words. The pleasure they afford is that of a concerto (ex. 14).

Orphée has in its text the making of a drama and it is the only cantata where dramatic intentions are evident: the middle section is in a free, declamatory style, with almost orchestral descriptive writing for violin and viol. But it is of little musical interest and the *air gai* which succeeds brutally the hero's loss of Eurydice is a heartless anticlimax. *Aquilon et Orithie* has one splendid fury air on a rising scale theme with a brilliant violin part,

> Servez mes feux à votre tour,
> Force indomptable, affreuse rage,

and a tender E minor one with occasional violin concerto figures. Rameau's formal qualities are well marked in *Thétis*, which is heralded by a slow prelude of thirty-two bars with dotted rhythm and rushes of thirty-seconds like an opera overture—quite imposing, in spite of

Ex.14

its miniature scoring.   Though the cantata is for solo bass two characters are impersonated, Neptune and Jupiter, and to each is given an air.   Both of these numbers are vigorous and spacious, but Jupiter's, with a *ritornello* of twenty-eight bars, is the more interesting, not only in itself but because it announces the "Tombez, tombez" chorus of *Castor et Pollux*, III, 4 (ex. 15).   In his letter to La Motte, Rameau

Ex.15

pointed out that both airs expressed anger, but with more passion in Neptune and more self-control in Jupiter.   In the tender concluding air, where an anonymous singer adjures Thetis to disregard her noisy suitors and make her own choice, a French and more personal Rameau is discernible.

A completely personal Rameau is present in the opening recitative and air of *Le Berger fidèle* (ex. 16).   This is more than the *ébauche*

of many an elegiac or tragic 3/4 air in the operas; it is a realization
worthy to stand beside them and the earliest member of the family to
which belong Castor's "Séjour de l'éternelle paix", Iphise's "Cesse,
cruelle Amour", Sapho's "Bois chéri des amours", Memphis' "Veille,
Amour", Délie's "Ah! qu'il est doux de pardonner"[1] and others.

It is followed by the most charming and mature of the Italianate
solos in this group of works, "L'amour qui règne dans votre âme",
which Rameau rated highly enough to use again eleven years later in
the third *entrée* of *Les Fêtes d'Hébé*.   It has an urbanity and a *souplesse* absent from the imitations of *Italianità* in the earlier cantatas.
The final air has an accompaniment for two violins which sounds like
concerto writing of the Leclair period.

All these works are written to serious themes.   I have left to the
last consideration of the one comic cantata, *Les Amants trahis*.   This,
the longest of the six, stages two lovers who have been betrayed by

their mistresses and react, one with tears, the other with sarcasm.
Tircis' opening lament sounds pathetic enough, but the mocking
intent becomes clear in the course of the duet "Ma bergère a trahi sa
foi", in which each character draws the emotional conclusion from
this statement, Tircis to weep, Damon to laugh (ex. 17).   In Damon's
"Lorsque malgré son inconstance" the Alberti figures of the *obbligato*
viol announce, then echo, his laughter; here the concerto writing is
well integrated with the dramatic conception.   A second duet opposes

---

[1] *Castor et Pollux*, IV, 1; *Dardanus*, I, 1; *Les Fêtes d'Hébé*, I, 1; *Les
Fêtes de l'Hymen*, II, 3; *Acante et Céphise*, II, 4.

the two swains by giving Tircis crotchets and Damon quaver triplets, a device probably borrowed from *opera buffa* (ex. 18). The jaunty figures of the viol again emphasize Damon's levity; they suggest that the singer indulges in capers when his voice is not engaged.

Musically the most attractive piece is yet another solo of Damon's, "Du dieu d'amour je prends tous les feux". I own that I am sensitive only to the musical qualities of this number and fail to detect the connexion that is intended between the viol's haunting undulations and Damon's fickleness. I realize that the delightful wavy figure must be meant to express mutability, but its formal loveliness banishes all suggestions of cynical behaviour.   This number, with "Faut-il qu'Amaryllis périsse?", is the crowning achievement of these youthful works (ex. 19).   The music rises to a passionate climax, not demanded by the words, in much the same way as *La Poule*, a few years later, was to start from a seemingly frivolous conception and similarly to

Ex.19

brush close to tragedy before it closed.   The passage in the cantata is too long to quote and too closely knit to be split up.   Some dozen bars from the end we hear a first hint of a strain in the Musette chorus, "Suivez les lois".[1]   Who would not prefer such a brand of faithlessness to Tircis' moist-eyed fidelity?

---

[1] *Les Fêtes d'Hébé*, III; at the words "On fait un choix".

In a closing duet Tircis is won over to Damon's side and joins him in vocalizing "Ri-i-ons"; the heroes achieve unanimity and the music ceases to be interesting.

These products of Rameau's first period are, therefore, worthy of attention, even though they pale beside the works of his years after fifty or beside the harpsichord pieces that are their younger contemporaries. If *Le Berger fidèle* is really the only one that could give La Motte, or anyone else, a convincing idea of what Rameau might do were a serious libretto put into his hands, *Les Amants trahis* is a rare product of that comic side of his genius that was to flower a quarter of a century later in *Platée*.

MOTETS

Till recent times we did not think of France as a country with a strong choral tradition. Little French choral music, apart from Gounod, was known over here and French choir singing was regarded with disapproval. Yet sacred music, solo and choral, was abundant there in the later seventeenth and eighteenth centuries. The number of distinguished organists and the output of music for church usage, especially motets, was prodigious. Several thousand survive, many of which are anonymous,[1] and many more must be lost. As late as 1764 a German visitor little inclined to praise anything French, Leopold Mozart, commented on the excellence of the singing in the Chapel Royal at Versailles.[2] The larger churches must have spent much money on their choirs, and the enjoyment of endowments made this possible. The economic foundation of this musical activity was wiped out by the Revolution, and in the comparatively few churches that opened after the storm[3] the tradition was not re-established. Tasteful and lively choral execution in France is a reconquest of the present century.

In 1700, when Rameau was reaching his formative years, the prevailing form of sacred music was the unliturgical motet. The word is much older than the form as it existed at this time, and it would be clearer to translate it by "anthem", in the sense of Anglican church music, since our anthem was its English counterpart. Though performed during a service, either mass or Benediction of the Blessed Sacrament, it was not liturgical since its words were not part of the service but were superimposed on the formal worship which went on while it was being sung or was interrupted till it was finished. At

---

[1] Charpentier alone wrote more than a hundred.

[2] Letter of February 1–3, 1764, to Frau Hagenauer.

[3] In Paris alone one hundred and thirty churches and chapels were destroyed between 1799 and 1860. See (128), 10.

its fullest it was a kind of small oratorio, with recitatives, solos, duets and choruses, marked with a strong dramatic cast, setting Latin words taken from Scripture, generally from the Psalms.   The influence of Carissimi, through Dumont and still more through Marc-Antoine Charpentier, as well as directly, predominates in the late-seventeenth-century French motet; later it yields to that of Buononcini.

The opposition between old and new, between French and Italian, was felt also here, though less violently than in secular music.   That champion of tradition, Le Cerf de la Viéville, has a lively and informative essay on church music in his *Comparaison*.   He goes at once to the heart of the matter and asks what the motet sets out to be and to achieve.   All it really does is "to lend the sounds of music to some-one speaking in church, and the perfection of these sounds will needs consist in being suitable to him to whom they are lent".[1]

Adapting Quintilian he asks the questions: *Quis, quid, ubi, quibus auxiliis, cur, quomodo* and *quando*.

Who is speaking?   A Christiãn.

What sentiments is he uttering?   Those of a sinful wretch, "now happy, now sad, according to the more or less hope which he has of winning the grace he needs".

Where?   "In a fane full of the majesty of an eternal and infinite Being."

By what means?   Sacred words.

Why?   To ask for graces.

How?   With fervour and respect.

When?   On a solemn feast day "which gives us the right to hope that we shall be heard".

What and *when* are variable circumstances; the others are fixed.

It is usual to dwell on the growing secularization of sacred music throughout the two centuries that followed the introduction of monody.

> The secularization of church music during the seventeenth century was not an isolated phenomenon but a part of the drift of European culture from the church to the stage.[2]
>
> It is usual to-day to proclaim that sacred music of the seventeenth and eighteenth centuries, contrasted with that of the Middle Ages and the Renaissance, bears no character of religious feeling.   It is considered theatrical, rhetorical and declamatory, incapable of satisfying the impulses of mysticism or even the needs of merely pious souls.[3]

But the identification of sacred with secular music was far from being as close in 1700 as it was three-quarters of a century later. Contemporaries felt strongly the difference between the two and the suitability of maintaining that difference.   Church music, says Le Cerf,

---

[1] (83), III, 38–39.   [2] (193), 146.   [3] (127), 83–84.

must be "vraie, juste", therefore "dévote". Sacred music in the theatre would be hissed; theatre music in church is worthy of contempt. The same opinion is expressed by Mably some forty years later. "The music of our motets is quite different from that of our operas and a piece we admire with Latin words would be supremely ridiculous with French ones."[1] Church music, says Le Cerf, must be "expressive, simple, pleasing"; so, no doubt, should secular music; but the former should be more expressive and less pleasing ("agréable") than the latter.[2]

Le Cerf debates the obvious importance of relating sound to sense. Should the musician be content with rendering the general sentiment of the work, or section of the work, that he is setting, or should he apply himself to describing details and single words? This problem was not confined to sacred music; it exercised also composers and critics of opera. In general, the critics seem to prefer the first alternative, while the composers, Rameau included, do not disdain the latter, while also complying with the former.

Le Cerf comes down emphatically in favour of rendering "the general meaning of the words" rather than "the particular expression of each line, of each word".[3] The composer should resist the temptation to paint a rushing river or the sound of thunder each time he meets *fluvius* and *fulgur* in his text. He ridicules a fugue of the Rouen organist Lesueur upon the words "Flagellum non appropinquabit" "which made a prolonged and piercing noise representing the clicking of fifty scourges". He cites as another ridiculous instance Campra's *Lauda Jerusalem Dominum*, where the words "ante faciem frigoris ejus" are set to music recalling the shiverers in Lulli's opera *Isis*.[4]

Abbé Dubos is of the same opinion. Though he is against what we call pure music he deprecates excessive interpretation of single words as, for instance, in the "De torrente in via bibet" of Psalm 110, where musicians

> cling solely to expressing the swiftness of the torrent instead of rendering the sense of the verse which contains a prophecy of Jesus Christ's Passion. Yet the expression of a word can never touch us as much as that of a sentiment unless the word contains only a sentiment. If the musician concedes something to the expression of a word which is only a part of a phrase, he must do so without losing sight of the general sense of the phrase he is setting.[5]

This point of æsthetics is not, of course, confined to French music and has been much discussed with reference to Bach.

In matters of practice Le Cerf is as conservative as in choice of

---

[1] (84), 139. [2] (83), III, 60. [3] (83), III, 68.
[4] (83), III, 135. [5] (64), 657.

music. He is doubtful of the fitness of string instruments for church use. "It is less than twenty years ago that we allowed strings in our choirs and Campra was the first who had enough influence to introduce them into that of Notre-Dame . . . Forty years ago we had in our temples only wind instruments, organs and serpents." It is more grievous still to use operatic singers in church.

> The latest abuse is to bring in actors to execute our motets. Lami, deputy choirmaster at Rouen cathedral, gave up his place because of the grief this caused him. . . . One of them, Antoine, nicknamed Phaéton, was tipsy when singing a lesson at Tenebrae in Rouen cathedral. . . . The Church excommunicates actors and yet she engages them to sing in her temples! Actresses, too, are engaged

to sing a lesson on Good Friday or a motet on Easter Day. "They are placed behind a curtain which they draw back from time to time to smile to listeners whom they know. In their honour the price paid at the door of the Opéra is paid for a seat in church."[1]

Some are even clapped in church.[2] After this we are not surprised to hear him own he is sensitive to the beauty of plainsong and would like to hear no other music at Tenebrae.

His general judgment on French sacred music is that it is "neither long enough to tire our attention, nor involved enough to absorb it entirely, nor playful enough to amuse it".[3]

He implies that Italian sacred music is all these regrettable things.

The fourth and fifth volumes of the *Œuvres complètes* of Rameau contain five motets: *Laboravi, In convertendo, Quam dilecta, Deus noster refugium* and *Diligam te*. Of these only the first two can adduce external evidence of Rameau's authorship; *Laboravi* was printed in the *Traité de l'Harmonie* and *In convertendo* exists in an autograph manuscript. The next two have been preserved in eighteenth-century copies which belonged to Decroix. The fifth exists in a

---

[1] (83), III, 178–188.

[2] La Bruyère's ironic account of a "beau Salut" is well known and chimes in with Le Cerf's complaints.

"Shall I declare what I think of what society calls a 'fine Benediction' [of the Blessed Sacrament]: the often secular setting, the seats booked and paid for, the librettos [of the motets] handed out as at the theatre, the frequent meetings and assignations, the babble of murmurs and conversation, someone on a platform speaking unceremoniously and drily, with no zeal except for bringing the people together and amusing it until an orchestra, nay, voices that have long been rehearsing make themselves heard?" ((77), Chapter XIV).

[3] (83), III, 200.

manuscript copy which belonged to Le Gros, who was conductor of the Concerts Spirituels in the 'seventies; a hand different from the copyist's has written on it: "Motet à grands choeurs par M. Rameau."

The third and fourth figure also in the catalogue of the library of the Académie des Beaux-Arts of Lyons. The academy was founded in 1713 and *Deus noster refugium* bears the number eleven, which places its acquisition early in the society's life and certainly not after 1715. A few years later *In convertendo* was purchased and *Quam dilecta* a little later still. The library, now long dispersed, possessed, without acquisition number, another motet of Rameau's, *Exultet coelum laudibus*, which has vanished. All four works are attributed to our composer in the catalogue and as he lived in Lyons from 1713 to 1715 there can be no doubt of their authenticity.[1]

There is really no external evidence that *Diligam te* is by him, and everything in it points to a date after the middle of the century. It is an attractive work and has a charming gavotte movement, *Cum sancto sanctus eris*, but the style is almost *galant* and shows no Ramellian characteristics. The attribution to him was probably made quite arbitrarily by someone in the Bibliothèque Nationale long after his death.

The Bibliothèque Nationale possesses another motet, *Inclina Domine*, which figures under Rameau's name in Écorcheville's catalogue. The manuscript does indeed bear the name Rameau, written in pencil and inked over, but the hand that wrote it is a nineteenth-century one; moreover, the original library number of the manuscript shows that in the oldest catalogue, drawn up by Roualle de Boisgelou in 1787, it was classed among the many anonymous motets that the library possessed. Style and handwriting suggest Rameau's date and if there were good external evidence of its authenticity there is nothing in them to preclude his authorship. The work, which is for barytone solo, is pleasing and the manuscript has some interesting features, but this is not the place to speak of it.

It was in the year of Rameau's birth that Louis XIV appointed Michel de Lalande to be one of the four choirmasters of his Chapel Royal. By the deaths of his colleagues he finally became the only one and in 1689 was made Surintendant de la Musique du Roi. The forty motets which he composed during the forty-odd years that he held this position and which were published after his death had spread far and wide during their composer's lifetime. They were to appear again and again in the Concerts Spirituels throughout the eighteenth century and were performed in many churches, in Paris and the

---

[1] He alludes to his "motets à grands chœurs" at the end of his letter to La Motte. — *Exultet coelum laudibus* was for three solo voices only and *symphonie*; it is the sequence for All Saints' proper to the diocese of Lyons.

provinces, which could muster the resources they required; in some conservative choirs they survived till the middle of the nineteenth century.[1]

In the 'teens of the eighteenth century, when Rameau was writing his church music, it was natural that the figure of Lalande should loom large in the mind of any young French composer of sacred works. Yet one hardly feels his presence in Rameau. Lalande knew the music of the Italians and may have taken from them the *aria concertato* in which one or two instruments *consort* with the voice. But his ancestry is to be found in Dumont rather than in Carissimi. In spite of the favour with which Louis XIV welcomed Lorenzani, Versailles was a stronghold of national art, less open to Italian influences than certain circles in Paris and the provinces.

Campra had been appointed to Notre-Dame one year later than Lalande to Versailles, and most of his religious music was written between that date and his resignation in 1700.[2] An increasingly Italian style is recognizable in his third book of motets, published in 1703, and was commented on severely by the conservative spirits whose opinions Le Cerf was voicing. Bernier's motets were also Italianate and Couperin's church music, like his chamber works, shows a combination of the two styles. It is this new Franco-Italian style, corresponding in church music to the change from Lulli to Campra and Destouches in dramatic music, that is evident in Rameau.

Rameau's few pieces written for the church have been called "undistinguished". If this means that his personality is less emphatically stamped upon them than on his operas and ballets the judgment is just, but the music is by no means dull. He was not devout, and the brand of feeling we associate with worship is one of the few he has never rendered. His temple scenes are solemn and grand but not expressive of awe. But this, though specific, is not the only *affect* required in sacred music of the anthem type.

Laboravi is in one movement and differs from the others in being uninterruptedly contrapuntal.[3] Its text: "Laboravi clamans, raucae factae sunt fauces meae. Defecerunt oculi mei dum spero in Deum meum"[4] is taken from Ps. 69, v. 3. The work was printed by Rameau

---

[1] (127), 112.

[2] In 1722 Lalande's partial retirement caused him to be appointed to a share in the succession and he wrote a few more motets. He was still holding this part-time post when he died, aged eighty-four, in 1744.

[3] Counterpoint, of course, survived longest in church music. Blainville says this happened "because the vast space whence we hear this musical mass, allowing the heaviness of this coarse *chant* to lose itself in the distance, causes us to hear it with a sort of pleasure" ((37), 97).

[4] "I am weary with crying out, my throat is parched" ("hoarse" in the Vulgate); "mine eyes fail while I wait for my God" (tr. C. Lattey).

in the *Traité de l'Harmonie*[1] to illustrate the chapter on *fugue*, a form
which he defines as consisting in "a certain continuance of melody
which is repeated at will and in whatever voice one wishes but with
more circumspection" than in mere imitation, "according to the
following rules". It is thus a much less strictly defined form than
the fugue we know. Rameau uses the word both for the movement
and for the subjects. Thus: "One may sound several different
fugues" (i.e. subjects) "together or one after the other; but as far as
possible they must not begin on the same beat or in the same key,
especially the first time they are heard."[2]

It is in five parts—two sopranos, two tenors and bass—with
figured bass for organ.[3] The whole text has been given out by the
end of the first third, and the sections into which it breaks up are
heard more or less concurrently until eight bars from the end, when
all join in singing the concluding words. We are far from the homophonic clarity desired by the Florentine reformers; it is as difficult to
recognize what is being sung as in the complex polyphonies of the
Renaissance.[4]

It contains, Rameau points out, four different "fugues", that is,
subjects, illustrating each one a clause in the text. Whether the work
was composed in the first place for performance in Clermont cathedral
or whether it was written as an example of the art of fugue cannot be

Ex. 20

said. Its austerity is undeniable, but austerity is evident in Lalande
and is a not uncommon feature of Louis XIV music, noticeable also
in chamber music and at times even in opera. Austerity, too, is a
characteristic of Rameau himself; it should not be considered as proof
of didactic origin. The music illustrates the chief details of the text
but with great restraint (ex. 20). The weariness of "laboravi" is
barely suggested; there is no attempt to render the hoarseness of

---

[1] Book III, Chapter 44; pp. 341 and ff. [2] (1), 340.

[3] In the *Traité* Rameau writes the *fundamental bass* beneath the apparent
bass.

[4] This motet and the two others published in vocal score have been
transposed down a tone in the edition. The original key is D minor.

"raucae", so tempting a word, nevertheless; the failing in "defecerunt" is expressed merely by a descending scale. It is the longing of "spero" which is depicted most clearly, especially near the end.   The tenor is very even and the style self-denying for such description-evoking words; the only break in the flow and the only dramatic moment is, after the close on F major, the sudden allusion to G minor in the passage back to the tonic (ex. 21).   Under this restraint lies emotional power, and the little piece, as one knows it better, is felt to be alive with a personality as unmistakable as it is unbending.

The three other motets are "à grands chœurs", with soloists, organ and orchestra.   They belong to the form evolved by Dumont, used by Lulli, Lalande and Campra, in which solos, duets, trios, choruses and recitative alternate one with another.   Like opera this form corresponded to the King's personal taste.   It was Louis who had favoured bringing string instruments and women's voices into church, thereby intensifying the trend of devotional music towards theatricality.[1]   The Chapels Royal in Paris and Versailles were the birthplaces of the form.

Deus noster refugium (Ps. 46), the earliest of the three that have survived if we can go by the entry in the Lyons catalogue, is at first sight the most forbidding.   It consists in nine complete numbers; of the tenth, a *récit*, *Vacate et videte*, only the flute part and the bass have been preserved; a note on the Decroix copy says: "On n'a point retrouvé les paroles de ce récit", nor, apparently, the rest of the music. A further note says: "On reprend le chœur *Dominus virtutum* par où finit le motet", which may indicate that the original final chorus is also missing.

Every one of the work's nine numbers is in the key of B flat.   It opens with a solo for counter-tenor accompanied by strings and haut-boys, which is followed by a trio for soprano and bass with strings only, *Propterea non timebimus* ; this latter has little imitative entries and homophonic sections.

The third, a four-part chorus on a large scale, also with strings only, *Sonuerunt et conturbatae sunt aquae*, is the most ambitious number.   It is built like a concerto grosso, with four orchestral *ritornelli* alternating with choral sections.   There is an underlying symmetry in the construction: thus, the first and second *ritornelli*, and again the third and fourth, are separated by short choral sections of some twenty bars each, whilst between the second and third *ritornelli*, themselves quite short, there extends a complex, modulating development of nearly a hundred bars, more than half the movement.   The key system resembles rather that of the later sonata rondo than of sonata form itself; the first chorus leads to the dominant; the second *ritor-*

---

[1] Lulli's *Te Deum* (1677) has not only strings but drums and trumpets.

Ex. 21

nello leads back to the tonic and closes upon it.   After the long middle section the work remains in the tonic, except for a short excursion in the last chorus into C minor.

In the first chorus the whole four parts are in operation, but in the middle section the vocal ensemble is constantly breaking up into passages for one, two or three only of the parts, and the third section also begins with a short duet for sopranos and counter-tenors.   A plan will make this clear.

1st *Ritornello* (or *tutti*).—B flat.   12 bars
1st Chorus.—B flat leading to F major.   18 bars
2nd *Ritornello*.—F major returning at once to B flat.   8 bars
2nd Choral section.—Begins in B flat; then : G minor, B flat, C minor, E flat, G minor, B flat.   95 bars
3rd *Ritornello*.—B flat.   6 bars
3rd Chorus.—C minor, B flat.   21 bars
4th *Ritornello*.—B flat.   11 bars

The long middle section is hinged on the relative minor and is not an unbroken flow of modulation.   The six bars of C minor with which the last chorus opens effect a gradual return to the staid ways of the tonic after the key exploration of the preceding division.   This device resembles the sudden brief modulation which is often found just after the beginning of the recapitulation in later sonata-form movements.

Though the resemblance is so marked with concerto grosso and with the solo concerto of the rondo-concerto type, like those of J. S. and C. P. E. Bach, it would be misleading to see here the influence of the instrumental form, since the development has been in the other direction.

The material of this powerfully articulated movement is simple and consists mainly in two contrasted types of themes.   One, a descending arpeggio of the common chord, is confined to the strings; the other, a series of wavy motifs first heard in the opening *tutti* as a trailer to the first theme, is the stuff out of which most of the choral contribution is compounded.   With unremitting four-square rhythm, the smooth undulatory parts peel off from one another against little percussive calls which save the music from sounding machine-made (ex. 22).   The strings do not completely double the voices but they use the same material, except for the arpeggio theme which is their own; only once, in the closing bars of the passage quoted, do the violins exuberate into a true concerto motif over declamatory pronouncements in the bass.

Though the first impression is one of regularity, even of something mechanical, more patient acquaintance shows it to be alive in every bar. Thus a codal passage which closes the *ritornello* theme and returns

Ex. 22

four times in all shows three different dispositions of the inner parts, even though the harmonization is the same each time. Those who have been nurtured on the most expressive pages of Rameau's dramatic music may feel disappointed at not finding trace here of his melancholy; the only Ramellian detail is an unexpectedly pathetic subdominant ninth in bar 111. But the force with which the movement pushes unrelentingly forward, without hurrying, unfolding without jerks or those awkward links of the type apologetically called "epigrammatic" when found in the great masters, will possess one and compel one's admiration if one does not set out with the idea that it is just conventional Handelianism and has been "done much better" by Handel and Bach.

Sonuerunt et conturbatae sunt aquae shows the sureness and experience of an old hand, and these qualities suggest that Rameau must have written much similar music which has perished; the technique is not that of a "first period". It emphasizes the mystery which shrouds his formation. Before these motets the only work we possess of his is the little harpsichord book of 1706, with which, of course, a chorus like this has nothing in common and from which the secret of its origin can derive no light.

This is the kind of chorus which he tried to have accepted on the stage when he introduced "Que ce rivage retentisse" into *Hippolyte et Aricie*. The mighty ensemble, which seems so unique when one confines one's attention to his operas, is seen to belong to a small but impressive family of contrapuntal choruses of which it is the last. In at least this respect the study of these neglected motets does explain an aspect of his dramatic work.

The tonic arpeggio opening of this chorus was perhaps remembered when he came to set "Aux portes des Enfers" in *Castor et Pollux*. It is interesting to set one beside the other and see in what ways one is dramatic as well as musical, whereas the other is only musical.

The fourth member is a soprano air, *Fluminis impetus laetificat civitatem Dei*, in which an almost constant succession of triplet figures represents the joy while occasional semiquaver rushes downhill evoke the river (ex. 23). The fifth is a bass solo, *Deus in medio ejus*, with imitation between voice and violin and a lot of doubling between vocal and instrumental bass which makes the music sound stiff.

The sixth is a quartet, *Conturbatae sunt, grave*, a not unpleasing curiosity. It is for a quartet of counter-tenor, two tenors and bass, and this dusky ensemble is not lighted up by any treble tones but is accompanied merely by the organ and bass viols, whose part is written in figured bass. The timbre is like that of the sixth Brandenburg, as far as voices and strings can be likened to each other. The writing is contrapuntal throughout, but in a pattern of Rameau's own devising. We begin with a fugal exposition of the following rather didactic

Ex. 23

Flu - mi - nis im - - - pe - tus

les autres Basses et l'Orgue

lae - ti - fi - cat

theme (ex. 24). Then the first tenor gives it out once again and after three homophonic bars of transition to G minor a second theme, expressive of a very stylized earthquake, is heard on each voice in turn, but the entries tread on each other's heels and come at irregular intervals, on D, low G, high G and C (ex. 25). This figure is prolonged by a few bars in one voice only and the first theme re-enters in D minor, with its counter-subject (see ex. 24, bars 6–11). The treatment is freer and the unbending subject is a little modified in some

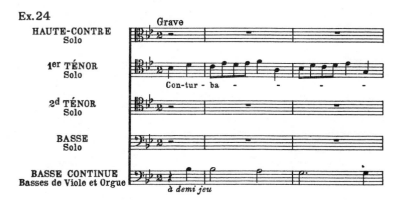

Ex. 24

HAUTE-CONTRE
Solo

1er TÉNOR
Solo

Con-tur - ba - - - -

2d TÉNOR
Solo

BASSE
Solo

BASSE CONTINUE
Basses de Viole et Orgue

Grave

à demi jeu

of its entries. Eventually, in F major, the second theme is heard
again. It is treated in similar fashion to the first and this time it
holds the stage much longer, in fact almost to the end. In the last
bars this austerest of numbers relaxes into expressionism in the form
of *tremolandos*, indicative of quaking, in the lower voices (ex. 26).

Ex.25

This is the kind of movement which one is apt to condemn at sight as an exercise in counterpoint; but this judgment would be superficial. Though extremely static, it is not flat and its sombre colour renders well the menacing words, even though much of it is in the major. Should we not admire, too, that Rameau sets to such sober yet not inexpressive music such impressionistic words: "Conturbatae sunt gentes, inclinata sunt regna, mota est terra"? Think of all the *affective* figures which most composers would have scattered over their score in presence of such a text. But Rameau concentrates on the effect of these terrors instead of doing the obvious and easiest thing: describe them pictorially.

Ex.26

We are not as far as we might think from at least one opera. The spirit of this piece lives again in even more grisly form in the instrumental introduction which was written for the third act of *Hippolyte et Aricie* on the occasion of one of the revivals. A comparison between ex. 24 and the introduction given in Appendix E will show at once the kinship.

The seventh number is another "grand" chorus, *Dominus virtutum nobiscum*. It is straightforward and generally syllabic, with occasional moderately contrapuntal passages. Its most expressive section is the minor one in the second half where we meet again Rameau's subdominant ninth.

Ex. 27

The eighth is quite different. It trips as lightly as a Boucher shepherdess, beckoning to those who would see the wonders God has wrought (ex. 27). It is in *da capo* form and the even measure is kept till near the return when it winsomely breaks step (ex. 28). Here, too, Rameau eschews the tone painting to which he might have been lured by the "prodigia" and "bella" in the text.

Ex. 28

The ninth and last complete number is a duet between tenor and bass on the verse *Arcum conteret et confringet et scuta comburet igni*. Description comes into its own here. Strings and voices clash as they rise and fall against one another, with a pitiless mechanism that befits the words (ex. 29).

Ex.29

This motet is a noble piece, unbending and at times forbidding except in the "Venite" interlude; if it lacks the fervour we expect of church music the psalm which it sets hardly calls for such a sentiment.

Quam dilecta is more genial but on more intimate acquaintance much less satisfying. It is scored for strings, with flutes in four of its seven numbers, and *continuo* in only one of them, a trio. It centres in the key of B minor, with numbers in D and G major and E minor. It is shorter and offers fewer contrasts. The text calls for gentler music: "O how amiable are thy dwellings, thou Lord of Hosts" (Ps. 84)[1]; it speaks of desire and longing, of the sparrow and the turtledove (instead of the A.V. swallow) and their nests, of God's altars, of them that dwell in God's house and put their trust in Him, and of their bliss. Only one number expresses supplication. The music is correspondingly mild, with faint touches of melancholy. Its strains are tender, sometimes *attendrissants*, and cumulatively a little weak.

There are two departures from this pervading gentleness. One is the second number, a chorus in D major on *Cor meum et caro mea exsultaverunt in Deum vivum*, where the *affect* is given by the "exsultaverunt". It is a resourceful contrapuntal piece in five parts, with string accompaniment, but marred by extreme rhythmical regularity, and though there is contrast on paper the prevailing impression is that the impersonally exultant theme (ex. 30) is never absent. The

Ex.30

insistence upon one single sentiment is no doubt intentional, but the movement is too long and too undynamic for the conception to be carried out without loss. This type of movement is highly conventional and we find it still represented some seventy years later in the *Cum sancto Spiritu* fugue of Mozart's C minor mass, which contains this same subject, though not in the place of honour.

The other exceptional number is the sixth, *Domine Deus virtutum*, an air for solo bass. This is the finest in the motet and the only one where the personality of the later Rameau speaks out. Its text is a supplication, its indication *gravement*, and its key E minor. The *ritornello*, with the recollected mood of its opening and lyrical, beseeching strain that rises at the end, reflects the expression of the whole piece. The declamation is of the kind found only in sacred music, but the mood is close to that of many a piece in Rameau's dramatic works (ex. 31).

---

[1] The verses set are 1 to 4, 8, 9, 13.

Ex. 31

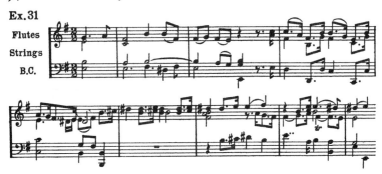

In convertendo[1] was purchased by the Lyons society some years after 1713 and was presumably performed at Lyons. It was revived at the Concerts Spirituels in February and March 1751, during Holy Week, when it seemed old-fashioned and met with nothing but criticism. The *Nouvelles littéraires*, at that time written by Raynal, said that even "Rameau's best friends had to agree that it contained neither brilliant recitatives, nor majestic choruses, nor symphonies, nor images, nor homogeneity".

Mondonville was at the height of his reputation as sacred composer, and Raynal added: "Mondonville has not been dethroned and Rameau's rivalry has but increased the esteem in which his motets are held."[2]

The *Mercure* sought to excuse the failure by saying that the motet was an old work, composed forty years earlier. This takes us back to 1711, which is too far; between thirty and forty would have been a truer statement.

The original scoring was for strings and woodwind; in 1751 horns were substituted for hautboys in *Facti sumus laetantes* ànd added in *Laudate nomen Dei*. Whether the autograph we possess is the original or a copy made for the revival is not certain. The handwriting is characteristic, but as no other musical autographs of the composer exist from this period no conclusion as to date can be drawn from it. The manuscript shows many corrections and pastings-over, especially in the fugue *Tunc repletum est* and the first number which originally began in three-time and was altered to 2/4; under the pasting is preserved an intermediate version.

This is the shortest of the three longer motets and the best. It has the vigour and contrasts of *Deus noster refugium* and many marks

---

[1] Campra had included a setting of this psalm in his third book of motets (1703) "à grand chœur et symphonie". His interpretation of the text differs greatly from Rameau's.

[2] (96), II, 46.

of Rameau's mature personality. It sets verses 1, 2, 4, 5, 6 and 7 of Psalm 126, intercalating between verses 5 and 6 a modified form of Psalm 69, v. 31. The key of all but one number is G (minor or major).

With the opening solo for counter-tenor[1] we are in the presence of the authentic Rameau. This is an almost tragic supplication which reminds one of "Coulez, mes pleurs" in *Zaïs* (III, 3) or of "Fatal amour" in *Pygmalion* (sc. 1); the key and musical sentiment are the same. A modulation (ex. 32) has a terseness more dramatic than

Ex. 32

declamatory which announces similar passages in the operas.[2] This, with the air quoted from *Le Berger fidèle*, is the clearest inkling we have yet had of the future dramatic master.

It leads into a rather pedestrian fugue, *Tunc repletum est*, in six parts, the minor section of which recalls that in *Sonuerunt*; it is interrupted by short *trio* instrumental interludes like those in many operatic triumph-and-dance choruses. The bass solo, *Converte Domine*, in D, is uninteresting. A duet for solo and bass, *Facti sumus laetantes*, with horns *obbligati* (originally hautboys) that amble canonically in triplets, imitating the voices, is somewhat static and always on the point of taking off without ever leaving the ground. *Laudate nomen Dei cum cantico*, for soprano solo and chorus, with horns and strings accompaniment, has a familiar outline[3]; it makes

Ex. 33

great play with a little leap for joy almost each time the words "cum cantico" return (ex. 33).

Qui seminavit is a trio for soprano, tenor and bass, with violins

---

[1] Originally for tenor. The modern vocal score prints "ténor".

[2] Cf. with bars 35 to 39 of "Coulez, mes pleurs" (cf. Chapter 12, pp. 455–456.

[3] Cp. with "Tu veux avoir la préférence" (*Fêtes d'Hébé*, III, 1).

and bass accompaniment (ex. 34).   The number recalls somewhat
Conturbatae sunt, but it is less forbidding, and has no need of weirdness to make an appeal.   Above this theme which, in various forms

Ex. 34

or allusions, never identical, and with varying degrees of exuberance,
is almost constantly present, the voices impose a freely fugal structure
quite independent of the ground.   The text suggests an obvious
contrast: "Qui seminant in lacrimis" and "in exsultatione metent"
(ex. 35) (the example shows the ground at its most extroverted).
This is a resourceful, lively movement, without a dull bar and with
none of the threat of rigidity felt now and again in the two earlier
motets.

The last movement, a five-part chorus with full accompaniment,
is the greatest piece in all Rameau's church music.   At the time it was
composed, towards his thirty-fifth year, it was the most ambitious
piece of music he had produced and it deserves a place among his
finest compositions.

Ex. 35

Its greatness lies in its combination of complex and consistent form and strong yet restrained emotion. Excluding a rather perfunctory coda, its eighty-five bars cover verse 7 of the psalm: "Euntes ibant et flebant, mittentes semina sua. Venientes autem venient cum exsultatione, portantes manipulos suos."[1] The plural of the Vulgate has afforded Rameau an occasion for contrapuntal complexity. The words indicate an obvious division and contrast between the slow-moving weepers and the joyful return, which the music reproduces.

The first part is a fugal exposition with a sombre, cramped theme into which a descending semitone introduces a tremor of light (ex. 36). The line of the counter-subject, to "mittentes semina sua", is a little freer and the exposition grows to animation as the mass swells with the entering voices. An orchestral interlude, with semiquaver scale passages, separates this section from the next and announces the coming liveliness of "venientes . . ."; it ends on D minor with a wavy motif destined to render the joy of "portantes" and, later, of "exsultatione".

The voices then come in with a bright B flat; the brightening in the mode is reflected in the homophony and in the lightening of the vocal and instrumental mass from which the basses are momentarily absent. Hardly have the lower parts re-entered with a rising scale reminiscent of the opening of the interlude when the fugal subject returns in G minor to "euntes" in the trebles, while second tenors and basses continue to rise and fall, with scales and rapid repeated quavers, to "venientes . . . , portantes . . ." (ex. 37). A few bars of C minor,

---

[1] "Who goeth his way weeping, bearing the trail of seed, shall return with glad cries, bearing his sheaves" (tr. C. Lattey).

Ex.36

in which all round off the verse with "mittentes . . .", close this section.

Leaving once more the "euntes" motif, all join in a fresh development of "venientes . . . (descending scales) cum exsultatione, portantes . . ." (wavy motif); this is an expanded and symmetrically inverted repetition of ex. 37; we move from C minor, with a breath of F major, to settle in D minor.

The second half of the number opens with a return of the "euntes" subject in D minor in a kind of *stretto*; it does not linger here and, again with a glance at the major, leads back to the tonic, when the second tenors bring in their waving sheaves of semiquavers before the sopranos have finished singing of tears; indeed, the second basses

The Jesuit Novitiate, Paris, in the seventeenth century

Ex. 37

belatedly emit one last "flebant" to part of the fugue theme when the first basses and tenors have been singing "venient" for a whole bar.

All tears are at length forgotten and for a score of bars the chorus gives itself up to a peroration in which the swirling scales of "venient", the waves of "portantes" and the emphatic statement of "exsultatione" belie the opinion that triumph is not expressible in the minor mode. At one stage the returning captives seem to be throwing up their sheaves into the air with joy and at length the music, which had hitherto resisted the allurements of a conventionally exuberant word and had set it merely to repeated notes, flings itself into two bars of vocalise on the "–o–" of "exsultatione", while four full bars on the "–tan–" of "portantes" bring before our mind's eye a vision of dancing harvesters (ex. 38). How could the writer of the *Nouvelles Littéraires* complain that this superb movement contained no imagery?

Our own taste would be to conclude at this point on the chord of G minor. But this movement resembles so many other grand minor key pieces in which the perverse promptings of a convention-loving imp have led the musician to tack on a commonplace coda in the major. So while we prepare for departure, picking up prayer-book or programme, the music traverses some fifteen bars of G major *allegro* in which orchestra and voices go through the motions of excitement to the familiar wavy motif, some on the "–ta–", some on the "–o–", of the Latin word for rejoicing.

I trust that the examples quoted will have shown that at least some parts of these motets are not "undistinguished". It is undeniable that they do not contain signs of "religious experience", but this does not prevent their best numbers being fine music of an abstract type, in which the words and their sentiments are present as occasions for the music rather than to be interpreted by it. Moreover, it does not make them unsuitable for performance in church. Except for their bulk—an objection which weighs even more against some of Bach's most deeply religious pieces—there is nothing about them which would make them sound incongruous when given during a service. *Quam dilecta*, the least personal and most unobtrusive, is probably the best suited for use at worship; the rather banal *Beati qui habitant* comes to life and fits perfectly into place when sung during Benediction. The polyphonic *Laboravi* makes an excellent Offertory anthem. The voluminous *Sonuerunt* and dramatic *Euntes et ibant* are too autonomous to fit in with our demands in liturgical worship but they are as rightly performed within a church as *The Messiah*, the *Passions* or *The Dream of Gerontius*. Even if they are lacking in fervour, their very gravity, passing so readily into austerity, brings them into sympathy with the emotional climate of a place of worship.

Secular and dramatic as seventeenth- and eighteenth-century music

Ex. 38

is often stated to be, its contemporaries, as we have seen, drew a sharp distinction between what befitted the stage and what the house of God. It is wrong to lump both centuries together and pass on the religious music of the earlier period judgments which are just only for the later, and say that all its music, whatever the words and destination, was equally secular. This may be true of the much maligned and little-known sacred compositions of Mozart and Haydn; it may begin to be true of Mondonville's once popular motets; but it is ludicrously inappropriate when said of Lalande, Couperin, Rameau and their contemporaries.

Laboravi, *Quam dilecta* and *In convertendo* are published in vocal score. The shorter numbers of *Quam dilecta* are the most suitable for performance during or after a service. Their more commonplace character makes them less suitable for the concert hall, whose musical standards are more exacting than those of God's house. *In convertendo* should be heard in concert performance as it stands, in the vocal version which leaves out the weak number, *Converte Domine*. *Deus noster refugium* could be given without numbers 1, 2 and 5. *Laboravi* is equally fitting in church or at a concert.

4. *Lulli's* Tragédie en musique

IT is usual to compare and contrast the opera of Rameau with that of Lulli, using the latter as the known quantity with which to determine the former. This procedure is unhelpful since most people know as little of one as of the other. It is therefore best not to attempt to define Rameau in terms of Lulli. French opera between 1730 and 1760, in its chief forms of *tragédie en musique, pastorale héroique* and *opéra-ballet,* is autonomous enough to be studied in its own right, without an account of its previous history. Nevertheless, as some of my readers might think I was shirking my duty if I began in 1733 with *Hippolyte et Aricie* and ignored the earlier years, I will outline briefly the course of its development before that moment.

The first opera in France deserving of the name—that is, which is not more ballet and display than drama—is Lulli's *Cadmus et Hermione* performed in 1673. Lulli or his librettist Quinault called it a *tragédie en musique.* It arose neither as a spontaneous growth like the post-Florentine school of Italian opera, nor as a direct imitation of the Italian forms. It was a deliberate creation, borrowing certain features from Italian opera as it existed in 1650–1660 and also incorporating other elements. These latter may be classified as ballet, spectacle, pastoral and tragedy.[1]

Though there was in France a long tradition of ballet we need not go back further than the 'seventies of the sixteenth century when the poet Baïf founded an academy of music and poetry which, among other aims, aspired to revive the drama of classical Antiquity. It performed ballets in which scenes of declamation alternated with songs and dances carried out by the chorus. "The dramatic ballet owes its origin to the performance of these classical fantasies at a court fête."[2]

In 1581, under the influence of Baïf's attempts, an Italian ballet master, Baldassarino di Belgiojoso, who had come to France in the 'fifties and had Frenchified his name into Beaujoyeulx, produced a ballet which is a landmark in the history of the form: *Circé,* also known as *Le Ballet comique de la Reine*—"comique" because associated with a comedy.

"J'ai animé et fait parler le Ballet et chanter et résonner la Comédie",

---

[1] See (159) and (162).   [2] (213).

he says in his Avant-propos.   He deliberately combined dancing and drama, and his work was the first of many *ballets de cour* which were given during the next forty years.   After 1620 fashions changed and a new form, the *ballet à entrées*, ousted the older kind.   This form consisted in *récits*, *entrées* and *vers*.   The *récits*, which answered to the dialogue of drama and the recitative of opera, were spoken by actors who did not dance.   The *entrées* were the ballet proper and corresponded to the acts of a play or opera; they formed self-contained plots and had no connexion with each other[1] except in that they were all related to some general theme which gave the ballet its name.   The *vers* did not enter into the performance at all but were short descriptions, sometimes just factual, sometimes humorous and satirical, of the characters in the *entrées*.   They were not recited but were printed in the *livres de ballet*, which resembled programmes rather than librettos[2].

The approximation to opera was made closer when the longer ballets came to be preceded by overtures consisting in a slow, pompous movement and a quicker one, such as that of the *Ballet de Mademoiselle* (1640).   The origin of this form goes back to the previous century and is found in the association of a pavan and a galliard. Already three ballets in the Philidor collection are preceded by overtures (not so called) with the Lullian *coupe*: slow (2/2): fast (3/2): repeated with changes.   They are the *Ballets de la Chienne* (1604), *des Sénateurs* (1607) and *de la Comédie* (1608).   The importance of the chorus also increased as the name *ballet aux chansons* indicates[3], though ballets danced to singing were less common than in England (e.g. Morley's) or Italy towards 1600.   The popularity of the ballet, which was almost entirely a court entertainment, was increased by the infatuation for it of the young Louis XIV, who danced his first ballet in 1651.[4]

The first intervention of the Italian Lulli, which laid the foundation of the king's friendship for him, was in *the Ballet de la Nuit*, in 1653, an enormous show with forty-five *entrées* which lasted all night and went on for thirteen hours.   One year later Lulli, then twenty-two, composed his first ballet, *Le Temps*, as a result of which he was appointed "compositeur de la musique instrumentale".   In 1664 began his famous collaboration with Molière in a new genre of the playwright's invention, the *comédie-ballet*—a play with ballet *entrées* as interludes.   During the next seven years Molière and Lulli co-operated in a number of such comedies as well as in some *entrées*; the

---

[1] Bukofzer calls this form of ballet "an almost incoherent series of danced tableaux" (125).

[2] They are alluded to in the closing ballet of *Le Bourgeois Gentilhomme*.

[3] An early instance of which is *Le Grand Ballet du Roi sur l'aventure de Tancrède en la foret enchantée*, 1619.

[4] See (179A).

most celebrated is *Le Bourgeois Gentilhomme*.[1]   One should remember
that Lulli was firstly a dancer and actor and only secondly a composer;
that he rose to fame as a ballet producer and kept his influence with the
King through his ability in this capacity.

Molière died early in 1673 and Lulli's first opera was performed
a few months later, so that we can leave the ballet at this point.   It
was not ousted by opera, however, and during the next twenty-five
years eight new ballets were given by the newly founded Académie
de Musique.   Most of these show the influence of opera; sung parts
increase in number and come to contain dramatic moments.   In 1697
appeared a fresh fusion of choreography and drama, the *opéra-ballet*.
It became the most popular form of opera in the early eighteenth
century, and two of Rameau's best-known works, *Les Indes galantes*
and *Les Fêtes d'Hébé*, belong to this class.

The importance of dancing in French opera of both seventeenth
and eighteenth centuries is a legacy from ballet.   Into the prologue
and into almost every act there enter *divertissements* of singing and
dancing.   In the earliest operas the prologue was always devoted to
a eulogy of the monarch and in form it was like an *entrée* from a *ballet
à entrées*.   Romain Rolland calls it the last refuge of the *ballet de
cour*.[2]   The praise of the King was given up later.   Luigi Rossi's
Palazzo d'Atlante and *Orfeo* both opened with prologues.   The form
of Quinault's prologues survived with little change till about 1750.
Some ballets, too, had prologues.   The great place taken by choreography in Lullian and Ramellian opera is obvious.

The element of mechanical display is also important.   It consists
generally in the movement of figures through the air and the imitation
of natural phenomena such as storms and floods.   This, too, has an
ancestry.   Italian opera in the first half of the seventeenth century
made use of machinery, and Italian stage engineers like Torelli and
Vigarani were celebrated.   The few Italian operas performed in
Paris between 1645 and 1662 showed marvels of mechanical con-
trivance.[3]

---

[1] The two parted company in 1672 and the music for Molière's last
comédie-ballet, *Le Malade Imaginaire*, is by Charpentier.

[2] (219), 180.

[3] They are as follows:

1645: March.   An unidentified opera sung without scenery in the
Palais Royal.   The *Nicandro e Fileno*, which Prunières had thought was
this opera, is the libretto by the Duke of Nevers, Mazarin's nephew, set to
music by Lorenzani and given at Fontainebleau in 1681; Prunières himself
corrected his mistake later.

1645: Dec. 14.   *La Finta Pazza*, a play with music rather than an
opera, by Giulio Strozzi, set to music by Sacrati; performed in the Petit
Bourbon with elaborate stage machinery.

Earlier than this, however, the French stage had produced examples of machinery, as in Chapoton's *Descente d'Orphée aux Enfers* (1640),[1] which was improved upon by the actors of the Théâtre du Marais in 1648 after the performance of Rossi's *Orfeo*; this second venture, *La Grande Journée des Machines ou le Mariage d'Orphée et d'Eurydice*, associated machinery and music. Boyer's *Ulysse dans l'île de Circé* (1650), Pierre Corneille's *Andromède* (1650) and *La Toison d'Or* (1662) also combine the two elements. In Corneille's and Molière's *Psyché* (1671)[2] spectacle and music were again combined with drama. The former consisted in Venus' descent "dans une grande machine" in the prologue, Jupiter's appearance "sur son aigle" amid thunder and lightning in Act V, sundry flights by Love, both up and down, and several transformation scenes in the interludes in Act IV; the latter, in singing in the prologue and interludes, the words for the songs being by Quinault except for the Italian lament after Act I.

The taste for such plays was lively in the 'seventies, and Lulli and Quinault played up to it in their new entertainment. Roman opera, at the time of Raguenet's visit, could still show magnificent scenery, and he speaks of a performance in Venice where an elephant came on to the stage and a whole army emerged from its inside. Le Cerf de la Viéville, so loath to concede anything to Italy, has to acknowledge her superiority in stage machines and settings. He considers that an opera without machines is a woman without "fontanges" (topknots)[3]. Later, Italian opera lost interest in display and concentrated on singing. Saint-Évremond, thinking of the French opera which he never saw since he was living in exile in England, was opposed to elaborate staging;[4]

1646: February. *Egisto* by Cavalli; given without elaborate setting or machinery in the Palais Royal.

1647: March 2. *Orfeo*, by Luigi Rossi (libretto by Buti); specially composed for the occasion and sumptuously produced in the Palais Royal; repeated several times in April and May.

1653: April 14. *Le Nozze di Peleo e di Teti*, by Cavalli, in the Petit Bourbon.

1660: November 22. *Serse*, by Cavalli (libretto by Minato); given in the gallery of the Louvre; several performances.

1662: February 7. *Ercole amante*, by Cavalli (libretto by Buti); specially composed; given in the Tuileries; several performances.

[1] Machinery had been used even earlier on the French stage: in Durval's *Travaux d'Ulysse*, acted in 1629 or 1630, which staged a boat, Rotrou's *Hercule mourant* (1634), Corneille's *Médée* (1635), Claveret's *Le Ravissement de Proserpine* and J. B. Lhermitte's *La Chute de Phaéton* (1639).

[2] Not to be confused with Benserade's ballet (1656) and Lulli's and Thomas Corneille's opera (1678) on the same subject.

[3] (83), I, 140.

[4] "Something foolish laden with music, dances, machines, scenery, is magnificently foolish, but it is foolish all the same."

La Bruyère was in favour of it. He was writing in its defence at a time when Lulli had cut down machinery after he had taken over Perrin's and the Marquis de Sourdeac's opera which had led to the latter's bankruptcy.

It is to be misled and to cultivate a wrong taste to say that machinery is just a children's amusement, suitable only to marionettes; it increases and beautifies the fiction, keeps up in the spectators that gentle illusion which is the whole pleasure of the stage, to which it adds the *merveilleux*. *Bérénice* and *Pénélope* need neither flights nor chariots nor transformations; opera needs them; and it belongs to this spectacle to hold mind, eye and ear all equally spell-bound.[1]

French opera did not cease to be spectacular, though on a less lavish scale, but it remained in the long run more dramatic than Italian; it was also more conscious of its essential unreality. That is why it took its characters from mythology or legend instead of from history, like Italian. "We should laugh in France at the mere title of an opera called *Titus, Themistocles*, etc."[2]

History, said Cahusac, implies facts too well-known, characters too serious, deeds too much like those of ordinary life for song, music and dance not to clash with them.[3] Abbé de Mably praised Quinault for excluding "les grands intérêts"—that is, major political themes—from opera and for concentrating on love, the most suitable theme for music.[4] The imaginary beings, with whom he filled his librettos, "of whom the spectator has no very precise idea, leave the composer free to give them a more musical speech".[5]

The defence of *merveilleux* was general. But the painful contrast between what one imagines and what one actually sees and hears often dispels its force. Quinault's conceptions, as expressed in his stage directions, were superb but they were often poorly rendered: "a frigid *symphonie*, an ill-painted piece of cardboard, a few handfuls of lighted tow" is all one had for the Proteus episode in *Phaéton*.[6]

[1] (77), I.   [2] (97), 267.   [3] (44), III, 5; 65.   [4] (84), 51.   [5] (84), 49.
[6] (44), III, 5; 84. "Protée disparaît et se transforme successivement en tigre, en arbre, en dragon, en fontaine, en flamme. Tandis qu'il prend ces formes différentes, il est sans cesse suivi et environné par les suivants de Triton, et Triton lui fait entendre qu'il ne le quittera point, malgré ses transformations" (*Phaéton*, II, 7).

Cahusac instances also the end of Act III in *Cadmus et Hermione* and Act IV, 2, when the hero sows the dragon's teeth. I quote the directions relating to the teeth. "L'Amour s'envole. Cadmus sème les dents du dragon et la Terre produit des soldats armés qui se préparent à tourner leurs armes contre Cadmus; mais il jette au milieu d'eux une manière de grenade que l'Amour lui a apportée; elle se brise en plusieurs éclats et inspire aux combattants une fureur qui les oblige à combattre les uns contre les autres et à s'entr'égorger eux-mêmes. Les derniers qui demeurent vivants viennent apporter leurs armes aux pieds de Cadmus."

The presence of pastoral is another important element in French opera. In the sixteenth and seventeenth centuries pastoral was frequently associated with music. Its sources in antiquity were not musical since, in spite of allusions to pipes, neither Theocritus' nor Virgil's eclogues were sung. But Tasso's pastoral play *Aminta* had been given with incidental music by Cavalieri in 1590 and by Monteverdi in 1628. There were pastoral scenes in French ballets, including Beaujoyeulx's *Circé*, and the pastoral play was one of the chief kinds of drama in the first half of the seventeenth century. As early as 1576, a pastoral play, with musical interludes, by Nicolas de Montreux, called *Arimène ou le Berger désespéré*, had been performed in Nantes castle. *Le Triomphe de Bacchus*, a pastoral given in 1615, also introduced music.[1]

After 1650 more of these plays were provided with music, among them Perrin's Issy *Pastorale* (1650), with music by Cambert, and Molière's *La Princesse d'Élide* (or at least the fifth interlude in this *comédie-ballet* (1664)) and *Les Amants magnifiques* (1670), both with music by Lulli. French opera had therefore a heavy pastoral heredity. Italian, too, was well laden with it; pastoral sentiment fills the works of Cavalli and Cesti. The new genre could not escape being "pastoralized" from one source or the other.

The influence of contemporary tragedy is not so easy to define and circumscribe as that of ballet, spectacle and pastoral. By "contemporary" I mean that of the years after 1630. This well-characterized and rather austere genre which we know through its two greatest exponents assumed its classical form in the 'thirties and answered to a need in the public for order, clarity and verisimilitude. The result was that clear-cut form of drama, bounded in space and time by twenty-four hours and one place, drawing its chief interest from the conflict of feelings rather than from exciting incident, although, with lesser playwrights, surprising and unlikely occurrences entered into it. Corneille's years of fame ran from 1636 to 1651; he was active again in the 'sixties and 'seventies but was no longer supreme. Racine's short career falls between 1664 and 1676; it coincides more closely with the period in which Quinault and Lulli were evolving the new opera.

The spectacle of machine plays and ballets was one of disorder; that of tragedy, one of order. The former could serve as entertainment, but the second was more admirable. In its most exalted moments the taste of the French public and particularly of the King

---

[1] It contains a comic scene of doctors announcing that of the apothecaries in Molière's *comédie-ballet*, *Monsieur de Pourceaugnac*.

and Court for whom Lulli was working was for something well organized, with a strong stamp of dignity and stateliness.   If classical tragedy had not existed, this taste might have been present but it would have been less clearly formulated in literature and there would have been nothing to which patrons could turn and say: Go and do likewise.   I do not say that Quinault, who was himself a tragic play-wright of talent, the most distinguished, with the younger Corneille,[1] of Racine's contemporaries, sought deliberately to equal, still less to imitate, tragedy in the field of opera; but the fact that either he or Lulli called their creation *tragédie en musique* shows that the existence of spoken tragedy was present to their minds and provided something of an exemplar.

No doubt almost all the elements of *tragédie en musique* existed in France, yet the stimulus to make a dramatic synthesis of them came from Italy.   But once Quinault had started from Italian example he aimed at bringing French opera nearer to tragedy than Italian was.   Already Lulli's first opera, *Cadmus et Hermione*, shows attempts to suit the foreign genre to French taste, with a fairly simple plot and more unity than in Italian librettos; and, while he still retained comic scenes after the Italian model, the comedy is more refined.   Later librettos cut down episodes, work the interludes more skilfully into the plot and eliminate comedy.   The ideal of tragedy is most nearly approached in *Atys*, his fourth opera and the first to eschew comedy. It has less spectacle and machinery than the first three, and the action is more inward and therefore more like that of tragedy; also it ends sadly.   Musically *Atys* ranks high among Lulli's works and is prob-ably the best with *Isis* and *Armide*.   It is true that this approximation to tragedy is not kept up equally through the remaining eight operas; there is no straight line of progress; still, Quinault and Lulli sought to introduce into the genre they had transplanted on to French soil more order, continuity, clarity, pathos and emotion than there was in the Italian forms, and to give it something of the analysis of feeling which had made the greatness of Cornelian and Racinian tragedy.

All this should not let us forget that it was opera and not a new form of tragedy or ballet that Lulli wanted to establish.   Cahusac regretted that Quinault should have called his creation *tragédie en musique*, a misleading title which concealed its novelty and laid it open to be criticized as if it were real tragedy.[2]   The increasing likeness to Italian opera noticeable in ballet, machine plays and *pièces en musique* was due to the example of the Italian works that were performed in Paris between 1645 and 1662; Italian opera was Lulli's model. *Cadmus et Hermione* shows the influence of Cavalli's *Ercole amante*, the last Italian opera to be given in the French capital.   The public had been

---

[1] Lulli's librettist in *Bellérophon* and *Psyché*.   [2] (44), 95–96.

carried away by the sumptuous setting, the innumerable interventions of gods, the changes of scenery and the interludes—more so, in fact, to Cavalli's great annoyance, than by the music of the old Venetian. So Quinault in *Cadmus et Hermione* multiplied machinery and ballet *entrées*, with dancing statues (as in Rossi's *Orfeo*) and an apotheosis. Throughout he remained faithful to the operatic tradition, seeking to satisfy the eye as much as the heart and mind; the ancestry of ballet and machine plays was also, of course, responsible for this visual appeal.   The French wanted opera such as Italy had; but they wanted an intelligible opera.   Lulli and Quinault gave it them.

It is inevitable that one's first and probably only impression of this composite art form should be obtained from a vocal score.   By reducing it to its musical components at least as much is lost as by reading the lyrics of the troubadours and trouvères without the music to which they were set.   This was recognized by even that determined foe of Lullian opera, Melchior Grimm.   "To judge of it, it is not enough to see it on paper and read the score; one must have seen the picture on the stage."[1]

But since this cannot be avoided we must accept it and begin our examination of the impressions that Lullian opera makes on us from the standpoint of someone who knows it only through the score, with the help, possibly, of a piano and his own voice.   One of the first of these impressions is the importance of the recitative.   Its musical interest is not always considerable, but musical and melodic it clearly aims at being, even when it has a declamatory cast.   The prominence of recitative has as its counterpart the unimportance of airs.   Moreover there are moments in the recitative itself where the outline becomes more tuneful and something like an air begins to be sketched.   Sometimes these embryo tunes are actually entitled *air*.

This is a feature very foreign to the Italian operas of the next century which have given us what notions we commonly have of pre-Romantic tragic opera.   The story of Hasse's wife Faustina, an Italian *prima donna*, related by Burney, is well known.   After half an hour's attendance at a French opera she exclaimed: "When are we to hear an *aria*?"—a cry echoed a century later by the legendary anti-Wagnerite who complained that he came away from a Wagner opera without having heard a tune.   But this recitative will at times render faithfully the slightest gradations of sentiment, its half-tints as well as its contrasts, and the result emotionally is not a succession of unmoving pictures, with sudden changes of slide, as it were, but a single, moving canvas, as in spoken drama.   Instead of appearing and vanishing with a click the affective states fade into and grow out of each other.

[1] (72), 291.

Italian opera of the generation before Lulli had also known this use of recitative.

> It is extremely interesting to compare a Florentine opera such as Vittori's *Galatea* (1629) with essentially Roman operas such as those of Mazzocchi or Stefano Landi. In Vittori, the recitative is the very backbone of the drama. Through this medium, feelings and passions are expressed; the airs, choruses and ballets serve only as a diversion.[1]

But with Alessandro Scarlatti Italian recitative was already moving towards the syllabic, non-declamatory and non-musical *recitativo secco* of later days.

The conflict over the respective merits of French and Italian music raged nowhere more fiercely or more tenaciously than round the question of recitative. Grimarest's *Traité du Récitatif*[2] shows how weighty the matter appeared in France. French literature is full of evidence of this, and down to the closing years of the century the nature and necessary qualities of recitative were debated by numerous writers.

The pre-eminence of France in this respect is one of the very few points on which Raguenet agrees with Le Cerf and his other fellow-countrymen. Raguenet praises French recitative and prefers it to Italian; Le Cerf sees in it a "juste milieu entre le parler ordinaire et l'art de la musique".[3] Rémond de Saint-Mard finds fault with Italian recitative because it goes on too long and is too uniform, and especially "because it paints badly or paints nothing at all".[4] In France there are few criticisms of French recitative before Rousseau. Jean-Jacques's opinion is well known. It was bad because it was foreign to the natural character of the language. French is "smooth, simple, restrained, devoid of song", whereas French recitative is a noisy and wild bawling "always leaping from high to low, racing without cause over the whole range of the voice and ever stopping the narration irrelevantly for the sake of beautiful held notes on syllables that neither have meaning nor require one to stop on them".[5]

The weakness of Rousseau's criticism is that it mixes up indistinguishably the nature of the music and the shortcomings of the performers. If French actors had always observed Le Cerf's advice to sing lightly, half of his complaints could not have been made.

D'Alembert is much more discriminating. He keeps apart deficiencies in the music and defects in execution. He makes against French recitative the same kind of reproach that is made against some

---

[1] (213), English edition, 170.   [2] (73).

[3] (83), I, 101. He says further on (II, 343) that "the recitative and *petits airs* should be sung lightly"—a recommendation destined to be frequently forgotten.

[4] (97), 260.   [5] (102).

of Handel's settings of English words. "It is a foreigner who created our recitative and one can see it; one knows how the prosody is deformed, especially in the final syllables." Why make the mute *e* more obvious in singing than in speaking? Much French recitative is excellent and if it were enunciated in the Italian manner it would gain greatly.[1]

Marmontel's answer to him touches on points not usually brought out. After complaining that Italian recitative is monotonous, he desires that no marked difference should be made between recitative and "airs chantants". One should blend into the other. The general rule should be to pass gradually from one sentiment and one degree of emotion to another and thus avoid monotony; only exceptionally "should the harmony cause a sudden revolution, an unexpected commotion. . . . I consider that musical declamation should follow approximately the same inflexions as the spoken tongue but should undulate more widely". This is one of the best definitions of the relation between declamation in speech and music to come out of this century-old discussion.

For him the only superiority of Italian recitative lies in the *accompagnato* or *obbligato* sort, provided all "the ridiculous wobblings they put into it are cut out. . . . The pathos of such pieces is the only real superiority" of Italian opera. Like d'Alembert he recognizes the bad style with which music is declaimed in France.[2]

A few years before him a conciliatory spirit, C. H. Blainville, whose *L'Esprit de l'Art musical* tries to be nice to everyone,[3] praising Rousseau and calling him more French than he realizes, had already drawn this new distinction between the two recitatives—the French being more sensitive and more varied, the Italian more sharply marked. Henceforward this difference is generally recognized and people are in favour of one or the other largely on grounds of personal preference.

As against Italian, French recitative

> comes infinitely nigh to the noble and lofty declamation which most tragedies unquestionably require. The accompaniment of a well conceived thoroughbass, indicating the foundation of the harmony, seems better able to give us an idea of the melopoeia of the Ancients than those frequent bows of the whole orchestra and those jerky accompaniments which cut across the meaning of the speech every instant and weary extremely the ear and attention of the spectator.[4]

---

[1] (29), 418–419 and section XXV.   [2] (86), 75–103.

[3] (37). He shows a commendable sense of relativity. "Before Lulli one looked upon the art of counterpoint as the *ne plus ultra* of music. We think of ours with the same self-satisfaction. Who will assure us that our great-grandchildren will not look on us as Goths whom none remembers?" (65–66.)

[4] (60), 102.

The writer, Decroix, a young man at the time, was writing during the Gluckist quarrel.   He was to some extent a modern but was also a devoted admirer of Rameau,[1] whose music he collected; it is in fact to him alone that we owe the preservation of some of the master's unpublished works.

Chabanon was another belated admirer but more unreservedly modern.   His ideal of recitative is nearer the Italian.   It should be "almost spoken and therefore delivered rapidly".   This will enable the poet to write longer scenes and the composer, "convinced that he has not written any music as long as he has written only recitative, will be able to rhythm, to time, to articulate his airs according to a definite and invariable character and rhythm in each piece".

This is an expression of preference for the clear divisions of Italian opera.   It will liberate the musician and will bring him

> a crowd of musical ideas of which he had never dreamt, and the execu-
> tants will no longer have time to delight in the excessive development
> of their voices; the accompaniments will follow of their own accord the
> melody and the cadence prescribed by the subject; everything will be
> *one*, easy and agreeable in our vocal art, as it is in our fine *symphonies*.

He looks upon recitative as the chief obstacle to this growth of French music and, with all his admiration for Rameau, regrets that he did not reform this side of opera.   He admires the *chants* of Télaïre in *Castor et Pollux* and of Dardanus in his prison, but would wish them to be "more measured" (i.e. in stricter time) "and more articulated; . . . they are two admirable recitatives; we would like to be able to call them two very beautiful airs".[2]

This small selection from musical opinion on the subject of recitative, gathered over a century, shows how important a part of operatic art it was considered.   Our examples have all been drawn from French writers.   Outside France opinion is almost unanimously against French recitative.   In Germany the only musicians able to understand it were Telemann and Scheibe; in Italy and England, as far as I know, it had no supporters at all.

As for the semi-airs, or *petits airs*, of Lulli's opera, they are found in Luigi Rossi, who excels in setting pronounced melodious strains in the middle of a recitative where they stand out against the background.[3]   In fact this "fluid stage of differentiation"[4] between recita-

---

[1] And also of Voltaire.   His *L'Ami des Arts* was written as a defence of both these great men.

[2] (53), 34–36.   [3] (214), 121.

[4] Bukofzer's expression.   The likeness with the ideal of Wagner, who probably knew nothing of Lulli's work, must strike all those who discover *tragédie lyrique* for themselves.   Wagner's "working formula was *arioso stromentato*, the fertilization of more or less melodious recitative by means

tive, air and *arioso* in Lulli existed also in Cavalli, and Lulli did not go beyond it. Older Italian tradition agreed in this with the later French desire for intelligibility. Already in French ballet of the sixteenth century "melody tends rather to comply with the suggestions of prosody than to satisfy the exigencies of lyrical declamation".[1]

Claude Le Jeune and Mauduit were less interested in harmony than in the relation between poetry and music which they desired to link indissolubly. So that Lulli, by choosing this particular kind of Italian practice, showed how faithfully he interpreted French taste.

The chorus was important in early Italian operas. Those of the Roman school began and ended with choruses. Some choral interventions were contrapuntal, some homophonic, in syllabic diction with precise and well-marked rhythms, and most dramatic. Often "voices combine with the instruments in choruses with dancing, in the French fashion".[2] The chorus often intervenes in Monteverdi. Later its importance declines, possibly for the same reason as the orchestra, for economy's sake. Alessandro Scarlatti confines it to short exclamations such as those of crowds. In 1704 Le Cerf could write: "It is well-known that choruses are out of use in Italy."[3] Apostolo Zeno, who was court poet and librettist at Vienna between 1718 and 1729, though he retained the prologue of seventeenth-century opera, reduced the chorus to an ornamental function. Nevertheless, the tradition of choral sections survived in the Viennese operas of Fux and Badia, and Metastasio reintroduced them. Hasse gave them sometimes a neo-antique cast which reminds one of Gluck, as in *Olimpiade*.[4]

Choruses had also played a large part in the *ballet de cour* where, for clarity's sake, they were generally syllabic. Luigi Rossi, whose works Lulli admired greatly, used choruses with vertical harmonies which occur again in the Florentine at a date when they had vanished from Italian opera. Prunières considers that it was in Rossi's art that "he learnt the art of building up great vocal ensembles".[5]

Lulli made of his prologues independent choral cantatas on a broader scale than any hitherto. With *airs* half merged in recitative and extensive choral sections it is not surprising that singers never exercised the same tyranny in France as in Italy. In addition to these

_____

of orchestral culture, with recitative and more musical development freely alternating according to the context instead of being imposed arbitrarily on the text in a series of prescribed numbers" (139). In Lulli and still more in Rameau the "more musical development" is provided by the *petits airs* which so bothered non-French contemporaries.

[1] (213), 19.   [2] (213), 67.   [3] (83), I, 71.
[4] (221), 160.   [5] (214), 124.

checks on their egotism they had to compete in popularity with the dancers.

In the eighteenth century foreigners were annoyed by the liking for frequent changes of bar length in French opera and especially by the alternation of binary and ternary beats.[1] This taste went back a long way, for the Renaissance composers of *musique mesurée* already used bars of varying length; neither was it confined to France, for Monteverdi did likewise in some of his *Scherzi musicali* and Cavalli was fond of intermingling 4/2 and 3/2. They also disliked the prevalence of ternary beats which was again an early Italian feature surviving in France. In Luigi Rossi's *Orfeo* three-time preponderates, as it does in early seventeenth-century opera generally, with frequent changes of time and bar signature.

Another characteristic that we notice is the presence of dance rhythms in much music that is not intended to be danced. This is perhaps more noticeable in the simple music of Lulli than in the more complex art of his successors. Here, too, was a feature of some early Italian works, like Rossi's *Orfeo*; it is another instance of an Italian influence, not undergone but chosen by the Florentine because of its kinship with French taste which had inherited from the ballet a fondness for these rhythms.

Lulli's own stamp was felt in the liveliness he put into dancing; he quickened the speed and introduced vivacious or jerky dances like the jig, the canari and the forlana, so that to conservative taste his dances seemed to partake of buffoonery. By dramatic pantomime he transformed ballet into drama and he retained these features in opera.

Still more characteristic are the many sung dances which still charm us, even when our contact with the opera is limited to the printed page. The union of singing and dancing is found in the Middle Ages; it occurs in the Renaissance *ballet de cour* and spreads to Italy. Monteverdi (or his brother Giulio Cesare) has a suite of sung dances in the ballets which conclude the *Scherzi musicali*, and the earliest oratorio preserved, *La Rappresentazione d'Anima e di Corpo* by Cavalieri (1600), contains a chorus intended to be danced.

In such numbers the music was generally composed before the words and these had to be adapted to it, a task often achieved with skill. This was known as "parodier un air de danse". Prunières considers that the poets knew better how to suit their words to the music than the composers their music to the words.

Of the fixed dance forms found in Lulli or that appeared after his death, the most highly organized was the chaconne. Lulli's movements in this form are perhaps the greatest monuments of his art. They occur first in some of his ballets, for instance *Alcidiane* (instru-

---

[1] In Rameau's *Zaïs* eleven bars on end have each a fresh time-signature.

mental) and the *Pastorale comique* (choral). They are not strict ground basses but variations of a rhythmic pattern, resembling rondos, with interludes for woodwind trio. The tendency for rhythm to predominate, already present in French music, was strengthened by Lulli, in whose musical temperament rhythm was the most forceful element. The rhythmical strength and intricacy of French music, so noticeable in Rameau and his century, was still triumphant in *opéra comique* where, says Abert,[1] it far surpassed in its variety the achievements of other nations. It has remained a national feature to this day and is still one of the most attractive qualities of modern French music.

Though so much Italian precedent entered into Lulli's realization, melodically his art is purely French. "Its spirit is as French as his opera is fundamentally Italian," says Prunières.[2] Its sources are in the vaudeville, *airs de cour*, *airs de danse*, tunes from the *comédies ballets* and a stylized rendering of tragic declamation.

The overture is the part of a Lulli opera that has kept its place most firmly in musical memory, thanks to the great expansion of its slow-fast form. Its history is well known and there is no need to repeat what is said elsewhere.[3] Though not identical, of course, and not even always fugal in the *allegro*,[4] there is a sameness about his overtures and d'Alembert was not unjust in his remark that "for more than sixty years there was only one overture at the opera".[5] Neither is there much connexion of form or of mood between overture and opera. This, however, was to change with Rameau.

With recitative and choreography, the presence of descriptive or evocative *symphonies* is one of the most obvious features of Lullian opera. Like the preceding, these had occurred in Italy, especially in the earlier Venetian operas. They had disappeared by the time of Alessandro Scarlatti. We know how firmly they remained in France and what a source of vitality and musical interest they still are. As we roam through the pages of Lulli or Campra at the keyboard, we find ourselves, against our better principles, turning rapidly over the pages of dialogue and hastening to the next non-vocal section. Far from

---

[1] (114), I, 646.   [2] (214), 368.

[3] The name was first used in the ballet towards 1640. The first complete example of the French type is the overture which Lulli wrote for the ballet introduced into Cavalli's *Serse* for its performance in Paris in 1662. R. Rolland ((219), 181) makes the interesting remark that Lulli's overtures sound best with large orchestras and quotes Marpurg to that effect.

[4] His overture to Molière's *comédie-ballet*, *Le Mariage forcé* (1664), resembles many eighteenth-century ones in that the fast section is not fugal. The dotted rhythm is not prominent in the *lent* of the *Armide* overture and the *vite* is not fugal.

[5] (29), XXXVIII.

disappearing, they were given fresh life when Gluck extended the structural principles of French opera to that of Italy, and they are the direct ancestors of the symphonic writing which almost submerges the vocal element with Wagner. These *symphonies* were the element in French opera that escaped with least censure from critics of the genre.

Their development in France is due, of course, to the presence of an efficient and well-disciplined orchestra, at least in Lulli's time. The King's band of twenty-four violins, "les vingt-quatre violons du Roi", were already famous under Louis XIII. They were the first permanent orchestra in history. Elsewhere, orchestras were just solo ensembles; this one consistently reinforced all five parts and thus established the practice of modern orchestral doubling, celebrated at the time as an amazing innovation. The doubling instruments all belonged to the violin family. Supplementary harmony was unnecessary and the *basso continuo* was late in appearing in France, becoming common only after 1650. The top and bottom parts were more heavily reinforced than the middle ones, the proportions being six : four : four : four : six. In 1725 the composition of the orchestra at the Opéra was as follows:

Eight first violins
Six second violins
Seven basses ('cellos)
Two double-basses
Five hautboys
Five bassoons
Two flutes
Two horns or trumpets
One pair of kettledrums
One harpsichord, for realizing the figured bass
A second harpsichord for accompaniment, whose task was to accompany the *récitatifs simples*, with the help of two 'cellos; it was generally the *maître de musique* who presided over it.[1]

Lulli's conducting was in "a dry, pointed style of utmost rhythmical precision, . . . later admired and imitated by all European composers. . . . He combined the unornamented, straight playing of the Venetian opera with the emphatically rhythmic style of French music."[2] This was the famous Lullian orchestral discipline.

Yet another feature present in earliest Italian opera which Lulli took over and France retained was the important part played by the

---

[1] (161), 16; Adam Carse (126) gives the numbers in 1713 which are slightly less.
[2] (125).

orchestra in the entertainment. In Monteverdi the instruments had been nearly as weighty as the voices. His operas contain orchestral *sinfonie*, like the *symphonies* so prominent in Lulli and his successors. In Luigi Rossi's *Il Palazzo d'Atlante* (1642) "the orchestra accompanies the airs; it represents the murmuring waves evoked by the air of the prologue and executes charming ballets which are danced by the sorcerers' captives".[1] Raguenet was impressed by the beauty and fullness of the accompaniments in the operas he heard in Rome.[2]

Later, the setting up of commercial opera, which dates in Venice from 1637, compelled composers to cut down their orchestras, so that harpsichord and strings became the pivot on which the whole orchestra rested. Only in the course of the next century did the ejected instruments return little by little to the bosom of the operatic family.

The importance of the orchestra in accompaniment strikes one forcibly in French opera. To say of Lulli, as one can say of sections of Rameau, that the accompaniment makes sense without the voice, would be an exaggeration, but the importance of much accompaniment in the Florentine comes near at times to self-sufficiency. And with his successors this is even more marked. An air from Destouches's *Les Éléments* will illustrate this and will show the degree of tone painting of which French music was capable in the early years of the eighteenth century (ex. 39).[3] The contrast is great with the later "Handelian" opera where the orchestra is important only in the *ritornelli* of the arias and does not form continuous strands of music as in France. Rousseau's gibe that Rameau reduced the voice to being merely the accompaniment of the accompaniment is well-known.

The frequent orchestral interventions in preludes, interludes, postludes, bring us in sight of the continuous dramatic symphony which Monteverdi had perceived and Wagner claimed to have invented. One can never forget the Wagnerish impression which one's first contact with a Rameau opera gives one. When we turn to the art form of Lulli and Rameau we are struck by its modernity. The continuous musical discourse of Wagnerian and modern opera is there; it is broken, no doubt, by the passage from orchestra to harpsichord and back again to orchestra but, while the accompaniment thus occasionally flops to insignificance, the vocal part retains its interest and the recitative remains expressive and moulded on the words and never lines up in the dead frame of Italian *recitativo secco* where, as far as the music is concerned, the words might signify anything.

It is easy, when going through a Lulli or Rameau score, to be so occupied with the music and words that one omits to read carefully

---

[1] (213), 172.   [2] (94), 53–60, 77–78.   [3] II, 2.

the detailed stage directions, given in small print at the head of each
act and elsewhere.   But it is important to do so since this is the only
way in which we can bring into our mental picture that essential
element of Lulli's and Quinault's complex creation, namely, the
spectacle.   It is revealing to read of the complexities that enchanted

Ex.39

the audiences of these operas—the same people, most of them, who
delighted in the austere settings of tragedy.   If we sometimes feel
surprised that the *palais à volonté* should have satisfied the theatre-goer
in the seventeenth century the answer is that it did not satisfy him and
that he got full amusement for his eyes in the realistic trappings, first

of machine plays, later of opera.　The Italian ancestry of this spectacle is well known.

Towards 1635, the fantastic subject of a Roman opera "gave occasion for constant changes of scene, and for *divertissements* in song and dance.　It was a splendid display for the delight of the senses, but appealing little to the mind or the heart."[1]　In Mazzocchi's *La Catena d'amore* (1626), taken from Marino's *La Prigione d'Adone*,

> many scenes already familiar to librettists of the time and destined to be repeated for more than a century in every opera performed in Europe, are already seen unfolding one after the other: enchanted gardens where unseen voices bewitch the hero; Vulcan's cave where Cyclops sing as they beat the anvil; deep forests where the echo answers the despairing lover.[2]

Later, in Italy, spectacle, like orchestras, tended to be cheapened away; yet it, too, returned with a vengeance in the following century. In 1773, at Milan, Mozart announced he was about to see an opera performed with "twenty-four horses and a great crowd of people on the stage, so that it will be a miracle if some accident does not happen".[3] We know, moreover, how well entrenched spectacle is in opera even to-day and how more so it was in the last century. "The greenish gauzes in which the Rhine Maidens float in mid-air hanging from invisible steel wires is an optical illusion which would have delighted the subjects of Louis XIV and Louis XV."[4]

It is usual to insist upon the decorative aspect of this art, and indeed that side is strong.　Naves evokes it as "a poetry of *fête héroïque et galante*, with which Tasso and Ariosto had enriched epic and of which the age of Louis XIV, especially with Quinault's operas, had given decorative examples".[5]

Paul Lang expands this to embrace the whole of Lulli-Quinault opera.　Opera in France "was an expression of decorative art; the decorative effect is its immediate aim.　It joined the other arts . . . in enlivening and decorating the court.　The searching for effect forms the basis of the ideas of the French artist."[6]　This decorative element, he continues, predominates abusively over "the essential condition of art, sincere emotion".

------

[1] (213), 171.　　　　　　　　　　[2] (214), 6.

[3] Letter to his sister of January 23, 1773.　It has been suggested that this opera was Mysliwecek's *Bellerofonte*.

[4] (172), 168.

[5] (197), 116.　He is referring to Voltaire's tragedy *Tancrède* (1760); its subject, from the *Gerusalemme liberata*, had been set as an opera by Campra in 1702, when the part of the heroine, Clorinde, had been taken by the celebrated Mademoiselle Maupin.

[6] (175), 384.

Its hedonistic spirit prevented it from becoming a medium for true tragedy.   Its object being pleasure, it had to be optimistic.   Thus love, the chief emotion in its realm, must be presented as a virtue to be rewarded, not as a vice or a scourge.   Hence its "lewd ethics" which Boileau castigated:

> . . . cette morale lubrique
> Que Lulli réchauffa des sons de sa musique[1]

agreeing in this with Prynne, who had already attacked "lust-provoking songs" in his *Histriomastix* in 1635.   Yet Rémond de Saint-Mard considered that "l'opéra purge les mœurs et les purge tout aussi bien que les genres de poésie qu'on regarde comme les plus moraux".[2] But he did not defend this opinion very forcefully.

We have seen that the austerer form of classical tragedy influenced the new genre and indeed Quinault's *tragédies en musique* do not always end happily.   The ancient belief that Lulli's operas eschew strong dramatic moments, expressed again recently[3], is belied by many a passage.   *Atys* closes with a funeral scene.   In *Phaéton* the story of the hero's disastrous end is left unaltered and the play closes on a chorus singing:

> O chute affreuse!
> O témérité malheureuse!

with no attempt to mitigate the catastrophe.   *Armide* concludes with the heroine lamenting the loss of her enchanted palace and her lover. In fact, tragic endings were commoner with Lulli than they became later.   In the eighteenth century they were unusual.   Metastasio's *Didone abbandonata* (1743) ends tragically with the heroine's death. Leclair's fine *Scylla et Glaucus* (1746), probably the best French opera of the century with Rameau's and Gluck's, closes with the lovers irremediably parted and Scylla turned into a rock by the jealous Circe; the curtain rings down on the sight of the petrified maiden and the sound of a "*symphonie* to express the barkings of the monsters that surround Scylla, and of the Abysses".   But Gluck never allowed his operas to conclude as tragedies.

The social interpretation of opera is more fully justified in France than anywhere else.   The genre was created deliberately for the entertainment of a well-defined social group.   Consequently, the reflection of that group is an important element in the emotional appeal this opera still makes.   Especially in pieces like the grand chaconne in *Phaéton*, Act II, it is the impression of a world, and of a way of life desired by that world, that we receive.   To seek in it,

---

[1] (38), X, lines 141–142.   [2] (97), 280.   [3] (177).

therefore, any direct expression of the poet's or composer's own personality is vain. From a frequentation of Rameau's operas and ballets one certainly does carry away a strong sense of personality; nothing comparable arises from Lulli's music or Quinault's verse. It is as idle to seek Lulli's "soul" in his music as it would be to seek Lenôtre's in his gardens. Only the quality of his intelligence can be judged in them. The emotion is collective and impersonal, but the embodiment of it bears the mark of one mind.

"Lulli", said Cavalli, "has the great quality of our classical century; he knows how to order." He shares the credit for this achievement with his gifted collaborator. Between the two there reigned the same co-operation, broken only for one spell, as between composers and authors of *opéra-comique*: Dauvergne, Duni, Philidor, Monsigny, Grétry on one hand; Vadé, Favart, Sedaine and Marmontel on the other. The unity that resulted from the collaboration of Lulli and Quinault is not, it is true, an organic one, like that of a growing tree. There is not in it the equivalent of the strong, abstract pattern found in French architecture and garden designing of the time or in Poussin or Racine, or later in the fugue and sonata. It is an external unity achieved by the skilful juxtaposition and intermingling of separate elements, all of which were already associated in varying degrees in opera and ballet, but which Lulli combined with harmony and proportion so that nothing stuck out, nothing predominated, neither song nor drama nor spectacle nor *symphonies* nor dance. It is as grave a mistake to imagine that French seventeenth-century classical operas were merely displays of dancers' virtuosity as to think that vocal virtuosity made up the whole of Italian *opera seria* in the eighteenth century. It is in this that French opera is so superior to its Venetian predecessor, to that of Cesti and Cavalli, with "its heap of airs piled up at random in each act, as in a drawer where one has tried to pack as many things as possible one on top of the other.".[1] In Italy, the true forerunners of Lulli and Quinault were the composers of the Barberini opera in Rome before 1650, Mazzocchi, Vittori and Landi.

Yet French opera remained drama and, like all true drama, it had its moments of tension and relaxation. In both French and Italian opera tension was broken at intervals, but in different ways. In Italy, when melody was wanted the *aria* provided it, arresting the progress and affording a moment of contemplation.[2] It was the choruses that

---

[1] (219). But, adds Rolland, as regards the actual music, there is more genius in one air by Cavalli than in all Lulli.

[2] That is one way of looking at it. But Rolland, referring to this combination of recitative and solo air, calls the former "an artificial band holding the different airs together like the string round a bouquet". For Pierre Lasserre recitative alternates with air "like desert spaces and flowering oases" ((176), 85).

gave these breaks in France; at the same time, as in Carissimi's oratorios, they also made up, by punctuating the scenes, for the lack of formal differentiation between air and recitatives.   Hence the unprecedented grandeur they assume in Lulli.   They become the main means of organization since the air is too small and too indistinct to fulfil this function.   In this, their only predecessors were in Carissimi's oratorios.

Writing in 1711 Addison declares that French audiences were apt to join in singing some of these choruses.

> The chorus in which [French] opera abounds gives the *parterre* frequent opportunities of joining in concert with the stage.   This inclination of the audience to sing along with the actors so prevails with them that I have sometimes known the performers on the stage do no more in a celebrated song than the clerk of a parish church, who serves only to raise the psalm and is afterwards drowned in the music of the congregation.[1]

Rémond de Saint-Mard has left us a definition of opera in terms of the spectator's feelings which I will quote in preference to the more satirical and external descriptions of La Fontaine and Voltaire.

> We are caught at the Opéra by so many sides that it is hardly possible to defend ourselves.   We are given what dishonours us and what we so dearly love—I mean, the *merveilleux* [enchantment and magic].   When it sets about it well, opera succeeds in moving us.   It enraptures our eyes, it flatters our ears at every moment; and out of it all there is formed a kind of spellbinding which, when the work is built and performed as it should be, inebriates us deeply, shuts our eyes to its defects and surrenders us wholly to its charms.[2]

It is needless to warn musicians that a Lulli score contains only part of the opera.   That is true, but since it is all, bar the imagination, by which we have to judge it, we must be content with it.   An undirected exploration of Lulli's operas based only on score reading may prove disappointing and anyone who desires to enter his world via score *and* keyboard—the latter very important—is advised to begin with *Armide*, Quinault's most picturesque libretto and Lulli's most romantic work.   After *Armide*, *Atys* should be tasted.   "Atys est trop heureux" (I, 4) is a good example of an elegiac air bordering on the tragic, close to declamation yet definitely melodic.   This kind of tuneful declamation, so characteristic of French opera, is well presented in the duet that follows, "Un amour malheureux".

The *ritournelles* at the beginnings of Acts II and III and the orchestral introduction to Act II, 2 show us the importance and value of his musical interludes.   The second is required for the goddess's majestic

---

[1] (28), April 3, 1711.   [2] (97), 246.

entry, but Atys could well have emerged without *ritournelle* and in many other musical interludes one feels that no dumb show is needed and that the music is there in its own right.   Atys' sleep in III, 4 is an enchanting example of almost self-sufficient orchestral writing, over which the voices seem to hover and wander without stringent relevance.   They feel superimposed; it does not matter whether or no they are present.   What matters is the beautiful through-composed sleep symphony itself.   The closing *divertissement*, as we have said, is a funeral scene in honour of the dead Atys.

The libretto of *Armide*, taken like Campra's *Tancrède* from the *Gerusalemme liberata*, is the same that Gluck was to set ninety years later.   The highlight is Act II, 3, the scene in which Renaud-Rinaldo finds himself in the heroine's enchanted gardens and succumbs to their charm.   There is the same through-composition as in Atys' slumber, and the languidly moving lines reflect an unmistakably pastoral mood. This is the most quoted scene in all Lulli and it deserves to be. Rameau knew it well and analysed it in his *Nouveau système*[1] and elsewhere.

It is not easy to get to know the dramatic music of the generation after Lulli.   The only nineteenth-century editions—there are as yet none of the twentieth—are those of Collasse, Lulli's collaborator and stooge, Campra and Destouches, by Michaëlis.   Of Desmarêts, Mouret, Marais and Marc-Antoine Charpentier, only single airs exist in modern editions, such as that edited by Gabriel Grovlez for Chester's.   Jeanne Arger has, however, edited a large number of airs from cantatas by these and other composers, including Clérambault, Montéclair and Rameau, and some idea of their style can be derived from these.   Heugel's are bringing out airs of Charpentier and the Éditions de la Schola Cantorum publish quite a number of smaller sacred pieces, suitable for modern church use.

Ex.40

Of Destouches I gave an extract earlier in this chapter.   His chief originality is in his *ariosos*, some of which, like the example quoted, are narrative.   *Les Éléments* contain some half-dozen examples of this form of his art.

Part of an air by Campra is quoted in Chapter 11.[2] It comes from

---

[1] Chapter XX.   [2] P. 425.

his ballet opera *Les Fêtes vénitiennes*, a work which gives a good idea of his attractive sparkle and melodic variety.   The contredanse which closes the *entrée* called *Les Sérénades et les Joueurs* in this work is an instance of a dance form recently imported from England and has an unmistakably English lilt (ex. 40).   The dates of these composers, several of whom were still living when *Hippolyte et Aricie* was performed, bring us to the period of Rameau himself.

5. Hippolyte et Aricie *and Rameau's* Tragédie en musique

*H*IPPOLYTE ET ARICIE has over Rameau's other *tragédies en musique* the advantage that its subject goes back, however indirectly, to a Euripidean model. Though between Euripides and Rameau there stand the works of two other men, something of the original survives and it is thus, in part, a Greek tragedy and not, like *Dardanus*, merely a fairy story with Greek names.

At the source of the libretto is Euripides' *Crown-bearing Hippolytus*. The subject of this play is a contest between Artemis and Aphrodite, the stakes of which are the happiness of Phaedra and of her stepson Hippolytus. Phaedra, wife of the absent Theseus, is consumed with an incestuous love for her stepson but dare not confess it. Her nurse draws the secret from her and reveals it to Hippolytus. Phaedra, overcome with shame and fearing lest her guilty love be made known to Theseus by her stepson, decides to hang herself, but before doing so leaves tablets on which she accuses the youth of having attempted her honour and declares that she is ashamed to live after such an affront. Theseus returns and, without allowing Hippolytus to clear himself, calls upon Neptune to fulfil a promise the god had once made and to compass the young man's death. Hippolytus, banished from his father's presence, is driving his chariot along the seashore when a monster sent from the deep attacks him and frightens his horses. He is thrown and mortally wounded. His innocence is vouched for by Artemis and, having been carried into his father's presence, he expires. The tragedy ends with the lamentations of Theseus and the chorus.

Upon this same theme Euripides had composed an earlier tragedy, now lost, the *Veiled Hippolytus*. He is said to have introduced into it a scene between the queen and her stepson in which Phaedra, in spite of herself, confessed her passion. This version was followed by Seneca who, in his *Hippolytus*, caused his hero, at the end of the interview, to draw his sword as if to kill his stepmother. The sword, forgotten, is picked up by the nurse and used as evidence of his alleged assault.

More than one French playwright of the sixteenth and seventeenth centuries set this story, but the genius of Racine has caused them all to be forgotten.[1] Racine's *Phèdre*, performed on January 1, 1677, was the last of his secular tragedies and the fruit of his genius at its highest. While following Euripides' first play, portions of which are recognizable in his text, he, like Seneca, made the queen herself own her love to her stepson in a scene which is the central point of the tragedy. Phaedra with Racine is a modern, tortured soul, torn between her conscience and her love, and she dominates the play, casting both husband and stepson into the shade. Her guilt is lessened by the announcement of Theseus' death which is made at the end of the first act. The king's return is all the more unexpected for this false report and its dramatic effect is heightened thereby. The queen's death takes place on the stage and she has time to make a full confession in the presence of her husband. The nurse is a more sinister figure than in earlier plays and her suicide is the first warning of the impending climax.

The chief change made by Racine concerned the character of Hippolytus. Theseus' son had been hitherto the darling of Artemis, the virgin goddess, a true child of his Amazon mother, untainted by love and hating women. The contrast between the votary of Artemis and the victim of Aphrodite was thus all the sharper. Racine considered that so boorish a hero would make no appeal to his audience and he introduced a new character, Aricia, for whom in his preface he alleged various authorities, notably Virgil.[2] Aricia is the daughter and only surviving child of Pallas, whose sons had been ousted by Theseus from the throne of Athens. The king, after murdering her fifty brothers, had spared her on condition that she never married. Hippolytus has conceived for her a passion which his father's decree causes him to conceal and which is not known even to Aricia till he discloses it in the second act.

The invention of this character and consequent change in the traditional figure of Hippolytus was much criticized, even by Racine's countrymen and contemporaries. Dryden's contemptuous and self-satisfied references to it in the preface of *All for Love* and his branding of the young man in his new guise as Monsieur Hippolyte are well known. To-day we are too well accustomed to transmogrifications of ancient themes, Biblical and classical, to be troubled by such trifles.

---

[1] Except Robert Garnier, who, however, has been revived rather than remembered. His racy *Hippolyte* (1573), based on Seneca, in which the long discussion between Phèdre and her nurse is rendered with vehemence, contains much fine poetry.

[2] Aricia is mentioned in *Aeneid*, VII, 762, as the mother of Virbius, son of Hippolytus, who was worshipped as a god in Diana's grove by Lake Nemi. She gave her name to the neighbouring town of Aricia, the modern La Riccia. (Cf. Sir James Frazer, *The Golden Bough*, shorter edition, 4–5.)

Moreover Hippolytus' loss was Phaedra's gain. Racine's heroine is not only the repelled and shamefast lover of Antiquity; her torture has been rendered more exquisite and her personality enriched by the pangs of jealous love, and it is this jealousy that drives her to sanction the nurse's false accusation of her stepson.

The story of Phaedra and Hippolytus alone, even as modified by Racine, would have been too stark for the optimistic convention of opera, in which tragedy could be but incidental and agreeable sentiments had to appear frequently throughout the action and normally to triumph at the close.[1] Abbé Pellegrin seized therefore upon the Hippolytus-Aricia idyll, which was a secondary element in Racine's play, and exalted it into the chief theme. His libretto is based on the chequered loves of these twain which takes the place of the ancient drama of Artemis, Aphrodite and Phaedra. But the Euripidean foundation was too well-known and too moving to fade away entirely and for us, at any rate, what is left of it in Pellegrin's work is the most vital part of the story and has inspired Rameau with his finest music.

Hippolyte et Aricie bears a specious likeness to Euripides' tragedy in that it introduces a chorus of huntsmen and appears to reinstate at least one of the two goddesses of the Greek play. Diana is a *dramatis persona* and takes part in the prologue and the *dénouement*. But she has nothing in common with the grim deity of Antiquity; in the prologue she is only a combination of a schoolmistress, concerned for the morals of her flock, and a *maîtresse de ballet*, and in the fifth act she is the usual god from a machine, intervening to bring about a happy ending.

Of the traditional story, as told by Euripides, Seneca and Racine, Pellegrin has kept Phaedra's passion, the nurse's accusation,[2] Theseus' invocation to Neptune, Hippolytus' death and Phaedra's suicide. From Seneca comes Phaedra's declaration to Hippolytus, which is more unblushing in the opera than in any earlier play. From Racine come the love of Hippolytus and Aricia, Phaedra's jealousy, and the reason given for Theseus' absence—namely, his descent to Hell in order to help his friend Pirithous to carry off Persephone. To these Pellegrin has added the episode of Phaedra's irruption into the temple in Act I, the staging of Theseus' adventures in Hell in Act II, the facts that the nurse knows of Phaedra's passion before the play starts and that the queen learns of Hippolytus' love for Aricia by his defence

---

[1] Biblical subjects like that of Jephtha's daughter had, of course, to be respected, but even the story of Dido was sometimes given a happy ending; e.g., in Cavalli's *Didone*, where the heroine finds consolation in marrying Iarbas. But see Chapter 4, p. 122 and Chapter 15, p. 566.

[2] As in Racine. In Seneca, the nurse accuses him to the chorus and Phaedra herself to Theseus.

of her in Act I—a far less dramatic form of revelation than with
Racine—and the resurrection of Hippolytus by Diana and his union
with Aricia.

The chief losses sustained by the story are Hippolytus' virginity
and tragic fate, Phaedra's avowal to the nurse and her discovery of
Hippolytus' love for Aricia by a casual remark of her husband's.

Phaedra's part is much shortened and her character is rather wood-
en.   She has nevertheless one great air, "Cruelle mère des amours",
in which the emotion, though not the words, are Racinian.   Theseus,
who paled before his wife in Racine, regains his Euripidean stature.
His scene in Hell, the situation in which he is placed in Act III and
his monologue in Act V all make him a lively and imposing figure.

Hippolytus comes to the front more than in Racine and resumes
the importance he had in Euripides, but this is due to the effacement
of Phaedra and not to any added interest in his own part.   Aricia, too,
is more prominent and both lovers gain by having some lovely music.
The nurse keeps her traditional character but is almost squeezed out
of existence.

The king and queen have tragic parts throughout; the lovers are
lyrical, sometimes elegiac.   The only conflict of sentiments is in the
scene between Phaedra and Hippolytus in Act III.   The contest
between Artemis and Aphrodite becomes an insignificant wrangle
between Diana and Love in the prologue—an instance of how Hellenic
forms survived into neo-classical literature voided of their content.

Despite these eliminations, the emaciated ghosts of Euripides and
Racine that stalk through the opera give it a tragic grandeur which
none of Rameau's other works possesses.   There is more subtlety and
complexity of feeling in *Castor et Pollux* but little real tragedy.
Dardanus, in its original form, is mainly a series of spectacles with
one convincing character.   *Zoroastre* depicts a struggle between good
and evil but is spoilt by a commonplace love plot and has too much
display.   In some of the ballet operas there are tragic fragments but
never a tragedy as nearly complete as here.   *Hippolyte et Aricie* is
in this respect unique.[1]

By 1733 the tradition according to which the prologue was devoted
to praises of the King had long been given up.   Instead, an opera was
prefaced by a short spectacle in the course of which mythological or
allegorical figures outlined a plot leading up more or less coherently
to the subject of the work.   With *Hippolyte et Aricie* this plot is
closely connected with the main story.   It opens with a chorus of
Diana's sylvan votaries singing their goddess's praises and thus puts
us more immediately into the action than most prologues.   The overture, in D minor, is in the usual Lullian form with a slow section

---

[1] Pellegrin defended his libretto at length in a preface.   See p. 193 for a
comparison between Racine's and Pellegrin's plots.

followed by a quick *fugato*. Though not programmatic it strikes, especially in the *lent*, an unmistakably pathetic note in sympathy with the climate of the subject. The *lent* is repeated and the *fugato* leads into the opening chorus, the notes of which repeat in D major the beginning of the movement. As there was no curtain the overture was played with a view of the stage, which represents the forest of Erymanthus.[1]

A lively *symphonie* accompanies the entry of the forest dwellers, heralding Diana who at once sings an air. This pleasant scene is interrupted by a short prelude of flutes and violins which Diana herself calls "doux concerts". Her suite is about to enjoy the entrancing sounds when Love is disclosed and the goddess orders a hasty retreat.

> Que vois-je? C'est l'Amour! Venez, suivez mes pas!
> Ce n'est qu'en le fuyant que l'on peut s'en défendre.
> Mais que vous fuyez lentement!

And indeed the chorus sings several more bars before it can tear itself away from the delightful vision. Diana, meanwhile, far from carrying into practice the advice she has just given, stays to begin an argument with the intruding godlet. This gives him the opportunity to establish his presence with an air in which, as in Diana's, his part, doubled by the violins, forms the bass whilst the flutes cap it with a two-part accompaniment. Diana counters with another air, and the arguments for and against the presence of Love are pressed home in a duet. The argument proves inconclusive and Diana appeals to Jupiter to order Love off her preserves. With Jupiter's appearance, descending in a machine, the music, which had hitherto moved in the domain of D and G and their relative minors, opens into the spacious key of E major, the character of which, according to Rameau's table, is "great and magnificent".[2]

We are by now far from the world of Euripides. This Jupiter is a *galant* monarch who cannot but make concessions to the tender passion. It is true that he shifts the responsibility for his decision on to Fate, but he is not acting against his own inclination when he grants permission to Love to "lancer ses traits vainqueurs" in Diana's woods one day in the year. Thereupon he withdraws skyward and Diana, unwilling to witness the desecration of her domain, does likewise.

The rest of the prologue celebrates this easy triumph of Love. From here on, the music, which had been somewhat cramped by the

---

[1] It was only in 1828 that the use of the curtain between the acts became the rule at the Opéra. Cf. Bapst in (225), 176.

[2] (1), 157. In Charpentier's table, some half-century earlier, it was called "querelleur et criard". For most of the other keys Charpentier agrees with Rameau. In the prologue of *Renaud* (1722, music by Desmarets) Pellegrin had staged a similar conflict between Venus and Minerva.

uninspiring subject, more suited to comedy than to the serious style, blossoms out and takes possession of the stage.   An *air en rondeau* in F sharp minor, a couple of gavottes and minuets constitute the ballet with which the prologue closes, and the first two of these are repeated to words sung by a follower of Love or by the chorus.   In the *air en rondeau pour les Amours* the sweetness is touched by that slight acerbity present in nearly all Rameau's music on voluptuous themes, and in the second minuet, in D minor, it is more marked still.

When the first act opens the stage shows the temple of Diana. Aricia is in it, alone.   In order to enforce his command that she shall never marry, Theseus has compelled her to dedicate herself to the goddess's service, and this day she is to take her vows.   She cannot do otherwise than obey and, in her solitude, she beseeches the sanctuary to shield her "troubled heart" from an unhappy love—her unrevealed passion for Hippolytus—declaring herself ready to sacrifice it to the goddess of whom both the prince and she are servants.

Her solo illustrates the main differences between the French *air* and the Italian *aria*.   It resembles an *aria* in that it is preceded by a *ritornello*, is in *da capo* form and modulates to the relative minor in its middle section.   But the first part is a mere repetition and not a development of the *ritornello*, as in an *aria*, and the middle section is as long as the first.   The differences are even greater in rhythm and melody than in structure.   The beat is the 3/4 time beloved of French opera which annoyed so many foreigners, who missed in it the firm pattern of Italian airs.   The vocal line, though melodic, is close to recitative.   The way in which it rises to its highest note on "Diane", falls to its lowest on "vœux" and "cœur", then rises again with "agité" to a second climax on "amour" and ends on almost the same pitch as it began, partakes rather of speech than of song (ex. 41).   The rhythm, however, does not follow the words but has its own regular pattern of two-bar divisions, apparently disregarding the poetry. Close to speech in melody, the music thus remains abstract in rhythm, striking a balance between total neglect of the words and subjection to them.

The accompaniment, too, is characteristic.   It is of the kind known as *concertant*, in which the instruments compete with the voice on equal, or almost equal, terms.   These accompaniments are still semi-polyphonic and differ completely from the familiar harmonic type in which a figure, such as reiterated chords or arpeggios, is repeated for bars on end.   Though it predominates in Rameau and separates him from his Italian contemporaries, it is itself Italian but of the later seventeenth century.   Many admirable examples of it are found in Scarlatti's cantatas.   Combarieu[1] says that Lalande was the first to introduce it

---

[1] (129), II, 255.

into France; this is wrong, and several instances of it occur in Lulli himself.[1] Rameau remained faithful to it when it had gone out of fashion in its original home. Old-fashioned Lullists reproached him

---

[1] In the enchanted garden scene of *Armide* and the sleep scene of *Atys*.

for these "accompagnements tumultueux" which, they said, sounded more like sonatas and concertos than airs, and the Italianists agreed with them, so that Rameau, in this as in other respects, fell between two stools, displeasing both the conservative and the advanced. Masson claims rightly that no eighteenth-century musician, not even Bach and Mozart, carried further than he the art of blending instruments and voice.[1]

The character is dignified and pathetic. Its solemnity is more expressive of the sacred precincts in which Aricia finds herself than of her own personality, and its religious cast announces worthily the august nature of the subject, with its story of divine intervention in a play of human passions.

Hippolytus[2] enters and, questioning Aricia, learns with dismay of her fate and of his indirect responsibility for it.

"A Thésée, à son fils, ces jours sont odieux," she declares.   This draws forth a passionate disclaimer and it is thence an easy step to an exchange of confidences.   This short dialogue, in which touching phrases express Hippolytus' emotion, is in the freest style of French recitative, almost as melodic as the air which had preceded it.   Our idea of eighteenth-century recitative is based on what we know of either Bach's and Handel's sacred music, or of Italian opera, remembered mainly through Gluck, Mozart and occasional revivals of *La Serva Padrona* or *Il Matrimonio segreto*.   Allowing for the difference between English and Italian, the recitative of Handel's oratorios is on the whole akin to that of Italian music.   Bach's sensitive and sometimes vehement recitative is remote from the *recitativo secco* of the Peninsula, with its unmusical and inexpressive patter of repeated notes, suitable to almost any words or to no words at all.   The difference between French and German and between Bach's and Rameau's subject-matter is very great; yet it is Bach's recitatives, rather than those of Italian opera, which can give the fairest impression of Rameau to ears ignorant of the Frenchman's art.

With *recitativo secco* the difference is enormous.   In the score of

---

[1] It was stated by Burney ((43), II, 968) that "nothing in Lulli's operas was imitated or adopted by the rest of Europe but the style of his overtures or in Rameau's but the dances".   This is too exclusive.   French *symphonies* with incidental voice parts occasionally crossed the borders; there is one in Handel's *Semele*, III (Somnus' first air).   Handel, of course, heard French opera at the court of Hanover where Cambert's son-in-law, Farinel, was music director.   Müller-Blattau (196) says he was acquainted with Rameau's music.

[2] He is a *haute-contre* or counter-tenor, "a natural tenor with an exceptionally high *tessitura*: neither the male alto nor the bass or baritone voice singing in falsetto can provide an adequate substitute for its limpid yet virile tone" ((193), 330.)   See also (224).

bars that precede the passage just quoted the line is constantly on the move, rising and falling by as much as an octave within the space of one bar as it follows the expression. Within the framework of B minor it modulates in almost every bar to one of the related keys of B, E minor or F sharp minor.

With Hippolytus' avowal the emotional pitch heightens and the recitative turns to song. This is indicated by the word *air* in the score, a word misleading to the reader acquainted only with Italian opera. Nothing like an *aria* or indeed like Aricia's opening air occurs here but just five bars of a more pronounced melodic nature than what had gone before. Musically the line is not distinguished, but when we take it together with the words we feel its expressiveness; indeed, these bars are a perfect example of a melody whose beauty consists in its admirable fitness to its text. The lovely downward line is but an idealization of the intonation of the spoken sentence, in which the voice would start at its highest point and gradually drop to "rendu" (ex. 42).

Ex.42

Peut - être vot-re in-dif-fé - ren - ce   Tot ou   tard   me l'au - rait ren-du.

The dialogue continues, Aricia leading, and again her recitative breaks into song, with a miniature *da capo* air of some twenty-five bars in which she explains that her peace of mind is gone and that, in her retreat, the memory of Hippolytus' love will haunt her ever more. The music is as sincere and expressive as hitherto till the arrival of the word "revoler" in the text causes it to forget its subject and to launch out into three bars of coloratura quite uncalled-for by the theme. Such a display is typical. Except for those airs definitely imitative of Italian models, coloratura for its own sake is not found in French classical opera.[1] The instances that do occur are illustrative and suggested by the text. This, it seems, is as it should be. Unfortunately, it is not the sentiment of the text as a whole that provokes the outburst but the presence of one or a few magic words[2] which alone have this power, such as "voler, tonnerre, lancer, gloire, chaîne, victoire, triomphe", and a few others. The coloratura is expressive of flight, or casting, or chains, but often not at all of the subject.

---

[1] "Flourishes based only on the convenience of a fine A or O and not on the meaning of a word are inexcusable" ((83), II, 202–203). See Chapter III, p. 73.

[2] Le Cerf calls them ironically "mots privilégiés". Later they were known as "lyriques". Le Cerf notes with approval that Lulli made little use of them. They were criticized by Dubos ((64), 657) and Mably ((84), 140).

The scene ends with a duet between the lovers in which they address a prayer to Diana, assuring her that, though they have yielded to love, they remain faithful to her.   Lulli's duets had been nearly always homophonic.   Campra was the first French composer to imitate the Italians and write polyphonic duets.   Both kinds are found in Rameau, the polyphonic preponderating slightly.   This one is mainly harmonic; the parts move in thirds and sixths with here and there a little imitation. The writing is stiff and archaic, and one is reminded of the seventeenth century rather than of a contemporary of Handel.[1]   The duet is not without beauty and its austerity is fitting to a prayer, but it is not the natural outpouring of two beings full of their newly discovered passion; the music suggests rather a penitential theme.

As it finishes a march strikes up and to its strains there enter the priestesses of Diana.   The first two scenes had been in D major and minor; what follows as far as Phaedra's arrival is in G.

The priestesses' entry heralds a *divertissement*.   In a chorus of which the most one can say is that, like the "paisible séjour" of which it sings, it is "aimable" and "innocent", the priestesses hymn the

Ex. 43 *Tendrement*

delights of their sacred calling and exhort each other to give homage to their queen.   Of all the shades of feeling that the treatment of his subjects has called on Rameau to express, this is the most alien to him. The chorus is interrupted by two *airs* in G minor, the first of which is the loveliest piece we have met hitherto.   Its theme is a variation in 2/4 of the D minor minuet in the prologue (ex. 43).   Its two-note phrases, contrasted in pitch and direction, are very Ramellian and the piece has a brother in the *rondeau du Sommeil* in *Dardanus*, IV.   A priestess *parodies* it to words celebrating Love's inability to disturb Diana's tranquil bowers.   The second air, marked *un peu gai*,[2] is less individual and, like the duet, rather archaic.

---

[1] For the 1757 revival a more modern number was substituted.

[2] Rameau makes little use of Italian terms.   With him as with the Italians musical terms have moved away from their original meanings and *gai*, *tendre* and *gracieux* have come to denote speed as much as expression.   If this is forgotten the presence of these indications at the head of movements which appear to be neither blithe nor tender nor graceful seems incongruous. In his *Traité de l'Harmonie* he used the Italian terms, prefacing them with "comme disent les Italiens" (II, 23).   See Appendix B.

Into this limpid environment there bursts the wrathful figure of
Phaedra, bringing with her the key of D minor.

Phaedra is already the jealous lover of the last two acts of Racine's
play though she has yet no proof of Hippolytus' love for Aricia.
Her purpose in appearing in the temple at this moment is to make sure
that Aricia pronounces the vows that will prevent her marrying.
But Aricia is no longer as docile as she was and much less disposed to
bind herself to eternal celibacy. She fears, she says, lest Heaven
condemn a love that is not given freely—a possible allusion to forced
vocations, a common theme in eighteenth-century French literature—
and an enlightened chorus replies with one accord: "Non, non, un
cœur forcé n'est pas digne des dieux." Phaedra appeals to Hippolytus to second her, but the prince withdraws politely under cover of
his respect for Diana who would be outraged if she were offered
unwilling vows. Phaedra sees through this ruse and replies sarcastically:

> Je ne sais qui vous touche le plus,
> De l'autel ou de la victime.

This is the first intimation we have that she has perceived the prince's
love for Aricia, but the absence of any surprise in her note suggests
that, in Pellegrin's mind, she has already guessed the truth. In any
case, she had foreseen this resistance and is come prepared to storm
the temple. After this moment of drama, spectacle again takes possession of the stage. Phaedra sings a brief fury air, in the tempo—
6/8—and key—F major—usual for such airs at this time; then the
trumpet sounds and the stage is invaded by soldiers. The priestesses
counter this with an appeal to the "dieux vengeurs" in a chorus and
solo where the presence of the words "lance" and "tonnerre" gives
opportunities for abundant flourishes.

The thunder duly peals and lasts for over forty bars of 2/2 *animé*.
Descriptions of natural phenomena were one of the many adornments
inherited by French from Roman and Venetian opera and, far from
losing their popularity as they had in their homelands, they became
more frequent and more ambitious as time went on. They were easy
to fit into the theory of imitation sacred to the æstheticians of the age.
Abbé Dubos recognized that at times "music uses only instruments
to imitate [natural] sounds in which there is nothing articulate",
and he included in these sounds "all those which are most capable of
impressing us when we hear them in nature".

Such music, though non-vocal, is most certainly "true imitation
of nature"; indeed, the sound it makes is "like to the din which the
winds make in the air and to the roaring of the billows", an extremely
literal interpretation of imitationist theory. He justified these *symphonies* on grounds of verisimilitude. "Those suitable to the subject

help us to take interest in the action and they may be said to play a part in it."[1]   Thus, the "fiction" of Atys' sleep is made all the more touching by the *symphonies* that precede and follow it.   He analyses the Logistille *symphonie* in *Roland*, the music which restores the hero's reason, and shows how true an imitation it is.   Its character is exactly right to calm a madman; it is highly "vraisemblable" that it should have this effect, and this suitability is what constitutes its imitative quality.   What is "vraisemblable" is good imitation.

In Diana's thunder there is no change of harmony for the whole forty-three bars, yet "the slow climb of the basses, the ever-rising chords, built in tiers on the centrally placed dominant, the progression of the very simple melodic designs, make the whole unexpectedly varied and threateningly expressive".[2]

Rameau was not afraid of modulation and it may seem surprising that in such a long, stormy *symphonie* he should have remained in one key. But he knew what he was doing.

"The expression of feeling requires a change of key," he wrote to Abbé Arnaud, "whereas the painting of images and the imitation of different sounds does not need it; . . . the mind will remain in the same mood . . . as long as the same key persists."[3]   Here there is agitation but no change of mood; consequently no change of key is wanted.

The presence of the *crescendos* and *diminuendos*[4] should be noted.

Diana appears to gentle strains in G minor and gives her full support to the priestesses, Hippolytus and Aricia.   Her entry to a smooth, close counterpoint gives us an unexpected glimpse of a Bach-like Rameau—unexpected, because it is very seldom that he recalls his great contemporary.   These few bars (Sc. 5; p. 64 of the vocal score) move in the same harmonic mood as the *fugato* of Bach's E minor harpsichord toccata.

> On peut servir Diane avec le même zèle
> Dans son temple et dans les forêts,

she declares with deistic sentiment.   Thereupon she enters the temple and all but Phaedra and the nurse follow her.   The rest of the act belongs to the queen and to D minor.

On finding herself baffled and deserted Phaedra gives vent to more fury in an expressive passage with a dotted quaver accompaniment.   Her thoughts are turned from her feelings by the entry of a messenger with heavy tidings, effectively marked by the change to F minor.   He comes—this incident is borrowed from Racine—with the news of Theseus' death.   Phaedra's exclamation on learning of it

---

[1] (64), I, 638–639.   [2] (190), 328.   [3] (235).
[4] Indicated by ◁━━━◁ and ▷━━━━▷ in the printed score of 1733.

affords one of the most dramatic uses in all Rameau of the chord of
the major seventh, the chord which, when used separately by him,
says Masson, "always indicates a peculiarly intense stress of the
musical discourse, either a heart-rending lament or a cry of terror or
a violent effect of passion".[1]

The messenger completes his report and the air clears for an
instant into the major as the nurse performs her evil task of kindling
hope in the queen's breast. Now, she says, Phaedra's love for
Hippolytus becomes lawful. She hints this too in Racine but more
discreetly[2]; here, the idea is expressed with brutal clumsiness; the
scene stands in the same relation to the Racine original as an ensemble
of tubas to a string quartet. The value of Racine's heroine lay in her
sense of sin; Pellegrin's dummy has no such subtlety; her only consideration is the very positive one, that Hippolytus' affections are
engaged elsewhere. The nurse pursues ingratiatingly and the music
assumes a warm, fondling tone that we had not heard since the scene
between the lovers. After resisting a little longer Phaedra gives way
to this gentle hope, responding in tones like the nurse's but more
passionate. Failure, however, she will not survive, and on this stern
thought the act ends.

From the usual description of a Lulli or Rameau opera, one would
imagine that the interruption of the action by *divertissements* was quite
arbitrary and bore no relation to the plot. This act proves that it was
not always so. The scene in the temple is necessary since without it
Phaedra's suspicions would not be confirmed and one of the motive
powers of the play, her jealousy, would not be set in action. What
is undramatic about Scene 3 is not its presence but its length.

It is worth while insisting how essential a part in the French conception of opera is played by the interludes. French opera is not a
form in which the progress of the action is the sole source of interest.
It consists in a succession of tensions and relaxations obtained by
pathetic scenes alternating with festivity.[3] By Rameau's time the
form had been well tested and his contemporaries had built an artistic
theory out of it.

> The excellence of the French plan seems to consist in this division
> of the poem into dialogue and entertainment. The dialogue is to
> absorb strongly the spectator's attention; it is a serious pleasure. The
> entertainment is a rest, a passage to pleasures of a different sort which
> are to amuse him without taking his mind off the subject.[4]

---

[1] (190), 475.—This dramatic scene was cut out for the 1757 revival.

[2] "Votre flamme devient une flamme ordinaire" (*Phèdre*, I, 5).

[3] "You must picture opera as a kind of concert composed of several
elements which should accompany each other faultlessly if they are to give
all the pleasure one may expect of them" ((97), 196).

[4] (98); in (190), 556.

Marmontel expresses this more philosophically.

The essence of tragedy requires that the action should not relax, that everything should inspire fear or pity and the danger or misfortune of the chief characters should increase from scene to scene. But the essence of opera requires that its action be only intermittently distressing and terrible; that its passions should have moments of quiet and happiness, like serene intervals on stormy days. It is enough if care is taken that all happens as in nature, that hope succeeds fear, suffering pleasure, pleasure suffering, with the same ease as in the course of life.[1]

The second act is entirely Pellegrin's invention. It is played at the gates of Hell and falls into four parts. In the first, Theseus battles unsuccessfully with the Fury Tisiphone in the attempt to advance into Pluto's realm, the entrance of which he has already penetrated. In the second, Pluto himself appears and Theseus beseeches him to be allowed to rejoin his friend Pirithous, on whose behalf he has come down to the nether regions. In the third, Pluto's court meets, as it were, *in camera*, without Theseus, and the god exhorts his attendant divinities to wreak their worst on the offending intruder. In the fourth, Theseus is readmitted, still guarded by Tisiphone. He begs for death but is told by the three Fates that he must await his hour. He appeals to Neptune, reminding him of his promise to succour his adopted son up to three times. Another vengeful chorus of Pluto's demons answers him but as it closes Mercury enters, bearing Neptune's request for the king's release. After a brief argument Pluto agrees but commands the Fates to warn Theseus of the horrible destiny that awaits him. The demon court withdraws and Theseus, sped by Mercury, regains the light of day.

Rameau has taken fullest advantage of the opportunities for display and for the expression of clashing and violent emotions, both personal and collective, which the libretto affords. Moreover, in the figure of Theseus he has created a character truly individual. Theseus' music is his and his alone; no other character in Rameau has any like it. The hero's emotional composition is, of course, simple; his chief elements are dignity and assurance and a restrained violence that contrasts with the uncontrolled fury of the jabbering chorus and the *staccato* soullessness of Tisiphone. But with these few qualities Rameau has built up one of the most monumental figures in tragic opera.

The music is more vital than in the first act and responds fully to the tension of the situation. It opens with an animated prelude in B flat, expressive of the Fury Tisiphone; although it suggests mimicry there is no indication that it is accompanied by dancing.

One of the greatest surprises which the study of earlier music

---

[1] *Encyclopédie*, 3rd edit. (1779), XXIII, 747: *Opéra.*

brings lies in the changes undergone by the emotional meaning of keys. In the later seventeenth and in the eighteenth centuries keys were fairly precisely defined from the standpoint of the feelings they connoted, but the attribution of keys to moods differed widely from later practice. Accustomed as we are to the characters of F and B flat in the Classical period and throughout the nineteenth century, no description more foreign to them could be imagined than that of "furieux et emporté", suitable to "tempêtes, furies et autres sujets de cette espèce", which are the labels affixed to them by Marc-Antoine Charpentier towards 1680 and by Rameau some forty years later.[1]

Such is clearly the significance of B flat in this opening prelude and the short *air* that follows it, a dry, syllabic piece in the same style as Phaedra's F major "Périsse la vaine puissance" in the previous act.

The monumental quality of Theseus is well seen in the opening phrases of his part. The recitative strides up and down the register, not with leaps of vocal virtuosity, intended to show off the singer's agility or the rich contrasts of his tone, but expressive of the big-heartedness of the character (ex. 44).

After a short argument king and Fury join issue in a *contradictory* duet—one, that is, in which they sing simultaneously but utter symmetrically antithetic sentiments:

> { Quoi? rien n'apaise ta fureur? }
> { Non! rien n'apaise ma fureur! }

The fashion of this form of duet came from Italy and spread in France in the first half of the century; it is commoner in Rameau than in his predecessors, and the parts move usually with more freedom than in the *unanimous* kind. This one is more alive than that of the lovers in Act I and it has a certain menacing bleakness, but the writing is still that of a motet rather than a dramatic piece. With it, the key moves to G minor and, on its conclusion, the infernal court enters to a slow fanfare in C major.

With Pluto's entry the music regains strength and personality. The two *airs* in which Theseus beseeches the god to unite him with Pirithous are masterpieces of rapid declamation, large-limbed and vigorous, in which the expression of the sentiment is cut down, as it were, to the bone, with a nudity worthy of Racine at his most *dépouillé*. The first of these follows the old practice of making the voice double the *continuo* which goes back to the origins of French opera. It occurs in Cambert's *Pomone* and was borrowed from Italian opera

---

[1] (1), 157.—Such attributions of meaning were already well established before Charpentier's time; for instance, the Witches' dance in Matthew Locke's *Macbeth* music is an F major 6/8 movement of the same type as Rameau's Fury dances.

where both Cesti and Cavalli had followed it. Lulli gave it an
emphatic rhythmical declamation, but his use of it appears to our
taste excessive.[1]   By Rameau's time it had become exceptional.   The

Ex.44

second *air* has the same striding measures as the recitative with a lively
leaping bass.[2]

The third scene consists of Pluto's exhortation to his court and
its choral and choreographic response.   In a syllabic *air*, made up
largely of repeated notes, Pluto calls upon the rivers of Hell, by name,
to avenge Proserpine and himself.   The voice part is hammered
out and devoid of melody, nearer to speech than to song, but over it
the orchestra weaves a feverish accompaniment with an undulating

---

[1] There is a familiar instance in Handel's "O ruddier than the cherry"
in *Acis and Galatea*.

[2] It has a bassoon *obbligato* in connexion with which Rameau wrote on
the score: "Recommandé aux bassons de nourrir les sons sans les détacher
et faites chanter de mesure" (this for the soloist); "on me l'a promis."
The last words allow us a glimpse of a long tussle at rehearsals with an
obstinate singer.

motion like the piano part of a Romantic *lied*.   There is no fixed
pattern and the wavy thirds and sixths of the violins keep moving
from beginning to end, but the key sequence travels from C minor to
the relative major and thence to the dominant, where there is a short
pause in the voice part and whence we return to the principal key.
The words, with obvious changes, are taken up by the chorus of
demons,[1] from which sopranos are absent.   The chorus is more
extended than the solo and the undulating design is occasionally
broken by repeated chords, whilst the key sequence is different and
the mode scarcely leaves the minor (ex. 45).

No one who has heard this chorus can be in two minds about its
beauty and dramatic power, yet this was the kind of number of which
Rousseau was thinking when he complained that the orchestra, in
French opera and especially in Rameau, so predominated over the
voice that the melody was drowned in accompaniment.

The complaint was neither new nor personal to him.   It had been
heard for at least a quarter of a century.   Old-timers regretted the
lightness of Lulli's accompaniments and complained that the heavier
harmony of those in modern operas distorted the expression and
prevented the words from being heard.   Rémond de Saint-Mard ill-
humouredly grumbled at the amount of "fugues, held notes, counter-

Ex. 45

---

[1] This French device is used by Handel in *Saul*, II and III, and *Acis
and Galatea*.

-cy - te, Le Phlégé - ton, Par-ce-qu'ils ont   de plus bar-

-cy - te, Le Phlégé - ton, Par-ce-qu'ils ont   de plus bar-

- cy - te, Le Phlégé - ton, Par-ce-qu'ils ont   de plus bar-

-ba - re,   Ven - gent Proserpine et Plu-ton!

- ba - re,   Ven - gent Proserpine et Plu-ton!

- ba - re,   Ven - gent Proserpine et Plu-ton!

points and a prodigious crowd of chords" in them that "stifled the sung part by excess of harmony".[1]   There is, he wails, too much "charivari" and not enough tune in modern music, a state of things for which he blames the Italians.   Several of the cronies represented in Mably's letters[2] have the same grievance.   One of them, it is true, a Chevalier, who is an accomplished amateur, "l'âme de nos concerts", defends harmony, "the principle of all music", and finds Lulli's accompaniments too simple, but he is alone in his opinion.   Madame de S . . . breaks out: "Je les déteste" (i.e. modern accompaniments); "c'est un vacarme affreux, ce n'est que du bruit, on en est étourdi." The richer harmonies of "opéras nouveaux" and especially of "ce chef d'œuvre qui a été tant vanté et qui nous a tant fait bâiller"—a probable hit at *Hippolyte et Aricie*—are looked upon as an indiscreet display of technique and the result of a search for the difficult and the abstruse. This "goût pour le difficile et pour les bizarreries les plus singulières" is a sign of the decadence of present-day music.

"La musique la plus difficile et la plus harmonique n'est que du bruit dès qu'elle est sans expression," says another of these ladies.

Rousseau's objection, on the other hand, was that of an admirer of the later Italians.   Judging by his *Lettre sur la musique française* the chief test of good vocal writing is whether the tune will make sense if you play it on the keyboard with one hand.   Such a test may be favourable for the composers of *opera buffa* and of early *opéra-comique* with whom Rousseau and the Encyclopædists were infatuated, and, indeed, for any musician who, like Jean-Jacques, looks upon the writing of his accompaniments as "hack work",[3] but it is fatal for a composer who relies to any great extent upon his command of harmony and orchestral colour.   *La Serva padrona*, *Le Devin du village*, even *Richard Cœur-de-Lion* may pass such an ordeal with flying colours but Wagner will fail to satisfy anyone who, in exploring his scores, confines his attention to the vocal line, and Rameau is as inadequate as Wagner in this respect.   Indeed, in this particular *air* and chorus, it is the orchestral part, not the voices, that can well-nigh stand alone. And this is true of many of Rameau's solos whereas it is exceptional in Italian operatic music of this century, including Gluck and Handel themselves.

The vindictive mood of the chorus is expanded into two *airs infernaux*, the only dances in this act.   The first of these, in F, has nothing we recognize as infernal but exemplifies the plastic quality of Rameau's ballet music which almost dictates the details of the dancers' mimicry.   Here we see the sweeping curves of the mantles and the

---

[1] (97), 198–201.   [2] (84), 152, 162–165.
[3] "Travail de commande."—See the chapter in the *Confessions* relating to *Le Devin du village*.

alternately slow and rapid gestures.   The second *air* is livelier and has
more intrinsic interest but suggests less plainly any particular motion.
It is repeated and a chorus superimposes on it another syllabic fury
piece, whose chief interest lies precisely in the combination of rhythmic, declamatory voice parts and scurrying accompaniment.   The
independence of this accompaniment is even greater than that of the
last chorus.

Theseus then re-enters.   His first words suggest that he has been
carrying out a search for his friend; though he has seen many unfor-
tunates, Pirithous was not among them.   Tisiphone warns him that
they cannot meet as long as he is alive and, in a moving phrase—note
the force of the rising fourth on "misérable"—he calls for his release
(ex. 46).

He is answered by the three Fates.[1]   This first trio of theirs,

Ex.46

though less spectacular than the second, is among the peaks of Rameau's tragic writing.   Its model is the *Trio des Parques* in Lulli's
Isis, IV, 7, which is worthy to stand beside it.   It is the kind of piece
we call Gluckian, not because it is really characteristic of Gluck nor
because his examples of it are the finest that exist, but because it is
only from his *Alceste* or *Iphigénie en Tauride* that we know it to-day.
With its dignified simplicity and hollow harmonies this measured
chant conveys a sense of impending doom (ex. 47).   Towards the
end the solemnity deepens and the music comes close, in both feeling
and form—a descending middle part framed between an upper and
lower pedal—to Sarastro's "Stärk mit Geduld sie in Gefähr".

Theseus again comes to the fore and calls upon Neptune to help
him.   This is the first and less weighty of his two invocations.   His
prayer is an *arioso*, sustained by an *arpeggiando* accompaniment which,
like that of Pluto's *air* and chorus, sounds more modern than its date.

---

[1] Their parts are sung by two counter-tenors and a bass.

Ex.47

Such harmonic accompaniments, consisting of a repeated figure, are Italian and always rare in Rameau; when they are used it is generally for not more than a few bars. Only in passages of great emotional stress do they persist from one end to the other as here. The style is more declamatory than melodic and maintains the dignity and foreboding present in the trio (ex. 48). (The quotation gives the closing bars.)

A lively chorus of protest answers the king's supplication. The contrast of mood is indicated by a sharp jerk from C minor to A flat and from *mesuré et pas vite* to *très vite*. This is another chorus where the voice part is syllabic and mainly homophonic and rhythmical and the orchestral part full and active.[1] In its thirteenth bar it plunges into D flat, a key which is made to seem more remote than it is by the close on the dominant that precedes it. The music moves quickly back to A flat and the chorus winds up smartly on the thrice-repeated warning: "On ne peut en revenir" (i.e., from the Underworld).

These words are at once belied by the appearance of Mercury, claiming Theseus in the name of Neptune. With this conventional solution of an insoluble problem the interest at once flops and Rameau's music, which for good and for ill is intimately linked to its text, does likewise. To Pluto's refusal Mercury opposes the argument: Jupiter is master in the Heavens, Neptune in the sea and Pluto in Hades, but the happiness of the universe depends on their concord.

"Le bonheur de l'univers dépend de votre intelligence."

---

[1] It begins like two of Philip-Emmanuel Bach's sonatas, No. 1 in F in the Prussian set and No. 2 in A flat in the Württemberg set.

Ex. 48

This unconvincing reasoning, put forth to unconvincing music, is deemed unanswerable by Pluto, who yields forthwith. "C'en est fait; je me rends." The happiness of Creation triumphs over my anger, says this enlightened despot, and Theseus may go free. But . . . —and here the sting of vengeance is heard again and the music revives—but his fate will not be as sweet as he thinks. And again the three sisters advance and address him.

This is the famous second *Trio des Parques*. When *Hippolyte et Aricie* was first performed by La Pouplinière's private orchestra and troupe[1] this trio was tackled successfully, but when it came up for rehearsal at the Opéra, singers and instrumentalists broke down over the enharmonic passage in the middle and were so incapable of negotiating it that the whole trio, to Rameau's disgust, had to be left out.

> We had managed to insert in the second Fates' Trio . . . a *chant* in diatonic enharmony of which we had expected much; but though a few singers were able to master it, all did not succeed as well; so that we had to change it for the stage, since what may be of the greatest beauty when perfectly rendered becomes unbearable when that perfection is lacking; however, we have always left it in the printed edition in its original form for connoisseurs to judge of it. But one should not hear it unless one is assured of perfect execution; many judge on a first impression without examining whether the defects are due to the work itself or to the performance.
>
> We do not despair of finding a favourable opportunity for making use of it, and also of chromatic enharmony, at least in *symphonies*; but for that we would need docile performers able to play in agreement and ready to give all the patience which such a novelty needs for unaccustomed ears.[2]

He never found this opportunity and never again wrote anything so far beyond the capacities of his executants. A good artist, no doubt, recognizes the limitations of his medium, but we have lost much thereby.

The trio is the grandest of those ensembles of his where the voice parts are fairly simple, rhythmic and syllabic, and expand over a florid and richly laden orchestral *symphonie*. The whole piece might be danced without the voices; I do not say that it would not suffer thereby, but the instrumental parts can stand alone and the message of the number—its prophecy of woe—would still be clear.

Though nothing in the score says so the *ritournelle* cries out for plastic interpretation. The long sweeps of demoniacal robes, the flapping of sable wings, are vividly suggested in the two phrases which alternate, on descending steps of the scale, in the first eight bars; it is not possible to visualize an immobile stage while this wealth of movement is being poured out in the music.

Assez lent is the mark but, whatever the exact tempo, the impression must be one of extreme deliberation, for the harmonies move but every other bar and then by only one degree (ex. 49). The scheme is

---

[1] "D'habiles musiciens et de bonne volonté" ((12), 94).

[2] (9), XIV, 154–155.—He returned to the subject in (12) and again expressed his disappointment.

Ex. 49

interrupted after the sixth bar and a new figure introduced, after which the concluding bars mingle both motives. The words are:

Quelle soudaine horreur ton destin nous inspire!
Où cours-tu, malheureux? Tremble, frémis d'effroi!
Tu quittes l'infernal empire
Pour trouver les enfers chez toi.

Each line is dealt with separately in slow counterpoint whilst the orchestra continues to unwind an accompaniment derived from the *ritournelle*. With the second line the runs and dotted quavers stop for a moment and the orchestra doubles the voices, throwing into relief the direct appeal of the Fates to the king. The runs begin again and the whole line is repeated in imitation in a magnificent passage of enharmonic modulation, leading us at length to a momentary close in D minor. These are the bars on which the Opéra singers foundered. In six bars the modulation slides down by semitones from G minor to D minor (ex. 50), six bars which are a vivid tone-painting of the horror announced by the Fates.

Rameau shows great interest in enharmonics in his writings. In spite, he says, of the abolition of the difference between the harmonies through equal temperament,

let us not think that the ear is taken in by it; it feels in the lack of relation [between the two keys] all the harshness which enharmony provokes; we are struck by the quarter-tone without realizing it; we are revolted by it because it is unnatural, because our ear cannot appreciate it; nevertheless, the common harmony by which this passage from one mode to the other is effected tempers the hardness of it, the moment of surprise passes like a flash and soon this surprise turns to admiration with finding oneself transported from one hemisphere to another, so to speak, without having had time to think.[1]

He adds enviously that "the Italian theatre shows admirable scenes of this kind, for instance, that in *Coriolano* beginning 'O iniqui marmi'.[2] We have given a few specimens of enharmony in two of our harpsichord pieces, *L'Enharmonique* and *La Triomphante*."[3]

---

[1] (9), 153.

[2] By Ariosti. The correct quotation is: "Spirate, iniqui marmi!"

[3] These examples contain diatonic enharmony, that is, a sequence of two major semitones between the beginning and end of which an additional quarter-tone slips in. "Diatonic enharmony is used to inspire dread and horror as in the *Trio des Parques*" ((21), 184). See Chapter 2, 34–35.—There is an instance of chromatic enharmony in *Les Indes galantes*, II (earthquake) and one in the 1744 version of *Dardanus*, IV, 1 ("Lieux funestes"). In the former, says Rameau, "I was so badly received and so ill served that I had to change it into ordinary music" ((12), 95). But the score retains the original.

Ex. 50

To return to the trio. The third line is set to canon-like imitations in which the orchestra doubles the voices; an air of false mildness falls on the scene corresponding to the seeming good news: Thou art leaving the halls of Hades (ex. 51). The fourth line follows without

Ex.51

a break, set homophonically, after which the flourishes return with the words: "Tremble, frémis d'effroi!" The symphonic as well as dramatic conception of the piece is shown in that it concludes with an important coda; the rushing thirty-seconds and iambic throbbings die away into the bass as Pluto, his court and the Fates withdraw from the stricken king.

No earlier Hippolytus play had staged Theseus' adventures in Hell, and indeed there is no close connexion between this act and the rest of the plot. Nothing in the opera would be unintelligible if it were omitted. But how much would be lost! The full grandeur of Theseus would not be grasped and his two remaining solos would seem disproportionately powerful for so secondary a personage. The great music which falls to him in Act II gives him a stature worthy of these later effusions. And to lose Theseus would be to lose a great deal. Phaedra's part is so compressed and desiccated that, though she still wears a tragic air, she is not a tragic heroine; indeed, she is not much more than an obstacle to the love of Hippolytus and Aricia. The two lovers are elegiac, not tragic; Theseus alone is fully tragic, battling against the gods in the person of Pluto and against the Fates themselves, bereaved of his friend, bereaved of his wife and his son. Rameau, admittedly far greater musician than playwright, nevertheless grasped fully the possibilities which Pellegrin's libretto gave him of shaping a monumental tragic hero.

Dramatically, therefore, the excision of this act would be a great loss. Musically, the loss would be even more grievous. Few acts in Rameau pass through such a succession of contrasted moods: heroic, vindictive, imploring, prophetically menacing. I have perhaps laboured this but it is important to counteract the impression that French classical operas are constantly interrupted by irrelevant spectacle and dancing and that Rameau, in particular, pure musician that he was, showed himself incapable of grasping the dramatic values of his texts and sacrificed his subjects to his love of abstract music. His deficiency lay in that he could not criticize a libretto as a whole and appeared to accept almost any plot; but he was as alive as any opera composer who has ever existed to the dramatic possibilities of given situations; if none of his *tragédies lyriques* is a complete tragedy, they all contain tragic fragments, and this second act of *Hippolyte et Aricie* is among the longest and grandest of them.

The third act is in this respect almost its equal. It incorporates material from the second, third and fourth acts of *Phèdre*, roughly rearranged at the expense of the heroine. The *divertissement* which divides it into two sections is a natural expansion of the theme of the king's homecoming.

The first half comprises Phaedra's confession to Hippolytus, the declaration of the prince's love for Aricia and the expression of the queen's jealousy. By far its most outstanding number is the magnificent solo "Cruelle mère des Amours" with which it begins. It is here that Rameau's music comes nearest to the substance of Racine's work. Though nothing in Pellegrin's words is quoted from his great predecessor the tenour of the lines is that of the queen's soliloquy in *Phèdre*, III; Rameau's setting is a commentary thereon and it will make the sense of his music clearer if I quote it.

> O toi, qui vois la honte où je suis descendue,
> Implacable Vénus, suis-je assez confondue!
> Tu ne saurais plus loin pousser ta cruauté.
> Ton triomphe est parfait; tous tes traits ont porté.
>   Cruelle, si tu veux une gloire nouvelle,
> Attaque un ennemi qui te soit plus rebelle.
> Hippolyte te fuit, et bravant ton courroux
> Jamais à tes autels n'a fléchi les genoux.
> Ton nom semble offenser ses superbes oreilles.
> Déesse, venge-toi; nos causes sont pareilles.
> Qu'il aime. . . .

The greatness of these lines lies, *inter alia*, in the way in which the queen, notwithstanding her deep sense of sin, beseeches Venus to wound Hippolytus as she herself has been wounded and to make him yield to her passion. This mingling of what is best and worst in her nature is retained by Pellegrin in dull, obvious terms; the queen's prayer is expressed quite unblushingly.

> Je ne te reproche plus rien
> Si tu rends à mes vœux Hippolyte sensible.

In addition he introduces an allusion to the goddess's persecution of the house of Minos, a theme which Racine had stressed in his first act. Pellegrin's couplets are therefore richer in material than Racine's monologue but are terribly flat. Rameau, however, has given them a setting worthy of Racine.

The opening words, "Cruelle mère des Amours", set the tone, which is one of tragic and suppliant love, smarting under harsh blows. This sentiment has frequently inspired Rameau with great music.[1] The queen's supplication has something of physical pain; she is not only sick at heart but ailing to death, and every word she utters, every gesture she performs provokes exquisite suffering.   Such an interpretation is not in keeping with her robustious appearance in Act I, but in Racine Phèdre is at the point of death and this conception of her has overridden that of Pellegrin and inspired Rameau.   All the pungency and acridity which are perhaps the most persistent characters of his music are present in the opening bars (ex. 52).

Ex.52

The middle section contains the queen's prayer and the tone, without ceasing to be suppliant, is less bitter; the sense of cruelty has gone and Phaedra, in the caressing line with which she leads off, almost cajoles the goddess into granting her request.[2]   The *da capo*

---

[1] See Iphise's "Cesse, cruel Amour" (*Dardanus*, I, 1) and "Fatal Amour, cruel vainqueur" (*Pygmalion*, 1).

[2] The chaconne in Act V begins with this strain.

is preceded by eight bars of new matter which is the orchestra's own expression of the queen's state of soul.

Soon after the first performance another air, with different words, was substituted. It sings of hope:

> Espoir, unique bien d'une fatale flamme,
> Pour la première fois viens régner dans mon âme.

The music is correspondingly gentler; the finest moment is in the first three bars where the glide on the C sharp is as caressing as Phaedra's hope and the mode as uncertain. With harmonies both pungent and delicate it gradually settles down to a 7/3 chord and B minor (ex. 53).

Ex.53

In 1742 yet another change was made. The significance of Phaedra, already not very great, was further whittled down and she was deprived of this, her chief solo. Scene 1 consists now in a few lines of recitative in which she explains drily that she has learnt of the king's death and intends offering her heart and her crown to Hippolytus. The emotional content of the mood formerly expressed between orchestra and voice is now concentrated in an extraordinary *ritournelle*, perhaps the harshest piece ever sprung from Rameau. The note of physical agony which could be heard in the background of "Cruelle mère" fills now the whole music to the exclusion of any other. It must be one of the earliest paintings in music of physical suffering.[1]

The recitative that follows "Cruelle mère" is lively and its changes of key show the care with which Rameau keeps close to the emotional phases through which the dialogue passes. At the point where Hippolytus reveals his love for Aricia and Phaedra hits back with a profession of hate for her rival the conflicting sentiments join issue in a duet and once again the music seems to step back fifty years. The voices sing in rather stiff imitation whilst a busy bass keeps going with broken scales. Archaic though this piece seems there is no denying its grim sturdiness; it expresses with rugged beauty the mutual threats of queen and prince. The parts assail each other with the symmetrical violence of a stage fight.

> { Ma fureur va tout entreprendre
> { Gardez-vous de rien entreprendre

---

[1] See Appendix D.—Compare bar 5 with bar 29 of the first movement in Bach's E minor partita.—In 1757 "Cruelle mère" was reinstated.

$$\left\{\begin{array}{l} \text{Contre des jours trop odieux!} \\ \text{Contre des jours si précieux!}^1 \end{array}\right.$$

The dialogue is pursued in a passionate tone indicated by the key of F major, and suddenly, as Phaedra is about to kill herself with Hippolytus' sword, Theseus enters.

Here, Pellegrin crushes Racine's II, 5 and IV, 1 into a few lines. Both queen and prince withdraw and Œnone, the nurse, accuses Hippolytus of having assaulted his stepmother's honour. Theseus at once recalls the Fates' predictions; he sends the nurse away so as to be alone, but as she departs a march is heard; his subjects are preparing to celebrate their king's return.

De mon heureux retour au Dieu des vastes mers
Mes peuples viennent rendre grâce,
Et je voudrais encore être dans les enfers . . .

The whole *divertissement*, joyful though it be, is overshadowed by the presence of the sombre king, and the contrast expressed in these lines gives the succession of chorus and dancing a grim irony that raises it far above the *festa teatrale* level of many such interludes.[2] No other *divertissement* of Rameau presents music so strong, so broadly conceived and so varied. It consists in a chorus, two danced *airs* and two rigadoons, the second of which is repeated by a singer. The chorus "Que ce rivage retentisse" is unique in his operas. It is not his most dramatic chorus but his most spacious and most sustained, and the most highly developed example of contrapuntal writing in them. The dramatist gives way to the pure musician and the result is some hundred and sixty bars of choral writing recalling Handel at his biggest, with a rhythm firm and square from start to finish.[3] The chorus falls into five parts, separated by short homophonic interludes; some of these are instrumental and accompany dancing, others are confined to the *petit chœur* of sopranos and contraltos.[4] It opens like a fugal exposition (ex. 54). Hardly is this complete when the counterpoint breaks off and the first homophonic interlude occurs.

---

[1] Omitted in 1742.

[2] It is said to have given Pellegrin much trouble.—The irony was not felt by the audience and a mistaken taste for symmetry caused this *fête* to be placed at the end of the act, so that tragedy and entertainment were kept in different bottles. This was done soon after the first performance. A writer in *Observations sur les écrits modernes* (XXXII, 165; March 30, 1743) could thus say: "I like to see the Dlle. Camargo come joyfully to wipe away the tears that Thésée has made me shed" (in (190), 556).

[3] Cf. Chapter 3, p. 86.

[4] An example, contemporary with Rameau and less unfamiliar to us, of a chorus embodying dance interludes, is "Crown with festal pomp" in Handel's *Hercules*, but here the dance bars are sung like the rest.

-tis-se De la gloi - - - - - - re du Dieu des

gloi -re du Dieu des flots! Que ce ri - va - ge re - ten - tis - se De la

flots, du Dieu des flots! Que ce ri - va - ge re - ten - tis - se De la

Que ce ri - va - ge re - ten - tis - se De la

flots, De la gloi - - - re du Dieu des flots!

gloi - - - re du Dieu des flots!

gloi - - - re du Dieu des flots!

gloi - - - re du Dieu des flots!

The second episode, much shorter than the first, is based on a new subject which each part takes up in imitation. The voices push upward step by step to a close on the dominant. The third episode combines the subjects of the two previous ones and modulates to E minor (ex. 55) (the quotation gives the last bars). The emotional tension is increasing and this time the singing is continued throughout the homophonic interlude which ends in A minor. The fourth episode introduces two new themes; the second is a motif of great vigour which thrusts upwards and finally takes possession of all the parts (ex. 56).

By this time the emotion is far too braced up for an interlude to be tolerable and as soon as this episode is finished the violins give out the first subject, the contraltos follow, and the opening fugue starts over again. Now comes the most exciting moment. The fugue stops on the dominant chord of G. There follows a half-bar of silence, then, *ff*, the chorus breaks out in harmony with a sixfold repetition of the chord of F, echoed by the *petit chœur* (ex. 57). Such brutal juxtapositions of foreign keys—and the foreignness is accentuated by the dominant harmony that preceded the change—are not uncommon in Rameau.[1] The practice was not new; it occurs already in Peri and Monteverdi[2] and in Purcell.[3] Rameau uses it with unrivalled force. The tonal opposition is enhanced by the contrast between counterpoint and harmony, between a regular smooth-flowing rhythm and the impact of repeated chords, between melody and rhythm reduced to its barest form.[4]

After this intrusion of F major the music slips back into G, appearing to end on a full close. But the end is not yet; the emotional tension is too great for the chorus to conclude so simply. A second time the chords return, this time in a less distant key, C minor. Rameau feels that a repetition would be pointless since the element of surprise would be feebler the second time. So he does not attempt to compete with himself and weaken his success by overdoing it; he is content with a less startling change and thus the dynamic contrast is thrown more sharply than ever into relief. The close is this time in D major and, now that some of the potential has been discharged, the music finds leisure for a dance interlude. For a third time the full chorus hammers out "Que ce rivage retentisse" on its repeated chords, but now there is no change of key at all; the *petit chœur* echoes and the chorus winds up to its real close.[5]

---

[1] Cf. *Castor et Pollux*, III, 4.   [2] See (240).   [3] See (241), 215.
[4] One is reminded of the outburst "God save the King" in Handel's Coronation anthem *Zadok the priest*.
[5] In the succession of keys F, C, D, Masson sees rather "un bel effet d'éloignement".

Ex.55

Ex.56

Ex. 57

The effect of this threefold intervention of the repeated chords, with a decreasing element of tonal surprise, is tremendous. The chorus had begun with something of the static character of a motet but as it progressed it acquired impetus and at the finish it is thoroughly dramatic. Its chief character, at least till the triumphal violence of its latter part, is one of tripping speed. The quick repeated notes of the main theme and the light broken scale of the counter-subject call up a picture of swift entries; the music runs on like wavelets racing before the breeze.

Despite its rising emotional strength and ultimate dramatic power there is no doubt that this chorus is too long for an opera. Since Rameau never wrote another like it he himself must have realized this. But his audiences would have been less ready than we to suffer from it; they were used to the spectacle of men and women standing on either side of the stage, singing without any action. The perusal of French classical operas suggests a most plastic use of the chorus singers; there are few choruses where the music does not call up in one's imagination a picture of concerted movement. One is all the more surprised to learn that, till well into the eighteenth century, opera choruses took no part in the action but stood stolidly in two rows, the men on one side, the women on the other.

> J'ai vu des guerriers en alarmes
> Les bras croisés et le corps droit,
> Crier plus de cent fois: Aux armes!
> Et ne point sortir de l'endroit

wrote the *chansonnier* Panard in *Le départ de l'opéra-comique*, performed the very year of *Hippolyte et Aricie*. Rameau's later librettist Cahusac, who in 1749, in the fourth act of *Zoroastre*, attempted to draw his chorus into the fray, complained of this immobility in his article *Chœurs* in the *Encyclopédie*:

> The choruses fill the stage and form thus a most pleasing sight but they stay motionless in their places; one hears them say sometimes that "The earth crumbles beneath their feet", that "They perish", etc., and meanwhile they remain quietly in the same spot without the least movement.[1]

The spectacle of a body of people, standing immovable, singing: "Que ce rivage retentisse" would have appeared less incongruous then than now.[2]

The chorus is followed by one of Rameau's most beautiful and

---

[1] Quoted in (190), 293.

[2] A term of comparison with this chorus is afforded by "Qu'à nos sons" in *Les Éléments*, II, 4.—This chorus was much cut down for the revivals of 1752 and 1757.

haunting instrumental *airs*. The dancers are sailors; whether those who have brought Theseus home or others is not indicated. The music advances *gravement* with a slight swing suggestive both of a sailor's rolling gait and of the undulation of a ship at anchor. In addition to this rhythmic quality there is an emotional significance. No particular sentiment is called for by the subject and we may feel here something of Rameau's own personality—that personality which is nearly always veiled behind the passing mood of the drama (ex. 58).[1]

Ex.58 *Gravement*

The second *air* is a complete contrast. It has the buoyant rhythms and light-heartedness of a folk-dance and resembles a hornpipe. Two rigadoons follow; the first one,[2] which Masson calls Handelian, is headed *rigaudon en tambourin*. The *tambourin* is the Provençal form of the tabor and has given its name to any dance in which the throbbing of the drum is present. Apart from its beat of two in the bar, it has no fixed form and can be combined with other two-time dances as it is here. Unknown to Lulli it appears in the eighteenth century; one of its earliest examples is in *Les Éléments*.[3] It is the most purely rhythmical of the dances in use in Rameau's time and some of his tambourins, like those of his contemporaries, are content with a dynamic effect. But often a deeper feeling and rich harmonic texture infuse them without weakening the Dionysiac appeal and we then have pieces which are unique, such as those in *Les Indes galantes*, I, 6, *Dardanus*, prologue, and especially *Les Fêtes d'Hébé*, I, 8 and III, 7; the last of these is a transcription of the well-known E minor tambourin for harpsichord.

The high jinks character of the tambourin is less obvious here since the dance is a rigadoon, but the full-bloodedness of the drum-ming bass is present. The second rigadoon is not *en tambourin* and is quite different. Its tripping measures, with no bass, contrast not only with the heavy drumming of the first one but also with the nostalgia which pervades the music and which Pellegrin's words, clumsy though they be, interpret rightly as an "invitation au voyage".[4]

---

[1] In 1757 several changes were made in this *divertissement* (see p. 191).

[2] Its opening notes recall those of the march.

[3] II, 4; *Troisième air pour les divinités*.

[4] The *matelote* who sings it is not a female sailor but a woman singer attired as a sailor.

Here the *divertissement* ends. The brooding figure of Theseus steps forward and, in dignified recitative, dismisses his faithful people. He is left to himself and the music follows him at once into his private world of torture. It passes into B minor, pivoting on the last words he has addressed to his folk, "d'autres biens", which he repeats with the exclamation: "Quels biens! Je frémis quand j'y pense!" There follows one of the most remarkable passages in all Rameau. The B minor phrase closes and, *ff*, the orchestra breaks out at once in the

major with four bars of vehement syncopation which step straight out of the *Mastersingers*, II, 5 (ex. 59). One feels impelled to continue with (ex. 60). A passing cry of tenderness is expressed by three bars like a slow movement from a violin sonata. After further

hesitation Theseus settles down in his determination to seek vengeance and prepare himself to call upon Neptune for the third and last time.

The mighty *arioso* that unfolds is the second and greater of the king's two invocations. "Puissant maître des flots" is not only unsurpassed in all Rameau but is one of the grandest solos in eighteenth-century music—grand in the truth and intensity of its emotion, in its breadth and sustained power, in the significant scoring that lights up the voice part. Like Phaedra's air at the beginning of the act it is in B minor. It opens with an ample prelude whose sinuous line

advances with deliberation, enlivened by syncopations (ex. 61). Over this meditation, adding itself to it instead of replacing a part, Theseus throws the melody of his prayer (ex. 62).

The strength of this piece lies largely in the contrast between the line of the violin melody, with a harmonic rhythm that moves rapidly, and a more slowly moving bass. Moreover, here as in the second Fates' trio, there is an antithesis between an instrumental part with marked rhythmic patterns and a *sostenuto* vocal section. Akin though this supplication be to Bach's *ariosos*, it is unmistakably Ramellian in its touch of rhetoric, of gesture and attitude, so that we not only feel the presence of a soul but catch darkly the glimpse of a majestic figure in a corner of the stage, with hands and head raised in prayer. The flow of emotion is constant and there is no climax, but just at the end, with an interrupted cadence,[1] the intensity rises slightly before dying down into the recitative that follows (ex. 63).

This soliloquy adds to the stature of Theseus. He is, indeed, a weightier figure in Pellegrin-Rameau than in Racine. As the play progresses it is less of Racine's Thésée than of his Mithridate that we are reminded. The opening of his monologue in this act (sc. 9) has a mood analogous to that of Mithridate in III, 3–4 of the tragedy that bears his name, though neither situation nor sentiment is the same.[2]

Here, to our taste, the act should end. Only intense admiration for stage machinery could enable one to enjoy the sight of Theseus standing by while the azure canvass of Neptune's realm bulges and billows and the strings run races up and down the scale of G major. In vain Rameau varies his descriptive efforts and replaces scales by rushes in 6/8 while Theseus utters bloodthirsty threats against his son. Neither plot nor music, in order to be complete, requires the responsive heavings of Poseidon.

---

[1] With passage from dominant harmony to that of the sixth degree.— Rameau uses such cadences to "lengthen a phrase which one is loath to end" ((21), 144).

[2]
       Mon fils, . . .
       Me préserve le ciel de soupçonner jamais
       Qu'un fils qui fut toujours le bonheur de ma vie
       Ait pu percer ce cœur qu'un père lui confie!
       Je ne le croirai point. . . .

       Je ne le croirai point? Vain espoir qui me flatte!
       Tu ne le crois que trop, malheureux Mithridate!
       Xipharès mon rival? et d'accord avec lui
       La Reine aurait osé me tromper aujourd'hui?
       . . . Tout me trahit ici?
       . . . Et toi, mon fils, aussi?
       Toi de qui la vertu consolant ma disgrâce. . . .
                 (*Mithridate*, III, 3–4.)

Ex.63

fois! En-tends ma gé-mis-san - te voix! Per-mets que ton fils t'im-por - tu - ne Pour la der-niè - re

fois! Per-mets que ton fils t'im-por - tu - ne

Pour la der-niè - re fois!

If I were asked to point out a portion of Rameau's work which gave the fullest picture of his musical powers I should not hesitate to name this act. We have in it a masterpiece of each of the three sides in which he excels: *arioso*, chorus and dance. The greatest depth of feeling, not only in Rameau but in all French classical opera, is found in its soliloquies, "the final and most organic development of recitative. . . . The French are unwilling to give dramatic airs a purely musical rhythm. The secret ideal is that the melody of these airs should draw as near as possible to the movement of impassioned speech."[1]

Of the chorus I have spoken at length. The first sailors' air and the rigaudons, though less outstanding than chorus and monologue, are nevertheless examples of Rameau's dances at their best, in their union of compelling rhythm and emotional strength. For sheer splendour and might no *divertissement* surpasses the fête with which Theseus' unhappy return is welcomed. All Rameau, of course, is not there, but what is present is so essential and so superb that it is the finest summary of his work that one can find.[2]

French opera, unlike French tragedy, was never tied down by the rule of the three unities of time, place and action, and the plot of *Hippolyte et Aricie* is not compressed within twenty-four hours. Neither does the scene remain the same. Each act is in a different place: the first in Diana's temple, the second in Hell, the third in a part of Theseus' palace near the seashore.

The fourth is also by the sea but in a grove sacred to Diana. Here Hippolytus is discovered, alone. He has been banished from his father's presence and from that of Aricia and he is musing:

Ah! faut-il en un jour perdre tout ce que j'aime?

His soliloquy is set in a free rondeau form, in which a melodic section alternates with measured recitative. A long prelude introduces the chief theme and evokes a mood of gentle melancholy, very different from the bitter supplication of Phaedra in Act III or Theseus' despair in Act V. Each of these acts opens with an expression of sorrow and the extent of Rameau's powers may be judged by observing the skill with which he renders each different shade of woe. Phaedra and Theseus, each in dissimilar ways, live in worlds of tragedy; Hippolytus, whose sadness, one feels, is not far from resignation, belongs to elegy.

The scene that follows answers to the first scene of the fifth act of

---

[1] (190), 216–217.—As late as 1773 an anonymous writer complained that an *aria* in which an actor is dogged by the rigid precision of the tempo destroys dramatic illusion.

[2] Its only rival in this respect is the third entrée of *Les Fêtes d'Hébé*.

Phèdre. Hippolytus announces his departure to Aricia and asks her
to come with him. After some hesitation she consents and both lovers
place themselves under the patronage of Diana. At this moment a
bruit de chasse is heard and their meditations are interrupted by the
arrival of Diana's hunters and huntresses. The change of mood is
underlined by the passage from A minor to D major.

The elegiac atmosphere that prevailed in Hippolytus' soliloquy
reigns throughout this scene. The conversation culminates in a
unanimous duet in which several features already noticed are present:
the rigid rhythm, 3/4, and the passages in thirds and sixths.

With the arrival of the huntsmen a *divertissement* begins. This
one has no dramatic justification, but contains some enchanting music.
It opens with a hunting chorus of a familiar type; we meet in it a
milder version of the C major to F major jump in "Que ce rivage"
and alternations of full and half choruses as well as nine bars of canon.
Its rhythm and descending outline carry into the delightful *air* that
follows. The melody ripples out, smooth and effortless as a folk-song
(ex. 64).[1] A tune like this, sparkling with life and spontaneity, con-

Ex.64

tradicts the opinion, still to be derived from certain judgments
expressed on him, of Rameau's "pompous artificiality".[2] It comprises two short episodes; the first is rollicking, the second combines
dynamism and melody. The *air* is *parodied* with variations to words
in which a huntress gives lovers advice which is the contrary of
Napoleon's "There is only one victory in love: flight", and sings:

> Osez sans alarmes
> Attendre ses coups;
> Si vous combattez,
> La victoire est à vous.

This *air* belongs to the well-defined category of the *fanfare de
chasse.* Séré de Rieux[3] gives a large number of these fanfares to which
words have been set; they are the mob of the tribe of which Rameau's
air is a chief.

---

[1] Compare with a similar chorus in *Les Éléments*, IV, 3.
[2] (228), 43: a work no page of which shows the least knowledge of his
music.
[3] (110).

The second *air* is a gavotte in which the 6/8 rhythm and repeated triplet notes of the hunt theme are cleverly combined with the 2/2 of the dance.   Upon it is built an ingenious chorus.

The entertainment closes with two minuets.   The repeated note, representing the huntsmen's horns, is present in both; indeed the first contains little else; it runs through the whole interlude like a leit-motiv.   The second of these minuets is tinged with familiar Ramel-lian wistfulness (ex. 65).

Ex.65

Drama returns at the end of the minuets.   A sudden drop from D to B flat announces the fact.   A *bruit de mer et de vents* arises; the sea grows rough and "un monstre horrible" emerges.   The descrip-tive music that accompanies this apparition could obviously count on receiving but little attention from an audience fascinated by the agitated muslin and cardboard terror; yet it will bear scrutiny.   The first six bars consist in a rising scale on a tonic pedal, involving ninths and elevenths and showing the little scurrying motif of three ascend-ing notes which was to signify terror for many generations to come. Over it a chorus of horror utters its feelings in appropriate terms. The description of the Neptune-sent creature as "une montagne humide" comes from Racine.   At this point the key drops from B flat to A flat; the modulation is made more expressive by being introduced through the subdominant chord of the new key, and the impression is heightened by the tumultuous accompaniment.

Hippolytus advances towards the beast while Aricia sings of her quivers and shivers.   Her recitative is punctuated by the *tremolandos* and *staccato* outbursts which are reserved in Rameau for moments of special intensity and which were to become an abuse in later opera. The chorus joins in after the fashion of its Greek prototype, and through it the reader of the score learns that a flame and thick clouds envelop the hero who, when the screen lifts, is no longer visible.

The end of this act is the most purely tragic moment in the opera.

Aricia leaves the stage, and the chorus in slow strains weeps for Hippolytus. Phaedra enters and on hearing of the disaster utters cries of remorse. Thunder peals and the earth quakes as if to encompass her doom, and she asks to be spared long enough to proclaim the innocence of the unhappy prince. As she leaves the chorus raises once again its lamentation.

The transition from the tumult of the monster's appearance to the expression of the chorus's sorrow is effected by slowly descending chords (ex. 66). The lament of the onlookers, full of dignified pathos, follows a pattern traditional in French opera (ex. 67). We find it in Jean-Baptiste Moreau's music to Racine's *Esther*.[1] In the scene with

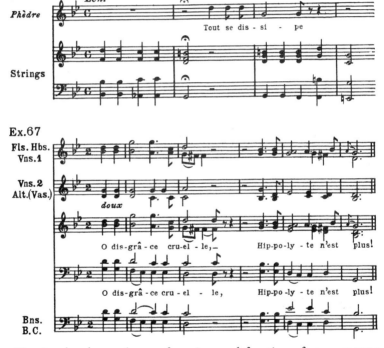

Phaedra the chorus departs from its usual function of commentator or spokesman of collective feeling and enters into dialogue like a character, anticipating Gluck's practice. The accompaniments to Phaedra's recitative depict the thunder and the quaking of the ground that mark Heaven's disapproval of what has occurred. Rameau's earthquake figure carries us as far forward as his duets carried us back;

---

[1] Racine: *Œuvres complètes* (Édition des Grands Écrivains), vol. *Musique*, 15.

the following quotation might come from a work of the next century (ex. 68) and reminds us of the debt which growth in the technique of expression owes to the devices of descriptive music.

The close of Phaedra's part, accompanied in semibreves, addressed to the "dieux cruels, vengeurs implacables", has the character of a

Ex. 68

solemn invocation—a form of which this opera offers us three different examples. When she has finished the chorus repeats ex. 67 with a change of words: "O remords superflus! Hippolyte n'est plus!"[1] The sense of meaningless loss, of youth and valour crushed by blind brutality, hangs heavy over this final scene and makes it one of the moments of sheerest tragedy in all Rameau.[2]

---

[1] A modification of Théramène's words in *Phèdre*, V, 6:

. . . O soins tardifs et superflus!

Inutile tendresse! Hippolyte n'est plus!

[2] It is incredible that this superb scene, from Phaedra's entry, was cut for the 1742 revival; it was probably reinstated in 1757.—Gluck must have known it: the scene where Clytemnestra surprises the plaintive chorus in *Iphigénie en Aulide*, III ("Puissante Déité"), is built on the same lines.

The fifth act is in two *tableaux*. The first unfolds in the same place as Act IV. In the wood where the chorus reminded Phaedra of the futility of her remorse stands now the lonely king. This scene—the last in which he appears—is as grand as any of his previous ones. Its continuity with what we have just heard is marked by the identity of key (G minor); were it not that a short time must elapse between the acts for Phaedra to make her confession to her husband, the end of Act IV and beginning of Act V could well be played without a break. The entr'acte music is the G minor sailors' *air* from Act III.[1]

The king has learnt the truth; accusing himself of his injustice he prepares to commit suicide by throwing himself into the sea. His solo is a passionate, despairing *scena* with no fixed form, in which, to full and agitated accompaniment—in itself a *symphonie descriptive* of his torments—the vocal line follows a pathway of declamatory melody (ex. 69). (The quotation begins at the end of the prelude.) When he comes to the mention of his son he falters and the music renders touchingly the tenderness that comes over him and the moment of loving reflection that follows the words "Mon fils" (ex. 70). There are few passages where the likeness between Rameau and Wagner, in the relations of voice and orchestra, is more evident.

The way to self-murder is barred by Neptune. The god explains to the unhappy father that his presence is still needed in the world; moreover his son is not dead; Fate has deigned to release the god from his oath and Diana has taken Hippolytus into her keeping. But Theseus may never see him again.

This news draws from the king his final and most moving utter-ance: an expression of renunciation, accepted willingly as a just punishment. In expiation of his fault he consents never more to embrace his son, and his last words wish Hippolytus the longed-for peace that the youth could not find in his father's bosom.

The verses are dull but the sentiment is not commonplace; a more stagy reaction would have been a fresh outburst of despair. So com-plete an acceptance of what, in the pagan world of opera, corresponds to God's will, raises the scene to an almost Christian level and it is therefore not just a coincidence that we should be reminded, in this last effusion of the suffering king, of the St. Matthew Passion (ex. 71). Formally, the likeness is with "The Saviour falleth low" (Part I, 28); the spiritual kinship is rather with later stages in the Passion story.

Rameau was very conscious both of his own value and of the rights of music. It is therefore all the more incredible that he should have sacrificed some of the finest numbers in his works so easily.

---

[1] As the curtain was not lowered between the acts the orchestra played a *symphonie* already heard while the scenery was being changed. Between the prologue and Act I the overture was repeated.

Ex.69

Ex.70

Vons.

Alt.

Th.

B.C.

Quel mystère o - di - eux!   Quel a - mour dé - tes -

- ta - ble La per - fide, en mou - rant,   vient de me dé-clar-

- rer!   Mon fils   O douleur qui m'ac-ca - ble!   Il était in-no-

- cent. Dieux, que je suis cou - pa - ble!

The three different openings of Act III, which he discarded successively, were all fine music; yet each one disappeared without a protest
whenever he fancied that his public's taste demanded it. The most
astounding of these sacrifices was the jettisoning of Scenes 1 and 2 of
this act. Less than a month after the first performance a note in the
Mercure de France tells us that these scenes were suppressed in order
to keep the unity of place within the act. The unities had never

Ex.71

Fls.

Vns.

Thésée

Je ne te ver-rai plus! O jus - te châ-ti - ment!

B.C.

reigned in opera and changes of scene were not uncommon between
acts. One of the speakers in the discussions reported in Mably's
Lettres objected that such changes were fatiguing.

> "I am obliged by them to use my reason, and reasoning is mortal to
> illusion. A poet should steal from me the use of my mind and my
> senses to leave me occupied only with my passions."[1]

Or, the writer adds in a note, if changes there must be, let them
never take place within the act. This opinion was obviously wide-

---

[1] (84), 22.

spread enough to make itself felt here, and so this magnificent music was thrown to the winds and not reinstated in any subsequent revival.

With Theseus' disappearance the tragedy is at an end. The second and last *tableau* breathes an air of bliss and enchanted gardens, with one moment of pastoral charm. The *symphonie* with which it opens is a descendant of the celebrated enchanted garden scene in Lulli's *Armide*.[1] Like its ancestor it is in E minor. The stage represents "delightful gardens" forming the drives in Aricia's wood; Aricia herself is "lying on a grassy bed and awakens at the sound of a gentle symphony".

The beginning forms one long orchestral prelude, falling into three parts. The first conjures up the spirit of peace which reigns in Aricia's bower. It reflects a feeling for Nature, for an artificial, dream-like Nature, born of the desires of the jaded court-dweller but infused with that yearning which so readily pervades Rameau's music. Its smooth imitations are woven on and around a theme of four repeated notes (ex. 72).

The second, in 3/4 dotted rhythm, fulfils a more concrete purpose and suggests the proximity of Diana's shepherds and of the goddess herself. It heralds a brighter light and inspires hope. It belongs to a type more fully represented elsewhere in Rameau and sounds therefore more commonplace.

At irregular intervals Aricia interjects a few words:

Où suis-je? De mes sens j'ai recouvré l'usage . . .
Quels doux concerts! Quel nouveau jour l'éclaire? . . .

They float above the glassy waters of the orchestral background which continues regardless of them.

The third section is more definitely a solo. It opens with some concisely expressive three-part writing for flutes and first violins, illustrating the words:

Mes yeux, vous n'êtes plus ouverts que pour verser des larmes!

There is about every great artist an emotional flavour, an affective tone peculiar to him and to no one else. Rameau's own brand is present in its most distilled form in these few lines. For those who cannot turn to his operas it can be perceived in the *Allemande*, *Courante* and *L'Enharmonique* in the third book of harpsichord pieces, in *La Timide* and *La Livri* in the trios. That it often expresses melancholy is evident from the words that accompany it in the operas, but its content is better described as unsatisfied desire and unsatisfiable longing. It may even happen, as in the chorus that concludes this

---

[1] Rameau knew the scene well; he quoted or praised or studied it at least three times, in (2), XX, 80 ff., (17), 69–115, and (21), 168–169.

Ex.72

very opera, that the music suggests its presence whilst the words indicate a different sentiment—a proof that the mood is the composer's own.

This flavour is too rare for me to call it anything but Ramellian. Outside his work we may perhaps recognize it sometimes in Ravel. The opening of his trio, the introduction of the septet breathe the same spirit with more ethereal grace and less acid tang. "Ravishing the senses without touching the heart," says Martin Cooper of the septet.[1] Is this not sometimes true of Rameau's most nostalgic strains?

All such subtleties are banished by the entrance of shepherds and shepherdesses singing "Descendez, brillante immortelle" to what, for Rameau, is very stolid music, in the stolid key of G major. Diana is not long in responding to the call and she addresses her "peuples toujours soumis" in an air of a type that not even a sense of history can make interesting. The audience, as well as Diana and the shep-

---

[1] (131), 130.

herds, guesses what is coming; Aricia alone sees nothing.   The goddess plots a surprise and promises to provide her with a charming
husband.   Aricia of course protests that nothing can make her
unfaithful to Hippolytus, whereupon Diana gives the signal and
fluttering quavers in the fiddles announce a flight of Zephyrs, bearing
Hippolytus down to earth.   At first the lovers, bashful and ignorant
of each other's presence, refuse to advance and be identified; when at
length they see each other, their feelings flow out in a *unanimous* duet.
While Diana is blessing them and they are expressing their gratitude,
a sound of pipes is heard and a throng of forest-dwellers enters the
presence of the newly appointed king and queen.

The tune to which they advance is entitled *marche* and belongs to
the family of movements called *musettes*.   Like the tambourin, the
musette takes its name from an instrument, the bagpipe.   "Innocente
et champêtre," this instrument was looked on as "too slender and
unrefined for the fashions that have prevailed in town life" as far back
as 1668.[1]   It was reintroduced for special effects in the early eighteenth
century, its first appearances in opera being in Destouches's *Callirhoé*
(1712) and Montéclair's *Les Fêtes de l'Été* (1716).   Conservatives
disliked it.   Bollioud-Mermet complained that *vielles* and *musettes*
were suitable only for village music and were deformed by being
introduced into "symphonies régulières".[2]

Like the tambourin again the musette does not correspond to a
definite dance form.   It is defined by its orchestration and characteristic bass.   It may occur combined with various fixed forms; thus we
have *menuets* and *gavottes en musette* just as we had a *rigaudon en
tambourin* in Act III.   Rousseau described it as

> a kind of air suited to the instrument of the name, in two or three time,
> gentle and naïve, rather slow, the bass of which is generally held, after
> the fashion of a bagpipe, and called for this reason *bagpipe bass*.   Upon
> these tunes are built suitable dances, also called *musettes*.[3]

To-day it is best known through German examples, those in Bach's
English Suites and in the finales of Mozart's violin concertos in D and
G.   It is, however, Rameau who has wrung from the form its fullest
emotional power.

What the pastoral style meant for Rameau will be discussed later.[4]
For the moment let us confine ourselves to this so-called *marche*.   It
is not headed *musette* but the indication "bruit de musettes" a few bars
earlier, when its opening strain was first heard, and the words of the
chorus that takes it up, would determine its character even if its
scoring did not.   For a march it has a strange and unearthly rhythm,
advancing as it does in two phrases of seven beats in all, grouped in

---

[1] Abbé Michel de Pure.   [2] (39).   [3] (100): *Musette*.
[4] See Chapter 10, pp. 377 ff.

five and two. This queer metre is enough to make an uncanny dynamic appeal and when combined with the evocative tones of the hautboys and the droning bass it is almost hypnotic. Its entrancing melody, winning and soothing, has none of Rameau's customary bite. The composer's favourite ninths are prominent in its harmonization. The two seven-beat phrases act as a refrain, their returns being separated by longer ones, the first of which has eleven beats, the second two groups of five and seven respectively. The bar time is 3/4 and we are conscious enough of the steady ternary beat for this rhythmical freedom not to become chaos (ex. 73).[1]

Ex.73

----

[1] Melodically this opening recalls the aria "Wohl euch, ihr auserwählten Seelen" in Bach's cantata *O ewiges Feuer*.

Everyone, even a Frenchman, approaches the eighteenth century through the Italo-German tradition of Bach and Handel, Haydn and Mozart.   Though the rhythms of these masters are not as monotonous as is sometimes stated, only in Bach is there any great variety.   In minor composers, especially those of the latter half, regularity amounts sometimes to rigidity.   One of the great surprises that meets us when we turn to French keyboard and operatic music of the periods of Louis and François Couperin and of Rameau is the constant suppleness and life of its rhythms.   It is in pieces like this march that we are most forcibly aware of these qualities, so refreshing after the pre-established beat systems of the Italian and German classics.[1]

One has to reach the post-Romantic age to find again such freedom and variety.   By Dr. Burney and his generation this was misunderstood; the firm measures which we know as classical, with their well-emphasized strong and weak beats, had blunted their sensibility to the subtle windings of the older French rhythms, and they condemned these as formless wanderings.   Burney could tolerate and even admire Rameau's dances only because there was in them "*some* determined measure and movement".[2]   But we, educated by what has appeared in Debussy's day and since, feel otherwise and enjoy the movement of the living line, whose rhythm is none the less firm for not conforming to a preconceived pattern.   Indeed, a sense of untrammelled rhythm, wiry rather than emphatic, is a feature of French music throughout its history.   It is most obvious, of course, in

---

[1] "Foreigners find that we manage movement and beat better than the Italians and that we succeed better than they in the domain of music which the Ancients called rhythm.   They are not as conversant with rhythm as we are and know less how to use it for expression and adapt it to the subject imitated" ((64), I, 660).

[2] (43), ii, 25.—Rameau knew well that one of the alleged superiorities of Italian music was its hard and fast rhythms which he calls "mouvements cadencés", but he considered that they were suited only to comedy because comedy "has scarcely ever *sentiment* for its object" ((17), viii–ix). "The expression of a sentiment, especially of a passion, makes its effect only with changes of beat. . . .   To praise Italian music for its constant observance of beat is to deny its expressiveness" ((21), 170).   Rhythm is less rigid with the French "because the main object of their music is *sentiment*, which has no (pre-) determined movement and therefore cannot be enslaved everywhere to a regular beat without losing that truthfulness which makes its charm" ((17), vii–viii).

Rousseau, so unjust to French music in his *Lettre*, spoke more fairly of its freedom of rhythm in his dictionary: "While Italian music derives its energy from its enslavement to a rigid beat, French music seeks it in controlling that same beat, in hastening or slackening it as is required by the character of the voice part or the flexibility of the singer's voice" ((100): *Chronomètre*).

Debussy, Ravel and their contemporaries, but it is present also in composers who are in the more direct line of descent from German classicism, such as Fauré and Chausson.[1]   Berlioz has been called unmelodic because his tunes are not four-square.   Ernest Newman's defence of him against this charge is valid for much of French music. Berlioz ignores the "conventional mooring-posts" of strong and weak points in the bar division; to sing his melodies in the "standardized four-square style" is to distort them.[2]

Abbé de Mably had already linked the difference between French and Italian music with the difference between the two languages.   Is not Italian music, he asked,

> so far removed from the simplicity which is the chief feature of ours merely because its language entails sounds more inflected and freer than the French which does not allow of inversions and has no tonic accent? . . . The music of our motets is quite different from that of our operas and a piece which we admire with Latin words would be highly ridiculous with French ones.[3]

It is well known that Rousseau coupled his attack on French music with one on the allegedly unsingable French language.   Burney, too, associated language and vocal music, relating "these eternal changes of measure which tease and disappoint the ear of all that are used to other music" with the limitations of French poetry.   "They seem as much the fault of the poet as the musician."

He compares a phrase of recitative to a French heroic verse:

> Each is an Alexandrine, through the song
> That like a wounded snake drags its slow length along.[4]

Without sharing his contempt one must endorse the association of music and verse.   In every land sung music is closely governed by the prosody of the language.   We are all habituated to the mould of German melody, itself based on German poetic rhythm and accent, and this has rendered other poetic rhythms, when we meet them in music, hard for us to grasp.   It is well known that French is alone among most European languages in having a weak tonic stress.   More-over, its prosody is based on syllabic count and not on feet.   (I speak, of course, of the orthodox classical tradition; there are in modern poetry plenty of experiments which contradict this assertion.)   As a result there are in French verse none of those strong beats so familiar

---

[1] E.g., the finale of the latter's *Concert.*—The character—strength and grace combined with litheness—of this musette march is precisely that of the opening strain of Ravel's trio.

[2] *Sunday Times*, August 1, 1943.   [3] (84), 139.

[4] (43), ii, 967.—These same "eternal changes", with the dotted-quaver rhythm, made Frederick II call French music "gigotante".

in our own and which, by confusion between stress and duration, we sometimes describe in quantitative terms: dactyl, iambus, trochee, and so on. In a language like English with strong and weak stresses it is possible to work to a pre-ordained pattern. In a French poem all syllables are not equal in length and stress, but accentual and quantitative differences depend much more upon syntax and expression than with us. The alexandrine or line of twelve syllables, which fulfils in French literature many of the functions of our pentameter, often appears monotonous to English readers because they do not know where to linger and where to hurry, and read every syllable as if it were of equal importance. In our own pentameter, they know well enough how it should scan; in fact, speaking generally, they know the scansion almost before they have begun to read; but in the alexandrine only the meaning will tell them which syllables are strong and which are weak. In reading French poetry, understanding of the meaning is as necessary to a rhythmically correct rendering as it is in prose, whereas in Italian and German it is possible to obtain a delivery satisfying to rhythmical requirements with an imperfect understanding of what the poem is saying. This may sound preposterous, yet many a beginner in German, whose slender vocabulary has still many deficiencies, derives pleasure from the well-marked rhythms of a poem whose sense he has only partially grasped.

There is little poetry in French which would respond to this treatment. A rhythmically correct rendering of French poetry requires a thorough knowledge of the language—more thorough than is needed, for similar correction, in German or Italian—and this is why so many people who are able to appreciate French prose find that the music of French poetry escapes them.

This fluidity of rhythm and stress in the verse is responsible for the lack of fixed rhythms in the vocal music based on it. Lulli intended to make his recitative the handmaid of his text; in point of fact he was far from following its rhythms with fidelity. His own declamation is often monotonous and, as even his admirer Romain Rolland has pointed out, consists for lines on end of a succession of anapaests. Rameau reproduces much more sensitively the rhythm of the very indifferent verse he sets, and it is in him, not in the Italian Lulli, that the French classical style of setting words to music should be studied. The absence of verse forms with fixed rhythms hindered the French from developing similar forms in music; in fact, regular rhythms enter music, in France, from dancing, not from song. Eventually the prestige of Italian voices and the greater freedom of the melodic line—not of the rhythm—in Italian airs caused the French, in their imitation of ultramontane fashions, to adopt hard and fast rhythms, but the square, strophic construction of German *lieder* has always been exceptional in France.   This freedom from cast-iron rhythms in vocal music is responsible for the greater elasticity of rhythm that is such a constant feature of French instrumental music at all periods since the sixteenth century, especially, of course, in those masters who have been least affected by Germany and Italy.[1]

The musette from which we set out on this long digression is repeated by a chorus in which the sopranos are divided and treated antiphonally, thus giving the impression of a double chorus.   On its last appearance the refrain is given to the tenors and basses under held notes in the sopranos.   The only fault in this enchanting piece is that it is so short and its brevity is scarcely compensated for by the fact that, if the directions are obeyed, it is heard three times.

Another solo of Diana's, more interesting than the last, leads to a noble chorus of congratulation in honour of the happily reunited lovers.   It is one of those pieces where Rameau's music seems too pungent for the insipid words set to it.

The tradition of concluding an opera with a *chaconne* goes back to Lulli.   The dance had come to Seville from the West Indies or perhaps Mexico late in the sixteenth century.   It was licentious in character and was associated with the saraband in the condemnation of moralists, being included in the dances whose performance was forbidden on the stage.   The period of its greatest vogue in Spain was from 1600 to 1625.   Sung chaconnes figure in Briceño's collection of guitar music published in Paris in 1626; their music is rudimentary and rhythmical.   As a dance it was known in France by 1625 when, on February 11, a *Ballet des Fées de la Forêt de Saint-Germain* included an *Entrée des chaconnistes espagnols.* We have no details of its steps at this stage; the earliest description of them, by Feuillet, dates from 1701 when it had long been established as a theatre dance.   The earliest instrumental chaconnes appear in Italy in the 1620s, also in guitar collections.   In 1627 Frescobaldi's second book of *Toccate e Partite* includes *Partite sopra Ciaccona.*   Some of those by Chambonnières may go back to 1630.   It seems that, as with

---

[1] The well-known *romance* has, of course, a fixed rhythm but its origin in *opéra-comique* points to kinship with danced songs.   It is first cousin to folk-song where the influence of dance rhythms is always strong.   In purely instrumental music Rameau's command of rhythm is seen at its most masterly in his second A minor *Courante.*

the passacaglia, Spain provided the dance and Italy developed the instrumental form.[1] The fusion of the two took place perhaps in France where it came to be used for prolonged displays of dancing on a large scale, especially at the close of an entertainment. Its instrumental form was originally strict since it consisted in a number of couplets on a ground bass which was repeated unchanged each time. Lulli first freed it from the constraint of the ground[2] and Rameau carried its freedom still further. With him the bass changes; there are modulations; episodes are of varying length; repeats occur irregularly and the first theme returns from time to time like a refrain. His chaconnes make up one continuous development, "free and shapely, ... not far removed from the form of variation by amplification".[3] The chaconne survived in French opera till Gluck and it is mainly through his examples and one or two of Purcell's that we know it to-day.

That of *Hippolyte et Aricie* opens with the same strain as Phaedra's "Je ne te reproche plus rien" (III, 1), and the first two couplets, which are in A minor, diffuse that Ramellian mood which I have tried to define (ex. 74). This pensive tone is kept up for some fifty bars. The rest of the movement is in A major. It is one of the shortest and most formal of Rameau's chaconnes, and its six couplets all subdivide into phrases of four or eight bars. It closes poetically with a smooth passage in pastoral mood on a dominant pedal.

Here in the score follows the *Nightingale air*. It has no place in the story, which is complete with the chaconne, but it is well known enough for a few words to be needed.

It is entitled *ariette*. This word was coined early in the century to translate the Italian *aria* in its specialized sense of operatic air. It did not acquire till later the meaning which its form suggests of a piece lighter and shorter than the *air*. It is given to solos, unconnected with the drama, inserted in the interludes to exhibit the virtuosity of a singer. French opera resisted up to a point the introduction of the Italian *bravura* air with *ritornelli*, *coloratura* and cadenzas, but the

---

[1] (180).

[2] I speak of the danced chaconne. Louis Couperin's chaconnes and passacailles for harpsichord show already this emancipation.

[3] (190), 418.

pressure of Italian fashion was too strong for virtuosity to be excluded altogether and it was let in, so to speak, by the side door, and flourished in *divertissements*. *Ariettes* are naturally more numerous in ballet operas than in tragedies where their place is in the prologue and final rejoicing. They are therefore devoid of dramatic significance but many are musically grateful. The conservative Rémond de Saint-Mard confessed that he liked them and acknowledged that they were very popular. "After the dances, ballets exist only for their sake."[1]

The *Nightingale air*, however, has not even musical interest. The title indicates its character. The soprano is supported by a flute and a violin and, if well performed, the whole affords the kind of pleasure we derive from watching a difficulty overcome with skill and elegance. It is one of Rameau's misfortunes that, with so many pathetic or stirring solos buried in oblivion, this untypical trifle should survive as a specimen of his vocal writing.

Two very lovely gavottes are also added to the *divertissement*; a place should be found for them earlier in the act, between Diana's second solo and the chaconne, for instance. The second one, another A minor piece, is a charming instance of what Noverre called the "conversations spirituelles" in which Rameau led his instruments to engage (ex. 75).

Ex.75

The first performance of *Hippolyte et Aricie* at the Opéra took place on October 1, 1733. The only name in the cast remembered to-day is that of Jélyotte who had just entered the Académie de Musique and was twenty-two; he sang the part of Love. Aricia was taken by Mlle Pellissier, Hippolytus by Tribou, Phaedra by Marie Antier and Theseus by Chassé. Musical reporting scarcely existed at the time and we have to be content with vague remarks such as that the music was "manly and harmonious" and had a "novel character".[2] So original a work provoked, of course, attack and defence. Abbé Dubos, it is reported, "who is a connoisseur, was not pleased

---

[1] (97), 257. The same music-lover who, though conservative, was not narrow-minded, adds: "We hear every day in France with admiration Handel's arias (les ariettes d'Handelle). How stirred we are by those fine airs of Tartini danced some time ago at the Opéra by mimes; every day the symphonies of Telemann and Hasse are played in our concerts" (towards 1740).

[2] *Mercure de France*, October 1733.

with it".[1]   Campra remarked to the Prince de Conti: "My Lord, there is enough music in this opera to make ten of them; this man will eclipse us all."[2]   It is curious to hear Gabriel Fauré pass somewhat the same judgment on the morrow of the revival in 1908 in an otherwise very laudatory account: "I will not deny that, here and there, one would have wished for a little air, so considerable is the musical substance."[3]   Looking back more than thirty years the *Mercure de France* for October 1764, the month after the composer's death, wrote of it:

> This opera was the time when the revolution took place in music in France and there was fresh progress.   People were at first astonished by music much more laden and richer in images than they were wont to hear on the stage.   But they appreciated this new kind and they ended by applauding it.

It had the honour of two parodies by Boissy.   After about forty performances it was dropped.   A revival took place in 1742 and another forty performances were given that year and the next.   It was revived a third time in 1757 and a fourth time, after Rameau's death, in 1767.[4]   Then began the long night in which no Rameau was heard.   Throughout the nineteenth century no work of his was staged.   The first performance in our age took place at Geneva in 1903; the opera was revived in Paris on May 13, 1908, and at Basel, in German, in 1931.

We have pointed out some of the changes made for the eighteenth-century revivals.   For that of 1757 several alterations were effected in the *divertissement* of Act III.   An *air gai* replaced the first *air des matelots*; for the *rigaudon en tambourin* were substituted a couple of minuets and three tambourins.   The first minuet, in G, came from *Naïs*, I, 8; it has a pastoral cast; the strings play in *pizzicato* double and triple stopping and the score includes piccolos.   The second is the original D minor one from IV, 3, transposed to G minor.   The first tambourin also comes from *Naïs* and is a companion piece to the first minuet; it has the same scoring and pastoral mien.   The second tambourin, which may have been composed for the revival, when Rameau was seventy-four, is one of his most impressionistic, with its crossing violin parts (ex. 76).   All these *génial* pieces lie buried in the appendix to the sixth volume of the Durand *Œuvres complètes*.

Hippolyte et Aricie holds a high place in Rameau's work and in eighteenth-century opera.   Like the hero of Corneille's *Le Cid*, Rameau wished his trial stroke—at fifty—to be a master stroke, and

---

[1] Letter from Abbé Leblanc to Président Bouhier, in (179), 169.

[2] (85), note 36.   [3] (146), 115.

[4] Abbate Frugoni translated and adapted the libretto and it was set to music by Traetta, who, however, retained some of Rameau's music; in this form it was given at Parma in 1759.

Ex.76

he succeeded.   Only personal preference can discriminate between
his first three tragedies, for they all contain great music.   The
differences are due mainly to their subjects and librettos.   Pellegrin's
book is neither the best nor the worst that Rameau was to set, but the
Hippolytus story afforded the only essentially tragic plot that ever
came his way and the presence of extensive tragic stretches in this
opera distinguishes it from the other two.   Tragedy is intermittent
elsewhere, but in *Hippolyte et Aricie* it reigns for several scenes at a
time and for the whole of the second act.   Moreover, in this his
first appearance before the opera-going public, Rameau dared more
greatly and conceived more broadly than later when he had gauged
the limitations of his performers and audience.   Never again did he
write a trio as gigantic as the second *trio des Parques* nor a solo and a
chorus as monumental as "Puissant maître des flots" and "Que ce
rivage retentisse".   Monumental, too, is his conception of the king.
No later tragic hero of his is designed on this scale and no other is not
a lover.   Even Zoroaster, in the opera that bears his name, has to be
in love.   Theseus alone is not amorous and his stature is all the
greater.   And him alone among all Rameau's heroes we feel to be
completely personal and not merely a vehicle for the expression of
emotion.   The ransom of this boldness is a discrepancy between the
tragic and heroic scenes and the idyllic and elegiac ones.   There is
an abyss between Hippolytus and his father, between Aricia and the
jealous queen.   *Castor et Pollux* and *Dardanus* are more homogeneous but also less daring and less brawny.

To stage a Rameau opera is a difficult enterprise, but it would not
be hard to revive portions of one for concert performance.   Scenes 8
and 9 of Act II—the welcome-home of Theseus and his *arioso*—

make a first-rate combination of singing and playing of the kind beloved of amateur music societies. Another excerpt full of vigour and beauty could be made by beginning with Pluto's air in II, 3, continuing with the chorus that echoes him, the chorus "Pluton commande", the first *trio des Parques*, Theseus' prayer "Puisque Pluton", the chorus "Non, Neptune aurait beau" and the second *trio des Parques*. The short fragments of recitative between some of these numbers could be retained or omitted at will. The beautiful "Chantons sur la musette" in Act V could be combined with the hunting chorus in Act IV and the invigorating first *air des chasseurs*.

Several of the solos possess enough vitality to stand alone as concert pieces. In Theseus' part "Puisque Pluton, Puissant maître" and "Grands Dieux! de quels remords", in Phaedra's "Cruelle mère" and "Espoir, unique bien",[1] in Pluto's "Qu'à servir mon courroux", in Hippolytus' "Ah! faut-il en un jour" and in Aricia's "Quels doux concerts" (beginning with the *symphonie*) all deserve and would justify presentation in this form.

The following passages in *Phèdre* are represented in *Hippolyte et Aricie*:

II, 2 "Moi, vous haïr . . ." (P) *by* I, 2 "Moi, vous haïr . . ." (HA)

I, 5 "Votre flamme devient une flamme ordinaire" (P)
by
I, 8 "Vous pouvez brûler d'une ardeur légitime" (HA)

III, 1 "Fais briller la couronne à ses yeux" (P)
by
I, 8 "Phèdre avec son cœur promet une couronne" (HA)

III, 5 "J'ai vu Pirithoüs . . ." (P) *by* Act II (staged) (HA)

III, 2 "O toi qui vois la honte" (P)
by
III, 1 "Cruelle mère des Amours" (HA)

III, 2 "Et l'espoir malgré moi" (P)
        by III, 1 "Espoir, unique bien" (HA)

II, 5 Phèdre's avowal to Hippolyte (P)
        by III, 2–3 (same scene) (HA)

III, 4–5 Thésée's return (P)   *by* III, 4–5 (same scene) (HA)

IV, 1 Œnone's denunciation of Hippolyte (P)
        by III, 6 (same scene) (HA)

III, 3 "Le peuple pour le voir" (P)
        by III, 8 (staged) (HA)

III, 2 "Et toi, Neptune" (P)   *by* III, 9 "Puissant maître des flots" (HA)

V, 1 Scene between the lovers *by* IV, 1–2 (same scene) (HA)

V, 6 "Hippolyte n'est plus" (P) *by* IV, 4 "Hippolyte n'est plus" (HA)

V, 6 Théramène's story (P)   *by* IV, 3 (staged) (HA)

V, 7 Thésée's lamentations (P) *by* V, 1 (HA)

---

[1] "Espoir, unique bien" is only in O.C., VI, appendix.

Among the guests who sat at La Pouplinière's hospitable board was Voltaire. At the time of the first performance of *Hippolyte et Aricie*, at which he was present, he had met Rameau and had not taken to him. "He is a man who has the misfortune to know more music than Lulli. In musical matters he is a pedant; he is meticulous and tedious."[1] But Voltaire could distinguish between the social bore and the composer. Impressed by the greatness of Rameau's music, he improved his acquaintance and less than two months later he had written an opera on Samson for him "during an illness".[2]

We are free to guess how he had got so far. No doubt he went to congratulate the "pedant" on his success. Rameau took advantage of this to beg for a libretto. Voltaire had already the year before "played" at writing an opera text, *Tanis et Zélide*, by which he set no store; perhaps he tried it on Rameau. I rather think that it was Rameau, stimulated by the recent success of *Jephté*, who said: "Why not a Biblical subject?" whereupon Voltaire proposed *Samson*.

The idea of a sacred opera was not new. In 1696 there had been talk of an *opéra spirituel* to be directed by Moreau, the music master at Mme de Maintenon's school at Saint-Cyr and composer of the incidental music to Racine's *Esther* and *Athalie*. The plan was to have sacred plays performed "as they were played at the Hôtel de Bourgogne, and with musical interludes and choruses", says J. B. Rousseau in a letter to Duché of November 13, 1696.[3] Francine, the director of the Opéra, succeeded in preventing the plan from maturing. But later a "spiritual opera" was given by the Opéra itself. Montéclair and Pellegrin's *Jephté* was thus the first sacred opera to be given publicly in France—since those performed in the Jesuit schools were not public and not "true operas", says Le Cerf de la Viéville scornfully, because the cast excluded women.[4] It met with success, partly perhaps a *succès de scandale*, and, as we have seen, was taken off after only a few performances.

In spite of *Jephté's* chequered career Voltaire may have thought of *Samson* because its story, less religious than that of Jephtha, had been staged by the Italian comedians in 1717 with L. Riccoboni's *Sansone* and revived in 1730 in a French translation by Romagnesi.

Rameau and he threw themselves heart and soul into the work. Rameau hoped to see *Samson* finished and performed that winter but Voltaire soon realized that he was ill-fitted for the task he had under-

---

[1] Letter to Cideville, October 2, 1733.
[2] Letter to Cideville, December 5, 1733.
[3] (179), 50, note 3.
[4] Le Cerf had himself written the libretto of a Christian opera which he published in the third part of the *Comparaison*. As he does not indicate the protagonists, it is impossible to judge of its dramatic interest.

taken and that the opera would not be ready till the 1734–1735 season. In June 1734 his *Lettres philosophiques sur les Anglais* were condemned and he withdrew to Cirey where *Samson* dropped into the background.

By October 1734, however, most of the text had been set to music and a concert performance was given at the house of the *intendant des finances* Fagon in rue Neuve des Petits-Champs. Mme du Châtelet, who was present, found the third and fifth acts "admirable".[1] After this Rameau cooled off. He got tired of waiting and, being on the spot, he saw better than Voltaire all the obstacles in the way of a public performance. He turned to ballet opera and produced *Les Indes galantes* with Fuzelier and d'Orneval, using perhaps parts of *Samson*. Voltaire, still at Cirey, followed its fortunes and, when it succeeded, exclaimed: "I knew that Rameau's music could never fail!".[2]

It was now his turn to ginger up his collaborator. He gave up writing to him for Rameau did not answer letters; he used as go-betweens Thiériot, another guest at La Pouplinière's, and Berger, secretary to Prince de Carignan, who had been inspector of the Opéra from 1730 to 1734. In February 1736 his text was ready and he sent it to Thiériot to be given to the composer.

But Rameau had lost interest. Though Voltaire besought him not to let such great music lie unused, he dallied with Paradis de Moncrif, a very light-weight poet. Voltaire was indignant. But it became clear that powerful interests were against *Samson*. "Intrigues that thwart the progress of the arts" and "the cabal that was later to stop the performances of *Mahomet*" prevented *Samson* from reaching the stage.[3]

What a waste! moaned Voltaire. If only Rameau would have his music printed! "I wrote *Samson* only for him; it is but right that he should enjoy the profit and the fame".[4] But Rameau, like so many creative spirits, never lingered over a work once it was completed. In the La Pouplinière circle he had found another librettist and *Castor et Pollux* was laid on the stocks. This was *Samson*'s death-knell.

But Voltaire did not forget. "I never think of his music without looking back wistfully to *Samson*. Shall we never hear at the Opéra

> Profonds abîmes de la terre,
> Enfer, ouvre-toi, etc., etc.?"[5]

---

[1] Letter to Maupertuis, October 23, 1734.
[2] Letter to Thiériot, October 13, 1735.
[3] *Avertissement* to *Samson* in the 1746 edition of the *Œuvres complètes*; id. in the 1752 edition.
[4] Letter to Thiériot, September 5, 1736.
[5] Letter to Thiériot, December 6, 1737.

After *Les Fêtes d'Hébé*, after *Dardanus*, he still wept for *Samson* and felt bitterly towards "les grands ministres" who had banned it because it mixed sacred and secular; "I dare to think that, in spite of a weak text, it is Rameau's masterpiece".[1]

This was the epitaph of Rameau and Voltaire's "still-born child".[2] We too are saddened by the loss of this "awe-inspiring and graceful" music.[3] What has happened to it? All we know for certain is that some of it was used again. The details given on this score are late and may not be trustworthy. Writing to Chabanon on January 18, 1768, Voltaire said that some went into *Castor et Pollux*. Later still a writer in the *Journal de Paris*[4] stated that "the finest pieces" in *Les Talents lyriques* (another name for *Les Fêtes d'Hébé*) contained music from it. He had this, he said, from someone who "had often heard the celebrated Rameau assert it". Voltaire quotes no authority and the context in which the remark occurs—the letter begins with a humorous reference to the flu from which he is just recovering and then chaffs Chabanon for still taking an interest in his Biblical heroes, Samson and Delilah, to whom he alludes in jocose and unprintable terms, and after a line or two about Rameau goes on to other matters—makes the memory seem very casual.

It is futile, if amusing, to try to fit music from these operas to Voltaire's lines. We may judge best of what *Samson* would have been by comparing the text with the music of *Hippolyte et Aricie*, the boldest and most vigorous of Rameau's operas.

Even if many fragments have survived this cannot console us for the loss of the whole, any more than fine sculpture that has been saved and housed in a building for which it was not intended can make up for the loss of the cathedral it once adorned. The loss is all the more lamentable in that Voltaire's libretto is the best that Rameau was ever to set.

----

[1] Letter to d'Argenson, January 4, 1739.—See (156).

[2] Letter to Thiériot, April 23, 1739.

[3] "Terrible et gracieuse"—two extremes between which all Rameau is contained; letter to Chabanon, January 18, 1768.

[4] January 5, 1777.

6. Castor et Pollux

BEFORE 1737 the only French playwright who had taken the sons of Leda for his heroes was Danchet, author of both tragedies and *tragédies en musique* whose *Les Tyndarides* had been performed in 1708. It bears little likeness to the text which Pierre-Joseph Bernard supplied to Rameau in 1736.

Bernard has left behind him a more luminous trail than Pellegrin. In 1736 he belonged to La Pouplinière's circle but was shortly to quarrel with his host; he was also a member of the Caveau brotherhood which included two other librettists of Rameau's, Fuzelier and Collé, Panard, the two Crébillons and Jean-Philippe himself. He was under thirty but already famous for his *Art d'aimer*, an imitation of Ovid, which he jealously declined to publish and would bring forth only in select readings to admiring friends. He was already hailed as a rising star and that wily flatterer Voltaire eulogized him thus:

> À. M. Bernard, auteur de *L'Art d'aimer*.
>
> En ce pays, trois Bernard sont connus:
> L'un est ce saint, ambitieux reclus,
> Prêcheur adroit, fabricateur d'oracles;
> L'autre Bernard est enfant de Plutus,[1]
> Bien plus grand saint, faisant plus de miracles;
> Et le troisième est l'enfant de Phébus,
> Gentil Bernard, dont la muse féconde
> Doit faire encor les délices du monde
> Quand des premiers on ne parlera plus.[2]

Whether he already enjoyed the nickname of "gentil" or whether Voltaire gave it to him is not certain, but the epithet has stuck, even though according to Prince de Ligne he was the reverse of "gentil". "This name always made me laugh. . . . He was a tall, rather fat, handsome, dark, genial, easy-going, obliging man of breeding, beloved by everyone, without show of either wit or compliments, greedy enough and excellent reader of his *Art d'aimer*".[3]

---

[1] Samuel Bernard (1651–1739), a celebrated financier. He came to the rescue of Louis XIV towards the end of that monarch's reign.

[2] What an unfulfilled prophecy! (*Œuvres* (Beuchot ed.), XIV, 368 (1730)).

[3] Quoted by F. Drujon, *Poésies choisies de Gentil-Bernard* (Paris, 1884), XV.

The masterpiece was not given to the world till after his death in 1775. By this time his reputation had waned and the poem's appearance did not enhance it. Bernard had cultivated, as well as written upon, the art of loving with an ardour that ended by affecting his health. At the end of his life he had a stroke, brought on, it was thought, by too generous a style of living, and he lost his memory. One of its last gleams was kindled by a performance of *Castor et Pollux* at which he was present. He asked the name of the opera and who was singing. On being told "*Castor et Pollux*, and Mademoiselle Arnould", he exclaimed: "Ah oui! ma gloire et mes amours!"

His collaboration with Rameau began in 1736. Voltaire, then in. semi-exile at Leyden, heard of it. "So, Castor and Pollux are under the other hemisphere until next year".[1] They emerged from it on October 24, 1737.

Though a very minor poet Bernard had more talent than Pellegrin and, as a play, his libretto is the best that Rameau ever set except for the stillborn *Samson*. Bernard adopted the version of the Twins' story that makes Pollux the son of Jupiter and a demi-god and Castor the son of Tyndareus and therefore mortal. Castor and a certain Lynceus are rivals for the hand of Telaira, daughter of the high priest of Jupiter, and have taken up arms to support their claims. Castor has been killed and, when the opera begins, a funeral ceremony is in progress about his monument. Pollux goes to avenge him and, having slain Lynceus, lays the spoils at Telaira's feet; then, with indiscreet haste, he offers her his love in place of Castor's. Telaira, at first a little ruffled by this inopportune declaration, quickly sees what advantage she can take of it and insists that Pollux must persuade Jupiter to restore Castor to life. Jupiter, summoned to his temple, informs his son that Castor can return to earth only if Pollux takes his place in Hades, thus resigning his immortality. In order to enlighten his judgment and to show him all he will lose if he makes this sacrifice, Jupiter calls upon Hebe, mistress of the Heavenly Pleasures, to give him a foretaste of the delights of Olympus. Notwithstanding this temptation Pollux remains firm. At the gates of Hell he has to resist, not only the opposing demons but also Phoebe, who loves him but whose affection he has spurned, and who strives to hold him back whilst Telaira urges him on. With Mercury's help he forces an entry, discovers Castor and discloses his mission. After a duel of generosity between the two, Castor consents to go back to earth to see Telaira once more and to tell her he will not accept Pollux's sacrifice. He does this, but while the lovers are exchanging

---

[1] Letter to Thiériot, February 4, 1737.

eternal farewells, Jupiter appears and announces that the Fates have relented; both brothers are to enjoy immortality and will be at once translated to dwellings in the skies, Telaira by special licence following Castor. The only victim of this *tragédie mise en musique* is Phoebe, who kills herself.

Such a plot gave less scope for outward action than *Hippolyte et Aricie* but much more for those conflicts of feeling which Corneille introduced into French tragedy and Racine carried to the highest pitch of intensity. Opposition of feelings between the two women; conflict in the heart of Pollux between inclination and duty—the kind of struggle misleadingly called Cornelian; struggle of generosity between the brothers, much more truly Cornelian and reminiscent of *Rodogune*: these emotional contrasts had no counterpart in *Hippolyte et Aricie*; they opened a new field to Rameau's powers in which he was as resourceful as he had been in dealing with the simpler issues of the earlier libretto.

The overture, in D minor, is more personal than that of *Hippolyte et Aricie* and is sufficiently self-assertive to form an agreeable concert piece. It is one of the earliest overtures to be organically connected with the opera that follows; the opening *fièrement* returns at the end, modified, as the *symphonie* accompanying the entry of the Heavenly Bodies. The *vite* begins like a three-part fugue and has but one theme which is ever present, in tonic, relative major or dominant, on strings or woodwind, right way up or inverted.

The prologue has no connexion with the story and refers to the Peace of Vienna which in 1736 had concluded the war of the Polish succession. Venus is besought to subdue Mars with her charms, so that the terrible god may cease harrying a distracted world. The recipe suggested for ensuring peace is desirably simple.

> Vénus! O Vénus! c'est à toi
> D'enchaîner le Dieu de la guerre:
> Il rend le calme à la terre,
> Quand il repose sous ta loi.

Arts, Pleasures, Minerva and Love all join in striving to enlist Venus's mighty support. To the strains of a "soft symphony, mingled with a few warlike noises and sounds of trumpets, . . . Mars appears on a cloud, bound by Love at Venus's feet"; he announces his surrender and the scene ends with singing and dancing.

Musically this prologue is full of beauties. Its choruses are short but well contrasted. The first strikes a note of earnest supplication in a tone more like that of the beginning of the *Elijah* than of a *fête galante*. Minerva's solo "Implore, Amour", is in the same vein; both are excellent examples of Rameau's G minor mood in its gentler form. A charming *ariette* tears us brutally from the climate of G minor and the tradition of Lulli and tumbles us, with a light-hearted C major, into that of *Italianità*.   The words show no contrast with the supplications that have gone before, yet the music expresses only joy in its own vitality; voice and violins throw themselves up in crystalline runs that have no object beyond their own exuberance.   This is Italian virtuosity at its cleanest, standing outside the opera and free, therefore, from the reproach of interference with the drama.

The *divertissement* contains some of the loveliest and best-known dances: a couple of gavottes, a tambourin and two minuets.   The first gavotte[1] and first minuet have sung repeats; the second gavotte, in A minor, is a slow movement with expressive imitations and prominent 'cello and bassoon parts.   The first minuet is taken, transposed from G to D, from the third book of harpsichord pieces where it had appeared thirteen years earlier with a different *mineur*; between the two minuets is inserted a tambourin in D, destined to reappear in A in the *Pièces en concert*.[2]   The second minuet is a mysterious piece harmonized in thirds and sixths in which much effect is made of opposing registers and changes in instrumentation (ex. 77).

Ex.77

The highlights in Act I are the opening chorus, sung at Castor's tomb, Telaira's air "Tristes apprêts" and the chorus "Que l'Enfer applaudisse", but the whole of Scene 2, between Telaira and Phoebe, is also admirable; in fact, at no point in the act does the music descend to the level of the commonplace.

Ex.78

---

[1] Pierre Lasserre gives an imaginative description of this gavotte:
"Its admirable theme, both sinuous and simple, a dance theme but also, like all Rameau's dance themes, one full of feeling, suggests the light tripping of a young woman who, as she steps forward, keeps the purest lilt in all her movements and smiles with enigmatic tenderness" ((176) 79).
[2] And in the 1744 version of *Dardanus* (III, 5).

The scene at Castor's mausoleum is one of those great ensembles in which Rameau excels. As the curtain rises the Spartans are seen moving slowly round the dead warrior's monument.[1] The music indicates the speed and mood of the procession. It uses the conventional but ever effective symbol of desolation: the descending chromatic scale,[2] alternating with a lament (ex. 78). For a moment the weight of grief lifts and a trio sings a more tuneful phrase; then lament and scale return and at the end the two combine (ex. 79). The departure

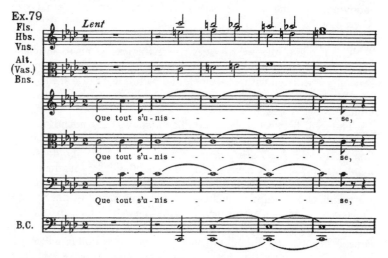

Ex.79
Fls.
Hbs.
Vns.

Alt.
(Vas.)
Bns.

Que tout s'u-nis - - - - - - - se,

Que tout s'u-nis - - - - - - - se,

Que tout s'u-nis - - - - - - - se,

B.C.

of the mourners after the ceremony is well suggested by the last enunciation of the chromatic theme in which the scale, hitherto always descending, now rises from dominant to tonic before the closing cadence.

Tomb scenes were stock numbers in French opera. Cambert's *Les Peines et les Plaisirs de l'Amour* had staged one in its second act, *Le Tombeau de Climène* (1672), the music of which is lost. This, however, except for a very short one in *Dardanus*, I, 2, is the only one in Rameau. The mood of lamentation relates the scene to the end of Act IV, *Hippolyte et Aricie*, but it has also the solemnity of a religious ceremony. It is, indeed, the blending of intense grief with ritual movement that makes it so affecting. As one dwells on it one's mind

---

[1] In a modern performance, that is; for the behaviour of eighteenth-century choruses, see Chapter 5, p. 165.

[2] Instances of this use familiar to us occur in Dido's lament and in the music to which Winter enters in the *Fairy Queen*. The opening of Winter's air is harmonically almost identical with the beginning of this chorus. Rameau explains that "the numerous descending chromatic intervals depict the weeping and wailing caused by keen regret" ((17), 67–68).

turns to another tomb scene, in one of the few eighteenth-century operas still within our reach: Gluck's *Orfeo*. The scene in *Castor* is a collective ceremony, not a lyrical song; the chief mourners are absent, whereas in *Orfeo* the hero interjects his cries with the chorus's lament. With Gluck the scene centres in a character; even the chorus is lyrical; it is an extension of the hero's person, not an independent people mourning its prince. In Rameau the lyrical moment will not come till Telaira has been left alone. The distinction between the anonymous throng and the bereaved Telaira is absent from *Orfeo*, where lover and chorus are one. What Gluck's scene has gained in sensuous melody it has lost in frieze-like solemnity.

This is one of the few passages where Rameau seems to anticipate the expressive Romantic handling of the hautboy, an instrument not generally associated with wistfulness and pathos in France at this time. The Romantic use of it originates in German practice with Keiser and Gluck.

The scene between Telaira and Phoebe shows how much Rameau's handling of recitative has developed since *Hippolyte et Aricie*. In his first opera and *Les Indes galantes* the recitative had a boldness unfamiliar to his hearers, many of whom were offended by it; the part of Theseus showed it clearly. But there had not been much opportunity for the display of subtler qualities, for the expression of finer shades of feeling. This is what we have here. The two women are opposed but not brutally contrasted; Telaira mourns her loss; Phoebe seeks to console her with the thought of the vengeance that Pollux will wreak on Lynceus. But vengeance is poor compensation when one loses one's good without hope of recovery; how favoured was Phoebe when she was chosen by the immortal one of the two brothers[1]; thus runs the dialogue. The two women are delicately characterized by the music; moreover, most of Telaira's part, like the chorus, is in F minor, whilst Phoebe generally sings in the major. In both parts the line of the recitative is varied and broken by the insertion of occasional bars of rhythmical melody in 3/4; though entitled *air* these are not, of course, independent numbers but just moments when the greater intensity of the emotion causes the latent melody to rise to the surface. The loveliest of these moments is Telaira's "Quelle faible victoire" (ex. 80).

Ex.80

B.C.

_____

[1] Phoebe does not know yet of Pollux's love for Telaira.

Phoebe withdraws and Telaira is left alone with her sorrow. She sings it in one of Rameau's best-known solos: "Tristes apprêts". "Best-known" is, alas! a relative term, for how many have ever heard, or even discovered for themselves at their keyboard, this great lament?

"Tristes apprêts" has those qualities of intense pathos united with great dignity which we have already admired in the end of the fourth act of *Hippolyte*. The utterance is personal, not collective; it is the complement of the anonymous weeping of the Spartan throng around the prince's tomb. Yet the individuality is kept within bounds; it retains that general, universal value which French art and literature at their highest—sculpture of thirteenth-century porches, tragedy of Racine—have in common with those of ancient Greece. This is something more than an expression of impersonal sorrow, a reach-me-down emotion fitting everyone and anyone; something more, too, than just the sorrow of one woman, compelling us to pity rather than to fellow-feeling. The sense of utter loss which pervades it is all the more overwhelming for the restraint and dignity of bearing. No rending chromaticisms, no dramatic suspensions, no minor mode even—the key is E flat[1]; the line is reduced to its simplest; just a broken fall from tonic to subdominant and thence again to tonic (ex. 81). Rameau's systematic use of the subdominant—a term which

Ex.81

Tris - tes ap - prêts,   pâ - les flam - beaux,

Bn.

he invented—as a means of expression was new. In his harmonic system the dominant, which belongs to the series of upper harmonics, is part of the natural resonance of the tonic, whilst the subdominant, which belongs to the lower harmonics, is "refused" by the tonic and therefore brings with it a feeling of strangeness.[2] "F is foreign to C", he says in 1760.

> Do we not feel naturally struck with the same solemn sadness[3] as the actress who is singing "Tristes apprêts" . . . when the lower fifth, that is, the subdominant, succeeds the tonic on the last syllable? And do we not feel relieved when the tonic returns almost at once on the last syllable of "pâles flambeaux"?[4]

---

[1] Described as "cruel" in Charpentier's table.
[2] See Chapter 14, pp. 521–522 and 538–539.
[3] Rameau's queer word is "componction", that is, a religious sadness.
[4] (21), 167–168.

A few years earlier he had connected the expressiveness of this air
with his use of the fundamental bass.   "The feeling of dull suffering
and of gloom which prevails here arises from the chromaticism in the
fundamental succession, whilst there is not a single chromatic interval
in any of the parts."[1]

Sorrowful and dignified as it is this air is also highly plastic.
Truly dramatic, if deficient in certain qualities of the complete playwright, Rameau *sees* his characters on the stage as well as expresses
their emotions.   His music not only reflects their feelings but indicates
their attitudes and motions.   Telaira's slow movement away from
where she had been standing, as Phoebe withdraws, and her dignified
bearing, are suggested in the prelude, with its shadow theme and slowly
pacing bassoon crotchets (ex. 82).   The line of her first notes (ex. 81)

Ex.82 *Très lent*

again suggests an attitude—a figure erect without stiffness, facing its
sorrow without fear.   The orchestra's concluding notes indicate a
movement similar to the prelude but *away* from the audience (ex. 83).[2]

Ex.83

---

[1] (17), 67–68.   See also (12), 97.

[2] As a term of comparison I quote part of an air in which is present one
of the most striking features of "Tristes apprêts", the broken fall of a fifth
and a fourth.   It is in Desmarêts's *Iphigénie en Tauride*, V, 2—an opera to
which Campra made some additions; this air is not one of them and is
wrongly attributed to Campra in Grovlez's *Les plus beaux airs de l'opéra
français* (ex. 84).

Ex.84

Seuls con-fi - dents de mes pei - nes se - cre - tes

It was great praise for so ardent an admirer of Gluck and contemner of all other Classics as Hector Berlioz to give when he wrote of this solo:

> Gluck himself has very few pages finer than Telaira's famous air. . . . Everything goes to make this air one of the sublimest conceptions of dramatic music.[1]

One of his most telling practices, the jumping of several fifths from one key to another, is seen at the end of this air.   From E flat he skips upward by three fifths to C major, justifying the instruction *hardiment* which heads the *symphonie guerrière* and shouts of victory. We emerge from the sombre world of flats in which the action has unfolded hitherto, and the chorus and games that follow are in C. The ensemble of athletes and warriors, accompanying the triumphant Pollux, is one of his most stirring dramatic choruses.   I say, *dramatic*, because I do not want to institute a comparison of value between this and the great "Que ce rivage retentisse" of *Hippolyte et Aricie*.   Unlike the latter, which might well find place in a secular oratorio, "Que l'Enfer applaudisse" is bound up with the drama, for the athletes, warriors and people who sing it are part of the story.

Its dramatic character consists largely in the contrast of two themes: triumph and vengeance, sorrow and mourning.   To these there correspond alternating contrasted sections, one *vif*, the other *lent*.   The first theme appears as a mere succession of repeated notes; its purely rhythmical appeal answers perhaps to a desire to represent Spartan austerity, more clearly suggested later in the *airs pour les athlètes*.   The mourning theme is no more melodic but is more richly harmonized.   Neither is remarkable when isolated; it is the rapid alternation that works on our sensibility.   On the first return of the *vif* the minor key of the *lent* is retained and vengeance substituted for triumph (ex. 85).   At intervals the lament interrupts this wild outburst and on each intervention the music modulates.   We thus traverse the variously desolate regions of C minor, G minor and F minor;

---

[1] *Revue et Gazette musicale*, 1842, p. 442; quoted in (190), 218.

the last appearance of the lament, in C minor, is followed by a return to the major and the repetition of the opening. The whole forms a magnificent series of oppositions, the constant modulation and melodic variation of which attenuate without destroying the strong symmetry of the design.

Rameau has clearly endeavoured to make the three dance *airs* stiff and austere and it is not fanciful to think that, like Gluck in *Paris and*

Helen, but more forcefully, he was aiming at reproducing in his music the conventional characteristics of Sparta.[1]

I would not speak of the last scene in the act, a dialogue between Pollux and Telaira, the substance of which has been already described, were it not the subject of an interesting correspondence between Telemann and Graun.[2] It disproves Burney's contention, that French opera "is displeasing to all ears but those of France".[3] Telemann was a convinced partisan of French opera, which he knew intimately and which he defended against his friend's attacks. Graun had written to him, picking to pieces the recitatives in *Castor.* He quoted a part of this scene[4] with many criticisms and then rewrote it after his own idea, in Italian *recitativo secco*! Telemann countered with an analysis of Rameau's scene in which he justified every detail. He then turned on Graun's stick-like *ersatz*, calling its harmony "mournful and sour" and its rendering monotonous; he was delighted to find a mistake in prosody, for Graun, whose knowledge of French was shaky, had counted "rendre au jour" as four syllables,[5] and he wound up, as if anticipating Burney's objection:

> You say that French recitatives please nowhere outside France. I do not know, because history books say nothing about it. . . . But I do know that I have met Germans, Englishmen, Russians, Poles and even a couple of Jews who could sing by heart whole scenes of *Atys, Bellérophon,* etc. On the other hand, I have not seen one single man who has said anything but this of the Italians[6]: "It is wonderful, it is matchless, but I couldn't remember anything of it."

The correspondence appears to have gone on at intervals for several years. One of the details which Telemann had praised in Rameau's scene was the presence of a mordant on "ressusciter". This word, he said, is "rendered by a rolled trill" (ein rollender Triller). Graun seized on this and, rather unfortunately for one who had composed a *Tod Jesu,* retorted: "In all the resurrections mentioned in Scripture nowhere does one read of anything having been 'rolled'. . . ."

---

[1] Thereby, like Gluck, committing an anachronism, since the "date" of the Heavenly Twins is earlier than the reform of Lycurgus which gave Sparta the qualities we associate with her name.

[2] *Denkmäler deutscher Tonkunst,* erste Folge, XXVIII (1907), lxix–lxx.

[3] (43), ii, 966. Burney himself quotes another instance which disproves his contention when he says reprovingly that "Avison exalted Rameau and Geminiani at the expense of Handel and was a declared foe of modern German symphonies" (ii, 7).

[4] Pages 170–171 of the Durand vocal score, bars 8–13 and 1–5; Act I, 5, not II, 5, as (221) states.—The correspondence took place in 1751–1752.

[5] Graun was not to be beaten and held out that "rendre" was pronounced "render" and consequently had two syllables, even before a vowel.

[6] He uses the scornful word "Welsch".

It may seem strange that the composer of a *Tod Jesu* should never have read of a certain angel who "rolled back the stone"; actually, in Luther's Bible the word we render by "roll" is "walzen".

Telemann's enthusiasm proves that the opera of Lulli and Rameau was not the insular, unexportable product that its adversaries would have us think.

The most remarkable moments in the second act are its opening and its conclusion. It is set in the hall of Jupiter's temple, where a sacrifice has been prepared and where Pollux is discovered in melancholy solitude.

The air which he sings is one of those *symphonies* with voice *obbligato* which make Rameau's operas seem now and again so much more modern than others less distant in time. The orchestral part consists almost entirely in a flowing line of notes linked in twos of a type that goes back to Venetian opera,[1] where it usually illustrates the murmur of trees and running water, and which survives well into the Romantic age. Here it expresses the mood of half-resigned sorrow, elegiac rather than passionate, into which Telaira's request has plunged Pollux. It flows on, rising and falling in gentle hopelessness (ex. 86),

keeping within the confines of D minor. A slight climax occurs towards the end in two bars with an insistent *appoggiatura* on the dominant.

To one brought up on Italian music, an orchestral introduction of this weight heralded an important voice part and Burney expressed the disappointment he felt when, "after ... symphonies that are extremely promising, [when] the ear has been made to expect a continuation of the prefatory strain, nothing is given to the vocal part but broken accents and dislocated measures".[2]

To us, trained by experience of Wagner and those who have learnt from him, we find it natural that the orchestra should not abdicate before the voice but should pursue its course while the human organ superimposes itself above the symphony. It is, indeed, in the instruments rather than in the singer that the soul of the moment is fully

---

[1] See for example the scene "Mormorate, o fiumicelli" in Cavalli's *Ercole amante*, quoted in (214), appendix, 27, and in (200), 141.

[2] (43), ii, 967–968.

embodied (ex. 87).[1] The form is that of the *da capo* aria, with a well-developed middle section in F major and A minor in which there is no change either of mood or of accompaniment. The smoothly winding stream of quavers pursues its serpentine course from start to finish, with an occasional half-bar's break, as in ex. 87. This is Rameau at

Ex. 87

his most lyrical and provides an obvious retort to those who still associate him with *Rationalismus* or call him "pompous and antique". A comparison with the solo given to Castor at the beginning of Act IV will show that even in this dreamy mood he has more than one style.

Debussy found this air so personal and so modern that he felt one should be able to go up to Rameau after the performance and congratulate him on it.[2]

The scene between Pollux and Telaira is in recitative and short airs and has the same qualities as that between the women in Act I. It is mainly in D minor but at one moment Telaira's part goes into the

---

[1] The very importance of the orchestra was a stumbling-block for the pro-Italian. See *Les Indes chantantes*, a parody of *Les Indes galantes*, by Romagnesi and Riccoboni (quoted in (237), 611).

> Que la Française [that is, French music]
> Me paraît niaise;
> Toujours à l'aise,
> Pour qu'elle plaise
> Il faut à tout moment
> Grand accompagnement.

[2] *Gil Blas*, February 2, 1903; reproduced in *Monsieur Croche, anti-dilettante*.

major with a melody, reminiscent of a well-known Christmas hymn, the associations of which intrude with irrelevant humour upon the English listener (ex. 88).　Pollux remains faithful to his promise but

Ex.88

deplores his fate and envies his brother's in an expressive phrase where the Ramellian broken fall of a fifth and a fourth is prominent (ex. 89).

Ex.89

The temple scene is more conventional than anything we have hitherto heard.　It has many predecessors, the earliest of which is in Lulli's first opera, *Cadmus et Hermione*.　Such scenes were common in French opera where "sacrifices, invocations, oaths", said Le Cerf proudly, were "beauties unknown to the Italians".　Gluck and Mozart have taught us to expect trombones in them, the usual concomitants of the oracular and the supernatural, but this convention had not as yet entered French opera and the Académie de Musique did not include them in its orchestra till after Rameau's death.

With the Lulli-ish *entrée* to which Jupiter makes his slow descent we seem to have moved back half a century.　This dotted-rhythm piece, like the first section of a French overture, is inordinately long: twenty-two bars of *majestueusement*; it gives the audience plenty of time to wonder at the god suspended in mid-air and leisure for the machinists to lower their precious burden with precaution.[1]

---

[1] In the argument and *examen* of *Andromède* (1650) Corneille alludes to "a concert of music which I have used only to satisfy the spectators' ears while their eyes are intent on watching some machines go up or down, or are fixed on something which would prevent them hearing what the actors might be saying, such as Perseus' fight with the monster".

The public withdraws and Jupiter is left alone with his son.   Pollux pours forth his prayer.   His tone warms up by degrees and at length he cries out despairingly (ex. 90), in strains that echo down the century to Tamino's "O ew'ge Nacht!"   His imagination becomes fired; in an animated passage with accompanied recitative and occasional *tremolando* basses he sees himself forcing an entry into Hell after

Ex.90

O mon pè - re, O mon pè - re, é - cou - te mes voeux.

the manner of Hercules, preceded by his father's thunder.   Jupiter quells this transport in the way we know and, before granting his son's prayer, calls on Hebe to display before his gaze all her attendant pleasures.

The end of the act consists in the *divertissement* of the Heavenly Pleasures.   The hero's presence, like Theseus' in Act III of *Hippolyte*, adds a note both human and discordant, but Pollux stands by less silent than the king of Troezen; from time to time he interjects an ironical query that adds a touch of bitter illusion to the lovely spectacle.

The display with which Hebe tempts him consists in a succession of dances, choruses and *airs*.   Except for a saraband these are not in fixed forms.   Hebe's entry and her first *air* are action dances or pantomimes, though the movements are not indicated with the same precision as, for instance, in the athletes' fight in Act I.   *Danses d'action* occur sometimes in Lulli, as in the funeral scene of *Alceste*, but they are much more frequent in Rameau.   His librettist Cahusac introduced *ballets figurés* of some length in several of his poems.[1]   In Rameau's later works there are elaborate pantomimes; in the *entrée* called *L'Enlèvement d'Adonis* of *Les Surprises de l'Amour* a long ballet, entirely without words, depicts the loves of Diana and Endymion.   It was Noverre who brought these attempts to fruition with his dramatic ballet.

The entry of Hebe and her suite is followed by a full-scale chorus of the Pleasures.   Except for the first *air* and the solo "Que nos jeux comblent vos vœux" set to it, the whole *divertissement* is in E minor. The various pieces melt one into the other, similar in their mood and pervasive in their charm.   The leaning notes and dragging motion which irritated Burney are here in force; so are those expressively bare harmonies beloved of Rameau when he wishes to conjure up intense

---

[1] E.g. *Les Fêtes de Polymnie, Les Fêtes de l'Hymen, Naïs, Zaïs* and *Zoroastre*.

emotion. A climate all its own envelops this apparition from the court of the gods, the like of which we have not yet found in his operas, though some of the harpsichord pieces from the second book, such as *Le Rappel des Oiseaux, Les Soupirs* and *L'Entretien des Muses,* diffuse one very like it.

The whole *divertissement* is surpassingly lovely but it is hardly our idea of the perfect *volupté* which, judging from the words,[1] it is meant to illustrate. Its beauty is overwhelming, almost excruciating; we feel that, like Chinese pleasure tortures, if it were prolonged it would turn to pain. It has the pungency of so much of Rameau's music and, entrancing though the vision be, this apparition of Hebe and her Graces seems tantalizingly unreal. No wonder Pollux repels it! It sings of love, *jouissance* and games, but there is no warmth in it, no passion, no true delight. Set it beside the voluptuous passages of *Paris and Helen;* how sensual and solid are the pleasures sung of by the Trojan lover and Eros, compared with Hebe's.

> Qu' Hébé de fleurs toujours nouvelles
> Forme vos chaînes immortelles!

writes Bernard. But the lovely *vocalise* to which Rameau sets the "chaînes" is expressive of infinite yearning, of undying melancholy, not of everlasting loves (ex. 91). His world of beauty and pleasure is a sceptic's; it has never existed and Rameau, at fifty-four, has no illusions about it.[2]

Ex. 91

[1]
> Venez, voyez, goûtez
> Les célestes voluptés!
> Nous aimons. Jupiter même
> N'est heureux que quand il aime.

[2] The audience is, no doubt, meant to see it through Pollux's eyes; hence its unreality.

I have referred to Pollux's interruptions. The first comes after the chorus "Connaissez notre puissance". It is in an affirmative E major and its opening rise, in three leaps, of one ninth, expresses vigorously his determination not to yield. The other two are more conciliatory though quite as firm; beginning differently, they end with the same pathetic and rhetorical question (ex. 92). Passively, he allows himself to be bound with nosegays but at the end of the act he tears them asunder and escapes, pursued in vain by the Pleasures.

Ex.92

The third act is fuller of external action than the others. It depicts the final discussions at the gates of Hell and the storming of the dark abode. About half of it consists of choruses, active and dramatic; the rest is mainly recitative and *symphonies*. There is a short trio but no solos; the story advances too quickly for them.

The prelude with which it opens precedes a scene for Phoebe and the Spartans in which she exhorts the people to turn back their king from his enterprise. Its striding theme is present throughout the number, except for the declamatory middle section; it is based, like many of Rameau's vigour motives, on the common chord.[1]

As it finishes, Pollux appears alone. He is in an intolerant and slightly hectoring mood; his flourish on "vole", as, in answer to Phoebe's "Où courez-vous?" he throws back "Je vole à la victoire", is for once more than an illustration of the single word and conveys something of the braggadoccio temper in which he is approaching his task. Like a Cornelian hero, his mouth is full of "la gloire qui me suit". Telaira soon joins them and encourages Pollux on his mission with the account of a dream vouchsafed to her in the temple of which her father is high priest. The report is made in that form, not common in Rameau, of narrative recitative which Destouches had introduced. It consists here in declamation with an accompaniment, largely made up of figures, which is more pictorial than the actual voice part. It opens dramatically with a sudden change from G minor to C major. As she lives again her vision the style expresses "transport"; against a scurrying treble and a *tremolando* bass she describes what she has seen. The music paints it briefly step by step: "la nuit" (heavy

---

[1] See the two *airs* in Act I and the first *air infernal* in this act; also the chorus "Tombez, tombez".—A writer in the *Mercure de France* (August 1778) says: "It resembles a *grave* of one of Geminiani's concertos that I have always heard called *The Gates of Hell*" (in *O.C.*, VIII, civ).

piano chords in the basses), "mille éclairs" (upward rush of arpeggios). The climax sounds like the aftermath of a *Götterdämmerung* (ex. 93), till we realize that she is referring to the transformation of Castor and Pollux into a constellation. The last words of her oracle adumbrate the death of the luckless Phoebe.

The warring interests of the three are gathered for an instant into a trio, the only one[1] and indeed the only solo ensemble, apart from the

Ex. 93

Et du fond des en - fers, j'ai vu de nou-veaux Dieux pas - -ser au - des - us du ton - ner - re.

interludes, in the whole opera. Each protagonist expresses a different sentiment: "Je reverrai donc . . ." and "Je ne verrai plus . . . ce que j'aime", and "O douleur extrême!" This is a *divergent* trio, a type unknown to Lulli that appeared in the eighteenth century with the gradual enrichment of French musical style under Italian influence. It has the austere and antique character of the duets in *Hippolyte*. At its close we pass from minor to major without a change of tonic as the day grows dim and Hell let loose springs out upon Pollux (ex. 94, with a fine eleventh on "-cit").

Ex. 94

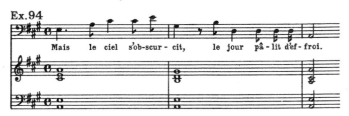

Mais le ciel s'ob-scur - cit, le jour pâ - lit d'ef - froi.

The rest of the act consists in two action choruses and two demon dances; the choruses, greatly superior to the dances, are among Rameau's finest of this type, in which *Castor et Pollux* is particularly rich.

The basis of the first one is a *divergent* trio in which the demons guarding Hell eventually join. Phoebe sings:

> Sortez d'esclavage, combattez, démons furieux!

Pollux and Telaira, on the contrary, command:

> Tombez, rentrez dans l'esclavage!

---

[1] Except for the beginning of Scene 4, which is really a chorus with trio of principals.

The demons, when their turn comes, naturally support Phoebe and sing:

Sortons d'esclavage!

A rapid stepping figure in repeated notes, suggestive of a running set, depicts the steady surge of the demons round the group of three (ex. 95). The whole chorus is set against this figure and one of dropping arpeggios with the same throbbing bass.

Ex.95

The chorus is in free counterpoint much broken by homophony. Though more static than "Que l'Enfer applaudisse" it has a basis of action and movement and its running-set rhythm suggests vividly the demons pouring forth from their abode to drive back Pollux.

Its three sections are separated by shortened returns of the prelude whose first bars are quoted in ex. 95. It modulates hardly at all and the obstinacy with which it clings to one key expresses the stubborn resistance of the demon host. It opens with a long solo phrase of Phoebe's which contains the few melodic and rhythmical elements of which it is built (ex. 96). Pollux and Telaira enter at close quarters

Ex.96

Sor-tez, sor - tez d'es - cla - va - ge,   Com-bat-tez,

with the dropping-triad subject and there is an ample development of (b) (ex. 96) interspersed with occasional returns of (a), now dropping now rising. The second section begins with the addition of the demons to the principals. Their part is musically not very important and consists mostly in punctuating the strong beats with cries of "Sortons", occasionally expanded into recalls of (b). The third section is more incisive than the other two and is chiefly made up of (a) in close imitation and of the rhythm of (b) on repeated notes. The chorus closes with ten bars of cadential harmony.

The first air des démons which follows it and the second which comes after the next chorus are excellent illustrations of the force and precision with which Rameau prescribes his dancers' movements through the music he writes for them. The dress of stage demons in earlier eighteenth-century opera shows that they were less terrifying than decorative and were, before all, dancers. Not till the increase in dramatic realism of which Diderot's theories and plays are portents do they come to correspond more closely with their title.

The remaining chorus, "Brisons tous nos fers", fully the equal of the others, is exceptionally violent and almost ostentatiously syllabic and mono-toned, surpassing in this respect the quick parts of "Que l'Enfer applaudisse". We are still in A major but there is more modulation. The devils are now thoroughly roused and everyone else is silent. They no longer surge forth in ever increasing numbers but rush headlong in battle array at their opponent and seek to rebut him by sheer weight (ex. 97). When the exposition is over each part

Ex. 97

enters afresh, one second above the last, "with an extraordinary effect of excitement and desperation".[1] As the fury rises the music loses what little melody it had and the triumph of repeated notes comes with

---

[1] (190), 462, note 5.

ex. 98. Hitherto the excitement has been only dynamic. The shock of repeated notes does not cease in the curt F sharp minor middle section, but there is added to it Rameau's favourite trick of laying side by side unrelated keys, of which he made such good use in "Que ce rivage retentisse". Here the excursion is less distant (to the key of

Ex. 98

Qu'au feu du ton-ner-re Le feu des en-fers Dé-cla-re la guer-re!

É-bran-lons la ter-re!

the ultra-dominant, G sharp minor) and less prolonged, since we are back in F sharp minor by the end of two bars; but the punch is strong enough to be keenly felt and it whips us up afresh just as the protracted effect of the reiterated notes and unmitigated rhythmical impact is running the risk of wearing off.

This chorus made a deep impression on contemporaries. As late as 1772 Chabanon wrote:

> The combination [of the vocal parts] is nothing but the effect is prodigious. We own with pleasure that this piece seems sublime to us. The diatonic progression which the artist has used from bar to bar strengthens the effect; never have we heard this passage without feeling the shiver which makes our hair rise on end. No doubt Aeschylus' Eumenides were singing a similar music when the people of Athens thought it saw Hell yawning before it and women's fright brought on the pains of premature delivery.[1]

This descent into Hell, from the nature of its subject, brings to our minds the great second act of *Orfeo*. But beyond the mere fact of the entrance into the kingdom of death by an intruder there is little in common between the two scenes. Orpheus comes alone to the dread gates; alone, though with the gods' permission, he faces the Furies and alone he overcomes them with the power of his song; no Mercury descends to force a way for him. He is inspired by love, the strongest of the passions and the least susceptible to reason. But Pollux is impelled by friendship and duty; he is in a more rational mood than Orpheus; he is sustained by Telaira and the path is smoothed for him by Mercury, who "strikes the demons with his wand and sinks with him into the cavern". Alone, he would achieve nothing; he has no song wherewith to ravish his foes and, till the god's arrival, their resistance shows no signs of abating. Rameau's scene is static; it is the repetition of the same gestures, the enactment of a battle without

---

[1] *Mercure de France*, April 1772; in (190), 307.

vicissitudes, the issue of which is a stalemate; Gluck depicts a gradual victory, and the stages by which Orpheus weakens his opponents and breaks down what we should nowadays call their morale are finely noted.   Rameau's demons are more violent and their attack is more massive; "Brisons tous nos fers" works with as powerfully direct a physical effect upon us as the technique of expression at the period allowed; even now, we can feel its bombardment if its full force is brought out by conductor and performers; but there is nothing of the horror, of the might of unnatural presences which make Gluck's Furies so sinister.   To convey a sense of mystery is within Rameau's powers,[1] but he has not done so here.   Demons and scenes at the gates of Hell were stock features in classical opera; they were far too common to be taken realistically.   The demand for ever greater truth in drama, including opera, led Gluck, in one of the last Hell-storming scenes, to associate with his devils the feeling which usually accompanies the thought of such beings.

The fourth act is played in the Elysian Fields where Castor sits, a little apart, deploring the loss of his love.   His solo is less sad than Pollux's in Act II, for he is, after all, in the realm of the Happy Spirits whence active sorrow is banished; in fact, he recognizes the pleasant nature of his lot:

> Que ce murmure est doux!
> Que cet ombrage est frais!

He experiences deprivation but his song has not the awareness of conflict from which Pollux suffered and still less the bitter smart of which Phaedra sang in "Cruelle mère des Amours".

Its dragging rhythm and enervated sixths give it a voluptuous tinge. Grace there often is in Rameau, though it is a quality of his period rather than of his own nature; but voluptuousness, though more than once indicated by his text, is seldom present in his music.   When such an expression is called for we are likely to find in its stead a strain of melancholy and disillusion.   From one to the other is but a short way, but Rameau usually travels the whole of it at a bound and presents us with the ultimate fruits of voluptuous enjoyment rather than the enjoyment itself.   Here, however, it is suggested in the heavy, drooping prelude, with its garland of cloying sixths and persistent dotted rhythm, and his characteristic nostalgia, though perceptible, remains in the background (ex. 99).[2]   This is more lyrical than anything we have met; there was nothing as deep and calm in *Hippolyte et Aricie* where all the most individual numbers had something external about

---

[1] As in the second Magicians' chorus in *Dardanus*, II.

[2] There is an obvious likeness with the opening of Bach's B minor violin and harpsichord sonata which goes deeper than mere formal resemblance.

Ex.99

them and suggested attitudes and movements. Rameau is never entirely calm, as Gluck is in the corresponding scene in *Orfeo*, and his instrumental music, whether orchestral dances or harpsichord solos, can be as nerve-racking as Chopin's; but this is his nearest approach to a sense of peace. His tranquillity, like Mozart's, is passionate, and the presence side by side of these two superficially contrasted moods is keenly felt in the passage near the end of this prelude which begins with a short dominant pedal (ex. 100).[1]

Ex.100

The voice part is more tuneful than in Pollux's air and the orchestra, though still symphonic, is a little less independent. The solo is in rondeau form. The first episode, though marked *récitatif*, is as melodious as the main section. On its first return the refrain concludes with the pedal and the mood these bars induce is that of the second episode into which it at once leads. In the words I have quoted and, for an instant, in the dreamy reflectiveness of the reiterated or sustained notes, we catch a foretaste of Orpheus' "Che puro ciel" (ex. 101; the quotation follows on the first beat of bar 3 in ex. 100).

---

[1] Bars 1 and 2 of ex. 100 show a favourite harmonic sequence of Rameau's; see *L'Enharmonique* (bars 21–19 counting from the end), *L'Égyptienne* (bars 5–3, do.), *La Boucon* (bars 7–5, do.) and *La Cupis* (bars 5–3, do.).

Ex. 101

The skill with which instruments and voice are blended in this piece makes it unique in French opera at this date.

As Castor finishes his plaint the Happy Spirits throng forward, ostensibly to induce him to be blithe like them but really to provide a *divertissement*. Here a second comparison with Gluck is natural. The situation is the same as in the famous ballet which precedes Eurydice's appearance and the chorus "E quest'asilo". Two of the dances in Rameau's ballet, the gavotte and passepied, and the sung air derived from the gavotte, are in their line equal to anything in Gluck, but as a whole this *divertissement* is inferior to the succession of minuet, flute solo and chorus that limn one of the most convincing miniatures of the joys of the Blessed to be found in all art. It is as if Gluck, though evoking "what eye hath not seen nor ear hath heard", believed in the existence of his subject, whereas Rameau does not. Yet there is here no *arrière-goût* of dissatisfaction and yearning, as in the *Plaisirs d'Hébé*; the picture, full of beauty and health, fills its frame without emotional irrelevancies or mental reservations.

The scene consists in an *air* danced by quadrilles of Happy Spirits; a chorus, nominally inviting Castor to share in the general felicity; a loure, twice *parodied*, as a solo and as a chorus; a gavotte, afterwards expanded into a solo, and a couple of passepieds. All this is excellent Rameau. The *air* to whose strains the Shades draw near suggests their movements admirably and is as limpid as its subject, but it is more plastic than expressive, unlike Gluck's ballet and so many of Rameau's own dances, in which expression and gesture are linked. The E minor gavotte is one of his most beautiful and a queen of gavottes, but it has the same illusory and sceptical sentiment; Rameau knows full well the unreality of all pleasures, even in the Elysian Fields, and disbelief is rendered more strongly than enjoyment.   Laloy puts what is perhaps the same impression in different words when he says that Rameau's smile is that of a man who is habitually morose.   His music has its own enchanted worlds, pastoral, celestial or Elysian, but there is no pretence that they exist outside it.

The passepied, a quick form of minuet, occurs late in the seventeenth century with Le Roux's harpsichord pieces and the operas of Campra and Destouches.   No other of Rameau's numerous examples has quite the roguish charm of the first of this pair.   The apparently harmless opening, *doux*, with seven repeated tonic chords, is mischievously belied by the break in the rhythm and sharp change from three to two and back again to three, typical of the dance.   Passepieds, like other fixed forms, vary in tempo though they are always fast; this one

Ex. 102

is among the fastest and should be taken at one in the bar if the full force of the change of rhythm is to be felt; for lack of this it sounds tame and the point is missed.   There is the usual *mineur*, more expressive but presenting the same clashes of rhythm.

Pollux's arrival causes a commotion among the Shades, who disperse with cries of indignation.   He discovers Castor, and the music, without departing from recitative, expands with appropriate warmth into a few bars of duet (ex. 102).   A long conversation ensues in which Pollux makes a clean breast of his affection for Telaira and of the sacrifice he is making.   A dramatic change of key emphasizes the confession.   The recitative keeps up its interest without the device of *petits airs* and is one of the best examples of Rameau's current style in a scene whose mainly argumentative character offers little scope to music.   The emotional tone rises here and there and almost reaches passion in Pollux's cry: (ex. 103).   In the end, Castor is carried off by

Ex. 103

Mon im-mor-ta-li-té t'ap - pel - le!

Mercury after declaring he will not stay on earth for more than one day. Pollux remains with the Happy Spirits who, having summoned up courage, return to invite both brothers to abide with them for ever. The invitation is expressed in one of the many "Revenez, revenez" airs of French opera—for once a completely happy one, with none of the longing that even Lulli displays in such pieces,[1] and on their serene A major tones the act ends.

The fifth act, like that of *Hippolyte*, opens with the tragic monologue of a character whose last appearance it marks.   The counterpart here of Theseus is the luckless Phoebe.   Tumultuous soliloquies are not common in French opera, where the monologue form is generally expressive of melancholy or sadness.   Nor are such moving accents often heard in quick tempo.   The scoffing Rousseau seized on the association of pathos with slowness in his dictionary.

> The whole expression of French music in the pathetic style consists in dragged, forced, yelping sounds, and in so slow a tempo that all sense of the beat is lost.   Whence comes that the French believe that all that is slow is *pathetic*, and all that is *pathetic* must be slow.[2]

Phoebe's scene breaks the rule.

The prelude sounds more like the exposition of a symphony of the Mannheim period than the work of an early-eighteenth-century Frenchman.   The abrupt, rhythmical statement of the common chord in a minor key, followed at once by a flowing line in the relative major, has the short-winded anger of certain works by Beck, Richter, Schobert, the young Haydn or the adolescent Mozart.[3]   It reminds us of two

[1] E.g. in the prologue of *Thésée*.   [2] Art. *Pathétique*.

[3] See Mozart's early G minor symphony, K. 183, or Haydn's quartet in the same key, Op. 20, III.

points that are often overlooked. First, that French opera, though
remaining, in its librettos, true to the lines laid down by Lulli and
Quinault, was far from impervious to influences from other genres and
lands. Secondly, that Rameau often looks ahead and announces the
music of later generations.

- ger cet ou - tra - ge?

This irate piece is played before "une vue agréable aux environs
de Sparte". Phoebe sums up her situation in unstable, modulating
recitative, punctuated by lashes of the strings. Her air is, as usual,
an extra part added to the prelude (ex. 104).[1] She moves from key to
key in frustrated rage and winds up with a splendid shriek on high G
and a sensational tumble of an eleventh in which we may see an attempt
to depict the collapse of her efforts to blight her rival's happiness (ex.
105). The orchestra winds up with the last bars of the prelude which
give the impression of a symphonic coda.

It is a pity, musically, that more is not heard of Phoebe. She
affords the same contrast to the gentlemanly, self-sacrificing brothers
as Theseus and Phaedra to Hippolytus and Aricia. This solo is the
only tragic outburst in the opera.[2]

With her ill-merited disappearance we return to the elegiac climate
of Castor and Telaira. The lately released prince has the difficult task
of persuading Telaira that duty compels him to leave her once more
and that she must share in his sacrifice. Rameau notes their feelings
with extreme delicacy, especially in Castor's part. The prince's tone
is that of a well-bred gentleman whose fibre is heroic without his
realizing it and who commits the noblest acts with the simplest words.
He strikes no attitudes; the recitative follows the movements of the
heart, idealizing them just enough to remain above the level of prose.
The scene is broken by the interruption of a crowd of Spartans who,
having heard that their prince is about to leave them again, enter to add
their prayers to Telaira's. For a moment Rameau makes use of the
chorus as protagonist and interlocutor. The voices enter in poly-

---

[1] The orchestral part was substantially the same in the prelude, except
that bars six and following were in B flat major.

[2] This fine scene was cut out at an early stage as being dramatically
useless.

Ex.105

phony, thereby conveying the sense of many separate people who at first utter their supplications with some disorder but eventually reach unanimity. Castor dismisses them and the discussion continues till closured by Jupiter's intervention.

Rameau's art in this kind of scene is perhaps best observed on p. 185 of the vocal score. Pierre Lasserre, who, in his *L'Esprit de la Musique française*, shows a keener insight into Rameau's music than any writer except Masson, admires the skill with which the master has here treated a scene in which the lovers are divided between delight at meeting again and sorrow at their coming separation. Other composers have expressed the two states one after the other, but Rameau, by his subtle mezzotint observation of every *nuance*, has rendered both elements of this hybrid mood and has remained within its bounds.

This psychological delicacy impressed Debussy when part of *Castor* was performed at the Schola Cantorum in 1903. Romain Rolland declared himself unable to recognize it and fortified his opinion by quoting Rousseau's well-known description of the noisy orchestra and barking singers to show that, in Rameau's own century, moderation and sobriety were not looked on as attributes of his music. Rousseau was, of course, referring to standards of performance which were far from perfect and his judgment is here irrelevant. Rameau's subtle recitative follows every change of sentiment without excess one way or the other, in a manner in which Italian opera and Gluck himself, with their broadly contrasted arias, could not. "His recitative follows nature with sincerity and attracts us by the unbroken spontaneity of its expression and the freshness of its inventive powers."[1]

Such a scene is the eighteenth-century equivalent of *Pelléas et Melisande* and the musical counterpart of certain scenes in the plays of Rameau's contemporary, Marivaux, and of later French playwrights like Musset and Giraudoux. It is perhaps not what an English listener will value most in his work, but it illustrates a quality peculiarly French. Phoebe's solo is more exciting, but Italians and Germans have done that kind of thing as well; this is Rameau's own game and he is unbeaten at it. Debussy was right in recognizing here his own ideal.

Jupiter's approach is heralded by the usual paraphernalia of thunder and earthquake, but his actual arrival is more interesting than his pompous entry in Act II. First, "a melodious symphony is heard"; then he is descried descending upon his eagle. The impressionistic *symphonie* aims at suggesting the floating movement of the monarch and his royal bird; its beautiful tone-painting receives little notice when competing with the divine machinery. It is wasted in performance unless the forewarned spectator closes his eyes at the right moment (ex. 106). The music becomes more matter-of-fact as the precious load reaches *terra firma* and it ends stolidly with a conventional two-bar cadence.

The action being now over all the rest is spectacle.

The Heavenly Bodies are called upon to join the party in a serene air by the father of the gods, repeated as a chorus, with smooth, spacious lines and the ever effective accompaniment figure of wavy semiquavers, "Descendez des sphères du monde". "Several fiery orbs come down from the clouds and their presiding genii join with the planets and stars to compose the *divertissement*."

The *symphonie* which accompanies the Twins' induction into the Zodiac is an extended version, in A major like the rest of this scene, of the *fièrement* of the overture. It is followed by a gigue and this by an *ariette*, a pleasing specimen of an unwanted genre, in F sharp minor, a key seldom used by Rameau for solos, suggested here by the A major character of the scene. The words are not helpful to the musician:

> Brillez, astres nouveaux,
> Parez les cieux, régnez sur l'onde!

---

[1] (176), 88.

Ex.106

but Rameau has concentrated on illustrating the first of them with reiterative semiquaver figures and syncopated grace notes expressive of scintillation.

The chaconne is more ambitious than that of *Hippolyte et Aricie*. It falls into four broad divisions and a coda but, except for the change to the minor in the fourth, the sections are not strongly marked and merge one into the other. Most of the phrases are in four or eight bars; a few are in six with now and again an irregular transition passage. The opening strain is retained longer than in *Hippolyte* and returns refrain-wise several times in the first section. Emotionally, the dance sums up the opera, expressing the prevailing temper, especially the transfiguration mood of the end. Only in the last bars do fanfare and rhythm run riot. A chaconne is meant for display and the lyrical and fanciful elements which we love in Rameau's other dances find little place in it. Here, the A major opening is perhaps what appeals most, but it is wrong to judge such a piece as pure music and to criticize it without seeing in one's mind the gorgeous spectacle of Jupiter, Twins, Planets, Stars and Zodiac revolving in their courtly orbits, to which it is a strength and stay.   In the score it is followed by a short chorus full of that diaphanous gaiety which Rameau sometimes expresses in A major, and akin to the "Revenez, revenez" appeal in Act IV, but it is hard to believe that the chaconne should not be the final number.

All the music of this scene, from Jupiter's descent onward and including the *ariette*, is ethereal and luminous, without becoming thin, and in sympathy with the sidereal apotheosis.   Lofty yet gracious, it is more reflective of joyful disembodied spirits than the ballet in Act IV.

There are more differences than likenesses between Rameau's two best-known *tragédies* and the works are so complementary that they give a comprehensive view of their creator as a tragic composer.

Hippolyte et Aricie is the more vigorous; it exhibits more physical action.   *Castor* is more ideal; elegy reigns over long tracts and the action is in the characters' hearts rather than in their deeds.

Hippolyte is full of a strong sense of place.   The settings are well reflected in the music: the temple, in the priestesses' entry; Hell, in the solo and choruses of Pluto and his court; Troezen, in the crowd that welcomes Theseus home; the woodlands, in the hunting chorus and, in Act V, in Aricia's solo and the concluding *divertissement*.   In *Castor*, though each act is headed by the description of its place, the sites are less clearly marked; the action seems remote from anywhere or, if it has a setting, it is an ideal one, like the Elysian Fields or the mysterious meeting ground of humans, gods and constellations in Act V.   People do not travel in it; they just *find* themselves.   In *Hippolyte* there were five marches or march-like airs; there is not one in *Castor*.

Both operas stage crowds, of course, but these are more indefinite in the second.   Either they are anonymous, like the Spartans who weep at Castor's tomb and of whom we do not know whether they are courtiers or people or priests; or else they are creatures of fancy, like Hebe and her Pleasures, the devils, Castor's companions in the home of the Blessed and the throng of stars at the close.   The crowds in *Hippolyte*, on the contrary, are much clearer.   Pluto's court is well characterized by its music; Theseus is welcomed by a massive concourse of his subjects who voice their joy in one of Rameau's most substantial choruses.   Substantial, too, are the huntsmen who sing in Act IV and, as for the woodlanders who receive Hippolytus as their king in Act V, though more ideal they too are given musical existence by the musette that accompanies them and to which they sing their song of welcome.   All these are more earthy than the ethereal beings of *Castor et Pollux*.

Hippolyte is rich in contrasts; *Castor* is homogeneous, though nearly as varied as its predecessor. Pellegrin's libretto afforded Rameau the chance for broad contrasts of tone, like those between each act, more widely different one from the other than those of *Castor*; for sharp emotional clashes, between Theseus and Pluto, Phaedra and Hippolytus, Hippolytus and Theseus; for geographical opposition, even, between the various phases of the action. All this makes *Hippolyte* more colourful and picturesque. Its force lies in its abrupt changes of emotional flavour; that of *Castor*, on the other hand, lies more deeply hidden in the truthful delicacy with which the music delineates kindred soul states and distinguishes between them; and in the sobriety of most of its pathetic passages. In spite of some vigorous choruses it has fewer contrasts; there is less difference between the characters, all but one of whom are elegiac, though the distinction between the two brothers and, in Act I, between Phoebe and Telaira, shows a fineness of touch not present in *Hippolyte*.

The native vigour of *Hippolyte* has been tamed in *Castor*.

Not only has Bernard's libretto a better constructed plot than Pellegrin's; the music betokens a surer hand. There are awkwardnesses—rather lovable ones—in *Hippolyte*; rough transitions, stiff dialogue, undramatic invasions of music for its own sake, like the second *Trio des Parques* and the chorus in Act III. Phaedra and Theseus both have something barbaric about them which is not unpleasing when we recall the grim myth out of which the plot was evolved. The opera leaves at times an impression of primitiveness, strengthened by such numbers as the duets and fury airs which sound like ghosts from the previous century. *Castor* has nothing barbaric in its plot and very little that is archaic in its music.

Between the resplendent beauties of *Hippolyte* there are a few dull patches; if nothing in Castor is as monumental as the finest numbers in the earlier opera its high quality is well sustained and there are no mediocre scenes.

Elements common to both works are neither numerous nor remarkable. Phoebe and Phaedra are kinswomen, but Phoebe is secondary and exceptional. The hero and heroine in *Hippolyte* are, like the twin brothers, elegiac, but they are, musically, far less distinguished than Castor and Pollux and it is not to them that our mind turns when we recall the opera.

The finest numbers in *Hippolyte* are unlike anything in *Castor*. Here, the choreographic ensembles of Acts I and III, the rendering of fine shades of feeling, the disembodied character of three *divertissements* out of five, and the penetrating loveliness of the heroes' solos are among the chiefest beauties and there is nothing similar in *Hippolyte et Aricie*.

There are perhaps more individual beauties in Rameau's trial stroke, more of those pieces which survive extraction and exhibition far from their setting; more purple patches and concert-platform numbers. For this reason I insist on the feasibility of giving selections from it in concert version. *Castor et Pollux*, a more perfect whole, is less suited to dissection. The third act is fairly autonomous and might be given separately. A presentable block could be carved out with the lament "Que tout gémisse", followed at once by "Tristes apprêts", one or more of the *airs pour les athlètes*, and ending with the chorus "Que l'Enfer applaudisse". It is, however, through its solos that it deserves to be better known. "Tristes apprêts", once so famous, Pollux's "Nature, amour", Castor's "Séjour de l'éternelle paix", Phoebe's "Soulevons tous les dieux" and the two *ariettes* can all stand on their own legs upon the recitalist's platform and deserve to be given the opportunity of doing so.

The first performance of *Castor et Pollux* took place on October 24, 1737. The cast included Mlle Fel as Love; Tribou, who had played Hippolytus, as Castor; Chassé (Theseus) as Pollux; Mlle Antier (Phaedra) as Phoebe; Mlle Pellissier (Aricia) as Telaira. The dancers included Dupré and Mlles Sallé and Mariette. It was given a score of times in the autumn of 1737, then not again till 1754, when it was used as a weapon, common to Lullists and Ramists, to oust *La Serva padrona*. After resisting with Leo's *I Viaggiatori* the Italians had to withdraw[1]; the French victory was resounding. Yet the minority was not silenced. The revival of *Castor*, wrote Montucla, a Lyonnais lawyer who had moved to Paris and enrolled in the ranks of the Bouffonists,

> is neither the triumph of French music nor the grave of Italian, and there are many like me who prefer certain airs of *Bertolde à la cour*[2] to all *Castor et Pollux*, where the only tune is at the end of the third act, imitated from Mondonville, with an Italian accompaniment,[3] and the work, if you remove the accessories of dancing and stage decoration, which are the illusions of fools, is only one everlasting recitative, that is, one bawling from high to low all the more boring that Jélyotte appears very little . . .[4]

This time the cast still included Chassé, "great actor but who can no longer sing at all",[4] but Jélyotte had replaced Tribou as Castor.

---

[1] Rameau's *Platée* at once took the place of Leo's opera.

[2] Performed by the Opéra-Comique on March 9, 1754. It was a parody by Anseaume and Lasalle d'Offemont of Ciampi's *opera buffa Bertoldo alla corte*. Montucla's choice is like preferring *Le Petit Duc* to *Tristan*! It reminds me of the remark, I trust apocryphal, attributed to Ravel, that he would give all Bach for a page of Chabrier.

[3] An *ariette*, not in the Durand vocal score, added for the revival to the ballet of the Heavenly Pleasures.

[4] Letter from Montucla to the Academy of Lyons; in (236A), 459.

Mlle Fel had now become Telaira. It was performed thirty times in the course of this year and at least ten times in 1755. At one of these performances Jélyotte made his farewell appearance. It was revived in 1764 with Sophie Arnould as Telaira; in 1765—ominous sign of a change of taste—Pierre Berton added several pieces to the act at the gates of Hell. There were further revivals in 1772, 1773 and 1778—this one against Gluck—1779 and 1780. Excerpts, if not the whole opera, were played in 1792 when Reichardt heard them and expressed the opinion quoted in Chapter XVI. Then it was heard no more in Paris till the twentieth century, though it was performed in Munich as late as 1805. The first modern revivals were a concert performance at the Schola Cantorum on January 29, 1903, and a stage performance in Montpellier in 1908.

The 1754 version differed considerably from the original; it is the text printed in the collected works of Bernard. The prologue was omitted. A new first act was written in which Pollux, about to marry Telaira, gives her up in favour of his brother, who loves her and is loved in return. Lynceus, his rival, attacks the brothers and Castor is killed. This change had the advantage, if it was one, of not beginning with a funeral scene and also of ennobling Pollux. It added spectacle since Lynceus' intrusion and the fight were shown on the stage. The new Act II is the old Act I, save for a fresh scene between Phoebe and Telaira. Act III is the old Act II; Act IV has two *tableaux*, corresponding to shortened versions of the original Acts III and IV; Act V is essentially the same in text but the music is largely new. These changes brought much fresh material, the best numbers being: in Act I, a solo for Telaira, a couple of minuets (ex. 107: second minuet), gavottes and tambourins; in Act III, two gavottes for the Pleasures ballet; in Act V, a C minor *ritournelle*, an *air léger* in A minor and two gavottes.[1] There is some loss; Pollux's soliloquy has been replaced by one shorter and less interesting; the loure in the original Act IV has also gone.

Ex. 107

à demi jeu   doux fort

---

[1] Some of these numbers are recorded in the *Castor et Pollux* suite published by Decca.

This was the version which Dr. Burney heard in one of his visits to Paris. He commented unfavourably on the new soliloquy for Pollux in III, 1.

> The *prélude tendre* at the opening of the third act abounds with too many of these drags, which being equally harsh to the ear and injurious to pulsation seem to prevent the performer from ever falling on his feet; and bar eleventh, the chord of the superfluous fifth,[1] which makes all nature shudder except our Gallic neighbours, is here continued so long that it distorts the countenance of every other hearer, like *hiera picra* . . .[2]

The offending number is not given in the Durand vocal score; I quote the relevant bars (ex. 108).

Ex.108

---

[1] In French usage, an augmented fifth on the third degree, with or without the third above. "In the minor mode, if one adds the third above to the dominant chord one has the chord of the superfluous fifth, composed of a third, a false" (e.g. diminished) "fifth, a seventh and a ninth; it is figured ♯5 or +5." (30), 134.

[2] (43), ii, 967–968.

7. Dardanus

THE librettist of Rameau's third *tragedie en musique* was Le Clerc de la Bruère, whose name is even more completely forgotten to-day than those of Pellegrin and Gentil Bernard.[1] He was a nobleman and a wit of twenty-three who devoted his leisure to literary pursuits. He is the author of four librettos, one of which, the ballet-opera, *Les Voyages de l'Amour*, set to music by Bodin de Boismortier and given in 1736, earned the praises of Voltaire, who was as prone to excessive amiability on some occasions as he was to unjust carping on others. A contemporary newswriter called him a "phénomène" and placed him above Gresset, no doubt on the strength of his comedy *Les Mécontents*, performed in 1734. He was also the author of an "elegant" *Histoire de Charlemagne*; he wrote most probably, some time before 1752, the libretto of Rameau's ill-starred *Linus* and he contributed to the *Mercure*, whose editor he was from 1752 to 1754. He later became secretary to the Duc de Nivernais, ambassador at the Papal court, and died of smallpox in Rome in 1754 at the age of thirty-eight.

The theme of *Dardanus* is another of those semi-mythological subjects which irritated the *philosophes* and provoked the scorn of Italians like Algarotti who said that most French operas were more like mascarades than dramas. Actually, although four lines from the *Aeneid* preface the libretto[2], mythology provides but few elements in the plot. Dardanus, son of Jupiter and of a certain Electra, and founder of Troy, and Teucer, king of Phrygia, are names found in ancient legend, and Dardanus' marriage with Teucer's daughter and his succession to his father-in-law's throne are also given by classical authors, but the daughter's name, the existence of Dardanus' rival, the magician and the war between Dardanus and Teucer are inventions of La Bruère, who himself suspected that "le merveilleux ... peut-être n'est que trop prodigué" in the play.

The story revolves round the love of Dardanus and Iphise, Teucer's daughter, whose feelings at the opening are unknown to each other. Teucer is at war with Dardanus and has promised his daughter to Antenor, a neighbouring king, whose love for the maiden has decided him to help her father against the son of Jupiter. With the complicity of a magician, Ismenor, a name that savours of Tasso rather

---

[1] His name was not given when *Dardanus* was first performed, but was made known four days later.

[2] VIII, 134-137.

than ancient Phrygia, Dardanus meets Iphise, surprises her secret and reveals his own.   His audacity costs him his freedom and would indeed cost him his life were he not saved by Venus, ever helpful to lovers.   Other gods, too, enter on his side and a monster is sent on a punitive raid to ravage the coasts of the offending Teucer.   With ungrateful gallantry Dardanus volunteers to annihilate the aggressor and, in carrying out his dangerous mission, saves the life of his rival who was succumbing to the monster's onslaught when the Trojan prince arrived.   After a further intervention of Venus, Antenor withdraws, Teucer relents, and Dardanus and Iphise are happily wedded.

The situation was perhaps suggested to the librettist by Duché's *Scylla* (1701), with music by Teobaldo Gatti (known as Théobald); in this opera the heroine, daughter of Nisus, king of Megara, is loved by her father's ally Dardanus but herself loves secretly his enemy Minos. The climax is tragic and of the five characters only Minos is left alive.

Dardanus was first given on November 19, 1739, and had twenty-six performances.   The cast consisted in Jélyotte (Dardanus), Le Page (Teucer and Ismenor), Albert (Antenor), Mlles Pellissier (Iphise), Eremans (Venus), Fel (a Phrygian woman) and Bourbonnois (Love); among the dancers were Dupré, Mlles Sallé and Barberine. Opinion was far from favourable though the work was not a failure. Dacier's examination of contemporary newsletters (*nouvelles à la main*) allows us to follow the shifting opinions almost day by day.[1]   There was a solid body of Rameau supporters—they were nicknamed "ramoneurs", a word which means "chimney-sweep"—determined to applaud the opera at all costs and turn its performance into a triumph. And there were the usual discontented reactionaries, with the old complaints of discordant harmony and no melody—the stock-in-trade of musical anti-modernists at all periods.   The work was so stuffed with music, they declared, that for three whole hours no one in the orchestra had time even to sneeze.   The later acts seemed frigid, especially the long slumber in Act IV which made people yawn, the chief theme of which was scoffed at because it resembled a popular lullaby.   Jean-Baptiste Rousseau lent the anti-Ramists his venomous pen and, in a letter of November 17, 1739, to Louis Racine, enclosed a satirical verse directed against Rameau and others.

Distillateurs d'accords baroques.	Lulli de la lyrique scène
Dont tant d'idiots sont férus,	Est toujours l'unique soutien.
Chez les Thraces et les Iroques	Fuyez, laissez-lui son partage,
Portez vos opéras bourrus.	Et n'écorchez pas davantage
Malgré votre art hétérogène	Les oreilles des gens de bien.[2]

---

[1] (135).

[2] The date shows that the poet is tilting at Rameau before anyone had heard *Dardanus*.   *Lettres de Rousseau sur différens sujets*, Geneva, 1749: I, 233.

To-day, when Rameau is approvingly labelled one of the great "baroque" composers, it is amusing to register, thanks to this lampoon, the road covered by this footsore and travel-stained epithet.   In the same letter Rousseau says he once tried to sing some of Rameau's music but had to give it up, "ayant perdu mon latin".   It is curious to find the same reproach of unsingability in the mouths of both Rousseaus, the conservative Lullist Jean-Baptiste and the modernist Jean-Jacques.

Average opinion, however, was not enthusiastic.   The poem was considered involved and much fun was made of Dardanus' sleep; many caricatures were sold of this scene,[1] with the composer as the slumberer. *Les Fêtes d'Hébé* were given on December 10 in the hope that they would revive the composer's waning fortunes; they proved to be only a too successful rival to the *tragédie*.   Finally, poet and musician set about rewriting the second half, and the veteran Pellegrin was called in for advice.   In a new form it was performed on April 23, 1744, and, after the last three acts had been recast, on May 15 of the same year.   This latest alteration seems to have been the most radical one. The new *Dardanus* came before the public as a fresh work; the title-page of the 1744 edition calls it *Nouvelle tragédie mise en musique par M. Rameau et représentée pour la première fois par l'Académie Royale de Musique le 17 avril 1744*.   The libretto gives the date as the 21st. The change of date to the 23rd shows that the performance had to be put off at the last moment for a reason we do not know.

Dardanus was revived in 1760 with Sophie Arnould and scenery inspired in part from Piranesi.   It was given again, after Rameau's death, in 1768, with additions by Joliveau to the libretto and Berton to the score, and yet again in 1771.   Finally, modified by Guillard, the poet of Gluck's *Iphigénie en Tauride*, it was set by Sacchini in 1784. It was given in concert version at the Schola Cantorum on April 26, 1907, and the same year in Dijon; in 1934 it was performed in Algiers.

In the 1744 version Dardanus, when captured by Teucer's forces, is threatened in prison by Antenor and visited by Ismenor, who foretells his liberation.   Iphise also enters his cell and is about to set him free when a successful counter-attack by Dardanus' own men brings salvation nigh.   Antenor, mortally wounded, warns him of a plot against his life and Dardanus sallies out to join in the battle.   He is victorious and Teucer becomes his prisoner.   The old king refuses at first to grant his daughter to his captor but at length gives way, and Venus descends to officiate at the wedding.

---

[1] One is reproduced in (167), 32.

Though better planned than in the first version the plot remains somewhat absurd. As a play it is without an atom of interest. But it is not a play, only a support for independent dramatic moments, for singing and dancing. Does this matter? It is true that the weakness of the libretto is more fatal in French opera than elsewhere since the music serves the words so faithfully. In theory and origin the genre was dramatic, but its bad luck lay in that its librettos, individually, after Quinault's death, were nearly always weak as dramas. The weakness is not only in the words but also in the substance. It is possible for a poor text to help its music to greatness if its content be weighty; Bach's cantatas and the *Magic Flute* are sufficient proofs of this. If Gluck's *Iphigénie en Tauride* is so superior to his *Iphigénie en Aulide* and if the monotonous rat-tat-tat of Italian recitative has given way in it to something alive it is largely because the music rests on a libretto, no better poetically, but of more import and better designed than that of the earlier opera.

Rameau is the loyal servant of an unworthy mistress. He is interested in the descriptive and expressive aspects of his text, not in its architecture. He is not without constructive power, and the ensembles of *Zoroastre* show that this power grew in the course of his life, but his organizing sense is never strong enough to cause him to criticize his plots as dramatic wholes.

Dardanus contains more first-rate music, and of greater variety, than any other work of Rameau's except perhaps *Les Fêtes d'Hébé*. It is regrettable that so alien a plot should overshadow such riches and should lock them up in a prison which not even Venus can open. *Castor et Pollux* and *Hippolyte et Aricie* have in their themes enough dramatic stuff to make revivals possible, but *Dardanus* is a musicians' opera, and operas that appeal only to musicians remain within their scores where not even musicians often seek them out.[1]

Ex.109

Although the overture still falls into the mould of the slow introduction with dotted rhythm followed by a quick *fugato*, it is more significant and more modern than those of *Hippolyte* and *Castor*. The pretence at fugal writing is hardly kept up. As soon as all four parts have entered, counterpoint is discarded and a few bars later there comes an unmistakable second subject (ex. 109). This is followed by

---

[1] Considered, that is, as operas. As suites for soloists, chorus and orchestra they have more chances of revival. Rameau's best operas, suitably translated and judiciously pruned, should prove successful in this form with choral societies.

a short development of (*a*) with one of its counter-subjects, from which all suggestion of fugue is absent. The second half, where (*b*) reappears, has somewhat the character of a recapitulation. The music is more "Italian" than in the earlier tragic overtures which looked back to Lulli; indeed, a piece like this, where one single set of rhythms and themes persists throughout, broken twice by a strongly contrasted motif of which no further notice is taken, points to the early symphony. The music is spritely and vigorous and, though short, this overture has enough character to deserve performance apart from its opera.

The prologue makes even less dramatic sense than that of *Castor*. Venus invites the Pleasures to "régner en ce séjour", that is, in Love's palace on Cythera, and this, despite a momentary interruption by Jealousy and her following, they proceed to do with such completeness that Love and his court, including the Pleasures themselves, all fall asleep. Venus, discontented by this turn of things, thereupon recalls Jealousy who returns in force and "continues her ravages". Love awakes; Jealousy's job being done, Venus again dismisses the intruder and mortals of all ages come and pay homage to her son. When this has gone on for some time, the goddess intervenes once more and calls on the Pleasures to "depict the story of a darling of Mars imprisoned in her court"; in other words, to perform the opera of *Dardanus*.

Futile as this opening sounds its contrasts offer scope for varied tone-painting. There are the oppositions between Pleasures and Jealousy, activity and slumber, *volupté* and wrath. Rameau has taken full advantage of these, and the music is richer and stronger than in any of his earlier prologues. About half of it belongs to Venus, who sings no less than four solos, three of which are expressive bravura airs. All four are well contrasted and tax the singer's interpretative powers. The first, "Régnez, Plaisirs", is a voluptuous, inviting air in 3/4 time and that key of A which predominates in the prologue. The second, "Brisez vos fers", calls to Jealousy to waken the drowsy loves and reminds us of the demon-unloosing chorus in *Castor*, Act III. "Quand l'Aquilon fougueux", a descriptive piece whose character is indicated by its opening words, is the most purely *virtuoso* of the four, and the last is a wistful A minor melody first played as a *symphonie*. Love's one solo is an angry piece in F sharp minor, banishing Jealousy; the bass motive of repeated notes, later so conventional, is felt here in its freshness as vehement and threatening.

Of the choruses the best is the "ravaging" piece of Jealousy and her minions. It has the rustic swing of so many 6/8 choruses and keeps up its energy by frequent modulations. It is the most vigorous vocal number of the prologue.

The two descriptive *symphonies* both stand out, especially the first, in which the dance of the Pleasures is broken in upon by Jealousy.

The slow measures of the dance continue, partly obscured, by the rushes of the thirty-seconds (ex. 110).

The two formal dances are among the most beautiful in the whole opera. The D minor minuet shows to a high degree that blending of pungent expression with precise indication of plastic movement which makes Rameau's dances so unique. Other dance tunes have one or

Ex.110

other of these qualities—I am thinking, of course, of formal dances—
but few have them both.   The tambourins deserve to become as much
household objects as the well-known E minor one for harpsichord.
The first is full of that "joie folle et endiablée" which Masson says is
the chief quality of the dance, and in the leaps of the second (ex. 111)

Ex. 111

we can see the bounds and gambols of *danse haute* which were
Camargo's triumph.   Through both pieces there throbs a Dionysiac
frenzy that carries us back to the fife and tabor of the dance's native
Provence.

The first act is laid in a spot "filled with mausolea" erected to
the memory of the warriors who have fallen fighting against Dardanus.
It introduces Teucer, his daughter Iphise, her suitor Antenor, and the
usual throng of people and soldiers.   Its chief mood is one of determination, strengthened by warlike song and the memory of the fallen.
Iphise's private sorrow, shared by none, upon which the act opens,
falls into the background with the entry of the kings but enriches and
sharpens with irony the very different mood of Teucer and Antenor.
The *divertissement* at the end, the occasion for which is the unwilling
girl's betrothal to her father's ally, dwells on the conventional theme
of the charms of love.

To each of these three moments there corresponds one outstanding
number in the music.   The work opens in sorrow with Iphise.   To
begin with a soliloquy, like the prologue of the Greeks, Gloster's
speech in *Richard III* or Emilie's "Impatients désirs" in Corneille's
Cinna,[1] is a device that strikes a modern audience as dangerously
undramatic in a play, even when a degree of formality, as in tragedy,
frees the playwright from the shackles of realism, but in tragic opera
its effectiveness is proved by the frequency of its occurrence.   One
of its advantages is the ease with which it allows for a long instrumental

---

[1] Already archaic in tragedy at that time (1640).

prelude.   It is difficult to keep two or more characters silent on a stage
at the rise of a curtain for any length of time while the music induces
in the listeners the suitable mood; their inactivity is liable to look
ridiculous.   But there is no difficulty in having a single character held
unoccupied while the orchestra, in slow measures, performs its task
of evocation.

This introduction, some twenty bars long, and the *arioso* that follows, show the tragic Rameau at his highest.   Our mind is carried
back to similar opening soliloquies whose theme was unhappy love,
sung by young characters, in earlier works: those of Hippolytus,
Pollux and Castor.   But Iphise does not travel over the same ground:
her sorrow, through the elements of conflict which it contains, is tragic,
and Rameau has not failed to bring this out.   The three earlier examples
were elegiac; here, Iphise is not merely in love with someone who
knows nothing of her love and who, as she imagines, cares nothing
for her; she is ashamed of her passion for her country's enemy and
rebels against the cruel god who has stung her with it.[1]

Cesse, cruel Amour, de régner sur mon âme!

She is not a violent nature and there is nothing vehement in her
music, but here and there a touch marks the distinction between elegy
and tragedy (ex. 112).   With horror she sees the "aveugle ardeur"

Ex. 112

that is carrying her away and, as she reiterates the plain statement of
her infatuation for the foe (ex. 113), the flute underlines with expressive counterpoint the force of her repetition.   Her shame is emphasized by the presence of the dead around her (ex. 114).

The second mood of the act, that of stern determination, is seen at
its best, musically speaking, in the duet sung by the two kings.   The
warriors' inflexibility is well rendered in the stark yet lively music
whose austerity is heightened by the fact that both voices are basses.
The scene, which opens with a short funeral ceremony, continues with

---

[1] Another Iphise, in Montéclair's *Jephté*, was in a similar situation.

Ex. 113

a chorus, an entry of warriors and a further chorus consisting in a hymn to Mars and Bellona. The D minor *entrée des Guerriers* is one of the finest descriptive *symphonies* in the opera; in outward form it is

Ex. 114

a march, suggestive of athletic strides, but, like so many of Rameau's dance movements, it expresses mood as well as gesture (ex. 115).[1]

The whole of this third scene, to the end of the "Mars, Bellone" chorus, is well sustained, without violence, suggesting great reserves of energy. In the prayer chorus we meet again the accompaniment

---

[1] In the 1739 version there followed here an attractive loure (*O.C.*, X, appendix 10).

Ex. 115 *Majestueusement*

motif of the repeated chord which appears so hackneyed because later generations have worked it to death; with Rameau it retains its meaning and conveys both the intense steadfastness of the crowd's purpose and the passion underlying that steadfastness.

The last part of the act consists in the dance interlude, introduced as a festivity in honour of Iphise's and Antenor's betrothal. The infectiously bouncing *air vif* in G minor with which it opens (ex. 116),

Ex. 116

expressive but impersonal, is repeated as an *ariette*: "Allez, jeune guerrier!" in a form more fiery still. Then come the celebrated rigaudons. In the days when Rameau was more unknown than now these two dances and the E minor tambourin from the harpsichord pieces[1] were his Prelude in C sharp minor by which, and by which alone, his work was judged. No single piece, however well chosen, could sum up a work as rich as his, but in their way this couple of rigaudons illustrate as aptly as any other single dance or *symphonie* the best features of his ballet forms. The first owes much of its originality to its instrumentation from which the bass is absent; fiddles, violas and hautboys make up the orchestra. The second, like so many of Rameau's *parodied* dances, combines lightness of step with wistfulness and contrasts with the rhythmical character of the first. Diverse as they are, the opposition was not marked enough in the composer's opinion, and in 1744 he replaced the first by a shorter one, more purely rhythmical and more martial but also more commonplace.

---

[1] Whose memory was kept green by the carillon of Saint-Quentin Town Hall which played its first bars once a day.

Iphise has withdrawn into the background, but the recollection of her sorrowful *arioso* at the beginning and her mournful figure haunt us and embitter the festive strains.   The crowd scatters and she steps forward, utters a few words that express her state, and decides to consult Ismenor.   Her presence throughout this spectacle and her lack of sympathy with it, known only to herself and the public, recall the situation on Theseus' return in *Hippolyte*, Act III.

The orchestra plays almost continuously throughout this act. There is very little recitative and most of it is *accompagnato*.   Drama's loss is music's gain; it was no doubt to this feature, which is present in two other acts, that the complaint already quoted was due.   It is precisely this that pleases us to-day when we unearth the score of *Dardanus*.

Act II is musically as interesting as Act I and better as drama, since what *divertissement* there is arises more directly out of the subject.   It unfolds in a desert place with a temple in the distance. This lonely spot is the haunt of the magician Ismenor,[1] priest of Jupiter.   Thither repair Dardanus, Antenor and Iphise, separately, on errands all concerned with love and with each other.

The prelude is not this time an introduction to a solo but a *symphonie* which appears too long to be accompanied by dumb show on the stage.   It is in the style of a toccata (ex. 117).   The development after the pause, with compact harmonies that never move more than one degree at a time, rises to a *stringendo* on which it breaks and, closing abruptly with three chords, gives way to Ismenor's first words. His solo "Tout l'avenir est présent à mes yeux" is an accompanied recitative mingled every few bars with stirring intrusions by fragments of the prelude.   A grim but lively air follows,[2] the chief feature of

Ex: 117

---

[1] Ismeno is the name of the magician in the Tancred episode of Tasso's *Gerusalemme liberata*.   It appears as Isménor in Campra's *Tancrède*, whence La Bruère took it.

[2] Compare with the similar but more sinister air of Arimane in *Zoroastre*, IV, 5: "Accable de tes chaînes."

which is a long descending scale expressive of the magician's far-reaching power.   All this scene is in D minor, the use of which corresponds to the "grave and devout" of Charpentier's classification rather than to Rameau's "tender and loving".

The service which Dardanus requests of Ismenor, namely, that he effect an interview with Iphise, *incognito*, cannot be granted without much display of "formidable mysteries".   These make up a *divertissement* almost entirely vocal and comprising two good choruses.[1]   The

Ex.118

_____

[1] It contains only two danced *airs*.   The first, slow, is noteworthy for its obvious indication of sweeping robes and impressive ritual gestures.   In 1744 Rameau substituted different *airs*, the second of which sounds like a scherzo of 1770 (ex. 118).

first of these picks up from a solo of Ismenor and begins with four
bars on one repeated note, to:

Hâtons-nous! commençons
Nos terribles mystères!

—a passage which Verdi would have marked *quasi parlando*. Throughout, the single-note theme alternates with an ascending strain in three-

Ex. 119

part writing (ex. 119).   The oracular pronouncement in which Ismenor declares the success of his incantations contains some impressive
jumps, but the highlight of the act is the second chorus in which the
magicians warn the venturesome Dardanus that he must

Obey the laws of Hell, else thy loss is sure,

and urge him to remember that,

> Under the flowers whither pleasures lead thee
> Deep abysses yawn.

This is one of Rameau's greatest passion choruses, and unfailing vigour is linked with a boding sense of danger. The vocal writing is scarcely melodic and almost constantly homophonic, one note to a syllable. In contrast with the syllabic character of the singing the orchestra flings out in diabolic swirls and builds up the mood with a

Ex. 120

part independent of the voices and individual enough to stand alone as an action *symphonie* (ex. 120). The composer's greatest strength is called out by the second part of his text; a modulation from D to C minor, emphasizing depth, corresponds to the "gouffres ouverts" (ex. 121). The climax comes with the last repetition of the warning: "Songe, songe!" (ex. 122).[1] Like "Que ce rivage retentisse" in *Hippolyte et Aricie*, once the climax is reached, not far from the end, it falls back to its original state of tension.

---

[1] The likeness between this passage and the climax of the first movement of Tartini's fine D minor violin concerto reminds us of the frequent identity of idiom in dramatic and instrumental music in the eighteenth century. For a term of comparison, see the temple scene in Collasse's *Thétis et Pélée*, III, 1–2.

A good deal of the act is in recitative. The dialogue between
Ismenor and Dardanus, between Dardanus disguised and Antenor,
then Iphise, covers a wide range of thought and feeling. Gratitude,
requests, instructions, avowals, passionate hope and fear, shame, supplication are the themes upon which the discourse turns, and the tone
travels from plain statement to passion. All parts are not equally
admirable; when Rameau, guided more by the pitch of his singer's
voice than the purport of his words, adopts with Antenor the archaic

Ex. 121

device of making the voice double the bass under a superstructure
more complex than beautiful, he is frankly remote, but the passage
lasts only a few bars. Neither do we appreciate the taste for tone-
painting which makes him give Iphise a strained solemnity foreign to
her nature when she informs the pseudo-Ismenor that

> Par l'effort de votre art terri-i-ible
> Vous ouvrez les tombeaux, vous armez les enfers,
> Vous pouvez, d'un seul mot, ébranler l'univers.

But when line and harmony aim at following the progress of
emotion in the speaker's heart he achieves a reserved but sensitive and
poignant beauty which recalls Racine's poetry more than anything
else in music.

When Ismenor thanks Dardanus for having protected his "tranquil sojourn" the music abandons the stiffness with which Rameau characterizes the magician's role and gives itself for an instant to the grace evoked by the words "asile heureux", and its supple melody denotes the momentary unbending of the austere magician.

The delicate and precise depiction of fine shades of feeling, in

which French literature, both prose and poetry, has so constantly
excelled since the seventeenth century, appears when the libretto's
"si tendre, si sensible" hints at a distinction which a less discerning
artist would have overlooked (ex. 123).[1]

Ex. 123

The finest moments are those in which Iphise and Dardanus, in
turn, own to their mutual love.   The music not only brings out the
difference in situation and sentiment between them but does so for each
one in a manner amounting to characterization.   It is not just a
difference between two brands of emotion; it is the outlining of

Ex. 124

different personalities.   Iphise's avowal is entitled *air* because the
rhythm stiffens imperceptibly.   The tone is dispassionate since she
does not know whom she is addressing and the important idea is the

---

[1] D'Alembert praised highly the recitative of this part of the scene in
(29), 430–432.

excess of her love—a point that Rameau lightly underlines by means
of two little scales (ex. 124).

Dardanus has not the same reasons for calmness, yet he must keep
his disguise.   The presence in him of passionate feeling held in check
by external restraints produces a line more eventful, yet remaining
short of agitation, expressive of a richer nature,[1] and with a melodi-
ousness that, in comparison with Iphise's under-statement, is almost
voluptuous (ex. 125).

In its original form the third act is musically the least interesting.

Ex. 125

It has, however, an opening as noble as any.   In a gallery of Teucer's
palace Iphise is disclosed alone, bewailing the capture of Dardanus.
Her lament is preceded by a majestic prelude in E minor, whose dirge-like
measures progress like an idealized burial march.[2]   The character is
more funereal than tragic and the feeling more reserved than in "Cesse,
cruel Amour".   Its contrapuntal texture and the short strands of
scale with which it is woven recall the opening of *Hippolyte*, V, 3.
The whole orchestra takes part and for once the violas, whose expressive powers Rameau does not as a rule call out, have here and
there melodic parts (ex. 126).   The solo proper takes the form of
accompanied recitative, mingled with echoes of the prelude.[3]

The rest of the act consists in the *obbligato* rejoicing over Teucer's
victory and the alarm spread by the announcement of the monster's

---

[1] In the original version little else in his part betrayed this richness, but
it was brought out in the 1744 music, especially "Lieux funestes".

[2] The original edition has no heading.   The Durand full score suggests
Sans lenteur; the vocal score has *lentement*.   The former should be preferred.

[3] This solo is published separately by Durand.

ravages.   In the *divertissement* we greet with a smile of recognition an
old friend, *Les Niais de Sologne* (without its undignified name), first
presented as an *air en rondeau* and then set as a delightful solo and
chorus upon the theme of "Paix favorable", the unheroic corollary of

Ex. 126 *(a)*

Ex. 126 *(b)*

which, "Le plaisir vaut bien la gloire!" is surely an operatico-ethical
variant of "Paris vaut bien une messe".

The two minuets, especially the second, show that blending of
choreographic gesture and emotional significance upon which it has
now become commonplace to insist (ex. **127**).   The tambourins,
though in the same keys as those of the prologue, do not resemble

Ex. 127   *Modéré*

them.   The diversity of life that Rameau was able to throw into this
form, whose conditions appear so liable to be stereotyped and whose
limitations are so narrow, is truly remarkable.   Preference for one
pair or the other is a matter of taste and both should figure in that
anthology of his dance numbers, chosen and grouped irrespective of
the works whence they come, which we would welcome.

With Act IV in its original form La Bruère's libretto reaches its summit of preposterousness and Rameau's music one of its heights of unearthly beauty. Unearthly it may well be since it has to depict the hero's slumber in conditions which, for any but the son of a god and the darling of a goddess, would prove most disturbing. "The stage shows the seashore, with traces on every side of the fury of the monster that is devastating the coast. Venus comes down in a chariot in which is discovered Dardanus, sleeping."

Dardanus continues to sleep for quite a long time whilst "flattering Dreams", summoned by Venus, now invite him to sleep on, now inform him that glory and love are combining to give him "the myrtle and the laurel", now bring the news of the devastating monster and warn him that "to obtain what one loves" is a reward reserved for those who have known how to merit it, now cold-douche and electrify him with the vision of the beast and immediately afterwards relax him under the tepidity of

> Ah! que votre sort est charmant!
> L'Amour même a formé vos chaînes,

and of a *symphonie* describing "le calme des sens". When relaxation is complete and he has, we would fain think, found integration once more in blessed slumber, conflict dire is aroused in his soul by two choruses, the first of which stirs him with the thought that "La gloire vous appelle", whilst the other soothes him with the promise that "Le plaisir vous attend". Agreement has just been reached by both choruses on the advice:

> Livrez-vous à l'espoir du sort le plus charmant!

when an *air de* (premature) *triomphe* stirs anew the perplexed warrior-lover's heart and more Dreams, or perhaps the same to a new tune, follow up the statement "Il est temps de courir aux armes" with the order "Hâtez-vous!" tempered by the discreet appeal to vanity "Généreux guerrier".

We have hinted at Dardanus' emotional state as alternating between integration and disruption but, *au fond*, this is baseless surmise since nothing in the directions shows him to have lain otherwise than as a valuable piece of timber in Venus' chariot (whence the goddess, in default of any sign of her continued presence, must have departed, vertically or horizontally, off the stage). Such profound slumber speaks worlds for the exhaustion wrought in him by the battles, military and amorous, of the last few acts.[1] It breaks at length, however, and he wakes with the question "Où suis-je?" The monster-damage about him convinces him of the veracity of the

---

[1] In Marais' *Alcyone*, IV, the famous tempest in which her husband perishes rages likewise before the sleeping heroine's vision in a dream.

dreams he has just enjoyed and gives him courage.   He gets up from his couch, preparing to meet the foe, when Antenor comes on the scene. . . .   And here a more realistic section opens.

In presence of such rubbish the question that comes to one is: How could any audience ever have accepted it?   The answer is, as we already know, that no audience did and that composer and poet had to devise other ways of leading Dardanus to his appointed triumph.   In fact, we should ourselves to-day be probably more tolerant of these *enfantillages* than the original public because the radiant music which Rameau wrote to them would shine, could we but know it, more brightly after two hundred years and blind us more effectively to the nonsense of the theme.   This act is unique in his work.   In no other part has he poured so much of that liquor of illusion, enchantment and *volupté* which is peculiarly his own.   There are "enchanted worlds" elsewhere in his music but a tang of nostalgia is nearly always present in them; in *Dardanus* alone has he called up—not for a few bars only but for pages at a time[1]—a mood and a climate where no hint of bitterness or scepticism dissolves the fairyland.

The numbers to which these eulogies refer are:

The prelude, during which Venus descends;

Venus' air "Venez, Songes flatteurs";

the *rondeau tendre* entitled *Sommeil* and the trio and chorus which are sung to it;

and, after the vision of the "monstre sortant des flots", the solo "Ah! que votre sort est charmant!" sung by a Dream;

the *symphonie* called *Calme des sens*;

and, at least in part, the conflict chorus "La gloire vous appelle".

All these are heard "en songe",[2] and in them Rameau has spun with uncanny craft the threads of a happy dream.   In spite of the simplicity of his means, in this achievement later artists, working with richer resources, have seldom equalled and never surpassed him.

The prelude is the longest piece of instrumental music in the play, apart from the overture and dances.   It is more through-composed than the ordinary descriptive piece which the precise gestures on which the music has to model itself tend to cut up, and it gives us a hint of the way Rameau might have written had he lived a little later, in the age of sonata and symphony.   The key throughout all the numbers enumerated is that of "douceur et tendresse", G minor.   The writing

---

[1] I apologize for measuring in bars and pages what should be told in terms of time.   The choice, alas! is a reminder that this great music lives in eyes that peruse scores, not in ears that hear it played.

[2] This removes the scene as a whole from the category of stage slumbers of which Lulli's *Atys* and *Armide* and Destouches's *Issé* provide distinguished examples.

is freely and smoothly contrapuntal and its formal qualities are those of the prelude to Act III, though their spirit has nothing in common (ex. 128). The feeling heightens a little as the semiquaver half of the

Ex. 128

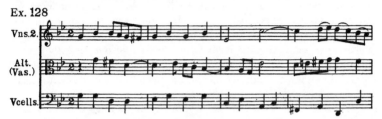

theme is developed. A full close on B flat, instead of ushering in a relative major section, is followed at once by the return of the opening G minor strain and, towards the end, a new element appears, very Ramellian in both shape and setting and of a pattern familiar elsewhere in his work (ex. 129).

Ex. 129

The music of the *sommeil* itself, which seemed ridiculous to some members of the sophisticated public because it recalled the *dodo des enfants*, is charged with an almost hypnotic drowsiness (ex. 130). We are far from the rocking 12/8 measure which an Italian composer

Ex.130

would have used here. This *sommeil* is all at once an inducement to sleep, a *berceuse* and an impression of the state of sleep. Music is packed with *berceuses, barcarolles* and *Wiegenlieder*, but evocations of sleep are much rarer and probably the most familiar example comes from another French composer, that of the Holy Family in Berlioz' *L'Enfance du Christ*. A chance discovery of this and a few other pieces of Rameau's[1] is a date in one's musical journey. The G minor close, as La Laurencie points out, interrupts felicitously the cradling rhythm and symbolizes the hero's slumber. It is important to take it without either hurrying or dragging if the music is to produce its effect. To quaff it too fast is to miss its flavour; to dawdle over it kills it and sends us as firmly to sleep as Dardanus himself. The trio of Dreams takes it up after the orchestra has played it, but on the whole it is best left unsung; words cannot avoid clipping its wings.

Instrumental refinements are not very common in *Dardanus*, but there are a few here, such as the flute duet that accompanies "Ah! que votre sort est charmant!" In the *trio des Songes* there is a threefold antiphonal opposition between the *basso continuo* only (first trio section), and *tutti* (chorus) and strings (second trio section).

Of the other pieces mentioned above the *calme des sens* is the most telling. It appeared no doubt less ethereal to its first hearers than to us and expressed more clearly the morrow of *volupté*; but we can still respond to the blissful weariness of its rhythm, and the tiny recrudescence of feeling in the fourth bar from the end[2] is very Ramellian.

The refinement in opposition of timbres just noticed is apparent again in the chorus where the whole band accompanies the full choir singing of "gloire" and the woodwind only the *petit chœur* singing of "plaisir".

The programme pieces depicting "le monstre sortant des flots" and "le ravage du monstre" are about as alluring as such pieces ever can be; the latter is in a brilliant toccata style that makes it good abstract music. The trio of Dreams based on the *air de triomphe* is a spacious, large-limbed piece, enlivened by the ejaculations "Aux armes! Hâtez-vous!" of the chorus. It is among the more successful of Rameau's specimens of that not very interesting type, the warlike song, and differs from most others by being almost entirely homophonic.

The second part of the act is "realistic" with a vengeance. The storm which forms a background to Antenor's struggle with the flame-throwing monster and to Dardanus' rescue is one of Rameau's most sustained tone-pictures, worthy of comparison with the earthquake in *Les Indes galantes*, II. The tempest-and-fury key of F predominates with a good deal of modulation. Besides Vivaldi-like passages of violin arpeggios there are others which carry us forward

---

[1] Such as the *danse des bergers devant Eglé* in *Les Fêtes d'Hébé*, III, for instance.

[2] Expressed in the characteristic rising sixth. Compare with the G minor gavotte in *Les Fêtes d'Hébé*, I, 8, second half. The whole gavotte is close in sentiment to the *calme des sens*.

well beyond Rameau's period, as so often happens in these descriptive
pieces where a composer's powers of expression were more severely
taxed than in passages of a merely sentimental significance.

The gem of this part is the solo in which Antenor compares the
respective merits, on grounds of *Schrecklichkeit*, of Neptune's monster
and love. Its swaying accompaniment, though its counterpart could
certainly be found in music of Rameau's contemporaries,[1] has a

Ex.131

Schumannish character (ex. 131) and, despite the declamatory line of
the voice part, the air, especially towards the end, might almost pass
for a Romantic *lied* (ex. 132).

Such is this unique act. Unique, without doubt, in Rameau;
unique, also, in a wider sense, if we take into account the peculiar
flavour given to the theme by the composer's personality. It plunges
us into sheer fairyland—a fairyland of ease and rest, of a discreet sweetness that never cloys, however often it is entered, with no aspirations
beyond itself, but with no reservations, either, with none of the
scepticism that poisoned the *Plaisirs d'Hébé* as they were unfolded
before the disenchanted view of Pollux.

There are other moments in Rameau where such a fairyland is
called up, but they are passing. Only in the original fourth act of
Dardanus has he dwelt on this theme and exhibited it under more than
one aspect. And this, I repeat, is one of the most personal achievements of this musician whom text-books teach us to consider as a pure
intellectual and an academic, a brain whose only interest in music was
to work out previously conceived harmonic theories and who to-day
can appear but "dry" or "pompous". One day in his courts is enough
to dispel this impression. I would fain insist here on the fact that,
whereas Rameau has many strings to his lyre, this one he shares with
few. Broad, vigorous choruses and airs of passion are found in
many composers; Rameau's, like all art worth anything, have of
course their own cast; they nevertheless belong to families well repre-

---

[1] E.g. the scourging music in the St. Matthew Passion.

sented elsewhere. The fairyland of *Dardanus*, IV, and its more evan-
escent appearance in other parts of his work, and pastoral worlds like
that of *Les Fêtes d'Hébé*, III, have few or no peers and, though we
may prefer other faces of his muse, none are so much his own.

Ex.132

In its 1739 form the fifth act begins with a light-hearted chorus,
acclaiming Antenor's supposed victory. It breathes an open-air
freshness not common in *tragédie lyrique*. The light, flexible lines
toss about like gossamer in the breeze or country-dancers on a lawn in
May. This is the second triumph chorus that the exigencies of the
libretto have required of Rameau's inventiveness[1]; here the emphasis
in the music, though not in the words, is on happy deliverance rather
than on victory.

Venus' descent, after the misunderstanding about the victor has
been cleared up, is accompanied by a beautiful *symphonie* in which,
with simplest means used with Racinian economy, Rameau paints for
an instant another "enchanted world" (ex. 133).[2] The tone-picture

---

[1] The other is in Act III, a more conventional grand acclamation in 2/4
time and with a square rhythm.

[2] Note the force of the flute entry on the leading note.

unfolds whilst Teucer expresses his wonderment. The G minor *air des Plaisirs*, close in feeling to the fourth act, shows an interesting example of flute and violin combination; the flute part is more consistently independent of the strings than usual.

In the final *divertissement* the most attractive pieces are the second gavotte and the chaconne. Of the four final chaconnes in his early operas this one is unquestionably the grandest.[1] In musical interest, it is the most independent of the attendant spectacle and can stand as an autonomous piece of symphonic writing. Even its most choreo-

---

[1] It is one of his longest: 283 bars.

graphic episodes are musically significant.   The scope and intensity
of expression are great.   The beginning is as grandly massive as that
of the chaconne in *Les Indes galantes* but more open, commencing as
it does on the third of the scale; a fine effect is produced by the first
three bars in which the harmonies move under a static treble.   Even
when contrasted the episodes are subtly linked.   For the first time
Rameau combines through-composition with the choreographic
variety required in a chaconne.   Each of the two long episodes that
separate the return of the opening theme has expressive minor sections in which he makes good use of his exiguous woodwind resources.
One couplet is given to the bassoons, playing alone with the support of
the basses (ex. 134).   His use of these instruments is remarkable; he calls

Ex. 134

on them to render a feeling graceful, tender or wistful like that associated
with the flute.   "Thanks to Rameau and Mondonville an instrument
hitherto appreciated only for its force has become pleasant and touching, capable both of pleasing the ear and affecting the heart."[1]   Exs.
135 (*a*), (*b*) and (*c*) show how Rameau, in other expressive parts of
this chaconne, blends strings and wind; note especially the cross-
tying in (*a*).   It is in a movement like this that we realize what an
advance his scoring shows towards independence, as well as counterpoint, of sonorities.

   Is it because it was impossible to be dramatic with such a libretto
that Rameau poured so much pure music of the first order into the
1739 version of this opera?   Scarcely a single number is commonplace, and there is even more variety and contrast between the sections than in *Hippolyte et Aricie*.

   The improvement in the plot effected for the 1744 performances

_____

[1] (36), 306; in (190), 523.

and the increase in dramatic power led to the cutting out of some good
music and, on the whole, the later version appears musically rather
less rich.   The greater dramatic quality shows itself mainly in the
long scenes of dialogue with orchestral accompaniment and in the
varied nature of this accompaniment; also in the small number of

Ex.135ª

Ex.135ᵇ

Ex.135ᶜ

separate pieces in the comparative fewness of which the later *Dardanus* resembles *Zoroastre*.

Of the music for the original third act only the rather commonplace triumph chorus "Que l'on chante" and the two minuets are retained. The chief loss is the E minor prelude and Iphise's "O jour
affreux". Dramatically the gain is for Antenor, who comes to life
and is involved in an emotional conflict between a desire for vengeance and a sense of honour.   Most of the act, apart from the
divertissement, is in recitative.   The disappearance of "O jour

affreux" is in some degree compensated by a magnificent chorus of hate sung by the Phrygians over the captive Dardanus.

> Dardanus gémit dans les fers.
> Qu'il périsse! qu'on l'immole!

It boasts an unusually long prelude, explained by its presence at the head of the act (ex. 136).[1] This rhythm, the homophonic imitation

Ex.136

and syllabic declamation are kept up throughout, with occasional malevolent syncopations. The onrush is continuous; there are none of those ponderous slowings up and halts on half or full closes, and breaks at verse ends, which check the movement in some of Rameau's earlier choruses—a feature surviving from the previous century.[2] The most striking moment occurs with the modulation from F to its dominant minor (ex. 137). It is a pity that this fine piece lies buried in an appendix volume where no one ever seeks it out, instead of being included in the vocal score, and the same regret applies to much else in the 1744 version.

The other highlight in this act is Antenor's "Le désespoir et la rage cruelle s'emparent de mon cœur", a semi-melodic, semi-declamatory utterance against a background of striding arpeggios. One is reminded of Orestes' "Le calme rentre dans mon cœur"[3]—an impression

---

[1] An attempt to shake the customary immobility of the chorus is visible in the stage directions for the 1744 version. "Le peuple vient en foule environner le palais de Teucer; les danseurs courent tantôt d'un côte tantôt de l'autre, pour épier de quel côté le roi pourra paraître."

[2] The step forward, historically as well as in expressive power, is unmistakable.

[3] *Iphigénie en Tauride*, Act I.

traceable to the harmony of bars 4 to 7 (ex. 138).   This is a vital piece that shows Rameau in a less familiar light.

Among the new dances written for the *divertissement* we recognize the tambourins from the *Pièces en concert*, transposed to D.[1]

Nowhere, surely, can there exist within the work of a single artist a greater contrast than between the two Acts IV of *Dardanus*.   The first was Rameau's most ethereal and fairylike composition; the second, his most grimly realistic.[2]   For Dardanus lying on Venus'

Ex.137

bed, unscathed by his foes, is substituted Dardanus lying bound in his enemy's dungeon; for the endearing curves of Venus' descent music, the harsh seconds and ninths of the new prelude; instead of the slumber and the *calme des sens*, a poignant duet by Dardanus and Iphise; and for Antenor, instead of an elegiac *Lied*, a dramatic death

---

[1] The first one had already been used in the prologue of *Castor*.   The first eight bars of *La Timide* were introduced into the prologue in 1744. Two new *airs vifs* composed for this revival were used again in *Les Sybarites*, II, 5.

[2] I do not forget the exceptions to this generalization: the monster music in the first version, Ismenor's incantation in the second.

scene, preceded and followed by "bruits de guerre". Were it not for
the inevitable *divertissement* there would be nothing in common
between one bar and another of the two versions.

Like nearly every other act in this opera the new fourth act opens
with a soliloquy, "Lieux funestes", preceded by a prelude as long as
those of previous acts. "Le théâtre représente une prison", say the
directions with unusual brevity. The key words of the text, "funestes, honte, douleur, désespoir, sombre, cruel, horreur, déchirent

Ex.138

mon cœur", express the dominant mood which is reflected in the
music with an intensity and a sustained savagery remarkable in a composer generally associated in musical history with *fêtes galantes*. In
earlier works we have found plenty of pieces full of passion, vigour,
or sorrow, but none as cruel. It is customary to call passages of this
sort Beethovenian but the term is misleading, if only because there is
so much to be found in Beethoven that one is never quite sure which
aspect of his art is intended; however, should it be used of anything
earlier than the generation of Haydn, this piece deserves it as much as

any. But it is a very special Beethoven that it recalls; in spirit, it comes nearest to the *Crucifixus* of the Mass in D and it has something of the almost physical anguish of that passage.[1] Like all the rest of the 1744 version it is well and truly interred in an appendix volume of the *Œuvres complètes*—a volume which is without the aids to the un-lettered, in the shape of a piano arrangement beneath the full score, which exist in the other volumes; I have therefore reproduced it in the appendix as quotations are merely tantalizing and, who knows? perhaps an enterprising singer may discover it there and allow us to hear it in public.

The bassoon part is so individual that it amounts to an *obbligato*. The excruciating harshness of the clashing seconds and ninths is[2] at first sight the most obvious feature of this prelude. The enhar-monic relations of bars 8 to 10 and 36 to 39 filled Rameau with satis-faction; they were the only place in his work where he was able to induce his public to accept *enharmony*.[3] The enharmonics add greatly to the poignancy of the passage, whilst the bitter sliding suspensions of the last bars give a false impression of rest.

The music has thrown off all trammels of external pattern from which French opera was in any case always freer than Italian. The only relic of *aria* form is the *da capo*. Free polyphony, as distinct from the imitation customary in choruses, predominates more than usual. The impression is one of unity and massive spareness.

Masson calls it Rameau's greatest height of monologue. No doubt it is hard to think of anything to place above it, though one may find Theseus' "Puissant maître" and Iphise's "O jour affreux" equally moving. Its great difference from others is its comparative lack of lyricism. One hardly thinks of it as a vocal piece. It is obviously conceived instrumentally; except for the few bars of declamation in the middle and the recitative between the *fine* and the *da capo* the voice merely travels over the same ground as the prelude, annexing most of the time the original first violin part, after the fashion of later instru-mental concertos. The music expresses a mood of despair but in the manner of a symphony, not of a lyric. This does not detract from its beauty; it merely emphasizes once again the appearance of Rameau the pure musician and makes one regret that he had not lived fifty years later. At the end of the century and in a less purely vocal tradition,

---

[1] Compare with the 1742 prelude to *Hippolyte*, III. The second act of *Fidelio*, of course, also opens with the hero in prison and a *grave* in F minor, but its likeness with "Lieux funestes" goes no further.

[2] Was a reminiscence of it in Clementi's mind when he wrote the intro-duction to the third volume of the *Gradus* (No. 51)?

[3] "L'enharmonie n'a encore eu lieu dans les opéras français que dans un monologue de *Dardanus*" ((17), 65–66). Also: "La dureté de l'enharmonie y fait bien sentir l'effet de la situation" ((18), 59).

he might have been that rare product: a first-rate pure musician who was also a dramatist.

There is a sudden change as the solo ends and the music heralds the magical entry of Ismenor, borne on shimmering sixths and thirds. The long scene that follows is intended as a substitute for the *sommeil* and *Songes* incident in the original version. "The stage lights up; the Spirits subject to Ismenor fly on at his call and the prison walls are hidden by shining clouds." But we are not in a mood for this after the strains of the opening and in any case Rameau had done this sort of thing much better in 1739. His interest now does not lie there. This half-hearted attempt at fairyland is not convincing and none of the dances and *ariettes* which spin out the *divertissement* are more than second-rate. The only interesting passage is some impressionistic bars inserted for the second 1744 revival (ex. 139).

The scene between Dardanus and Iphise, who comes to deliver him, culminates in a very beautiful duet, "Frappez! frappez!" The key is G minor but we are far from the passionate melancholy which Rameau so often pours into that key. Here, the feeling is more elevated; the text, indeed, includes the word "ardeur" but the chant-like, semi-religious music sings of a resignation and a renunciation in which the sorrow is so calm that it is hardly more than a memory. Its tranquil pathos is infinitely penetrating, all the more, perhaps, for not containing any touch of longing. The grief is almost too deep for words, certainly for attitudes. French vocal music of this period is always sober, almost austere, compared with Italian; but here the sobriety is absolute and the neck of eloquence has been well and truly wrung. The piece is so unlike the conventional Rameau that I have reproduced it in the appendix. The line remains smooth; it is the absence of any vocal jumps that reminds us of a chant. Much of the effect depends on the uncertainty of the third, hovering between major and minor (bars 8 to 14 contain instances of instability, heightened by the consecutive fifths of bar 13). The rhythm has all the freedom of French music with none of that occasional hesitancy which upsets foreign ears. By the felicitous lengthening of the line in bars 25 to 28 we are led to think we have reached the end, so that the fresh start in bar 29 has a force quite out of proportion to the music in it. Rameau is often said to show no signs of development after his first opera. It is enough to place this duet beside that in *Hippolyte*, III, to see how unjust is this judgment and to measure the distance travelled in twelve years, from the stiff archaism of the one to the freedom of the other.[1]

---

[1] It is incredible, but this lovely duet was cut out soon after its composition, in the second revival of 1744. For a term of comparison see a not dissimilar duet in Collasse's *Thétis et Pélée*, I, 5: "Faut-il que tout s'unisse?"

Ex. 139

Les dieux vont re-ti - rer le bras qui vous op - pri-me;

Mais en bri-sant vos fers, de la ri-gueur du sort, Vo-tre li-bé-ra-

-teur de-vien-dra la vic - ti - me, Et vo-tre vie est l'ar-rêt de sa mort

The last scene of the act illustrates the same progress in a more external way.   Antenor comes in, mortally wounded, to confess his treachery to Dardanus and to warn the Trojan prince against the traitors that surround him.   This message once delivered, he dies. The almost breathless recitative is punctuated by bugle-call rushes in the strings which, on the word "tumulte", clash with a suspended resolution in the voice part (ex. 140).   The excitement is carried on

Ex.140

Ce Tu - mul — te des ar - mes.

through the brief dialogue between Iphise and Dardanus after his death and leads into a stirring "bruit de guerre" of over fifty bars which serves as entr'acte.[1]

The battle music is more musical than most descriptive passages of the kind; it resembles a fragment from an overture.   Advantage is taken of the contrast between strings and bassoons in an expressive passage (ex. 141(a)).   Towards the end, as the battle ceases abruptly with Teucer's defeat, there comes a sudden break (ex. 141(b)).

By the time the clamour has stopped the scene has changed to the hall of Teucer's palace, where once again Iphise is revealed disconsolate.   The solo with which she opens the last act has not the grim,

Ex.141a

Vns.

Bns.

Basses

---

[1] In earlier operas Rameau followed the usual custom of directing that some *symphonie* or dance from a *divertissement* already heard should be repeated between the acts.   Here, for the first time, he composes a special entr'acte piece and links it with the action.   This is all part of the increase in dramatic quality shown by the 1744 version of *Dardanus*.   Other special entr'actes exist in *Castor* (1754 version), *Naïs*, *Acante et Céphise*, *Zoroastre* (1756 version) and *Les Boréades*.   Mouret's *Pirithoüs* (1723) has one which must be among the earliest.   Entr'acte music was given up by Gluck.

Ex.141^b

sustained force of "Lieux funestes" but is more modern and deserves
more justly the well-worn title Beethovenian. The form is completely
free and the recitative follows no pattern; there is no prelude and no
theme, only a motif (obvious in the example), recurring at intervals
throughout (ex. 142).

The only other number to which I would draw attention brings us
back to the familiar world of Dreams, Loves and Goddesses. It
accompanies the *descente de Vénus* without which no one can marry
in the circles whence *tragédie lyrique* draws its fictional sustenance.
Rameau, after three acts in which his music has been predominantly
dramatic, throws himself once again into his task of spellbinding with
as much zest as formerly and leads down his goddess to strains quite
different from those of 1739. The scene is on a grand scale. "Le
théâtre change" and Venus is disclosed "dans une gloire" with her
retinue. From two to three minutes elapse between the beginning
of the descent music and Venus' first words. No detailed instructions
are given, but from the words of the spellbound onlookers it is pos-

sible to reconstitute the order of the proceedings. First come the
"doux Plaisirs" and "mille nouvelles fleurs qui parfument les airs";
the "melodious sounds" are attributed to the "bruit flatteur" of their
wings. About half-way through the scene appears the goddess herself; at least, that is when reference is first made to her; and it is clearly
stated that "elle descend dans ces lieux", which precludes any entry
on the flat; whilst the "gloire" refers to her transport. Teucer,
Dardanus and Iphise supply the commentary from which these conclusions have been drawn, now singly, now in trios, whilst the violins,

Ex.142

with a seesaw movement of broken scales or octaves, suggest the
"flattering sound of wings" which continues as a background to the
voices (ex. 143).

Once Venus has touched earth the enchantment ceases, at least for
us, dispelled by a stolid G major duet of Teucer and Dardanus, combined with a chorus, grand and Handelian in the least favourable sense
of these epithets. For the second revival of 1744 Rameau substituted
a more poetic chorus in G minor, conventional but pleasing, with
downward fluttering *vocalises* on "volez . . . volez!" The chaconne
was kept with slight alterations.

It is hard to generalize about *Dardanus* as if it were a single opera,
since the two versions amount almost to two different works. The
contrast between them—the one spectacular and full of "pure" music,
the other rich in action—is one of the most remarkable things in our
composer. It is a proof of the ease with which he could on occasions adapt himself to his public's requirements—a trait sometimes

forgotten by those who dwell on his unbending and intolerant attitude towards his collaborators.

One may, however, assert that strength and martial vigour are predominant qualities of both versions. There is no character as rock-hewn as Theseus and consequently no music as brawny as in *Hippolyte*, but the presence of Teucer and Antenor, even in the first version where they are quite impersonal, entails vigorous strains, and Dardanus, too, in the second version, adds to this effect. Theseus was the strongest character Rameau was ever to draw but he was the only one in the opera where he figured; the presence of these three helps to make strength one of *Dardanus*' chief characteristics. The total impression is thus more consistently forceful than either *Hippolyte* or *Castor*, though it contains nothing as violent as the two most violent choruses of the second and third acts, respectively, of those two works.

The other general feature that remains in one's mind after study-ing *Dardanus* is its emotional range. From the extreme dreaminess of the original Act IV, the tragic laments of Iphise and, in 1744, of Dardanus, on the one hand, to the martial or daemonic power of the duet in Act I, the magicians' chorus, the fury chorus "Dardanus gémit" and Antenor's "Le désespoir et la rage" in the new Act III, on

Ex.143ª

Ex.143^b

the other, there runs a tremendous range of feeling and all points along the scale are marked by first-rate music. Rameau always rises fully to the opportunity afforded by the text and sometimes, as in the Dardanus-Iphise duet in the new Act IV, goes beyond the actual words.

The dramatic qualities of the second version are obvious. In this form the opera is better constructed and its action less interrupted than *Hippolyte et Aricie*. Its main weakness is the unreality of the subject. In both earlier works, under the mythological externals, themes of universal interest were discernible. Here, apart from the conflict between love and patriotism in Iphise, nothing is of any significance; or at least, what might have been significant, like Antenor's jealousy, is not significantly presented. For this reason the only part where there is anything like character study is that of Iphise. The music does succeed in imparting a certain unity to the various solos in which she expresses herself though the Iphise of 1744, with her share in the hymn of renunciation "Frappez, Dieux tout-puissants" and her *arioso* "Dieux, que pour Dardanus", is a fuller personality than in the first version.

It is not only in that part of the music that expresses personal sentiment that *Dardanus* excels. In the interludes—choreographic, descriptive, decorative—it is also at least the equal of the two earlier *tragédies*. As for the recitative, if the second version is taken into account, this is the most interesting of all its composer's works. It has variety, expressive power, intelligent interpretation of the text. No more favourable examples could be found of the capabilities of classical French recitative than in the new fourth act.

In addition to covering a wider gamut of emotion *Dardanus*, in the sustained interest of its music, is in no way inferior to *Castor et Pollux*. It is deplorable that so much life and beauty should lie unknown, and one wonders whether a modern version, based on that of 1744 but incorporating some of the best parts from the earlier score which Rameau omitted, could not be put together. A prolonged acquaintance with his three greatest *tragédies* convinces me that much in them is still alive, awaiting merely the magic wand of an arranging and transcribing Ismenor.

8. *The Later* Tragédies en musique

RAMEAU's fourth *tragédie, Zoroastre* exists like *Dardanus* in two versions, of 1749 and 1756. No printed full score of the first has appeared since the middle of the eighteenth century; a vocal score was produced by Michaelis in the 1880's. But a scholarly edition of the later version, prepared by Françoise Gervais, was brought out by the Office de Radio et Télévision Françaises in 1964.

Its subject was more novel than most French operatic plots in that it drew for its setting on ancient Persia; yet it had been treated already several times.[1] It had the making of something more real and more profound than any other of Rameau's subjects except *Hippolyte et Aricie*. A struggle between the founder of Zoroastrianism and an evil magician might have been presented as a conflict between good and evil; the dualist character of the Persian religion lent itself to such a development and at another period and with another public we might have had a worthy treatment of this Manichean theme.

Zoroastre, unaided, and the magician Abramane, with the help of Arimane—the Angra-Mainyu of the Zend Avesta, one of the two primaeval powers that came together to create, the one, matter and evil, the other, spirit and good—and the spectacular assistance of Vengeance and her attendant demons, wrestle for mastery. The stake of their battle is the gentle and lovely Amélite. Good and Evil contending for a human soul: such, in our view, should have been the theme of Cahusac's libretto. Rameau could certainly have risen to such a conception, but anything so utterly serious would have been alien to the tradition of the operatic stage. Opera, as distinguished from spoken tragedy, had inherited from its origins in the ballet the character of a spectacle and a recreation, which must not move profoundly, however violent the emotions roused *en passant*. So it happens that what might have become a story of Archangel and Devil is just another unreal love plot, enhanced by an exotic setting and stage magic. The soul whose salvation is the stake between Zoro-

---

[1] In Italy by Alessandro Scarlatti; in France by the playwright Le Brun whose libretto was never set. Masson quotes three other French eighteenth-century operas, all earlier than Rameau's, in which the character of Zoroastre appears ((190), 48, note 2).

astre and Abramane is just another princess, beloved by two rivals, persecuted by the one and saved by the other.   It seems almost blasphemous to depict a figure like Zarathustra in love; it is the height of the ridiculous to put into his mouth the words of the bravura air which he sings in the second act.   Nothing in the libretto raises the tone above that of a purely secular and recreational story like *Dardanus*.

One can nevertheless detect at times in the music something which is not present in Rameau's other *tragédies*.   The profane passions of hatred and jealousy are rendered more intensely and with a stronger sense of reality.   Abramane and his accomplice Erinice are sinister figures almost able to make our flesh creep.   The fifth act lifts us above the *Ancien Régime* world of pasteboard property enchantments into a realm of pure feeling.   Here we have not merely Rameau the craftsman, "imitating" this or that *affect*, but Rameau the wizard, conjuring up good and evil presences.   It is no doubt of such passages, especially of the ethereal, unvoluptuous love music sung by Zoroastre and Amélite and of the chorus "Douce paix" in Act V, that Masson is thinking when he makes the very flattering claim that this opera is Rameau's *Magic Flute* and *Parsifal*.

Zoroastre is the only major work of Rameau whose libretto came from the pen of Louis de Cahusac.   This man was our musician's most constant collaborator and the author of most of his librettos after 1748.   Such mutual fidelity is remarkable for in the first dozen years of Rameau's operatic career he had changed his librettist with every new work.   He was difficult to work with; no *galant homme*, says the sharp-tongued Collé, would put up with his rudeness; Cahusac alone held out and became, continues Collé, a sort of word-flunkey—"un valet de chambre parolier"—to him; "his meanness of spirit bent him to everything that Rameau willed".[1]

Cahusac had certain qualities.   He sought to unite dancing with plot so that the interludes enhanced the action instead of breaking into it; he was in this respect a forerunner of Calzabigi and Gluck. He also took a close interest in the scenery and, according to the *Mercure de France*, invented and constructed himself the chief machinery in *Naïs* and *Les Fêtes de l'Hymen*[2].   He had his own views on music which he expounded in several articles of the *Encyclopédie*,[3] and he wrote a history of dancing.[4]   His long liaison with Mlle Fel, the singer, who was his mistress but steadfastly refused to become his wife, has given him a small niche in the temple of eighteenth-century anecdote and gossip.

Compared with the three earlier *tragédies* the difference which

---

[1] (56), II, 375; in (190), 110.   [2] *Œuvres complètes*, XVIII, xxxiii.
[3] *Ballet, Danse, Décoration, Opéra.*
[4] *La Danse ancienne et moderne*, 1754.

strikes us first in *Zoroastre* is its heightened dramatic character.   The contrast between recitative and set pieces, never very marked in French opera, is less pronounced than ever; recitative shades ever and again into a few bars slightly more melodic; airs and even duets break off into recitative.[1]   The chorus intervenes more often and more intimately; its usual appearance is in short outbursts which do not form independent *ensembles*, detachable from their background, like those of the earlier operas.   The kind of piece like "Que ce rivage retentisse", during the singing of which all action stops and audience and characters listen, or watch the dancing, occurs only twice in the 1749 version and neither time on a large scale.[2]   We recognize here the hand of Cahusac seeking to integrate drama and spectacle.   The music never arrests the action and the dialogue is more natural and realistic.   In III, 3, recitative, solos and choruses intermingle with no formal pattern and few orchestral interludes.   This further levelling of the barriers that separated the various elements of the music was already noticeable in the 1744 version of *Dardanus*; it is carried further in others of Rameau's later operas, such as the pastorals *Zaïs* (1748), *Naïs* (1749) and *Acante et Céphise* (1751), all three contemporary with *Zoroastre*.

Drama's gain is music's loss.   Such a conception is Wagnerian and, *a priori*, should mark a step forward.   But what is lost in formal shapeliness in the voice parts is not gained in the orchestra because the band's resources were still too small to allow for this compensation.   The absence of formal pieces, of "tunes", is more than made up for in Wagner by the sumptuousness of the scoring, so that it is often possible to abstract the voice altogether and to enjoy what is left as something complete.   We have seen that Rameau's treatment of the form he inherited from his predecessors came near to Wagner's in this respect, and that his orchestral accompaniments were sometimes individual enough to stand alone.   But this autonomy can be sustained only for short spaces.   His instrumental resources are too meagre to compete for long with the charm and expressiveness of the voice.   When the power and formal appeal of pure music in sung parts are subordinated to the necessities of dramatic action, as they are here, there is no orchestral splendour and variety to assert music's claims elsewhere, and the result is a certain tedium.   The opening scene of Act I is a very favourable example of ordinary conversational recitative, in which no emotion is strongly expressed but plans and projects are discussed; but it would be better spoken.   In their conception of the art, Cahusac and Rameau were too far ahead of the means at their disposal.

---

[1] E.g. in I, 2; pages 21–22 of the Michaëlis edition.
[2] In "Zoroastre, vole à la gloire", II, 5; and "Douce paix", V, 4.

Yet *Zoroastre*, as a result of integrating chorus with story, is rich in exciting ensembles, of which those in the fourth act are among the most dramatic in all Rameau.   The duet and chorus in Act V in which Abramane is finally vanquished by Zoroastre has a tempestuous descriptive accompaniment, which reminds one of the introduction and first scene of *Iphigénie en Tauride*.

The importance of the *ballets figurés* is another result of this increase in dramatic power.   Cahusac's ideal was to make each dance entry a separate action connected with the main one.   He began carrying out his plans in the first opera he wrote for Rameau, *Les Fêtes de Polymnie* (1745); he went further in *Les Fêtes de l'Hymen et de l'Amour* (1747), where he brought *ballets figurés* into each of the three *entrées*.   By *ballet figuré*, Cahusac meant a dance in which a group "figures", that is, mimes, some action related to the drama.   In this sense the word "figuré" had already been used by Gentil-Bernard in *Castor et Pollux*, I, 4.   Here is Cahusac's programme for one of the *ballets figurés* in *Les Fêtes de l'Hymen* :

> The priests of the God Canopus erect a turf altar on the banks of the river and put on it all that is needed for the sacrifice.   Egyptian women surround Memphis and adorn her with wreaths of flowers bewailing the victim's fate.[1]

The fourth act of *Zoroastre* has two such ballets.   One "is made up by Hatred, Despair and their retinue.   Hatred gives Vengeance a handful of snakes; Despair, a dagger dyed in blood."
The other stages the

> spirits of Hell who, led by Hatred and Despair, run to the call of Vengeance.   Vengeance stands at the foot of the altar; the demons, armed with serpents and daggers, cast terrible spells over Zoroastre's statue; they draw nigh, raise their arms as if to strike; a whirlwind of flame rushes forth from the altar and the statue vanishes.   Hatred, Despair and their retinue remain as they are.

The fine choruses in the fourth act are part of the second of these ballets; there are others, less dramatic, in the fifth act.   The contemporary operas of *Naïs* and *Zaïs* are also rich in such ballets.

Zoroastre was the first large-scale French opera to discard the prologue.   In its original form its second act was too empty and too remote from the story; in the much altered version staged in 1756 Cahusac went to the other extreme and overloaded it.   To make the hero a counter-tenor was a mistake but quite in accordance with Cahusac's conception of the theme.   The only interesting characters are the two evil confederates, Abramane and Érinice; there is unmis-

---

[1] Later the term took on a rather different meaning and even came to be opposed to *pantomime*.

takable unity in them but this is due to Rameau, not to his librettist. Abramane, especially, is an excellent example of our musician's power of characterization.

Zoroastre was given on December 5, 1749. The chief parts were sung by Jélyotte, Chassé, Mlles Fel and Chevalier. It was staged with great magnificence. "Decorations, machinery, lighting, costume, everything . . . was of a tastefulness, a magnificence and a splendour exceeding the greatest beauties that had been seen" at the Opéra since its foundation. The fifth act showed a superb temple "whose fluted columns were of gold, adorned with masses of carbuncles and rubies, flashing like the brightest fire". An immense dome formed the sanctuary "which was separated from the rest by a golden balustrade"; and on a magnificent altar shone the sacred fire. On either side were gorgeous galleries, with wreaths of laurels, myrtles and flowers. Here took place the crowning and wedding of Zoroastre.[1]

In spite of all this the opera was not a success.[2] A ballet by Fuzelier and Mondonville, *Le Carnaval du Parnasse*, which had been running since September, competed victoriously with it and it was withdrawn fairly soon. Yet it had its defenders. D'Alembert, then an ardent Ramist, considered it was the best thing the composer had done.[3] It was revived on January 19, 1756, with largely new second, third and fifth acts. This time the success was greater. "*Zoroastre* has great success; the fourth act is very fine and nothing could be better than the ballet and staging" (January 31). "*Zoroastre* is still a great success" (February 7). "People still go to *Zoroastre* with delight" (May 8).[4]

Grimm reserved his usual sarcasm for Cahusac's libretto.

> In *Zoroastre* it is day and night alternately; but as the poet . . . cannot count up to five he has got so muddled in his reckoning that he has been compelled to make it be day and night two or three times in each act, so that it might be day at the end of the play.[5]

The opera was revived a third and last time on January 26, 1770, for the opening of the new Opera house, the old one having been burnt down in 1763. It was well received and was performed some

---

[1] (81), in (207), 4–5.
[2] "The Hôtel de Ville [that is, the city of Paris], which administers the Opéra, has spent fifty thousand livres on a worthless opera called *Zoroastre*", growls d'Argenson in his *Journal* ((34), VI, 79).
[3] Letter to Cramer, February 12, 1750; in (190), 51.
[4] From *nouvelles à la main*, in (210).
[5] (71), 26; May 15, 1756.

twenty times. The director of the Opéra, Berton, made some cuts and added music of his own.[1]

It had the doubtful honour of being translated into Italian by Casanova and given in Dresden on January 17, 1752. Doubtful, because, though the overture and some of the choruses and *symphonies* were kept, the rest was recomposed by the ballet master Adam.[2]

In addition to the sacrilegious absurdity of depicting an august figure like Zoroastre as an amorous theocrat, Cahusac's libretto is structurally weaker than those of Pellegrin and Bernard. Musically *Zoroastre* is not the equal of Rameau's three earlier *tragédies*. The most dramatic act is the fourth in which Abramane, faced with disaster, makes a supreme appeal to the powers of darkness and is promised support by Vengeance, Discord, Hatred and the prince of devils Arimane. The music here is physically exciting; its sheer animation compels our approval and seizes us with its vigorous bustle. But it seldom comes within sight of the significance of these evil enchantments. Cahusac is not to blame. He does his best. "Venge-toi", sing Abramane's henchmen to Vengeance and her demons:

> Ce n'est qu'à la terreur
> Que tu dois l'encens de la terre.

Vengeance herself sings:

> Nous offrons pour secours, dans leurs maux rigoureux,
> Aux cœurs outragés la vengeance,
> Et le trépas aux malheureux,

while the Furies chuckle:

> Quel bonheur! L'Enfer nous seconde.
> Qu'ils dévorent la terre et l'onde!
> Que tout se confonde!

The words provide sentiments dire enough to inspire music like that of the second acts of *Hippolyte* or *Dardanus*. But there is nothing terrible about Rameau's choruses, broad, muscular and rhythmical though they be. The drama in them is in the movement, not in the harmonies. That is why the act leaves us disappointed, with the sense that an opportunity has been missed of which, in happier days, the ageing composer would have made magnificent use.[3] None of the music is uninteresting, but little of it is adequate to its purpose.

Yet there are three passages which are exceptions. Abramane's opening solo is a superb rendering of the lines:

---

[1] *Mercure de France*, May 1752. See also (153), 108–109.

[2] It was given in concert form at the Schola Cantorum on November 26, 1903.

[3] One thinks of the second magicians' chorus in *Dardanus*.

Cruels tyrans qui régnez dans mon cœur,
Impitoyable haine, implacable vengeance,
Des remords dévorants épargnez-moi l'horreur
　　Ou cédez à leur violence.
Dans le fond de mon âme une importune ardeur
　　S'irrite par ma résistance.
　　Pour me reprocher ma fureur
Le crime unit sa voix aux cris de l'innocence.
De l'abîme où je cours je vois la profondeur.
Tout m'alarme et me nuit, tout jusqu'à ma puissance
Fait voler sur mes pas le trouble et le malheur.

The verse is prosaic but the sentiment interesting. Rameau grasps the spiritual disorder within his hero's soul and expresses it in accents which reflect a suffering intense and almost physical. The essence of the piece is contained in the prelude (ex. 144).

Ex.144

The *syllabé* chorus of demons with running semiquavers, in Scene 5, which announces the immediate advent of Vengeance, is another sinister piece but it soon gives way to a dry, 6/8 solo of Vengeance herself, of a type already mentioned[1] which the seventeenth century

---

[1] See Chapter 5, p. 141.

Ex.145

liked to use for this sentiment and which to us appears so remote from it.

Arimane's air in the same scene is the third highlight in this act. It too belongs to an ancient type but it is lively and thoroughly malevolent. Its nearest counterpart in Rameau is the air of the magician Ismenor in *Dardanus*, II (ex. 145).

The fury chorus in Act I is not arresting in melody and harmony but its rhythm is original in that it contrasts 6/8 in the voices and basses with 4/4 in the treble.

The climax of the struggle between good and evil is attained in the grandest pages of the score (V, 4). Abramane and Zoroastre, after a short challenging duet, engage in conflict whilst the two camps sing a warlike chorus[1] whose chief purpose is to provide an emotional background to the struggle. It is the best chorus in the play and the only one, indeed, worthy to be compared to the best passages with a similar inspiration in *Castor* and *Dardanus* (ex. 146. The basses are Abramane's followers).

Elsewhere the best in Rameau is called forth by those moments in the drama where the mood is elegiac or voluptuous, or the theme is tender anguish, chaste love and the triumph of good. The first of these moods prevails in that part of Act I where Amélite is on the stage. The *chœur gracieux* "Rassurez-vous, tendre Amélite" is typical of Rameau's treatment of this theme and has an independent accompaniment with prominent flute parts. The two G minor gavottes in the interlude that follows, the first of which comes from *La Princesse de Navarre*, are in the very front rank of his dances. They are not only graceful—all French music of this date is graceful and grace is no distinguishing mark of Rameau; with a rhythmical precision which almost dictates the dancers' movements they combine an uncanny interpretation of the prevailing mood. "Rassurez-vous", the chorus has just sung to Amélite and, though Zoroastre's absence makes her sad, she knows no reason for fear, trusting as she does in Abramane's protection and Erinice's friendship. But we, who are in the secret of the two accomplices, know otherwise; and we feel that the mood which results from the mixture of gentle lovesickness and innocent trust with a hint of treacherous cruelty to come, is reflected in them and in the duet which is sung to the second one (ex. 147: the second G minor gavotte in the scoring of 1756).[2]

A more definitely pathetic mood is expressed by two *symphonies*,

---

[1] Zoroastre's camp sings "Lancez la foudre!"; Abramane's "Quels terribles éclats!"

[2] The beginning of the first gavotte (ex. 148) occurs in the gavotte of the overture to *Semele*, where its pronounced French character stands out prominently.

Ex.146

- dre,   qu'ils soient ré-duits en   pou - - - - - - dre!

- dre,   qu'ils soient ré-duits en   pou - - dre,   ton - nez,

—   Ton - nez

                    Ah!

147

Fls.

Vns. 1

Vns. 2

B.C.

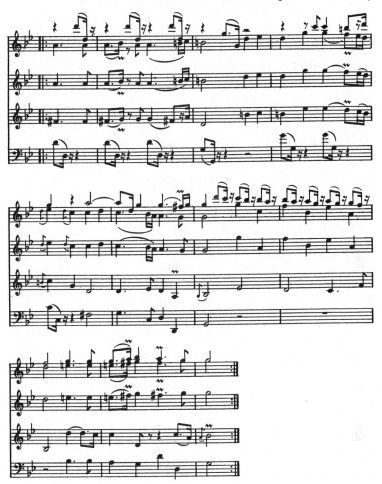

both borrowed from the composer's harpsichord works.   One is the haunting *La Livri* from the *Pièces en concert*, in C minor, which appears in III, 7 as a *gavotte en rondeau gracieux* in A minor, shorn of its expressive cross-rhythmed tolling accompaniment.   The other is *Les Tendres Plaintes*, transposed into G minor.   The *symphonie* omits the second episode and the first is set entirely in the treble. One often wonders how far old music was intended to convey the mood it calls up in us.   In many cases, of course, the title puts us on the right lines towards understanding it, but one frequently wishes that one had the composer's commentary.   Here, for once, we have almost such a thing in the stage direction which gave Rameau the idea of using this piece and which is, therefore, a reliable clue to its signi-

ficance: "Accablée de douleur, Amélite s'asseoit sur un gazon." The word "accablée" shows that the gentle pathos, as it seems to-day, of *Les Tendres Plaintes* was more overwhelming before time had passed over it and given it that spurious quality of old-world quaintness which is all that some perceive in it.

Zoroastre contains in all four pieces taken from the harpsichord recueils or *Pièces en concert*—more than any other opera. The other two are the A major saraband from the *Nouvelles pièces*, transposed to G (III, 7) and *L'Agaçante* from the *Pièces en concert* (II, 4); the chorus that precedes it also contains allusions to it. No later opera borrows music from this source. A caricature, published by La Laurencie,[1] shows the composer as a devil threatening a man writing, no doubt a librettist; on the floor lies a book bearing the title: "Vieilles pièces de clavecin pour faire des opéras nouveaux." This suggests that he had been twitted for his frequent re-use of his keyboard music and may account for his giving up the practice.

The third act opens with the expression of a keener sorrow. It is a chorus of supplication sung by the victims of Abramane's power. The discouragement and suffering are realistically rendered by the drooping, broken phrases and by the pleading tunes of the flute's upper register (ex. 149).[2]

The most individual music in *Zoroastre*—peculiar, that is, not only to Rameau but to this opera—is found in Act V, especially in Scene 4, after Abramane's overthrow. Some of it is triumphant[3]; some of it sings of love[4]; some is just pure and ethereal.[5] But it all

---

[1] (166), 600.

[2] Compare with *Pygmalion*, Sc. 1, bars 1–5; *Zaïs*, III, 3 (both of 1748). Compare also with the first number of *In convertendo*. bars 1 to 5, where the likeness is less close.

[3] Chorus "Douce paix" (p. 242 of Michaëlis edition); *air majestueux* (p. 286).

[4] Love of subjects for ruler: "Règne sur cet empire" (p. 257); love of Zoroastre and Amélite: "Présent des cieux" (p. 289) and *air gracieux en rondeau* (p. 306).   [5] Rigaudons (p. 295); second gavotte (p. 308).

has a disembodied loveliness which puts us at times in the mood
called up by the end of the Diabelli variations and other parts of
Beethoven's latest works and which, no doubt, explains why Masson
says that one of the rigaudons in this act is "not without analogy
with the seraphic melodies at the end of Schumann's *Faust*",[1] though
the likeness is not obvious to me.   The magnificence is of the same
quality as in the apotheosis of the Heavenly Twins in *Castor*.[2]   The

Ex.150

love numbers almost reconcile us to the idea of Zarathustra in thrall
to the tender passion, so spiritual a union do they reflect.   They
might serve as a commentary to the mystical wedding of the soul of a
saint with its Maker.   The beginning of the chorus of Zoroastre's
subjects is pregnant with this "third period" sentiment (ex. 150).
The other-worldliness becomes poignant, unsuitable though the
term may sound, in the rigaudons and the second gavotte.   The
obsessing first rigaudon conveys a feeling of discomfort, with its
persistent semi-canon (ex. 151).   We are not quite sure whether we

----

[1] I presume he means the final chorus ("mystical choir"), the beginning
of which, like much of the above, is in A minor.

[2] *Entrée des Astres* and chorus.   In the 1764 version of *Castor* these
rigaudons were inserted in this scene.

are in the body or out of it.[1]   The second rigaudon and gavotte[2] and
the *air gracieux* which comes between them and is on the same plane,
are all in A minor.[3]   Rigaudon and gavotte are akin and yet unmistakably different.   Both dances are worthy of disembodied spirits
but, whereas in the rigaudon the joy is unclouded and without a
touch of anything else, a familiar, insistent longing penetrates the
gavotte.   The difference in feeling is indicated chiefly by the melodic

Ex.151

tonic, on which it relaxes to rise again with resilience (ex. 152); in the
gavotte it remains below it, with a gradual downward trend.   There
are in Rameau many strains grander and more stirring and expressing
more fundamental emotions; but they are strains to be paralleled in
pages as grand and stirring, and more so, in Bach, Handel, Mozart—
not to move outside his own century.   Though it be not fair to limit
his claims to recognition to his dances alone, as Burney and foreigners
of his way of thinking tended to do, it is nevertheless in his *symphonies
de danse* that he is least like anyone else and most completely triumphant over all other musicians who have used similar forms.   In this
gavotte we can hear and taste something found nowhere else and see
most clearly illustrated what is most essential, if perhaps not most
precious, in him (ex. 153).

Cahusac's alterations for the revival in 1756 entailed the rewriting

---

[1] A believer in such things might say that its astral body did not quite
fit its physical body.

[2] The first gavotte is a more conventional piece, witty and vigorous,
like many another dance of its composer's.

[3] The rest of this scene is in A major.

Ex.152

of most of Acts II, III and V.   A new character was introduced, Oromasès, king of Genii, whose high priest Zoroastre now is.   He is Arimane's adversary and the operatic avatar of Hormuzd, the good Spirit of Zoroastrianism.   Rameau treats him as Bach treats Christ in the St. Matthew Passion and always gives his words instrumental accompaniment.[1]

As with *Dardanus*, the production of a new version entailed loss and gain.   The new opera is more lively and more unified, though its second act remains unsatisfactory.   The loss was in the music.   The sunrise in Act III in 1756 kept part of its original music in Act II of 1749 but omitted the imposing chorus "Ciel! de feux ce mont étincelle!" (Michaëlis, p. 90).   Gone is the chorus of supplication in III, 1 (ex. 149).   Arimane's impressive air in IV, 5, "Accable de tes chaînes" (ex. 145), is replaced by an exhortation from a Voix Souterraine, an example of oracle music less archaic than the air, more concentrated

Ex.153

* 1756 Vns.2

---

[1] This is not the only peculiarity of recitative accompaniment in this opera.   Abramane's threatening words of command to Zoroastre in II, 4 (p. 264), "Fléchissez en tremblant", are accompanied by two bassoons and the basses only.

and at the same time externally more expressive (ex. 154). In Act V the chief losses are the nostalgic little chorus "Régnez sur cet empire", of which only a few bars are kept as *annonce*, heard during a conversation between Zoroastre and Erinice (V, 2), the duet between Zoro-

Ex.154

astre and Abramane, and the superb chorus "Dieux tout-puissants" that followed it, whence ex. 146 was taken.

When one knows these later operas of Rameau the passage from him to *Orfeo* and *Alceste* is seen to be gradual.   The music for 1756 intensifies the break-up of set pieces by integrating *petits airs* and choral interventions even more closely with the background of dialogue, for instance at the close of Act II, where short interventions of the chorus are mingled with Amélite's soliloquy and with her conversation with Zoroastre, and in III, 8, when Amélite swoons. Rameau wrote a short entr'acte piece—two dance-like movements in 2/4—to link this act with the next.

There are two good short airs for Erinice in Acts II and III, both expressive of hate and jealousy; the second has an active accompaniment of arpeggios and scale fragments in the strings of the kind used in Antenor's "Le désespoir et la rage" in the 1744 *Dardanus*. Abramane's reply, pointing out that Erinice's expression of hate is but the mask of wounded love, like his words in II, 4, of 1749, is sustained only by bassoons and basses (ex. 155). And, to put her out of harm's way,

Ex. 155

he places her under a cloud, at which she very naturally exclaims "Ah! le perfide!" (III, 1). Having thus disposed of his indiscreet ally, he surrenders himself to an air quite in *opera seria* manner—a feature which would not have been found in Rameau's earlier *tragédies*. It is but one instance of the creeping Italianism that was invading even *tragédie lyrique* and it belies such remarks as Burney's "this nation, so frequently accused of more volatility and caprice than their neighbours, have manifested a steady persevering constancy to their music, which the strongest ridicule and contempt of other nations could never vanquish",[1] which is the source of gibes at the "Chinese-like fidelity" of French eighteenth-century music to its Lullian prototype by modern writers [2] who have not looked further than *Hippolyte* and *Castor*.

Lullian opera used the set soliloquy generally at the opening of an act or after a change of scene, and most often in slow tempo. This one is quick—*vivement*—with a bravura swagger that makes it more external than the traditional French solo. Italian in spirit, the vocal part remains in the tradition of declamation and though the syncopations of the accompaniment suggest *opera seria* the figuration does not depart from Rameau's usual practice (ex. 156). French, too, is the middle section in unaccompanied recitative.

Act V opens with a dramatic scene for Erinice, whose part is affectively more subtle than in 1749. It begins with a pleading, sighing figure in the strings and flutes which returns at intervals like a leitmotiv, and ends in impressive "pronouncement" style (ex. 157).

Many of the *symphonies de danse* were retained from the 1749 performance, the most regrettable omissions being the gavotte adapted from *La Livri* in III, 7, the elegiac *air gracieux en rondeau* in A minor in the final *divertissement* and the rigaudons, which were used again eight years later for the 1764 revival of *Castor*. Of the new ones the best are a pair of rigaudons in II, 7, the first of which makes witty use of those wide leaps that are perhaps more frequent also in the vocal parts of this version (ex. 158). The second, in G minor, is up to the standard of Rameau's best movements in that key.

In *Zoroastre* clarinets were used for the first time at the Paris Opéra. Rameau wrote no special parts for them and they no doubt doubled or replaced the hautboys. The Opéra pay-rolls show that the executants were two Germans, Johann Schieffer and Franz Raiffer, who probably belonged to La Pouplinière's private orchestra which we know to have contained two German clarinettists in 1748.[3]

Historically, if not musically, one of the most interesting parts of *Zoroastre* is its overture. In his earlier *tragédies* Rameau had remained close to the Lullian model. Indeed, for sixty years there was little change in the form and I have quoted elsewhere d'Alembert's well-known gibe in 1758. He added: "M. Rameau was the first to throw off the yoke and to try another way."[4] *Zoroastre* will therefore give

---

[1] (43), ii, 966.

[2] (144). As if "fidelity" to a satisfactory art form, even when that form is neither Italian nor German, were something ludicrous or contemptible!

[3] Excerpts from *Zoroastre* were given by Vincent d'Indy at the Schola Cantorum early in the century. In 1964–65 it was performed several times at the Paris Opéra with much criticized re-orchestration; a concert performance of the 1756 version from Françoise Gervais's edition was given by the Office de Radio et Télévision Française in November 1964.

[4] (29), Chapter XXXVIII.

Ex. 156

Ex. 157

A - mour,   Cru-el   A - mour,   Cru-el!

Et creu - ser mon tom - beau.   Et creu - ser

mon tom - beau.

Ex. 158

us an opportunity to consider his nineteen overtures as a whole.

The Lullian overture was in two linked movements, slow and fast, and it had little connexion of mood and none of theme with the action it prefaced. Departure from it was to take place along two lines, form and content, and it will be best to separate them.

In Rameau's first five operas—*tragédies* and ballets—the outward form of Lullian overture is present, though the musical texture is increasingly different. *Hippolyte*, the first, is closest to it; *Les Fêtes d'Hébé* and *Dardanus* are furthest. With *La Princesse de Navarre* there is a change. This play is a *comédie-ballet* and the music is merely incidental, though indispensable. The Lullian formula is given up and the overture unfolds gaily in three short movements, *gravement*, *gracieux* and *assez vite*. The *gravement*, though in dotted rhythm, is light-hearted and recalls the overture to *Les Fêtes d'Hébé*; the *gracieux* is utterly Italian, in that modern style which Pergolese's trios and

Ex. 159

Sammartini's *sinfonie* were spreading, and which is found also in Gluck's trios—a style sentimental without solemnity (ex. 159). It is a movement that takes us far from the Paris Opéra—and indeed the play was composed for a court function—and from Rameau himself, not a trace of whose personality can be caught in this commonplace little *cantilena*. But at sixty-one Rameau was not too set to be unable to write in a foreign style as if to the manner born. The finale, a *presto* in 3/8, is just as Italian. This is the first appearance in him on a large scale of the *new* Italian music; of the *old* he had given examples in his cantatas and his *ariettes*.

Six later operas revert to the slow-fast formula, but without any real resemblance to the discarded Lullian model. That of *Les Fêtes de l'Hymen* is like an Italian *sinfonia* in that it contains no allusion to the opera; the others will all be mentioned further on.

Two operas, one a pastoral, one a ballet, *Le Temple de la Gloire* and *Les Surprises de l'Amour*, open with two separate movements, in each case a dance-like *allegro* and a minuet. *Les Fêtes de Polymnie* and *Les Fêtes de l'Hymen* return to the traditional *coupe* but neither is Lullian; dotted rhythm and fugal writing are given up.

Most of the later works follow the Italian practice inaugurated by *La Princesse de Navarre* and begin with three movements; the only exception is the *Anacréon* of 1754 whose opening *symphonie*, though entitled *ritournelle*, is really an overture in one movement, ending on a half-close in preparation for the first scene.[1]

It is more relevant to inquire how these movements are connected with the drama they announce.

The need to connect overture and action was felt generally towards the middle of the century. The lack of connexion between overture and subject must have been much greater in Germany than in France, since J. F. Schutze, writing as late as 1794, complains that in Hamburg it was not uncommon to play "unsuitable *angloises* before tragedies, and *adagios* before comedies".[2]

Yet Hamburg was the city where Johann Adolf Scheibe had laboured in the 'thirties and 'forties—he left for Copenhagen in 1744— and had attempted to attune overture and play. He wrote incidental music to Corneille's *Polyeucte* and Racine's *Mithridate*, in German guise, in 1738, which he intended to bear special relation to these tragedies. He does not say that they were definitely programmatic overtures, and as the plays were not operas the overtures could not stand in thematic kinship with what followed; but it is clear he was seeking some sort of relationship between the two.[3]   A contemporary, Christian-Heinrich Schmid, looking back on this attempt, calls it "a great and memorable thing of the year".[4]   It is perhaps due to Scheibe's influence in Copenhagen that Gluck's earliest programme overture was composed in that city for *La Contesa dei Numi* in 1749.[5] It is not likely that Rameau was aware of these experiments.

Already in *Hippolyte* both the *grave* and the *vite* are thematically related to the first number, the chorus of nymphs. The *fièrement* of the *Castor* overture, in D minor, returns, expanded, in the key of A major as the *Entrée des Astres* (V, 7). The *lents* in those of *Platée*

---

[1] The evolution away from the Lullian overture did not always lead to the programme piece.   The influence of the *sinfonia*, visible in *La Princesse de Navarre* and several other overtures of Rameau, is strong in other composers, such as Leclair and Mondonville.   The overture of Leclair's *Scylla et Glaucus*, though beginning with a *lentement* of twenty bars, is a sturdy piece with only glimpses of *fugato* and, as one might expect with Leclair, solo passages for the fiddles (1746).   Mondonville's *Titon et l'Aurore* (1753) is in two movements, *vivement* and *vite*; it is homophonic with brilliant violin solos, and noteworthy *galant* details.   Neither overture is allusive or descriptive.

[2] (108), in (217), 487, note.   [3] (106), ii, St. 67, in (217), 487.
[4] (107), in (221), 85.   [5] (130), 62.

and *Les Fêtes de Polymnie*, both of 1745, the same year as *La Princesse de Navarre*, announce music which will be heard in the body of the opera; in *Platée*, as the *symphonie extraordinaire* in II, 4 that heralds the entrance of Folly; in *Les Fêtes de Polymnie*, as the *symphonie* in the prologue that accompanies the raising of the trophy to the glory of Louis XV (ex. 160), a majestic prelude in which the harmonies build up slowly with splendid suspensions to the chord of the ninth.

Ex. 160

The overtures of his last works all contain sections that return in the operas.   That of *Les Surprises de l'Amour* contains jumping unison octaves which foreshadow Vulcan's hammer and leads into Vulcan's air "Que la flamme nous environne".   *La Naissance d'Osiris* has three movements, the first of which, *un peu gai*, is heard again as a contredanse at the end of this one-act ballet.   *Les Paladins*, also in three movements,[1] ends with an *air gai* recalled at the beginning of the last scene (III, 4).   *Les Boréades* consists in a fast movement, common time, in F, *da capo*, with horn calls and a theme in unison octaves, a minuet in F, with important horn parts, and another quick movement in 6/8, a true *chasse*, though not so headed, with rapid passages from instrument to instrument.   The first words are "Suivez la chasse" and in the recitative that follows short horn calls are heard to remind us that the hunt is continuing; the overture is thus clearly linked to the

---

[1] The first of which, *très vite*, contains much 6/8 against 16/32 and alternation of 6/8 and 8/8.   This overture is contained in a stage copy preserved in the Bibliothèque Nationale; the autograph has a quite different one, also in three movements, none of which appears in the opera.

opening scene and is as much a prelude to this act as an overture to the whole opera.

A closer union still is achieved when the overture, though musically independent, calls up a mood in harmony with that prevailing in the work as a whole or seeks to emphasize its chief aspects—when it is, in a word, a programme of what follows.   This is so in *Zoroastre*. The task was made easier by the absence of a prologue, and the composer's object is explained by the note found in all editions of the text.   The piece is in three parts.

> The first is a strong and pathetic picture of Abramane's barbarous rule and of the groans of the peoples oppressed by him.   A gentle calm follows: hope is born again.   The second is a bright and joyous image of the beneficent power of Zoroastre, and of the happiness of the peoples whom he has freed from oppression.[1]

The first, corresponding to Abramane's perversity, is largely made up of repeated notes and upward rushes of thirty-seconds.   The second is an artless little *andante* of a score of bars in 3/4.   The third, which is the longest and answers in importance to the fugal *vite* of Lulli, is a rapid 2/4 movement, completely homophonic, in a style where it is hard to discover any trace of French dramatic writing and even, save for a brief moment, of Rameau's own imprint.   Its pert and short-winded phrases, with rapid changes of mood, remind us of Philip-Emmanuel Bach's keyboard writing; it is, in fact, a typical Italo-German *presto* of the mid-eighteenth century.

Zoroastre is not the only one, nor the most significant, of Rameau's programme overtures.   *Acante et Céphise* (1751), an occasional work written to celebrate the birth of the Duke of Burgundy, opens with a series of three movements: *Vœux de la nation*, *Feux d'artifice*, *Fanfare*, which form an original and exciting picture of the national rejoicing. The second is heralded by five bars of tocsin and punctuated with cannon fire.   The third contains a rhythmical imitation of the cry "Vive le Roi!"   It impressed deeply those who first heard it, and one of them even found it recalled to him "les grands efforts d'imagination de l'étonnant Milton".   It is more of a curiosity than a work of art and our jaded ears are no longer likely to find, like the writer just quoted, that "sound of cannon, bursting of shells, speed of rockets, sparkling sky, tumult, shouts of joy, are all depicted in the manliest hues".[2]

Three others, all a little earlier than *Zoroastre*, are of a higher order.   The most purely musical is *Pygmalion*, a brilliant movement

---

[1] This note is also written on the MS. score of the 1756 version in the Bibliothèque Nationale, Vm.² 376.

[2] (33), I, 75–76.

in 6/8 with themes of repeated notes representing, according to d'Alembert, the chipping of a sculptor's chisel.[1]

The two *pastorales héroiques*, *Zaïs* and *Naïs*, both have spectacular overtures, which nothing in the conventional tales of the rival loves of gods, genies, nymphs and shepherds seemed to demand. Each pastoral has a prologue and it is this, and not the actual opera, that suggests the programme.

The prologue of *Zaïs* "paints the unravelling of chaos" and the creation of the world. Oromasès, king of genies, awakens the various elemental spirits; Zaïs, the hero, is the genie of the air. The overture is an interesting attempt to render the unrenderable. As absolute music it reads like a fantasia, very disjointed in the early stages of the "unravelling"; it is eccentric but ineffective. It has not the shapeliness of Haydn's *Creation* overture, which one unfortunately cannot keep out of one's mind, nor its evocative power. The reason is perhaps that Rameau was concerned only with *painting* what he thought were the *external* attributes of chaos and not in calling up the mood which the idea of chaos induces in us, as Haydn has done. It has nevertheless points of interest and even deserves an occasional performance in an "historical" concert, or better still a recording. Some passages sound as if they came out of a pre-Romantic work of 1790 to 1800 (ex. 161); they are like excerpts from a later work put back into an earlier setting.[2] They show how such descriptive writing furthered the advance of the technique of expression.

> I consider [said a contemporary] that the overture paints so well the unravelling of chaos that it is unpleasant, for this clash of elements separating and fitting together cannot have composed a very agreeable

Ex. 161ª

---

[1] (29), 460.

[2] The menacing rising figure, so popular later, is prominent.

Ex.161^b

Ex.161^c

Ex. 161ᵈ

concert for the ear; happily man was not yet there to hear it; the Creator spared him such an overture which would have burst his ear drums.[1]

The prologue of *Naïs* stages the storming of Olympus by the Titans.[2]

> The stage shows the skies.   On the earth are seen the Titans and Giants piling up mountains to scale the Heavens, led by Discord and War.   In the skies is disclosed Jupiter, armed with thunder and surrounded by the gods.   The overture is a warlike alarum, depicting the shouts and tumultuous motions of Titans and Giants.

After a short introduction, marked *modéré*, which seems to illustrate the preparations and advance of the enemy, the *bruit de guerre* starts in earnest.   The movement is on a large scale; it has one hundred and forty-four bars of 3/2, *vif*, and the chorus into which it leads is nearly as long again.   It is a better musical whole than the last and does not require for its appreciation an indulgent sense of history.   Overture and chorus would make an exciting, as well as instructive, number in a choral concert.

The subject calls for rhythm rather than melody, for clash and impact rather than harmonic refinement.   Yet the movement is not without those expressive modulations which occur in Rameau's descriptive *symphonies* and look beyond his age (ex. 162).   The rhythmical violence is far from monotonous.   In addition to the ♩♩ ♩ figure shown above there are two types of quaver figures, one of which, flowing, is contrasted with syncopated minims (ex. 162, bar 1).   The other is seen in ex. 163 which contains also a vicious clash of seconds in the minim figure (ex. 163).   The chief weakness is that there is no

---

[1] (55), Jan. 5, 1748; in *Œuvres Complètes*, XVI, xlvi.   Grimm's uninspired comment was: "On dirait l'enterrement d'un officier suisse" (1748). The task of painting chaos had already been undertaken by Jean-Ferry Rebel (1664–1747) in his ballet *Les Éléments* and his foreword explains how it was done.   See (152), 143.

[2] The attack and defeat of the Titans figured on a smaller scale in the prologue of *Enée et Lavinie* (1690), by Collasse and Fontenelle.

Ex.162

Ex.163

climax; although the overture leads into the chorus the voices do not, as one would have liked, enter on a wave of fury but are preceded by a full close without expectancy.

In the chorus itself the words are mostly *syllabés* but additional animation is given when "at-ta-quons" becomes "at-ta-quons". The orchestra consists of strings, bassoons, hautboys, trumpets and kettle-drums—flutes and piccolo are rather surprisingly absent—and a muffled drum ("tambour voilé") which Rameau had used also in *Zaïs*. These limited resources are utilized with his customary elasticity of grouping.

Chabanon in his *Éloge* has two interesting passages about Rameau's overtures. He was a warm defender of absolute music and an adversary of the merely descriptive and programmatic. He should, it seems, have passed condemnation on pieces like these overtures. His thesis, however, is that they are really pure music and not descriptive.

> Nothing is so dangerous . . . as this project to paint, especially in *symphonies*. This intention merely cramps the composer's imagination, rivets it to a few little doubtful likenesses to which he sacrifices every-thing and turns him away from seeking beautiful melody . . . The overture of *Naïs* paints . . . the Titans' attack. One should therefore hear in it the seditious shouts of these children of the earth, see the rocks uprooted by their hands pile up like storm-clouds. Let me perceive these scenes, not traced but merely indicated in a single passage of the overture and I condemn it. [Whereas] this overture, to my mind, is a powerful and daring music whose peculiar incisive character is streng-thened by a few unusual harmonic devices. Those who are too untrained to grasp this music call it baroque; those capable of feeling it find it new and conceived with vigour; it moves them; and these harsh, wild intonations, these abrupt passages, this so to speak bristling harmony are for them a more than sufficient analogy with the Titans' fight that they are witnessing.[1] This analogy is the only painting that music should afford us.

If Rameau had painted more he would have sung less, and "without melody there is no music".[2]

The virtue of absolute music is that, even if it has been composed to illustrate a particular situation, it will be effective in any other situation. He illustrates this with an anecdote of a performance of the *Pygmalion* overture.

> A few years ago I was listening with several musical friends to a

---

[1] As there was no curtain the stage was visible from the beginning of the performance.

[2] (53), 25–27.

concert by night; the concert room was open on all sides, we were outside, and a mighty thunderstorm was going on.   The overture to *Pygmalion* was being played, and at the *fortissimo* of the *reprise*[1] there came a terrific flash of lightning, with thunderclaps.   We were all struck simultaneously by the marvellous relation between the storm and the music.   Assuredly this relation was not intended by the composer; he did not even suspect it.   What he had conceived as a brilliant *symphonie* became for us a picture by the play of circumstances.   One can make a music *that sings* say almost everything one likes; a music that fails to do so, however imitative, is essentially deficient and is always the very imperfect image of an object deformed and grimacing under a clumsy, coarse brush.[2]

As we look back over Rameau's overtures we see that he broke loose from the Lullian tradition and integrated the movement with the action, sometimes by introducing passages to be heard later in the opera,[3] sometimes by linking it with the first scene,[4] now by expressing in it the festive mood of the occasion,[5] now by summing up the chief aspects of the drama.[6]   One of these movements is actually continuous with the opening chorus which is thus a kind of *parodie* of it.[7] Gluck's four programme overtures were anticipated by one or other of them: *Alceste*, by *Pygmalion* and *Zoroastre*; *Paris and Helen* by *Castor*, *Platée*, *Les Fêtes de Polymnie*, among others; the two *Iphigénies* by *Zaïs*, *Naïs* and *Les Boréades*.   When one reads in as recent a standard reference book as the 1927 edition of Grove of "Rameau's inelastic orchestral preludes", which the writer contrasts with Gluck's, "intended to prepare the audience for the action of the piece",[8] one feels that it is still justifiable to insist rather heavily on his achievements in this field.

A small memorial tablet must be put up here to *Linus*.   Some time before 1752 this *tragédie en musique*, whose libretto was by Le Clerc de la Bruère, was being rehearsed at Mme de Villeroi's house, where it was to be given privately.   Some deficiencies in the music or the executants delayed the performance and it was laid aside.   So much can be gathered from Abbé de la Porte's *Voyage au séjour des Ombres*.[9] Soon afterwards the mistress of the house fell very ill and the plan had to be shelved.   This illness "mit beaucoup de trouble et de confusion dans sa maison" and when Rameau made a search for the

---

[1] Presumably the beginning of the *vite*, repeated.   [2] (53), 29–30.
[3] *Castor*, *Platée*, *Les Fêtes de Polymnie*; this is the practice followed in the overtures to *Don Giovanni*, *Cosi fan tutte* and *Leonora*.
[4] *Naïs*, *Zaïs*, *Les Boréades*.   [5] *Acante et Céphise*.
[6] *Pygmalion*, *Zoroastre*.   [7] *Naïs*.
[8] Art. *Opera*.   [9] See (60), 154 to 157; (166).

score and parts all he could find was two copies of the first violin part. Whether the rest was destroyed by ignorance or malice is not known.[1]

A first violin part is not much by which to judge of an opera. From the libretto, however, we see that it was a full-scale work in five acts. The violin part begins with a *ritournelle* in D minor, followed by a recitative in G; whether Rameau intended to compose an overture later we do not know. The gavotte in III, 2, in C minor, comes from *La Princesse de Navarre*, and one or two other dances look familiar but I have not tracked them down. There are several descriptive *symphonies*: a storm and alarums in Act II, a conflagration at the end of Act III, an "annonce des forgerons", imitating blows on the anvil, in Act IV, an interesting thunder effect in Act V, with exclamations by the chorus and solos; and a truly gigantic "tempête" of seventy-five bars for orchestra alone, in G minor, leading into a chorus, in the same act: one of Rameau's largest single *symphonies*. These numbers alone, as well as the outline of many dances, make one regret keenly the action of the conscious or unconscious malefactor responsible for its loss.

Ex 164

This memorial may be illustrated by a quotation from a gavotte in Act III not found elsewhere (ex. 164).

When Rameau died he had completed *Abaris ou les Boréades*, a *tragédie* in five acts, to a libretto which Decroix asserts to be by Cahusac, though neither autograph nor copy gives any name, and one of the copies says that the poet's name is unknown. The story is quite in Cahusac's manner, with its elaborately contrived *merveilleux* and close association of *divertissements* and action. The story is laid in ancient Bactria, a kingdom ruled by a queen, Alphise, who is bound by tradition to marry a descendant of Boreus, god of the north wind. She is in love with a gallant adventurer, Abaris, of unknown origin, who has been brought up by the high priest of Apollo. As she may not marry him and keep her throne she decides to abdicate. Boreus will have none of this and shows his displeasure through tempest, thunder and earthquake. Polymnia, with Muses and Zephyrs, and finally Apollo himself, intervene in favour of Abaris, whose resistance is strengthened by the possession of a magic arrow, given by Love to Alphise and by her to Abaris. His triumph is determined by the

---

[1] Decroix's note on the first violin part in the Bibliothèque Nationale, Vm.[2] 381.—The manuscript of the libretto has been preserved (Bibliothèque Nationale, ms. fr. 9253).

revelation of his birth: he is the fruit of Apollo's love for a nymph, daughter of Boreus.   He may therefore reign over Bactria and everyone is satisfied except other Boread pretenders, who had played their part in the troubles.

Within the conventions of the art Cahusac's libretto is well constructed.   The plot advances steadily and there are none of the turns and twists which made *Dardanus* and *Zoroastre* so undramatic.

The music certainly deserves to be accessible and repays study. It does not show signs of exhaustion, though similar words call up similar strains.   Texts like "Vole, triomphe" and "Triomphe, Hymen" had been set so often that we can hardly expect Rameau to be more novel than his poet.   But this is true of many other operas. The amount of conventional writing is no greater than elsewhere.

On the other hand, much of the writing is vigorous.   Choruses and airs are generous in size and the *divertissements* more varied than in some earlier works.   There are more *symphonies* and fewer set dances.   The emotional range is as great as ever.   The tender feelings find vent in the music of Alphise, Calisis, Orithie and some of Abaris'; there is terror in Alphise's "Songe affreux" and in several choruses; wonderment in the chorus that greets Love at the end of Act II; misery in Abaris' "Lieux désolés".   Fury resounds in Boreus' part and in the fifth act his followers deliver themselves of Rameau's last torture chorus, "Qu'elle gémisse!"   An air is sung in honour of Apollo (II, 6), an oracular pronouncement is made (IV, 3).   A hymn is sung to light; an invocation is addressed to the implacable god of the north wind; we are treated to the agitated narration of a vision (II, 5) with a full and rhythmically varied accompaniment, and of course an address is delivered to Hymen.   Music like Alphise's "Un horizon serein" (I, 4) or the Muses' chorus "Parcourez la terre, franchissez l'espace" (IV, 4) breathes a spaciousness which is new. And the nature-descriptive music is richer than ever.

On first acquaintance it is, as usual, the dances and *symphonies* that win our hearts.   We meet many features which are familiar and unchanged, and others which, though not unknown, have altered their appearance a little, and yet a few more that seem new, though it is always rash to assert, in presence of an unfamiliar trait, that Rameau has not been up to this particular trick somewhere else already.

Emotionally there is a mellowing which excludes the old tang and turns what would once have been sharp nostalgia into a soft plaintiveness, sometimes enhanced by rich harmonies or expressive overlappings (ex. 165).[1]   The *entrée des Peuples* for Alphise's and Abaris' wedding (III, 2) has a *démarche* of old-world Lullian solemnity which

---

[1] This gavotte (II, 6) has been published in a piano arrangement by Diémer (Heugel, Paris) with an added middle part.

Ex 165

at this late date makes it almost a pastiche.   But into it intrudes twice
over a strain of pre-Romantic tenderness that Rameau himself could
hardly have uttered thirty years earlier; after which it draws itself up
and ends with a gesture of impersonal pomp (ex. 166).

Ex 166

The key of A minor keeps its old evocative power, and four
gavottes exhibit various shades of that wistful sentiment that Rameau
expressed so often through it.   That in the same *divertissement* as
ex. 165 conveys this flavour with a most compelling rhythm, at once
vigorous and enervating, which settles on us and would reduce us to
moral paralysis if we did not resist it (ex. 167).

Ex 167

There is compelling rhythm of a different kind in what must be
the queen of all his many contredanses; I know of none where the lilt
is so possessive or the line so weird (ex. 168).[1] Weirdness of line, to
a point of strain, occurs several times in *Les Boréades* dances and may,
if one likes, be put down as the result of a barren genius lashing itself
into novelty.　The favourite drop of a fifth and a fourth, the classic

Ex 168

example of which is in "Tristes apprêts", gives asperity to the second
rigaudon in IV, 4, the *divertissement* in honour of Apollo over which
Polymnie presides with her Muses, Zephyrs, Seasons, Arts and Hours
(ex. 169).　A sense of strain is felt, too, it seems to me, in part of a

Ex.169

curious *air vif* which occurs in the scene where Boreus and his henchmen seek to terrorize Alphise into submission (V, 2).　Its key of
E flat seems strangely inoffensive for this purpose, but Charpentier
classed it as "cruel et dur" and it must have kept this character for
Rameau.[2]　The *air* is interesting for its scoring.　Rameau has

---

　[1] The line, though not the rhythm, recalls Couperin's *La Distraite*.

　[2] Rameau does not include it in his own list.

tended to group his hautboys, violins, violas and bassoons close together so that they are perpetually crossing and recrossing each other's paths, treading on each other's toes, and sometimes the lower instruments overtop the higher (ex. 170).   The tension and sense of search in this piece may well be meant to represent the cruelty of the situation, and the writing has a modernity which shows once again how sensitive Rameau remained up to the last to the musical climate

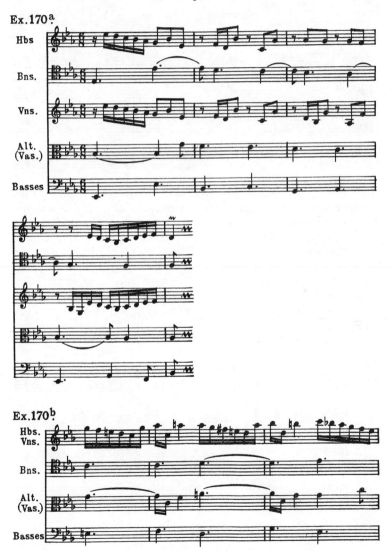

Ex.170ᵃ

Ex.170ᵇ

about him.   The page has the appearance of a Haydn quartet.   I do not suggest that such an appearance is astonishing in 1763; it is significant only because of the composer's great age.[1]

This quotation shows another feature more apparent in this opera than in earlier ones—an alternation between broad semiquaver runs and gasping fragments which, scattered through the different parts, build up into a mosaic pattern.   The same interest in fragmentary themes, with lightning exchanges between trebles and bass, is found in a rigaudon, the partner of ex. 169 (ex. 171), and in a gavotte in A major (III, 3) scored for hautboys, bassoons and basses, whose *mineur* I have quoted (ex. 167), and in yet another A minor dance—a gavotte

Ex.171

---

[1] The substance of this *air* is present throughout the succession of chorus, air and chorus in which it is embedded.

in I, 4, the first half of which is scored for flutes, bassoons and basses; in the second half the violins relieve the flutes which re-enter near the end. The abruptness of the exchanges is tempered by the diminutions as they are repeated; the dance is a miniature example of Rameau's picturesque orchestration (ex. 172).

Ex.172

His resourcefulness in scoring has not deserted him and there are still many *trouvailles*. He takes advantage of the opportunities in the poem to indulge to the full his taste for impressionism, as in the opening of the fifth act, when the chorus of subterranean winds is about to lend its support to Boreus; we see again here the build-up with short

Ex.173

fragments which eventually form a theme for the voices' entry (ex. 173). The chorus illustrates another modernism in an accompaniment figure new in his writing (ex. 174). In Alphise's lovely air, to the suggestive words:

> Un horizon serein, le doux calme des airs
> Invitent à voguer (I, 4),

which are well rendered by the soaring line, the flutes enter in crotchets,

Ex.174

then burst into sixteenths and thirty-seconds in the seventh and eighth bars (ex. 175).

In Polymnie's *entrée* and in the not quite unknown *gavottes pour les Heures et les Zéphyrs* in IV, 4, he has grouped his strings and wood-

Ex.175

wind and given them contrasting functions—the strings to sustain, the wind to move, which is less common than the contrary practice. The *entrée* is a freely contrapuntal piece whose rich chains of suspensions and *appoggiaturas* give us a last taste of Rameau's sensuous writing (ex. 176).[1]

The gavottes are included in Heugel's *Les Vieux Maîtres*, arranged by Diémer, a series which includes also the gavottes from II, 6, already mentioned, two commonplace *airs très gais* from IV, 4, and a supple, caressing *symphonie* in G, transposed to A, the *air andante et gracieux pour Orithie et ses compagnes*, from II, 3. Not only do the strings sustain; as they represent the hours they are directed by a note in the score to imitate the clock "en faisant retentir la fin de chaque blanche et noire". Long before, Roy had staged dancing Hours and Zephyrs in his *Éléments*, but he had kept them separate (I, 2); Destouches, however, had clearly intended his repeated minims in the *air pour les Heures* to represent the striking time-piece. Flutes were traditional for Zephyrs; Rameau makes them piccolos and disciplines a shade their wayward triplets with the staid arpeggios of the bassoons (ex. 177). If any single dance number of *Les Boréades* deserves to be rescued it is this ravishing child of Rameau's eightieth year. Diémer's transcription is faithful and one may catch from it something of the charm of its colouring.[2]

I have not stinted either admiration or quotation. Perhaps the former will be voted rather naïve and I shall be told that Rameau may well have taken his dances from a store composed long before. But there are no borrowings from earlier operas in *Les Boréades* and there is unmistakable kinship between a number of them which proves them children of the same vein and the same hour. Moreover, a piece like the last must have been written for the opera in which it is inserted; it is not a reach-me-down which could be turned to account in any ballet. There is no evidence for believing that he used up here music lying handy. The strains, never, alas! to be heard, belong to his last years; he conceived them on the edge of the grave; they, much more than his *Nouvelles Réflexions* on the infatuating "principle", are his true testament.[3]

Rameau's and his librettist's determination to build up great wholes is seen at its most spacious in the third and fourth acts. In the

---

[1] Is it not admirable that after so many entries of nymphs, muses, godlets and *hujus generis omnis* for which he had indited music for thirty years he should renew himself at the age of seventy-nine and compose one of his best at the very last?

[2] The second gavotte, in B minor, is like a variation of the gavotte in A minor quoted above (ex. 165), or rather both are variations of the same unexpressed original.

[3] I must qualify this by saying that Cahusac was dead since 1759 so that if the libretto be really by him it may have been in Rameau's hands for some years. But there is nothing to show that he began work on it before the last years of his life.

Ex.176

Ex.177

fourth scene of Act III Alphise decides to give up her throne and
marry Abaris. With her companions she invokes the mercy of the
wrathful Boreus, who hears her prayer by unleashing the elements.
The chorus raise their wailing while "the *Aquilons* take possession of

the stage. A whirlwind carries off Alphise; another counters Abaris'
efforts and as soon as he has finished singing Alphise is borne up in the
air." The music carries through the entr'acte with a descriptive
symphonie which leads into a terror chorus, "Nuit redoutable".[1]
The tempest continues to rage in the orchestra throughout the first
scene of Act IV, with exclamations from Borilée and the chorus, and
does not abate till Abaris' return in Scene 2.

This symphonic development is of a size unprecedented in Rameau,
except for the storm in *Linus*. The first fifty-seven bars of "orage,
tonnerre et tremblement de terre", in an emphatic C major, seem

Ex.178

disappointingly diatonic until we realize that Rameau is holding himself back for later on. The volume builds up with the entries of
Abaris and Alphise, then of the chorus, in the sixteenth and twentieth
bars. When Alphise has been spirited away, Abaris and the chorus
sing a plaint in C minor in which the latter's role as protagonist recalls
the end of Act IV in *Hippolyte*. The entr'acte music, headed concisely *Suite des vents*, is in C minor and the excitement is considerably
heightened; the reason for the comparative tameness of the *orage* is
now clear. Though it contains nothing so purple as the ninths and
elevenths at the beginning of the *Indes galantes* earthquake its fifty-
five bars are not unworthy to stand beside that act of God. Towards
the end the mark drops to *doux* in distant preparation for the C major

---

[1] At the beginning of the entr'acte the violin line bears one of Rameau's
many detailed instructions: "Adoucissez insensiblement pour être toujours
doux avec les flûtes."

on which the *symphonie* will conclude, then rises to *à demi* (*mf*) in the transition passage (ex. 178) to the chord of G, whence, after a pause, C major bursts out *fortissimo*. The most dramatic single moment is when, after a close in C major, the chorus enters afresh in C minor (ex. 179). Violin scales keep the winds present throughout Borilée's song of hate; a final chorus with full-blast storm music brings us back to C major and the lesser emotional tension of the beginning.

The storm breaks off suddenly on a dominant seventh chord to "Nous périssons tous" as Abaris returns to survey the damage. He registers his dismay in ten bars of recitative, then settles down to an

Ex.179

air. Its words, "Lieux désolés", challenge a comparison with Dardanus' "Lieux funestes" and indeed it does not pale beside the earlier piece. It shows in an extreme form that building up with tenuous wisps of themes—here, no more than sighs—which is a feature of the latest Rameau. Further comment is unnecessary as the piece is given in Appendix E.

It is unlikely that *Les Boréades* will ever emerge from the caverns of its two manuscript scores, one largely autograph, one a copy, with their simultaneous use of six different clefs. And yet publication of a vocal score, with indications of the orchestration, would bring musical pleasure to many in addition to providing historical interest. In the absence of such a thing I have quoted more liberally from the work than its obscurity would have seemed to warrant.

9. Les Indes Galantes *and Rameau's* Opéra-Ballet

W E tend to think of classical opera as falling into two kinds: tragic and comic, *opera seria* and *opera buffa*. While such a division may hold good for Italy it is as incomplete a classification of French opera during the first hundred years of its existence as a division into tragedy and comedy would be for French drama of the seventeenth and eighteenth centuries.

We have seen how important a place the dance carved out and maintained for itself in *tragédie lyrique*. The tradition of ballet survived independently and, in the eighteenth century, under the shape of *opéra-ballet*, came to rival Lullian opera in popularity. Out of the seventeen surviving works of Rameau which have more than one act, only five—the fifth of which was never performed—belong to the class of tragic opera; two more are comedies; one consists in incidental music to a comedy; three are pastorals; whilst the largest genre is that of *opéra-ballet* which comprises six works, including two of his best and most famous. Of his ten works in one act, seven are *actes de ballet*, in no way different from the acts which form the *entrées* of an *opéra-ballet*. It is thus clear that works where dancing predominates are as important in him as those where the interest is divided between dance and drama or is predominantly dramatic. This is typical of French classical opera as a whole.

The *ballet à entrées* was not ousted by opera and survived the competition of the new form of entertainment. From it derives *opéra-ballet*. This was the creation of Houdar de La Motte and Campra, the appearance of whose *L'Europe galante* in 1697 was the birth of the genre, though Lulli's *Le Triomphe de l'Amour* in 1681, to words of Benserade worked up by Quinault,[1] and *Les Saisons*, by Collasse and Pic, in 1695, were well on the way towards it.

"*L'Europe galante*", wrote Cahusac in 1754, "is the earliest of our lyric works which was not like a Quinault opera."[2] He defined it

---

[1] It was in this ballet, so it is generally thought, that women dancers first appeared on the stage.

[2] (44), 110.

as "a spectacle of singing and dancing made up of several different actions, each one complete and with no link one with the other except a vague and indeterminate relation".[1]   Its subjects were not always taken from mythology or legend, as in opera, and comedy was not excluded.   Thus, in *L'Europe galante*, though two *entrées* are laid in an imaginary or exotic setting, another takes place on a square in contemporary Spain and a fourth in an Italian ballroom.   All the *entrées* of Campra's *Les Fêtes vénitiennes* are set in modern Venice and several have frankly comic scenes.   Thanks to these elements of realism and comedy "ballet opera, before the advent of *opéra-comique*, helped to bring verisimilitude and truth into our musical drama".[2]

This new genre was entirely French.   In the work of Lulli and Quinault, with its mixture of French ballet and Italian, especially Venetian, opera, the dramatic element predominated.   In ballet opera, dancing and spectacle take first place and opera is reduced to a few scenes of recitative and singing.

> The old French passion for dancing has again a free run, whereas in Italy vocal virtuosity ends by banishing choreography almost entirely from opera.   Moreover, so varied a spectacle, sensuous and easy to follow, agrees perfectly with the average taste of the French public of the time [the declining years of Louis XIV's reign] which was not inclined towards entertainments which required concentration.[3]

"The pathos and seriousness of opera suit us much less well than dancing," said Rémond de Saint-Mard in 1749.[4]

"It corresponds to French impatience," wrote Roy in 1753.[5]

No Lulli and Quinault ushered it in and gave it fixity of form; no distinguished inheritance weighed it down.   Lack of rules allowed for experimentation and made it popular with artists and a public ready for novelty.   By cutting down the drama and increasing dance and display it gave further scope for symphonic music of a descriptive and impressionistic kind and hence for innovation in orchestration.

Serious opera was not superseded, but the new genre became a strong rival.   Before 1735, the date of Rameau's first *opéra-ballet*, the first thirty-eight years of its existence had seen some forty examples produced by the Académie de Musique.   With the two by Campra that I have named the most notable musically was *Les Éléments* (1725), by Destouches (with Lalande's collaboration in the prologue) on a libretto by Roy; its music is still as fresh as some works of Purcell's.[6]

---

[1] (44), 108.   [2] (190), 23.   [3] (190), 24.

[4] (97), 275.   [5] (104), 130.

[6] It was published in vocal score by Michaëlis, Paris, edited by Vincent d'Indy.   The reader who is able to obtain this now rare edition will find much enjoyment in studying this charming work.   There is attractive

From time to time attempts were made to strengthen the operatic part by making the plots of the *entrées* more dramatic. These attempts were indicated by the addition of *héroïque* in the title and it is to this category of *ballet héroïque* that *Les Indes galantes* belongs.

Rameau's second dramatic work was performed on August 23, 1735, two years after *Hippolyte et Aricie*. The librettist, Louis Fuzelier, a man over sixty, was well known as a writer of comedies, some of which had been given by the Comédie Française, some by the Italians, and others by the theatres which flourished in May and August during the Fairs of St. Germain and St. Laurent and caused considerable anxiety to the Comédie Française actors by trespassing on their privileges. Out of the fairmen's attempts to dodge the regulation which forbade spoken acting elsewhere than on the two privileged stages arose in 1724 the earliest form of *opéra-comique* in which Fuzelier played an important part, collaborating with Lesage, of *Turcaret* and *Gil Blas* fame, Piron and d'Orneval. He was born soon after 1670 and died in 1752. His work includes the texts of thirteen operas, all performed by the Académie de Musique, six comedies given by the Comédie Française and eighteen by the Italians. The earliest of the numberless sketches and *opéras-comiques* which he wrote for the Fair theatres from 1705 onwards, *Le Ravissement d'Hélène*, is an attempt to evade the edict which forbade unprivileged theatres to perform "comédies ou farces", broke all rules of space and time by extending over many years and many square miles. In a parody which he made of La Motte's and Marais's *Alcyone* there occurs the following pronouncement: "A reasonable opera would be a white raven, a silent wit, a candid Norman, a modest Gascon, a disinterested attorney, a faithful fop and an abstemious musician."[1] Near the end of his life, in 1744, he became joint editor of the *Mercure de France* with La Bruère, the librettist of *Dardanus*.

The title of *Les Indes galantes* speaks of love and exoticism commingled, and each *entrée* unfolds a tale of amorous intercourse in a remote part of the globe—one of those magical lands comprised under the name of Indies. The first is laid in Turkey, the second in Peru, the third in Persia, the fourth in a North American forest.

The settings are intended to be modern; the prologue, however, makes use of mythological figures. It treats of the universal appeal of love, exemplified by the youth of four nations, French, Spanish,

---

descriptive writing in *L'Eau* and original orchestration in Neptune's air in this *entrée*: *Le Feu* contains a good discussion, an effective terror chorus, a narrative *arioso* and a well-developed chaconne. The numbers are more sharply characterized than in Lulli or even in Campra. Cf. Chapter 4, pp. 119 and 125.

[1] *La Rupture du Carnaval et de la Folie.*

Italian and Polish, "who run on to the stage and form graceful figures". The ballet mistress is Hebe, minister to the gods' pleasures, and she is supported by a chorus of nameless singers who, to judge from their words and the nature of their music, seem to be shepherds. The prologue develops dialectically; to the thesis of concord in the first two scenes is opposed the antithesis of Bellona's invasion and her appeal to Glory.

> La Gloire vous appelle; écoutez ses trompettes.

Two flag-bearing warriors perform, "gravement", a recruiting dance, and "call to the lovers of the allied nations. These generous lovers take their stand near Bellona and follow the standards." But Love in person comes to the assistance of Hebe and the forsaken ladies; though no further stage directions occur the words of Love's air and of the last chorus prove that some sort of synthesis is achieved.

The overture, in G major, shows how ready Rameau was to depart from the tradition of Lulli. There is still a slow introduction and an apparently fugal *allegro*, but the introduction is more melodic than in earlier French overtures and the *allegro* soon leaves the paths of fugue. So melodic, indeed, are the opening bars of the *lent* that the librettist's son wrote words to them[1] (ex. 180).

Ex.180 *Lent*
Quel plaisir pour moi   quand je bois   le vin de mon voi-sin.

The *vite* is built on a spidery theme with witty jumps of sevenths that turn to octaves in the answer (ex. 181); it skips in and out every few bars. It has a counter-subject of scales and a second part which appears later on as a kind of second subject, first in A minor, then in

Ex.181 *Vite*

G major. The principle of contrast which was to characterize early sonata form is there but not the key sequence, since the first close—after an excursion into D major and a return to G—is in E minor and the middle portion in A minor, whence we return via D to G. One of the happiest moments is when, after this "second subject" has been given out, the spidery theme returns to a counterpoint of part of the counter-subject, tumbling down upon it inverted (ex. 182). It is a spritely and highly-strung movement of some hundred bars, long enough for concert performance.

---

[1] Rameau then set them as a duet "with a bass specially composed", according to the *Mercure de France*.

Ex.182

The best vocal number in the prologue is Love's air, "Ranimez vos flambeaux". It is scored for two violins only; though the words "avec clavecin" are added the score shows no bass. The three treble parts weave delicately in and out of each other to a firm, square-cut rhythm which would have pleased Dr. Burney; the solo, indeed, is more Italian than French. Its decided opening recalls Bach's D minor harpsichord concerto (ex. 183). This is one of Rameau's many airs well suited to chamber-concert performance.

Ex.183   L'Amour

The *symphonies* are the most attractive numbers. I would draw attention to the musette, *air grave* and minuets in Scene 2 and the *air pour les amants et amantes* in Scene 3. The musette is one of the earliest of those pieces with pastoral inspiration which impress us so deeply when we travel any distance into Rameau's world. Picturesque, indeed, all pastoral music is expected to be and there is always charm in the many examples found in Rameau's predecessors and contemporaries, but Rameau's pastoral music has much more than charm.[1] The minuets combine the harmonic power of the musette with a grace of outline that reaches its peak in bars 13 to 16 and 21 to 23 of the first. Rameau was so pleased with this strain that he took it up in the second minuet and built that dance almost entirely upon it (ex. 184). In the *air pour les amants* we see the skill with which, in the narrow limits imposed by his small orchestra, he paints the mood of each group by his choice of accompanying instruments; the *amants* who

---

[1] See Chapter 10, p. 387ff.

answer Bellona's call are sustained by fast-running fiddles; the *amantes*, who hold back and sigh, are symbolized by slow flutes.

A "generous" pasha, Osman, who is in love with his slave Émilie, a French captive, but yields her to her lover, Valère, who has been washed up (after a tempest and a "We perish" chorus) upon the shores of the pasha's domain and has retrieved his Émilie in a cynically unemotional recognition scene: "—Étranger, je vous plains . . .—le reconnaissant:—Ah! Valère, c'est vous!—C'est vous, belle Émilie!—" where the music is as unconcerned as the words: such is the hero whose character gives its title to the first *entrée*, *Le Turc généreux*. Spectacle is provided by a storm; terror by a chorus of sailors, perishing unseen; ballet by African slaves and the "Provençaux et Proven-

Ex.184

çales" of the fleet.   Of properly dramatic interest there is none. Neither is there much dancing; a short march, used again as a tambourin, an *air* for the slaves, and rigaudons and tambourins to mark the sailing home of the lovers, and that is all.   Music easily predominates over words and even over dance and spectacle.   In the preface to his libretto Fuzelier claimed that this *entrée* was founded on "an illustrious original, the grand vizir Topal Osman, well known for his abounding generosity.   His story is told in the *Mercure de France* for January 1734."

The *entrée* opens with a *ritournelle* of some forty bars.   Each of the first three *entrées* does likewise and the presence of *symphonies* of this length, which have not their like in any other of Rameau's ballet operas, is perhaps a sign that the "young" composer had not yet learnt to contain his music within the limits required by an impure art. This *ritournelle* is merely a fugal exposition in four parts followed by a short episode and two more entries of the subject; it owes an incisive character to its key of D minor and to the leaps of sixths, sevenths and tenths in its theme.   Too ephemeral, perhaps, to live alone, but assertive while it breathes.

The earlier part of the *entrée* is uneventful.   As in most movements of ballet opera the action takes some time to warm up and is not ready for its injection of song and dance till after a stretch of recitative has been traversed.   As we cross it, we notice a pleasing air sung by Osman, "Il faut que l'amour s'envole".   The pasha is a bass, but his melody remains distinct from the true bass and moves about with rapid and expressively sinuous lines up and down the register accompanied only by the continuo and violins.

Our excitement is first roused by the tempest. Storms are stock phenomena in the weather of opera. Lulli's pupil and successor, Collasse, provoked in his *Thétis et Pélée* (1689) one of the earliest to break upon the French stage. His tempest scene (II, 7), which shows more originality in figuration than in harmony, describes cleverly the motion of the waves and comprises chorus and dialogue. Another was in Desmarêts's *Iphigénie en Tauride* (III, 5), with Thoas and the chorus as human elements. The most celebrated of these early storm scenes in French opera was that in Marais's *Alcyone*, Act IV, where orchestration, as well as figuration, is impressive.

> Marais conceived the idea of having his bass performed not only by the bassoons and bass viols, as is usual, but also by loosely strung drums whose continuous roll produced a dull, lugubrious sound; this, combined with harsh and piercing notes on the violins' first string and the hautboys, makes one feel both the fury of a rough sea and a raging wind rumbling and howling.[1]

The tempest, twice broken by solo and chorus, lasts for about a hundred bars. *Alcyone*, first given in 1703, was revived in 1730, when Rameau may have heard it.

Ex.185 *Lent*

Sous les on - des pé - ri - rons nous,

The storm scene in *Le Turc généreux* begins with a startling change from D minor to B flat[2] and a descriptive *symphonie* of tremolos and up-and-down rushes on the common chord, with some dramatic changes of key towards the end. The words of Émilie's soliloquy,

---

[1] (111), art. *Marais*.—The opening bars are quoted in (165), 1370–1371.

[2] A key which, according to Rameau's classification, "is suitable to storms, furies and suchlike subjects" ((1), 157). A similar change from minor to major on the sixth degree (G minor to E flat) occurs when Émilie speaks after the chorus.

which begins in the sixth bar, declaimed against the background of tremolandos and scales—the key is now G minor—interpret the fury of the elements as a symbol of her own agitation. The sailors' chorus adds physical terror to elemental fury and moral perturbation; its most telling moment comes towards the end when, with a sudden enharmonic change, a gentler note is sounded (ex. 185). In the recitative which marks the subsiding of Nature's anger, all the string parts except the basses are in double stopping, a device which Rameau is said to have been the first to use in orchestral writing. A movement like the overture and opening chorus of Gluck's *Iphigénie en Tauride* is a descendant of this tempest of Rameau's where mingle descriptive *symphonie*, recitative and chorus.

All this is effective and masterly. But the Ramellian *fin gourmet* will savour the object of his love at its purest in the G minor section that corresponds to most of Scene 6 and in the tambourins that conclude the *entrée*. Here we find a beautiful duet, "Volez, Zéphirs", full of unquiet tenderness, where the agitation is in the music, not in the words, and bears Rameau's hall-mark; here, too, is a no less beautiful chorus which develops the mood of the duet and embodies quotations from it. Into such G minor choruses in three-time, marked *gai*—but no more gay than every *allegro* is blithe—Rameau has poured his most personal music. This one should be compared with the "Volez, Zéphirs" of *Les Fêtes d'Hébé* (prologue) which is as close to it in music as in text. The power of this particular chorus lies largely in its contrasts: between the parts, one of which sways and flows while the others interpellate, assert (ex. 186) or sustain (ex. 187),

and between the sections, when counterpoint is succeeded by homophony. Further variety is obtained by expressive abstentions of the basses, who ever and anon leave the upper parts to float or declaim in mid-air. The return, half-way through, of Émilie's and Valère's duet, is a lovely episode; it lasts for only seven bars; then the upward flow

Ex.187

of the sopranos' "Volez, Zéphirs" is resumed and the whole chorus
re-enters.   After another duet interruption the chorus concludes with
the most Ramellian bars in the movement with typical upper held fifth
and emphasis on the subdominant ninth (ex. 188).   Typical, too, is
the way in which the outer parts begin far apart and close in upon one

Ex.188

another; there are hundreds of instances of this procedure which is
French as well as Rameau's but which, in our composer, is always
significant.   Just before Émilie's and Valère's entry there occurs an
effective use of another of his favourite devices: the building of the
harmony by adding thirds upwards and downwards from a central
point (ex. 189).[1]

Such writing, where airy lines are wreathed against a firm back-
cloth of strong beats, reminds us of those pictures of Botticelli where
the flowing grace of the figures stands out against the hard, geometrical lines of the background.   A chorus like this one, even more
Ramellian than French, represents a form of beauty which is missed by

---

[1] Another instance, with upward building only, occurs in Valère's
ariette "Hâtez-vous de vous embarquer", just before the *da capo*.

those whose knowledge of early eighteenth-century music does not go outside the circle of Bach, Handel and Domenico Scarlatti.

Something of the outlines of this piece, with heavier rhythm, persists in the *air pour les esclaves africains*, with massive harmony, that follows.   With Valère's *ariette* "Hâtez-vous de vous embarquer", the alternation between sinuous line and repeated hammerings returns.

Ex.189

This solo recalls also the D minor *ariette* of the prologue, "Ranimez vos flambeaux".   Lively, too, but less characteristic, is the B flat *ariette* "Régnez, Amour", where the accompaniment is noteworthy for the sonata- and concerto-like writing of the violin part and its interesting combinations with the flute.   Masson opposes these two *ariettes* as examples of the two different kinds of *aria di bravura*: the older, musically richer, more refined in expression and more polyphonic in its accompaniment, represented by Alessandro Scarlatti, and the later, that of Pergolese, simpler and more flowing, more purely tuneful, with somewhat slick figuring and passage work.[1]

The *entrée* ends with the only set dances it contains, two rigaudons and two tambourins, all of which in their mixture of passion and grace are among the best examples of their forms; each of the two *minor* dances is repeated as a solo or a chorus.   The sinuous lines of exs. 186 and 187 are present again in the G minor rigaudon.

Of the four *entrées* that make up the final form of *Les Indes galantes* the second, *Les Incas*, is the only one with any dramatic interest and also the most spectacular.   Perhaps for these reasons it has inspired Rameau with his finest music.   Adaptable though he was to all sorts of situations he responded more readily to those in which drama, or at least the depiction of definite emotional moods, was required.   Considering as he did that the music was the libretto's

---

[1] (190), 234–235.

handmaid, it was natural that an exciting text should call forth exciting music and a dull text something as near to dull music as he could produce.

The story of *Les Incas*, though no more convincing than most others in ballet opera, affords contrast of character and even of civilization, conflict of personalities, diversity of passion and grand spectacle. As in *Le Turc généreux* there are three heroes: Huascar, high priest of the Sun, Phani, a maid of the royal Inca race, and Don Carlos. "The scene is in a desert of the Peruvian mountains shut in by a volcano." Phani and Don Carlos are in love with each other. Huascar is concerned with saving what can be saved of Inca religion and race and with keeping up the pretence of his priestly powers. His attempts to thwart the union of the Inca girl and Pizarro's gallant countryman are the most dramatic part of the act; needless to say, they are frustrated. The spectacle is twofold: one half, the first, is peaceful and consists in the Sun god's festival; the second contains the eruption of the volcano and Don Carlos' struggle to save Phani from the cataclysm and from Huascar's rule.

Like *Le Turc généreux* and *Les Fleurs*, this *entrée* opens with an extended *ritournelle*. It begins like the exposition of a five-part fugue, continues with an episode in which the parts never reach five and concludes without any return of the theme in its original form. It has no kinship with what is to come but is a pleasant piece, and it is rather surprising that it was replaced soon after the first performance by one shorter and much less characteristic. Clearly Rameau had underestimated his audience's impatience with pure music.

The earlier part of the *entrée* is uneventful. Not till Huascar appears does the music quicken its pulse. Huascar, the villain, stands out in relief; he is one of the few *dramatis personæ* in Rameau with whom it is possible to speak of musical characterization. There is no doubt that the music of his part is forceful and unlike that of any other hero; he has been conceived as a whole and is not just a succession of emotional states.

His first solo enjoins Phani to "obey without hesitation when Heaven commands" and is set to a 6/8 rhythm uncommon in our composer. The vocal line is broken into short scale passages and leaps of fifths, sevenths or octaves, and the impression of a blustering and domineering character is well rendered. I quote the concluding bars, in which the little breathless phrases of the violins, bassoons and basses will be noticed (ex. 190).

Phani is less sharply depicted; nevertheless the abrupt change from hard C minor to soft, warm A flat corresponds to the difference between her nature and Huascar's.

The Festival of the Sun and the earthquake episode are the most interesting parts. The first is a succession of *symphonies*, airs and

Ex.190

choruses, lasting some fifteen minutes, and moving within the circle
of the key of A.   The prevailing impression is one of breadth and
solemnity.   The worship is depicted in its external aspects only; this is
not sacred music in the accepted sense but the accompaniment to a
gorgeous spectacle.   The slow unfolding of the parts in the polyphonic A minor *prélude pour l'adoration du soleil*, the animated un-
spinning of long lines of conjunct melody in the A major air and chorus
"Brillant soleil", the unearthly sweeps and swoops of the loure which
brushes its skirts up and down over more than two octaves in a bar
and a half, and the more urbane but equally agile leaps of the first
gavotte, appeal to us as pure music, not as an interpretation of worship.   Perhaps what is rarest, because least possible to match elsewhere, are the A minor prelude and the loure.   The prelude, the
second half of which is acrid with ninths, has a slowly unfolding free

Ex.191

polyphony and a delicacy of scoring just imaginable in the piano arrangement (ex. 191). The uncanny opposition of registers in bars eleven to sixteen, which reminds one of the Fire and Water scene in the *Magic Flute*, may be intended to call up the unfamiliarity of an esoteric cult. A desire to express strangeness is unmistakable in the gaunt, agile outline of the loure (ex. 192).

The rest of this *entrée* contains some of Rameau's grandest impressionistic writing. It describes the earthquake which Huascar

Ex. 192

provokes artificially by causing rocks to be hurled into the volcano, the villain's attempt to frighten Phani into recognizing the phenomenon as an expression of the Sun god's will that she shall flee with him, Carlos' intervention, and Huascar's final suicide of despair in the flames of the volcano.

The first seventy bars depict the earthquake. The words of the chorus which enters at the twelfth bar describe the details of the erup-

tion which accompanies it. There is no mention of fear and this is
not a terror chorus; the music is expressive of awful might and
physical catastrophe, but untinged by personal emotion. Tremolandos, rushes of scales and repeated figures in the strings make up its
outline over a threatening seesaw rhythm in the bassoons. Slowly,
degree by degree, starting with a clash of seconds, the harmony builds
up with menacing rumblings to a chord of the thirteenth, bursting
forth complete in the sixth bar (ex. 193). After the first choral section

Ex.193

the music dies down to a unison, the first of several. The power with
which Rameau uses unisons in his dramatic music could be already
imagined from the end of the G minor minuet in the 1724 book of
harpsichord pieces. The device was comparatively uncommon in his
time; it became more frequent after the middle of the century. It is
followed by another outburst, with enharmonics, which was so badly
played and so ill received at its first performance that it had to be

changed, complains Rameau, for "une musique commune",[1] but the original is preserved in the *Œuvres complètes* and the vocal score. A chorus in 6/8 follows; then the crowd scatters and Huascar and Phani remain alone. Scenes 6 and 7 have exciting accompaniments, with much tremolando, which proved too difficult for the orchestra of the Académie de Musique and had to be replaced almost at once by a simpler one with mere continuo.

The dialogue in these scenes is in *récitatif accompagné pathétique*. In this kind of recitative the orchestra intervenes to emphasize by descriptive devices the features of a dramatic narrative. It was common in soliloquies, but Rameau appears to have been original in using it for scenes with more than one character.[2] The declamation keeps its expressive outline, however, and the composer is far from relying entirely on the orchestra. It is hard to think that Rameau sacrificed without a pang such a strain as this (ex. 194). After a short

Ex.194 *Huascar*

Que l'on est cri-mi - nel lors-que l'on ne plaît pas!

air of Huascar's characterized by giant leaps like those of the loure, Carlos enters and Phani at once informs him of the eruption—a seemingly needless act which gives Rameau an opportunity for more impressionistic writing and a striking unprepared second.

The agitation of the scene resolves itself into a *divergent* trio in which the feelings expressed are contradictory. Here the *divergence* is incomplete since Phani and Carlos express the same sentiment in identical words, so that the number consists in a *unanimous* duet and a *divergent* bass. The situation and sentiments are not unlike those in the trio, "The flocks shall leave the mountains", in *Acis and Galatea*

---

[1] (12), 95.—Indeed, according to Noverre, the whole earthquake music had to be left out in 1735 and this is borne out by the fact that, in the score, this part is either crossed out or has had pieces gummed over it or pages have been sewn together. Some parts were kept but with a simpler accompaniment.

[2] Rousseau's *Dictionnaire de Musique*, art. *Monologue*, says that Italian operas use this kind of recitative only in monologues.—There is another fine instance of it in the 1744 *Dardanus*, IV, 4–6; to the words of Dardanus, Iphise and Anténor the orchestra provides an accompaniment which calls up both the sound of battle and the turmoil of passion.

but there is little similarity in the music. To the lovers' "Pour jamais, l'amour nous engage" Huascar opposes his "Non, non, rien n'égale ma rage". The tempo is *modéré* but occasional repeated chords keep up the rumble of the earthquake and the undercurrent of Huascar's "rage". The lovers sing most of the time in harmony; the bass moves with independence (ex. 195). As the trio finishes "the

Ex.195

volcano lights up again and the earthquake begins afresh". The epilogue is a soliloquy in which Huascar declares his intention of throwing himself into the flames and his words are once more punctuated by an agitated accompaniment. His last strain contains another of those leaps which characterize his part. While "the volcano vomits flaming rocks which crush the villain" the orchestra delivers a final *symphonie* of fury in which the highlight is a bar of grinding seconds (ex. 196) and the *entrée* ends on another of Rameau's dramatic unisons.

I cannot insist too emphatically that all this latter part of *Les Incas* is far from being just childishly pictorial. Masson is right to say that

it is of the same order as the climaxes in Rameau's *tragédies*. And indeed, apart from the second act of *Hippolyte et Aricie*, it is hard to think of any passage in these where the emotion is sustained for so long at such a pitch and where the technique of expression is so superbly elaborated. The aesthetic interest of these pages is undeniable and they may be enjoyed fully as pure music, without reference to the scenes they were composed to accompany.

One cannot but be struck by the modernity of much of the writing. It is, indeed, in descriptive passages of battles, storms, monsters, "frémissements des flots", that Rameau is most modern and that we find strains and progressions that carry us on fifty years or more. The piano version of the opening of the earthquake music might almost be mistaken for a page from Liszt. The practice of description, even more than the desire to depict new emotional states, impelled eighteenth-century musicians to develop the expressive resources of their art.

There is a great difference between the third *entrée*, *Les Fleurs*, and the last. Nothing is dramatic here and the only spectacle is that of dancing, which occupies the second half. The plot is insignificant and had to be changed three weeks after the first performance because of the absurdity of a hero disguised as a woman which had aroused sarcasm. The setting was by Servandoni. It contains nothing even remotely tragic and the emotional climate is throughout of moderate intensity, devoid of the majesty and terror of *Les Incas*, of the sense of longing so common in Rameau's music and of the boisterous joy of some of his hunting or triumph choruses. While the music seems tamer than that of the earthquake scene, it is actually very personal and this *entrée*, quiet and mezzotintish as a whole, has a character of its own and it is impossible to confuse it with any other of the composer's many *actes de ballet*. The earlier part is in A, F and D minor; the ballet proper moves entirely within the latitudes of D major and minor—two keys which Rameau, in his *Traité de l'Harmonie*, describes as "lively and joyful" and "tender and loving". Such indeed are the qualities of the long *Fête des Fleurs* (Sc. 3); both vigour and poignancy

are absent, except perhaps in the B minor gavotte, the most arresting
of the many dance numbers in this ballet.[1]

Like the two earlier *entrées*, *Les Fleurs* opens with a contrapuntal
ritournelle, scarcely fugal; its light-footed gait announces the atmosphere of the act.   The dramatic part of the *entrée* was, I have said,

Ex.197

entirely rewritten early in its existence.   Of what was lost thereby
the best numbers are a touching air in A minor—Ramellian, but similar to many other A minor tunes of his in 3/4 time; one in F with
flute *obbligato*; some effective recitative in which we find the double
leap of a fifth and a fourth which he had used so tellingly elsewhere[2]
(ex. 197); and a quartet—the only one in all his work.   The loss of
the quartet was regrettable.   It is a quiet contrapuntal piece, with a
number of closely related themes that wave and wind languishingly
to illustrate the chain of love of which they sing.   The tradition of

Ex.198   *Tendrement*

---

[1] A doubtfully authentic story about this ballet was told nearly twenty
years later.   Rameau "had interrupted the charming soft *air* for the Rose
with unpleasing muffled buzzing; he said it was the bees and hornets settling
on the rose.   Fuzelier had difficulty in making him feel that though music
can paint everything, there are paintings which taste forbids" (*Jugement de
l'orchestre de l'Opéra*, 1753, 4–5; in (190), 426).   For once the "pure
musician" was not the composer.

[2] I.e. in "Tristes apprêts", *Castor et Pollux*, I, 3.

depicting musically "douces chaînes" and "dolce legami" goes back to madrigals, where they are represented by festoons of thirds and sixths as they still are in Lulli and Rameau (ex. 198). The voices are accompanied only by the continuo. After some fifty bars of tranquil meanderings we come surprisingly to a halt on an unresolved discord, the suspense of which is emphasized by the bar of silence that follows it; a close of three bars ends the movement.

In the second version this quartet was replaced by a less significant duet, also in B minor. But on the whole the numbers which Rameau wrote for the later text are more interesting. A fresh *air* in A minor takes the place of the first; it has an attractive flowing accompaniment with beating thirds to illustrate a murmur. The F major *air*'s place is taken by one in D minor, also with flute *obbligato*, and a very fine 6/8 *air*, depicting inconstancy, with harpsichord and violins but without bass, light, witty and aerial, is the finest solo in either version. The Durand vocal score gives only the earlier version and the full score prints the second version in an appendix to Vol. VII.

The ballet is musically the most interesting part. It opens with a march in 3/4 whose spirit is continued in a fine chorus evocative of night. This is the most spacious number in the *entrée* and the most personal. It contains a short swaying theme of five notes which the orchestra interpolates ever and anon between the vocal entries and which acts, as Masson says, as a sort of leitmotif of darkness. The writing alternates between the flowing counterpoint so typical of Rameau (ex. 199)[1] and massive homophony. The spirit of this impressive piece pervades also the lovely tenor air, with continuo accompaniment, that follows:

> L'éclat des roses les plus belles
> Disparait bientôt avec elles.

Here indeed Rameau's bitterness pierces for a moment in all its intensity as if to tell us that his roses are never without thorns. In the strain with which this tiny song opens and which makes up half its matter, we have Rameau at his purest (ex. 200).

The ballet has many dances: for Persians (the scene is laid in Persia), for flowers, for Boreus and Zephyr; some twelve numbers in all, including a bravura *ariette* for Fatime, a miniature storm and two gavottes. It is an early example of the *ballet d'action*. Save for the first gavotte, none of these dances stands out individually but it is easy to see, even from the vocal score, how delicately blended in them is the musical and the choreographic interest. Rameau, says Noverre, who admired his music greatly,

---

[1] The example shows the leitmotif at the end.

Ex.199

Ex. 200

L'e-clat des ro - ses les plus bel - les Di-spa-raît bien-tôt a-vec el - les.

had laid down wisely the limits suitable to music written for dancing; his melodies were simple and majestic; he avoided his predecessors' monotony of tune and movement and varied them; realizing that legs could not move as quickly as fingers and the dancer could not possibly perform as many steps as the air had notes, he phrased them tastefully.[1]

We are reminded of this judgment of the great ballet master as we run through, keeping in our mind the purpose for which these pages were composed, the *airs* and gavottes which conclude this *entrée*.

Les Indes galantes as first given consisted of the prologue and the first two *entrées*. At the third performance *Les Fleurs* was added; after the eighth the new version of this *entrée* was substituted. By the beginning of 1736 it had received twenty-eight performances. Rameau and Fuzelier then added a fourth *entrée*, *Les Sauvages*, first given on March 10.

The scene is laid in the grove of an American forest, "near the French and Spanish colonies where the ceremony of the Pipe of Peace is to take place". A Frenchman, Damon, and a Spaniard, Don Alvar, are courting Zima, an Indian girl, who rejects both and marries Adario, a native warrior. Each of the two Europeans and Zima symbolizes a quality of love: Don Alvar stands for constancy, Damon for its opposite, Zima for innocent nature, and these simple oppositions are rendered in the music allotted to each. The first half is as usual devoted to the miniature drama; the Pipe of Peace provides the ballet in the second, which concludes with a spacious chaconne.

The *ritournelle* which opens the act is little more than a perfunctory prelude and its breezy straightforwardness makes one think of Purcell at his most naïve. The dramatic half of the act has several good airs and the music as a whole remains more constantly interesting than in *Le Turc généreux* or *Les Fleurs*. The different outlooks of the three heroes are expressed in a series of solos which are good examples of simple characterization. Damon's represents inconstancy; the long notes of the vocal part suggest fatuity while the inconstancy motif is in the orchestra (ex. 201). There is in this number the sketch of an excessive extrovert which reminds one of a sonata or rondo by Philip-Emmanuel Bach. It helps one to realize Rameau's originality if one

---

[1] (90), 167.

Ex. 201

compares this solo with the very staid air in which Silvandre, in the first *entrée* of Campra's *L'Europe galante*, sings of the same theme.

Zima, to whom Rameau gives the most bewitching music in the whole opera, counters Damon's boasting of fickleness for fickleness' sake with a more subtle and qualified judgment.

> Le cœur change à son gré dans cet heureux séjour:
> Parmi nos amants, c'est l'usage
> De ne pas contraindre l'amour;
> Mais dès que l'hymen nous engage
> Le cœur ne change plus dans cet heureux séjour.

The bassoons, which played in Damon's solo, are replaced by the gentler hautboys, and the music becomes sinuous and caressing. The power of Rameau's melody to express not only a sentiment but also a person is seen at its clearest here (ex. 202).

Alvar's turn comes last. He is a firm believer in constancy and his song is a criticism of the Frenchman's creed; the characterization is in the bold, square-cut melody (ex. 203). After some twenty bars Damon, the more talkative of the two, bursts in again and there follows a second inconstancy air, with accompaniment of fluttering seconds grouped in triplets.

For sheer beauty and power to move, the palm must go to Zima's second air, "Dans ces bois l'amour vole". Here, as in "L'éclat dès roses", is distilled the essential Rameau: his grace, his limitless poignancy, his nostalgia, his power to bring the infinite within a simple

eight-bar phrase (ex. 204). I am perhaps unduly swayed by sympathy with certain strains and moods of his personality, but I would
give all the rest of *Les Indes galantes*, if need be, for these two songs.

The ballet is danced by Zima and Adario, the rejected suitors
having vanished, by "Françaises en habits d'amazones, guerriers
français et sauvages, sauvagesses, bergers de la colonie". It opens
with an air of Adario which is expanded into a fine chorus of savages.

Ex.204

The chorus, like many others of its kind, sings of peace and pleasure:

> Bannissons les tristes alarmes!
> Nos vainqueurs nous rendent la paix.

It announces both "Connaissez notre puissance" of *Castor et Pollux*, II, 5, and "Dansons tous, dansons, chantons" of *Les Fêtes d'Hébé*, I, 5, both of which sing of pleasures. Such a commonplace theme might have inspired one of Rameau's more commonplace choruses; yet this is one of his most personal, especially in those parts where rising and falling scale passages oppose or complete each other (ex. 205). Was it a desire to write savages' music that inspired such strains, full of sturdiness and passion, more original than was called for by the words? Some of the rhythms rather suggest it.

The feast of the Pipe of Peace, *Danse du grand Calumet de la Paix*, consists almost entirely of a dance *en rondeau* known to most of us from his harpsichord pieces, where it figures as *Les Sauvages* in the *Nouvelles pièces* of c. 1730. It is the most exotic number in the *entrée* —the only one, indeed, which to our ears speaks of exoticism. The suggestion is most marked in the second episode, where there occurs twice over an instance of diatonic-enharmonic change.

The piece is given first as a dance by the full orchestra except for

Ex. 205

trumpets and drums; it is repeated as a duet by Zima and Adario, each return of the refrain being taken up by the whole chorus. The vocal line is simpler and more peaceful than that of the instruments; it seems to hover above it. In the second episode the instrumental part is also

Ex.206

Jou - is - sons dans nos a - si - les,

Jou - is - sons des biens tran - quil - les! Ah!

peut - on être - heu - reux, Quand on

for - me d'au - tres vœux?

varied; this is the most moving section in this very beautiful number (ex. 206).

The rest of the *entrée* consists of a minuet and *ariette* and a majestic chaconne which, according to a statement in the *Journal de Paris* for January 5, 1777, had been composed for *Samson*, where it was destined "to call the people to worship at the feet of the True God".[1] If this is correct the chaconne must have been greatly expanded; the original consisted probably only of the opening section of sixteen bars in D minor, which is indeed of a much more inward and even religious nature than the rest and where the music seems to compel repeated prostrations (ex. 207).

Ex.207

This much-admired chaconne is one of those numbers which helped to break down the rigidity of traditional dancing. The celebrated Dupré himself, we are told, was much embarrassed by it and Rameau had to sketch the outlines to be followed, according to La Dixmerie.

> Dancing in the last century was like Pygmalion's statue; life was lacking to it. It owes a part of its advances to the illustrious Rameau. He caused in dancing the same revolution as in music; by strengthening the one he strengthened the other ... It is stated that the fine chaconne in *Les Sauvages* embarrassed greatly the famous Dupré; Rameau had himself to sketch out its execution for him.[2]

This was his second chaconne. It is much more varied than that in *Hippolyte et Aricie* and more broadly developed. Its opening is heavy with splendour, but this mood is not sustained and in many episodes the appeal lies more in rhythm than in tune and harmony.

---

[1] Opening of Act I.　　　　　[2] (78); in *O.C.*, VII, xxx.

Indeed, the preoccupation with choreography seems stronger here than in either its predecessor or that of *Castor et Pollux* which followed it. After the beginning the most purely musical sections are the duet between hautboy and bassoon, repeated near the end, and a D minor episode which returns to the mood, though not to the text, of the opening. It comprises just over two hundred bars and unfolds in some dozen episodes, most of which link up with the next and none of which plays the part of a refrain. Nothing remains of the rondeau-like construction and ground bass of earlier chaconnes.

Ex. 208

Operas were seldom repeated unchanged in the eighteenth century. Thus, quite early, the *ritournelle* of *Les Incas* was replaced by one shorter and more commonplace. A lively contredanse was inserted in the prologue and two danced *airs*, for the Persians and for Boreus, were added to *Les Fleurs*. All these additions are published in the appendix of the Durand full score. The only one to deserve comment is a mysterious Italian *aria*, "Fra le pupille". It is a witty and spritely display piece, with simple coloratura on "va volando", by no means commonplace, yet without one trace of anything characteristic of Rameau. It is proof of the Picasso-like versatility with which he could, on occasion, adapt himself to any style and yet produce work of distinction. The bars I quote from the *ritornello* will give an idea of the character of this solo, which deserves to be sometimes heard. It must be the only page in Rameau where the nose and eyes of Rossini may be seen, so to speak, winking over the wall (ex. 208). This *aria* is not found in any of the scores or parts in the Opéra library; it is preserved in a manuscript now in the Bibliothèque Nationale and was printed in an edition of selections of *Les Indes galantes* prepared by Rameau himself for concert performance; its authenticity is thus certain, but its purpose and the occasion of its composition are unknown.

The boldness of certain scenes and the novelty of the recitatives aroused opposition when *Les Indes galantes* was first given. The usual reproaches of noise and cacophony which are the stock-in-trade of those who object to what is new in music were addressed to it.

> Un Amphion dont le luth ne se guinde
> Que par le bruit, le fracas, les clameurs . . .

was the *Almanach du Diable*'s reference to Rameau in 1737. The gist of these complaints is found in a paragraph of Desfontaines, the editor of *Observations sur les écrits modernes*.

> The music is a perpetual witchery; nature has no share in it. Nothing is more craggy and scabrous; it is a road of constant jolts . . . What an excellent joggling chair[1] this opera is! Its airs are fit to stir up the benumbed nerves of a paralytic. How different are its violent shocks from the gentle stirring that Campra, Destouches, Mouret, Montéclair, etc., know how to cause in us! I am racked, flayed, dislocated by this devilish *sonata* of *Les Indes galantes*; my head is all shaken up with it.[2]

On the morrow of the first performance Prévost's *Le Pour et Contre* wrote: "I find the music truly Indian, allowing that this nation is capable of producing good music, for this extraordinary music is not without beauty."[3]

Voltaire had championed Rameau from the beginning; on October 13, six weeks after the first performance, he wrote to Thiériot: "I am well satisfied with having guessed that Rameau's music could not meet with failure." Cahusac, who was later to become Rameau's most constant librettist, tells us that in 1735 the opera appeared in-

---

[1] "Trémoussoir." It was the "name of a kind of armchair with springs invented by Abbé de Saint-Pierre to joggle himself [se trémousser] as a varied form of exercise which he considered necessary for health" (Littré, *Dictionnaire: Trémoussoir*).

[2] II, 238; in *O.C.*, VII, lvi.   [3] VII, 22; in *O.C.*, VII, lvi.

surmountably difficult to understand, that most of the audience came out raging against music overburdened with semiquavers, nothing of which could be remembered. "Six months later, every tune, from the overture to the last gavotte, had been *parodied*[1] and was known by all. At the 1751 revival the pit sang 'Brillant soleil' as easily as our fathers chanted 'Armide est encor plus aimable'."[2]

Except for the early alterations in *Les Fleurs* and the addition of *Les Sauvages* no changes were made in the libretto. In part or as a whole it was often revived till 1761, the date of the last complete performance. After that date single *entrées* were given for another twelve years; the last stage appearance of any part of it till the revival of *Les Fleurs* at the Opéra-Comique in 1925 was that of *Les Sauvages* in 1773, nine years after the composer's death. Concert performances of selections still took place for some time after that date. "L'air fameux des Sauvages de Rameau" was played at the Champ de Mai held on June 1, 1815. On December 18, 1904, excerpts were given at the Concerts Colonne. In June 1952 a complete performance on the most lavish scale was given at the Paris Opéra.

---

[1] Set to words.   [2] *Encyclopédie*; art. *Expression*.

10. Les Fêtes d'Hébé *and* Rameau's Pastoral Music

WE know how important was Rameau's acquaintance with La Pouplinière and the farmer-general's patronage for the origin of his operas, since without them he might never have ventured on dramatic composition. *Samson* nearly came to birth in the financier's circle; *Hippolyte* originated there. Both Rameau and Pellegrin were protégés of his, and five or six years after their joint production we again find them associated. The offspring this time was a ballet opera, *Les Fêtes d'Hébé.* Since his first *tragédie* Rameau had seen performed *Les Indes galantes* and *Castor*, each at two years' interval. After a further two years, this new work was given to the stage on May 25, 1739.

The earliest editions of the libretto mentioned no author's name, and an unsigned explanatory letter printed on it coyly justified this anonymity by stating that all the merit of the work was the musician's and that the nameless author had aimed merely at providing "a series of scenes lending themselves to music and spectacle and, in sooth, without claim to be read". The historical dictionaries, Dubuisson's *Lettres au Marquis de Caumont*[1] and *Le Postillon français* for June 30, 1739, all give Antoine Gautier de Montdorge[2] as the author. According to Dubuisson he collaborated with La Pouplinière and Gentil-Bernard; according to *Le Postillon français*, with Abbé Pellegrin. Another collaborator is said to have been a Mme Bercin who is hinted at by *Le Postillon*: "Une aimable dame et un joli cavalier, . . . à ce qu'on dit, se partagent la gloire de ces vers." One month after the first performance the second *entrée* was revised, the "needy" Abbé Pellegrin having been called in for this task.

"La dame généreuse a eu soin de parer le réparateur," mocked *Le Postillon*, saying that his fee had been a new outfit, including bedsocks, which he mistook for mittens.

Gautier de Montdorge, under whose name the libretto now appears, was according to Bachaumont a "financier", more accurately "maître

---

[1] *Lettre VI*, June 8, 1739.
[2] Spelt variously Mondorge, Montdorge, Mont Dorge, Mont d'Orge.

à la Chambre aux deniers du Roi". Born at Lyons in 1707, he died in Paris in 1768. He was a man of letters with an interest in painting; one of his books is the *Réflexions d'un peintre sur l'opéra* (1741); another deals with colour printing: *L'Art d'imprimer les tableaux en trois couleurs* (1755). He frequented La Pouplinière's society but not as a beneficiary, for he was well off. The two were neighbours; Montdorge lived from 1734 to his death in the Hôtel Boutin, which stood in the Rue de Richelieu on the spot where that street is now crossed by the Rue du Quatre-Septembre.[1]

It is probable that the idea of the ballet arose collectively in the farmer-general's circle and that several minds contributed to its genesis, none of them daring to claim the parenthood of the mediocre result. "Let the music of our ballet be enjoyed as much as it deserves, and for this once let us ask for nothing further," concluded the unsigned letter.

The ballet aims at presenting three forms of art: poetry, music and dance, personified by Sappho, Tyrtaeus and a shepherdess, Eglé, pupil of Terpsichore. These are the three *Talents lyriques* which give the ballet the sub-title under which it came to be known. Into this bottle any sort of wine could be poured, and Rameau gave of his best. No work of his contains more variety or gives so kaleido-scopically complete a view of his range in lyric, tragedy and pastoral.

Like his three earlier overtures that of *Les Fêtes d'Hébé* is in the Lullian mould of slow and fast sections, but the slow, or rather *modéré*, has no dotted rhythm and the fast can scarcely be called fugal. The *modéré* consists in slow rising triads in unison, with violin semiquavers, changing at each bar, opening in F major and modulating to C. The final C, repeated eleven times in dotted rhythm, constitutes the first subject of the *vite* and not till the third bar is it evident that we are back in F; the momentary ambiguity enhances the levity of the move-ment, with its pompously vacuous beginning and disrespectful parody of a fugal exposition on a ridiculous theme. This is the first appear-ance of comedy in Rameau's dramatic music. The frivolity is con-trasted briefly with a more pensive strain, recalling certain solemn or pathetic episodes in the chaconnes of *Les Indes galantes*, *Dardanus* and *Naïs*; it might be considered as a second subject, since the prin-ciple of contrast is well established by it, but neither its manner of alternation with the repeated-note theme nor the sequence of keys resembles sonata pattern.

The simplification and wilful triteness are startlingly modern when one compares this overture with Rameau's earlier ones. Polyphony

---

[1] (218), 225–226.—He is no doubt the Mondorge of the tambourin in Michel Blavet's E minor flute sonata *La Dhérouville*.

has vanished and we are conscious of that impoverishment in style for which the triumph of the new Italian music was to be responsible and which was apparently the price to pay in advance for the flowering of the classical age. In his cantatas Rameau had shown the influence of Scarlatti's and Buononcini's Italy; now, for the first time, there strikes in him the note of the later Italian music which was to take Paris by storm in 1752.

The learned author has prefaced his libretto with the argument: "Hebe was wont to pour out the nectar at the gods' table but their inconstancy having compelled the goddess to leave Olympus she sought a more fortunate asylum upon earth (Natalis Comes)." The name in parentheses is that of a Venetian scholar of the sixteenth century from whose Latin mythology, published at Padua in 1616 and translated into French, this information was derived.

Rameau has chosen to interpret the earlier part of the prologue, which begins with Hebe's arrival here below and her pursuit by Momus, in the tone of comedy. The words left him full choice, since they could have been treated equally well on a passionate note:

> Non! ne suivez point mes pas!
> Je hais, je fuis, je déteste
> Toute la troupe céleste!

Indeed one feels throughout this prologue, as so often in his music, that it was Rameau, not his librettists, who decided what mood to evoke; the words, in their colourless simplicity, might have suggested any or none.

The action is slight. Hebe, pursued by Momus, soon gives way to his entreaties, seconded as they are by the Graces and by Love, and confesses:

> Je ne regrette plus le séjour du tonnerre.

This stage is reached when the prologue is only one quarter of its way through; the rest is padding. Clearly, therefore, the musician cannot rely upon the plot to make this section one whole. Yet a whole it is, and not a mere suite of airs, ballets and choruses. It is infused by a principle of structure and a sense of direction, and as these are present in other prologues or *entrées* where nothing in the text calls for them, we may examine here how Rameau induces unity when his words offer him none.

The principle is here a sequence of moods. The music moves through a chain of recognizable affective states leading one into the other; the simplest is at the outset and the most complex at the end, though the progress from simple to complex is not regular.

If the overture had left us in any doubt on the matter the first notes of the prologue, depicting Momus' entreaties and Hebe's refusals,

Ex.209 *Tres vif*

would show us that we are in the world of comedy. This first scene, so completely in the vein of *opera buffa*, reminds one of the opening of *Fidelio* where the theme is not dissimilar. Rameau's scene is more truly a duet than Beethoven's, since after the first two bars Hebe and

Ex.210

Momus sing together, but when Jaquino and Marzelline join issue they do so with the same rhythmic counterpoint of chattering, overlapping short notes as do Rameau's minor gods (exs. 209 and 210). The long sustained F with which the scene opens indicates that the altercation has been continuing for some time and has reached a climax. We have here an adumbration of the complex chatter numbers in *Platée*.

Momus' reply, in D, is more tender and leads to the caressing strains to which the Graces descend. With their arrival, we leave comedy behind. A more sentimental mood prevails throughout Hebe's and Momus' duet (in G, with an E minor episode). The appearance of Love marks no change but when the three join in a trio it is enlivened by a more playful note and, though we do not revert to comedy, we find the same overlapping phrases in short notes as in the first scene.

A short recitative in E minor heralds a group of Thessalians who, once installed upon the stage, launch out into a chorus. This piece, if not the climax of the prologue—there can hardly be a climax where there is no action—is at least the weightiest moment and one of Rameau's more impressive pieces of choral writing. It is neither long nor complex and is entirely homophonic. It commands our admiration through its condensation. It is well known that Rameau declared that harmony should govern melody and not the other way about. Superficial critics drew the conclusion, from this statement rather than from his music, that he was no melodist. Now Rameau is the hardest artist in the world to enclose within generalizations. However sure we feel of the truth of some judgment we are tempted to make on him, once we have made it instances come crowding to our memory to contradict the rash pronouncement. And so it is here. Dance after dance, air after air enter singing on to the stage of our mind, mocking us for having dared make such a statement. What remains true, however, is the close relation between harmony and melody, and if the judgment is altered to mean that his tunes are never set to trivial harmony, then it stands its ground and no bar from his work reproves us for advancing it.

The melody here moves in smooth, broad waves that rise and fall unhurried,[1] illustrating nobly the words (ex. 211). The dense texture is ever and anon set off by the echo effect visible in this example; the tight motion of all four parts is maintained in nearly every bar. Rameau has taken advantage of the verse, which is better than usual, and has exploited the sonorous nasal syllables which are the most musical sounds in the French language. The climax comes in a great passage at the end where the melody sweeps down, step by step, for an octave and a half, thence to lever itself up effortlessly, in steps of a third and a fourth, with Rameau's favourite interval of a ninth, detaching thereby, as it were, the line of the bass voice from that of the real bass to which it does not return for another nine bars (ex. 212).

This is less a change of mood than the existing mood deepened and made more solemn. This massive yet luminous piece introduces rather suddenly the key of E major, in which we remain for the dance that follows. The sturdiness of the chorus is carried over into it and

---

[1] Did Handel borrow its opening bars for "And the glory of the Lord"?

Ex. 211

still more into the E minor bourrée.   E minor was the key of much of Hebe's wistful ballet music in *Castor et Pollux* and it is perhaps connected with her in the composer's mind, for he gives her now an air where the same pensive note is perceptible through the rapid coloratura. Closer still to the mood of the *Castor* ballet is her duet with Love.

Ex. 212

With Love's air in G major we return to the playful mood which had
been overlaid since the Thessalians' entry and, with Zephir's arrival,
to the sentimental, dreamy climate of the Graces' entry in the second
scene. The cast is now complete and the right frame of mind has
been induced in the audience, so Rameau concludes with a *vif* 3/2
movement, given out thrice, each time enriched and expanded, as a
solo for Hebe, a duet for Love and her, and a chorus. It is the only
movement in the prologue in his favourite key of G minor, and it
exhales the pungent mixture of delight and longing, of voluptuous
nostalgia, so common in his G minor numbers. The mood of this
key is often ambiguous with him; we are not quite sure whether to
smile at the delight it promises or to feel sad because that bliss is so
unattainable. This rich ambiguity is present here; it is Rameau's
own, for the words themselves are far from ambiguous:

> Volez, Zéphirs! tout vous en presse,
> Transportez la jeunesse
> Au séjour des plaisirs!

The "volez" has suggested the fanciful, unseizable line, but Rameau alone is responsible, as he was in the Hebe ballet of *Castor*, for the hint of unreality that underlies the command (ex. 213).   And in this spirit of nostalgic enchantment we are ready to enjoy the pleasures of poetry,

Ex. 213

music and dance that the purveyor of the gods' pleasures has prepared for us.

Thus, without stiffness, without a step-by-step advance from mood to mood, Rameau has woven the parts of this prologue together by means that are essentially, though not formally, musical.[1]   It is this capacity for organizing on a basis of musical interest, independently of what the libretto may have given him, that raises him so high in the history of opera between Monteverdi and Gluck and makes us regret that he did not live at a time when broadly conceived instrumental forms were in existence.   Thanks to this unity of mood, the whole act hangs together as music, no matter who is singing or what is being said.   It is, indeed, a tone poem, like so many stretches in his compositions.   His dramatic and choreographic quality is undeniable, and yet, as we dwell longer with him, knowing him away from the stage, in the score and at the piano—and indeed there is hardly another way—we realize ever more strongly that he is greater still as a pure musician.   His art does not need the theatre to come alive; it carries its own evocative magic and but a small measure of adaptation would suffice to make it presentable, without actors, without dancers, even—for much of it—without singers, by the sole medium of instruments.

Sappho and Alcaeus are taken as the representatives of Poetry, to whom the first *entrée* is dedicated.   Sappho, we are told by the libretto, is "not as Story depicts her in the waning years of her life but still young, moved by the talents of Alcaeus, tasting the charms of mystery and worthy of the homage of an enlightened court".   The court of the isle of Lesbos, under the guidance of its enlightened despot Hymas, is honoured by the poetess with an allegorical entertainment, but as this does not provide action a sketchy love plot has been invented.   The affections of poet and poetess are crossed by a jealous

---

[1] By "not formally" I mean that there is no strict key sequence.   Though G major and its relative minor predominate, neither of them begins or ends the section, neither opening nor close is in its domain, and it is idle to seek any structural significance in the fact that we begin in F major and end in G minor.

rival who denounces Alcaeus to Hymas and obtains his banishment. Sappho has no difficulty in winning from the king the repeal of this unjust decree; the jealous Thelemus disappears and Alcaeus and she are united. The libretto apologizes for these daring inventions. "Alcaeus' exile has been imagined to bring interest, if possible, into a ballet *entrée*." The "if possible", in its naïve scepticism, betrays the poor dramatic value and the little "interest" which the genre of ballet opera was held to possess. It is a revealing sign of the authors' lack of faith in their own art.

Whether or not it was shared by the composer, it is certain that what is liveliest in this *entrée* has gone into the *fête allégorique* and is not of a dramatic order. In the would-be dramatic scenes the best music is lyrical. The *ritournelle* to the *entrée* and Sappho's solo derived from it are one of those expressions of desolation that wring one so vehemently when one first explores Rameau; the same theme was to be rendered more powerfully in Iphise's two solos in *Dardanus*[1] (ex. 214). His love for coloristic orchestration is seen in the air where,

Ex. 214

after the bars quoted, the voice is accompanied by violin and flutes only.

"An attempt is made", says the libretto, "to keep the impetuous character which Horace attributes to Alcaeus", and this is more successful in the music than in the words. Alcaeus' vengeance air "Par les horreurs du noir Tartare" is a vigorous, menacing piece in C minor ("Alcaer minaces Camoenae", quotes the libretto), short but strongly characterized, and perhaps the most distinctive vocal number in the opera. It is certainly unlike much else in Rameau; Huascar's "Obéissez" in *Les Indes galantes*, II, comes nearest to it. It belongs to the archaic form in which the vocal part doubles the continuo— a form much beloved of Lulli and still occasionally found in Rameau.[2] An unbalanced form, it seems to us, and adapted to only very special conditions. Here the coincidence of voice and continuo is not persistent and at times the latter abandons the voice, leaving it on a high note, and makes a fresh entry lower down. Rameau has combined

[1] Bars 4 to 7 occur in *La Dauphine* (1747), Rameau's only piece written for harpsichord solo after he had turned to opera.

[2] The music most like this air which I know is Polyphemus' "Vengez-moi d'un fatal vainqueur"—also in C minor, 2/4—in Clérambault's cantata *Polyphème*.

the stiffness inherent in the form with subtlety in feeling, afforded by
the highly individual violin part, and Alcaeus' personality is clearly
outlined (ex. 215).

The water-pastoral *divertissement* is fresh and springlike.

> The back of the stage opens and discloses a distant prospect struck
> with light seen through portions of greenery; the vista is bounded by
> a river and a Naiad reclining upon her urn is seen in front of the
> setting.

Ex. 215   *Très vif et détaché*

Vns.

Alcée

Par les hor - reurs du noir Tar - ta - re,

B.C.

Que l'a-mour ou-tra gé   Soit ven - gé, Que l'a-mour ou-tra - gé soit ven - gé!

The entertainment contains an exhilarating mariners' chorus, the
repeats of which are separated by a couple of tambourins in F; the
lament of a forsaken Naiad; a second chorus of mariners, accompanied
by a river in flood; and a solo and short chorus of the "Revenez" type,
recalling the Naiad's inconstant brook-lover, whose return to his
mistress concludes the *fête*, dubbed, one knows not why, "allégorique".

The freshness and full-bloodedness of much of this music is most
infectious and comes as a surprise to those who think of Rameau in
terms of Roi Soleil, full-bottomed wigs and geometrical parterres, or
even in association with Watteau shepherdesses. If the words did
not convey a touch of vulgar heartiness, I would call the first mariners'
chorus and tambourins "Maypole music". The chorus has the vigorous unsophistication which we enjoy in much English folk-music, and
to meet such a piece in Rameau shakes one's belief in the exclusive
Englishness of much of what we consider most national in our musical
heritage. It is in a vein not often worked by him but which we found
also in *Hippolyte* (dances of Act I) (ex. 216). The source of this in
folk, or at any rate carol, music is visible in the likeness with the

Ex.216

Gloria refrain of *Les anges dans nos campagnes*.[1]   The more normal
Ramellian climate is felt in the episode.   The tambourins are almost
exaggeratedly chordal and rhythmic; there is no opposition between
the major and minor dances.   They continue the breezy unself-con-
sciousness of the chorus.   When this is repeated the first strain is
varied and developed and the episode is omitted.   Except in this very
brief episode there is no trace of pungency; all is wholeheartedly
joyous.

The terror piece of the mariners expressing alarm at the threatening river, though only make-believe, has been taken as seriously by
Rameau as the small scale allowed.   The strings rise and fall in unison
quaver scales while the chorus sings in syllabic crotchets.   The rush
of quavers is lulled for a space near the end and the strings sustain the
voices that rise step by step, with expressive progressions, falling back
as the scales begin again (ex. 217).[2]

Ex. 217

[1] See *Oxford Carol Book*, No. 119.—It is the line already heard in "Que
jusqu'aux cieux" (ex. 211).

[2] According to an anonymous correspondent in the *Journal de Paris*
for January 5, 1777, this piece came from *Samson* where it accompanied the
water gushing from the rock in Act II, 2.

cou-rons, cou - rons,   em - pres - sons nous!

The "Revenez, tendre amant" chorus belongs to a familiar type, found already in Lulli.   In key, time-signature and mood, it is close to "Volez, Zéphirs".   We approach the end of the *divertissement* on the same plane of wistful delight.   A very *unanimous* duet between the Naiad and the brook concludes the *fête*.

Alcaeus' pardon is granted and fresh revels begin, this time in honour of Sappho.   A four-square chorus sings her praise—a competent but rather wooden piece, more Italian than French, with adumbrations of the noisy, empty cadences of *galant* music and promises of polyphony that are not kept.

Of the dances and *ariette* which make up this second entertainment the best are the tambourins and the gavotte danced by the ever present mariners.   The tambourins are as melodious and expansive as the

Ex. 218

first pair were curt and rhythmical.   They are perhaps the loveliest of their kind in all Rameau.   The first, in G major, is akin to the mariners' first chorus; the second is in G minor and has an expressive bassoon part which answers the violins (ex. 218).   It is in such examples of the form, as well as in the first of the earlier pair and in the celebrated E minor tambourin of the third *entrée*, that one grasps to what extent

Rameau has taken advantage of the insistent repeating of the tonic in the bass to enrich his harmony by making all the chords of the key pass over it. If the presence of the drone prevents him from modulating, he is rewarded by the richness of the ninths and elevenths that arise quite naturally when dominant harmony passes over the tonic pedal.[1]

One realizes, too, how admirably his dances unite melody and rhythm; neither of these essential though sometimes conflicting elements is sacrificed to the other, so that his finest dances are both affectively and physically stirring.

Out of the blue, after an uninteresting *ariette vive*, full of Italian vocalises and "French levity", there falls one of his most G minorish pieces—a short gavotte of twelve bars, repeated as a song by the Naiad. Here everything is beautiful: the line itself, the semi-contrapuntal accompaniment, with its perpetual alternations between flattened and sharpened leading note, its extremely lively and expressive bass (ex. 219; the example shows the beginning of the second half).

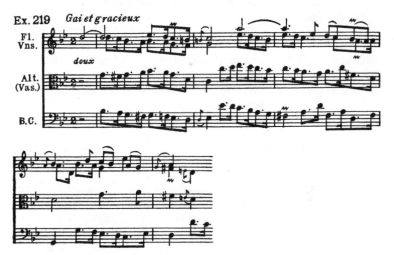

The sadness with which it is laden outweighs the *volupté* expressed by the words of the Naiad's song. Only in the gavottes of *Zoroastre*, Act I, has this mood, so recurrent in him, been rendered with such haunting intensity.[2]

The beauty of the first *entrée* lay in its *fête*; that of the second is in its story. Here, for once, is an act the interest of which, as far as the music is concerned, is dramatic. Scenes 4 and 5 form a miniature drama close to tragedy; indeed, in no passage in Rameau outside *Hippolyte* is the taste of tragedy so strong. If I had to give a sample

---

[1] From an unpublished study by Cecilia Campbell.

[2] The rigaudon that follows is thematically and, to some extent, affectively akin to it.

of Rameau the tragic it is from Scene 4 of this *entrée* that I should take my examples.[1]

The *entrée* begins with a *ritournelle*, *doux et tendre*, not unlike that of the first *entrée*. Its key is G minor and it is like two other G minor *ritournelles* at the heads of acts, those of Iphise in *Dardanus*, I, and of Castor in Act IV of his opera, but it is smaller and less distinguished. The difference between it and them is the difference between *tragédie*, even *lyrique*, and ballet. In a long recitative, Iphise, princess of Sparta, informs us that a "pompeux sacrifice" is about to be offered for her marriage to Tyrtaeus,[2] leader of the Lacedaemonian host and a gifted singer. As she recalls amorously

> L'instant où mon âme agitée
> Reconnüt un vainqueur

she breaks into song and rehearses the *ritournelle* from which, however, she diverges after the fifth bar; the rest of her air, though in keeping with it, is new. The words are pleasantly reminiscent but the music has that cast of sadness which Rameau seems incapable of avoiding when he turns to a solemn style. Lycurgus, whom the libretto makes king of Sparta,[3] enters to tell her that an oracle is causing a hitch in the arrangements and has declared that Heaven

> Destine à la princesse
> Le vainqueur des Messéniens.

"Que n'ai-je différé l'aveu de ma tendresse!" exclaims Iphise, and through the music of this cry there passes the first breath of tragedy. With an arresting jump from C minor to A flat Lycurgus comforts her with the news that Tyrtaeus is preparing himself to overcome the city's foes and to claim her hand. The next event is the singer's entrance.

The sequence of keys here is remarkable. The dialogue between Lycurgus and Iphise had passed from A flat to F minor and closed there. Tyrtaeus' entry is made to a bold C major and his address to the people is firmly in that key. But the fanfare solo "Qui te retient, Lacédémone?" with which he drives his point home, is in A major and the skip of three fifths upwards gives a forceful impression of resurgent energy.[4]

The iterative chorus "Marchons, commandez-nous" which responds to his appeal, also said to come from *Samson*, is much too long. When it is over the men withdraw and Iphise is left with her women to eat her heart out in suspense.

---

[1] Or perhaps from Zélidie's air "Coulez, mes yeux" in *Zaïs*, III, 3.

[2] Neither lame nor a schoolmaster, as in ancient tradition.

[3] He was never king; moreover he lived two centuries before Tyrtaeus.

[4] According to the *Journal de Paris*, art. cit., this comes from *Samson* where it set the hero's reproaches to the Israelites for their cowardice.

The air in which she does this is intensely tragic. The orchestra
is reduced to strings; harmonies are spare, melody meagre (ex. 220).
After this desolate appeal the music gains vigour as it cries for the

Ex. 220

destruction of Sparta's enemies (ex. 221).[1] The terseness and *dépouillement* of this air are found elsewhere, but not often, in Rameau;
it is the carrying to great lengths of a quality inherent in much of his
work which seldom sins through padding or loquacity. This solo is
on the plane of "Tristes apprêts" in *Castor et Pollux* and the "Frap-

Ex. 221

pez!" duet and "Lieux funestes" in the 1744 *Dardanus*. Something of
the starkness of death passes through it, perhaps inspired by the

---

[1] The air is in *da capo* form with written-out reprise; I quote from the
reprise.

opening words: "O mort, n'exerce pas ta rigueur."   After ex. 221
Iphise turns to the Oracle, beseeching it to relieve her uncertainty
(ex. 222).   Her entreaty becomes more pressing and is at its sharp-

Ex. 222

est with the question (ex. 223) where the clash of cross relations
on the "il"—a strong word in the context—is piercing.

A height of tragic intensity has been reached and it is maintained
in the panting chorus of women that follows.[1]   Iphise herself breaks

Ex. 223

in once more and all pause as she repeats her question; the Oracle's
ambiguous reply, with an impressive halt, "tien", on the sixth degree,
lessens the tension by promise of delay rather than aversion of disaster
(ex. 224).   I knew someone who said that in Purcell's *Dido and
Æneas* he went through all the emotions of the *Götterdämmerung*.
Here, too, emotional states crowd into a minute space, from desolate
passivity to fury, supplication and the anguish of expectancy.   Emotionally, it must be one of the most tightly packed successions of bars
in all music.

Most of us have come to love and admire Rameau first through his
keyboard music, and there is an almost private delight in meeting at

---

[1] The list of characters says Iphise, Lacedaemonian women and Oracle,
yet the parts of this chorus include tenors.   I cannot explain the discrepancy.

Ex. 224

Iphise. Tir-tée est-

Ré-ponds, O - ra - cle de nos dieux!

Des fiers Mes-sé-ni - ens   Ly - curgue est-il le maî - tre?

Ré-ponds, O - ra - - - cle de nos dieux!

-il vic-to-ri - eux?   *Marqué*

L'Oracle

Son des-tin et le tien vont par-aître á tes yeux.

this point the lovely *Entretien des Muses*, disguised as an *air tendre* in the *oracle figuré*.   The Oracle's promise is to be carried out ballet-wise.

> A Love comes out of the Temple and joins the Genius of Apollo; the Genius of Apollo draws on the Genius of Mars; both combine to attract the Genius of Victory; finally, the Genius of Victory is followed by a Love bearing the torch of Hymen.   These various *entrées* make up a ballet whose sequence informs Iphise of the issue she may expect.

The *Entretien*, which opens this charade, is scored for flutes, violins and continuo and is even lovelier in its colours than in its keyboard black-and-white.   It unfolds as Love fetches the Genius of Apollo but, alas! it breaks off half-way, ousted by the Genius of Mars.   This personage dances to a vigorous number, *pas vite et bien marqué*, fine in itself, but to which we give a rather sour welcome with the enchantments of the unfinished *Entretien* still working in our ears.   Grand, however, it is, if we will turn to it oblivious of what has gone before. It is in a dance like this, melodically and harmonically insignificant, that we see at its clearest Rameau's rhythmical ability.   Scarcely two bars running have the same *coupe*.   It contains in all fifteen different patterns.   Victory's air, on the other hand, is rhythmically unvaried and belongs to the commonplace fanfare class.   Two rigaudons follow; the second, in D minor, is a distant relative of Iphise's "O mort" solo.   All five protagonists—Oracle, Genii of Apollo, Mars and Victory, with Hymen who enters at the end of the second rigaudon —join forces in an animated chaconne.

Of some fifteen chaconnes by Rameau this is my favourite.   This is a very personal matter, for I fully acknowledge that the famous ones of *Les Indes galantes* and *Dardanus*, and the rather less renowned of *Hippolyte* and *Castor*, are quite as grand.   But when I come to it after what has gone before I am always carried away by the skill with which it combines the lithe vigour and speed of the Genii's dances and the melancholy of the "suspense" scene and of what we were allowed to hear of *L'Entretien*.   It is also more closely knit, less episodic, than most chaconnes.   Not till the eightieth bar does it change key and *allure* and even then, in spite of the passage into D major and a suspiciously fanfarish opening, smacking more of Mars and Victory than of the other confederates, it retains or recalls much of the melodious pensiveness of the earlier section.   This change of key is the only break in this magnificently through-composed piece of nearly a hundred and sixty bars.   Such constancy may be against the rules of chaconnes, but it is most exhilarating after the anguish of suspense through which we have been passing.   It was certainly Iphise's experience for, as it ends on six bars of honest rum-ti-tum, she exclaims:

Ah! le plaisir s'accorde avec la gloire!

After which, to say that all is over bar the shouting would be a little unfair, for there is much spritely, vigorous music, full of rhythmical *trouvailles*, as well as a touching "Aimes, aimes!" trio; but I feel tempted to say so when I come out of this particular *Götterdämmerung*. And so, as nothing in the rest of this *entrée* illustrates what is not as well, or better, illustrated elsewhere, let us pass on.[1]

On the first performance of *Les Fêtes d'Hébé* it appears that the third *entrée* pleased the public most. Its theme is inexistent rather than commonplace: a shepherdess, through the excellence of her dancing, earns a place at the court of Terpsichore. To put a little stuffing into it the librettist introduced Mercury and made him the shepherdess's successful swain, for which he apologized in timid, interrogative style. "Mercury, according to several mythologists, was the god of all the arts. Would it appear unlikely if he was represented in love with a shepherdess whose talents earn for her admission to the court of Terpsichore?" The answer is, of course, that nothing matters as long as the music is good. And that requirement is fulfilled, for Rameau has conjured up for this *entrée* some of his most unearthly strains. The music for the *divertissement* is said to be yet another survival from the stillborn *Samson* and to have accompanied the festival of Adonis in Act III, 1, and indeed a piece like the dance of the shepherds in love with Eglé is more suggestive of forgotten rites and esoteric cults than of pastoral measures.

As in the first *entrée*, where the action was nearly as slender as here, the best music is in the *fête* and the least interesting part is the would-be dramatic first five scenes. Like the *entrées* in *Les Indes galantes*, this one opens with a *ritournelle*, lightly contrapuntal with bell-like effects of broken thirds and sixths which remind one of the closing bars of *L'Égyptienne*. It is an independent *symphonie*, not connected with any air, and the action begins with a recitative of Mercury's. We will mention, in these opening scenes, the charming air with hautboy *obbligato* for Mercury, "Tu veux avoir la préférence", with its graceful swing between major and minor,[2] and the drowsy, voluptuous duet

---

[1] But not before quoting the stage directions at the beginning of Scene 8. "Clouds laden with trumpets, kettledrums, hautboys and bassoons alight upon the stage; the orchestra joins in this further concert," a phenomenon which Tyrtaeus interprets as:

Apollon veut aussi prendre part
Au succès de son art.

[2] Its opening line is the same as that of Venus' descent in the prologue of *Castor* and recalls also the opening of *Laudate Dei nomen* in the motet *In convertendo*.

between Mercury and Eglé, with dragging bass and slow-moving
vocal line.

As the lovers' avowals die away we hear the strains of pipes,
heralding the shepherds who come to compete for the hand of her
whose heart has already been given to the unrecognized god.   From
this moment on the music is one long enchantment.   This may sound
banal and, indeed, short of bringing the music to the reader, there is
no way of expressing its beauty, its peculiar mixture of delight,
nostalgic unreality and mystery.

The entertainment is in two parts.   In the first, shepherds and
Eglé sing and dance; in the second Terpsichore and her court join
them.   The key system remains steady: C major for the shepherds
and Eglé, E major and minor for the Muse.

The throng enters to a solo, repeated as a chorus, invoking Hymen
in the name of Love.   Much is made of the vocative "Hymen!" and
the line has a kind of irregular hemiola rhythm which is extremely
plastic, though there is no indication of dancing (ex. 225).   The

Ex. 225

orchestra includes musettes, hautboys and bassoons, horns *ad libitum*[1] and strings without harpsichord. The dance that follows, in which the music seems to depict the shepherds, drunk with love, circling blindly round Eglé is certainly more evocative of a mysterious Eastern cult than of rural innocence. It is one of the most impressionistic pieces in eighteenth-century music, and the magic, so often unconvincingly rendered, is here overwhelming. The effect it makes as one turns the page and comes upon it without warning is unforgettable, even when one does not know how it is scored. Musettes and hautboys play in unison, sustained by the thick packing of strings. Relief is given in bars two and three by the rising of the violins above the wind, and in the second episode by the silence of the strings (ex. 226). It is remarkable how few dissonances are present here; Rameau obtains his "atmospheric" effect by thickening the inner parts, by the droning fifths in the bass, by the uncanny dragging rhythm. The insistence on the supertonic in the refrain and the way in which each episode begins on its own supertonic increase the impression of weirdness. This exotic piece gives one the taste which Russian and Spanish music, now so hackneyed, must have given in their novelty to nineteenth-century audiences. A short air of Eglé's, addressed not to the shepherds but to Mercury, intervenes, after which the ignored shepherds repeat their evolutions.

Eglé herself now joins in the dancing "with a nosegay in her hand" and the measures take the more customary form of gavotte and rigaudon. The gavottes, in C major and minor, perpetuate the spirit of the earlier dance but without its intensity. Eglé then

Ex. 226

---

[1] Rameau's note in the score at this point is a reflection on the inability of horn players at the Opéra to play softly. "These horns are not absolutely indispensable, no more than those added to the next airs; they can do no harm provided they control their sound so as not to cover the orchestra."

presents the nosegay to Mercury, who reveals his identity, and this
part of the entertainment concludes with a mysterious little chorus in
A minor, *syllabé* and almost *parlando*, which acknowledges her triumph.
E major thereupon makes a brilliant intrusion; "the scene changes and
shows an ornamental garden".

The first strains are heard off-stage and are interrupted by speech.
The Muse and her nymphs "appear dancing to the sound of their
drum" and the orchestra strikes up a square-cut quick march, akin to
the spirit of post-1752 *opéra-comique* rather than to *tragédie lyrique* or
to *opéra-ballet*.[1]   The musettes are silent; flutes take the place of
hautboys.   The company next dance a rather Elgarian loure, one of
Rameau's best examples of this form.   The slow measures of the
strings are ever and anon broken into by the piccolos (ex. 227).
After the minuets, the first in quick time, and an air by Mercury, we

---

[1] Its first four bars occur as a fleeting episode in the finale of Mozart's
G minor quartet for piano and strings.

experience again the same sort of joy as when we discovered *L'Entre-tien des Muses* in the second *entrée*.   The well-beloved *Musette* in E major from the 1724 book of harpsichord pieces strikes up as Terpsichore's own dance, scored with flutes and horns but no haut-boys.   It is shorn of its last, clavieristic episode.   The equally well-loved *Tambourin* from the same book follows it, for the same instru-

Ex. 227

ments and unchanged, save for the repeat of the last five bars, but much enriched by the addition of two inner parts.   Then the musette returns as a chorus and here it achieves its full power.   The seeds contained in what Rameau had conceived, fifteen years earlier, for his gracile instrument, are now brought to fruit and stand revealed in all their force.[1]   The lute-like chords of the clavecin turn into sustained four-part vocal writing with the complement of the full band *minus* the flutes.   The addition of two solo voices allows for some delight-ful descant in the repeat of the refrain upon its first statement and in each of the episodes, where Mercury has the theme and a companion the descant (ex. 228).   Terpsichore, at the god's request, receives Eglé into her court and two passepieds seal the transaction.   Mer-cury's *ariette*, also in E, preceded by a long instrumental *ritornello* in concerto style, is the only piece which Rameau ever borrowed from

---

[1] It is, of course, possible that these and other pieces first published for harpsichord may have been composed originally for the Fair theatres.

Ex. 228ᵃ

Ex. 228ᵇ

his early cantatas.[1]   Unfeignedly Italian, it stands out almost brutally from the background of French pastoral music and sounds stiff after the swaying musette.   The Italian climate is maintained in the final piece which appears thrice: as an orchestral *air*, a solo for Mercury and a chorus.   Its 6/8 *siciliano* measure is not a French *coupe*.   The solo and chorus, which shorten the second half by a few bars, afford the usual delightful changes in line and, in the choral version, parts are added.   The haunting coda is unchanged each time; its *berceuse* lilt is redolent of Alessandro Scarlatti, in whom it occurs, rhythm and line, in the final number of the *cantata pastorale, O di Betlemme altera povertà* (ex. 229; ex. 230).

Les Fêtes d'Hébé was first performed on May 25, 1739.   Mlle Sallé took the part of Terpsichore, the Mlles Bourbonnois those of

---

[1] The original, in E flat, is in *Le Berger fidèle*.

Ex. 229

Ex. 230

Love; Mlle Fel was Hebe, Mlle Eremans Sappho, Albert Alcaeus, Le Page Tyrtaeus, Mlle Mariette Eglé, while Jélyotte played Thelemus and Mercury. According to Rameau's obituary notice in the *Mercure de France* this opera, with *Les Indes galantes* and *Zoroastre*, is the only one of his which enjoyed great success at its first appearance, a success due to the music, since the libretto was universally criticized. In August 1739 Mlle Barberine (Barbara Campanini) figured for the first time among the dancers, Rameau adding a few dances for her benefit.

It was revived in 1747 with the Camargo in the part of Eglé. Jélyotte was still in it and the *Mercure* reports that he sang the *ariette*—no doubt Mercury's in *entrée* III—"making it seem new at each performance by the variations which he put into it".

A further revival took place in 1756. Mlle Fel was still acting, seventeen years after the first performance. Vestris and Lany were in the ballet; Jélyotte and the Camargo had been replaced by Poirier and Mlle Puvigné.

The last complete revival was in 1764, the year of the composer's death. The sets had been superintended by Boucher. Sophie Arnould appeared as Iphise, drawing much applause. After 1770 the work was given only in selections, but without the prologue and first *entrée*. The last of these partial revivals was in 1777.

As soon as it appeared the opera was given in concert form before the Queen; it was acted before the court at Fontainebleau in 1753.

One month after the first performance, in June 1739, changes were made in *entrée* II. Scene 1 was given with new music and words and was shortened; this version is musically less interesting, as often happens when Rameau is compelled to abridge his original. Lycurgus is omitted from Scenes 2 and 3; in this latter a *douce symphonie* and an appeal from Tyrtaeus assembles the people. Tyrtaeus is given a new air with effects of *douceur* (D major) and *ardeur guerrière* (A major); it is long and is followed by the same long chorus, "Marchons". There appears to be no gain in these changes. The tragic Scene 4 was unchanged in purport but the music was rewritten, in E major instead of D minor, and voided of tragedy. This scene and the first have lost greatly by the change; it was felt, no doubt, that they contained too much tragedy for a ballet opera. The overpowering gravity of the *oracle dansé* must also have proved displeasing since a new scene was substituted with priestesses of Apollo and Spartan women; the warlike steps were replaced by a saraband for the priestesses, a chorus for Iphise and them, a gavotte and a *prélude gai*, and also *guerrier*, because it led into the next scene. Of all this, only the E minor gavotte is significant. The last two scenes were telescoped into one and contained a short duet for the lovers with continuo only, and the tedious and noisy "Éclatante trompette" chorus of the original Scene 7. Then, not to waste too much of the better music that had been discarded, "one plays the *airs* one likes, both those of the *pas de deux* [the *oracle dansé*] and the others, and between the last rigaudon and the chaconne is sung the following duet", which duet—very short, in D minor—was also new. Modern taste would have improved this act very differently. We should have kept the serious and tragic parts and got rid of the *guerrier* choruses.

Later alterations in this *entrée* included a number of dances added for the Barberine and a substantial cutting down of Iphise's solo "Éclatante trompette".

The prologue and first *entrée* remained untouched. The chief change in the third *entrée* was the addition of a gavotte for flutes and fiddles in E minor which, as *gavotte des Talents lyriques*, has survived in gavotte collections for piano solo and piano duet, representing the opera at the bar of posterity as the celebrated rigadoon represents *Dardanus*. Later still it was replaced by the E minor gavotte from the prologue of *Naïs*, another favourite of anthologies. Other changes were unimportant.

It is clear that much of the second *entrée* was felt to be beyond entertainment music. The great chorus in *Hippolyte*, III, was musically, but not emotionally, unsuited to its settings; Scenes 4 and 5 in *Les Fêtes d'Hébé*, II, were emotionally, not musically, incongruous. They were too strong for the delicate cadre in which they were inserted; while we enjoy their strength we recognize its irrelevance to their text and theme, but the first audiences, who knew exactly what they expected and demanded, who had a well-defined, pre-formed notion of what ballet opera should be, were offended by the irrelevance. Its virtue to us was a blemish to them, and on the grounds of artistic keeping and consistency they were right. This is not the only time that parts of Rameau's ballets are, as Masson vividly puts it, "des

Rembrandt dans un dessus de porte", but the discord is seldom as violent as it is here.   And so it was resolved.[1]

Those few who have penetrated into Rameau's world have been struck by the individuality of his pastoral music.   In a period of some two centuries during which almost every composer, at one time or another, dealt in pastoral, it is remarkable how original his inspiration is.   One would have thought it impossible, after so much dramatic pastoral in ballet and opera, to renew the themes and express the sentiments connected with it in so personal a manner.   Yet Rameau's shepherd *symphonies*, airs and choruses are among his most original pieces; they impress us most strongly and remain with us longest. Varied as were the *affects* he could render, those associated with the eclogue and the idyll have been given such vividness that one is sometimes tempted to think of him as first and foremost a pastoral artist and an effort is needed to redress the balance and to remember both the small space that pastoral occupies in his operas and the importance of his achievement in other fields.

A chapter devoted to *Les Fêtes d'Hébé*, whose third *entrée* is the first occasion for us to meet him in this vein, is a fitting place to discuss this aspect of his art.

In what follows, my considerations will be based on the pastoral music of some ten works, in four of which it is important.   I have confined myself to pieces where indications in the text show clearly that a pastoral sense is intended; otherwise fancy could extend the list to include compositions not so denoted whose inspiration seems to be in the same vein.   I have excluded, also, music evocative of nature but not of pastoral life in particular, such as that in *Hippolyte*, V, 3. The character of all this music is so marked that one is impelled to inquire what significance the theme had for the composer.

When speaking of pastoral in art and literature it is important to circumscribe the subject and not make it co-terminous with a love for the country.[2]   It is not only legitimate but necessary, for any useful handling of the question, to limit it to a well-defined stream of poetic inspiration, bearing evidence of historical continuity.   This stream arises with Theocritus, in whom it is born of the contrast felt between the pastoral life of Sicily and the more complex civilization of Alexandria.   It appears in Rome with the Augustans, and here takes shape the notion of a Golden Age, associated by Virgil with the

---

[1] In modern times only the first *entrée* has been revived: at Brussels in 1910, Monte Carlo in 1914 and Dijon in 1939.

[2] A rough and ready distinction is that pastoral nature is always a humanized nature; a "love for Nature", on the other hand, may well prefer the absence of man.

simplicity of pastoral life. It is responsible for the "outburst of pastoral song which sprang from the yearning of the tired soul to escape, if it were but in imagination and for a moment, to a life of simplicity and innocence, from the bitter luxury of the court and the menial bread of princes".[1]

This is what the word calls up for us to-day, but this description does not account for allegorical, realist and satirical pastoral. These forms, in which the shepherd setting is merely a cloak for another purpose, were the earliest in which pastoral was reborn in modern Europe. Petrarch's Latin eclogues were "ecclesiastical" and satirical; Boccaccio's, conventional, historical, satirical or religious; those of Battista Spagnuoli "il Mantuano", also satirical and religious. It is the form that prevails in Spenser's *Shepherd's Calendar*. In all these poets the note of longing for escape to an ideal life is heard hardly at all. Sannazaro's *Arcadia*, though far from being the earliest modern pastoral work, is therefore more of a source than these since it localizes the ideal and gives pride of place to primitivistic and Nature-loving, as well as amorous, elements, with little of the allegorical and political. "Mantuan's shepherds meet to discuss society; Sannazaro's to forget it."

The impulses and instincts, as well as the philosophical conceptions whence sprang this stream, were never made explicit at the time when it flowed its strongest. Theorists and theories about pastoral literature arose only in the later seventeenth century when the creative power of the original impulse was quite spent in drama outside opera, and nearly spent elsewhere. Within Rameau's own lifetime Fontenelle had analysed the chief elements of the enjoyment offered by pastoral works; he spoke, of course, for his own day, but much of what he said holds good for the two previous centuries as well.[2]

It is not the description of actual peasant life which pleases, he says, but "the idea of tranquillity attached to the life of those who tend sheep and goats".[3]

It is the idea of the

> few cares with which one is laden, . . . of the idleness one enjoys and the little it costs to be happy [in the country]. For men wish to be happy and they would fain be happy at little cost. Pleasure, and quiet pleasure at that, is the common object of all their passions and they are all ruled by a certain slothfulness. The most restless are made so not exactly by

---

[1] (157), 6.   [2] (68); 1688.

[3] Here is the link with religious pastoral which centres on the theme of Christ's Nativity. Religious Christmas music is indistinguishable from secular pastoral music. The cult of the Crib, whose great extension is post-mediaeval, is a manifestation of this element—the glorification of quiet, simplicity and innocence—in the pastoral appeal.

the love they bear for action but by the difficulty they have in finding contentment.[1]

Ambition is not a widespread passion, neither is it "fort délicieuse".

At the same time this idea of tranquillity is not enough. Montesquieu's brief analysis of the attraction of pastoral literature in the *Lettres persanes*[2] is inadequate.

> The authors of idylls and eclogues ... please even courtiers because of the idea they give them of a certain quiet they do not possess and which is shown to them in the state of shepherds.

Some activity and even some agitation are desired by men, provided they do not disturb their indolence, and they are afforded by love, "provided it is understood in a certain manner . . . tender, simple, delicate, faithful".[3]

Now, in the imaginary state of shepherds, there is agreement between love and indolence, man's two strongest passions. "This is what we imagine above all else in pastoral life." It harbours no ambition and nourishes no impulse capable of agitating us violently; indolence is content. It favours a love which is simple, absorbing (because there are no other passions), faithful (because there are no imaginings, whims or caprices), discreet (because there is no vanity). It is "love purged of all that is foreign and evil mingled with it by the excesses of human imaginings". What matters, therefore, is "the picture of a tranquil life taken up only with love; . . . goats and sheep are useless". Pastoral existence is the laziest and hence the best suited for "ces représentations agréables".

A hundred years earlier Pierre de Laudun in his *Art poétique français* (1598) had said already with a touch of sarcasm: "In *bergeries* it is love which is always, or most often, treated, because shepherds are idle and idleness is the mother of *volupté*." And a century later than Fontenelle, Corniani summed up thus the advantages which poets found in choosing pastoral scenes.

> It has seemed to poets that these advantages could be found united in pastoral life. The care of flocks requires an activity mild and gentle, far removed from hardship and excessive fatigue which offer unpleasant images. While the flocks graze the shepherds watching over them can

---

[1] A passage of which the third *entrée* in *Les Fêtes d'Hébé* "and a score of other pages in Rameau" are, says Masson, "an admirable illustration" ((190), 548).—See also (105); Roy was one of the most prolific opera librettists of his day.

"Pastoral poetry depicts the innocence and peacefulness of earliest ages; amidst the agitation of our own this picture wins and pleases us" (the quotation is from the first sentences of the book).

[2] Letter 137.   [3] (68).

contemplate the flowers, grass, brooks, plants, breezes, etc., and observe in themselves the pleasure which objects so fair and so simple awake in their hearts.   And it is natural that they should share in the mildness of the flocks, ever present to their eyes and thoughts.   They know not, therefore, the sophisticated passions which rend society.   Their passions are reduced to love and to emulation in games or songs or playing instruments.   These were the subjects of Theocritus' idylls and Virgil's eclogues and also of Sannazaro's *Arcadia*.[1]

Tasso more than anyone else is responsible for the invasion of pastoral by eroticism.   "The extravagant and conventional *pudor*, . . . one of the most abiding features of pastoral drama", is due to him. Voluptuousness does not lie deep beneath this exaggerated modesty. He has been accused of "fiddling harmonies on the strings of sensuality", and Greg adds that "the ear is constantly catching the fundamental note".   The sheer hedonism of the ideal presented in *Aminta* is expressed quite openly in the chorus that closes the first act, the theme of which is an attack on the concept of Honour which has thwarted the freedom of innocent and untrammelled love.   The beauty of the lost Golden Age does not lie in the charm and fruitfulness of Nature but in that the rule of Honour was unknown; the only law then observed was that "happy, golden one, engraved by Nature: *What pleases is licit* (S'ei piace, ei lice)".   No clearer and more seductive expression of the voluptuous ethics of erotic pastoral—Boileau's "morale lubrique"—can be found than these seventy lines of mellifluous verse.

There is thus a marked moral difference between the two elements, "tranquillité" and "douce volupté", which Fontenelle sees as the basis of the pastoral ideal.[2]   If the former is beneficent or at least harmless, the latter, with its insistence on sloth and hedonism, is liable to corrupt. Fontenelle is none the less true in his analysis.

But more than this had been sought and found in the pastoral dream.   At its loftiest, it was the conjuring up of a way of living pure and noble, from which everything base had been removed. Under the name of shepherds and the guise of rural images, says Abbé Genest, whose *Dissertation sur la poésie pastorale* (1707) is partly a rejoinder to Fontenelle, eclogue and idyll evoke the conditions and feelings of refined persons in loftiest stations.   They are one expression of a Renaissance ideal of which Rabelais's abbey of Thelema had been a more fantastic as well as material embodiment, an ideal that implied a wisdom, the poetic and pastoral wisdom of the Italian Renaissance, born in Florence, expressed by poets like Poliziano,

---

[1] (132), xiv.
[2] "A combination of sensuousness and innocence which is captivating" (Eric Newton, *Sunday Times*, January 30, 1944).

"an inner state in which the soul is analogous to that of the shepherd or the peasant", in which, however, the wise man is aware of the good which shepherd and peasant enjoy without knowing it; "sua si bona norint".

The ancient pastoral ideal was exclusively ethical; the Italian adds an aesthetic element of material beauty. Arcadia was the place, Orpheus the hero of this Renaissance dream. Orpheus is the hero whose soul is above ambition, greed, brutality, who charms through poetry and music and is the symbol of the civilizing power of mind and beauty as well as the expression of love faithful unto death. Pastoral love overcomes animal nature and low schemings. From the fifteenth to the eighteenth centuries, Arcadia is

> the ideal place where lives the dream of the Platonist Academy of Fiesole; the kingdom of Saturn is in the heart of man; music's and poetry's highest mission is to scatter the maleficent dream of common-place existence and to waken the inward Orpheus that sleeps in the best among men.[1]

A noble interpretation, but in how many pastoral writers was it even implicit? Fontenelle's humbler one was undoubtedly that of the great bulk of those who prosecuted the art of *bergeries*.

There was yet another appeal, morally not ignoble but artistically deplorable, namely the utilitarian one. Historically, this had been the first to be made when the Latin eclogue revived under the pen of Petrarch. Abbé Genest, intent on filling in the gaps in Fontenelle's theory of the eclogue, underlines it at length. In pastoral poetry, he says, "one may suggest the love of innocent pleasures and the lessons of a wise and gentle morality".[2] And on his last page he emphasizes that

> the pleasure and usefulness [of pastoral song] consist mainly in that one may insinuate in it many truths disguised beneath this pastoral veil, which are like as many parables. Such has always been the most suitable way of speaking delicately to great kings and it is still in use in the East. Finally, our eclogue, without having such lofty pretensions, may at least help sometimes to soften violent passions and to teach us to enjoy guileless delights, through the example of these simple herdsmen, content with the least presents of nature and fortune, and whose tranquillity and happiness, were they indeed as they are painted, no one would not envy.[3]

We have travelled far from poetry, far from moods susceptible of being rendered in music, with this Benthamite theory of pastoral.

Since real life did not correspond with the *mythus* of the pastoral state the cultivation of pastoral art involved a certain attitude of flight.

---

[1] (116).　　　[2] (70 A), 246.　　　[3] (70 A), 249.

At the end of the last section of *Arcadia*, dedicated to his pipe, Sannazaro concluded:

> He who dwells most hidden and furthest from the throng lives best, and he who is modestly content with his own lot without envying others' greatness may, among all mortals, be counted most truly blessed.

Concealment, as well as simplicity and innocence, is here given as an element of pastoral wisdom. Even the prosaic and unrufflable Fontenelle feels this need for flight and invites us to the enjoyment of unreality.

> Mais pour nous consoler de ne les trouver pas,
> Ces Silvandres et ces Hylas,
> Remplissons nos esprits de ces douces chimères,
> Faisons-nous des bergers propres à nous charmer.[1]

Unreality, indeed, is recognized by all as a quality of pastoral—recognized by some to be applauded, by others to be criticized, by yet others to inspire regrets. In *Aminta*, Tasso conjured up Arcadia without believing in it and created a pastoral mournfully conscious of its fictional nature,[2] as sceptical as Pollux in presence of Hebe's pleasures. This disbelief had sometimes been expressed by the juxtaposition of a mocking realistic counterpart. Herberay des Essarts, in translating *Amadis of Gaul*, added certain episodes to appeal to his French readers. They centred mainly in the hero's brother Galaon, whose "légèreté joyeuse" was preferred by La Fontaine to the nobler virtues of his brother, and, as a type, he descends through pastoral tales or comedies to Belleforest's *La Pyrénée*, where he is the Drion who mocks those whom the author calls "les philosophes amadysés", and to Molière's *La Princesse d'Élide*, where he is the grotesque Moron.

Already in Montemayor's *Diana* there was play-acting in that some of the shepherds and shepherdesses were frankly lords and ladies in disguise. In Tasso and Guarini, with the desire for a freer and more genuine life is found the representation in pastoral guise of actual persons and surroundings at the court of the Estes at Ferrara. It is as if they sought to find a place for their earthly affections in their land of pure ideal. In d'Urfé's *Astrée* the element of conscious artificiality is strong and it must be remembered that for French writers of the later seventeenth century Theocritus and Virgil were in a very distant background; the immediate model and inspiration was d'Urfé. It is the feeling and climate of his great novel that they seek to recapture. This is clear, for instance, in Fontenelle's first eclogue. The only themes available were love and the praise of indolence; the subject-matter is therefore much more restricted than with the Ancients

---

[1] Fontenelle, *Églogues*, II.　　　　　[2] (155), 75.

or even Sannazaro, Ronsard or Spenser, for whom politics and moral reflexions were also part of their repertory. This narrowness and unreality often excited derision or impatience. One recalls Boileau's outburst in his ninth satire:

> Viendrai-je, en une églogue, entouré de troupeaux,
> Au milieu de Paris enfler mes chalumeaux
> Et dans mon cabinet assis au pied des hêtres
> Faire dire aux Echos des sottises champêtres?

But it also had its defenders. Both Fontenelle and Genest maintain the necessity for this artificial limitation. Theocritus' realism is distasteful. "Pastoral poetry must neither be as coarse as nature nor turn on nothing but country things." It is not amusing to talk of sheep and goats. "We are not concerned with the meanness of the cares that occupy shepherds in real life but with the lack of trouble that these cares give them." A half-truth is good enough for imagination as long as it is presented vividly. "The illusion and at the same time the pleasure of *bergeries* consist then in presenting us only with the tranquillity of pastoral life and in concealing its meanness; its simplicity is uncovered but its wretchedness hidden."[1] Theocritus sometimes shows both at the same time; d'Urfé's people are often too much like courtiers. There is a middle way to follow between the vulgarity of the one and excess of wit of the other.

Some, when they realized how false was this beautiful ideal, were saddened by the thought and their dream was shot through with nostalgia. We feel it already in Sacchetti's

> O vaghe montanine pasturelle,
> D'onde venite si leggiadre e belle?[2]

and Lorenzo de' Medici is on the brink of dimming his happy scenes with the shades of contrast and regret. The vogue for pastoral in *cinquecento* Italy goes deeper than mere literary fashion and embodies the Golden Age ideal which cast such a spell over the time[3]; its expression may be the "gentle bookish melancholy" of *Arcadia* or the "profound bitterness" of the pastoral episode in *Gerusalemme liberata*.[4] It has even been sensed in Poussin for whom, according to Seznec,

> meditating in Rome amid the silence of ruins, . . . one feels that . . . this world of fable represents the golden age that will never return; everywhere is exhaled the regret for this age and its calm *voluptés*. The Ancient world . . . has become a kind of enchanted isle, lost in a misty distance, for ever unattainable. This feeling of nostalgia that infuses

[1] (68).
[2] Fourteenth century.
[3] (230), V, 168–171.
[4] VII, 1–22. Cf. (155), 75.

Poussin's work is the delicious and bitter fruit of the Renaissance; it comes from the change of perspective of humanism.[1]

The pastoral world was often, though not always, merged in that of Antiquity; for Poussin it was so, and realizing, with the late Renaissance, the distance in time that sundered him from it, he seemed to make "a conscious effort to bring into harmony two universes separated by centuries". The effort failed and the classical past became an "imaginary kingdom, a serene Arcadia where the great sorrowful heart of modern man seeks a refuge among the gods".[2]

Nostalgic regret for a lost Arcadia is thus sometimes a by-product of pastoral. It is a sentiment easier to express in music than the utility of the eclogue for moral improvement and political advice, and may well loom there larger than in literature. As we advance into the eighteenth century, we hear its note again. It is sounded at the end of Gresset's *Le Siècle pastoral*.

> Ce n'est donc qu'une belle fable!
> N'envions rien à nos aïeux;
> En tout temps l'homme fut coupable!
> En tout temps il fut malheureux!

Love of pastoral scenes blends sometimes with regret for the poet's youth spent amongst them, and the theme is then enriched with something more directly lyrical. Chaulieu's *La Retraite* (1698), *Loin de la foule* (1705) and *Les Louanges de la vie champêtre* (1707) unite the themes of old age and rural charm, foreshadowing Housman's "That is the land of lost content".

Until d'Urfé's talent had made narrative pastoral palatable to the French public it was mainly in dramatic form that this public had been able to enjoy its unreality. As we move towards 1700, dramatic and narrative pastoral die out and only eclogues and ballet survive. At the turn of the century it is still present in ballet and opera; the eclogue by this time is practically extinct. Abbé Genest, writing in 1707, deplores the loss of interest in pastoral literature. Pastoral poetry had enjoyed favour with Segrais and Mme. Deshoulières, and Fontenelle, who was not one to be unfashionable, had published his eclogues in 1688. But now it seems entirely false.

> Pastoral ideas . . . have faded out more than ever. The pictures that one can draw of this innocent and delightful life have no longer anything that chimes with men's feelings nor with the objects that the country shows us. The luxury, passions and anxieties that prevail in cities cause rustic simplicity and occupations to be despised; the state in which we see peasants cannot give us the least desire to resemble such shepherds. . . . Everyone is not capable of reaching back to an idea which no longer exhibits anything real.[3]

---

[1] (227), 290.   [2] (227), 290.   [3] (70 A), 109–110.

And he laments, like many in our own day, that

> People are no longer ready to see what demands peaceful attention. They want to be roused by turbulent objects full of variety or by the bitter, wounding shafts of satire.[1]

How different is this view of human nature from that of Fontenelle, for whom indolence was the most natural thing in the world! But the "Neustrian shepherd" was generalizing from his own placid temperament; Genest was the better observer. Some interest in pastoral writing there still was but *Astrée*, whose popularity was phenomenally long-lived, sufficed to satisfy it, while the pastoral play had long ago merged with the *ballet à entrées* and the opera.

The desire was not dead but its form of expression was changing. It was beginning to assume a primitivistic attitude that finds the pastoral ideal, not in the past, but in the present day and, *pace* Fontenelle, in village life, and it mingles with love for the countryside. This had perhaps been its original form in Theocritus and it had never been wholly distinct from this love. The *proema* to *Arcadia* is unmistakably primitivistic. It praises nature above artifice, prefers rugged scenery to cultivated lands and "woodland songs" to "cultured verse written on the blank pages of gilt-edged books".

Fontenelle's friend La Fare contrasts the happiness and tranquillity of present-day shepherds with "ourselves"; he deplores "our" state and lack of simplicity.

> Ici je rêve à quoi nos pères
> Se bornaient dans les premiers temps.
> Quel fut ce temps! quel est le nôtre!

The exclamatory last verse of his ode looks back to *Astrée*.

> Heureux habitants de ces plaines,
> Qui vous bornez dans vos désirs,
> Si vous ignorez nos plaisirs
> Vous ne connaissez pas nos peines.
> Vous goûtez un repos si doux
> Qu'il rappelle le temps d'Astrée,
> Enchanté de cette contrée
> J'y reviendrai vivre avec vous.[2]

Here is longing, but for *present-day* pastoral life, seen perhaps through the rose-coloured spectacles of literature.

Gresset, too, in his Epistle to Père Bougeant, draws a picture of the innocence of peasant life as he knows it: a primitivistic scene without the Parthian arrow that poisoned *Le Siècle pastoral*.

---

[1] (70 A), 108.
[2] (79), Ode I: *Réflexions d'un philosophe sur une belle campagne.*

Genest has some judicious comments on the fitness of pastoral motifs for opera. He has been speaking of songs with pastoral images and pursues:

> One would have thought, from the taste that prevails for these ditties, that *bergeries*, returning to their original foundation, which is music, would make marvels in opera. The idea we have of pastoral life makes it most suitable to song; the shepherds depicted have nothing to do but sing and talk of love from morning to night, by springs, under the elm trees' shade; and nothing would be as natural as to make them sing upon the stage instead of the knights and heroes or even gods and demons who are much less suitable for doing so and whom it becomes not to sing so long and so mawkishly.[1]

This is well noted. In Italy, after *Aminta* and *Il Pastor fido*, pastoral declines and enters the path of a romantic, spectacular, involved tragi-comedy. Poetry's loss is music's gain. In music the qualities of pastoral literature "recover all their value; its defects help the action".[2]   G. B. Doni, a theorist of the early opera, author of the *Compendio del trattato de' generi e de' modi della musica* (1635), said that no kind of drama was not the better for singing. And indeed many pastoral operas have been based on Tasso's and Guarini's plays. The earliest French opera was a *pastorale*; so were *Pomone* and *Les peines et les plaisirs de l'amour*. Lulli's first joint work with Quinault, in 1672, was the *Pastorale des Fêtes de l'Amour et de Bacchus*. There had even been, in 1630, a comic *pastorelle*, *Les Noces de Vaugirard*. The early Italian dramatic eclogues must have been very like the later pastoral cantatas and the third *entrée* of *Les Fêtes d'Hébé*. So that we are surprised to read in Abbé Genest that "shepherds appear now only in a few dialogues or *entrées*". One thinks at once of Lulli's *Acis et Galatée* (1686), of Destouches's *Issé* (1697), both of them pastoral. But round about 1707 the taste for operatic pastoral may have flagged. When Genest was writing pastoral was limited to *divertissements*. Though frequent these were brief and in the nature of ornaments; they did not belong to the subject. After 1700, though pastoral scenes are common, they are introduced as episodes into opera-ballet and do not often form the substance of any work. This makes all the more remarkable the musical significance attached by Rameau to them.

It is well known how deeply the tradition of pastoral and nature scenes is ingrained in dramatic music. From the outset these were evoked for their affective value. Monteverdi's "Ecco mormorar l'onda" conjures up an atmosphere and is the delicate suggestion of a

---

[1] (70 A), 106–107.   [2] (181), 426.

mood. Pastoral sentiment fills the works of Cavalli and Cesti in Italy, of Cambert, Lulli and Destouches in France, of Keiser in Germany. Lulli "has hardly written an opera that does not breathe the poetry of nature, of night and of silence".[1] His brook music in *Armide*, the "forest murmurs" of Destouches's *Issé* and the waves in his *Les Éléments* (III, *L'Eau*) have the undulating thirds of Monteverdi's scene. Tasso's *Aminta* had been set by Cavalieri. *Ballets de cour* like the *Ballet des Bergers* (1604) and *Tancrède dans la forêt enchantée* (1619) contained pastoral scenes. After 1650 music enlivens the dying pastoral play; Charles de Beys' *Le Triomphe de l'Amour* (1655) has music by Michel de la Guerre; Molière's *La Princesse d'Élide* and *Les Amants magnifiques* (1664 and 1670) both have pastoral interludes with music by Lulli.

A study of the pastoral in seventeenth-century music, its significance and its manifestations and means of expression, remains to be undertaken. There is no doubt that the genre had an immense stock in trade by the time Rameau turned to opera in the second third of the following century. So numerous and unavoidable, seemingly, were its commonplaces that it must have been difficult to be other than conventional in it.

We have heard Abbé Genest's regrets. Where shall we find pastoral in Rameau? Mostly, it is true, in "a few dialogues or *entrées*". Hardly at all in the *tragediés* and, as these are the least unfamiliar part of his output, his pastoral pieces are little known. Before *Les Fêtes d'Hébé* we find scarcely a piece in his dramatic music that can be called pastoral; only the musette-march in *Hippolyte* and another musette in the prologue of *Les Indes galantes* can be classed as such. In the third *entrée* of *Les Fêtes d'Hébé* pastoral inspiration floods his music for the first time. After 1739 we have to wait another six years before we hear any more pastoral music of consequence. Then, in less than five years, between 1745 and 1749, there arise two ballet operas, *Le Temple de la Gloire* and *Les Fêtes de l'Hymen et de l'Amour*, and two *pastorales héroïques*, *Zaïs* and *Naïs*, in which pastoral *divertissements* play important parts, and it is in these four plays, after *Les Fêtes d'Hébé*, that we find the bulk, and the best, of his pastoral music. The insignificance of the libretti seems to have liberated his fancy. He is no longer held to a text, a situation, a precise *affect*; he can let his imagination roam, stimulated only by the pictorial and impressionistic aspects of the setting.

This music is vocal and symphonic. The *symphonies* are all accompaniments to action; none is independent of movement on the stage. Some are *ballets figurés*, accompanying and underlining dumb show, such as homage paid to the statue of a pastoral deity; some, but

---

[1] (219): *Lulli*.

fewer, are cast in the forms of set dances, minuets, gavottes and tambourins.   The most expressive and most highly characterized pieces
are those that make up the *ballets figurés*.   Here are the directions for
some of these ballets.

The shepherds and shepherdesses enter the temple.   The high
priestess, preceded by the priestesses and followed by Zaïs and Zélidie,
follow them.   The god's statue is crowned with garlands of flowers; the
shepherds and shepherdesses return to the front of the stage (*Zaïs*, I, 4).

Lidie, Arsine, shepherds and shepherdesses consecrated to the
Muses coming forth from the caves of Parnassus, dance to the sound of
rustic instruments (*Le Temple de la Gloire*, I, 2).

The shepherds, bearing baskets full of flowers, strew them before
Tiresias' grotto.   They embellish the setting by hanging up garlands
that compose the monograms of Tiresias and Naïs (*Naïs*. II, 5).

Shepherds and shepherdesses form a ballet around Tiresias; they
offer him fruit and flowers (*Naïs*, II, 6).

A young shepherdess tries to approach Tiresias; she is turned
aside by two herdsmen who bar her way and wish to be heard first
(*Naïs*, II, 6).

The shepherds drive off the herdsmen; the young shepherdess
comes near and sings the following musette (*Naïs*, II, 6).

In addition to the third *entrée* of *Les Fêtes d'Hébé* I base my
attempt to appreciate what the pastoral dream meant to Rameau on
some ten or twelve *ballets figurés* in *Les Fêtes de l'Hymen*, *Le Temple
de la Gloire*, *Naïs*, *Zaïs* and *Daphnis et Églé*, since these ballets are
more definitely pastoral than the dances that are mingled with them.

The virtue they possess in common with other pastoral music is
their calm.   We have seen the stress that Fontenelle laid on "tranquillité".   Calm and slow—*musette lente*, *musette tendre* are common
titles—these movements are often in 3/4 time, beginning on the third
or the end of the second beat.   They are richly orchestrated and
harmonized; the standard five parts of the Opéra's orchestra are
represented and the voices are individual and move in free polyphony.
Sometimes the instruments are treated in opposing groups, like
miniature *concertinos*; thus, in the G minor tambourin of *Naïs*, I, 8,
piccolos, bassoons and violins separate and answer each other in rapid
changes.[1]   Expressive inner dissonances arise from this independence
in the parts.   Harmonization in sixths is common.   Even when
accompanying the voice, as in *Les Fêtes de l'Hymen*, III, 3, the full
orchestra is used.   Effects of instrumental colour are important and
of course the musette itself is included in the band.

But the impression of calm is nearly always superficial.   Rameau's
pastoral music, at its most typical, leaves behind a feeling of disturb-
ance, not of peace.   The expression, whatever it be, is too intense for

---

[1] See ex. 235.

true calm.[1]   The full scoring and part writing are largely responsible
for this result.

One quality that dispels calm is the penetrating languor so often
present in his 3/4 pieces.   In the well-known harpsichord musette in
E, used in *Les Fêtes d'Hébé*, the cloying heaviness is more than just
quiet; it is overpowering.   The mood which this very lovely piece
embodies can hardly be called pleasant: it is too oppressive for that.
In the refrain everything tends downward, drowsily, remorselessly,
towards the tonic.   In the episodes there is an upward motion, an
aspiration towards the tonic, but each time with the refrain we fall

Ex.231ᵃ

Ex.231ᵇ

back to the lower E, dazed with a druglike stupor.   The episodes
bring but momentary relief; the refrain is the real thing.   If this is the
beatitude of the fields and flocks, it is an opiate blessedness and it
leaves us unhappy.

The musette in *Le Temple de la Gloire*, I, 2, is as heavy-lidded and
languorous and here the second episode, far from relieving, merely
heightens the prevailing feeling and raises it to a pitch of intense longing, starting as it does on the third of the minor scale and descending
to the dominant (ex. 231).   The refrain is saturated with dissonances

---

[1] Did Rameau ever express any *affect* without intensity?   Whatever he
rendered, he rendered intensely, even gentleness!

and appoggiaturas. To reach such a state a previous condition of overwrought weariness is needed; this is not *délassement* or *détente* but sheer exhaustion.

The beautiful *ballet figuré* in *Zaïs*, I, 4, suggests in its rhythm and line the act of crowning the god with garlands. But the languorous sixths in the accompaniment are not part of this action and again languor and indolence are poignantly expressed; and poignancy is incompatible with "tranquillité". Would Fontenelle have recognized here the qualities he had enumerated in his *Discours sur l'Églogue*? The result of this pungent loveliness is neither consoling nor restful but intensely sad.

The musette in G in the fourth act of the same opera has an extremely expressive line, leaning heavily on the leading note as it falls, as if too far, below the tonic, seemingly too heavy to hold up. It lifts itself in steps but the ascent is expressive of longing, increased with each rise, not of deliverance. The rich singing counterpoint of the middle section pierces as it caresses (ex. 232). Here, too, sixths figure prominently in the harmonization.

Naïs has two musettes, both in C. The first, in II, 5, is weighted with inner dissonances and appoggiaturas. The beginning on the fourth, with the fall to the tonic, is highly emotional; it expresses intense abandon, especially in the codetta. Yet the decorating of Tiresias' cave, which this piece accompanies, requires no such feeling; it is of Rameau's own invention. There is more expressive counterpoint between hautboys and violins in the middle section. Though excessively weary the music is harmoniously and graciously so. One feels strongly the longing not only for a state of indolence so overwhelming that it becomes painful but also for a noble way of life. And over it all, as over most of these pieces, as over *Aminta*, there hangs the feeling that "this never was nor could ever be".

The second musette, describing the shepherdess's attempt to approach Tiresias, reflects the awe inspired by the seer and is less oppressive.

Languor is not so pronounced when the rhythm is square-cut, as in the *musette lente* of *Zaïs*, I, 4, in E. But the sentiment is quite as intense and there is no joy, in spite of the upward moving line; or perhaps merely the joy of contemplating a beautiful picture that "never was". This piece succeeds the *ballet figuré* in G just mentioned; the passage from G to E is a skip upwards of three fifths and it owes its sense of deliverance to this change, and for the conveyance of its full import it needs to be heard or played immediately after its predecessor.

In the fourth act of *Zaïs* is a very affecting piece in 2/2 time—a *rondeau* with one episode, entitled *air des bergers*. The dumb show is not indicated and the movement is more regular than in the *ballets*

Ex. 232

Hbs
Vns

Alt.
(Vas.)

Bn.

doux (un peu marqué)

B.C.

figurés. It denotes the union between Elemental Beings and Shepherds. Warm and full it is, yet its threefold lift "yearns" unmistakably. The five-part scoring is rich and the harmonization in sixths heightens the feeling of nostalgia. The bassoon in the episode has a part of unearthly beauty, far from tranquil (ex. 233). When, with the *air des sylphes* which follows, we pass into G minor and the usual climate of that key, we realize how near we were to this climate even in the G major of the *rondeau*.

I have often written the words "languor", "yearning", "nostalgia." Indeed, these are the dominant impressions of Rameau's most personal pastoral music. And, I would add, scepticism, disbelief. His ideal, as Masson says, is "un idéal nostalgique". Or rather, it is thus that shepherd life appears to him. The eclogue, at least in its Neoclassical form, was too optimistic, too much like that Wolffian philo-

Ex. 233

sophy of which Voltaire was to make fun some ten years after
Naïs.   Life is tragic, not idyllic or pastoral; hence the lifelessness of
so much pastoral literature.   But Rameau gave meaning and truth to
his eclogues by the tang of longing which he imparted to them; he
brought them nearer to tragedy or, at least, to elegy; that is his contribution to pastoral music.   There is no promise of happiness in his
strains, no sense of beyond, as there is, for instance, in the art of
Botticelli or Mozart, two other singers of nostalgia.   His shepherd
music rings true, not because it expresses a love for Nature as, maybe,
Vaughan Williams' Pastoral Symphony does, but because it bears a
profound and sincere longing for something out of reach and beyond
belief, and known to be so.   It is as unbelievable as the stage magic
of which his opera is full.   This sceptical nostalgia, felt at its keenest
in his musettes, pervades much of his music.   Laloy said, with some
exaggeration, that melancholy was the only feeling he expressed in his
own name; he could depict many others, as his subjects required, but
only when rendering melancholy and yearning was he himself and truly
lyrical.

The nostalgia that sweeps over his music, even when he is setting
words expressive of calm happiness, is seen in the final chorus of
Naïs, in which the sea divinities welcome to their ocean depths
Neptune and his bride.

> Coulez, ondes, coulez, mêlez votre murmure
>   A nos accords harmonieux.
> Plaisirs, faites régner cette volupté pure
>   Que vous répandez dans les cieux,

they sing.   But the music to which he has set this invitation is
piercingly sad.   Few of his choruses are so full of haunting disillusion.

Ex. 234

At no moment is the sentiment of the *ritournelle* belied in the piece (ex. 234).

Some of the set dances included in pastoral *divertissements* confirm this composite impression of languor, yearning and disbelief, expressed with intensity in forms rich and graceful, that I have been endeavouring to put into words. The writing, in many of them, is as rich as in the *ballets figurés*; in the minuets and tambourins *en musette* of *Naïs*, I, 8, the quadruple stopping of the strings gives an exotic colouring. The second tambourin, in G minor, is weird and mysterious; the bassoon dashes up from the depths and is answered by the piccolos. Within the limits of Rameau's orchestra the full colour is exploited and there results an eerie combination of mystery and Dionysian energy (ex. 235).

The A minor gavotte for the shepherds in *Naïs*, II, 5,[1] with its threefold plaint, also sings of abandon, like the musette which goes before it. The same gentle but quite disillusioned nostalgia prevails in the A minor saraband.

"Atmosphere" and impressionism are definitely intended in all this music. They reach their height in the minuets in *Platée* and in one of those in *Le Temple de la Gloire*. *Platée* is a comedy and it would be dangerous to seek to interpret the minuets in its second act on lines of languor, indolence or yearning. Though not placed in a pastoral setting they are headed "dans le goût de vielle" and may therefore be classed as bucolic. The imitation of the hurdy-gurdy through string arpeggiandos is acutely expressive, though what it expresses, beyond weirdness, it is hard to say; and probably strangeness and rusticity are all that are meant.[2] The second, the more melodic of the two, is also mournful. But how strange was this quasi-folk music to a French audience of 1745? Did its members not hear it commonly played in the country? It must have had a more normal and more functional existence than for us who never hear it except in a make-believe or picturesque local setting. We should therefore be careful not to attach as much strangeness to rustic music of a couple of centuries ago; it seemed no doubt countrified but much less evocative and "atmospheric" than to us. Nevertheless, we may enjoy the unearthly effect of Rameau's imitation *vielle* as much as we please and, even strummed on the piano, these minuets can be creepy.

In the second of two minuets in G in *Le Temple de la Gloire*, I, 2, a similar "atmosphere" is excruciating. The setting is a pastoral *divertissement* and we have just had the "heavy-lidded" musette in G major and the first minuet in the same key. Quadruple stopping

---

[1] No. 1 of the first pair in this scene.

[2] The *musette-vielle* combination was popular in the 'thirties and Bodin de Boismortier wrote many pieces for it.

Ex. 235

is used and the string arpeggiandos tear at us with the chord of G
minor and follow up with a strain that cleaves to the tonic, as in so
many 3/4 musettes, and is given pathos by the lift of the diminished
fourth.   The condensation in these sixteen bars is terrific (ex. 236).
The *major* minuet is good, too, with its blending of harmonic strength,
near-declamatory melody and plastic sense, but it has nothing particularly pastoral, except the use of musettes.

   I will bring in here a gem from *Daphnis et Églé*.   I will not seek

Ex. 236

to characterize it for it combines the feelings I have been labouring to
define and is yet beyond all of them—beyond yearning, desire, bitterness, scepticism, though they can all be perceived in it, together with

Ex. 237

unearthly peace, according to one's mood at the moment.   The
directions throw no light upon it; almost anything would have done
to play while "Love's attendants lead, dancing, the shepherds in the

different parts of the Temple [of Love] and invite them to pay homage to Love". What Rameau has expressed here is purely of his own (ex. 237).

I have kept for the end of these characteristic pieces one extraordinary *gavotte en rondeau* from *Naïs*, IV, 6,[1] certainly one of the most miraculous dances Rameau ever wrote. It is a *pas de deux* for shepherds and shepherdesses. Grace, unreality, suspense, satisfaction, longing, calm, agitation: here, too, everything can be sensed. The climate is given by the suspension in the opening bars (ex. 238).

Ex. 238

More than a century will elapse before we hear again music so charged with evocative power.

A few of Rameau's pastoral pieces have none of the characters I have been discussing. The enchanting march in *Hippolyte*, V, 8, "Chantons sur la musette", is sophisticated in its rhythm but its joy is quite unalloyed; it is one of the happiest things in him. The gavotte in G in *Le Temple de la Gloire*, I, 2, is brisk and vigorous, with the string chords hammering on every strong beat. The second gavotte of the first pair, in A, in *Naïs*, V, expresses—a rare thing with Rameau—the naïve merriment conventionally associated with bucolic

---

[1] It is the first of the second pair of gavottes in this scene; its A minor companion, for two violins and flute only, comes from *Les Fêtes de Polymnie*, prologue, 2.

sport. The lovely final air and chorus of *Les Fêtes d'Hébé* has no *arrière-pensée* of bitterness; the Italian model took Rameau out of himself. And indeed, all through his work, the most characteristic features of his musical personality are absent from his Italian *ariettes*, however unconventional they be.

In *Zaïs*, I, 4, are a couple of gavottes which are pastoral only in their setting, and I mention them here merely to draw attention to the

Ex. 239

curious clashes, *piano*, soft and cruel, like treacherous caresses, which can be heard in the second one (ex. 239).

One may be tempted to say: There is nothing peculiarly personal in all this; as music it is perhaps better than much contemporary output but the same sentiments of languor, indolence, longing, disbelief, disillusion, and what not, are found in them. Experience of pastoral passages in music of Rameau's age does not bear this out. Lulli's nature music—for instance, the scene in Armide's gardens—is graceful and even evocative, but the strains he gives his shepherds are no different from those he gives his other ballet characters. Destouches's *Issé* is a *pastorale héroïque*, yet we seek in vain through its scenes, many of them expressive, for music of a pastoral stamp. "Charmants hautbois, douces musettes" in the prologue, the shepherds' chorus in Act I, their march in Act II, the *divertissement* of Fauns and Dryads in Act III produce nothing distinctive. Campra's *Tancrède* has an interlude into which shepherdesses enter without affecting the character of the music. Destouches's *Les Éléments* has some unmistakably pastoral touches in the fourth *entrée*, *La Terre*, particularly a played musette in G and a sung one in the same key, "De nos fleurs les vives couleurs". But they are conventional imitation-bagpipe music, such as Couperin had written in his keyboard musettes, and their rather hypnotic charm is neither more nor less than that of all such pieces, common in the literature of *noëls*.

If we turn to his peers or betters and ask how Bach and Handel treat pastoral themes, we find again that, though indeed they create their own pastoral worlds, they are very different from his. In neither do we find a disturbing undercurrent; their worlds are spacious, tranquil and innocent. When they move us, they are benevolent and never Dionysiac. It should be enough to refer to *Acis and*

Galatea, to the Christmas music in the *Messiah*, to Bach's organ *pastorale* in F, to the lilting 12/8 chorus of cantata 104, *Du Hirt Israels, höre*, and to the *sinfonia* and relevant scenes in the Christmas Oratorio. There is here none of the scepticism of Rameau's pastoral. Only once do we experience something akin to the tang of Jean-Philippe's music and that, significantly, in a French dance, the musette of the G minor English Suite.

Some of Rameau's own music will afford a foil to his best pastoral pieces. Take the song from the cantata *La Musette*[1] or the movements entitled *musette* in the 1744 version of *Dardanus* (IV, 5) and in the third act of *Platée*; they are pieces whose pastoral character lies on the surface; it is confined to a drone bass and appropriate scoring, and their moodlessness sets off all the more strongly the *ballets figurés* we have been considering.

A generation later than *Les Fêtes d'Hébé* Piccinni composed his *Roland* for the Paris stage and his pastoral music, while recognizably of the genre, has no trace of Rameau's moods or indeed of any mood at all. None of it does more than reflect externals; it never, like Rameau's best shepherd strains, creates an inner world for the mind and heart to roam in, that "region of the mind" symbolized "by rural scenes and occupations . . . which does exist and which should be visited often".[2]

Rameau is sometimes likened to Watteau and it is in his pastoral music that this comparison is most apposite. He, like Watteau, has a "Hamlettish detachment"; like Watteau, he can be "heartrendingly sad".[3] Like him, he can "hint at depths beneath the neat, formal pattern of his" music. The pastoral ideal for Rameau's public was not more than one of "infinite leisure, endless round of love-for-love's-sake, elegance and careful avoidance of material discomfort"[3]; but behind that he, like Watteau, sensed and expressed a piercing melancholy.

---

[1] If authentic! But if it is not, this makes no difference to my argument.
[2] C. S. Lewis, *The Allegory of Love*.
[3] (199), 102–103.

11. Platée *and* Comédie Lyrique

A T the foot of Mount Kithaeron, somewhere in Greece, there lies "a great marsh, full of reeds, encompassed by ancient willows",

> . . . monument du déluge
> Que vit jadis Deucalion.

Here amidst paludean divinities, frogs and cuckoos, a nymph has established her retreat—a nymph as uncouth as her habitat and her companions. Though "laughable, and from all time proscribed by Love", she is credulously blind to her comic features and daily expects "a thousand lovers coming in turn to woo her". Among others, a neighbouring king, Kithaeron, she is convinced, is in love with her.

> . . . Je le vois,

she exclaims,

> Du plus loin quelquefois
> Comme un amant timide éviter ma présence.

One day, to conquer his shyness, Plataea calls on her attendant chorus of frogs and cuckoos to give voice in his honour. The king is attracted and, coyly, is upbraided for his timidity. The nymph's elephantine advances are repulsed and she is forced to recognize that he spurns her. She pursues him with fury while her frogs echo her question:

> Tu n'es qu'un perfide envers moi;
> Dis donc pourquoi?
> Quoi? quoi? quoi? . . .

Her anger is dissipated by the arrival of Mercury, the purpose of whose visit is hidden aloft on Mount Olympus. Jupiter, weary of his spouse's unrelenting jealousy, has deputed him to find a way of curing her of this trying defect. Mercury consults Kithaeron and the two together draw up a scheme to amuse their master and placate their mistress. Jupiter is to feign love for the ludicrous Plataea and pay her mock homage. Juno shall be informed of this new betrayal but will realize it is only a game as soon as she beholds the nymph and all will be well again on high. Only the ill-favoured and tiresome queen of the marsh (whom we will henceforth call by her French name,

Platée) will be disappointed.   But as an unlovely physique is a crime
in the erotic and hedonistic world of opera, this is as it should be.

The second and third acts of the opera stage the mock courtship
and its issue.   Juno, having been put on a false scent by Mercury,
flies off towards Athens, thus leaving her royal spouse full opportunity
to carry out unobserved his pursuit of the nymph.   Jupiter and
Momus descend in pomp and at once wrap themselves in a cloud,
which Platée investigates with curiosity.

> A l'aspect de ce nuage
> Je ne saurais m'abuser.
> Jupiter sait tout oser;
> Mais aurai-je le courage
> De recevoir son hommage
> Ou de le refuser?

Whereupon the cloud moves slightly.

> Le nuage s'entr'ouvre,
> Je vois du mouvement,

exclaims the delighted nymph.

> Je crois qu'il me découvre
> Mon adorable amant.

The lower part of the cloud breaks off and fits into the upper, disclos-
ing Jupiter in the shape of a "quadruped", i.e. a donkey, which Love
is wreathing with flowers.   Platée looks on with "tendresse" and
makes endearing commentary to her disguised lover, interpreting thus
the animal's braying:

> Vous soupirez, et je soupire;[1]
> Il suffit d'un si doux accent.
> Vous dites tout sans me rien dire.
> Ah! que l'Amour est éloquent!

Jupiter changes his shape and becomes an owl, flapping its wings in
mid-height, and Platée calls upon "les oiseaux de ce bocage" to sing
its praises.   Instead, they proceed to mob the intruder, making a din
("charivari") which Platée takes for a sign of jealousy.   The owl
escapes unnoticed by her.   When she discovers its absence, she weeps
loudly and rushes everywhere seeking it and keeping up the while a
commentary on the changed situation.   The next alarum is a thunder-
clap and a rain of fire which terrifies her.   Finally, Jupiter appears in
human form and engages her with caressing discourse, to which she
listens, "tongue-tied and trembling".

---

[1] A parody of the well-known line in Corneille's *Psyché*, III, 3: "Vous
soupirez, seigneur, ainsi que je soupire".

Seriez-vous insensible à mes tendres feux?

inquires the god. To which all she finds to answer is "Ouffe!", an expletive which shocked some of the more pedantic members of the audience, according to Rémond de Saint-Mard, who called it "une expression ignoble", especially as she follows it up with the apology:

Pardonnez-moi! j'étouffe;

even though she tempers this by adding:

Et je soupire en même temps.

Jupiter then offers a revel to his conquest; organized by Momus, it is quickly interrupted by the arrival of Folly, carrying Apollo's lyre, who takes charge through the succession of dances, airs and choruses. It culminates in a mocking chorus in honour of Platée, who does not perceive the raillery and herself leads the sarcastic "Hé bon, bon, bon!" which resounds all through it.

Juno, meanwhile, has failed to find Jupiter in Athens and comes to vent her wrath on Mercury. He reassures her and she goes into hiding, an unseen spectatress of what is to follow.

What she witnesses is the travesty of a nuptial feast. Platée, covered by a veil which conceals her distressing features, is seated on a chariot drawn by frogs while Jupiter and Mercury escort her on foot. Dryads, satyrs, nymphs, naiads surround, precede and follow the bride-to-be. Platée steps down from her chariot and boldly takes the god by the hand, expressing meanwhile her disappointment at the absence of Love and Hymen, which is explained by Mercury in discouraging terms:

Ces dieux, vous le savez, vont rarement ensemble;
C'est un hasard qui les rassemble.

Platée's impatience grows. She is made to sit down and watch Jupiter and Mercury work through an interminable chaconne, danced "dans le genre le plus noble" in order to increase her restiveness. After two hundred and thirty-two bars a "symphonie extraordinaire" interrupts the slow measures and Momus, the god of raillery, and Folly make their reappearance, the former impersonating Love who, engaged elsewhere, has entrusted his grotesque substitute with all the favours for the happy nymph, and the latter still strumming Apollo's lyre. Momus is a parody of Cupid; he is blindfold and carries an outsize bow and quiver. His gifts to Platée are "pleurs, tendres douleurs, cris, langueurs".

Fi!

she cries;

> Ce sont là des malheurs;
> Et, s'il faut que j'aime, je veux des douceurs.

The final gift is "la flatteuse espérance", which Platée refuses in a spirited 6/8 air:

> Eh! fi! votre espérance
> N'est que souffrance,
> Un vrai signe d'ennui!

Folly intervenes and, mocking Momus, "who looks embarrassed", sings him an *ariette* in the conventional "Amour, lance tes traits" style, a parody like much else in this *divertissement*.

The parody is continued by the appearance of the three Graces, represented by followers of Momus; they set about dancing "comically" a loure which Folly enlivens with her lyre. Cithéron and a troop of country dwellers offer their congratulations and a mock-pastoral note is added to the mock-courtly tones of Momus-Love and Folly-Apollo. Finally all are invited by Folly to sing the praises of Platée.

The time has come to close the festivities with the mock marriage. Jupiter, apprised of Juno's hidden presence, takes the nymph by the hand and prepares to swear. "Je jure . . ." he begins, looking round anxiously for Juno to interrupt him. Juno is late and there is a moment of comic anxiety while he puts off pledging himself with a fatal oath. At last she rushes in and the rejoicings are wound up with the uncovering of Platée by the furious queen of Olympus, who at once bursts out laughing. The expected reconciliation takes place; the gods go up to the sound of thunder, with Iris and Momus; Mercury flies before them; only Folly is left with the sovereign of the marsh. The rest of the unkind farce is taken up with pitiless mockery of Platée. She is pushed to the front of the stage by the rustics, their wives and children, and is surrounded by the jeering crowd. The opera closes to the reiterated strains of "Chantons Platée", more and more cruel in its laughter, against which break the threats and imprecations of Platée's mounting fury.

> Je troublerai mon onde,

she threatens;

> Et c'est du sein de ma grotte profonde
> Que je vous porterai, je lancerai mes coups.

She turns and grasps Cithéron by the throat; he is the prime malefactor, she declares.

> Qui, moi?—Oui, toi!—Moi?—Toi!
> Non, non!—Non, non!

And again we hear the echoing "oi, oi" of the earlier frogs' chorus and the "on, on" of "Hé! bon, bon, bon". The yokels dance; Platée gathers impetus and rushes headlong into her marsh. Folly leads off those who are left "to rejoice at the patching up of Juno's and Jupiter's quarrel", and with three ironic strums of her lyre the opera ends.

Even the climate of unreality in which this story unfolds cannot make us forget entirely that the basis of the comedy is physical ill-favour. That the unsightliness of an unweddable female should be the ground of such prolonged sport is not wholly pleasing, and it is hard not to be repelled in the long run by the inhumanity of the theme. Ugliness is no longer the source of comedy it could be two centuries ago, and the lack of geniality and the cruelty of the data give *Platée* a bitterness which lessens its appeal. The heroine's grotesque appearance is the foundation of the humour, if one can call it thus; much of the comedy in the music consists in suggesting ridiculous attitudes and movements; the most lively choruses are mocking and the opera closes with scoff and impotent rage. Surely it is not utterly Mrs. Grundyish to find such a tale somewhat distasteful. Such constantly cruel fun reminds us of Racine's *Les Plaideurs*, the subject of which is the madness of an aged judge[1]; it is derisive, pitiless, without the sympathy with which habitually comic playwrights like Molière give warmth to their creations. Both *Platée* and *Les Plaideurs* are the works of artists whose normal activity lay in, or near, the field of tragedy. The theme, moreover, is somewhat monotonous and the constant mocking of an unfortunate creature whose appearance debars her from the affection normal between men and women tends to pall.

Having criticized the subject from this moralistic standpoint it must be said that *Platée*, thanks to its music, is much more attractive than its story would suggest. Within the limits of the tale Rameau shows himself extremely resourceful and his music is as varied in its raillery as the situation allows. The sharp edge so constantly present in him, even when he is evoking gentle moods, is of course prominent here. Though the occasion be so different, it is still the composer of *Hippolyte* and *Dardanus* that we recognize, just as we feel the future creator of *Bajazet* and *Phèdre* in *Les Plaideurs*.

If we examine those passages where a humorous intention is present—and they cover most of the opera—we shall see that in some the music aims merely at evoking an atmosphere of comedy, without any person or object being the butt of mockery; the overture, for instance,

---

[1] Granted that the theme comes from Aristophanes, it was Racine's choice. The story of *Platée*, too, was not invented by Rameau but he bears the responsibility for having selected it.

the prologue and the music associated with Folly are of this kind. Others, while not directed at Platée, serve to make her background ridiculous or to underline the farcical nature of the honours rendered her, which is another way of ridiculing the nymph herself.   And, finally, a great many seek to present Platée's person in a ludicrous light.   The best way to reach the essence of Rameau's comic art will be to examine some of the devices which he uses for these purposes.

The simplest and almost the first we meet is the rhythmical trick of repeated notes.   We find it in the first bars of the overture in the six-five chords which return later, without the added sixth, in Folly's entry.   It is present in the *vivement*, in both subject and counter-subject.   The mechanical nature of these two themes and their constant repetition remind one of the overture to *Cosi fan tutte*, where a like theme, likewise repeated, serves a similarly derisory purpose (ex. 240).   The mocking chatter, as malevolent and witless as that of

Ex. 240

monkeys, is a sharp characterization of the opera as a whole.   It is prominent again in the D minor rigaudon, the contredanse and chorus which conclude the prologue; the last of them begins with a succession of eleven repeated D's, with obvious comic intention.   It recurs in the acclamation chorus that welcomes Folly in II, 5, and the humour is marked by the words, where the reiteration of "la ly-re la ly-re" ("Qui tient la lyre d'Apollon") recalls the stock refrain "lan-li-re lan-li-re" of folk-song.

Another device is the use of wide intervals in the vocal line. Suggestive of high skips, they evoke exaggerated and ridiculous movements.   They occur, *inter alia*, in the *air pour les fous* and Folly's solo "Aux langueurs d'Apollon" in II, 4.   The mock pomposity of the interminable chaconne in III, 3, is broken from time to time by absurd high-jinks passages of skips of octaves and elevenths, preceded by repeated notes in which the dancers, as it were, gather impetus for the ungainly leaps.   Wide intervals are present in the second passepied of I, 6 (original version),[1] and at the end of the mocking chorus "Chantons Platée" in III, 8 (ex. 241).

The element of mock solemnity and even of deliberate parody is, of course, prominent.   The surprising chords with which the chatter-

---

[1] Not in the vocal score, which gives those composed for the 1749 performance.   See ex. 280.

Ex. 241

ing overture ends can be only derisive in their context; they sum up in a few bars the spirit of the entertainment where mock pomp and ceremony play a large part and chromaticism is important in the arousing of humour.   The dotted-crotchet rhythm of Love's entry in the prologue, Scene 3, and still more of Mercury's at the end of Act I, are instances of false solemnity since the music, or at least its rhythm, is patently unsuited to the character; this distemper between music and personage is also the source of much of the comedy in Platée's part.

Direct parody may be recognized in Folly's "Aux langueurs d'Apollon", in her "Amour, lance tes traits" (to Momus "en se moquant de lui"; III, 4) and in the chaconne (III, 3).   This gigantic

Ex. 242

symphonie de danse, one of Rameau's longest, shows the composer's notion of tediousness.   The piece is written with his tongue in his cheek and is, intentionally, as dull and pompous as are, unintentionally, the chaconnes of *Orfeo* and *Alceste*.   "On danse dans le genre le plus noble pour impatienter Platée davantage," say the directions. Although it lasts for two hundred and thirty-two bars, eighty-two of these are sheer repetition, a much larger proportion than in Rameau's other chaconnes.   There are, besides, humorous intentions in the rhythm of bars thirteen to fifteen, in the scratchy figure of bars forty-four and forty-six (ex. 242) which has parallels elsewhere in the opera, in the great leaps and in the general tendency to wander and waste time instead of progressing.   The deliberate absence of any sense of direction is obvious.

Another comic device is the use of emphatic counter-rhythms in the rigaudons of the prologue, in Platée's "Quittez, Nymphes" (I, 5) and in the *air pour les fous gais* (II, 5).

The same devices are used to spread the comedy over Platée's background and over the honours so ironically conferred on her. Thus, the witless repeated notes occur in the chorus of marsh nymphs calling to the clouds to rain down on them (I, 6).   The style of

solemn summons is parodied in Platée's call to her subjects the frogs,
whose arpeggio accompaniment recalls that of Theseus' "Puisque
Pluton" in *Hippolyte*, Act II (ex. 243). "Hymen, l'Amour t'appelle"

Ex. 243

(II, 5) might come from a temple scene; it is an example of the invocations to Love which abound in final *divertissements*, and is humorous
only through its context, for its music is splendid, with sumptuous
chains of ninths, and it contains none of the grosser devices mentioned (ex. 244).

The D minor loure in III, 5, is another piece whose strange beauty
might blind us to its satirical intent, in spite of the suggestion it contains of grotesque movements; it is "danced comically" by three of
Momus's followers disguised as Graces, while Folly excites them by
touching them with her lyre (ex. 245). Away from its setting it
appears as a rich, solid piece with a serious cast. (The "pantomime
niaise" in *Pygmalion*, Sc. 5, is another piece where the facetious intention is easily overlooked; its "niaiserie" is much less apparent than its
warm caressing tone.) In Clarine's solo "Soleil, fuis de ces lieux"
(I, 6) the charm veils a sarcastic temper and the only grotesque touch
is in the chromatic warblings on "naïades" (ex. 246).

The most obvious form of humour applied to Platée's entourage is
the imitation of animal noises, for which Rameau has exerted his
instrumental inventiveness to the utmost. Frogs, cuckoo, donkey,
small birds are all conjured up at one time or another by the music.
Platée's appeal to her frogs is met by a response reflected first in the
accompaniment to her solo "Que vos voix m'applaudissent", itself a
parody of a form common in serious opera,[1] and next in the chorus of
invisible singers that answers her. The wobbling strings represent
the mass response of the frogs, the flutes that of the cuckoos, while
part of the latter—another case of the counter-rhythm device—
adds to the lopsided effect (ex. 247). Musically, this chorus is
impressive; the imitation is stylized and in nowise grotesque. The

---

[1] For instance: "Que ce rivage retentisse" in *Hippolyte*, Act III.

Ex. 244

frogs give voice again when they echo Platée's indignant question to
Cithéron:

> Tu n'es qu'un perfide envers moi.
> Dis donc pourquoi?

The last syllable, pronounced "kwè" at this time, is taken up by the
chorus with opposing rhythms (ex. 248). The donkey has its brief
moment of lustre when the master of the gods borrows its humble
shape to pay court to the nymph (ex. 249). The burlesque is idealized by the beauty of the harmonic sequence.

The richest of these Nature murmurs is heard when the birds,
alarmed by the presence of the owl into which Jupiter has changed,
assemble as if to mob it. Rameau's resources here are confined to

violins and flageolets[1] with bass, yet with this meagre arsenal he suggests utter confusion, thanks to the cacophonous succession of octaves, fifths and sixths and to the contrast of rhythm between strings and flageolets (ex. 250).

Though clever, and unusual in Rameau, these passages are not what hold our attention longest in *Platée*. It is in the part of the heroine herself that the composer's devices for arousing mockery most repay examination.

There are certain interesting attempts to depict the nymph plas-

---

[1] Flageolets were used by trainers to teach birds to sing. See La Bruyère's bird collector: "Il donne pension à un homme qui n'a point d'autre ministère que de siffler des serins au flageolet et de faire couver des canaries" ((77), XIII: *De la Mode*).

Ex. 245

tous,   cri - ons   tous,   cri - ons   tous

Ex.248   *Gaiement*

Hbs.

Vns.   *doux*   *un peu fort*

Alt.
(Vas.)

Platée   (pour-)quoi, quoi, quoi,   Dis donc pour-quoi?

Quoi?   quoi? quoi?quoi?   quoi?

Quoi?   quoi?   quoi?

B.C.

Ex.249

tically, attempts unparalleled in Rameau in the field of characterization. Her awkwardness, her massive, mannish gait, her poverty of
self-expression, are vividly bodied forth in such pieces as her *ariette
badine* in I, 3, with its long descriptive prelude, and in the opening
bars of II, 3, where she is shown going up to the cloud which conceals
Jupiter and "considering it". The *ariette badine* is at once graceful

and grotesque, like heavy attempts at banter or an elephant trying to
be mincing. The middle section is superbly felicitous when the
violins reflect mockingly the flutterings of "Mon cœur, tu t'agites"
and the simpering demeanour, and evoke, or impose, the appropriate

Ex. 251

gestures (ex. 251). The rendering of ungainly movements is done
again in the loure of III, 5.

The *ariette badine* and the solo in II, 3, are ludicrous, moreover,
in that this unsentimental music is the vehicle for sentimental words,
such as:

> Que ce séjour est agréable
> Pour qui veut bien perdre sa liberté . . . (I, 3).

> Puis-je en être assez sûre
> Pour soupirer tout bas? (I, 5).

> Je crois qu'il me découvre
> Mon adorable amant (II, 3).

Let one imagine the kind of music to which these lines would be set
in a serious work; the difference with the setting in *Platée* is the
measure of the ridiculous effect these airs produce.   The second quotation is set to a motif of dropping fourths frequent in the opera but
generally associated with Folly and her chorus[1] (ex. 252).

Ex.252

Sometimes it is the contrary and the incongruity is caused by the
contrast between the lightsome music and the lumbering person of the
singer.[2]

A subtler form of ridicule consists in examples of inappropriate
emphasis.   By underlining a word or syllable which, in normal speech,
would never receive emphasis, or by distorting the natural melody of
the sentence, irresistibly funny effects are produced.   Instances are
numerous in Platée's part and in references to her by others.   In the
ariette badine a wrong emphasis is laid on "est, ag*ré*able, *ai*mable,
li*ber*té"; and the rhythm of "perdre sa liberté" is quite unsuitable.

An instance of wrong stress is introduced in the prolongation and
repetition of the descending notes in "Qu'elle est ai-ma-a-a-able" in
the chorus of Momus' followers "that surround Platée with amazement" in II, 4 (ex. 253).[3]   Platée's tremolo on the word "Terpsicho-
o-o-ore" in III, 5, shows the same trick, but the intention here is to
depict the naïve and shambling artlessness of her excitement.   When
(II, 3) she dwells on the little word "ou" in

> Mais aurai-je le courage
> De recevoir son hommage
> *Ou* de le refuser?

---

[1] Cf. "Honneur à la Folie" (II, 5); "Chantons Platée" (III, 8).

[2] Cf. "Pour un amant qui sait plaire" (I, 4).

[3] That Platée is not wholly taken in by this mock applause is evident
from the direction: "Platée est tantôt fâchee et tantôt aise selon ce que lui
dit ce chœur."

Ex.253

N.B. Instruments double the voices.

there is an ironic intention attributable to the singer herself which goes deeper than the surface grotesqueness of the preceding examples.

More often Rameau upsets the melodic line itself and sets a word

Ex.254

to the wrong pitch. The following instances show how insignificant syllables are thus thrown into irrelevant relief.

> Non, tu n'es qu'un perfide en*vers* moi (I, 4) (ex. 254).

(The line should drop regularly from "perfide" to "moi" or, if any word is to be emphasized, it should be "perfide" or "moi", not the unimportant "envers".)

> Mais ce dieu plein d'ardeur,
> *Pour* attaquer mon cœur
> Se fait longtemps attendre (I. 5) (ex. 255).

(In addition to the unsuitable melodic line and wrong emphasis on "pour", the vast skips give an exaggerated impression of the undertaking.)

Ex.255

Ex. 256

C'est pour mon divertissement
Que Jupiter emprunte une forme nouvelle (II, 3) (ex. 256).

(Unwanted emphasis on the insignificant "que", like a hiccup.)

Qu'elle *est* belle! (II, 4) (ex. 257).

Ex. 257

(The "est" should be on the same level as the "qu'elle"; another hiccup effect.)

Dans *cette* fête
Mon cœur s'apprête (III, 3) (ex. 258).

(The insignificant "cette" has received emphasis of both stress and pitch; it is "fê-" that should be emphasized.)

Ex. 258   *Mouvemt. de Menuet: légerèment*

The air whence this last quotation is taken has extremely prosaic lines, with other examples of wrong emphasis and inflexion. Note the comic detachment of "Pour mon bonheur" (with wrong inflexion), stressing Platée's childish self-centredness. "Et pour le vôtre" is set as if it was an afterthought with a comic portamento on "et". Note also the repetition and stressing of the silliest word in the stanza, "ou du moins". In

Le croirai-je, *beau* Mercure? (I, 6) (ex. 259)

Ex. 259

the word stressed is of slight importance and the hiccuping leap is an
exaggeration.   In all these examples it is Platée's awkwardness and
lack of control over gestures and voice which are conveyed except, of

Ex. 260

course, in the examples from the chorus "Qu'elle est aimable, qu'elle
est belle!" (II, 4).

A number of ridiculous *vocalises* add parody to the risible presentation of the nymph.   Sometimes the word chosen is normal and the
melisma grotesque: "tendre" (ex. 260), "adorable" (ex. 261); "lance"

Ex. 261

(ex. 262); "s'envole".   The sentiment in this last word is Platée's
disappointment when the owl flies out of sight; it is followed by the
bathetic "Je ne le vois plus" (ex. 263).

Sometimes it is the word itself which is unsuitable or the syllable
which carries the melisma; e.g. the unpoetic "inonder" in Platée's
"Quittez Nymphes" (I, 5), which is otherwise not comic and is a
beautiful piece of vocal concerto writing.

The primitive comic device of repeated notes occurs in the prosaic

Ex. 262

Ex. 263

music to which Platée's delight before the opening cloud is expressed:

> Le nuage s'entr'ouvre;
> Je vois du mouvement (II, 3),

and in her mock-terrible threat at the end:

> Je troublerai mon onde (III, 8) (ex. 264),

where the music reaches an almost tragic intensity anent a laughable theme, just as it did at the climax of *La Poule*.

Ex. 264

Only once, I think, is something deserving the name of wit found in Platée's part. Here the characterization goes deeper than the notation of gesture and posturing (ex. 265). In the shrug of the repeated "si froid" there is a critical detachment which quite dispels what pathetic effect there may have been in the complaint. The tone of the spoken voice is audible here. Platée herself is capable of mockery as we see in the far from ridiculous reply she makes to Momus in III, 4 ("Eh! fi! votre espérance").

Though Platée and the elaborate practical joke of which she is the victim are the chief sources of fun, and though for that reason the main character of that fun is a rather cruel derision, there are forms of

humour in the opera where the characters provoke laughter without
either pouring ridicule on others or appearing themselves ridiculous.
The whole of the prologue, for instance, comes into this category.   It
is a much more friendly affair than the comedy itself and is certainly
the most attractive and best constructed of all Rameau's prologues.
More independent than most, it survived in separate performance
when the opera itself had gone out of fashion.

A troop of satyrs, maenads and vine-harvesters is holding its
revels when one of them espies the poet Thespis sleeping off, we
gather, the effects of deep potations.   Thespis, whom tradition con-

Ex. 265

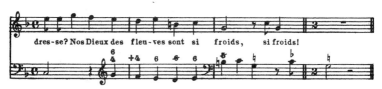

nects rather with tragedy, is here conceived as the inventor of comedy
and the owner of a biting wit—the inspirer, in fact, of tales like that of
Platée.   A lively chorus, in which the repeated-note motif is prominent, rouses him and claims a song.   He consents and sings in praise
of Bacchus an air which is the highlight of the prologue.   He then
turns to the maenads and throws suspicion on their fidelity to their
lovers.   The suspected damsels immediately seek to silence him and
beseech him to return to slumber.   Thereupon he addresses the
satyrs, throwing on them similar suspicions; they too seek to drown
his indiscretions with a "Rendormez-vous" chorus in which the
maenads join.[1]   Thalia, the muse of comedy, comes to reinforce his
satirical purpose but suggests, with Momus, who is by her side, that
he aim his shafts not at men but at gods.

> La raison dans l'Olympe est souvent hors d'usage.
>   Eh! qui pourrait résister à l'ennui
>   D'être immortel et toujours sage?

"Et toujours sage", he repeats with arch emphasis.   In this very spot,
he declares, Jupiter himself, unbending from his gravity, once cured

---

[1] The first of these three interruptions is unaccompanied; the second is
accompanied by the bass only; the third by all the strings.

his spouse of jealousy and pride; and he proposes to stage the adventure. This is spiced with sententious claims of "corrigere ridendo mores" in the style of seventeenth- and eighteenth-century dramatic critics. Love, whose appearance is inevitable in a prologue, claims to join the party and the act broadens out into the expected *divertissement* of chorus and dance.

Spirit and speed reign throughout this prologue, especially in the scene between Thespis and the forest dwellers. Nothing is slower than *modéré* and there is much variety of rhythm, especially in the *air*, pantomime and rigaudon; in the second of these occurs the chatter of repeated notes and, in both the last two, comic syncopations.   There

Ex.266

is merriment in the "Rendormez-vous" choruses, wit in the air in which Momus proposes to make fun of the gods, especially in the setting of "et toujours sage" (ex. 266).   The most remarkable piece is Thespis' air, extolling the benevolent influence of Bacchus and the permission he gives for satire.

> Aux dépens des mortels tu nous permets de rire.

It is a glorification of sarcastic laughter.

> Dans mes chansons je n'épargne personne.

The music renders this theme with the most *cocasse* clashes between violins and voice (ex. 267).

Not till the entry of Folly and her escort do we meet with this amiable and shaftless humour in the opera itself.   Up to this point (II, 5) the fun is founded wholly on mockery and on the contrast

between physical appearance and illusion, for Platée, like many comic
characters, wears a mask, figuratively speaking, and the comedy
consists largely in tearing it away.   With the arrival of Folly and her
crowd appears a fresh kind of humour, neither derisive nor grotesque;
it is nearer to wit, though still rooted in movement and expressed
through it.   What makes so weird the *symphonie extraordinaire* that

heralds her entry is the alternation and juxtaposition of totally different phrases and the use of harsh effects; it expresses incomplete dance measures, wild mirth and sadness, like the incoherent ramblings of an amiable madman.

Though very short the chorus of welcome "Honneur à la Folie" is one of the most bewitching moments in the whole opera.   If I was allowed to keep only three numbers from the work, this, with the minuets *dans le goût de vielle* and "Aux langueurs d'Apollon", would be one of them.   The interval of the fourth, so characteristic of *Platée*, is prominent in the tune.   The primitive nature of the har-

Ex.268

mony in the second half, the repeated notes and the bugle call, or rather *vielle* effects, give it a near-folksong twang which was already present, to a lesser degree, in the mocking "Le charmant objet que voilà! ah! ah! ah! ah! ah! ah!" heard just before Folly's entry.   Here, and in much of what follows, we find Rameau's powers of impressionism put to a new purpose.   As a standard of comparison I quote an air from Campra's *Les Fêtes vénitiennes* which belongs to the same type[1] (exs. 268 and 269).   It is intended to be grotesque but not mocking, and grotesqueness may well be the traditional character of this kind of air.   The interruption it suffers and its fragmentary but insistent returns resemble Rameau's chorus "Chantons Platée" in III, 8.

The newcomer is followed by two kinds of Fools, the merry,

Ex.269

Honneur, hon-neur à la Fo - li - e, Qui tient la ly - re d'A-pol-

Hbs.Bns.
Quat.
(Str.)

B.C.

---

[1] In the *entrée L'Amour saltimbanque*, Sc. 2: p. 87 of the Michaëlis vocal score.

-lon! Honneur, hon-neur à la Fo - li - e, Qui tient la   ly-re, la ly-re, la

ly - re, Qui tient la   ly - re d'A-pol - lon, Qui tient la   -lon!

dressed like children ("poupons"), the sad, like Greek philosophers. The *air* for the merry is of the high-jinks sort with a spidery outline. Typical counter-rhythms are present in it; they, too, are a hall-mark of the opera. Four bars of this music, as well as much of Folly's *symphonie*, had formed the introduction to the overture—an early instance of the practice of including in this piece portions of the work. The sad Fools are given little rope and are quickly interrupted by the merry ones. The figure of the dropping fourth or fifth is heard in the opening bars and the merry Fools' interruption has characteristic skips. The movement of their second intervention reflects a helter-skelter scattering (ex. 270).

Folly's great bravura air "Aux langueurs d'Apollon Daphné se refusa" is so absorbingly beautiful that one does not at first realize that it is intended as a comic piece and is partly a parody. It makes use of devices and effects whose object is primarily aesthetic, such as *coloratura* and giant leaps, to express a spirit of comedy. The humour no longer rebounds on the singer; it is deliberate. The element of parody is present in the misuse of *coloratura*, in the setting of *vocalises* to ridiculous words like "métamorphosa", or to sounds not usually set such as the "ou-" of "outragé". But the air is beautiful in its own right and precious for the expression of the spirit of

Ex.270

Folly—the consciously whimsical Fool, with the merest touch of the
buffoon, who infects us with his vigorous gaiety.   The 6/8 beat and
arpeggio accompaniment which savours of the jig, is more Italian than
French and the style is that of the *da capo aria*.[1]   The writing is in
concerto style, with spread-out harmonies, much figuration and a
strong dance rhythm.   Though Folly is not a dancer one can imagine
her leaping about the stage.   The whole piece is wiry, alert, highly
strung, constantly on pins, yet without the least sign of strain;
captivating in its resilience, it is one of Rameau's most easeful movements; its consummate self-mastery is in contrast to poor Platée's
shambling.   No opera expresses to this degree two opposite poles of
his talent for evoking character, and indeed "Aux langueurs d'Apollon" is the only one of his *ariettes* which is a characterization.

It is not, however, an individualization, the portrait of a Gilles or
an Arlequin, but an idealized representation of folly itself; it is therefore above and beyond mockery.   No victim is ridiculed; the play on
"métamorphosa" does not mock at Daphne's unfortunate transformation into a laurel.   It breathes the spirit of banter, wit and frolic; it is
true that there is an edge to its sporting and one feels that it could cut
if it chose, but in fact the blade is not unsheathed (exs. 271 to 274).

The *menuets dans le goût de vielle* are introduced by Folly's remark:

J'attriste l'allégresse même
Par mes sons plaintifs et dolents.

---

[1] Compare it with the Italian air "Fra le pupille", which Rameau wrote
for a revival of *Les Indes galantes*; the spirit is very similar (ex. 208).

Ex. 271

La Folie

Aux langueurs d'A-pol-lon ____ Daph-né se re-fu-sa, ____

Quat.
(Str.)

B.C.

Daph-né, Daph-né se-re-fu-sa.

Ex. 272

La Folie

la mé-ta-mor-pho-sa, ____

Ex. 273

Ex. 274

If, therefore, we find them heartrendingly nostalgic, we may rest
assured that this interpretation is not fanciful and that plaintive sorrow
is what they are meant to express. The fact that they are given as a
specimen of Folly's virtuosity and not as the expression of someone's
mood does not, of course, detract from their interest. We have already referred to them in speaking of pastoral music. Their intense
impressionism and power of evocation lie in their instrumental
associations and in their skeletal, strumming harmonies, like those in
"Honneur à la Folie". The harmonization remains unchanged for
bars on end (exs. 275 and 276).

Ex. 275

Ex.276

The *airs* that follow turn as frankly outwards as the minuets
turned inwards.   Poetry and "magic" again invade the music with
the invocation to Hymen.   A chorus, solid and straightforward as
music but ludicrous in words, closes this display and the second act.
Though the mock nuptials in Act III are an elaborate joke at
Platée's expense the music is not continuously derisive and much of it
has the disinterested bantering of Folly's pageant in Act II.   The
march and chorus which open the ceremony are diatonic, woodenly
but not grotesquely so.   They might illustrate a Spartan war triumph;
perhaps their austerity is humorously indicative of the small enjoyment
which the nymph is to derive from the festivity.   Platée's welcome
to Momus, "Puisqu'il vient pour moi tout exprès", has echoes of
"Honneur à la Folie" and her air "Fi! fi! votre espérance", deliberately
sarcastic, suggestive of nothing ridiculous in the singer, is a spritely
6/8 tune.   Folly next takes the stage with Momus and sings to him
the kind of "Amour, lance tes traits" air common in ballet opera.
Momus, in his disguise, "appears embarrassed" and the picture is
certainly farcical, but nothing comic transpires in the music, which is
developed out of the lyre-chord effects heard in the opening bars.
The piece is more instrumental than vocal, and one can imagine it as a
violin or even a harpsichord solo; its *coloratura* falls more readily to
the fingers than to the voice (ex. 277).   It is less extravagantly romp-
ing than "Aux langueurs d'Apollon" and also less characteristic.
Clearly Rameau knows better than to keep comedy to the fore in his
music the whole time.
Of the fine D minor loure I have already spoken.   The musette is
not comic but it lacks the convincing power of musettes in scenes
where the setting is genuinely pastoral and is meant to be taken
seriously.   The effects are there, not the soul.
Platée boasts four tambourins (prologue and Act III).   All four
are among the least melodic and least harmonically interesting in
Rameau; their appeal is wholly dynamic.
The final chorus, "Chantons Platée", is first heard as part of the

Ex. 277

nuptials. When, therefore, it returns after Platée's discomfiture it is ironic, yet there is nothing in the music that can be called mocking. It has the same vigorous rustic swing as "Honneur à la Folie", with the lilt of a forlana; it is racy and bucolic, with an aftertaste of folkishness, and is one of the most haunting tunes in the opera (ex. 278).

Ex. 278

Its 6/8 beat occurs more often in *Platée* than in any other Rameau work, a mark of the fact that the music of this *comédie lyrique* is more consistently choreographic than that of his other operas. The comic device of repeated notes in the couplet illustrates the "sautons tous" of the dancers and is not derisive.[1] The fun becomes bitter again only when, under the impact of Platée's interruptions, the refrain, which

---

[1] To put this piece beside Osmin's first air in *Die Entführung* is to perceive the essentially French quality of this latter; the link must be the later *opéra-comique*. There are hints of Osmin's air in Boismortier's cantata *Actéon*: "Quand le silence et le mystère" (*O.C.*, III, 168 ff.; published also by Jane Arger), and still more in Philippe Courbois's *Don Quichotte* (final air).

had been returning as remorselessly as "Hail the bridegroom, hail the bride" in *Ruddigore*, falls apart into separate pieces. And in the concluding duet between Platée and Cithéron it is the words "Qui, moi? —Oui, toi!" and not the music that underline the farce. This duet, the earliest example of its kind according to Masson,[1] breaks with the tradition of the simultaneous duet of serious and ballet operas and models itself closely on the rapid give-and-take of contradiction in real life, in which the speakers do not wait for each other to finish but are constantly tripping each other up (ex. 279). The underlying

Ex. 279

_____

[1] (190), 273.

rhythm is that of the "Chantons Platée" chorus that precedes it and returns mockingly afterwards.

The relation of key to character and mood is recognizable in *Platée*. F major is the favourite key for the heroine, and on one occasion its appearance is almost dramatic. The second act begins tamely with a conventional *ritournelle* in A major—a key used also for the heavy chaconne and nowhere else[1]—and continues with an explanatory soliloquy of Mercury. The uneventfulness of the music is not broken by Jupiter's descent in a chariot and subsequent immersion in a cloud. Then, suddenly, with Platée's appearance, we jump down into F major, a drop of four fifths, and into comedy. We are back on the ground; the effect is bathetic though startling. G minor is characteristic of Folly's company; Folly herself ranges over many keys but her best music—first solo, invocation, minuets and *airs vifs*—is in D major or minor. A minor, chosen for the highly individual overture and Folly's second solo, plays no great part in the rest.

I have mentioned most of the *symphonies*. There are two sets of passepieds; the best is the G minor dance of the first set which contains in its short span two of the opera's hall-marks: the dropping fourth or fifth and the wide skips (ex. 280).

Ex.280

The first act opens and closes with storms. The first is of no interest but the second is a remarkable piece of through-composed symphonic writing, savouring more of Mannheim in 1760 than of Paris twenty years earlier. The following through in the bars quoted shows that Rameau, at the age of sixty-two, was well aware of the direction which symphonic writing was taking. It is natural to

---

[1] Though once in the prologue.

Ex. 281

Hbs.

Bns.

Vns. 1 & 2

Alt. (Vas.)

B. C.

á 2 cordes

attribute this awareness to his experience of German music at La Pouplinière's house (ex. 281).

Always very generous with his marks, Rameau has been particularly so in *Platée*.   Unfortunately the vocal score omits many of them. Several indicate with preciseness the characters' movements or attitudes.   Others mark the expression that accompanies the music: "faisant l'agréable, en gracieusant, en pindarisant" (that is, "mincingly", altered in the vocal score to the commonplace "avec affectation"), "irritée des refus de Cithéron, le regardant tendrement, Platée interdite et tremblante, Platée marque une joie folle, à Momus en se moquant de lui, à Junon avec un sourire".   A few refer to the execution: "en coupant un peu les premières notes, filez en adoucissant", and especially "en glissant le même doigt et faisant sentir les deux

Ex. 282

quarts de ton du mi au fa" (ex. 282).   Examples from other operas comprise "en sentiment, ironique, avec toute la tendresse possible, très vif en peignant néanmoins le sentiment amoureux, adoucir toujours en mourant".   Rameau's manuscript parts are rich in dynamic and expressive annotations and prove how precise was his conception of the way his music should be played.

Lulli's earliest operas, *Cadmus* and *Alceste*, contained comic scenes mixed with serious or tragic ones.   Lulli had a great gift for comedy; he was a first-rate comic actor and his ballet music shows it.   But the mixture of comedy and tragedy was too alien to seventeenth-century taste for it to meet with approval even in a new and largely tradition-less genre like opera. Mythology and magnificence, not humour, were to be the realm of opera as the Académie Royale de Musique knew it. Comedy squeezed itself in here and there in a few ballet operas such as Campra's *Les Fêtes vénitiennes* (1710) and Mouret's *Les Fêtes de Thalie* (1714), but there are not more than half a dozen entirely comic operas earlier than *Platée*.[1] None of these works attains the high musical level of Rameau's work.

Jean-Philippe's *comédie lyrique* is therefore without a predecessor and is, indeed, unique, since the new genre of *opéra-comique* was to produce very different works. The librettist, Le Valois d'Orville, had used a libretto of Jacques Autreau, *Platée ou Junon jalouse*, as yet unpublished (it was to be included in the fourth, posthumous, volume of its author's plays in 1749). This had been written, so we are told in Pesselier's preface to the edition, as "a comic play in the style of Cariselli,[2] to be performed at Carnival time or during slack moments in the summer as a substitute for the selections which are made up of the flower of two good plays, which are thereby ruined".

Jacques Autreau, who was born at Paris, in the Cité, in 1657, was a painter who turned playwright, without deserting his former art, at the age of sixty. When the Italian comedians who had been banished nineteen years earlier returned to Paris in 1716 they found that their Italian repertory was unintelligible and their French one out of date. Autreau, who knew their leader Riccoboni, undertook to supply them with a play in French and produced in 1718 his *Le Port à l'Anglais*[3] *ou les Nouvelles débarquées*. This three-act comedy depicted the impressions made by French life on an Italian family lately arrived in France; as in the company's Italian plays the actors appeared under their real names, Lélio, Flaminia, Silvia. Autreau introduced into French drama this practice, which was to be followed by Marivaux. The play was a great success and it set the Italians on their feet. We owe to him the survival of Riccoboni's troupe and hence, at least indirectly, an important part of Marivaux's work. He died in 1745, aged

---

[1] The list is: Campra, *Le Carnaval de Venise* (1699); Destouches, *Le Carnaval et la Folie* (1704); La Barre, *La Vénitienne* (1705); Mouret, *Les Fêtes de Thalie* (1714) and *Le Mariage de Ragonde et de Colin ou La Veillée de village* (1714); the text of this last is by Néricault-Destouches; it was performed at the Duchess du Maine's "grandes nuits de Sceaux" and given at the Opéra in 1742 as *Les Amours de Ragonde*; Bodin de Boismortier, *Don Quichotte* (1743).

[2] "Cariselli, divertissement comique extrait des fragmens de M. de Lully, ajouté à *La Princesse d'Élide* le lundy 28 février 1729": words by Danchet, music adapted by Campra.

[3] The name of a landing-stage and an inn at Vitry-sur-Seine.

eighty-nine, a few months after the performance at Court of Rameau's setting of his text.[1]

The story is taken from Pausanias, but the original differs from Autreau's version in that Jupiter's mock love was only a wooden statue, manufactured on the advice of Kithaeron, king of the land where the future town of Plataea was to be built.   The statue is dressed up and passed off as Plataea, daughter of King Asopus, whom Jupiter is about to marry.   Juno arrives, tears off the bride's trappings, and forgives her spouse.   Autreau substituted the nymph for the statue.

Rameau had bought the rights of the play, which allowed him to modify it as he liked.   He engaged the services of d'Orville, who left unchanged the charming prologue, adding a chorus, and replaced a conversation between Jupiter and Platée in Act II by the scene of Jupiter's metamorphoses into cloud, ass and owl.   Juno's presence was cut down in Act II and her part altogether much reduced.   Folly is d'Orville's invention; so are the chorus of frogs and the mock nuptials.

Rameau's *ballet bouffon*, as it was first called, surpasses greatly the few humorous operas already in existence.   The orchestration is as important as in his serious works; the choruses quite as ambitious; Folly's invocation "Hymen" is followed by a seven-part ensemble—four-voice chorus and three soloists—which grows to eight when Platée joins in with her "bon! bon!"

The uniqueness and great musical importance of *Platée* should not, nevertheless, lead us to dwell on it at the expense of other works of its composer.   This would be like emphasizing *Les Plaideurs* and neglecting *Andromaque*.   It is a rich museum of his resources but the greatest Rameau is not there.   A work built on so heartless a theme and whose dramatic interest is drawn exclusively from this theme is bound, however consummate its artistry, to exert a very limited attraction.   It is too evidently the reflection of a society for whom a woman with an unprepossessing physique not only has no claim upon affection but is a legitimate butt for aggressive mockery.   We miss in it the warm geniality, the sombre passion, the caressing voluptuousness of his serious operas and ballets.   It is all spikes and prickles. Once we have admired the skill with which the musician has character-ized his conception of Platée—she is indeed one of his few characters who is a personality and not just a succession of situations—we have exhausted its appeal.   It is precisely in the sections in which this con-ception is most completely forgotten, like the wonderful Folly music of Act II and similar numbers in Act III, that the music becomes most captivating.   The latter part of Act II, in particular, from the entry of

---

[1] (226), 498.

Folly onward, is an inexhaustible source of a delight of which Platée's own part, the choruses of frogs and birds and the braying of donkeys, are bereft.   Folly's music, which presents itself, indeed, as a concert, a display of the protagonist's creative ability, "le chef d'œuvre de l'harmonie", is what comes nearest in the opera to pure music.

It is only there, in such an ensemble as the "Hymen" chorus and such a solo as "Aux langueurs d'Apollon", that music regains all her rights and banishes the inhuman data on which the story is based. There, indeed, we have music worthy to stand beside the loftiest passages in the three great *tragédies lyriques* and *Les Fêtes d'Hébé*.   Elsewhere, what is most admirable is the intense plasticity of the presentation.   For Platée is a character whose chief feature is her ungainliness. Moral traits she has none; the conception of her is above all physical. Rameau, always plastic, has here excelled himself in shaping a part whose every movement and gesture is delineated through the music he gives to it.   None of the serious operas is so devoid of sentiment, but none is so vividly physical.   Folly's music apart, this gives it an unusual degree of something which, for lack of a better term, I would call extroversion.   *Platée* has precisely the momentarily invigorating charm, the infectious vitality, the dynamism, and the capacity for rapid and utter boring, of the compleat extrovert.

When I open its pages it is to the rigaudons in the prologue that I turn, to Platée's *ariette* "Quittez, Nymphes", to the second storm, to the whole of II, 5, to Folly's *ariette* "Amour, lance tes traits", to the loure and "Chantons Platée"—precisely to those parts which are neither grotesque nor mocking, whose inspiration is most generalized and partakes most of the nature of pure music.

Incredible though it seems, this story of a mock marriage between an ugly woman and a god was first performed at Versailles, on March 31, 1745, for the wedding of the Dauphin Louis and Maria-Theresa of Spain, a lady reputed to have herself been uncomely.[1]   That anyone should have been obtuse enough to select such an entertainment for such an occasion passes all understanding.[2]   Only one performance was given and no attention seems to have been paid to the work. In 1749, with a few changes,[3] it was performed at the Opéra and met

---

[1] "Cette princesse me fit à la première vue l'effet d'une figure de marbre dont le statuaire aurait manqué les proportions" (quoted by Malherbe, *O.C.*, XI, ix, from a contemporary memoir which he does not specify).   She died the following year.

[2] The festivities comprised seven works, the first of which was Voltaire's comedy, *La Princesse de Navarre*, with incidental music by Rameau, and the last *Platée*.

[3] Such as new passepieds for I, 6, less grotesque and more melodious than the first.

with some success, as Rameau pointed out at length and with acerbity in his *Lettre à M. Rémond de Sainte-Albine*,[1] to put right someone who had written in the *Journal des Savants* that it was the only work of its author, that is, Autreau, which had been staged and that it had not succeeded, "although it had been set by M. Rameau". The part of Folly was taken both times by Mlle Fél; Platée, a man's part, by Jélyotte at the court and La Tour at the Opéra. The number of performances shows a certain success but there are few references to it. Rémond de Sainte-Albine and Collé both censured the libretto severely, though the latter wrote later, in 1760, that *Platée* contained the most striking, the finest and strongest music Rameau had written. It was revived in 1754 in opposition to Leo's *I Viaggiatori* and the *Mercure* commented on it in praisefullest terms, saying that "les connaisseurs le regardent comme le chef d'œuvre de M. Rameau. . . . Le prologue . . . est le plus agréable et le plus gai que nous ayons", though an anonymous newswriter said it appeared "tasteless and frigid" after Leo's *opera buffa* and the theatre was almost empty.[2] The enemies of traditional French music, the Rousseaus, Grimms and d'Holbachs, all praised it highly. Grimm, in his *Lettre sur Omphale* (1752), the very year in which *La Serva padrona* was to be given in Paris, declared: "I arrive in Paris as prejudiced against your opera as all foreigners are; . . . to my great surprise I hear a sublime work,[3] *Platée*, then a ravishing ballet, *Pygmalion*." To which Rousseau answered: "Call it divine; . . . never repent of having considered it as M. Rameau's masterpiece and the most excellent piece of music that has been heard as yet upon our stage."[4] D'Alembert was to dub it "son chef d'œuvre et celui de la musique française",[5] and d'Holbach, writing three months after the arrival of the Italian *buffoni* in 1752, looked upon the "innovator" Rameau as their forerunner. "The fatal event with which *Platée*, that terrible phenomenon, threatened us has happened at last. The Frenchman has forsaken the music of his fathers."[6]

The reasons for the favour found with the foes of *tragédie lyrique* are clear. Three years before the performance in Paris of Pergolese's trifle Rameau had created there the form of "humorous imitation"[7] and made straight the way for the revelation of Italian *opera buffa*.

---

[1] *Mercure de France*, July 1749; 116–118.   [2] (210), 568.

[3] "As Molière can be in his own genre as well as Corneille," he explains a little further on.

[4] (101).

[5] (29), 388. "He gave it an originality neither Italian nor French, though related to both" ((32), 177).

[6] *Lettre à une dame d'un certain âge sur l'état présent de l'Opéra.*

[7] (150), 87.

The favour which the *philosophes* show for *Platée* is explained largely by its naturalness and vivacity of expression which were not present in the same degree in the somewhat conventional nobility of French grand opera.[1]

D'Alembert suggests that it may have paved the way for the success of the Italians in 1752. "Who knows whether *La Serva padrona* would have pleased so greatly if *Platée* had not accustomed us to that kind of music?"[2]

Rameau was no doubt himself aware of this. He felt the influence, man of sixty-odd though he was, of the new Italian music, so different from that of 1700, which may be symbolized by Pergolese as the earlier was by Alessandro Scarlatti. Some of his *ariettes*[3] are soft and rounded like those of the second Neapolitan school. Daphnis' "Oiseaux, chantez" in *Daphnis et Églé*, Scene 6 (1753), is close to the late rococo of Louis XVI.[4] Maret tells us of his admiration for the new *opera buffa*-inspired *opéra comique*, in particular for Dauvergne's *Les Troqueurs*. "Forecasting the degree of perfection to which this genre might in the long run be brought, he pondered with emotion on the progress which the taste for this kind of opera would cause good music to make."[5]

"If I were thirty years younger", he is alleged by Grétry to have said to Arnaud, "I would go to Italy and Pergolese would be my model. But when one has turned sixty one must stay as one is."

Platée's last performance in the eighteenth century was in 1759. After that date the prologue was given from time to time, mixed with other "fragments", till 1773. "Thenceforward", says Charles Malherbe wittily,[6]

it is no longer on the stage but on paper, in the pages of registers, that one finds material traces of our opera. Thus, in an inventory of March 30, 1767, we read:

The flat of Marseilles harbour . . . one of gardens, one of reeds in *Platée*.

Two altars in relief . . . the crown of the chandelier of the mosque in *Scanderbeg*, the chandelier in *Anacréon*; a sun of wire and golden gauze; three pieces representing soldiers' heads and pikes in *Alceste*; Iris's machine in the ballet of *Les Sens*; a flying dragon in *Amadis*, the owl in *Platée*: estimated 80 livres.

One finds the same objects, reeds and owl, in inventories from 1768 to 1771 and the owl still figures in 1780. Thus at the Opéra, by a

---

[1] (190), 61.   [2] (32), 178.
[3] Such as Emilie's "Régnez, Amours", in *Les Indes galantes*, I, 6; Pygmalion's "Règne, Amour", in *Pygmalion*, Sc. 5.
[4] (190), 87.   [5] (85), note 48.   [6] *O.C.*, XII, xxxvi–xxxvii.

strange irony of fate, within the murk of the storeroom, among so much worthless and almost nameless jetsam, an owl alone remained to recall the ancient memory and vanished glory of *Platée*.

Platée was not performed again till 1901. In this year it was given at Munich in German. The music had been adapted by Hans Schilling-Ziemssen, the libretto by Felix Schlagintweit; their edition was published the following year. The parts of Folly and Momus were cut out and "contrapuntal enrichments" inflicted on the score. One shudders to think of the result!

It was given in French at Monte-Carlo in 1917 and at Como and Milan, in Italy, in January 1921[1] and at the Aix-en-Provence Music Festival in July 1956.

Rameau returned to *comédie lyrique* in 1760 at the age of seventy-six with a libretto by Monticourt, in comparison with whom, said Collé, "the late Cahusac was a Quinault".[2] Monticourt took the subject of *Les Paladins* from a La Fontaine *conte*, itself based on Ariosto, but he padded and transmogrified it with incidents of his own invention. The impossibly intricate plot is laid in mediaeval Venetia and contains a castle; a captive damsel with a watchful, cowardly and risible jailer, Orcan; a *paladin* disguised as a pilgrim; a fairy (a male part); a faithful soubrette; mock demons and furies; magic; a palace in Chinese style; dancing pagodas, that is, living statues (as in Quinault and Lulli's *Cadmus et Hermione*); and other embellishments, spun out to three acts.

All the characters are comic: some, like Orcan and Anselme, the jealous guardian, unconsciously so; others, like Nérine the soubrette, Argìe, Atis the lover, and the mock pilgrims, intentionally. Much of the humour is contained in the scenes of mock love in which Nérine seeks to beguile the jailer. The old device of inappropriate *vocalises* is used, as in her "L'Amant peu sensible" (I, 1), in her "L'Amour auprès de toi nous paraîtra moins beau, ♪♪ moins beau, ♪♪ moins beau" (I, 3) and her declaration in II, 7. With Orcan, the likeness to *Platée* is close since he, like the ugly nymph, is the butt and not the source of the derision (I, 3). The heroine herself, captive though she be, indulges in this sport, as in "Est-il beau? beau comme le jour?" and "Un instant de félicité est toujours bon, bon, bon à prendre" (I, 4). The aged tutor Anselme is given a ridiculous love monlogue (II, 1) and Orcan (II, 6) sings a would-be tragic air, a parody that outstays its welcome. Most of this buffoonery ceases after the middle of Act II when the arrival of the pseudo-demons and furies shifts the source of interest. An echo of the Franco-Italian *buffo* war is heard in I, 5 where

---

[1] (178), 103. [2] (56), II, 211.

an *air un peu gai à la française* is followed by a mocking *duo amoroso* in the Italian style.

Many of the *symphonies* are as good as ever, and thanks to the Oiseau-Lyre, several are now accessible in print and in recordings. A lively loure (III, 4) was used again in the 1764 revival of *Naïs* and, transposed from C to D minor, will be found in the appendix of *O.C.*, XVIII. The gavottes in C in Act II come from *La Naissance d'Osiris*, where they are in D. The final dance is a *contredanse en musette* in 6/8.

Les Paladins was a flop and was criticized by all. The *Mercure* summed up the criticisms in its *Essai d'éloge historique de feu M. Rameau* when it spoke of "les plaisanteries d'un comique trop chargé". Others had spoken more severely at the time. Only Decroix did his best to defend it. The opera held the stage at intervals between February 10 and March 20, 1760, after which no more was heard of it till June 1967 when, thanks to the enlightened enthusiasm of Renée Viollier, who had already achieved the revival of *Platée*, it was given a triumphant resurrection at the Lyons festival.

In this incredibly juvenile production of his old age, the septuagenarian passes with astonishing ease from the tender to the burlesque. In 1760 the ancient reproach of mingling seriousness and comedy was made against it. In this it was some twenty or thirty years too early, and the *opéra comique* of Grétry and Sedaine, not to mention that of Offenbach a hundred years later, was to achieve the same mixture. Rameau parodies *tragedie en musique* and *bel canto*. What was most admired at Lyons was his "unceasing verve, with a melodic invention and an art of modulation full of surprises, ironic, quick, lively and whimsical".[1] The return to life of this unique little masterpiece is the most sensational single result of the Rameau revival which has been stimulated by his centenary.

---

[1] Claude Rostand in *Le Figaro littéraire*, July 2, 1967.

12. *Minor Works*

I AM calling "minor" all those works of Rameau not already studied. Some I term thus because they are short, some because they are of less artistic interest, some for both these reasons. They include one *comédie-ballet*, four *pastorales héroïques*, four three-act and eight one-act *opéras-ballets*, and through these I purpose to take the reader on a conducted tour at Transatlantic speed.

The *comédie-ballet* is *La Princesse de Navarre*, the second of the three works born of the collaboration of his genius with that of Voltaire. Here their shares are unequal, for Rameau had merely to write the incidental music for a "heroic" play set in mediaeval Spain and providing a mixture of comedy and transparent allusions to the occasion for which it was written—the wedding of the Dauphin with his first wife, the infanta Maria-Theresa. It was given on February 23, 1745 in the Grande Écurie at Versailles, turned for the nonce into a theatre, and was the first event in the long series of entertainments of which *Platée* was the last.

It was the Duc de Richelieu who, as first gentleman of the chamber, had to organize the festivities, and the kind of play which Voltaire was to write seems to have been his choice; it was certainly he who insisted on Rameau being called in. His links with that ardent "Ramiste", Mme de La Pouplinière, are well-known and her favourite musician benefited from them.

The writing of the comedy took from April 1744 to January 1745. The worry it caused its author can be seen in his letters. Richelieu had pronounced views, mostly negative, it seems, and as with *Samson* a number of more or less competent and self-appointed advisers were always chipping in. Only the importance of the occasion made Voltaire keep his patience. His collaboration with Rameau began when the play was nearly finished. For merely incidental music Voltaire would have been content with a lesser light; he would have preferred, in fact, "les petits violons" (probably Rebel and Francœur), but Richelieu would have none of them.[1] For so slight a work Rameau's conceptions were too grand; "this music continually interlacing with

---

[1] Letter of President Hénault to d'Argenson, July 9, 1744, written after a visit to Cirey.

the actors' declamation is a new *genre* for which great instrumental pilings up are unsuitable", groaned the playwright.   Cannot Richelieu be made to understand this?   Let him compensate Rameau by reserving him for some completely musical work—a suggestion which perhaps gave rise to the order for *Platée*.[1]

But Rameau did not confine himself to "piling up" *symphonies*. As with everything he put to music, he set himself up as "a wit and a critic" and began correcting Voltaire's verse, to President Hénault's indignation.   "This madman is counselled by the whole rabble of poets"—meaning no doubt the gay spirits of the Caveau.   Hénault wrote twice to Richelieu about this scandal.[2]

"This weird Rameau . . . poor Rameau is mad . . . Rameau is as great an eccentric as he is a musician . . ."—these remarks occur more than once in Voltaire's letters.   He was exasperated and yet forbearing "for after all the man who composed *Les Incas* has the right to be mad".

The worst was that Rameau demanded that Voltaire "should put into four lines what is in eight and into eight what is in four. . . .   If M. de Richelieu does not have him severely spoken to I begin to tremble for the celebrations".[3]   But a month later things had improved: "Rameau is at work . . .".[4]

The music is made up of an overture and three *divertissements*.   Of the overture I have already spoken.[5]   The *divertissements* contain much beautiful music; Rameau, at sixty-one, was at the height of his powers and almost everything he was producing was first-rate. The scenario allowed no scope for drama, but in some of the vocal numbers he has squeezed to the utmost from his text the sentiment implicit in it—in the beseeching chorus "Dieux ennemis" in A minor (I, 6), in the soothsayer's erotico-hortatory air "Jeune Beauté" and in the mocking duet "En mariage un sort heureux" (id.) which shows him in *opéra-comique* vein.   The G minor *ariette* in II, 11, "Vents furieux", is worthy of a *tragédie lyrique*; it has a sumptuous violin part with concerto-like passages that outdo the voice in brilliance.   A short chattering chorus in the final *divertissement*, "Disparaissez, tombez"—an injunction addressed to the Pyrenees—is a crowd effect that reminds us from afar of Bach's mobs.

La Princesse de Navarre affords a rich harvest of dance symphonies many of which Rameau rescued and used again.   Among them I would "recommend" the minuets in E, in I, 6, especially the minor

---

[1] Letter to d'Argental, July 11, 1744.
[2] Letter to d'Argenson, July 9, 1744.
[3] Letter of Voltaire to Hénault, September 14, 1744.
[4] Letter of Voltaire to Hénault, October 6, 1744.
[5] Page 297.

which, scored for bassoons, 'cellos and basses, with hautboys in the
second half, begins like the G minor minuet for harpsichord but forks
off cheekily just as we are beginning to recognize it.   The entry of
the Graces in II, 11 is marked by a good saraband, a vocal trio for
soprano and a gavotte in C minor, used again in the ill-fated *Linus*;
from this *divertissement*, too, comes the first of the entrancing G minor
gavottes in *Zoroastre*, I, 3.

The concluding rejoicings comprise a lengthy chaconne, varie-
gated with chorus and duet.   Good, but not excellent, Rameau, it was
deemed worthy of preservation by its composer who kept it, transposed from D to C, in the first *entrée* of *Les Fêtes de Polymnie*.   The
rarest things here are the five tambourins, all of them first-rate; one
of them wastes quite a part of its short life in finding its key (ex. 283).

Ex. 283

Les Fêtes de Polymnie (October 1745) and *Les Fêtes de l'Hymen
et de l'Amour* (March 1747) are both *opéras-ballets* in three *entrées*, the
first fruits of Rameau's collaboration with Cahusac.   The former
keeps almost consistently just below the level of good Rameau, rising
very occasionally to the surface of his best work.   The opening of the
overture is probably its most original moment.   The fast section is
interesting in that it proves how unwedded Rameau was to a narrow
Lullian tradition; it is thoroughly modern and its empty, noisy cadences and tonic-dominant reiterations carry us into a world of Italian
overtures and German *galant* symphonies and sound surprising in a
contemporary of Handel and Bach.   The best numbers in this opera
can all be paralleled, and bettered, elsewhere; much in it sounds like
feebler versions, or echoes, of fine pieces in earlier works.[1]   Worthy,

---

[1] Thus, Stratonice's air in II, 4, is like "Cruelle mère des Amours" with
the edge blunted and the bitterness watered down.   In fairness to Rameau,
however, I should say that Masson's opinion is more favourable.

were there space, of more than "brief mention" are the minuets in I, 4, the second of which comes from the *Pièces en trio*, the exciting prelude to Act III, like a fragment from a Bach concerto, and the fleeting instant during which Argélie contemplates her lover sleeping, from which I cull these bars (ex. 284).

Les Fêtes de l'Hymen et de l'Amour is scarcely more interesting. It was already composed and destined to appear as *Les Dieux de l'Égypte* when an entertainment was ordered for the Dauphin's second wedding,[1] so it was used for this purpose with a special topical prologue and given at Versailles in March 1747.

The first *entrée*, *Osiris*, attempts a musical contrast between the rough Amazons and the refined Osiris, like that which Gluck drew between Spartans and Phrygians in *Paris and Helen*; its most interesting pieces are a saraband in G minor (Sc. 5) and a spikily scored *contredanse* (Sc. 7; ex. 285). The two highlights are in the second

---

[1] To Maria-Josepha of Saxony, the mother of the future kings Louis XVI, Louis XVIII and Charles X.

entrée. One appeals by its quality; the other by its volume. The first is Memphis' poignant air "Veille, Amour", in Sc. 3—the one personal utterance in the whole opera; for the short space of her air this character becomes a living being. The second is a curiosity; a ten-part double chorus that accompanies the overflowing of the Nile (Sc. 5). It is a majestic example of the chorus with soloists the development of which was one of Rameau's innovations. The origin of this form is in the motet; before Rameau, the only example of any size in drama was in Montéclair's "Tout tremble devant le Seigneur", in *Jephté* (1732), which had much impressed him. The two protagonists are the god Canopus and his following, and his high priest with the worshippers. Canopus, offended by the offering of a human sacrifice, causes the Nile to rise in flood. The god is seated in a chariot drawn by crocodiles and, in this amphibian vehicle, rides the cataract, plunges into the river and emerges on the further bank. He sings, while engaged in this exploit,

> Impétueux torrents,
> D'un dieu vengeur signalez la colère!

The terrified devotees supplicate:

> Quels débordements!
> Écoute nos gémissements!

The music reproduces the downward sweep of the god upon the wave and the panting exclamations of the crowd. The moment has to be

Ex. 286

short since the crossing of the river cannot last long, and the chorus has only thirty bars. It is good spectacle but musically not very interesting in spite of its complexity (ex. 286). The *entrée* ends with a dull chaconne of immense length.

The first *ballet figuré* has more value, especially a saraband in G minor and a musette, "Ma bergère fuyait l'Amour", which is among the best examples of Rameau's pastoral pieces.

The recitative is as good as the uninspiring text allows, and distinctly melodic, and there is an instance in III, 4, of that full accompaniment which pleases us and so offended his Lullist or Italianate contemporaries (ex. 287). As usual, many of the set dances are full of charm.

Le Temple de la Gloire, the second fruit of Rameau's collaboration with Voltaire, was ordered as part of the official celebration of the victory of Fontenoy. It was first given at Versailles in November 1745—the same year as *La Princesse de Navarre*, *Platée* and *Les Fêtes de Polymnie*—in the Grande Écurie and in December and January at the Opéra. Voltaire declined any retribution and left his share to Rameau. The original five acts were condensed into three with a prologue. Three heroes illustrate the whims of glory: Belus, Bacchus and Trajan. The Roman emperor is a thin disguise for Louis XV, whom Glory had just crowned at Fontenoy. Voltaire was then in the midst of his career as a courtier and, though its authenticity is very doubtful, the story of his anxious inquiry: "Trajan est-il

Ex. 287

content?" is in keeping.   A more authentic remark is Abbé de
Voisenon's reply to the author's inquiry whether he had seen the
Temple of "la Gloire".   "I called," he said, "but she was not at home.
I left my name."

The Italianate overture, in three sections, ABA, is an extension of
the opening fanfare and is no doubt intended to be triumphal.   The
prologue begins with the most majestic piece in the whole opera,
Envy's air "Profonds abîmes du Ténare", one of the pieces which
merited the commendation of Diderot-"neveu" (ex. 288).   It is
interesting to compare this with the Jealousy chorus in Handel's
Hercules, II.   The *air pour les démons* and *air vif* that follow are worthy

Ex. 288   *Gravement*

of its proximity. The *air vif* leads into a delicious *air tendre* for flute
solo and pizzicato string accompaniment, where we recognize *La
Cupis* from the *Pièces en trio* (ex. 289; in the repeat a second flute part
is added).

The richest music is in the pastoral sequence of the first act to
which I drew attention in Chapter X.[1]   Its occasion is the ferocious

Ex. 289

[1] Pp. 389, 394, 395, 397.

Belus' visit to the Temple of Glory, guarded by shepherds whose mildness disarms the bloodthirsty tyrant and converts him to the practice of justice and mercy. It consists in a musette, two *airs* in G major and minor, two minuets, and a couple of gavottes. In the second act a solemn loure in D would deserve to stand beside them in a pastoral suite drawn from this work, and for the 1746 performances a pensive entr'acte in the same climate of feeling was placed between the first and second acts. The third act, which opens with an appealing love solo, "Reviens, divin Trajan", contains a disappointing chaconne with chorus and solo and two "celebrated" gavottes, doubtfully perpetuated in piano anthologies, the first of which was quoted by Mozart in an early symphony.[1]

Les Surprises de l'Amour was ordered for the Théâtre des Petits Appartements at Versailles and acted there in November 1748. It consisted then in a prologue in honour of the peace of Aix-la-Chapelle, *Le Retour d'Astrée*, and two acts, *La Lyre enchantée* and *Adonis*. Nine years later, in May 1757, it was given at the Opéra, without the prologue and with the addition of a third act, *Anacréon*. The text was by Rameau's old collaborator, Gentil-Bernard.

While most of the dances are good, the two outstanding pieces are a chorus and a *symphonie de sommeil*. The chorus of Cyclops has a vigour worthy of its theme, though nothing except the key resembles Rameau's youthful harpsichord piece on the same subject (ex. 290). Anacreon's sleep, in the act added in 1757, owes nothing to the various slumbers that Rameau had set in the past and renews the well-worn theme (ex. 291).

The *pastorales héroïques*, as a category, come for musical interest

Ex. 290 *Vif*

---

[1] K.76 in F, finale.

at once after the best *tragédies*, *opéras-ballets* and *Platée*. *Zaïs* has an independent origin; *Naïs* and *Acante et Céphise* were command pieces; *Daphnis et Églé*, ordered for a Court performance at Fontainebleau, is in one act and I will consider it with the other short pieces.

Zaïs has a story of elemental beings, one of whom, the hero, loves a shepherdess and has assumed the pastoral disguise the better to be loved in return. Much of the four acts consists in the tests to which the sceptical genie puts his loved one's fidelity. She emerges triumphant, and un-irritated, from all of them, and after a final trifling episode, involving the collapse of a magic palace, they are united.

Cahusac has brought in his usual prescription of *féerie* and *pastorale*, and the musician's inspiration has been best stimulated by these drugs. The overture, as we know, describes chaos. In the opera

Ex. 291

itself the interest is overwhelmingly in the pastoral sequences of the first and fourth acts, of which I have already spoken. Delightful suites could be made out of a choice of these pieces, and of similar ones in *Le Temple de la Gloire*, *Naïs* and elsewhere.

The standard of the dances is very high and the list of first-rate gavottes, minuets and sarabands would be long. The almost symphonic *ballet de la légèreté et de l'inconstance* in III, 4, is one of Rameau's comparatively rare 12/8 movements. Curving scales and bounding arpeggios chase each other through violins or flute or imitate each other's gambols, without it being possible to discriminate between inconstancy and levity. Through the chorus broken by solos that follows, and through the *ariette* "Dans nos feux", echoes of the motifs persist and give unity to the whole sequence. This, too, would make a charming concert piece; it would be as well, for performance, to round it off by repeating the ballet after the *ariette*.[1]

The vocal numbers are less arresting. Yet one of them is exceedingly beautiful and contains one of Rameau's most pungent "foreshortened" harmonies.[2] The much-tested and ever patient Zélidie bewails her lover's feigned treachery and the music suggests a stylized imitation of sobs and sighs (ex. 292), with cruel little *appoggiaturas*. The air is *da capo* and the middle section closes in D minor. This is how the return is effected (ex. 293).[3] Did one evaluate music by the unit I would say that these bars were the most precious in all Rameau, and the third of them the costliest of the five. But let us not hyper-

---

[1] *O.C.*, XVI, 289–304.   [2] III, 2.

[3] In this terse transition is there not a parallel, in the same emotional field, with the economy of a Racine?

bolize. We will end, rather, on Masson's sober summing up:

> C'est ce mélange de grandiose, de gracieux et de touchant, dans une œuvre de demi-caractère, qui fait encore pour nous le charme particulier de *Zaïs*.[1]

Naïs was an *œuvre de circonstance*, ordered to celebrate the peace of Aix-la-Chapelle, but it was not ready to be played till one year after the treaty had been signed. The prologue contains allusions to the war of the Austrian Succession and the unwise generosity of the French.

> Jupiter is seen in it, with his thunderbolt, surrounded by his gods and smiting the giants; he is Louis XV, by your leave; but do not worry; you will see George the Second, represented by Neptune and sharing the Universe with his brother.[2]

The prologue, as we know, stages the storming of Olympus by the Titans, vividly described in the overture and first chorus; their defeat, and the "sharing" of empire with Neptune and Pluto.

The opera, which is in three acts, relates the story of the loves of Neptune and the nymph Naïs, daughter of the blind seer Tiresias, whom he courts *incognito*, triumphing over a king and a shepherd; he carries her off under the wave where, in a submarine palace, the sea gods welcome his return, brided, with song and dance.

The plot is less substantial than in *Zaïs*, but opportunities for spectacular and evocative art are many and the work contains some of Rameau's choicest music in these veins. The Isthmian Games in Act I, the shepherd festivities in Act II have inspired him particularly happily, and the chorus of sea divinities in Act III, "Coulez, ondes", is one of his loveliest (ex. 234). The pastoral sequence in Act II, like that in *Zaïs*, should be exploited by arrangers and transcribers; the music here is as poignant as when it was new—perhaps more so, because it is enhanced by unfamiliarity—and needs no sense of history to go straight to the heart. I have spoken of the overture in Chapter VIII and of this shepherd music and "Coulez, ondes" chorus in Chapter X. But there are other beauties.

Ex. 294

---

[1] (190), 54.
[2] Clément, *Les cinq années littéraires*, I, 214, May 20, 1749; in (190), 54, note.

The prologue contains two rigaudons, the first of which is *parodied* in an unusual manner; instead of taking up the dance tune, the chorus overlays it with a slow chant in semibreves while the orchestra repeats its lively strains. The second rigaudon has a familar outline (ex. 294); it is the original, or one of the originals, of an episode in the rondeau of Mozart's violin concerto in A.[1]

Naïs, like *Zaïs*, is a work of *demi-caractère* and does not exclude comedy. Neptune's light-hearted air in II, 1, "Je ne suis plus ce dieu volage" is set in almost *buffo* spirit and its opening recalls "Prenderò quel brunettino" of *Cosi fan tutte*. This act contains a remarkable chaconne to accompany the Isthmian Games. It is described in the text as "ballet figuré: dispute du prix de la lutte, du ceste et de la course". Its episodes include a quadrille of Greek girls who vie with one another in the race and one in which an athlete competes a second time; "none dare contest with him; he dances a second entry and Naïs crowns him". Musically the best part is the minor section; the rest is too long and too closely wedded to the action to stand alone as pure music.

The second act contains another humorous air to unpromising words:

> Les ennuis de l'incertitude
> Sont le supplice le plus rude
> Des tendres amants,

which Rameau has adapted to a witty line (ex. 295). The third brings a good battle chorus, unexpected in so light a play, "Allumez-vous, rapides feux!", with marching quavers and semiquaver scales in the accompaniment. It is in five real parts and, when Neptune and Naïs join in, seven.

When the stage has been transferred under water the local deities, "sous des déguisements agréables" and led by Proteus, engage in an extraordinary dance,[2] whose character reflects their leader's nature; it is full of twists and turns, distorted rhythms and alternations between *pizzicato* stopping and bowing.

Neither *Zaïs* nor *Naïs* is stageable but entertaining concert versions could be made out of parts of them. . It is sad to see so much lovely music, that shrieks to be allowed out, lying immured in Volumes XVI and XVIII of the *Œuvres complètes*.

The captivity of *Acante et Céphise* is even straiter since its only

---

[1] It had been used in his ballet music for Noverre's *Le gelosie del Seraglio* (K.Anh. 109 and K.E. 135 A), where it occurs twice; the ballet was intended to accompany *Lucio Silla* (Milan, December 1772). Saint-Foix calls it Hungarian; Einstein ((145), 207) says it is meant *alla turca*; in Rameau it can hardly be either!

[2] *Air gai*, III, 5.

Ex.295

edition is that of 1751, which as usual omits the middle parts. Two dance suites have been published by Roger Desormières, who has conducted performances of the overture and most of the dances. It, too, was an occasional work, ordered for the birth of the Duke of Burgundy, eldest son of the Dauphin and elder brother of Louis XVI, Louis XVIII and Charles X. Marmontel, the librettist, congratulated himself on having worked this happy event into the plot instead of merely referring to it in the prologue. The subject is the love of a shepherd and a shepherdess, crossed by a wicked genie and saved by a good fairy. The day of their deliverance, which had been foretold, is that of the royal birth, which the chorus acclaims:

> Triomphe, victoire! Un Bourbon voit le jour.
> Rendons grâce à l'Amour!

and

> Un Bourbon qui reçoit le jour
> Est un astre qui luit pour le bonheur du monde.

The ending sounds bathetic but the story is more dramatic than those of *Naïs* and *Zaïs*.

Of the ultra-occasional overture I have spoken in Chapter VIII. The opera as a whole is more varied and goes deeper than the subject would suggest. The presence of the genie is dramatically an advantage, and Rameau has put into his part more than a touch of the evil he had rendered in Abramane. Indeed, the scenes of terror and persecution recall similar ones in *Zoroastre*. The third act opens with a passionate *symphonie* in G minor, nearly thirty bars long, during which, "dans un désert affreux", the north winds (Aquilons) chain the lovers to rocks.   Before it is over a chorus of the genie's henchmen sing "Tremblez" and threaten inconceivable torments.   This climate is maintained throughout the next scene, as the genie contributes in person to the sufferings of the innocent couple; contrast is given to the pervading *Schrecklichkeit* by their laments, which take shape at one moment in an affecting duet recalling the "Frappez!" duet of *Dardanus* (ex. 296).   Solos—the genie—, duets and chorus intertwine in this

Ex. 296

scene with great *souplesse*; in the breaking down of the divisions between the different combinations we feel the neighbourhood of *Zoroastre*.   There is a great difference between a scene like this and one in the first act (I, 7), on one hand, and the stiff unanimous, contra-dictory or divergent trios of older practice, still found in *Hippolyte* and *Castor*, on the other.   This progress in dramatic ensemble writing is the most striking feature of the *pastorale*.

The range of emotion is much greater than in *Zaïs* and *Naïs*. The warning that the heroes are to pass through tribulation to a joy which will be announced by a sign holds an almost religious signifi-cance of which, to be sure, neither Marmontel nor Rameau was aware; but it enabled the musician to use the mediocre text to build a structure of emotional contrasts.   Beginning in a tranquil, slightly elegiac mood, we pass, with a halt on a stage of splendour—the genie's court —, to sorrow and the approach of tragedy (end of Act I).   Some relaxation, or postponement, of evil marks the second act, as the genie attempts to overcome the lovers by gentleness and cunning; there is even psychological subtlety in the perplexed monologue in which the evil spirit debates his course (Sc. 1).   The consultation at the temple of Love keeps us in this intermediate state between woe and deliver-ance; the dance of the lovers who flee from each other weeping ("qui se fuient en se plaignant") sums up the character of this section (Sc. 4) (ex. 297) and illustrates an aspect of Rameau the mezzotintist not often met hitherto.   It opens into a poignant little chorus, "Ah! qu'il est doux de pardonner!" where again we catch echoes of the "Frappez" duet.   A pastoral sequence of musettes, minuets and gavottes intensi-fies this intermediate mood which breaks in the last scene and rises to terror with an air of *vocalises* on "sup-pli-i-ces!"   The third act is largely on this plane of passionate tragedy, seasoned with gentler

Ex. 297

lamentation; the climax is reached in the scene of solo, duet and chorus I have mentioned (end of Sc. 2). The unprepared return of the good fairy dispels all this, and a prolonged coda rejoices over the deliverance of the lovers and the birth of the Bourbon babe. The mood of tragedy is prolonged but there is variety in its expression, and this final *divertissement* contains many a good *symphonie*, such as a dance for the aerial spirits[1] and another musette, *parodied* by solo, duet and chorus. Even the closing chorus, "Vive la race de nos rois", is a favourable example of a type that generally makes little musical appeal.

The pastoral music in *Acante et Céphise* shows the usual rich scoring and harmonic suspensiveness, but I do not detect any longing in it.[2] It is attractive but less original than in some other operas. Among the set dances, the first gavotte in I, 2 has an opening of characteristic subtlety, beginning as it does in a straightforward impersonal manner and then affirming gently its individuality at the end of the second bar (ex. 298). In the same act (Sc. 6) is a loure which must be the most thickly scored piece in all Rameau, with sumptuous

---

[1] Included in Desormières's suite for wind quintet.

[2] The musettes are in Desormières.

Ex. 298

clashes in the early bars and an evocative pedal point at the end[1] (ex. 299). The excellent *chaconne vive* in I, 6, is in the character of that in *Les Fêtes d'Hébé*, Act II; it was used again in *Les Sybarites* (Sc. 4).

Ex. 299ᵃ

Ex. 299ᵇ

Acante et Céphise is the first French opera in which clarinets were given individual parts. They play in the overture (*Feu d'artifice* and *Fanfare*), in the *divertissement* of Act II, in the entr'acte between Acts II and III which is scored for clarinets and horns only[2] and in the closing contredanse and chorus.

---

[1] Traditional at the close of a loure, but Rameau has stressed it more here.
[2] Masson quotes it in (190), pp. 524–525.

From this *pastorale*, too, it would be a grateful task to make a concert and choral version from the best numbers.

Of the eight one-act pieces which Rameau composed at various times between 1748 and 1754 *Pygmalion* is far and away the best. In quality it is easily the equal of the greatest *tragédies* and *opéras-ballets*. The librettist, a member of La Pouplinière's circle, was Ballot de Sovot (or Sauvot), the brother of Rameau's solicitor and a fervent partisan of French dramatic music, in defence of which, during the *guerre des Bouffons*, he fought a duel and was wounded; his opponent was an Italian castrato called Caffarelli who had said that the French ought to imitate Italian music if they wanted to improve their own.[1] A few years earlier, Graun had written a dramatic ballet on the same subject, about the time when Noverre first appeared in Berlin, but Sovot drew his inspiration from an earlier source; he adapted a libretto of La Motte—the fifth *entrée*, *La Sculpture*, of *Le Triomphe des Arts*, set by Michel de La Barre in 1700.[2]

As is usual the drama comes first and the ballet last. The drama, so often perfunctory, is here treated very seriously and for a while the music is close to tragedy. The delightful overture, with its suggestion of the chipping chisel, has been mentioned.[3] The act opens with one of Rameau's most searching expressions of grief, harmonically akin to the "Dieux, soyez touchés" chorus in *Zoroastre*, III, 1, and from the same vein as the first number of *In convertendo*. Pygmalion is apostrophizing Love:

> Fatal Amour, cruel vainqueur,
> Quels traits as-tu choisis pour me percer le cœur?

The music renders the "cruel" and the "percer" (ex. 300). Note two points of likeness with Beethoven: the rising third in the violins like the beginning of the *andante* of op. 81 a, and the falling seventh that reminds one of the *allegro* of op. 31, III. The scene is a superb *récitatif accompagné*, with recalls of the opening bars, worthy of *Dardanus*, but not closely paralleled in any of the *tragédies*. The vocal line remains as good in the dialogue with Cephise (Sc. 2); the accompaniment here is for thoroughbass only; the orchestra enters near the end as the temper rises. When Pygmalion is left alone we hear

---

[1] According to Marpurg, *Legenden einiger Musikheiligen*, 1786; in (153), 138.

[2] Mlle Sallé danced a *Pygmalion* ballet in London in 1734 and the same year a *ballet-pantomime* on this theme, with airs by Mouret, was given in Paris.

[3] *Pygmalion* is not only published in the *O.C.*, XVII, but has the honour of a vocal score (Durand; transcribed by Henri Büsser).

Ex.300

again ex. 300, returning like a leitmotif, and his sorrowful musing is pursued. As he decides to turn to Venus there is a simple but effective change from G minor to G major. His prayer is granted; a series of sustained chords precedes the coming to life of his creation; "Love crosses the stage in rapid flight, unnoticed by Pygmalion, and shakes his torch over the statue" whose first steps are accompanied by the sculptor's enraptured comments. "Quel prodige! quel Dieu! par quelle intelligence un songe a-t-il séduit mes sens?" His amazement

Ex.301

is expressed by the weird scoring of this passage (ex. 301), which is for flutes and violas only, answering each other with minim chords. The recitative remains highly expressive; the climax is in the last words of the statue (ex. 302; the accompaniment is for thoroughbass only).

Ex. 302

An *ariette* by Love, "Jeux et Ris qui suivez", serves as transition from drama to ballet; with its caressing flute triplets it is one of Rameau's most charming achievements in this despised field; its 12/8 rhythm reminds us of the *ballet de l'inconstance* in *Zaïs*. Then follows a chain of dances, a kind of sample book of the composer's gavottes, minuets, chaconnes, loures, passepieds and rigaudons—each one a little longer than the last; while the statue tries the steps of each in turn. When she has gained experience she launches forth into a complete saraband, the queen of the series, in which it is not fanciful to recognize a transformation of ex. 300 (ex. 303). She then throws herself into a tambourin, less Dionysiac than some but original for the way in which, at the start, the outer parts remain stationary while the motion is confined to the inner ones.

With Scene 5 the throng enters to acclaim the prodigy. The *symphonie* which accompanies their appearance is not the customary

Ex.303

march but a piece in which both sentiment and gesture are so generalized that it is no more than mood painting—the mood of tender
exaltation that has prevailed since the statue's awakening.   Interest,
for us at least, flags somewhat with a long solo and air to which both
Rameau and d'Alembert returned several times in their later correspondence, to praise it because in it the composer had disposed the
harmonic parts in "the order commanded by nature".[1]   It is followed
by "L'Amour triomphe" for Pygmalion and people, and another
expressive *symphonie*, surprisingly entitled *pantomime niaise et un peu
lente* and danced by two half-witted yokels, whose introduction into
a Greek ballet was later to be criticized.[2]   It is hard to see anything

Ex.304

but ineffable tenderness in bars like these (ex. 304).   An excellent jig-
like *pantomime très vive* follows, with leaps reminiscent of the orchestra's in Folly's "Aux langueurs d'Apollon" in *Platée*.   Pygmalion
then delivers himself of a majestic *ariette*, "Règne, Amour", unattrac-
tive yet masterful.   After which a short *air* and a contredanse wind up
the entertainment.

---

[1] (12), 28–29.   See also: "The chord formed with the major twelfth
and seventeenth united with the fundamental is for this same reason" (i.e.
because it is founded in nature) "extremely pleasing when the composer
can combine voice and instruments in such a way as to give it all its effect,
which does not always happen: M. Rameau has achieved this in a well-
known chorus of *Pygmalion*" ((12); report of the Académie des Sciences,
vi).   The writer is d'Alembert.

[2] *Journal des Théâtres*; December 1777.

Pygmalion had the most immediate and unequivocal success of all Rameau's works and, with *Castor et Pollux*, was his most performed opera in the second half of the century. It more than held its own against the Bouffons and *opéra-comique* in 1752–1754 and 1760–1762. Grimm and d'Alembert praised it. Rameau, according to Collé, was greatly moved by its reception, "weeping for joy and inebriated by the welcome the public had given him".[1] Only later, during the vogue for Gluck, was criticism heard. For us, the charm of its recitative lies in its melodic character. But for the writer who had found fault with the "paysans niais" in the *pantomime* it was defective. "The dialogue should be spoken; Rameau almost always makes it sing; I ask unprejudiced people whether that method is according to nature."[2] The same number of the *Journal des Théâtres* contained a defence of the master.

> I who am speaking, Sir, I have heard Rameau's airs (he is referring to his dances) admired and executed, truth to say very poorly, on all the stages of Italy and Germany. The famous Jommelli confessed that without Rameau Terpsichore would have had to forsake Italy.[2]

Pygmalion was revived in 1913. It was given at the Château de Grammont, near Tours, in 1952, during the Semaine musicale de Touraine. It is now (1968) often broadcast.

Of Rameau's remaining works all but one contain good music, the two most satisfying as dramatic wholes being *La Guirlande* and *Zéphyre*. It was with *La Guirlande* that the Rameau revival began on June 22, 1903, when it was played in the garden of the Schola Cantorum, together with the prologue of Campra's *Fêtes vénitiennes* and Duni's *Les Sabots*. Rameau had not been staged in his native country for more than a century. After this performance Debussy, with understandable enthusiasm, exclaimed: "Vive Rameau! à bas Gluck!"

> How much nearer this is to us [wrote a spectator] than the heavy-handed platitudes, the trivial clowneries and the poor harmony to which we were condemned later by a theatre corrupted by the contact of a degraded Italy.[3]

It is surprising that no further revival has taken place and that the little work remains unpublished. It is a flawless piece of Dresden-china Rameau. This is not, in my eyes, the most precious kind of Rameau nor, fortunately, the commonest; indeed, it is seldom that he abides successfully within the slender framework of the *bergerie*; but he has done so here and the result is perfection, even though the perfection be of a modest order. With finesse and a certain realism of

---

[1] (56), March 1751; 299–300.
[2] *Journal des Théâtres*, December 1777.
[3] (242).

sentiment *La Guirlande* keeps delicately to a middle path, verging a
little more to the happy than to the unhappy side of life's road.   Scene
6 is particularly sensitive.   A descriptive *ariette* in Scene 4 and the
usual "Triomphe" chorus at the end are the only numbers that smack
of the conventional.   Of the *symphonies*, all pastoral, the most personal is the *air gracieux* for flutes and strings in G minor (Sc. 6).   The
librettist was Marmontel and the work was given, without much success, in September 1751.   It clearly deserves revival, in stage, concert
or broadcast version.

Zéphyre is quite as good and has the advantage of existing in a
modern edition.[1]   Its origin, like that of *Nélée et Myrthis* and *Io*, is
quite unknown.   They were discovered in the last century and their
authenticity is certain, but no one has ever found out when they were
composed nor why, nor who wrote the librettos.   The autograph of
Zéphyre shows that its first title was *Les Nymphes de Diane* and that of
Nélée et Myrthis bears, deleted, the title *Les Beaux Jours de l'Amour.
Myrthis, entrée.*   No ballet opera of this name is known, but perhaps
both acts were destined for one which was never completed.

Zéphyre is as perfect as *La Guirlande* and considerably more varied.
The hero, whose nature is indicated by his name, loves Cloris, a
nymph of Diana, and the little work stages the courtship which no
storms traverse and over which the possible disapproval of Diana
casts the only shadow.   But Diana, converted by Endymion, gives
her consent and all rejoice.   The tale allows little scope for drama,
but Rameau has made up for this by indulging his love for impressionism.   The prelude of Scene 1—there is no overture—, for flutes and
strings, evokes flights of Zephyrs in wavy wreaths of semiquavers.
As Cloris advances (Sc. 3), "flowers are born beneath her feet" (ex.
305).   Scene 5 contains descriptive scoring of "murmure des eaux,
ramages des oiseaux" and an *air pour les groupes de fleurs*, with much

Ex.305

---

[1] *O.C.*, XI.

responsibility laid on the combination flutes-violins.   The sequence
which begins in Scene 5 with a saraband,[1] *pas d'un zéphyr et d'une
nymphe*, is continued during an air for Zéphyre and concludes with a
symphonie in G, 12/8, with comments by Cloris ("Quels sons!"),
which comprises hautboys, bassoons and horns with strings, and is
interesting for its colouring.   The last scene includes a saraband for
the Flowers, with fluttering thirds in the strings and semiquaver scrolls
in the upper register of the flutes and two gavottes in G major and
minor; in the second, up-scurrying sixty-fourths in the flutes represent the little breezes.

    The best vocal number is a short G minor *ariette* for Zéphyre,
"Vous ne devez l'éclat des fleurs" (Sc. 5), with a violin motif reminiscent of *Les Niais de Sologne* and expressive of the singer's nature
(ex. 306).   This motif is something of a signature tune since it returns

Ex.306

in the G major gavotte in Scene 8 where the likeness with *Les Niais*
is accentuated by the mode.

    Masson considers that *Zéphyre* belongs to Rameau's best period
and is "from the same vein as *Pygmalion*".   It is certainly free from
the feeling of weariness born of having done the same thing so often
already, which one detects at times in his later writing.   Musically, as
far as comparisons mean anything, I would place it between *Pygmalion*
and *La Guirlande*.   As perfect as the latter, it ranges further but does

---

[1] Not the saraband reproduced in (190), 449, which comes from *Daphnis
et Églé*.

not approach tragic utterance like the former and its choreography is less varied.   It was revived at the Aldeburgh festival in June 1967.

Nélée et Myrthis is another love tale, crossed this time by not very serious pique and jealousy.   It includes a ballet of the Argive Games and an imposing chaconne of one hundred and seventy bars to accompany them; as ever, the best portion is the *mineur* in the middle. The scoring is at times very full; the fanfare that heralds the games is for piccolos, hautboys, bassoons, trumpets, kettledrums and strings. The other dances have less distinction and the chief merits are in the sung parts.   Nélée's *air tendre* (Sc. 1) is constantly changing key and tempo and his dialogue with Myrthis in Scene 3 is a lively example of melodic recitative turning at times into an air.

The most attractive solo is Nélée's "Un amant rebuté", in a vein of "sour grapes, it was nice while it lasted" and "you won't catch me weeping" that carries us back to *Les Amants trahis*, Rameau's first portrayal of the cynical lover.   In the first bars of the following quotation (ex. 307) one hears an echo of the very notes of Damon's

Ex. 307

"Dieu d'Amour, je prends tous les feux" in that early work of his dramatic Muse.

The third of these mysterious one-acts, *Io*, is an unfinished fragment of very little interest, preserved in a copy from the Decroix bequest and therefore probably genuine.   It depicts the loves of Jupiter and the nymph Io; Jupiter's semi-*buffo* air, "Du doux plaisir je suis la loi", is the only piece with any claim to originality; its *vocalises* on "ri-i-re" faintly recall *Platée*.   Masson suggests that *Io* may be Rameau's last work.

Daphnis et Églé calls itself a *pastorale héroïque* though it is in only one act; its libretto is by Collé, who complained that Rameau made him cut it down.   Ordered for the Court and played at Fontainebleau in October 1753, it was the first opera that Rameau had written since the wave of Italianism unleashed by the Bouffons, and its overture shows his attempts to keep pace with modernity.   The earliest sketch for its first movement was discarded in favour of something more frisky and Italian (ex. 308 (*a*); ex. 308 (*b*)).   The second movement is

Ex. 308ª

Ex. 308ᵇ

only a slow transition of fifteen bars; the third consists in two minuets, the first of which, transposed from D to E, returns in Scene 6.   The second is the best part of the overture; it opens with that air of simple nobility of which Rameau has the secret (ex. 309).

Ex. 309

The story stages the usual innocent lovers; a Temple of Friendship and one of Love, each with its high priest; and Love himself with attendant Graces, Frolics and Pleasures.   "The theatre represents the main entrance of the Temple of Friendship, in the midst of a forest of tall trees.   They form an avenue leading to the Temple, the doors of which are shut."

The text is rich in stage directions for the *ballets figurés* which adorn the action at every turn.   Among the vocal airs my own preference goes to Daphnis' "Bergère, comme vous j'ignore quel est le trouble qui nous suit" (Sc. 3), in which he confesses his "trouble" in terms that plagiarize shamelessly Hippolyte's words to Aricie in

Phèdre, II, 2.   The *symphonies* are in the pastoral or near-pastoral vein
and are all excellent; the rarest of them is the musette in E quoted in
Chapter X (ex. 257).   Next to it I would place the *sarabande très
tendre* and, I would add, *infiniment triste* which Masson has reproduced
in facsimile, attributing it by mistake to *Zéphyre*.[1]   A long gavotte
with three *reprises* has some of those passages I can only describe as
weird which occur more frequently in Rameau's last works (ex. 310).

Ex. 310

Other beauties are less grim.   The *ballet figuré* which precedes the saraband mimes the return of the shepherds who express their astonish-
ment at finding the Temple of Friendship replaced by that of Love.
An elaborate *pantomime* accompanies two shepherdesses who enter
separately, meet, embrace and are joined by two shepherds whom they
approach suspiciously.   A minuet in E minor lets us hear more grinding appoggiaturas and the second of the tambourins restores to us a
large-limbed Rameau whom we had missed from these dreamy wanderings through pastoral groves; it shows in a new light his inexhaustible resourcefulness in handling the bassoon (ex. 311).   The contredanse at the end has five *reprises*; its refrain is a *moto perpetuo* that
suggests a running set.
     Daphnis et Églé is not a candidate for revival in any form, but its

---

[1] (190), 449.

Ex. 311

symphonies ought to be rescued and combined in a suite, not necessarily together, but mixed with others. It is, by the way, pointless to confine oneself to a single work when compiling suites of old opera dances; the dances themselves were so often moved from opera to opera that they suffer no harm from being mingled with others; the compiler is less cramped and can give a wider view of the composer's genius if he allows himself to choose and combine as he lists.

Another ballet had been ordered from Rameau and Marmontel for the following month, and they turned out *Lysis et Délie*. Though the libretto says it was performed at Fontainebleau on November 6, the fact is that it was never given because it was found to be too like *Daphnis et Églé*. Rameau no doubt made use of the music elsewhere.

The very next week the indefatigable pair produced another ballet, *Les Sybarites*, also given at Fontainebleau. In 1757 it was included in a revival of *Les Surprises de l'Amour*. It depicts the legendary struggle between Sybaris and Crotona; the latter city, led by a king, attacks the former, whose chief is a queen; Sybarites meet Crotoniats with flowers and song; the king falls in love with the queen and all ends well. The music represents the opposition between rough and gentle, but offers less for us to cull than the works just considered. Hersilide's address to Love to implore his help, "Tendre Amour, prête-moi tes armes", is a pathetic supplication in *récitatif accompagné*, as good as many earlier pieces but no better; it proves that Rameau could still do, and as well, what he had so often done in the past. Two of the best *symphonies* come from earlier works: a saraband in D minor from *La Princesse de Navarre* (originally in C minor, *entrée des Grâces*, II, 11) and a gavotte in G minor from *Acante et Céphise*, I, 2.   The first of two bright passepieds begins as if it was Bach's English suite in G minor.   The ballet closes with an inventive contredanse with the usual kaleidoscopic turns and tumbles.

La Naissance d'Osiris is an occasional piece for the birth of another Bourbon; Osiris is none other than the future Louis XVI, born on August 23, 1754.   There is practically no story and the interest is almost entirely in the *symphonies*, nearly all of which deserve quotation.   The Italian overture has a touching D minor *andante* for its second movement with curious broken rhythms.   Pastoral strains are prominent; there are three musettes, all good.   The most sustained movement is a *rondeau gracieux* in Scene 1, which is a kind of gigue. Of all the dances, the A minor tambourin is perhaps the least like its predecessors.   This ballet, too, is a mine of good *symphonies* for the explorer and rescuer of Rameau's buried treasures.

The *Anacréon* which Rameau and Cahusac produced at Fontaine-bleau in October 1754, "with great success", must be distinguished from the *entrée* of that name which was added to *Les Surprises de l'Amour* in 1757.   It opens with a long *ritournelle* which is really an overture, leading into the first number.   This *moderato* piece in E minor begins with a long scale in unison and develops in a leisurely way with much conjunct motion.   It is well worth rescuing; formally, it reminds one of the prelude to *Dardanus*, III, but the mood is different.   It is the most original piece in the ballet and possibly the best. *Anacréon* contains fewer *symphonies* than usual and the best vocal numbers are to be found among the airs.

13. Life : The Last Thirty Years

THE story of the last thirty years of Rameau's life is that of his operas and his writings. After his return in 1723 he never left Paris for any length of time and most of his existence was spent in the square mile bounded to-day by the Boulevard Sébastopol, the Seine, the Rue Royale and the Grands Boulevards—the district which by 1730 had replaced the Marais as the chief residential quarter. Here La Pouplinière had his abode before his banishment; here, in his house in the Rue Neuve des Petits Champs, where he dwelt from 1726 to 1739, Rameau's first opera was given. His private orchestra must have come into being soon after his return from Holland in the fall of 1731, and Rameau no doubt became its conductor at this time. He was to retain this post for twenty-two years. The orchestra was excellent and was able, as we have seen, to do justice to the difficult *Trio des Parques*.

Rameau and his wife occupied an influential position in La Pouplinière's household. It was strengthened towards 1734 by the financier's liaison with Thérèse Deshayes, whom he was to marry three years later. This lady, who came of an artistic ancestry—Mimi Dancourt was her mother, Manon her aunt, and Florent Dancourt the playwright both her grandfather and great-uncle—, was a good musician, of sounder tastes than her husband, whose loves in music as in amours were changeable; she studied harmony and the harpsichord with Rameau and "like her friend Mme du Châtelet belonged to that category of great ladies who were capable of enthusiasm for the most scientific discussions".[1] In 1737 she was to give an analysis of her teacher's *Génération harmonique* in *Le Pour et Contre*.[2] With her support La Pouplinière's house became a stronghold of *ramisme*. "Rameau's will", says Rousseau malevolently, "was law in that house."

In 1739 La Pouplinière bought a larger mansion in the Rue de Richelieu[3] and Rameau and his family lived there for a time in an apartment of their own. Deeds of 1746 and 1751 and the printed editions of *Acante et Céphise* and *La Guirlande* give his address as

---

[1] (134), 94. [2] Tome XIII, 34–49.
[3] On the site of the present No. 59.

"Rue de Richelieu, vis à vis la Bibliothèque du Roi". In 1747 La Pouplinière purchased the château of Passy and until the break in 1753 the Rameaus spent every summer there.

We have very little information about the musician's duties, but they can be imagined. Concerts seem to have been given several times a week at one period and Mme Rameau would play her husband's compositions on the harpsichord. At Passy, where there was an organ, he presided at it on Sunday mornings. There must have been much arranging of music for these concerts and no doubt much composing of lighter works, since La Pouplinière's tastes extended to *opéras-comiques*, *vaudevilles* and occasional pieces for weddings and namedays. Two instances of such arrangements have been preserved. When Samuel Bernard the financier married his grand-daughter to the Marquis de Mirepoix in 1733 Rameau, thanks to La Pouplinière, was given charge of the musical arrangements. During the wedding supper

> a melodious symphony was heard in the gallery, interrupted from time to time by fanfares, trumpets and cymbals. Half-way through the meal, Messrs. Charpentier and Danguy, famous executants on the *musette* and the *vielle*, came [into the body of the hall] to play pieces which Rameau had composed for the occasion.

The wedding took place in St. Eustache at midnight and Rameau had obtained leave from Forqueray, the organist, to play during the service, which he did "with great mastery"; this, adds not quite correctly the writer, "was his farewell to the instrument". The next day Bernard sent him an honorarium of twelve hundred livres.[1]

When the King recovered from a serious illness in 1744 a wave of gratitude swept over the land and many services of thanksgiving were held. The body of *fermiers-généraux* ordered one at Notre-Dame des Victoires, hard by La Pouplinière's house. Lalande's *Te Deum* was sung and it was preceded by a kind of lament the Latin words of which were fitted to the first chorus, "Que tout gémisse", of *Castor et Pollux*. Between the lament and the *Te Deum* a song of hope effected a transition, "Sperate non in vanum", and this was set to Huascar's "Clair flambeau du monde" from *Les Indes galantes*. It is obvious that Rameau had been lent by his patron to La Pouplinière's colleagues for this purpose.

Rameau, whose nature was not very sociable, must have met there more people than he would otherwise have done. La Pouplinière was on good terms with all the bright spirits who founded the Caveau

---

[1] (134), 313–314.

dinners in 1733: Collé, the two Crébillons, Panard, Gresset, "Gentil" Bernard, La Bruère, Duclos, Moncrif, Fuzelier, François Boucher, Jélyotte and a few others.

It was no doubt through Piron that Rameau came into touch with the Comte de Livri or Livry. Louis Sanguin, Comte de Livri, born on April 5, 1679, whose family descended from an *échevin* of Paris, was the son of a *premier maître d'hôtel* to the King and succeeded in due course to his father's charge; he became also a *maréchal des camps et armées* and, in 1731, a lieutenant-general. (His family was unrelated to the actress Suzanne Catherine Gravet de Corsambleu de Livry, who figures prominently in the chronicle of Voltaire's amours and came of a much less exalted stock, in spite of the length of her name.) His Paris house was in the Rue du Pot de Fer, near St. Médard, and he owned a château at Le Raincy, in that forest of Livry whence he took his title. He is best remembered to-day as the patron of Piron, who dedicated to him his tragedy *Gustave Vasa* and who, mentioning him several times in his works, calls the estate at Livry a "true Pindus and Helicon". The Comte was the centre of a theatrical and literary circle to which the actresses Mlles Quinault and Dalicourt also belonged. He was extremely generous to Piron, whom he often helped discreetly without his beneficiary being aware of it. His son, the Marquis de Livri, who lived in the Rue de Condé, continued the pension which the Comte had paid the writer and preferred him, it is alleged, to Voltaire, whereas the Marquise preferred the latter. The pension continued to be paid, though irregularly, after the Marquis's death.

We have no record of Rameau's presence at the Rue du Pot de Fer, and the only evidence of his acquaintance with the Comte is the fact that he dedicated to him one of his most beautiful *pièces en concert*. The recueil of these pieces came out in 1741, after the month of August, which is the date of the *privilège*; as the Comte had died on July 3 of that year the piece must be meant as a lament or, as the lutenists would have called it, a *tombeau*, in memory of the deceased patron.

It was at La Pouplinière's that Rameau met most of his librettists: those already mentioned, Gautier de Montdorge, Ballot de Sauvot, whose brother Sylvain Ballot was his notary, and Marmontel, who entered the circle in 1749, after La Pouplinière and his wife had separated. Cahusac is almost the only one who does not seem to have frequented the tax-farmer's house. Hither, too, came Carle Vanloo and Quentin de La Tour.

Other acquaintances, some of whom he does not seem to have met at La Pouplinière's, were his fellow-countryman Vennevault, a painter,[1] and Jean-Baptiste Forqueray, the viol player and composer, a cousin of the organist of St. Eustache; later, another Dijonnais musician, Balbâtre, who came to Paris in 1750, entered his circle; both he and Vennevault gave Maret information for his *Éloge*. Balbâtre played the *Pygmalion* overture on the organ at Passy and Rameau expressed his admiration of the performance.

Since 1737 relations had cooled off between Voltaire and the financier; Voltaire fancied that La Pouplinière looked critically on his works and was to be classed amongst his enemies. But Rameau was not included in this disfavour. In 1740 we find Voltaire seeking a composer for his *Pandore*, which Mme d'Aiguillon called "un opéra à la Milton". He entrusted his friend Berger with the task of deciding between Mondonville and him, and by June the text was in Rameau's hands. Rameau presumably had said that he was too busy to do anything quickly, for Voltaire wrote to Berger that he should take all the time he needed "to do a work that may crown his fame".[2] He asks Berger to put Rameau on his guard against any criticisms his patron may make. Rameau had seen his *Dardanus* staged the year before but had neither opera nor theoretical work on hand, and it is rather surprising that the matter dropped.

A less welcome acquaintance was to enter La Pouplinière's comprehensive mansion. Jean-Jacques Rousseau, who had arrived in Paris in 1741, probably met the financier in the following year; Mme Dupin, his protectress, was Mme de la Pouplinière's first cousin, and Dupins and La Pouplinières were at that time on good terms. But it is not till 1745 that we have proof of Rousseau's entry into the establishment. He had composed a ballet opera, *Les Muses galantes*, which La Pouplinière was induced to have performed in his house. The score was submitted to Rameau who, alleges Rousseau, said he was too tired to look at it. However, La Pouplinière got together a number of singers and instrumentalists and the work was given. Rameau showed his disapproval openly; he became impatient during the very overture and when it came to a certain air he cried out "that a part of what he had just heard came from a man who was master of his art and part from an ignoramus who did not know the first word of music". Ten years later, when criticizing Rousseau's article *Accompagnement* in the *Encyclopédie*, he inserted the following anecdote which clearly refers to the same occasion.

> Some ten or twelve years ago an individual had a ballet of his composition, which later was offered to the Opéra and rejected, performed at M . . .'s; I was struck by finding in it very beautiful violin airs in a purely Italian taste and at the same time all that was worst in the

---

[1] 1697–1775.
[2] Letters of April 26 and June 29, 1740.

French taste in the vocal and instrumental parts, including *ariettes* with the dullest voice part supported by the loveliest Italian accompaniments. This contrast surprised me and I asked the composer a few questions which he answered so badly that I saw clearly what I had already guessed, that he had written only the French music and had pillaged the Italian.[1]

It was reported that Rousseau was so overcome that he broke down and cried and fell into a ridiculous sulk.

La Pouplinière seems to have enjoyed *Les Muses galantes* but his wife, who was a staunch supporter of Rameau and also a better musician, frowned on it. She heard it first, it seems, at the Duc de Richelieu's, when she held her peace. But the next day, says Rousseau, "she gave me a very cool welcome, went out of her way to run down my piece and said that though a little tinsel had at first dazzled M. de Richelieu, he had changed his mind and she did not advise me to count on having my opera performed".[2]

Mme de La Pouplinière's hostility towards the newcomer, in whom she may have sensed not only a rival to Rameau but a representative of a form of art that threatened what she liked best,[3] was shown when Rousseau was given the job of completing *Les Fêtes de Ramire*. This was a libretto by Voltaire written to make use of some of the music which Rameau had composed for his *Princesse de Navarre*; as both Rameau and he were busy with *Le Temple de la Gloire* it was given to Rousseau to fill in a few gaps and arrange it for performance. Though what he did pleased Richelieu, she criticized it so bitterly that the Duke sent the work back to Rameau. It was performed, says Rousseau, with his overture and recitatives, but no mention was made of him and Rameau and Voltaire got all the credit. Thus, he complains, "I lost my time, my work and my money".[4]

In this wise was sown Rousseau's unalterable hatred for Rameau.

La Pouplinière and his wife separated in 1748. Nevertheless Rameau remained with his patron and was still living under his roof in

---

[1] (18), 41–42.—It is no doubt on *Les Muses galantes* that Rameau expressed the judgment that Laborde quotes as referring to *Le Devin du village*: "This little opera is a whole composed half of things well done, according to the principles, and half of bad ones against the rules. It is therefore not by the same hand; therefore if Rousseau has done the good ones he has not done the bad" ((74), 468).

[2] (99), II, 7; 99–101.

[3] There were perhaps yet other reasons. Mme de La Pouplinière was then on bad terms with her husband and had quarrelled with her cousin, Mme Dupin, Rousseau's patroness, with whom La Pouplinière continued to be friendly.

[4] (99), II, 7; 102–108.

1751. But an estrangement was preparing.   The actual break seems
to have had two causes, one artistic, the other domestic.

In 1752, when Manelli and la Tonelli, members of Bambini's
troupe, performed *La Serva padrona*, this unloosed the conflict known
as the Guerre des Bouffons, La Pouplinière's tastes were on the side of
the Italians.   In a play by Patu and Portelance, *Les Adieux du goût*
(February 1754), the actor who played the part of Plutus imitated his
tone of voice and arrogant manner and the god was pictured as a lover
of the Bouffons.[1]

Rameau was not a bigot and we shall see that he never took sides
openly in the quarrel and always admired what was good, whence-
soever it came, and La Pouplinière's liking for Pergolese and Leo
would not have sufficed to bring about an estrangement.   But, since
his separation from his wife, the financier had drifted from mistress
to mistress, till in 1753 he fell into the clutches of an *intrigante*,
Jeanne-Thérèse Goermans, the daughter of a harpsichord maker and
herself a musician.   She had married an ex-soldier, son of an inn-
keeper, who lived on her earnings, and it was this disreputable husband who advised her to seek fortune with the unattached and ageing
financier.

Having played her cards well she was installed as reigning favourite
at the Rue de Richelieu in November 1753.   She took the name of
Mme de Saint-Aubin and at once proceeded to clear the deck about her.
Vanloo, the Rameaus and several others soon found life impossible
and had to leave.   According to Maret, the actual break was caused
by La Pouplinière's action in bringing another composer into his
house.   If this is true, Cucuel conjectures that it may have been
Stamitz, who was to succeed Rameau as conductor of his band a year
or two later.   But Mme de Saint-Aubin's action is probably sufficient
to explain his withdrawal.   Rameau was now seventy; he who had
never known patience could hardly be expected to learn that virtue
at the hands of an interloper; and so a friendship of twenty-five years
came to an end.

Absorbing as his functions may have been with the farmer-
general they were not his only occupation.   He taught a group of
private pupils, among whom was Voltaire's niece Louise Mignot, the
future Mme Denis; indeed, as late as 1737 he opened, at his house in
the Rue des Bons Énfants, "a school of composition where it *was* proposed to bring together twelve pupils thrice a week, from three to five
o'clock, at twenty francs a month per head".[2]   And we have seen that
he remained organist at Ste. Croix as late as 1738.

As for his operas, the rate at which they follow each other, once
he entered the lists, is overwhelming.   Between the ages of fifty and

---

[1] (210).

[2] Announcement in *Le Mercure de France*, December 1737.

seventy he composed nearly twenty operas or ballets, amounting to some seventy acts. They appear at irregular intervals but with only one long break: in 1733, *Hippolyte et Aricie*; in 1735, his first ballet opera, *Les Indes galantes*; in 1737 another *tragédie lyrique*, *Castor et Pollux*; in 1739 a second ballet opera, *Les Fêtes d'Hébé*, and a third *tragédie*, *Dardanus*, three acts of which were rewritten for the revival in 1744; in February and March 1745 two comedies, *La Princesse de Navarre* and *Platée*; in October and November of the same year, in which he turned sixty-two, *Les Fêtes de Polymnie* and *Le Temple de la Gloire*; in 1747 *Les Fêtes de l'Hymen et de l'Amour*; in February 1748 an heroic pastoral, *Zaïs*; in August, *Pygmalion*, a one-act ballet, and in November *Les Surprises de l'Amour*, a ballet opera in two *entrées* and a prologue; in April 1749 a second heroic pastoral, *Naïs*, and in December his fourth *tragédie*, *Zoroastre*; in September and November, 1751, *La Guirlande*, a one-act ballet, and *Acante et Céphise*, another heroic pastoral; and in the course of 1751 and 1752 a *tragédie*, *Linus*, the music of which is lost. Such a list makes one giddy to contemplate.[1]

And this is not all. He considered his study of theory at least as important as his composition and he pursued his researches without ceasing to his very death. One year before *Hippolyte* he published a *Dissertation sur les différentes méthodes d'accompagnement pour le clavecin ou l'orgue*; in 1737, the same year as *Castor*, his *Génération harmonique*; in 1750 his *Démonstration du principe de l'harmonie*, followed two years later by *Nouvelles Réflexions sur sa démonstration du principe de l'harmonie*; besides a number of articles in the *Mercure*, the *Journal de Trévoux* and *Le Pour et Contre*.

It was worth while giving this list so that the man's tireless activity should be seen at a glance.

One may well imagine the shock that *Hippolyte* administered to the musical world of Paris. Here was a man known for his immense learning in acoustico-musical theory, a theoretician with a couple of cantatas and three small volumes of harpsichord pieces to his credit (but what did they signify? everyone produced *recueils* of harpsichord pieces); a learned man forsooth, and respected as such, but whom no one suspected of being a "creative artist" (the distinction was present to the mind, though the expression did not exist). And one day he takes it into his head to turn composer. It was as if a Hugo Riemann in his later middle age should have written an opera or a couple of symphonies. But this was not enough. Our Riemann's opera was very good, as good as anything that had been heard since 1687, the year of the death of the immortal Lulli; in fact, some felt it to be even

---

[1] The unperformed *Zéphyre* and *Nélée et Myrthis* probably belong to this period.

better than anything since that event and more stuffed with excellent music, well written and stirring, than anything that anyone then living in Paris had ever heard.   The effect was stunning.

By degrees it wore off as people could obtain nearer and repeated views of the monster.   Opinions began to shape themselves and critics to mass at opposite poles.   The result was one of those battles with which the history of French art and literature is marked, that of the *lullistes* and the *ramistes*.   From the performance of *Hippolyte*, "two violently extreme parties were to be found in France, enraged against each other; the older and the newer music was for each of them a kind of religion for which they took up arms".[1]   On the side of Lulli were the elderly and the unprofessional; only a few musicians like Mouret joined with them, more out of jealousy of the rising star than from devotion to the memory of Baptiste.   Theorists like Père André, author of an *Essai sur le Beau*, and Abbé Pluche, of *Le Spectacle de la Nature* fame, were also among the conservative.   Their leader was a poet, it was said: probably Roy who had worked as librettist with almost every composer except Rameau.   Roy had been introduced to La Pouplinière about the same time as Bernard; he was later to turn against him and satirize him.   Rameau and he had a spectacular quarrel in 1737, as a result of which Rameau gave up wearing a sword "on the advice of his friends, because he is stubborn and bad-tempered and would have either got himself killed or branded as a coward".[2]

Roy's coolness towards his former patron was due to the fact that the financier's mansion was the chief centre of *ramisme*.   Voltaire, Fréron, and at one time Desfontaines, more catholic than the *lullistes*, were all supporters of the newer music.

The attack was repeated over *Les Indes galantes*, whose recitatives were called "baroque", and *Castor*, whose poor success cheered the old guard.   The gist of what it disliked in Rameau is found in an amusing *Lettre de M. X . . . à Mlle X . . . sur l'origine de la musique*.[3]   The writer imagines that Venus had ordered a ballet for her stage and that even "les géomètres" had competed.   When their effort was performed people declared that

> nothing flowed naturally, no genius inspired them, they turned their backs on nature and feeling. . . .   Most of the spectators exclaimed that the instruments were out of tune; their sounds wounded the least refined of ears; they were told point blank that the discords had been made on purpose and were the height of art. . . .   All keys were traversed at high

---

[1] *Observations sur la littérature moderne*, I (1749); in (188), 202.

[2] MS. memoirs of Canon de Mondran, brother of La Pouplinière's second wife; in (134), 121.

[3] *Mercure*, May 1734; in (188), 201–202.

speed, discords were strewn incessantly; sometimes two notes were obstinately repeated for a quarter of an hour; much noise, many scraps of melody; when by chance two bars occurred which might have made a pleasing tune, key, mode and beat were quickly changed. Always sadness instead of tenderness; what was singular became baroque; fury became shindy; instead of merriment, turbulence; never any prettiness; never anything to go to the heart.

Rameau was labelled "learned", a fatal appellation, the antithesis of "artist". His harmonies, says Cartaud de la Villatte, "take on a geometrical tone which frightens the heart . . . and gives nothing but great algebraical truths".[1] Lulli's airs, groans Pluche, could be heard on the Pont-Neuf (an echo of Le Cerf); modern airs are no longer within the understanding of the bourgeois. This is an allusion to certain Ramists who called Lulli and his successors bourgeois, because their airs were the delight of the multitude. In this quarrel, Lulli's music was popular, in the broad sense of the word, whereas Rameau's was that of an *élite*, of a narrow circle: a correction of the notion sometimes expressed that Lulli's opera was aristocratic and courtly and Rameau's was more broadly based on the middle classes.

The revivals of Lulli's works called forth similar sarcasms from the Ramists. *Persée* was given in February 1737; "those who dare not remove their masks say that it is beautiful but boring."[2] *Atys* was put on a year later; "our young women found it dull and antique."[2] In Boissy's *Les Talents à la mode*, which came out the year of *Dardanus*, the old man Géronte is a Lullist but his three daughters are pro-modern.

Rameau himself, always a sincere admirer and, later, defender of Lulli, deplored these attacks. His preface to *Les Indes galantes* and a reply to Père Castel in *Le Pour et Contre*[3] laboured to prove that he had the utmost respect for his predecessor and not the scorn he was accused of expressing.

By 1745, the year of *Platée* and *La Princèsse de Navarre*, both command pieces for a royal wedding, Rameau had become a kind of court musician. He was granted a pension and the title of Compositeur du Cabinet du Roi in May 1745, after *Platée*, and a further pension, chargeable to the Opéra, was given him in 1750. The Lullists now cut a reactionary figure and began to fall away. Yet Mme de Pompadour, according to Collé, liked neither his music nor his person, and d'Argenson, who shared these feelings, was able in 1749 to forbid that more than two of his operas should be given in one year.

Plenty of people held a middle course and were able to see some-

---

[1] *Essai historique et philosophique sur le goût*, 1736; in (188), 202–203.

[2] MS. news sheets for 1738–1739; in (188), 193.

[3] 1738, Vol. XIV.

thing good in both composers.   Thus d'Aquin de Châteaulyon, son
of the organist and composer, called Rameau's music "lively, thunder-
striking, majestic" and Lulli's "engaging, caressing, a little effeminate".[1]

This quarrel resembles the discussion between Raguenet and
Le Cerf thirty years earlier.   The Lullist arguments are those of the
partisans of French music at that time and we have seen that Rameau
was praised, or blamed, for working according to Italian taste and
remaining open, in his music, to influences from beyond the Alps.
This will not save him from passing, in his turn, for a narrowly French
and out-of-date old fogy.

Perhaps the most readable, and reasonable, survey of the position
in 1745 comes from the pen of Diderot, who was later to be so bitter
a scorner of Rameau's art.   The thirteenth chapter of *Les Bijoux indiscrets* (1748) contains an account of opera at Banza, that is, Paris, in
which the merits of Utmiutsol and Utrémifasolasiututut are contrasted.
The very names indicate the greater richness or, as some complained,
the excess of music of the later composer.   (In the following quotation, I have substituted Lulli and Rameau for the cumbersome pseudo-
nyms.)

> Lulli and Rameau, famous musicians, one of whom was beginning
> to age while the other was just born, occupied by turns the lyric stage.
> Each of these original composers had his supporters; the ignorant and
> the greybeards were all for Lulli, the young and the executants for
> Rameau; and the connoisseurs, both young and old, held both in great
> esteem.
>
> Rameau, said these latter, is excellent when he is good but he nods
> from time to time, and who does not?   Lulli is more sustained, more
> even; he is full of beauties; yet he has none of which examples, and even
> more striking ones, are not found in his rival, in whom qualities are
> found which are his own and occur nowhere else.   Old Lulli is simple,
> natural, even, too even sometimes, and this is a defect.   Young Rameau
> is singular, brilliant, complex, learned, too learned sometimes; but this
> is perhaps a defect in his listeners; Lulli has only one overture, beautiful
> in truth but repeated at the beginning of all his operas; the other has
> written as many overtures as operas and all pass for masterpieces.
> Nature has led Lulli in the paths of tunefulness; study and experience
> have laid bare to Rameau the springs of harmony.   Who has declaimed
> and recited as the elder has?   Who will give us light *arias*, voluptuous *airs*
> and character *symphonies* like the younger's?   Lulli is unrivalled in his
> grasp of dialogue.   Before Rameau no one had discerned the delicate
> shades that mark off the tender from the voluptuous, the voluptuous
> from the passionate, the passionate from the lascivious; a few supporters
> of this latter claim even that, if Lulli's dialogue is superior to his, this is
> less the fault of any inequality of talent than of the difference between the
> poets they have used.   "Read, they cry, the scene from *Dardanus*, and

---

[1] (33), I, 63.

you will be convinced that if Rameau is given good texts the ravishing scenes of Lulli will reappear." However this be, in my time the whole city ran to the tragedies of the one and crushed to the ballets of the other.[1]

In the world of theory Rameau's precision-loving nature, as well as his pernickety temper, led him into several discussions, evidence of which has come down in print.

On Sunday, May 8, 1729, "two fairly well-known musicians met in the house of someone whose daughter is an excellent clavecinist to discuss together upon several articles of harmony on which their opinions are opposed". The first one, that is, Rameau, had brought with him seven or eight friends. The second accused him of considering himself the only expert in the art of accompanying (that is, of playing from figured bass); "you say that what all other masters teach is worthless". Rameau replied in October, claiming that the system of the fundamental bass, "more and more followed throughout Europe, owes its inception entirely" to his *Traité de l'Harmonie*, where it was first expounded, and criticized the "second musician". He complained, moreover, that the discussion had been inaccurately reported in the June number of the *Mercure de France*.

The second musician retorted in May of the following year.

> What you pretend to have recently brought to birth has been common knowledge in Paris these thirty years and more; I know the man who taught it you when you were about thirty. You know that he lives in the Rue Planche-Mibray, next door to a sempstress.

Rameau, stung once again, took up the cudgels the next month.

> I have always taken pleasure in making known that M. Lacroix, of Montpellier, whose abode you have indicated, gave me precise knowledge of the octave rule when I was twenty. . . . But it is a far cry thence to the fundamental bass of which no one can boast to have given me the least notion.

(This stay in Montpellier, otherwise unrecorded, must date from 1702, between his temporary appointment at Avignon and his post at Clermont.)

> Do you not know [he drives home] that music is a physico-mathematical science, that sound is its physical object and that the relations between different sounds are its mathematical or geometrical object?

Thereafter the second musician held his peace but Rameau, to drive all possible nails into his coffin, returned to the charge in September 1731 with a *Lettre de M. à M. sur la musique*, in which he published an imposing "carte générale de la basse fondamentale avec une explication de cette carte".

---

[1] Chapter 13: *De l'opéra de Banza*.

I surmise that the "particulier" in whose house the acrimonious discussion took place may have been Boucon, whose daughter, a distinguished harpsichord player, was later to become Mme de Mondonville. As for the second musician, Michel Brenet thought it might be Bournonville, whom Laborde calls "the best teacher of accompaniment in his day", and who was held in esteem by Rameau. But a marginal note in the Bibliothèque Nationale copy of the *Mercure* for June 1729 says it was Montéclair, author of *Principes de musique* and a rival of Rameau; I think this is more likely than Bournonville, since it is clear from Rameau's tone that he did not hold this second musician "in esteem".[1]

Rameau's relations with Père Castel, the Jesuit mathematician who is remembered to-day for his *clavecin oculaire*, are more interesting and deserve more detailed study than I am able to give them here.

Castel, who was born at Montpellier in 1688, entered the Society of Jesus in 1703 and belonged to the Toulouse house. In 1711 he was sent to teach humanities at Clermont; at that time Rameau was in Dijon, and when he returned to Auvergne, Castel had left. His early eminence in mathematics reached the ears of Fontenelle, who, together with Père Tournemine, induced his superiors to send him to Paris in 1720. In the course of his life he was to contribute some three hundred articles and reviews to the *Journal de Trévoux* published by the Society and to write a number of books. His chief interests were threefold: gravitation (*la pesanteur universelle*), the development of mathematics, and music in colour. His *Traité de la pesanteur* sought to prove that the doctrine of gravitation was the key to the system of the Universe. In this age of "keys" and "secrets" to vast worlds, we are not surprised to hear that he was a friend of Abbé de Saint-Pierre, who was a kindred spirit in the field of political theory. His *Mathématique universelle* won him membership of the Royal Society, an honour accorded "without contradiction, solicitation or intrigue".[2] This work was highly praised in London, but in France it was criticized for not being sufficiently dry and austere. His best-known work,

---

[1] *Conférence sur la musique* (*Mercure*, June 1729, part 2).

Examen de la conférence sur la musique insérée dans le second volume du Mercure de juin, 1729 (*Mercure*, October 1729). (By Rameau.)

Plan abrégé d'une nouvelle méthode d'accompagnement pour le clavecin (*Mercure*, March 1730). (By Rameau.)

Réponse du second musicien au premier musicien sur les deux écrits qui concernent l'accompagnement du clavecin insérés dans le Mercure de février et de mars de la présente année (*Mercure*, June 1730, part 1).

Réplique du premier musicien sur l'harmonie (*Mercure*, June 1730, part 2). (By Rameau.)

Lettre de M. à M. sur la musique et l'explication de la carte générale de la basse fondamentale (*Mercure*, September 1731). (By Rameau.)

[2] *Éloge historique du Père Castel*, in *Journal de Trévoux*, April 1757. See also (225A).

Le Clavecin oculaire des couleurs, came out in 1740; he had been thinking of it since 1724 when Rameau encouraged him to publish it; he
first made it known in a letter to the *Mercure* in November 1725.
The clavecin was actually manufactured "several times over and at
great expense", but it

> did not realize the author's specifications nor satisfy the public's ex-
> pectations.... His person, books, innumerable writings, and workshop
> for the *clavecin oculaire* all lived in one same den, and one had to possess,
> like him, a mathematical sense to make out anything in that prodigious
> heap of objects of all value which made up his physical and mathematical
> treasury.[1]

He died in 1757.

When Rameau published his *Traité*, Castel wrote an enthusiastic
review and when the author settled in Paris the two met with interest
and formed a sort of mathematical friendship. But as the Jesuit
investigated further, he waxed less enthusiastic and began to doubt the
originality of Rameau's theories. His review of the *Nouveau Système*
was less warm and the musician was somewhat disappointed; yet they
remained friendly. In 1735, three articles entitled *Nouvelles expériences d'optique et d'acoustique adressées à M. le Président de Montesquieu*[1]
implied that Kircher and Zarlino both knew more about the fundamental bass than Rameau had allowed. This drew from Rameau a
Lettre,[2] in which one feels that the musician is straining to remain
suave and courteous; its ingratiating and circumlocutory style sounds
unnatural. In the course of his reply in September 1736 Castel noted
with disapproval that his correspondent's "genius had turned him
completely towards practical music against *his* [Castel's] opinion";
since 1734 Rameau "had been unable to reconcile our former intercourse of speculation with his new practice of the stage". Music for
Castel, it is clear, meant the theory of sounds, not the art itself. For
Rameau, fortunately, it meant both.

Rameau did not reply, and in 1737 Castel reviewed his *Génération
harmonique*. The review was considerably less favourable than his
earlier ones; he said quite frankly that when Rameau's first book came
out, fifteen years earlier, he was younger and still a novice in the subject, and that what he had learnt since had modified his opinion concerning both the originality and the value of the musician's theories.
This was too much for Rameau. . He threw to the winds all pretence
at suavity and wrote one of his most heavily irate retorts. He did not
entrust it to the Jesuit journal but sent it to Abbé Prévost, who printed
it in the 1738 volume of *Le Pour et Contre*.

The subject of the discussion is involved and remote, but this

---

[1] *Journal de Trévoux*, August, Parts 1 and 2, and September 1735.
[2] *Id.*, July 1736.

riposte brings us so directly in presence of Rameau's thorny, passionate personality that I cannot refrain from quoting from it.

> If the sole love of truth had moved the learned journalist of Trévoux in his reflexions on *La Génération harmonique*, he would have confined himself merely to the limits of the review, without entering into baseless discussions. Why has this celebrated mathematician, all together geometer, physicist, metaphysician, physico-mathematician, not used his learning otherwise than to fall into errors of which he would never have been suspected, did not the proof follow closely upon them? Should not this rare talent which he says he has, p. 2143, for "clarified exposition", for "methodical arrangement", for "systematic reconciling", for "full, correct and physico-mathematical demonstration" suffice him? Why forsake it in order to give himself up to "personal details, in which", as he says very truly, p. 1999, "the public takes no interest and whose only use is to feed the proper pride of those interested"? This lesson, which he gives me, concerns only him. . . . He dares claim that he gave me lessons of very geometry, that he has even communicated to me harmonic generations. . . . What! is it the author of *Universal Mathematics* who contests with me for the glory of my own poor discoveries—me, a mere musician? I must have succeeded; that is the proof of it. . . . "I agree readily", he says elsewhere, "that fifteen years ago I was younger by as much." The calculation is geometrical; so let us not hurry. Fifteen years hence he will perhaps have the same excuse.[1]

If Castel's memory is to be trusted—his good faith is not in doubt—in 1733, in the first flush, that is, of operatic parturition, Rameau had declared that he could not pursue "speculation" any further and had offered the father his papers "where everything would be found". Castel declined the offer because his views diverged by this time too widely from Rameau's. In particular, he respected the opinions of the Ancients; Rameau despised them. In any case, Rameau did not absent himself for more than a while from the felicity of "speculation".

In this passage from friendship to enmity we catch, I think, a clearer glimpse of Rameau's character than in the endless wrangles with Rousseau and d'Alembert later in life. It shows, among other things, that author's vanity affected Rameau the theorist more than Rameau the composer.[2]

Soon after his arrival in Paris he had met another mathematician, Dortous de Mairan, and had discussed with him his theory of harmon-

---

[1] *Le Pour et Contre*, tome XIV, 74–78.—Is it a coincidence that about this time Rameau ceased to be organist at the Jesuit Novitiate?—Castel let the matter drop. He returned to music in 1754 in connexion with Rousseau's *Lettre* in his *Lettre d'un Académicien de Bordeaux sur le fond de la musique*.

[2] Castel's papers, in the Bibliothèque Royale at Brussels, do not appear to contain any letters from Rameau.

ics.   No doubt about the same time he came to know Abbé de Gamaches, another member of the same Academy, author of several semi-
philosophic works, of a *Nouveau Système du Mouvement* (1721) and of
a treatise on physical astronomy, an attempt to reconcile the Cartesian
and Newtonian cosmogonies.[1]   It was Gamaches who made him see
the connexion between Mairan's theory and his own.[2]   All this must
have been taking place in the middle 'twenties, when he was also discussing his researches with Castel.   Gamaches was a canon of Ste.
Croix de la Bretonnerie, and it was no doubt thanks to him that, not later
than September 1732, Rameau was appointed organist of this church.

Of his private letters that have survived, several concern the defence of his theories.   One of the longest, dated November 1741,
is addressed to Christin, secretary of the Academy of Lyons, in order
to rectify certain misstatements made by Bollioud-Mermet in a
Mémoire published by the Academy.   It has not the acrimonious tone
of other defences and did not lead to a discussion.   A few years later,
a young musician in the provinces called Mongeot wrote to the great
man asking for advice and, in particular, "by what means a youthful,
inspired and willing musician could succeed in composing an opera"
(Rameau's words).   A difficult order, and Rameau might have had
cause to answer curtly so naïve a correspondent.   He did indeed begin
by saying that he was too busy to reply at length, but he then gave a
neat summary of all that was needed: familiarity with the stage, prolonged study of Nature "in order to paint her as truthfully as possible"; knowledge of every passion and great sorrow—imaginative
knowledge, presumably, not experience; sensitiveness to dancing,
knowledge of voices and actors, and the ability to command an
orchestra "and sometimes even the public"; knowledge of the possibilities of every instrument, "a little genius" and still more "a little
taste".   Nothing must be left to chance and it is best to begin on a
small scale with cantatas, *divertissements* and "such small nicknacks
which feed the mind, foster its spirits and gradually make it capable of
greater things".   He ends with a charming confession in which he
sums up his professional life: "I have attended the theatre since I was
twelve; I worked first for the Opéra at fifty, and even then I did not
think myself capable of doing so; I risked, I had luck, I went on.   In
a word I was brave . . . rash, and I have succeeded."   Mongeot
turned up in Paris in 1749 but never composed an opera.   In 1765,
when he published Rameau's letter in the *Mercure*, he was music
master to the children of the Princesse de Guéménée at Versailles.
Nothing more is known about him; he may be the Abbé Mongeot

---

[1] *Astronomie physique*, 1740.
[2] (12), 3–4.

whose motet *Cantate* was sung at a Concert spirituel on September 8, 1752,[1] and who appears to be equally unknown.

Strange though it seems to us, who enjoy his music but do not read his books, it was through his theories rather than his compositions that Rameau hoped to win renown.   He dedicated his *Génération harmonique* (1737) to the Academy of Science, and three of its members were given the task of reporting on it.   Two of them, Mairan and Gamaches, were as we have seen already familiar with his theories and thought well of them; the third was Réaumur.   Their report was printed as an appendix to the book.   Twelve years later he submitted another work to the Academy, a manuscript of forty-three pages; the reporting committee again included Mairan, the other two members being Nicole and d'Alembert.   The work was published in 1750 as *Démonstration du principe de l'harmonie* and this time the Academy's report was printed at the beginning.   It was extremely favourable.

> Thanks to M. Rameau's labours, harmony has become a more geometrical science and mathematical principles can be applied to it more usefully and more accurately than hitherto.

Rameau sees himself on the way to becoming an acknowledged figure in the French mathematical world.   Not content with this, he reaches out to enlist also the suffrages of foreign scientists.   As soon as the *Démonstration* appears he sends a copy to Jean Bernoulli (the second Jean), professor of mathematics at Basel, with a letter begging for "the seal of *his* approval".   Bernoulli must have answered favourably and have asked for another copy, for Rameau wrote again in April promising one and offering others.—If you want more, do not fail to ask; "I have plenty; I do not sell them, I give away as many as are wanted, only too happy if success crowns my expectations".   Two years later he writes again, sending the *Nouvelles réflexions . . . sur la Démonstration de l'harmonie.*

He scored less well with Euler. He had sent him the *Démonstration* but had received no acknowledgement.   Unabashed, when the *Nouvelles Réflexions* appeared, he tackled the Berlin academician again. This time Euler answered, putting him right on certain points.   After which snub Rameau judged that public correspondence was preferable to private and countered with an *Extrait d'une réponse à M. Euler sur l'identité des octaves* in which he disregarded Euler's criticisms.   It is clear that Euler set more store by Tartini's theories than by Rameau's. Whereas he expounded Tartini's *Trattato di musica* to the Berlin Academy of Science in 1758, "during all the time he was director of

---

[1] *Mercure de France*, October 1752.

the mathematical section (1746–1766) Rameau's name never appears in the reports".[1]

One last acquaintance may be mentioned in this chapter. He is the architect Charles-Etienne Briseux. Rameau refers to him without naming him in his second letter to Bernoulli. "Nous avons ici un architecte qui ne se conduit que par les proportions harmoniques, et qui vient de nous donner un bâtiment dont les dehors ont du neuf et de l'agréable". He is mentioned in the *Nouvelles Réflexions de M. Rameau sur sa démonstration du principe de l'harmonie*, a lengthy post-script to his book of that name. In 1752, the date of these reflexions, he was becoming more and more convinced that the study of proportions was the secret of . . . everything, "toutes les sciences", he was to claim later, to d'Alembert's horror and amusement, and he turned to architecture for confirmation of his belief. "The most celebrated architects . . . consider the length of the ground plan as the basis of every part of the building; from this length, by the divisions one makes of it in the same proportions as those of music, are drawn the beauties of elevation." He added:

> I have this last remark from M. Briseux, architect, who is about to give us a learned treatise on this subject, in which he reckons to demonstrate, *inter alia*, that the beautiful buildings of the Greeks and Romans . . . are founded on all the proportions drawn from music, which justifies the idea that I have long had that in music dwells most certainly and most sensibly the principle of all Fine Arts.[2]

He gave the architect's name and address two years later to an Italian correspondent, the Marchese di Poleni; the simplicity of the address is a comment on the growth of cities: "A M. Briseux, architecte, à Paris."

I suspect that Briseux's works would repay investigation. He was a man of Rameau's generation and part of France, born in 1680 at Baume-les-Dames in Franche-Comté. He had written upon his art; his first book was *L'Architecture moderne ou l'art de bâtir pour toutes sortes de personnes* (1728); he had specialized in the construction of country houses, one of which, an elegant little château for one of La Pouplinière's colleagues, the farmer-general d'Augny, erected at the gates of Paris in the Rue Neuve Grange-Batelière,[3] survives in the present Rue Drouot where it serves as the Mairie of the ninth *arrondissement*; he published in 1743 the results of his experience in this field, in *L'Art de bâtir des maisons de campagne*. Finally, he had reflected upon the principles of his art and in 1752, the same year as Rameau

---

[1] See E. Jacobi, *Nouvelles lettres inédites de J.-Ph. Rameau*, in *Recherches sur la musique française classique*, III (1964), 145–158. The dates are: to Jean Bernoulli, February 18 and April 27, 1750 and April 30, 1752; to Euler, September 12, 1752. Euler's letter is published in *Autographes de Mariemont*, part I, tome 2.

[2] (13), 50.   [3] Briseux lived in the same street.

referred to him in the preface of the *Nouvelles Réflexions*, he brought out his *Traité du Beau essentiel dans les Arts, appliqué particulièrement à l'Architecture*, followed by a *Traité des Proportions harmoniques*. He died two years later.

This last work, which is handsomely produced and headed with a most engaging portrait of the author, is printed in a type that imitates script—artistic enough but trying to the eye, at least in the light of a public library, and suggestive of a refined but idiosyncratic personality. Its theme is a defence of proportions against the attack of Claude Perrault who, himself reacting against excess of attention paid to Vitruvius, had belittled their importance. Though Rameau is mentioned only once,[1] the book shows familiarity with his theoretical writings and it is the work of a mind sensitive to music, ready to draw examples thence and to establish analogies between the two most abstract of the arts. One can imagine that the two elderly gentlemen, baroque survivors in an age of rococo, must have had much in common and must have met and discussed their kindred ideas about proportions more than the scanty evidence can prove. But whether, as Rameau announced,[2] Briseux's work demonstrated "that the fine buildings of the Greeks and the Romans *were* founded on all the proportions drawn from music" is more than I am able to assert.[3]

Rameau's relations with his family will be mentioned later. Other contacts with his native province seem to have been unimportant. "All his life", says Piron, "he honoured his countrymen" (the Dijonnais) "with the most perfect indifference and the deepest neglect, as his dearly beloved countrymen, without his reputation, would no doubt have honoured him."[4] Yet indifference and neglect gave way in July 1752 when the Société littéraire founded at Dijon by President Richard de Ruffey made him an honorary member. Rameau sent it his *Réflexions sur la manière de former la voix*[5] and shortly afterwards his *Réponse à M. Euler*. Ruffey's society was wound up in the early 'sixties and on May 22, 1761, the Academy of Dijon elected him a member; four years later, after his death, the secretary, Dr. Maret, delivered the obituary eulogy to which we owe much of our knowledge of his early life.

In the course of 1748 and 1749 six of his works had been performed; this was unprecedented for any composer.[6] It was this

---

[1] In an allusion to "the experiment that the celebrated Rameau has recorded in his *Traité de la Génération harmonique*"; I, 43.

[2] (13), 50.

[3] Cf. Louis Hautecœur, *Histoire de l'architecture classique en France*, III, 176, 199, 209, 276, 459, 464–465, etc.

[4] (92).

[5] *Mercure de France*, October 1752.

[6] *Les Fêtes d'Hébé* (*Les Talents lyriques*), *Zaïs*, *Les Fêtes de l'Hymen*, *Pygmalion*, *Platée*, *Naïs*.

quasi-monopoly of the operatic stage by one man that gave d'Argenson the opportunity for the limitation already mentioned. The turn of the half-century marks the climax in his fame. The Lullists are silenced; the new moderns have not yet arisen to class him in his turn as a back number. In 1748 Diderot, who was later to side against him, praised his theory of harmonic generation and expressed the wish that "someone should extract this admirable system from the obscurities that enwrap it and put it within everybody's reach, less for its inventor's glory than for the progress of the science of sounds".[1]

In 1752 d'Alembert did him the honour of presenting his theories in an easily intelligible form and in the most elegant and limpid prose style of the century by publishing *Éléments de musique théorique et pratique suivant les principes de M. Rameau*, for which the composer thanked him in a letter to the *Mercure* in May 1752.[2] D'Alembert had submitted his manuscript to Rameau beforehand; his accompanying letter is published in *Autographes de Mariemont*, part I, tome 2. He requests Rameau to look through it carefully and to make any comments he thinks needful. He suggests having it read by Ballot de Sauvot (the librettist of *Pygmalion*). Much of the letter is reproduced in the preface to the *Éléments*. Speaking also of a possible meeting at dinner at La Pouplinière's, the letter shows mathematician and composer on friendly terms. The *Discours préliminaire de l'Encyclopédie* put Rameau beside Descartes, Newton and Voltaire. "At this stage the Encyclopaedists are all more or less Ramists."[3]

In 1749 Melchior Grimm arrived in Paris and entered quickly into the cultural life of the city, mixing with advanced circles. He felt no reticence as a foreigner in judging the country whose guest he had become, and early in 1752 he published a letter on Destouches's opera *Omphale* (1701), which had just been revived. For long this letter has been looked upon as the first blow struck in the battle of the Bouffons. But *La Serva padrona* was not performed till August 1 of that year and the great final onslaught of Italian music had not begun. Grimm's letter is an attack on Destouches's opera, it is true, but it is as much a eulogy of Rameau,[4] for whom Grimm professes a veritable cult. In speaking of *Pygmalion* he exclaims: "The author of the monologues [in this ballet] must have been kindled by the divine fire we call genius."[5] He praises his variety: "What a Proteus, ever new, ever original, always grasping what is true and sublime in each character!"[6] So excessive, indeed, did his praises appear that Raynal reproached him for their exaggeration.[7] Rousseau replied in a well-

---

[1] (63a), IX, 115.

[2] Rameau expressed his gratitude in a letter to the *Mercure* (May 1752).

[3] (186), 17.

[4] This has been shown conclusively by P. M. Masson in the article just mentioned.

[5] (72), 304–305.   [6] *Id.*, 307.   [7] *Mercure*, March 1752.

known *Lettre* in which he attempted with a wry face a would-be impartial judgment of Rameau.

Grimm's letter of February 1752 is the last episode in the Lulli-Rameau quarrel. For a short while, Rameau, having silenced his enemies and conquered the esteem of thinkers and music-lovers, is at the height of his fame. Two years later, all this has changed and Grimm has become one of his most violent critics.

In 1753 the Rameaus spent the summer at Passy for the last time. Already the year before they had returned to that Rue des Bons Enfants where Couperin had died nearly twenty years earlier, where Abbé Dubos had dwelt, where Rameau himself had lived from 1735 to 1744. It is not known whether the house they now inhabited was that Hôtel d'Effiat where he lived then, but it was on the same side of the street and backed on to the gardens of the Palais Royal. These gardens were more extensive than at present and they were open to the surrounding streets; the galleried buildings which now surround them on three sides were not erected till 1781 when the landlord, the Duke of Orleans, the future Philippe-Égalité, laid out three streets and the galleries as a commercial undertaking. He curtailed thereby the spacious park where Rameau had so often walked, where he had observed the little whirls of dust which he attempted to render in *Les Tourbillons*, and where, too, after his death, when the musical climate was already very different, the youthful Mozart came to say his chaplet of thanksgiving after the successful performance of his Paris symphony.

His existence during these last twelve years of his life was externally uneventful. "The emptiness which he found in society made him avoid it."[1] Never ready to make contacts, he drew in more and more upon himself, husbanding his strength for "literary and learned disputes"[2] and, to a lesser extent, for composition. For to the very end he produced operas and ballets, though at a slower tempo than between the ages of fifty and seventy. In October and November 1753 three one-act ballets, *Daphnis et Églé, Lysis et Délie* and *Les Sybarites*; two more in 1754, *La Naissance d'Osiris* and *Anacréon*, which must not be confused with the *entrée* of the same name in *Les Surprises de l'Amour*. All five were ordered for performance at Fontainebleau; *Lysis et Délie*, however, was found to be so similar to *Daphnis et Eglé* which had been given a week earlier that it was cancelled and the music, which Rameau may have used elsewhere, has not been preserved. In 1760, for the first time for nine years, a new work of his was given on the stage of the Opéra. This was his second *comédie lyrique, Les Paladins*. It was also his last new work to be performed. In 1764 he worked at a full-scale *tragédie lyrique, Abaris ou Les Boréades*, which he completed and which was to have been performed at the Opéra in the autumn of that year. But his

---

[1] (59), 8.   [2] (26).

death in September stopped the rehearsals and the work, which seems
to have been ordered largely out of respect for the venerable musician,
was not given and remains unperformed and unpublished to this
day.

The court pieces amounted to only six acts, so that his musical
production had dropped considerably.   On the other hand, his literary efforts were unflagging.   In 1754, 1755 and 1756, stimulated
and irritated by Rousseau's and d'Alembert's articles on musical
topics in the *Encyclopédie*, he produced *Observations sur notre instinct
pour la musique et son principe, Erreurs sur la musique dans l'Encyclopédie* and *Suite des erreurs....*   A reply by d'Alembert called
forth in 1757 a *Réponse de M. Rameau à MM. les Éditeurs de
l'Encyclopédie sur leur dernier avertissement*, and the energy and heat
generated in this polemic condensed in 1760 into one last book, *Code
de musique pratique*, to which some *Nouvelles Réflexions sur le principe
sonore* were added as a postscript.   Two further letters to d'Alembert
and a final *Lettre aux Philosophes* bring us to 1762; for this last he had
recourse to that *Journal de Trévoux* where, a quarter of a century
earlier, he had had his bitter-sweet correspondence with Père Castel.
To the very end he wrote, hammering and re-hammering his assertions
in the face of d'Alembert's courteous disdain.   When he died, he left
three unfinished works on the origins of science, sixteen pages of one
of which, *Vérités intéressantes peu connues jusqu'à nos jours*, with a
fearsome array of erasures and interlinings in his small, nervous hand,
are preserved in the Conservatoire library in Paris.[1]

He was an unclear writer and he knew it.   He had a mathematician's but not an author's pride and he readily sought help from others
in the expression of his ideas.   Diderot is said to have had a hand in
drafting the *Démonstration du principe de l'harmonie* in 1760.[2]   Later,
another friend and collaborator came into his life.   This was Abbé
François Arnaud, a Provençal from Carpentras with literary and
scientific ambitions who turned up in Paris in 1752.   A friend of
Suard, he was much esteemed for his conversation and high spirits.
In 1754 he had published a *Lettre sur la musique à M. le comte de
Caylus*; at this time he was already in touch with Rameau, who on
occasions opened his heart to him.   It is to Arnaud, according to
Grétry, that he said: "If I was thirty years younger, I would go to
Italy; Pergolese would be my model. . . .   But at over sixty one
realizes that one must stay where one is."[3]

His letter to Caylus, which contained the criticism of a *minutia* in
Les Fêtes d'Hébé, did not antagonize the old composer and two years
later he turned to him for help.   In 1756 the *Code* was on its way to
completion and Rameau wished to herald its appearance with a pros-

---

[1] See (25A).
[2] According to Raynal, *Nouvelles littéraires*, I, 313.
[3] In Grétry's *Mémoires* (1797), I, 426–427.

pectus. D'Alembert had recently praised Rousseau for his ability "to think and express himself clearly" and Rameau, who knew that this was a hit at his own obscurity, alludes to this remark in a letter to Arnaud, the gist of which is to enlist the Abbé's help in drafting the prospectus. A second letter, of August 19, 1757, somewhat rambling, turns on the same subject; the prospectus came out that same year. It is possible that not only the prospectus but the *Code* itself benefited by Arnaud's advice. He is stated to have helped later another musician in the throes of literary expression, Padre Martini.

In a third letter, dated June 7, 1758, he asked advice for one of his works[1]—doubtless the *Code* still; but this letter, which appeared in a sale early in this century, has been lost sight of. Possibly there were others. A private correspondence existed also between Rameau and d'Alembert, in addition to the unamiable public exchanges, but it too is lost.[2]

In one of these letters to Arnaud Rameau speaks of his ill-health. Already in 1750 the preface of the *Démonstration* mentions the "peu de santé" he had enjoyed for some years.[3] But, as with Voltaire, whom he resembled physically and with whom it became commonplace to compare him, this chronic ill-health did not restrict his activity.

A pamphlet, the work of a self-important *inconnu* who plagued the old man with views on his theories and, receiving but short shrift, revenged himself in print, has preserved another letter and perpetuated an incident which was probably typical.[4] One does not attain to Rameau's celebrity without being written to by all and sundry, some of whom use this opportunity to air opinions otherwise unairable and to snatch for themselves a reflected ray from the great man's light.

M. Ducharger "de Dijon" had written from St. Malo on December 12, 1753, criticizing certain points in his theoretical works. Receiving no acknowledgment, he endeavoured to enlist Maupertuis's help but the Breton mathematician alleged his incompetence and made the obvious suggestion that Ducharger should approach Rameau directly. This he did and he received a reply by a circuitous route—via Abbé Trublet, who passed on the message to his brother, M. de la Flourie, who gave it to Ducharger—saying that Rameau "would insert his reply in the book which he was writing to refute M. Rousseau who had attacked him". Thereupon Ducharger wrote to Rameau to inquire when this book would appear. He received the curt answer which he published and for which, Rameau's letters being so few, we are duly thankful.

SIR,

The book in question is at present in print: it is entitled *Observations sur notre instinct pour la Musique*. I have neither time to write nor

---

[1] According to a sales catalogue mentioned by Tiersot (235).
[2] (235); (187).   [3] (12), xxii.   [4] (66).

CHARLES ÉTIENNE BRISEUX
From an engraving in his *Traité des proportions harmoniques*

health to think, to reflect; forgive me, Sir, I am old, you are young, and I am your very humble and very obedient servant,

RAMEAU

At Paris, this 13 June 1754.

When the *Observations* appeared, Ducharger found indeed an allusion to his contribution on p. 11, but without mention of his name and lumped with other nameless contributors. Moreover, the terms of the allusion were unflattering. "The authors of these writings will perhaps thank me for not naming them." Ducharger was offended at being baulked of his crumb of fame. "I do not thank him (*Je ne lui sais point gré*)", he declared. He therefore decided to print his St. Malo letter which had received such unfitting acknowledgment and to give the *historique* of his relations with the composer. The pamphlet is the result. It is, of course, an attack on Rameau who, he asserts, has incurred a debt to him and whom he accuses of contradictions and "fausses idées". Rameau disdained to reply and the matter dropped, but Ducharger has nevertheless entered the House of Fame under a few square inches of the great man's cloak, and perhaps, in the Elysian Fields, "il lui en sait gré".[1]

Rameau's touching *billet* is not the only expression of regret at his age. To another fellow Dijonnais, the young organist Balbâtre, he confessed:

> Music is perishing [*la musique se perd*]; taste is changing every moment. I should not know how to manage if I had to work as I did in the past; there is only Daquin who has had the courage to resist the torrent; he has always preserved for the organ the majesty and graces which befit it.[2]

His fame involved him in correspondence with people abroad such as the Paduan Marchese di Poleni who had written asking about the work by Briseux to which Rameau had alluded in the *Nouvelles réflexions* and enquiring whether Rameau was preparing anything else. Rameau hastened to "submit a new work for his scrutiny", probably the *Observations* of 1754, and to give him the desired information about the architect.[3]

---

[1] It is perhaps unfair to call Ducharger an *inconnu*. He is the author of an *Entretien d'un musicien français avec un gentilhomme russe sur les effets de la musique moderne ou tableau des concerts de province* (Dijon, Defay, 1773), containing an interesting account of concerts in his native town, in whose orchestra he played the 'cello. Leopold Mozart, who heard him there in 1766, noted him as one of the people in the musical world to see on his son's behalf, adding the appreciation *misérable*; the context shows that this refers to his playing. His name was written also De Chargey and Du Chargé (*Mozart en France*, Paris, 1956, 19).

[2] (74); III, 377.

[3] Facsimile in Erwin Jacobi's edition of Rameau's *Pièces de clavecin*, xviii.

A few years later we find him in touch with Padre Martini.

At the age of seventy-five he was again possessed of a desire for the approval of a foreign institution, perhaps to offset the attacks against him in Encyclopaedic circles.   Early in 1759 he submitted to the Accademia delle Scienze dell'Instituto di Bologna a manuscript entitled *Nouvelles réflexions sur le principe sonore* which was to be published in 1760, with many alterations, as postscript to the *Code de musique pratique*.   It was some time before the manuscript was acknowledged and in April he wrote again, at very great length, heading his letter with the request "have the goodness to read all, or to have it read so that an account of it can be given to you".   This was dealt with by the distinguished scientist J. B. Beccari who passed the manuscript on to Padre Martini, the only musical member of the Academy, asking him and another member to report on it.   Martini had known Rameau's theories since the later 'forties and, though he did not agree with them, he considered them worthy of consideration.   There ensued a correspondence of which have survived five letters of Rameau (two to Beccari, three to Martini) and seven from Martini to Rameau, besides several others between Martini and Rameau's brother-in-law Jacques-Simon Mangot, since 1756 *maestro di cappella* at the court of Parma, who acted as go-between while a quarrel of the Paris and Geneva posts held up communications.

Martini took his task very seriously.   He not only translated Rameau's manuscript; he also translated, or caused to be translated, the whole corpus of his published works.[1]   This took time, and on August 7 Rameau wrote to Beccari with polite impatience, suspecting an unfavourable report. — Criticize me, he said, if I am wrong; but at least let me know your criticisms so that I may profit by them. — But Martini would not be hurried and a letter to Mangot of April 8, 1761, shows that the work was then still unfinished.   Rameau did not make things easier by sending twice over batches of insertions and excisions. Moreover, he was as bad a correspondent as ever.   One of Martini's letters (January 3, 1760) he coolly passed on to someone else to deal with, perhaps the obliging Arnaud, with the instructions:

Vous voyez de quoi il est question, j'ai des idées sur le Tétracorde, son auteur est-il cité, c'est ce que je voudrais savoir, aussi bien que celui qui donne à entendre que Pythagore était fondé en progressions, dont cependant il n'est nullement question dans le Denarius Pythagoricus.[2]   Par-

---

[1] He also translated into Italian Rameau's letters, and one of them into Latin!

[2] By Jan van Meurs (Johannes Meursius), Leyden, 1631.

don si je n'ai pas l'honneur de vous aller voir, notre éloignement me prive de vous voir aussi dans le quartier, du moins à dîner.

When Martini's report was finally ready it was by no means an eulogy or an endorsement.   There is no record of its presentation; in fact Rameau's name is as absent from the Bolognese as from the Berliner academy's archives, but the style of its fifteen and a half pages of roughly forty lines each suggests that it was intended to be delivered as an address.   Though he disagrees with Rameau he gives his theory a fair exposition and shows he understands it.   His estimate, says Jacobi, is that "his system is thoroughly modern and a far cry from the excellent old Italian school; it would be grossly unjust towards that school if to-day's Italians were to follow Rameau, for Italy has given its laws to all the nations beyond the Alps but has never itself adopted the laws of any other school.   Martini feels that Rameau's system can be of value in the secular and theatrical styles but not in the polyphonic and church ones where he even considers it to be harmful".[1]

What Rameau, now verging on seventy-nine, thought of this is not known but is easy to guess.   Correspondence on the topic ceased but in May 1762 Martini asked Rameau to help Goldoni who was settling in Paris, and he wrote again in August.

Yet one more acquaintance is left to be mentioned—one who entered his life in its closing years and whom he always welcomed. This is Chabanon, a young Colonial born in 1730 in Santo Domingo, who had devoted eight years of his existence to the study of music, then several more to that of letters.   He entered the Academy of Inscriptions in 1760 and the French Academy in 1780, and died in 1792.   In his latter years he wrote two books on music: *Observations sur la Musique* (1779) and *De la Musique considérée en elle-même* (1785).

Attracted by the great man, he had watched him taking his solitary walks in the Tuileries and the Palais Royal, never speaking to anyone, unless it were to some lady the bark of whose dog jarred on him.[2] For a long time the admiring youth thought he was "plunged in learned meditations" and never dared disturb him.   One day, however, he obtained an introduction.   Far from being lost in deep thought, Rameau assured him that he was thinking of nothing whatever and that he would always enjoy being addressed and taken out of

---

[1] See (161C), 473.

[2] A little dog in the Palais Royal gardens barked each time Rameau passed.   "Madame," said he to the beast's mistress, "de grâce faites taire cet animal; il a la voix on ne peut plus désagréable" ((59), 8)—quite possibly as apocryphal an anecdote as Bachaumont's about the priest who came to hear his confession when he was dying.

his empty idle life. Chabanon took him at his word and had no reason to regret it, but he noticed that Rameau always seemed startled when he was first accosted, as if he had been far away, and sometimes he did not recognize the visitor until he heard his name, although they had been speaking together but a short time before. The musician was at that time nearing eighty. Against the almost universal judgment of unsociability, unapproachability and habitual bad temper, this glimpse of a more genial and quite unassuming old Rameau is precious.[1]

From time to time he would attend the Opéra, usually trying to pass unnoticed. Sometimes he failed and would be applauded. Now and again he had to pay a visit to Fontainebleau for a performance of one of his works on the Court stage. The year before his death *Castor et Pollux* was performed there and Chabanon espied him, walking up and down a sequestered and ill-lighted room.

> I ran towards him to embrace him; he started abruptly to take flight and came back only on hearing my name. Then, excusing the weirdness of his welcome, he said that he avoided compliments because they embarrassed him and he never knew how to reply.[2]

His temper, which had never been easy and had led to many unpleasant exchanges between other artists and himself, remained the same when it came to securing a good performance. When rehearsing *Les Paladins*, some actress complained that the accompaniment was so full that no one would hear what she was singing. He is alleged to have retorted: "No matter whether one hears your words as long as one hears my music."[3] People have tried to build an aesthetic of pure music upon this sally, maintaining that Rameau was quite indifferent to the meaning of his text. It is clear that the reply, if authentic, must be understood in its setting as a way of shutting up a self-assertive *virtuosa*.

The great event in his life during this period, as in that of every Frenchman interested in music, was the quarrel concerning the *buffoni*, or Italian comic-opera actors. The story has been told too often for me to go over it yet again. The incident that unleashed the war was the performance, in August 1752, of *La Serva padrona*, followed by several other Italian *opere buffe*, among them being Leonardo Leo's *I Viaggiatori*. Strange to say, *La Serva padrona* had been given in Paris six years previously and had fallen flat. No one has explained what change of factors made the climate so very different when the work returned.

---

[1] (53), 52–53.   [2] *Id.*, 53–54.
[3] First reported in the *Journal anglais*, I (1775). Decroix, Rameau's last and most determined champion, hotly denies its authenticity in *L'Ami des Arts*.

These performances brought to a head the old opposition between pro-Italians and pro-French. All the emotions and arguments that had fluttered and flickered to and fro since the days of Lulli hardened now round a few points and the issues appeared suddenly in heightened light. Instead of enumerating once again the principles at stake, I prefer to quote from a contemporary whose words will express imaginatively what this Italian *buffo* music could mean to a young Frenchman.

After a few weeks of illness

> a few doses of Italian music . . . have set my machine again in order. Italian music has been a lucky specific for me. So you will not be surprised if, in the quarrel which divides music-lovers to-day, I have sided with the pro-Italians. I owed this as a debt of gratitude and as I pride myself on this virtue I have sported the colours of the Queen's side.[1] . . . There are there half a dozen confederates, people of genius, who have sworn to wipe out French music or to make it change so greatly that if Lulli and even Rameau come back in half a century they will not recognize it.[2]

There were two sides to this and they are both found in this passage. It has been said, I believe by Cocteau, that one never cries: "Vive X. . . ." without implying "A bas Y . . .". And enthusiasm for the Bouffons implied hostility for French opera of the Lulli-Rameau tradition. It was, indeed, hard to separate them if only for the very practical reason that there was in Paris only one operatic stage and that you could not accept one without excluding the other. Moreover, the intransigence of the upholders of national glories provoked a corresponding intransigence and violence in those who attacked them. We sometimes think of French patriotism as particularly exclusive, but there are in France other brands of sentiment that are astonishingly anti-national and delight in running down everything home-grown and praising up everything foreign—the meaning of "foreign" varying according to the period. This failing, which we sometimes consider to be also British. has been endemic in France since the end of the seventeenth century. One extreme has begotten the other.

Rousseau, of course, was a foreigner; so was Grimm; but there were plenty of Frenchmen who, like Montucla, saw no good in French dramatic music and all good in Italian (which included German composers like Hasse and Handel-Endelli who passed in France for Italians). This provoked the antagonism of other Frenchmen, such as Piron, who were not particularly musical but were piqued by the

---

[1] "Le coin de la Reine": the side on which the queen's box was and where the pro-Italians grouped themselves.

[2] A letter from Montucla, a Lyonnais lawyer, to the Academy of Lyons, read at a public meeting of that body on January 25, 1754; in (236A), 459.

onslaught on a national institution.　　And so the battle at once passed over the bounds of aesthetics and committed deep-seated passions.

The labels were not clear to everyone, at least as time went on. Mme de Genlis, who tells us that she often saw Rameau in her youth, loved *Le Devin du Village* which she called

> a charming work which will always please those who like what is natural, for one finds in it a musical expression singularly suited to the words, and which since then has been seen in this degree of truth only in Monsigny's *opéras-comiques* and Gluck's grand operas.

This would seem to class her as a Bouffonist.　　But in a footnote she adds:

> The celebrated Rameau had already given examples of so desirable an agreement, notably in *Pygmalion*: "Fatal amour, cruel vainqueur". The most perfect declamation could not express better the words of this *ariette*.[1]

To this catholic-minded young lady there was no incongruity in coupling in the same praise the two men who were at the opposite poles of the conflicting tastes.

Rameau was a dogmatic character but not a fanatic, except, in his extreme old age, where his "principe" was concerned.　　He was not swept off his feet by the crying up of *opera buffa* and the crying down of the art form to which he had given the best twenty years of his life. In the *Code de Musique pratique*, which had been preparing while the battle raged and was partly a reply to Rousseau, there is the significant declaration: "To embrace one national taste rather than another is to prove that one is very much a novice in the art."[2]　　The remark made to Abbé Arnaud quoted higher up, that if he was younger he would take Pergolese as his model, shows the same open-mindedness.　　He is known to have admired certain works of the new French *opéra-comique* which arose as an acclimatized form of the Italian import, especially Dauvergne's *Les Troqueurs*[3] and Philidor's *Le Maréchal*.[4]

> Forecasting to what degree of perfection this form might be carried in the future, he would think with emotion [*avec attendrissement*] of the progress which taste for this opera [i.e. *opéra-comique*] would bring about in good music.[5]

In 1758 or 1759 an unidentified private stage performed a comic opera entitled *Le Procureur dupé* in which there occurs a burlesque edict, a caricature of the royal decree which had dismissed the Bouffons. The inclusion of this piece shows clearly on which side were the

---

[1] (154), II, 1–2.　　　　[2] (21), xvi.　　　　[3] (85), note 48.
[4] (59), 11.　　　　　　　[5] (85), note 48.

sympathies of the author and his audience.   The music for this little play is not preserved but the manuscript of the text says it was by Rameau, whose task amounted probably to arranging rather than composing, since the comedy was "mêlé de vaudevilles"—ditties sung to well-known airs.   His co-operation in a pro-Bouffon piece is proof that he did not side with the extremer defenders of the national style.[1]

Yet he could not but be irritated by Rousseau's *Lettre sur la musique française* which is to-day the only literary survival from the contest.   Here his own views on his art must have chimed in with his antipathy to the writer.   Rousseau knew a lot about music, just as Gladstone knew a lot about Homer; but his opinions on the art have about as much intrinsic worth as the statesman's on the Greek poet. Unfortunately, he had been entrusted by d'Alembert and Diderot with some of the articles on musical subjects in the *Encyclopédie*.   In the earlier volumes the articles *Accompagnement*, *Chœur* and *Enharmonique* were by him, and *Cadence*, *Dissonance*, *Fondamental* and *Gamme* by d'Alembert.   All of these contained statements with which Rameau could not agree and, in spite of his hitherto friendly relations with the editors, he was impelled to collect his criticisms of them in *Erreurs sur la Musique dans l'Encyclopédie*, a publication of which neither the title nor the content[2] were calculated to preserve this friendliness.   I allude in the next chapter to such points in this work, and in the *Suite des Erreurs* which followed it and which was devoted entirely to Rousseau's *Enharmonique* article, as they concern Rameau's aesthetic theories.

The practical effect of this was to throw d'Alembert into the anti-Rameau camp, to which, as an admirer of Italian music, he was already prone to belong.   An anonymous *avertissement* by the editors affected to reply to him; it was short, disingenuous, and distorted some of his statements.   Rameau, who seldom let anything pass, retaliated with a *Réponse* in 1757.   The attack on Rousseau's contribution arose directly from the Querelle, but those on d'Alembert's concerned the deeper and dearer subject of his own acoustico-musical speculations, and thus was initiated the final stage of this unhappy discussion. Parts of the *Code de Musique pratique* and still more the *Nouvelles Réflexions sur le principe sonore*, the two letters to d'Alembert and the final *Lettre aux Philosophes* are in a wrangling tone *ad hominem*— the *homo* being, of course, d'Alembert, generally alluded to as "les géomètres".   The first of the two personal letters to him (1760), "sur ses opinions en musique insérées dans les articles *Fondamental* et

---

[1] (220).

[2] E.g., remarks *ad hominem* such as: "A lack of ear is a great obstacle to whoever sets up as a legislator in music" (p. 13).

Gamme de l'Encyclopédie", opens hopefully with the accusation: "It is clear enough that you have chosen the articles *Fondamental* and *Gamme* to declare open war against me."

"Speculation", personalities and debating points are mixed in this distressing letter. That same year, the mathematician, who was not, he says, accustomed to reply to what was written against him, broke his rule because of Rameau's reputation and published a brief acknowledgment, promising a fuller answer later. It was published, bound with a *Réponse* by Rameau in which he re-expounded at length his theories. D'Alembert had said that he generally contented himself with "démentis laconiques" to his critics; Rameau retorted: "You are as laconic on the subject of your misdeeds as you are diffuse in your criticisms." One may doubt whether the mathematician troubled to read all this. His real answer appeared in 1762 with a second edition of the *Éléments de musique*, preceded by a *Discours préliminaire* which both acted as a reply and effected a restatement, clever and elegant, mingling praise and blame. At the end, twenty pages answer more directly Rameau's letters, with allusions that show that the writer had at least glanced at other recent productions of the ageing genius. When one has fought one's way, gasping and oppressed, through the eiderdown opacity of Rameau's turgid prose, the relief one feels on emerging into the crystal air of d'Alembert's easy writing is inexpressible! The chief allusion to the Querelle is in this sentence where eulogy and belittlement are insidiously interwoven: "Before hearing your operas I thought that no one could go further than Lulli and Campra; before hearing the music of the Italians, I imagined nothing above ours."[1] And when we realize that "the music of the Italians" means mainly *opera buffa*, this gives also the measure of the distinguished writer's judgment as a critic of music!

It is regrettable that the Querelle and its issues could not have been kept separate from the squabbles about the "principe sonore". When Rameau bestrode his domineering hobby-horse he twaddled; on the points raised by Rousseau he had right on his side. He was, in brief, defending the cause of good music. He hit the nail on the head when he branded the critics of French music as untrained *littérateurs*.

> To know the limits where one should stop [in judging of melody] great experience is needed, and to acquire it one has to have listened often and long to music full of harmony, so to speak from the cradle. Your *philosophes, gens de lettres, artistes,* whom you take for judges of your opinions in your *Mélanges de Littérature,* IV, 443 [that is, *De la Liberté de la Musique*] have perhaps never listened to anything but ditties [*chansons*], even at a ripe age.[2]

---

[1] (30A), 228.
[2] (20), 12. For the ins and outs of this final quarrel between d'Alembert and Rameau see E. Jacobi, (161B), 100–108.

The Encyclopaedists had one reason

for celebrating Italian music: its mediocrity. . . .   The Querelle des Bouffons is a quarrel of bad music against good.   Foreign or hostile to music, or, like Jean-Jacques, only remotely familiar with it, all they looked for in it was a facile amusement and, as one said in those days, "cadences and refrains favourable to the digestion of good dinners". Grimm declared frankly: "Italian music gives pleasure to all men who have ears; no more preparation than that is needed" . . .   Rousseau owns ingenuously that "it is very tiring for me to follow scores which are rather heavily laden"; he condemns without appeal Rameau's operas "where one hears several simultaneous themes which destroy one's attention by dividing it because it is impossible for the ear to lend itself at once to several melodies and because one effaces the impression made by the other and the only result is confusion and noise".   Thus does an overweening and simple-minded philosopher turn his mental weakness into a law of art.[1]

The Querelle, in fact, and the triumph of the facile, the senti-mental and the unprofessional which it heralded, is but the fall of that night which was to descend upon French music for more than a hundred years, which even Berlioz was unable to penetrate, and which persisted till it was dispelled in the closing years of the nineteenth century.

What is curious in Rousseau's criticisms is that he appeared in-capable of distinguishing theory from practice, intention from realiza-tion.   There is no doubt that the orchestra of the Paris Opéra at this time was composed of indifferent executants and, in particular, that it was unable to play otherwise than *forte*.   Hence the continuous din of which so many listeners complain.

Imagine an unending and tuneless uproar of instruments, a perpetual dragging droning of the bass; the most mournful, the most boring thing I have ever heard and that I have never been able to bear for more than half-an-hour without a violent headache.   It all makes up a sort of chanting in which there is as a rule neither song nor beat.   But when by good luck there comes a rather tripping tune, everything begins stamping; you hear the whole orchestra pit in motion follow with difficulty and great noise a certain man in it.   Delighted to feel for a moment that rhythm which they feel so little, they torture their ears, their voices, their arms, feet and whole body to run after the beat always ready to evade them.

And in a footnote: "I think it a good comparison to have likened the light airs of French music to a cow galloping or a fatted goose trying to fly."[2]   In this passage the two things are mixed up and the criticism of the execution merges with that of the music.

---

[1] (170), 26.   [2] (103), II, letter 23.

Jokes about the noisy playing of the Opéra were traditional. Abbé Galiani, the noted wit, had said it ought to be re-erected outside the city gates, at the Barrière de Sèvres, opposite the bull-ring, because loud noises should be banished from the town.[1]

D'Alembert's solemn voice was added to the chorus and his judgment was as undiscerning as that of others.

> The fury of our French musicians is to pile part upon part. They make effect consist in noise; the voice is covered and drowned by their accompaniments which it impairs in its turn. It is like hearing twenty different books read at the same time.[2]

Defenders of French music recognized the shortcomings of instrumentalists and singers but endeavoured to keep the two things separate.

> It is not to our national music but often to the way of playing it that one should attribute the ridicule which foreigners who know it badly or fellow-countrymen who decry it disingenuously wish to shower on it unreflectingly; this is particularly true of the récitatif.[3]

When Rameau defends a rich accompaniment against those who prefer Italian meagreness, he says that it is not fair to blame the composer for an orchestral part which the band plays too loud.

> A true proportion should be kept between voices and instruments, a proportion the lack of which [in performance] is never suspected by those whose intention is to criticize, otherwise there would be much bad faith in their criticism.[4]

Still having in mind Rousseau's letter and defending the fullness of orchestral writing he repeated in his *Lettre à M. d'Alembert*: "It would have been much more fitting to lessen the noise of the instruments than to deprive Nature of a part of what she prescribes in the resonance of the Sounding Body."[5] When one bears in mind this defect of the Paris orchestra, much of the attacks on French opera and of the preference given to the thinly accompanied vocal music of the *buffonisti* becomes intelligible.

---

[1] (71), I, 351 (April 1763).—The artistes were included in this criticism. The complaint that they sing much too loud returns again and again in visitors' accounts of the Opéra.   That this tradition is not extinct may be inferred from the following (private) opinion of the revival of *Les Indes galantes* in May 1952.   "Quelques artistes du chant exagèrent leur rôle de 'derviches hurleurs'.   C'est une maladie héréditaire et contagieuse sur notre première scene lyrique.   Elle conduit à chanter faux dans le registre élevé."

[2] (29), 448.—But in an earlier *fragment* ((32), 188), written, he says, about 1752, he asserts that the Opéra orchestra played sometimes loud, sometimes soft, but never *à demi jeu* (*mf*).

[3] *Mercure de France*, March 1762; 182–183.

[4] (18), 38.   [5] (23), 12.

Attacks on Rameau extended to his person.   The best known is
the particularly venomous one, put by Diderot into the mouth of his
nephew, near the beginning of *Le Neveu de Rameau*.   It is too
familiar and too slanderous to be quoted.   Rameau showed himself a
good husband and, except perhaps at the very end, a good father.
Malevolent caricatures depict him as interested solely in music and
money, insensitive to affection and miserly in the extreme.

There are enough instances to show that he was not ungenerous.
In his youth and middle age he was a poor man.   Voltaire recognized
this when, in 1745 and 1749, he gave up to him all the payment for
La Princesse de Navarre and *Le Temple de la Gloire*.   A pension in
1745 and another in 1750 were granted him, and by degrees, through
much careful management, he became comfortably off.   His family
was included in this care.   In 1740 he took out an annuity of a hundred
and sixty livres for himself, his wife and his daughter Marie-Louise.
Tontines were taken out in 1745 for his wife, daughter and second son
Alexandre who died shortly afterwards.   In 1750 Marie-Louise went
into a convent of Visitandines at Montargis and her father gave her
a dowry.[1] Further investments for his eldest son and younger daughter,
Claude and Marie-Alexandrine, were made in 1758.   He had already
purchased for Claude the post of king's *valet de chambre* for the sum of
21,500 livres.   In 1739–1740 he sold his house in Dijon to a certain
Bazin and three letters relating to this transaction have survived; they are
the only private letters of his known to us.[2]   The third of them shows
him giving up to his sisters a sum which his correspondent owed him.

> If you would give my sisters the little treat of giving up to them the
> rest of the last year which comes to an end on February 15, I should be
> much obliged to you on my own account; I have already relinquished
> all the rest to them and would do more if I could.[2]

And Maret tells us that he gave an allowance, always paid punctually,
to his sister Catherine, whose infirmities had made her incapable of
earning her living.[3]

That this carefulness may, in his extreme old age, have turned to
avarice, is possible.   Though he lived in a comfortable flat of ten
rooms with his wife and two children, the inventory drawn up after
his death shows poor furniture and wardrobe.   The only instrument
was "un vieux clavecin à un clavier en mauvais état".   His clothes
were well worn; his wife possessed few jewels.   He had scarcely
any books: the *Mercure de France, Journal de Trévoux* and a few works
of piety; not much music: among it sixteen copies of the "premier
livre de pièces de clavecin" (certainly that of 1724), twelve of the
"second livre" (the *Nouvelles pièces* of c. 1728) and twelve of the

---

[1] But was not present at her clothing.
[2] (235) and (161A).   [3] (85), note 3.

Pièces en concert. There was a small stock of Hérissé wine (a Burgundian vineyard). But in his bureau there was coin in bags amounting to 40,584 livres; that is, 1691 louis d'or.[1] Simple furnishings,
poor clothing, and money in bags: have we not here something
suspiciously suggestive of the traditional miser?

The only discreditable detail told of him comes from his enemy
Collé. "Je suis Dupuis," he is alleged to have declared. Now,
Dupuis is a hero in Collé's comedy *Dupuis et Desronais* who boasts
that his daughter shall not marry while he is alive. This comedy
dates from 1763, and Rameau was then in his eightieth year. Did
Rameau prevent Marie-Alexandrine from marrying, either because he
disliked her suitor or because he wished to retain her services for
himself? Or was the remark simply a joke on which the malevolent
Collé was only too glad to pounce? Be this as it may, the girl married
François de Gaultier two months after her father's decease, a haste
from which each one may draw his own conclusions.[2]

According to the *Raméide* of Jean-François Rameau, Jean-Philippe
and his brother Claude were rivals for the same woman, Claude being
successful. There is no other evidence for this and certainly it is not
borne out by the fact that Jean-Philippe came up from Lyons to
Dijon for the wedding nor by the friendly relations that always
existed between the two musicians.

Jean-Philippe's brother Claude deserves a biographical study all
to himself. In him we find exaggerated some of his elder brother's
characteristic features. Like Jean-Philippe, he took a long time to
settle down. Six years younger than his brother, brought up in the same
musical surroundings, he left home, enlisted, was hanged for looting,
saved by rain which prevented the noose from closing, was cut down
by some passing hussars, took refuge in a country inn clad only in a
torn shirt, staged a marionette show with puppets cut out of this shirt
with twice-daily performances running for a week, at the end of which
he was rich enough to cross the frontier . . . at least according to that
gossip Sébastien Mercier, reporting that other gossip, Claude's son
Jean-François.[3] Returning home, he became organist of Notre-
Dame, Dijon, where, as we have seen, he emulated his brother's
exploit with the canons of Clermont. At the age of sixty-five, in
1755, he became organist of St. Lazare's cathedral, Autun, and remained
there till his death six years later.

He was twice married; his first wife was Marguerite Rondelet, at
whose wedding Jean-Philippe was present in 1715; she bore him three
children, of whom the eldest, born in 1716, was the notorious Jean-

---

[1] The louis d'or at that time was worth twenty-four livres.
[2] (166).
[3] *Tableau de Paris*, 1788 edit.; XII, 110–114; reprinted in (63), 252–253.

François. In 1756, at sixty-six, he married again one Jeanne Guyot and began founding a fresh family. The eldest of his four children by this second wife was Lazare, another remarkable "neveu". The youngest of them was born in 1760, his father being seventy, so that he was exactly forty-four years younger than his eldest brother!

Claude was clearly an eccentric and awkward character. Jacques Gardien has written the account of an absurd lawsuit which he brought against one Publot, *directeur des bureaux des carrosses de Dijon*, who had refused to pay for the music lessons which Claude had given to his daughter.[1] It is therefore all the more remarkable that between Jean-Philippe and him peace and concord should always have reigned. He was chosen to be godfather to the composer's eldest son, who was called after him. The two brothers must have exchanged a lively and humorous correspondence, judging from the sole relic of it. This is a *cantatille*, the only printed composition of Claude's, dedicated to Jean-Philippe, the frontispiece of which runs: "Le Buveur devenu Amoureux. Cantatille. Par Rameau le Vigneron à Dijon, dédié à Rameau Opérateur à Paris, en attendant Le Maître de Musique imposteur." The promised piece either never took shape or is lost.[2]

Claude was a staunch supporter of his brother's reputation. The year after its appearance on the Paris stage he had *Hippolyte et Aricie* performed in Dijon.[3] When, in 1752, an anonymous critic in Soissons printed a prospectus announcing a *Traité général de la musique* in which he criticized some of Jean-Philippe's theories, Claude took up arms and published a *Lettre* in defence of his brother.[4]

His son Lazare, the first-born of his autumnal love, deserves commemoration. Born in 1757, he was playing the organ in Autun cathedral at the age of nine and at seventeen set off for Paris. He collected some pupils there and lived by giving lessons, but his irregular habits and debauched life caused him to lose them all. He was taken in by the porter of the Jardin du Roi (now the Jardin des Plantes), who was a Burgundian, and stayed with him for a while. He frequented the Couperin of the time, Armand-Louis, organist of St. Gervais, for whom he professed great admiration, but knew nothing of his uncle's works. Later, he drifted to Étampes, where he was organist in two churches; then to a troupe of actors at St. Cloud; then from town to town, occupying a number of church organs, in Montfort l'Amaury, Bordeaux, Pithiviers, the Sainte Chapelle of Dijon and, finally, the cathedral of Mâcon, in which town he died in 1794.

"An unhappy wretch, stupefied by the most crapulent debauch, despised by all and indifferent to esteem," his friend Gautherot calls

---

[1] (148).   [2] (149).
[3] (120), 189.   [4] (191).

him. "In spite of all his vices, he has a kind heart which completes his ruin and makes him an indefinable ethical monster."[1]   He had, in fact, all the traits which Diderot gave to his elder brother.   If Diderot wrote *Le Neveu de Rameau* as late as the 'seventies, he may have known Lazare and have been inspired by him as much as by Jean-François in creating his hero.

Jean-François himself is well known, thanks to the biography written by E. Thoinan and published in Monval's edition of the *Neveu*, the first one to give Diderot's authentic text.   Like his father, he had been a soldier; he had left the army to embark on a clerical career, had given this up and gone in for music.   Somewhere about 1740, or perhaps earlier, he came to Paris where he was well received and looked after by his uncle, who helped in his musical instruction and found him some pupils.   But his unstable character made him unfitted to agree for long with the settled bourgeois which Jean-Philippe had become.   In 1748 he was involved in a scuffle at the Opéra and insulted the director, as a result of which he was imprisoned in the For l'Évêque.   His uncle must have been privy to this captivity, for a letter from the *secrétaire de la Maison du Roi* to M. de Tréfontaine, the *concessionnaire* of the Opéra, contains the words: "You will see with his uncle how long he deems it fitting that he [the nephew] should stay there, and you will let me know."

Rameau's idea was to have this cumbersome relative shipped overseas, where his adventurous character would have found better outlet than in Paris, but he was told that the young man could not be deported against his will.   He was therefore set free after three weeks in the For l'Évêque.   He continued to wander about Paris but seems no longer to have frequented his uncle's respectable household, although the two met on amicable terms in public places.[2]   In 1756 he was living in the Rue des Cordeliers, in the district where his uncle had first lodged when, fifty years earlier, he had arrived in Paris and settled near to where Louis Marchand played the organ.

That same year he produced a book of harpsichord pieces published by Veuve Boivin.   No copy of them is known, and we can judge them only through a lively account given in Fréron's *Année littéraire*.[3]

The pieces were divided into six suites with "character airs", and titles such as *Le Génie français*, *Les Gens du bon ton*, *Les Magnifiques*, *Les Petits Maîtres*.   They provided descriptive and programmatic writing on a grand scale; one whole suite was devoted to *Le Général d'Armée*.   It was to be played "fièrement et avec feu" and pictured the hero at all stages of his activities.   "Ici, il entre en campagne; ici,

---

[1] Quoted in (117), 62–63.   [2] (166).
[3] Vol. VII (1757), 40.   Reprinted in (63), 243–246.

il fait prendre les postes; il marche à l'ennemi; il livre la bataille"; at this moment repeated notes progress "with great intervals and cascades" (says the journalist) in order (says the composer) to "imiter le chamaillement des armes". Then follow "cris et plaintes", the enemy's flight, "coups de canon"; after which "le Général retourne Vainqueur" and, at the end, "reçoit de la main de son Roi la couronne destinée aux héros".

Le Génie français contained a minuet called L'Encyclopédique, whose sub-title was Menuet intra-ou ultramontain. The fifth suite was a ballet on Love and Psyche; as for the sixth, Les Trois Rameaux, the writer assures us that "elle doit faire un effet prodigieux sur l'instrument". The first Rameau was Jean-Philippe, "notre grand Rameau", says the journalist; his piece is played "avec beauté, sagesse, profondeur". The second is Claude, to be played "d'un air libre, assuré, d'un toucher beau et précis". The third is the composer's self-portrait; it should be "vive" and "d'un air content de tout, d'un toucher à la Française, à l'Italienne et à l'Allemande"; each kind of touch being recognizable in the music.

Fréron's description makes us hope to find one day this strayed masterpiece among some pile of unsorted second-hand music.[1]

In 1757 he took a wife and was married in St. Séverin, uncle and cousins being absent. His biographical epic La Raméide shows that he admired his uncle's works and bore him no grudge, as indeed he had no reason to do. His wife died a few years after his marriage and he was taken into a religious house where he died at a date unknown. His friend Cazotte, who is our chief authority for his life, published an account of him in the preface to La Nouvelle Raméide, and a hilarious evocation of him by Piron, quite the equal of Diderot's, occurs in a letter to the said Cazotte.[2] It is well known that Diderot's portrait of him and account of his opinions is largely fanciful. The references to his uncle's works which Diderot puts into his mouth are so inaccurate that it is not always possible to be sure what they refer to. "Profonds abîmes du Ténare" is Envy's air in the prologue to Le Temple de la Gloire; "Nuit, éternelle nuit" may be "Dans le sein de Thétis" in Les Indes galantes, III, 8, in which the line "Nuit, étendez vos voiles" occurs; "Pâles flambeaux" are the third and fourth words of "Tristes apprêts" from Castor et Pollux, I, 3; "Dieu du Tartare, Dieu de l'oubli" seems an invention of Diderot's.

Rameau had no illusions about the decline of his forces as death drew near. "My friend," he said to Chabanon, "I have more taste

---

[1] His music to Le Calendrier des Vieillards, a one-act opéra-comique, is contained in Nouveau Théâtre de la Foire ... Année 1761 ... (Nouvelle édition, chez Duchesne, Paris, 1763, 8°).

[2] In (63), 249–252.

than formerly, but I have no longer any genius at all."[1]

Président de Brosses had pressed him more than once to set the texts of Quinault and La Motte, and he owned that he had indeed thought of doing so but had always been deterred by the fear of appearing conceited, as if he thought he could excel the old masters (Letter 51, fol. 237, ms. fr. 14665, Bibl. Nat.; in *Jean-Philippe Rameau: Bibliothèque Nationale*; catalogue of the 1964 Rameau exhibition, 44). Maret adds another reason: "imagination is worn out in my old head; it is unwise to want to work at my age at arts which are purely creative [*qui sont entièrement d'invention*]".[2]

As he felt his creative strength wither he clung more tenaciously to his powers of reasoning.   He pursued his theoretical studies and the defence of his opinions to the very last.   In fact, as if to spite the faithless Muse he would say that "he regretted the time he had devoted to composition because it had been lost for research into the principles of his art".[3]   Great must have been his delight when Dupleix, on his return from the East, brought him an "orgue de Barbarie" from the Cape of Good Hope "which was able to play all the Chinese tunes in the third tome of Father Du Halde's work and on page 380 of the twenty-second tome of Abbé Prévost's *Histoire des Voyages*".[4]

He was a few days short of his eighty-first birthday when death came to him.   Four months earlier he had been ennobled, a somewhat belated tribute, one feels, and the *lettres de noblesse* registering the honour were entered in the Chambre des Vacations in the very month of his death.   Calumny, always harping on the theme of avarice, was to say that he refused to pay the fees and never took out the letters; the contrary is the truth.

On August 23, 1764, he was attacked by a "putrid fever accompanied by scurvy".   Towards the end of his life he had enjoyed fairly good health which he declared he owed to a certain *baume de Le Lièvre*,[5] but he did not resist the fever and died on September 12.   He was buried the next day in St. Eustache in presence of his son and a friend, Le François de Villeneuve.

---

[1] (53), 54.—Cf. with Vaughan Williams's: "I have struggled all my life to conquer amateurish technique and now that perhaps I have mastered it, it seems too late to make any use of it" (words reported to have been said in 1949), and with T. S. Eliot's

   . . . One only learns to get the better of words

  For the thing one no longer has to say, or the way in which

  One is no longer disposed to say it. . . .

[2] (85), note 49.   [3] (53), 50.

[4] (22), 192.—The "orgue" does not figure in the inventory of his belongings taken after his death; it was by then in the possession of Abbé Arnaud, at whose house Burney saw it (see (43), I, 46).   André Schaeffner (see (224A)) considers it to have been a Javanese or Japanese xylophone. Laborde illustrates it in his *Essai*; Schaeffner reproduces the picture.

[5] (26), 199.

His passing was marked with pomp in Paris and several provincial towns.   A first memorial service was celebrated at the church of the Oratorians in the Rue St. Honoré[1] on September 27; the invitations, to the number of sixteen hundred, were sent out in his widow's name; Gilles's celebrated Requiem was sung, interlarded with passages from *Castor* and other operas.   A second service was held at the Carmelite fathers near the Luxembourg[2] on October 11; Philidor's *Te Deum* was sung.   A third was held at the Oratoire on December 16.   At Orléans, the service included a *De Profundis* set to passages from *Castor* (no doubt the Temple scene); in Marseilles, at the Dominican church,[3] well-known passages of his music were performed.   Masses for him were sung also at Dijon and Rouen.

The *Mercure* published an *Éloge* in its October number; Chabanon's appeared before the year was out.   Maret pronounced his eulogy before the Academy of Dijon on August 25, 1765, after research into his hero's biography, and published it in 1766 with many notes.

His widow and son lived on awhile in the Rue des Bons Enfants. After 1768 Mme Rameau moved to Andrésy, near Poissy, where her son-in-law François de Gaultier had bought an estate, and there she died in 1785.   Claude married in 1772 and is known to have had a son, born in 1773.   He had musical inclinations and among the Decroix papers in the Bibliothèque Nationale is a *première suite* by him for what seems to be several instruments though it is written on two staves.   Nothing is known of his descendants, but La Laurencie traced those of his sister, Mme de Gaultier, to the beginning of the present century, when they were represented by a family called Baudet, living at Mazan near Carpentras.[4]

Rameau's physique is familiar.   His long, thin body resembled Voltaire's[5]; his features, too, were not unlike his contemporary's; they also recalled those of another contemporary, Tartini, like him both a composer and a theorist.

"He had a sharp chin, no stomach, flutes for legs," says Sébastien Mercier.

> He was singularly thin; his features were large and marked, announcing his firmness of character; his eyes sparkled with the fire which kindled his soul; if this fire sometimes seemed to die down, it would rekindle on the least occasion and Rameau showed in society the same enthusiasm which caused him to compose so many ·sublime pieces.[6]

---

[1] Now the Temple de l'Oratoire.

[2] Now the church of the Institut catholique.

[3] Now St. Cannat.   [4] (168).

[5] It was customary to compare them.   A pen drawing, almost a caricature, of the two meeting, signed "G. de Tersan: A Belleville en Beaujolais en 1763", is reproduced in *O.C.*, XIV, xxxviii.   There is no evidence that they met at that time; the inscription must refer to the place and date of the drawing, done from memory or imagination.   The artist is the Marseillais antiquary Abbé Charles-Philippe Campion de Tersan (1737–1819).

[6] (85), 34–35.

"His stature was extremely tall," said Chabanon; "he was lean and skinny and more like a ghost than a man . . .",[1] an expression which was heavily and pedantically slated by Grimm, who pointed out that you could not be like something that did not exist.[2]

The most vivid evocation of him in life comes from Piron, whom Maret had consulted, together with de Féligonde, Vennevault, Balbâtre and La Condamine.   Piron's answer was so outspoken that Maret dared not print it, but he kept the playwright's letter and it was published many years later.

> As regards talent, Rameau lends himself more easily to the panegyrist than Abbé Leblanc [whose eulogy Maret had also to pronounce].   There remains the personal side.   This, I own, is more tricky.   In this respect, Rameau was too singular and too out of the ordinary to make things easy for you; good luck to you! your art will have all the more glory to jump the obstacle. . . .   For forty years that this great man and I have been living under the same sky we have not seen each other in all for more than the space of one day and we have never confided to each other anything intimate.   Here is all I can tell you for certain on my own knowledge and on that of others.   His whole heart and soul were in his harpsichord; once he had shut it there was no one at home.   At eleven in the morning he would go to the Tuileries to acquire an appetite and show off fittingly at the table of some big financier[3] who, in his early youth, had been smitten with the fiddles of our *guinguettes*, had refined his taste in cooking and music, and failed not to consider it a mighty honour to drink with your illustrious associate.   I was sometimes in the garden alone with him at the same time; he would see me first, would hail me from afar, and run up; I saw him coming through my *lorgnette*, like a long organ pipe with the blower away.   After he had smited my cheeks with the impact of his own, each one of us would endeavour to lead off with the conversation; his booming voice got him in first.   He would talk music and fundamental bass; I would talk Homer and Corneille.   We belaboured each other's ears with algebra, by turns; in the end he would grow impatient and send poetry where I dare not say but where I at once sent music.   It all ended by us sending both of us whither we had sent the two fine arts, with a "So long!   Good friends, eh?", ready to begin again at the next meeting.   That is, Sir, all the connexion I have had with the celebrated bard whose Orpheus you are about to be and whom, from I know not what idea, you have thought to call my former friend.[4]

Though his foes accused him of avarice, no one ever suggested he could act basely.   Indeed, his frankness as well as his pride in his discoveries were one of the reasons for his unpopularity.   Always upright and outspoken, he was full of contempt for anything under-

---

[1] (53), 52.   [2] (71), IV, 283–284.   [3] No doubt La Pouplinière.
[4] (92), 5 ff.—Piron had once spoken more warmly of his fellow-townsman.   See p. 7.

hand. He was ready to receive attacks provided they were given openly. In his second book he hints at a kind of whispering campaign that was being carried on against him and dares the whisperers to come out into the open. "If those who are jealous for the early masters' fame" (that is, the authorities he had criticized in the *Traité*) "wish to undertake their defence, I beg them to speak their mind openly and not rest content with giving their reasons to persons incapable of countering them."[1]

In tones suitable to a panegyric Maret evokes his unbending dignity. His temper might be thorny and short; his soul was haughty and independent, incapable of time-serving or trimming his sails to suit the wind. "He would have judged it debasing for himself to ask for favours, and though he was accused of liking money this passion never led him to bend for any reason whatsoever."[2]

At the same time, he did not overestimate himself and was ready to take advice. More than once, so Balbâtre told Maret, Rebel and Francœur, directors of the Opéra, induced him to modify passages in a score to which he appeared much attached. Indeed, the way, shocking to us, in which he sacrificed some of his best numbers for revivals, is proof of his modesty. In later life, he criticized himself readily. Thus, he is alleged to have declared that he could never write either good *ariettes* or good duets, a statement which, when published, called forth from his young admirer Decroix the comment: "Has one the right to use thus the modesty of great men to run them down?"[3] Decroix, in his hero-worship, even refused to believe Chabanon when he wrote that Rameau had said: "Je n'ai plus de génie."

Vennevault, a Dijonnais painter fourteen years his junior, and his still younger compatriot Balbâtre told Maret how he composed. To what extent the oft-repeated account is reliable I do not know.

> When the poet had given him the text, he would read it through several times, thinking it over, declaiming it, and very often obliging the author to make changes in it, thereby taxing greatly his patience [Voltaire had experienced this; so had Collé]. He composed his music with a violin in his hand; sometimes he would sit at his harpsichord; and when he was at work he suffered none to interrupt him; woe to the intruder who came into him!

He found vocal music harder to write than instrumental.

> He had never had a teacher of composition and had learnt it by himself. When he composed he was truly in a state of enthusiasm; he would give himself up to joyous declamation when his genius responded, and to a kind of furious chagrin, if it refused. . . . At rehearsals . . . he would sit in the *parterre* where he wanted to be alone; if anyone came

---

[1] (2), viii.   [2] (85), note 44.   [3] (60), 171.

to disturb him he waved him off with his hand without speaking and even without looking at him. At times he had to talk a lot; he did this with so much fire that his mouth would become dry and he had to eat some fruit to enable himself to go on; the same thing would happen in conversation and then, at the very instant that he was most excited, he would be seen to fall into silence, open his mouth and indicate in dumb show that he could not speak.[1]

Rameau's name and fame lingered, declining, till the end of the Ancien Régime. In the nineteenth century the name was still remembered at least as much as theorist as composer, but it was only a name; the music was forgotten and the books unread. In the night that overcame French music as a result of the Bouffonists' triumph, the great era of the sixteenth, seventeenth and early eighteenth centuries was as if it had never been. Critics like Castil-Blaze, Fétis and Scudo knew nothing of it; it was as barbarous for them as the Middle Ages for d'Alembert and Condorcet. "Before Duni", wrote a certain Delaulnaye in the *Biographie Universelle*,[2] "our music was merely a succession of meaningless chords, the fruit of sterile learning or else a languishing and mournful psalmody."[3]

It may be appropriate at this point to present the reader with a posy of absurdities anent our composer culled in writings of the last two centuries.

From Mattheson's *Philologisches Tresespiel* (1752): "Rameau: infatuated, pedantic and affected imitator of Lulli."

From J. A. Hiller (1770): "An art difficult, frigid, strained."

From Castil-Blaze: "Rameau possessed no taste . . . He never understood anything of Italian music. . . . His choruses and orchestra were very badly constructed and often incorrect in point of harmony."[4]

From F. H. Jenks, "of Boston, Mass.":

> Gluck enriched his scenic effects with an orchestral background with which the most ambitious attempts of Rameau would bear no comparison whatever. In place of Lulli's formal fugue and Rameau's scarcely less inelastic orchestral prelude, he introduced an overture intended "to

---

[1] (85), note 51.   [2] 1855; art. *Duni* (XI, 566).

[3] This opinion had already been expressed by a German as early as the time of Gluck. Before Marie-Antoinette came to France and mended matters, says Weber, her foster-brother, "the land knew only a semi-barbarous music. The art was in its childhood, whereas all the others had passed their age of maturity. Marie-Antoinette saw French opera and resolved at once to set national taste right. . . . It is she who brought Gluck to Paris", etc., etc. (*Mémoires*; in J. F. Barrière, *Bibl. des Mém.* VII (1847)), 177–178.

[4] *Histoire de l'Académie royale de Musique*, quoted with approval by Sutherland Edwards, *History of the Opera* (1862), I, 222.

prepare the audience for the action of the piece, and serve as a kind of argument to it."[1]

From R. A. C. Streatfeild's *The Opera*: "Rameau's pompous artificiality . . ."[2]

From E. Markham Lee's *The Story of the Opera*: "Rameau's music is pompous and antique; nor does it compare in interest with that of the versatile J. J. Rousseau,"[3] a pronouncement which I would fain set beside the following anonymous judgment: "Brahms's music is heavy and long-winded, nor does it compare for spirit and sparkle with that of the gifted Gilbertonsullivan."

From Cecil Gray's *History of Music*: "Rameau is far more important as a theorist (with evil results) than as a composer. His music is unenterprising, stiff, archaic, lacking in spontaneity and charm ; . . ." And Burney is quoted as an authority, which is like quoting Hanslick on Wagner!

And from Jean Chantavoine: "Expression . . . guindée, monotone et précieuse."[4]

It is just over a century ago, in October 1852—one century, too, after the year that saw the peak of Rameau's glory and the beginning of his decline—that the first study devoted to him appeared. This was an article by Adolphe Adam in the *Revue contemporaine* for October 15, reprinted in *Derniers Souvenirs d'un Musicien*,[5] in which he stresses how little is known about the composer.

"He is the author of *Castor et Pollux* and the inventor of the fundamental bass," and that is all. Yet "his portrait is engraved on the gold medal that the Institut awards to its laureates".[6]

When Farrenc, of *Le Trésor des Pianistes* fame, died in 1866, his collection included the autograph scores of *Nélée et Myrthis* and *Zéphyre*. The auctioneer in charge of the sale had never heard of

---

[1] Grove's *Dictionary*, 1st edition (1880), art. *Opera*; an article which does not mention one single work of Rameau and which, shortened by Rockstro, was reprinted as late as 1927.

[2] (228), 43.—No page of this book shows the least knowledge of Rameau's music.

[3] P. 82.

[4] *L'Affaire Rameau*, in *Le Courrier musical*, May 15, 1908.

[5] Paris, 1859.—Adam knew some of Rameau's music, since he introduced "Eclatez, fières trompettes" (from *Castor*, I, 4) into his *Le Bijou perdu* for a humorous effect. He also knew *Hippolyte* and rated it highly.

[6] Rameau, of course, was not the only great musician of his century to be unknown in nineteenth-century France. This is how Elwart, writing the *Histoire de la Société des Concerts du Conservatoire de Musique* in 1860, referred to one even greater: "Sébastien Bach, dont un prélude récemment arrangé par un compositeur enthousiaste, a mis le nom à la mode" (quoted in (208)).

Rameau, "not being a musician myself"; neither, apparently, had any of the bidders except Weckerlin, who was thus able to acquire them for the modest sum of seven francs.[1]   Ten years later there appeared the first book on him, the little biography by Arthur Pougin.   That same year a statue was erected to him in his native city[2] in presence of a representative of the Government whose remark, that in Rameau's music he could hear "comme un ressouvenir de Gluck",[3] bore out Adam's testimony as to the prevailing ignorance.   The still uncompleted edition of the *Œuvres complètes*, associated with the name of Saint-Saëns and Charles Malherbe, began to come out in the last years of the century.   Since then the studies of Quittard, Michel Brenet (Marie Bobillier), La Laurencie and Masson, the books of Laloy, La Laurencie, Migot and Gardien, Masson's great *L'Opéra de Rameau*, and many revivals have made him an almost familiar figure.   In this country, several first-rate broadcasts of his great operas have also played a part in breaking down the barriers of ignorance and prejudice.

---

[1] *O.C.*, XI, introduction.
[2] Melted down by the Germans and now replaced.
[3] (150), 50.

14. Theories

THERE are several reasons why this already large book is not being
swelled still further by an exhaustive inquiry into Rameau's
acoustico-harmonic theories. The first is personal: I am not competent to discuss them in detail and they hold little interest for me.
The second is an extension of this: they are to-day of little interest for
anyone except such as study the history of acoustico-harmonic theory.
The third is that they have never lacked expositors and are to be found
more or less adequately presented in most books dealing with music
theory. The fourth, and chief, is that Rameau lives for us through
his music, and through his music only. Most of those who in late
years have come to know and love him want to know more about his
music and, perchance, about his life, and about the music and life of
his times, but not at all about his speculations.[1] If he had never "specu-
lated" at all, we should not feel impoverished and the history of music
would not have been very different. All this has emboldened me to
write a book about him that speaks scarcely at all of that side of his
production which won him his earliest and widest fame.[2]

That is not to say that one may neglect altogether the dozen books
and as many pamphlets and articles that stand to his credit. All in
them is not acoustics and harmonic theory. From them can be
deduced the attitude which he took up towards his art, his unconscious
aesthetics, which is more relevant to his music than his cogitations on
the "phénoméne du corps sonore". From them, too, we catch in
snatches, and can build up over long reaches, a likeness of what he was
and, though I do not think that the knowledge of artists' life-stories
adds essentially to our enjoyment of their work, I do not regard as
irrelevant the contact with their day-to-day being or believe that an
impenetrable barrier separates their mundane from their artistic
personalities. Much of Rameau's writings is interesting because in
them we can see what manner of man he was in ordinary relations.

Nevertheless, in deference to I am not sure what canon, I have
included a few pages on his harmonic theories. They are summary
and unblushingly second-hand. The reader who wishes to know

---

[1] Thus belying Burney's pronouncement that Tartini and he would be
remembered only as theorists, which is untrue of both ((43), I, 706).
[2] For recent studies of Rameau's theories, see (126A, 161D, 205A).

more can turn to the kind of book I have mentioned.   And if he can read French and is within reach of a complete d'Alembert, he will find this writer's *Éléments de musique . . . suivant les principes de M. Rameau* still the most luminous and most elegant presentation of the subject.

Rameau claimed priority in several respects for his system and claimed it rightly.   He was the first to justify harmonic practice by explaining it on a coherent system derived from the nature of sound. Before him there had been many treatises on harmony but they were entirely practical; they were rules for the putting together of music without reference to principles.   They were empirical, not philosophic.

He was convinced that it was necessary to get away from the superstition of numbers and from the numerical artifices of the Pythagoreans and find a principle given in nature which should take into account both sounding bodies and our organs of hearing.   He was to some extent preceded in this search by Mersenne, but it was Sauveur's acoustic discoveries which served as his basis.   Sauveur, the inventor of the word and the science of acoustics, laid down the physical theory of harmonics and was the first to make a consistent use of them in establishing a musical theory.   He showed that they existed in nature but did not inquire how and why they passed into us.

Rameau began, in this respect, where Sauveur left off.   In the course of his life, he presented his principle as founded on the nature of our psychology, on a general conception of the method, on a physiological hypothesis, on physical experiments and on the facts of musical practice.

All earlier theoreticians, following the example of the Greeks, had started with the scale, which was natural in a monodic system of music. Rameau brought theory into line with practice; realizing that the days of pure melody were over and that much of the expressive power even of counterpoint was due to significant clashes of sounds, he began his investigations with the chord given by the vibrating string, in the sound of which can be detected the upper octave, the twelfth, the second octave, the major seventeenth, and higher harmonics.   This phenomenon was already well known; Mersenne was familiar with it and claimed to have heard up to the ninth harmonic, the major twenty-third, three octaves and a tone above the fundamental!

The sound given by the total length of string is the fundamental or "générateur" (root) of the chord—the "basse fondamentale" which plays so important a part in Rameau's system and in all discussions about it; the second and third harmonics, together with this fundamental, give the major triad.   He thus finds the unity of harmony in one principal sound instead of seeking it, as hitherto, in the divisions of the octave.

Ste. Croix de la Bretonnerie, Paris, in the seventeenth century

The principle of harmony does not reside only in the common chord, whence is derived that of the seventh; but more precisely in the bass sound of these two chords which is . . . the *harmonic centre* to which all the other sounds must be related.[1]

He was led to consider as one and the same the chords that arise from different combinations of the same notes and to introduce the idea of inversions of chords. The notion of inverted intervals had long been current, but that of inverted chords was Rameau's own discovery. By thus classifying as one and the same harmony all the varieties of position and inversions of a chord he greatly simplified harmonic theory.

He derived dissonances from the triad by the addition of thirds, but they are deduced with less immediacy than the triad itself from the vibrating string and Rameau's explanations here were never quite satisfactory; the origin of dissonances was always recognized as the weakest part of his system.

Its most original part, at least if we take it in relation to his dramatic writing, is his theory of the two sets of fifths, the ascending and the descending. In addition to the upper harmonics the lower series was also known in his time. When one stretches alongside a vibrating string other strings twice, thrice, four and five times its length, they can be seen to quiver though the vibrations are not audible. Thus, the string twice as long gives the octave below, that thrice as long gives the twelfth below, those four and five times as long give the second octave and minor seventeenth. When reduced within the octave these notes give the minor triad. Thus, if on the one hand the upper harmonics, with progressions by fractions (or sub-multiples) of the vibrating string, supply the major triad, the lower ones, with progressions by multiples of the vibrating string, supply the minor triad.

When he was working at his first two books he seems not to have known of the lower series and his explanation of the minor triad was less satisfactory; the explanation based on the undertones occurs first in the *Génération harmonique* of 1737. With it comes the explanation why the dominant and subdominant stand in such intimate relation with the tonic, a fact no earlier writer had explained; with it, also, the explanation of the psychological effects of these keys. On the ascending series, revealed by the vibrating and sounding string, is founded the dominant, the realm of joy, light and strength; on the descending series, revealed by the strings that remain silent and merely quiver, the subdominant, the realm of sadness, gloom and weakness.[2] As these lower harmonics

---

[1] (1), 127.
[2] (17), 52–53.

only quiver C is sounded and do not sound with it as do [the upper], it
follows that the minor mode is given by nature less immediately and less
directly than the major.[1]

The division of a single sound implied a physical principle which
was made explicit in the *Génération harmonique*. This book, contemporary with *Castor et Pollux*, brings experience into Rameau's
theory. It enunciates the twelve acoustical propositions based on
seven experiments of the resonance and quivering of sounding bodies
and explains them by an hypothesis of Mairan's on the elasticity of air
which makes feasible the production and perception of several simultaneous sounds, a fact that had much perplexed Mersenne. Rameau
had discussed this and other points some ten or twelve years earlier
with the illustrious mathematician who had published a study of it in
1720.[2] It was, said Rameau, M. de Gamaches who made him see the
connexion between Mairan's theory and his own.[3]

This is completed by a physiological hypothesis, the likeness
between the inner ear and a sounding body, an anticipation of Helmholtz.

> What has been said of sounding bodies should be understood also
> of the fibres that line the back of the concha; these fibres are so many
> sounding bodies to which the air imparts its vibrations and whence the
> sense of sounds and harmony is borne to the soul.[4]

The *Démonstration du principe de l'harmonie* (1750) is the most
readable and the most genial of all his writings; this may be due to
Diderot's help. The work was submitted to the judgment of the
Academy of Science, and Rameau clearly tried to make it presentable.
The report of those appointed to examine it, Dortous de Mairan,[5]
Nicole and d'Alembert, drawn up by the latter, is prefixed to it and is
most flattering. His own introduction has an unwontedly literary air.
It sums up the work of his predecessors and makes the usual criticisms,
leading up to his own starting-point.

---

[1] (30), 20–21.

[2] *Mémoires de l'Académie des Sciences*, 1720; 11.

[3] (9), 3–4.—The existence of the difference-tone or third sound discovered by Tartini and made known by him in a treatise of 1754 is first mentioned by Rameau in 1761 ((24)), when he contests the accuracy of Tartini's
experiment which, if genuine, would have disturbed his own theories by
introducing a new factor. D'Alembert refers to it in the *Discours préliminaire* of the 1762 edition of his *Éléments* and accepts it, but Rameau was too
old to take it into account and recast his system.

[4] (9), 7.

[5] Mairan had been the censor for the *permis d'imprimer* of the 1724 book
of harpsichord pieces.

Tel était l'état des choses, lorsqu'étonné moi-même des peines que j'avais eues à apprendre ce que je savais, je songeai au moyen de les abréger aux autres, et de leur rendre l'étude de la composition plus sûre et moins longue. . . . Je compris d'abord qu'il fallait suivre dans mes recherches le même ordre que les choses avaient entre elles. . . . Éclairé par la méthode de Descartes que j'avais heureusement lue et dont j'avais été frappé, je commençai par descendre en moi-même; j'essayai des chants, à peu près comme un enfant qui s'exercerait à chanter; j'examinai ce qui se passait dans mon esprit et dans mon organe. . . . J'imaginai . . .; et je conclus. . . . Je me mis cependant à calculer . . . et je trouvai. . . . Je vis donc. . . . Je me plaçai donc le plus exactement qu'il me fût possible dans l'état d'un homme qui n'aurait ni chanté, ni entendu du chant, me promettant bien de recourir à des expériences étrangères, toutes les fois que j'aurais le soupçon que l'habitude d'un état contraire à celui où je me supposais m'éntraînerait malgré moi hors de la supposition. Cela fait, je me mis à regarder autour de moi et à chercher dans la nature ce que je ne pouvais tirer de mon propre fond. . . .

"and I found three things: noise, a fundamental sound and accompanying sounds."

J'appelai le son primitif ou générateur *Son fondamental*; ses concomitants *Sons harmoniques* et j'eus trois choses très distinguées dans la nature, indépendantes de mon organe et très sensiblement différentes pour lui; du bruit, des *Sons fondamentaux* et des *Sons harmoniques*.[1]

Is it Diderot or Rameau himself who is responsible for this pleasing adaptation of the beginning of Descartes's *Discours de la Méthode?*

It is all there; the methodical and even hyperbolic doubt; the revelation of a *cogito* which is here an *audio*. Only this allegedly Cartesian method leads Rameau, contrary to Descartes, to *experience* and to a principle of certitude whose value lies entirely in that it exists *outside him.*[2]

The *Démonstration* is the account of an achievement and a taking of bearings; with the *Observations sur notre instinct pour la musique* (1754) the march forward is resumed. The instinct mentioned in the title is assumed lest all our musical system appear to be merely something acquired through habit. "Habit does not command instinct; on the contrary, it is on instinct that habit is formed."[3]

By dint of going deeper and deeper in his search for a unifying principle, Rameau arrived at a dead end. "To give these precepts all their necessary force I had to prove instinct by its principle, and this principle by the same instinct; they are both the work of Nature."[4] Which is perilously like a vicious circle. We are thus brought back

---

[1] (12), 6–13.

[2] (169), 86, note 2.

[3] (17), 28.

[4] (17), xiv.

to that "nature" the invocation of which covered up so many obscurities in Rameau's century.

The "principle" played a great part in Rameau's last years. At first it had been merely the principle of harmony, that is, of consonance, dissonance and the sequence of the fundamental bass, and also of melody which derives from harmony. Then it explained the relationship of the major and minor modes and of keys. In the *Démonstration* it was extended to the structure of instruments and the invention of new ones and to the improvement of singing. It is in this book that there rings the first warning of later divagations. When d'Alembert, as one of the judges, appended his signature to the Academy's flattering report he cannot have grasped the significance for future developments of a passage like the following, in which alarming ambitions are thinly disguised behind a diffident question mark and an expression of modest doubt.

> When one sees Music given by Nature in so complete a manner; on one hand, these qualities and powers that we can no longer ignore in sounding bodies, on the other, the conformation of our organs to receive the effects of these bodies and make us enjoy them; may one not believe that this art, apparently reduced to mere pleasure, is destined by Nature to serve us with a usefulness better proportioned to her intentions? Forgive this reflexion, Gentlemen; I own it is much more of your domain than of mine; you alone are able to feel all its consequences.[1]

Two years later the tone had hardened, the voice grown more rasping.

> It will be recognized in these . . . further reflexions that the principle in question is effectively drawn from nature herself and perceptible to three of our senses, that there is here no question of conjectures or hypotheses and that everything written earlier is absolutely useless to reach the knowledge and practice of the Arts; . . . I say, the Arts, because there is every reason to presume . . . that this principle affects also all the Arts of Taste which have the senses for judge and proportions for rule.[2]

The *Observations* mark a further step forward. Alluding to Briseux's *Traité du beau essentiel* he declares: "The principle in question is not only that of the Arts of Taste, as this *Traité* confirms . . .; it is also that of all the Sciences subject to reckoning."[3]

> Music is natural to us; we owe only to pure Instinct the pleasure it brings us; this same Instinct acts in us at the instance of several other objects which may well have some relation with music, which is why persons who cultivate sciences and arts cannot be indifferent to knowing the principle of such an Instinct.[4]

---

[1] (12), 103.   [2] (13), preface.
[3] (17), xv.   [4] (17), 1–2.

In another three years its sway had become universal. "Le principe de tout est un."[1] The Ancients had sought for it in music but had not found it for lack of knowing the phenomenon of resonance.

Occasionally discrepancies troubled him. Thus, he was puzzled by the scales of the Greeks and the Chinese in which "the ear" was not in agreement with "nature" and showed "the false relations of which all ancient systems are made up",[2] but these difficulties never amounted to one doubt. In fact, in these same reflexions he launches out into interplanetary space, borne on the wings of the principle, in one of the most revealing passages, for his personality, that I know.

> To bring before us an infinite whose beginning and end are both unimaginable, the principle places itself exactly in the centre of its multiples and sub-multiples—a law that it imposes at the same time to the ordinators 2, 3 and 5, whence follow more progressions *ad infinitum* towards each extremity of their proportions. And then to prove that it is the first and only one, that none surpasses it, it compels the bodies greater than itself to divide in its emissions, to unite with its unity, to incorporate themselves, so to speak, in its whole; so that, remaining always whole without the least disunion, it generates nevertheless an infinity of parts which it therefore contains without being itself contained. What shall we think of such a prodigy? . . . Would such a principle be communicated to us with such overwhelming evidence, generating all proportions and progressions and assigning to each one of its first products particular and subordinate prerogatives according to its order of generation—a point to be noticed—if an infinity of useful knowledge were not to flow from it? So many philosophers, ancient and modern, who have devoted themselves to the study of music, have watched so late and worked so hard to succeed in penetrating the depth of its scientific side, would assuredly not have done so if they had not felt that advantages far more precious than those resulting from Art alone could be derived from it.[3]

Is this a study of the mathematics of resonance or a pantheistic theodicy?[4]

How, he wonders, did the first men discover the laws of music? How did Adam do it, how Noah after the Flood when all learning had to begin afresh? "The era of the Chinese is not far from that of the Flood since it is earlier by thirteen years than the time when the Tower of Babel began to be built."[5] A phenomenological approach seems to be indicated. "What I have supposed in the operation of the first man on the subject is exactly what I have experienced myself in the

---

[1] (22), 189.   [2] (22), 192–193.   [3] (22), 213.

[4] "Peut-être l'enthousiasme de M. Rameau qui croyait voir dans la musique l'origine de toutes les sciences ressemble-t-il un peu à celui du Père Malebranche qui voyait tout en Dieu," said Palissot ((91), 104–105).

[5] (22), 225–226.

progress of knowledge that my studies and my researches have pro-
cured me."[1]

All this is mixed up with hits at the "géomètres" who deny the
primacy of the "science du corps sonore". It drove d'Alembert to
write scathingly of "the furious mania of musicians to give what they
write a pseudo-scientific air which impresses none but the ignorant",[2]
a remark which rankled, since Rameau alluded to it more than once.
This phantastifying accompanied some very pertinent criticisms of
erroneous statements and perverse judgments made by d'Alembert
and Rousseau in the *Encyclopédie*, unfortunately buried in the flow of
conglomerate.

Rameau taxed d'Alembert with inconsistency since he had praised
his *Démonstration* a few years earlier. D'Alembert's reply was
simple. The Academy of Science did indeed approve, he says, on
my report, the book in question; "that did not commit it, nor myself
either, to adopting the more than singular opinions that you have
hazarded since." And he refuses, as Rameau had defied him to do,
to "prove seriously that geometry is not founded on music or to
examine whether Pythagoras ought to have interested Nature in
favour of the number seven rather than of the number three".[3]

D'Alembert's final answer came when he republished his *Éléments*.
It is divided into two parts: a *Discours préliminaire* and the answer
proper, added at the end. It is vain, he says, to assimilate geometry
and musical theory as Rameau persists in doing. The latter can never
have the forceful evidence of the former and nothing can be demonstrated in it; and a footnote recalls that the work of Rameau which the
Academy of Science had approved in 1750 was then called a *Mémoire*,
and that the author substituted the misleading term *Démonstration*
only when publishing it. He distinguishes, moreover, between
"approving" a work and "adopting its principles as demonstrated".
He acknowledges Rameau's chief claim; he "will always have the
honour of having been the first to make music a science worthy to
occupy philosophers". But it is useless to seek why certain chords please
more than others, to try and discover "chimaerical relations" between
music and the other sciences; these attempts are the "vagaries of men
of genius when they talk of what they do not know".[4]

---

[1] (22), 227.   [2] Quoted in (23), 4.   [3] (31).
[4] D'Alembert returned to this when in May 1777, long after Rameau's
death, he read to the Academy of Science a paper called *Réflexions sur la
théorie de la Musique*. He spoke more cruelly now: "Rameau ended by
wishing to find in musical proportions the whole of geometry, in the major
and minor modes the two sexes of animals, and finally the Trinity in the
threefold resonance of the sounding body" ((32), 138).

An obsession with one tyrannical belief, a brooding on the injustice of wilful misunderstanding and wounding remarks can be felt behind the old man's reiterative involutions and give them a pathetic interest out of proportion to their intellectual content.

If we return now to his days of sanity, we recognize the true significance of his principle. It lies in the passage from the mathematical to the physical.[1]

> It is in Music that nature seems to assign for us the physical principle of these purely mathematical first notions upon which all the sciences are based; I mean, the harmonic, arithmetical and geometrical proportions.[2]

These two notions, abstract and concrete, are indissolubly linked, but the abstract is grounded in the concrete.

Rameau's theory was satisfactory inasmuch as it explained consonance but it failed to explain dissonance, and Rameau himself added to it a different theory of dissonance which could not be reconciled with his main theory—a weakness which his critics were not slow in pointing out and upon which turned much of the discussion that occupied his old age. It left unexplained the possibility of reducing all sounds to within an octave, and the dissonance of sounds which are not harmonics and which therefore do not enter into the framework of his theory. These were the gaps that Helmholtz, in his turn, endeavoured to fill.

Rameau's aesthetics are nowhere formulated systematically but are implicit throughout his writings and are expressed piecemeal on many of his pages. The absence of a systematic exposition is no drawback since his philosophy of art is not different from that of his time, and to know the views on music held by La Motte, Le Cerf, Dubos, Pluche, Père André and others is to know his.

The phenomenon of music entered late into literature. Before 1700 it had been studied only in the folios of learned men like Zarlino, Kircher, Descartes and Mersenne. Then, near the turn of the century, the pleasure that music afforded and the very object of the art began to interest non-specialist minds and a theory of musical aesthetics took shape. It was natural that the earliest theorists should transfer to music the theories already recognized as valid in other fields of the Beautiful.

For thought, at this period, art is a fiction—no doubt, often a sublime fiction—but nothing more. It is not an absolute; it is subordinate to something of primary value which it is its function to

---

[1] (169), 88.   [2] (12), vi.

imitate, to wit, Nature.   The imitation of Nature is the object of all art, whatever its medium: language, colour, sound.

The chief merit of poetry and painting consists in imitating those objects which would have roused real passions in us.   The passions which these imitations rouse in us are only superficial

(compared to those which the real objects would rouse).[1]   And yet

it sometimes happens that the imitation interests us more than the subject of the imitation.[2]

The test of its success is verisimilitude which reconciles and joins together this fiction and this reality.   A fictional imitation of truth, checked by the standards of verisimilitude: such is art for Dubos and his contemporaries.

This theory presents an appearance of objectivity most satisfying to reason.   The soundness of this rationalism, however, turns on the meaning of the key word "Nature".   Basil Willey has shown what changes this word underwent and all that it ended by embracing throughout the eighteenth century.   "Nature" should mean all things natural.   But La Motte limits it to "characters worthy of attention and objects able to make pleasing impressions".[3]   This is, of course, highly arbitrary and a theory of art which sets out to be objective and realist leads rapidly to pure subjectivism.   Imitation for La Motte is "the art of taking from things what is fit to produce the effect one sets oneself".   In fact he confesses that "what I please to call natural is my measure".   It has the advantage of allowing one to indulge one's fancies under the respectable cover of an apparently scientific philosophy.

This theory of imitation is applied boldly to music.   Imitation in music must "conform to the general rules of poetry and painting on the choice of subjects, on verisimilitude and on several other points".[4] "Music which paints nothing is like speeches full of sounds wherein the speaker displays pompous words without treating any theme."[5] It must paint and the proper object of its painting is the feelings of the heart.   "Pure music is a marionette which flits about uselessly."[6]

Lucian was right in saying that a music which is not understood is useless.   A *symphonie* which does not speak to the soul is like a speech made in German before someone who knows only French.[1]

It is a principle received in France as in Italy and everywhere else that music should express and depict . . .   A music which depicts nothing is insipid.

---

[1] (64), I, 3.   [2] (64), I, 10.   [3] (80), 189.
[4] (64), I, 656.   [5] (93), VII, 116.   [6] (32), 155.
[7] (86), 73 and 75.

La musique est un art qui, tel que la peinture,
Retraçant à nos sens le vrai de la nature,
Doit surprendre, émouvoir, et par de doux ressorts
De l'esprit et du cœur exciter les transports.[1]

There is a close relation between a feeling and the music fit to render it.

"Every movement of the heart has a tone to express it."[2]   In theory, there are two stages: to imitate the feeling which is the model, then to express it.   But in practice the two are inseparable though imitation keeps a kind of priority of honour over mere expression. This latter, the true field of creative activity, is subordinate to the nobler act of imitating what already is given in Nature.   All expression is thus imitation—even self-expression, since when he expresses himself the musician is really imitating that eternal Nature of which he carries the model within himself.   Thus the objective, rationalist theory of imitation could be safeguarded even while allowance was made for the freedom of individual taste.

Music, subordinated to an absolute, could be considered only as an *art d'agrément*, a pleasant diversion; not as something valid in its own right.   French and Italian music, in appearance opposed, were both agreed on this principle; no one questioned it at this time.[3]   The only difference between the two is that the Italians travel further along the path of pleasure than the French; Alessandro Scarlatti and Pergolese are more exciting, more flattering entertainers than Lulli and Campra, who have stopped half-way.

Of course, in all this, it must be remembered, music means primarily sung music, particularly opera.   Music without words is a poor relation which theorists can justify only by invoking the imitationist doctrine and claiming that it paints this or that object, this or that feeling.   Which implies that music is the handmaid of poetry.

"Music must be made for the poetry rather than the poetry for the music."[4]

"An air must accommodate itself to the words."[5]

Rémond de Saint-Mard, a great lover and defender of opera, lays down a number of conditions for perfect opera; one of these is that the music should be "the slave of the poetry".[6]   The painting of external

---

[1] (110), 27.   [2] (46), in (142), 28.

[3] "This time" covers over a century, roughly 1640–1760.

[4] Saint-Évremond, in (229), 42.—Striffling quotes Théophile Gautier, who saw somewhere on a theatre bill the announcement: "La musique a été retranchée comme nuisant à l'action."

[5] Molière, *Le Bourgeois Gentilhomme*, I, 2.

[6] (97), 248.—Its task is to "complete, enliven, quicken the expression it has received from the verse".   Others would add: and of the situation. "Generally music is appreciated, especially at the opera, only in relation to

objects or scenes was legitimate; the painting of moods was less so. For Abbé Pluche, the feelings depicted in "sonatas" are meaningless because they are unmotivated, unlike those depicted in opera where they are provoked by a pattern of circumstances. At best, sonatas are exercises performed in the imitation and expression of an emotional attitude or a passion, of much the same status as an exercise in harmony or fugue. Fontenelle's "Sonate, que me veux-tu?" expresses this opinion.[1]

Écorcheville sums up ironically the teaching of these aestheticians regarding music. For thinkers like La Motte and even genuine music-lovers like Le Cerf there is no place for her in their philosophy; morality reprobates her, logical thought fears her; no good reason can be found in her favour.[2]

For these thinkers, then, the representation of feelings and emotional states was the proper function of music. The general term for them was "affections", which corresponds to the "affetti" of the Italian and the "Affekten" of the German theorists, of whom David Heinichen (1683–1729) is a younger contemporary of La Motte and Fontenelle and an exact contemporary of Rameau. The imitation of "affections" means "rendering into music the temper, disposition or frame of mind, passions and mental reactions characteristic of man".[3] It was because "sonatas" could not render the "affections" clearly that La Motte and Pluche denied them any value. The affections were not personal, psychological feelings but rather attitudes of a permanent, static nature, which could be attached, so to speak, to any fictional character, and so were peculiarly fitted for musical representation.[4] Each one has its "right" expression; in music as in poetry there are at most three or four ways of expressing it, and a search for variety in doing so is as ridiculous as the attempt to vary "Belle Marquise, vos beaux yeux me font mourir d'amour" in *Le Bourgeois Gentilhomme*, says Le Cerf.[5] Uniformity should be feared no more here than it is in speech; identical states imply identical expressions. Lulli was looked on as a repertory of these expressions and, for the conservative, this led easily to an *Ipse Magister dixit* (or *cantavit* or *sonuit*) which might have cramped disastrously later musicians if it had been taken literally by them. We find this narrow outlook maintained as late as 1778 by Gluck.[6]

The French expositors of this would-be rationalist and objective imitationism are the most lucid and orderly, and the doctine is most

the interest of the words and to the effect produced on us by the situation" (*Observations sur les écrits modernes*, 1743, XXXII; in *O.C.*, IX, xxxii); a statement of fact rather than a judgment.

[1] In (29), Chapter XXXVII.   [2] (142), 157.
[3] (175), 436.   [4] (125), 389.
[5] (83), II, 125.   [6] In (57).

easily studied in their writings, but it was general: Marcello in Italy, Kuhnau, Printz, Mattheson, Heinichen in Germany upheld it firmly. But none of its French exponents, except Le Cerf, could be called a music-lover and none was a practising musician. It is indeed essentially a theory of scientists, not of artists. Their hard-and-fast systems, as Bukofzer reminds us, are not reflected with the same absoluteness in the music of their time. Did the composers who were contemporary with La Motte, Dubos and Pluche believe what these pundits told them about the philosophic foundation of their art? Did they hold that it was merely an "art d'agrément", that instrumental music was inferior to vocal, and that in vocal music Euterpe was the handmaid of Melpomene and Polymnia? Rameau's opinions will be examined later; no other French composer has left any views on the question. None seems to have been interested in it. Montéclair's *Principes de musique* contain no reference to it and we cannot imagine that easy-going southerners like Campra, Mouret and Mondonville troubled their heads about it. Bukofzer warns us rightly that "the intuitively creating musician remained 'irrational' to a considerable degree" and we should forbear from mistaking the "puerile 'realism' and 'symbolism' apparent in . . . even the greatest baroque musicians for the essential stylistic feature" of their art.[1]

With the public of music-lovers we know that in practice, if not in theory, the doctrine of the subordination of music was not held universally. We know it, first, through the criticisms of highbrows like Abbé Dubos who, strict imitationist that he was, deplored that certain people should be more sensitive to the colour of a picture than to the expression in it and that, likewise, in music certain should attend only to the melody and harmony without "noticing sufficiently if the *chant* imitates well the sound it should imitate or if it is suitable to the meaning of the words to which it is adapted".[2]

This deplorable attitude is shared by many musicians.

"The number" [of them] "who comply with this taste, as if music were incapable of doing anything better, is only too great."[2] One of the speakers in Mably's *Lettres* complains that three-quarters of French opera-goers "are true Germans[3] . . . They look upon opera only as a concert", an attitude which encourages bad acting and vocal exhibitionism. This, says a writer in the *Nouveaux Amusements*, is "false and ridiculous prejudice, to think that the music alone makes the whole merit of an opera".[4]

A more august witness than any of these to the existence of the taste

---

[1] (125), 440. [2] (64), I, 656–657.
[3] Why? Because they are lacking in taste or because Germans were more interested in pure music than Frenchmen? (84), 137.
[4] IV (1739), 403.

for pure music, to the exclusion of what words it was supposed to interpret, is no less a person than the great King himself. According to Mme de Maintenon, music, particularly the music of opera, was "le seul vrai plaisir du Roi" in his old age. But, though he so enjoyed operatic music, he paid no attention to the words, "in which one hears nothing but maxims absolutely opposed to the Gospel and Christianity", as his spouse very truly remarked. These pernicious maxims made no impression on the aged monarch; "he is taken up only with the beauty of the music, of the sounds, the chords, etc., so that often he even sings his own praises without realizing they are his, solely from love of the songs."[1]

The partisans of pure music are known to us not only through these disapproving allusions of their critics but also through declarations of their own. Writers in the *Observations sur les Écrits modernes*[2] assert roundly that "music is the true foundation of opera; the lyric stage is in truth music's theatre". Before Rameau "no one would have thought that a music independent of words could have any expression", but he has "created a music which has character, which expresses on its own account without any extraneous help". He has succeeded in characterizing feelings; his music is intelligible without the help of words. An ardent defender in the *Postillon français* for June 30, 1739, went even further—further, probably, than Rameau himself would have done.

> Poetry has her stage; let her go and display thereon all her accomplishments! Music must have hers, too; let no one deny it her; let her reign there alone; let her expel thence any rival who ventures to contest with her and admit only those whose deformity may serve to enhance her lustre.[3]

And a contributor to the *Mercure* for September 1749 declared that "imitation of nature" had not much meaning when applied to music.

Instrumental music also had its champions. One of these was the Chevalier in Mably's letters of whom we have already heard. He is a good violinist.

> He plays us on his fiddle sonatas which have neither character nor harmony. He awakens no passion in me; not even my ears are pleased, and if I feel any pleasure . . . it is in the eyes in watching the agility of his hands. His music has no style, the ear never finds rest in it; it is

---

[1] (151). She adds that "formerly he took an extreme pleasure in the beautiful hymns of *Esther* and *Athalie* and now he is almost ashamed to have them sung because he feels that it bores the courtiers". This remark is undated but must be after 1691, the year of *Athalie*.

[2] IV, 139–141; XXXII, 159; in (188), 208.

[3] In *O.C.*, IX, xxvi.

all the time unexpected turns; everything goes by leaps and bounds; everything is harsh and precipitous.[1]

One recognizes here a caricature of the virtuoso sonata of the Locatelli type.

Positions remained much the same throughout the century. D'Alembert was "advanced" in some respects; he believed in modern music, though he disliked the Bouffons;[2] he mocked the "superstitious timidity" of Lulli's votaries. But pure music was a closed door to him. Admirer of *opera buffa* and Italian dramatic music in general though he was, a sonata was for him "literally a dictionary of words, the collection of which makes no sense."[3]. He

> *counts* for nought the prodigious quantity of sonatas we receive from the Italians. All this purely instrumental music, without intention or object, speaks neither to the mind nor to the soul and deserves to be asked Fontenelle's question. Composers of instrumental music will produce nothing but vain noise as long as they do not have in their heads (like, it is said, the famous Tartini) an action or an expression to depict. . . .[4]

And he quotes with approval that composer's *Didone abbandonata* sonata.

> In general, one feels the full expressiveness of music only when it is linked to words or dancing. Music is a language without vowels; it is for action to supply them. . . . The eyes, always in agreement with the ears, must be for ever acting as the interpreters of instrumental music.[4]

Diderot did not share this hostility to sonatas and, according to *Le Neveu de Rameau*, he admired those of Locatelli. But his preconceptions were quite as literary and music was no freer for him than it was for his colleague.

> I have never heard a good *symphonie*, especially *adagio* or *andante*, without interpreting it, and sometimes so felicitously that I hit precisely upon what the musician intended painting. So I shall never withdraw the advice I gave one day to a clever harpsichordist: "Would you compose good music? Would you have your instrument always speak to me? Put Metastasio on your desk; read one of his *arias* and let your imagination give your fancy free play!"[5]

At the same time, he did not enslave music to words. The poet, he said, should never forget the musician, for whom he is made. "If the poet draws all the bedclothes to his side, they will both spend a bad night." The ideal would be a great poet who was also a great musician.[6]

---

[1] (84), 163–164.　　[2] (199A).　　[3] (32), 155.
[4] (29), 455–457.　　[5] (62), 508 (1771).　　[6] (62), 509.

It is time to inquire where our composer stands in all this.

Rameau, I have said, never expounded this aesthetic as a whole but he took it for granted with the docility of a classic.   He does not adjudicate between pure and applied (*riservata*) music, neither does he dwell at length on the music's subsidiary function as the purveyor of pleasure.   He does not question the hedonistic-utilitarian conception of the art.   "Music's aim is to please and to arouse in us diverse passions."[1]   Indeed, he sees no alternative to it except that of the scientific mind that studies musical phenomena.

> For the common of mankind music is but an art destined to amuse and it pertains only to taste to beget and judge its productions; for you [gentlemen of the Academy of Science], it is a science founded on principles which, teaching us to please the ear, also gives reason material to work upon.[2]

Many musicians, he continues, are unconscious of the means they use; yet these can certainly be reduced to theory by people like these gentlemen.

As a rule, his acceptance of the hedonistic approach was implicit; there was no need for it to be expressed since no one attacked it.

The chief preoccupation of Rameau the aesthetician, as distinct from the acoustician and student of harmonic theory, is how to render with truth and intensity the *affection* implied in a text or a situation. (The terms corresponding in French to the German "Affekt" and the Italian "affetto" are "sentiment, caractère, passion, émotion, affection", all of which are synonymous.)

"The words one sets to music always have a certain expression, either sad or gay, which one cannot dispense oneself from rendering...; and he who does not take words for guides always imagines a subject which holds him in much the same subjection."[3]   This was written in 1722 when he was close on forty; his opinion was unchanged thirty years later.   "Expression is the musician's only object."[4]

Of all the parts of music which are at his disposal the most elementary is the rhythm or beat.   Rameau dwells more than once on its importance.   "It is the first effect that strikes us in music"; it is "natural to all animals . . .   The feelings of the heart, the passions, can be well rendered only by altering the beat."[5]   This is part of his defence of the free rhythms of French dramatic music which had been attacked by Rousseau in his *Lettre sur la Musique française* and in the article *Accompagnement* of the *Encyclopédie*.   He returned to its

---

[1] (9), 30.   [2] (9): *Épître* . . .: opening sentence.

[3] (1), 162–163.

[4] (21), 161.—"Musician" comprises, of course, executants.—Cf.: "Expression should be the soul of dramatic music" ((37), 74).

[5] (18), 24– 32.—Cf. also (21), 23.

defence in his *Observations sur notre instinct pour la musique*, where he identified the strong, regular beat of the Italians with the portrait of what is physical and with comedy, whereas French music, "whose object is sentiment, which has not these decided movements, . . . cannot therefore be subordinated everywhere to a regular beat without losing that truth which makes its charm".[1]   Next to rhythm in the order of refined sensibility comes melody.

> Rhythm is the first effect that strikes us; we become sensitive to the relation of sounds [that is, to harmony] only when we have listened to music for some time; at first our sensibility has only melody for objects and only after a certain number of years, according as one is more or less, well organized, as one hears music more or less often and gives more or less heed to it, does harmony begin to come to the fore.[2]

This, too, is part of his reply to Rousseau.   Rhythm has to be defended because it is primordial, but melody has to be put in its place. Our sensitiveness to it comes early and it is a mark of an untrained mind to go no further and to make it supreme as Rousseau does. The Genevan, like all upholders of Italian music, refuses to "recognize as good any music which does not sing, however harmonious it may be and whatever trouble it may have cost to compose."[3]   It was to this that Rameau was replying.

He had long been accused of sacrificing melody to harmony.   The grounds for this accusation lay largely in some rather unguarded statements which, taken without the necessary discretion and understanding, seemed to make little of mere tune.

"Melody arises from harmony."[4]   The first division of a vibrating string gives harmony, not melody.[5]

"The song that we imagine is suggested to us by a principle of harmony that is within us and this principle is none other than the chord which we hear in a single sound of our voice."[6]

"Success" in a melody is linked with a change in the fundamental, that is, in the harmony.[7]

And in the eyes of the vulgar the composer who gave as hirsute a definition of melody as the following could hardly be esteemed a melody-maker.

> The diatonic order joined to the fundamental succession, and all the arbitrary orders between the harmonics drawn from the fundamentals according to our enunciation in Chapter IV, form what is called the melody, that is to say the canto of a single part.[8]

---

[1] (17), vii–viii.   [2] (18), 24–25.   [3] (100), *Trio.*
[4] (1), 138: title of II, xix.   [5] (1), 139.   [6] (2), 48.
[7] (9), Chapter IV.   [8] (9), 61.

The supremacy of harmony was reaffirmed in the *Observations* of 1754.

"It belongs to harmony alone to stir the passions; melody derives its strength only from that source whence it springs directly."[1]

"It is mainly from the fund of harmony, whence is drawn the melody set to the words, that the singer receives the impression of the sentiment he must depict."[2]

It was pronouncements like these and not his actual music which gave his enemies the weapon which they wielded so perseveringly. On the other hand, it is easy to cull remarks which show the utmost regard for melody. Though harmony be the "principle" which is in us, the composing musician cannot begin with it. He must start with his bass and this he must "compose with the most beautiful *chant* that he can imagine".[3]

"The superiority of harmony lessens in nowise the value of melody, I myself set more store by it than any of your colleagues."[4]

It is true that one finds in his writings few or no statements that help the composer to render a given sentiment by this or that turn of melody. He does not connect forms of tune with types of feeling as he does with harmonies and modulations. He gives the reason for this deficiency in his very first book, written before he had acquired any experience of dramatic composition.

> Melody has no less strength in expression than harmony but it is almost impossible to give definite rules about it for good taste has more share in it than anything else; thus we will leave to favoured geniuses the pleasure of distinguishing themselves in this domain on which depends almost all the strength of sentiments.[5]

Nearly forty years later, in the *Code de musique pratique*, he voiced the same judgment. "However worthy of commendation be the fullness of harmony, the taste of the *chant* should triumph."[6]

The appreciation of harmony and the realization of its importance come last in time. And yet it is harmony which "determines the character of the expression",[7] says Marmontel, echoing Rameau. "There are chords which are sad, languishing, tender, pleasant,

---

[1] (17), 11.

[2] (17), 102.—Harmony is generally contrasted with melody, but in the course of defending French music, less concerned than Italian with "l'imitation des bruits et des mouvements" and more with "le sentiment qui n'a point de mouvements déterminés", he was led to contrast it with rhythm. "The physical is expressed by rhythms and tempo [*mesure et mouvement*], the pathetic . . . by harmony and inflexions; one should weigh this well before deciding which is to predominate" (at a given moment) ((17), viii).

[3] (1), 291.   [4] (20), 12.   [5] (1), 142.
[6] (21), 163.   [7] (86), 90.

merry and surprising."[1]   The attempt to relate types of emotion and dissonances is worked out in a whole chapter of the *Traité*.[2]   Thus, joyousness and magnificence are rendered by concords, or by discords "that arise naturally, that are prepared", in which upper part and bass are always concordant; sweetness and tenderness by prepared minor discords; tender complaining by discords "par emprunt et par supposition",[3] preferably minor; despair and fury by unprepared discords of all kinds.   These suggestions are qualified by "sometimes, rather good, most often"; there is nothing hard and fast in these equivalences.

Succession—that is, consistency—is as important as fullness.

> The regularity of the harmony consists as much in its succession as in its plentitude. . . .   The lack of succession . . . is like a man whose voice fails him in the middle of a sentence.[4]

Coherence of harmony is one of Rameau's most precious qualities and here, as indeed everywhere, he practised what he preached.

He never loses sight of the need to stir and "penetrate" the soul. Thus he notes that the more lasting a harmony the more chance it has of "penetrating to the soul and affecting it according to [the musician's] intention".[5]

One of the most fruitful springs of emotion lies in modulation. In fact, "the strength of expression depends more on modulation than on mere melody".[6]   One should know the "*chants* and modulations . . . which best suit the most marked expressions",[7] and be conscious of the danger which threatens all composers of falling into mechanical habits of modulation which destroy the expressive value of the music.[8]

I give elsewhere his list of keys in relation to their emotional significance.[9]   Such equivalences are of course arbitrary but he is on safe ground when he writes:

---

[1] (1), 141.   [2] (1), II, xx.

[3] "*Borrowed* discords" [dissonances par emprunt] "are chords without a fundamental such as the diminished seventh, because these chords *borrow* their completeness from a sound which does not appear in them.   Chords by *supposition* exceed the limits of the octave, such as the ninth or the eleventh" ((165), 1400, note 11).   See also (1), livre II, Chapters 10 and 12.

[4] (18), 14–15.

[5] (17), 92.—"Pénétrer jusqu'à l'âme" is an expression that recurs more than once.   "Cela peut quelquefois pénétrer jusqu'à l'âme," he says of an effective use of inversions in (21), 160.

[6] (2), 43: title of Chapter viii.

[7] (2), 43.—"Expressions" is here the equivalent of "affects".

[8] (2), 43.—"Un accord routiné", for "hackneyed", is an expression he uses elsewhere, e.g. in the *Dissertation*.

[9] Appendix B, p. 603.

Music, like speech, has its sentences; changes of key give the same impression as changes of sentence. . . . The different key relations which one may use produce in this impression a difference similar to those of the different relations of feeling expressed in successive sentences.[1]

He attempts for the modes what he had done for keys and chords.

From the closer or looser relation between successive modes arise the more or less strongly felt impressions, and only thus are strong effects produced. To the diatonic falls what is pleasant; to the chromatic what is varied, and in the minor mode it breathes tenderness and still more sadness. The enharmonic upsets the ear, carries to excess all the passions, frightens, terrifies, and scatters disorder over all when one knows how to compose it with relevance of diatonic and chromatic and support it with a movement that suits the expression.[2]

This was written in 1750. Some thirteen years earlier he had entertained some hopes, with suitable help, of reducing to something like a table of equivalences the correspondence between "modes" and "effects" and voiced them with his usual clumsiness but with an unusual wistfulness. "I should be too rich if I possessed this manner" (that is, the ability to know on what mode a given expression was dependent);

I own that I still seek it, I catch sight of the object from afar; I cannot reach it without the help of an able philosopher who would put me right on the exact difference between the relations of feelings, on which difference I might perhaps discover analogous differences between the modes and between the different ways of passing from one to the other.[3]

Anticipating Herbart, he had here a glimpse of relations between music and psychology but, for lack of a suitable guide, he never entered that domain, the day for exploring which had not yet dawned.

One of the chief discoveries which he owed to his acoustic musings is the succession of keys that follow each other in chains of fifths, above and below the tonic. In many places he dwells on the importance of this discovery for expression,[4] but never more fully than towards the end of his life, in those *Observations* in which he took up his much-worked pen to defend French music and his own against the attacks of Rousseau and the other fans of Italian opera.

Is it not natural to appropriate to joy the throng of descendants afforded by the sub-multiples whose existence is revealed by resonance? There take their source the major third, the major mode, the sharp keys; the *chant* whose strength doubles as it rises, and the dominant, the fifth above. And for the opposite reason, may one not appropriate to tears,

---

[1] (7), 20.   [2] (12), 99.
[3] (9), 226–227.   [4] E.g. (12), 82.

regrets, and so forth, those multiples whose dreary silence is awakened only by the divisions in unison of the body that makes them vibrate? . . . Well, it is on this side that take their source the minor third, the minor mode, the flat keys, the *chant* that relaxes as it goes down, the subdominant, the fifth below, and, moreover, the chromatic and the enharmonic.[1]

One of the accusations brought against French music after the storm had broken in 1752 was the overloading of its scores. Rousseau praised the simplicity of Italian accompaniments. "The Italians despise figures; they hardly even need a score; the promptness and delicacy of their ear make up for it and they accompany very well without all this apparatus." Rameau retorted that the Italians were constantly violating "the fullness of harmony and its natural succession".[2] Before Rousseau's attack he had never felt the need to defend a rich accompaniment and orchestration was still too simple for it to become the subject of theorizing, but now he was cut to the quick and over and over again he returned to the defence of a rich, full harmony. In the article *Accompagnement* in the *Encyclopédie* Rousseau had said that "certain chords would be unbearable with all this filling" (that is, the inner parts which were usually omitted from the printed score). This provoked Rameau's rejoinder: "A chord is a chord only with its filling; it must be complete."[3] He developed this in the *Code* a few years later, laying down that the harmony of the accompaniment

> should always be complete and regular both in its succession and in its fullness; otherwise the irregularity on this point would be liable to distract the attention and ruin the finest moment of the effect. To truncate the harmony because an instrument is too loud is the attitude of a Midas, when there are several ways of lessening the noise without harmony suffering.[4]

He might have added, as did Pierre Lasserre when he reviewed the battle a century and a half later, that it was precisely the excess of accompaniment, the "trop de musique" with which Rousseau reproached Rameau and French opera generally, which made it possible for his art, in the greatest hands, to indulge in fine shading, so that Rameau, because of the fullness of his orchestration, shows himself at times to be a great mezzotint artist as well as capable of bright, strong

---

[1] (17), 52–53.—Also more briefly on pp. xii–xiii.—Masson ((190), 469) sees in this opposition between the two slopes "almost all the secret of Rameau's expressive palette".

[2] (18), 5.

[3] (18), 13.

[4] (21), 73.—See also his words to d'Alembert quoted on p. 504.

hues, "just as in painting it is only a rich palette which can shade and grade the colouring".[1]

Only once did he write at length on the recitative, and this was in his early *Traité*, written while he was still organist at Clermont, eleven years before his first opera; yet his opinions are affirmed with an assurance which impresses and imposes respect for this church musician who had not had the opportunity of practising what he was preaching.

"One should be more circumspect in recitatives than in airs"; (who is he, one might ask, to lay down the law to practised opera composers?)

> for when some story, or some such thing, has to be narrated or recited, the *chant* must imitate speech, so that one appears to be speaking instead of singing. Thus, full closes must be used only where the meaning comes to a stop, and here one needs all we have said that a good musician should know; he should attend to expressing the long syllables of the speech by notes of a suitable length and shorter ones by shorter notes; so that the number may be perceived as easily as if someone were declaiming. It is nevertheless possible to pass several long and short syllables on notes of equal length, provided that the long ones sound at the beginning of the beat, and especially on the first beat.[2]

The close resemblance of recitative with declamation was a tenet of Lulli and his followers. Experience brought Rameau a wider outlook, and thirty years later Marmontel could state that "M. Rameau himself does not believe that the modulation of the melodic line should be slavishly accurate imitation of natural declamation".[3]

As it has so often been said, Rameau is a conscious artist who wants to know what he is doing and why he is doing it. The superficial view is that preoccupation with the principles underlying one's art is incompatible with creative activity and that the springs of inspiration are dried up by too clear an understanding of how they flow. This opinion, still common, is not a product of Romanticism; it was current in the eighteenth century and was responsible for the criticisms of Rameau's music as that of a geometer, as mathematical music, as what would be called to-day "une musique cérébrale" in which the heart spoke no word. No doubt the greater complexity of his music, compared with that of his predecessors, was responsible for the strangeness felt by his hearers, but it was the existence of his writings and his reputation as a theorist that caused the hostility provoked by his music to express itself in this form.[4]

---

[1] (176), 90.   [2] (1), 162.   [3] (86), 90.

[4] For an account of the musical theorizing of the 1670–1730 period and an explanation of the fact that such theorizing did not imply the stifling of spontaneity and imagination, see the excellent pages in (175), 433–444.

Here again an occasional unguarded statement did harm. In 1760, this is the impression which his *Observations* made on at least one reader.

> . . . One hundred and twenty-five mortal pages where the author repeats what he has said in his books of theory . . . M. Rameau proves clearly that he only thought of making harmony, believing he was making music, and that if he did fine things in a genre I think bad, it was without realizing it and without knowing his true worth. One of the most natural consequences of his principles is, that to make music genius is the last thing needed, and if M. Rameau is right, every petty musician will be able to write the finest things in the world once he has mastered the learning and knowledge of chords. M. Rameau is exactly like a mason or a carpenter who, writing a learned dissertation on the way to cut stone, or ratiocinating deeply on the cutting of planks, thinks he has enabled us to judge the beauty of a building.[1]

It is, however, unlikely that many of those who found his music difficult had fuddled their wits in the dense undergrowth of his books. Had they done so, they would have found many a passage precluding an intellectualist theory of music. The foundations of his art, like those of the French classical writers, are hedonistic. The ear is the final arbiter of what pleases or displeases; reason is subordinate to it; her task is to discover *why* the pleasure is produced, not to say that pleasure must or must not be produced according to a code of rules.

> One can judge music only through the medium of hearing; reason has authority only inasmuch as it agrees with the ear; let us therefore judge of everything with their mutual assistance.[2]

He has often emphasized what is primordial, unanalysable and instinctive in artistic creation, calling it now "l'ouïe" or "l'oreille", now "le bon goût, une certaine sensibilité, les talents, le cœur, l'imagination, partir de source, le génie, le sentiment, l'inspiration": terms which all refer to the same thing, the *given* in art, upon which reason and experience can build but behind which they cannot go and for whose absence they cannot make up. From the *Traité* of 1722 to the *Nouvelles Réflexions* of 1761 he never wavered. As he is still sometimes suspected of intellectualism in this field, it is important to quote chapter and verse to support what I am saying.

"Talents are not acquired."[3]

---

[1] (71), I, 1; 189 (June 1754).—The title of the *Dissertation sur les différentes methodes d'accompagnement* contained an even clearer boast and taken literally would certainly lead one to suppose that Rameau thought that all music was contained in rules, since it claimed that by its aid "one can become a learned composer and clever accompanist, even without knowing how to read music".

[2] (1), 125.   [3] (2), 91.

"As for taste and genius, they are not acquired."[1]   Music does not live by rules alone.

"Even if the rules known were beyond criticism, what are rules that enslave genius?   It is for imagination to give orders."[2]

"The various sentiments and events that can be rendered in music give rise every instant to novelties not reducible to rules. . . .   The choice of roads depends on our taste."[3]   In melody, "taste is also the prime mover."[4]

"Fugue" (that is, fugal writing) "is an ornament in music whose only principle is good taste."[5]

"One may excel in the practice of music without knowing the theory.   Without a certain native sensibility for harmony, one is never a perfect musician."[6]

"A *chant* produced and pursued by imagination without reflexion seldom sins against harmonic relations; such is the rule of nature."[7]

The converse is true.   Weaknesses occur "in *chants* which do not flow as from a spring, which have not come naturally, which are due only to reflexion.   What comes from the source recalls readily the principle that suggests it; let reflexion have her say and inspiration vanishes."[8]

The more anti-rationalist pronouncements come late; they are partly the result of the desire to prove the instinctive nature of the "principe" ("notre instinct pour la musique et son principe"), partly the outcome of the attacks of pro-Italians whose case was that Italian music "coulait de source" and was not, like Rameau's, the fruit of reflexion.   This drove him to emphasize more than he had done the rights of "inspiration" and the weakness of mere reason in order to counter the accusation of cerebrality.   There is in the following passage, aimed at Rousseau and his criticism of Lulli's *Armide*, an unmistakable taunt of "a little learning" as well as an expression of trust in feeling.

---

[1] (9), 170.   [2] (21), xv.

[3] (1), 358-359.—Cf. with Ravel's remark quoted by Paul Landormy: "There are rules for making a building hold up but none for linking modulations together.   Yes, only one—inspiration" (174).

[4] (1), 142.   [5] (1), 358.

[6] (2), vii; also Chapter xxi.   [7] (21), 141.

[8] (23), 10-11.   This holds good for execution.   "However well an ornament may be rendered, there will always be lacking the *je ne sais quoi* which gives it all its merit if it is not guided by feeling.   Too much or too little, too soon or too late, more or less duration in the suspensions, in the increase or decrease of sound, in the trills, in a word this fitting precision required by the expression, the situation—once this is missing, the ornament becomes pointless" ((21), 13).

One should always mistrust one's judgment when someone ignorant of the principles [of music] seeks to distinguish it [that is, the judgment] from the impressions he has received. . . . Let us surrender to pure feeling, let us listen without thinking of it [in order to judge of Armide's soliloquy].[1]

In 1760 he declared that "true music is the language of the heart".[2]
Out of the same quarrels came the vicious hits at "geometers' music". The geometers were well defined; indeed there was only one, his former admirer and expounder, now a partisan of the Bouffons and a supporter of Rousseau, Rameau's critic in the *Encyclopédie*. It is amusing to hear him use against others the opprobrious term once levelled at him. He spurns "the music of the geometer who is guided only by reckoning; the musician has never wanted to listen to it".[3] And: "It is not enough to be a geometer and physicist to be able to go deeply into the science of music; ears most consummate in the art are needed, so that one may express no judgment on it in which reason and feeling are not in absolute agreement."[4]

This last remark reminds us that a judicious choice of quotations should not lead us to believe that Rameau was a pure inspirationist. The bulk of his work shouts the contrary. The preface of his first book regrets that, although music has progressed through the ages and the ear has become more "sensitive to the wondrous effects of this art", while experience was thus acquiring authority reason was losing "her rights" because

the mind has not had the curiosity to investigate its true principles. . . . It is true that certain perfections depend on genius and taste for which experience is even more useful than learning; but it remains that perfect knowledge should always enlighten us. . . . It is desirable that the knowledge of musicians of our age should be as great as the beauty of their compositions.[5]

In his unacknowledged letter to La Motte he contrasted "the musician who prides himself less on his learning than on his taste" and "the musician who studies Nature before depicting her".
In his early *Nouveau Système* he wrote:

Talents are not acquired; they are perfected only by dint of being cultivated. But science is acquired, and let there be no mistake; it is with the help of this science that one finds the means to cultivate one's talents and bring them to blossom much more quickly than if one relies entirely on the passage of time.[6]

[1] (17), 77. [2] (21), 93.
[3] (20), 47. [4] (22), 70.
[5] (1), preface: first, third and fifth pages (unnumbered).
[6] (2), 91.

In 1760, in the heat of the quarrel that embittered his last years, he expressed afresh the idea he had stated in 1727, but directed *ad homines*, to those countrymen of his for whom Italy was the source of all light. "Talents are not acquired but they develop as by degrees the ear is educated; and to that end one should listen often to music of all tastes" (that is, styles)[1]—an obvious hit at Rousseau, Grimm and those who listen only to Italian music.

These quotations will suffice since no one has ever doubted that Rameau believed that study and learning were as necessary as taste and genius; the prejudice has been rather in the other direction.

Unlike the Pluches, Saint-Mards, Duboses and other less than amateur musicians who laid down the law to unheeding composers, unlike Gluck himself, Rameau never made any pronouncement regarding the primacy of words over music or of music over words. What his feelings were must be guessed from his practice. He was, it seems, indifferent to his plots but not to his texts. Indeed, some of his librettists found him exacting on the score of words. Voltaire, at the time of *La Princesse de Navarre*, complained humorously that he was made to reduce eight-syllable lines to four syllables, and vice versa, and Collé voiced his rancour against his collaborator in his *Journal*. Music was possibly the servant of plot and situation but verse was at times the handmaid of music. It had somehow to be amenable to musical treatment, and all verse, it seems, was not. Yet Rameau could be—perforce had to be—very open-armed. I do not know whether he boasted that he could set *La Gazette de Hollande* to music—the source of this anecdote is in Clément's *Les cinq années littéraires*[2]—but if he had he would not have been the only musician in his century to perform a similar feat. J. Benj. Laborde's setting of a *privilège de librairie*, for voice and orchestra, is preserved in the Bibliothèque Nationale[3]; it was probably inspired by the remark attributed to Rameau. But some of the lines which our composer had to set were no less prosy than the "Louis, par la grâce de Dieu, Roy de France et de Navarre, à nos amez et féaux Conseillers, les Gens tenans nos Cours de Parlemens . . ." on which Laborde showed his mettle. One of the least poetic comes from an illustrious pen:

> Il est une vaste distance
> Entre les noms connus et les noms glorieux,

which sounds like a quotation from a dictionary of synonyms but is a distich from Voltaire's *Le Temple de la Gloire*. How did Rameau treat this monster? Did he shy away from it and write "pure music"

---

[1] (21), xvi.   [2] III, 4 (1761).
[3] The beginning is quoted by La Laurencie in (165), 1424.

that bore no relation to the words? Certainly not. He looked for what "expression" it could afford; he marked the rhythm with its long beat on "vaste", the most important word; and he painted the "distance" by leaps of a sixth and a seventh, and the "glorieux" by a little swaggering descent. Only with the "Entre les noms connus" do we feel that he was nonplussed and so resorted to pure musicianship with a mildly surprising rise of an augmented fourth whose connexion with the distinction marked by "entre" I have failed to discover (ex. 312).[1]

Ex. 312

His great *tragédies* show a power of gripping a situation, a mood or even a character, though the psychology, from the nature of the plots, remains generalized. Long before his first opera he had expressed himself on the duties of a dramatic musician with as much assurance as if he had the authority of a long and successful career behind him.

> A good musician should surrender himself to all the humours [*caractères*] he wishes to depict; and like a clever actor put himself in the place of the person speaking, believe he is in the spots where the events he wishes to represent are taking place and take as much part in them as those whose interests are most engaged; be a good declaimer, at least in himself; feel when the voice should rise or fall so that he may conform his melody, harmony, modulation and tempo to it.[2]

Which is what Ravel said in more direct language to Jules Renard anent the latter's *Histoires naturelles* which he had set. "My intention was not to add but to interpret ... To say in music what you say in words when you stand, for instance, before a tree. I think and feel

---

[1] II, 2.   [2] (1), 148.

in music and I want to think and feel the same things as you do."[1]

This appeal to creative imagination, this attempt at identification with the character and the mood is, of course, a tenet of classical doctrine.

> Il faut dans la douleur que vous vous abaissiez;
> Pour me tirer des pleurs il faut que vous pleuriez,

had written Boileau; and Rameau echoed this when he said to his pupil Laborde: "Mon ami, faites-moi pleurer."[2]

There is an aspect of Rameau's outlook which is as much of his age as imitationism. In the standing quarrel between Ancients and Moderns he was unquestioningly on the side of the Moderns. "Our music is in its last degree of perfection and the Ancients did not attain such perfection by far," he boasted on the second page of his first book.[3] "We live in a century where light has at length scattered darkness" (in musical theory), he wrote to Christin, quoting from memory from his *Génération*.[4] He stands on his own legs and makes it quite plain that he owes nothing to his predecessors, by whom he is not impressed and whom he mentions mainly to criticize them. Of Plato and Aristotle he speaks in his *Traité* only by the way and at second hand; later, he made a good deal of play with the name and doctrines of Pythagoras, basing himself on the *Denarius Pythagoricus* of Johannes Meursius,[5] and he endorses the doubts already expressed by Zarlino on the stupendous effects of music quoted by writers of Antiquity. Zarlino is his oldest authority; he knows the *Istituzioni armoniche* (1558) in their 1573 edition, thinking them wrongly to be later than the *Dimonstrazioni*; then Mersenne[6] and Descartes[7] and a number of contemporary practicians, L'Affilard, Loulié, Masson and Frère, and the dictionary of Sébastien de Brossard. He gives to Zarlino, somewhat sarcastically, Brossard's title of "prince of modern musicians", and shows surprise that he should still remain "the oracle of a few musicians".[8] He pays scant attention to Zarlino's important

---

[1] (174); the passage is quoted from Renard's *Journal*, January 12, 1907; p. 748.

[2] The story comes from Palissot's *Mémoires sur la littérature* (article on Laborde), quoted in (150), 57, and is repeated here with the usual reservations about authenticity. The remark was directed to Laborde as harpsichord pupil, not as budding composer.

[3] (1), preface.

[4] November 3, 1741; first published by Vallas (236A); reproduced in (150), 97–99.

[5] Leyden, 1631.

[6] *Traité de l'Harmonie universelle*, 1627; *Harmonicorum libri XII*, 1635.

[7] *Compendium*, written in 1618, published in 1650; French translation as *Abrégé de la musique*, 1668.   [8] (1), 18.

notion of dual harmony, which he tries to refute; yet he returns to it several times, in the *Traité* and later, as if, says Riemann, with an uneasy conscience.

Of earlier music he had as little knowledge as a Fontenelle or a d'Alembert had of mediaeval art, and as little respect for what he knew. Historical science, then in its awakening, had not yet extended its field to music, and Rameau was deficient enough in historical perspective to criticize Zarlino for not figuring his basses and for not introducing the semitone "in places where it would be most effective". His allusion to Gregorian plainsong, or rather to what passed for such in his time, is full of scorn. He desires the reform of church music: "Music is made only to sing God's praises; how unpleasant for a man full of this truth not to be able to use his genius on so great a subject",[1] the only passage in all his work, as far as I know, with one in his last publication, the *Lettre aux Philosophes*, in which God's name is mentioned.

In all this he is in nowise exceptional; his ignorance of the past and contempt for it were, like his aesthetics, those of the generation of the La Mottes, Trublets, Terrassons and Marivaux to which he belonged.

Even his references to modern music are few. He pulls to pieces a movement of Corelli's, the bass of which he finds defective,[2] and a few of his formulas are taken from Masson.[3] Armide's soliloquy is praised and quoted in the *Nouveau Système*,[4] in the *Observations*[5] and the *Code*.[6] The only other works illustrated are his own: the motet *Laboravi* and the two canons "Ah! loin de rire" and "Avec du vin" in the *Traité*.[7]

Musicians who have also been critics are not uncommon, but Rameau is unique in that he is a great creative musician who spent as much as he could of his life in probing to their roots the scientific presuppositions of his art. For him, as for the theoreticians who had preceded him, "music" meant both a "physico-mathematical science, whose physical object was sound and the relations that are found between different sounds", and an art whose object was "to please and arouse diverse feelings (or passions) in us".[8] Though in later years he used Sauveur's word *acoustique*, which the physicist had coined on the pattern of *optique*, he never distinguished clearly between the two things; they were both "music", one speculative, the other practical. It is not clear that he thought the latter nobler than the

---

[1] (1), 147.   [2] (2), 94–106.
[3] *Nouveau Traité des Règles pour la Composition de la Musique*, 1694.
[4] 80 ff.   [5] 69–115.   [6] 168–16ç.
[7] 341–355, 360–362.   [8] (9), 30.

former; indeed, certain statements attributed to him and made at the end of his life would show the contrary; in any case, his one-time friend Père Castel was undoubtedly pained when he saw him desert, as he thought, the one for the other. This confusion under one banner of two things which we consider shriekingly discrete is not just poverty of nomenclature; the science and the art were *one thing*, seen now with the mind, now with the imagination ("le goût, le génie")

The example of other theorists, from Zarlino to Castel, who all considered they were studying music when they were studying the mathematical and physical basis of music, shows that Rameau was of his age in this; yet, as with all great minds, he was personal even while remaining of his age.   In practice, though not in thought, there *was* a distinction between the two meanings of the word; Zarlino, Kircher, Mersenne were not composing musicians; Morley, Monteverdi, Froberger, Kuhnau, Marcello and others who wrote about music as well as made it, were not "physico-mathematicians".   In fact, most "simple practising musicians", as Jean-Philippe complained, "look down on the source of the science that adorns them . . . saying: What is the use of all these calculations, all these commas, etc., when I make good music without all this?"[1]   In Rameau alone were the two sides of "music" united.

The union reflected something very deep in his personality and he was conscious enough to express it in a memorable passage in the year that saw the performance of his most accomplished masterpiece.

> With regard to practice, when I devoted myself to it on working for the stage, I was carried away by the pleasure of realizing, *as artist*, many pictures of which I had conceived the idea, a thing which flatters infinitely taste and imagination; but I was carried away *even more so* by the pleasure of seeing, *as thinker*, the interplay of all these phenomena of which the principle was not unknown to me, and to produce an infinity of effects whose causes I had fitted myself to know.[2]

Is it possible to evoke, I will not say more elegantly, but more clearly and pungently a picture of self-duplication, in which the observant, analytical self looks on fascinated while the instinctive self gets going with "creation"?   He is, of course, in the line of critico-creative writers like Corneille, a couple of generations before him, like Paul Valéry and T. S. Eliot in our own time; he is also a descendant of philosopher-artists like the Leone-Battista Albertis and Leonardos of the early Renaissance, or his elder contemporary, Christopher Wren, a type of mind not uncommon in the plastic arts more closely allied to literary expression, but not yet found in music.

---

[1] (9), Chapter xix.   [2] (9), 111–112; my italics.

Irritatingly turgid as is their style and unlovely their individual pages, the mass of his works compels admiration and even awe. There runs through their succession a unity of purpose more ethical than aesthetic, to which, nevertheless, it is hard to deny the name beauty. The obstinate outpouring has a forbidding grandeur, a *terribilità*, almost Michelangelesque. How far they take us from the one-time picture of a *dessus de porte* Rameau, a boudoir composer of imitationist miniatures, with a faded perfume and an old-world quaintness! Here is a soul grim in its persistence, pursuing one quest through half a century of a life to which neither "calme" nor "douceur" was ever granted.[1] From "earliest youth" he sought the "true principle" of the art to which he had found himself "destined" and with which his whole life was "solely occupied".[2] He was conscious, perhaps with some exaggeration, of having penetrated where none had preceded him, and, far more than the merit of his music, for which he never battled, he defended this claim whenever it was attacked. It was on this ground that he fell foul of his friend Castel. And if in old age the distortion, the mental ossification inseparable from the oncoming of eld made his single-mindedness stiffen into a kind of *rigor mortis* and involve him in mathematical metaphysics which even d'Alembert owned he could not follow—sweet consolation to lesser minds who have failed likewise!—there is a grandeur in his ultimate reiteration of the oft-made boast:

> Depuis environ cent cinquante ans, je veux dire depuis Zarlino et plusieurs autres qui n'ont rien ajouté de neuf à ses découvertes, *je suis le seul* qui ait écrit scientifiquement, bien ou mal, de la Musique, excepté quelques sectateurs de mes principes.[3]

To-day, the perusal of his writings is of far greater interest for what it reveals of him as a man than for a knowledge of his theories, which are more conveniently mastered in d'Alembert's *Éléments*. Such is at any rate the fruit won by the writer of these lines from a study undertaken from a stern sense of duty and pursued with determination. From the mass of these twenty-four books and articles there emerges in retrospect the figure of a personality. Not a very complete one, it is true; one from which the most genial qualities are absent; one to whom urbanity came with effort (as in the strainingly courteous letter to Père Castel), one always grimly in earnest, who could be scathing but never humorous, who would not have understood St. Thomas More's saying that nothing he said was "well spoken except he had ministered some mock in the communication". Was this the whole of Rameau's personality?

---

[1] (12), *Épître dédicatoire à M. le comte d'Argenson.*
[2] (12), 110. [3] (24), 35. My italics.

What his family saw of it we shall never know. Not a document, not a reported remark has come to us from his wife or his children to show him *dans l'intimité*. In his early life he is completely shrouded. Our imagination finds it easier to picture him as an old man of eighty, in his flat overlooking the Palais Royal, with a wife in late and a son in early middle age and a daughter not turned twenty, chafing to take flight in wedlock, but what we fancy cannot be checked. The core of mystery remains impenetrable.

It is after all in his music that we come nearest to his personality and see him at his completest. Here, too, when we live long enough with it and are acquainted with enough of it, we perceive the same figure as in the books, the same single-mindedness and persistence, the same dignity and disdain of trickery, the same inflexibility, honesty and contempt for the slick and easy, for the cheap effect, for the merely habitual. If this is what is connoted by the term "baroque", if "rococo" implies a relaxing of standards, then it is fitting to call his works "baroque blocks isolated in a rococo surrounding".[1]

But the tenderness, the sense of *nuance*, the caress, the *volupté* even, of which the writings give no hint, the conjurings up of pastoral nature, and here and there a gentle humour—not just the harsh mocking of *Platée* which comes from the same vein as his taunts at Jean-Jacques—these and many other qualities which escape enumeration clothe this personality without hiding it. Rameau the musician is a poet and a magician, the greatest, in music, of the century, and of this Rameau the prose writer gives no hint. Nevertheless, the knowledge of the one gives substance to the other. When we have soaked in his prose we turn to the music to recognize there aspects of the man which we would have perceived less clearly did we not know the *Traité*, the *Démonstration*, the *Code* and the gaggle of *Erreurs*, *Réflexions* and *Réponses*.

Book III of the *Traité de l'Harmonie* was translated into English (translator unknown) and published in 1737 by J. French; a reprint came out in 1752. Book IV was translated by Griffith Jones, organist of the French Chapel, Soho, and published by Longman and Broderip about 1795.

A complete French edition of Rameau's theoretical writings, undertaken by the distinguished scholar Erwin Jacobi, is being brought out by the American Institute of Musicology; the first volume, consisting of the *Traité de l'Harmonie*, came out in 1967; the edition will be complete in six volumes.

An English translation of the *Traité* by Philip Gossett is being brought out by Dover Publications, Inc. (1970). Both these editions have valuable introductions.

---

[1] A modified quotation of Bukofzer's "His *tragédies lyriques* stand like erratic blocks isolated in a rococo surrounding" ((125), 255).

15. Rameau and Gluck

Few composers have had their names so "sicklied o'er with" literature as Ritter von Gluck. He has been moralized upon; hailed as the achievement of something virtuous, as the triumph of Good over Evil, of common sense over absurdity, of nature over artifice; as a source of purification; as the first to express in music a beauty not aesthetic but ethical: "ses mélodies sont parfois médiocres et la beauté de son art est surtout morale; une grande âme y est empreinte".[1]   Add to this the advantages that spring from the virtues attached to national sentiment; he is the torch-bearer of Germanism in an age of Italian and Gallic decadence; "Hier ruht ein rechtschaffener deutscher Mann" is inscribed on his tomb.

These non-artistic judgments have called forth contrary ones: some as completely non-artistic, some tinged with an appearance of aestheticism, but always with ethical categories—a good thing, a bad thing—in the background.   The germ of "Wagnerian formulas" is in him; Wagner is a bad thing; *ergo* Gluck also.

> He prepared the victory of Donizetti and Meyerbeer. . . .   *Alceste* blazed a trail for *Robert le Diable*, and *Armide* for *Lucia di Lammermoor*,[2]

both, of course, incontestably "bad things" . . .

It is thus hard to approach him with an unbiased mind, influenced, repelled, irritated as one inevitably is by all the judgments that have been pronounced on him, by all the axes that have been ground on the anvil of his drama and all the bees that have been fed on its honey.

Yet an attempt to grasp the relation between him and Rameau is unavoidable at the close of a study on the elder dramatist—to grasp this relation not only historically but also, with due critical diffidence, artistically.   After all, there *is* a category of greatness in art though no one has ever defined it; and certain figures enter into it and others do not; and of those who do it is legitimate to recognize some as higher than the rest, though everyone knows that to pursue this recognition far leads to arbitrary and sometimes absurd judgments.

---

[1] (219), 179.—See also: "He was a man.   The others" (Hasse, Graun, Telemann) "were only musicians" (in (221), 150), an echo of Gluck's: "I should have been only a musician and untrue to nature" in Corancez (57).

[2] (171), 9.

It is still widely believed that Gluck's celebrated "reform of the opera" involved all opera and not merely Italian, and that the abuses against which he fought were to be found in all forms of the art in the eighteenth century.   As long ago as 1935 Martin Cooper emphasized that "reform" was a misnomer and the right word "reaction".[1] Yet even he asserted that "Gluck was the first clearly to formulate and then to put into practice this principle" (that is, of "the tradition which emphasizes the drama and regards the music as secondary and subservient").[2]   If this means that he was the first to do *both* things, then the claim is correct; but separately each had been done long before, the first by the Le Cerfs and Pluches and other rationalist theorists of music, the latter by Lulli and all the composers who followed him, including Rameau.

Now one of the first discoveries we make when we begin to explore Rameau is that here was an opera which not only needed none of the reforms enumerated by Gluck and Calzabigi in the famous preface of 1768 but even supplied to some extent the ideal implicit in that manifesto.   Let us note first of all that Gluck says explicitly that the abuses he proposes to correct are those "which have disfigured *Italian* opera". The points of the celebrated document are the following:

(1) "I have striven to limit music to her true function, which is to serve poetry by means of expression and by following the situations of the story."

How familiar this rings!   We are back with the rationalist aesthetics which we were outlining in the last chapter, with the Saint-Évremonds, Le Cerfs, Duboses and Mablys.   Le Cerf had written: "I call *expressive* an air whose tones suit the words perfectly and a *symphonie* which expresses perfectly what it wishes to express."[3]

Had not Dubos shaken his head at certain people who "do not by any means require of the musician that he should fit his melodies with the feelings contained in the words he is setting", who "are content that they should be merely varied, graceful songs; it is enough if these render in passing a few words in the text"?[4]

Had not Rémond de Saint-Mard said that music should be "l'esclave de la poésie"? So had many others.   "The French theory of expression enslaved music to speech or at least to thought.   Italian art overflowed the framework of this theory."[5] But in France, at any rate, those who spoke thus had been *honnêtes gens*, men and women

---

[1] (130), 15.   [2] (130), 282.

[3] (83), III, 378.—Also: "To devise tones so completely proportioned to the words that the poetry becomes an undistinguishable and living part of the music and the latter will then transmit directly to the heart of the hearer the emotion of every phrase uttered by the singer: this is what is meant by expression" (II, 169).

[4] (64), 657.   [5] (189), 544.

who had views but were not professionals. No practising French musician had made such a statement. It was left to Gluck to sell the pass.

In music as in poetry there are only three or four ways of expressing a given thought. This limits the musician, but he must abide by these limits; so much the worse if uniformity results. To vary for the sake of variety would be to "forsake nature", had declared Le Cerf.[1] Gluck was of the same opinion. One should not fear to repeat the same *chant*, such as the soldiers' chorus in *Iphigénie en Aulide*, when one is rendering the true accent of an elemental passion. Starving people will all ask for bread in the same way. One should follow nature and not vary what is not varied in nature.[2]

It is true that these prescriptions had not been strictly followed by musicians, even in France; nevertheless, the reproach of putting the music before the verse was much less deserved by French than by Italian opera. The backbone of Lullian *tragédie lyrique* had been the declamation, embodied in the recitative; and Rameau had preserved the importance of the recitative, even while he developed both the melodic and the choreographic sides.

(2) The music should not "interrupt the action nor stifle it with superfluous ornaments. . . . I have therefore refrained from interrupting an actor in the heat of the dialogue to wait for a tedious *ritornello*."

In Lullian opera there are sometimes preludes but not *ritornelli*. The prelude announces the emotional character of the piece and refers to the situation more closely than the concerto-like *ritornello* of the Italian *aria*; it is also generally shorter, except when it is the prelude to the act. The undramatic Italian *ritornello* has, however, full play in the *ariette* which is the *aria* transplanted.

(3) ". . . To break up a word on a favourable vowel . . ."

This abuse was absent from Lulli but had entered French opera later and was prevalent before Rameau's time; Rameau accepted it and never seems to have been aware of its anti-dramatic character, though criticisms of it were many. From the days of Lecerf the anti-Italians had protested against "mots lyriques" and "mots privilégiés"; later, pro-Italians like Rousseau joined with them, without seeing the illogicality of their action.

It is perhaps a slight defence of French practice to say that there is always an at least external connexion between the word chosen and the coloratura laid on it; it is never just the "favourable" quality of the vowel, as in Italian, that decides the moment for the *roulade*.

(4) "I have not passed lightly on the second part of an air, which may be the most passionate and most important, to have the oppor-

---

[1] See p. 530.   [2] Gluck's reply to Corancez, in (57).

tunity of repeating regularly four times over the words of the first part, and finish the air when the meaning is incomplete, to give the singer the means of showing how whimsically and in how many ways he can vary a passage . . ."

The attack here is against the *da capo* air with varied repeat of the first part.

This form is found in the *ariettes* of the *divertissements* and, as time went on and pressure from Italian influence became greater, occasionally within the discourse of the drama, as in Zoroastre's "Ai-mez-vous sans cesse",[1] but it is always exceptional. The ABA form of the French monologue does not sacrifice the second part and does not allow for extemporized variations in the reprise.

(5) "I have considered that the overture should warn the specta-tors of the action to be performed and be, so to speak, its argument."

I have discussed this question in Chapter 8. By 1768 the French overture was usually a reflection or an announcement of the action, and a writer in 1773 said with some surprise: "If it be true (as is reported) that the Italians play only an unrelated symphony as introduction to their operas, they are far from the perfection we desire on our stage; they are musicians, not artists."[2]

Rameau had linked overture and opening chorus by using identical material in both some twenty years before the preface to *Alceste*, and Gluck merely followed his example in the overtures of his two *Iphi-génies*. On the first performance of *Iphigénie en Aulide* in 1774 some Gluckists had asserted their hero's originality. Castillon recalled Rameau's priority. "An injustice has been done him by bringing forward this idea as entirely new."[3]

(6) "I have refused to allow an incongruous break in the dialogue between air and recitative."

The existence of an almost "continuous melody" was the most obvious difference between French and Italian opera. What Gluck was calling for here had always existed in French opera; Italian had given it up long ago. France had remained faithful to Lulli's practice of blending the more melodious moments with the declamatory back-ground by incorporating *petits airs* in the recitative, called *airs de mouvement* because they had a more precise "mouvement", or tempo and beat, than the unmeasured recitative. Le Cerf considered them to be one of the adornments of French opera and justified them.[4] Throughout the century the traditional "continuous melody" re-

---

[1] II, 4; where, however, the repeat is much cut down.

[2] *Réponse à la critique de l'opéra de* Castor *et observations sur la musique*, 26; in (190), 317.

[3] *Journal des beaux-arts et des sciences*; in (192), 475.

[4] (83), I, 60.

tained its defenders. Marmontel, who was to become one of Gluck's most determined opponents, deprecated any marked difference between recitative and *cantabile* air. "Is it not the height of art to prepare ear and soul *imperceptibly* for a keen emotion?"[1]

This view generally went with disapproval of Italian *recitativo secco.*

> Le plat récitatif des Romains adopté
> Est le simple discours du bas peuple emprunté;[2]

a couplet quoted approvingly by Decroix when he declared that, though *Orphée* and *Iphigénie en Aulide* had met with success in Paris, it was in spite of their Italian recitative.[3]

On the other hand, Chabanon, though as ardent a Rameau-lover as Decroix, regretted that his hero never reformed French recitative, that "sort of amphibious monster, half song, half declamation, which being neither one nor the other represents them both and prevents them from being what they ought to be".[4]

These two quotations show the extreme poles of taste and prove that the two points of view are, at bottom, irreconcilable. There is an appearance of ethical rectitude about the French "continuous melody" solution which Gluck pressed upon Italian opera and which Wagner, with his *Sprachmelodie*, ignorant of French anticipation and ignoring Gluck's priority,[5] carried to extreme lengths; it seems more in keeping with the dramatic quality of opera, and therefore more honest. One detects a sense of moral superiority about those who advocate it, or who applaud past advocates of it, such as Gluck. But the sectional conception can also be justified and if it is ethically inferior its defenders can snap their fingers at morals, whose right of concern with matters of artistic form is at best very doubtful. With the few operas that have survived the terrific shipwreck of three and a half centuries, it is in every case their musical appeal that has secured their life, whatever other merits they may have possessed, whether they were closely knit artistic wholes or whether their construction was of the compartment kind.

(7) "I considered that my greatest effort should be to seek a beautiful simplicity, and I have forborne from making a display of difficulties at the expense of clarity; I judged that the discovery of a novelty was precious only inasmuch as it was called for naturally by the situation and the expression."

---

[1] (86), 82. [2] (52).
[3] (60). [4] (53), 32.
[5] "Jealous of his honour as a revolutionary of music, he tried to make out that the preface to *Alceste* was little more than a protest against the influences of singers of Italian opera of his day" ((130), 139).

The difficulties are those which the composer has overcome and is proud of showing he has overcome, not those which he puts in the way of the singer.   There may be here an allusion to harmonic innovations for innovation's sake, which merely disconcert the average listener.   Rameau's originalities of expression could generally be justified dramatically, but in their newness they certainly did baffle and irritate conservative Lullists.   But this was only for a time.   "He was accused of having given us too learned a music, too difficult, too recondite; to-day for a little he would be accused of a plainness almost equal to that of Lulli,"[1] wrote Palissot in 1767.   French operas as a whole, between *Cadmus* and 1770, followed their way with a greater simplicity than Italian; the expression was more direct, the music remained closer to the words and there were few display pieces to obscure their meaning.   "A beautiful simplicity" is a loose term, but the ideal which it calls up is that of Lullian rather than of Italian opera.

(8) In the dedication of *Paris and Helen* to the Duke of Braganza Gluck added a further point: "I believed that song in opera was merely a substitute for declamation."

There is no doubt that here, too, the ideal is that of Lulli.   Was it not precisely that his operas and those of his successors were nothing but declamation, without any singing, which was the chief burden of the reproaches levelled against them?—"When are we to have an *aria?*"—"This eternal psalmody"—and suchlike remarks all bear witness to the impression which French opera made on those who loved, in Italian opera, the very feature which Gluck was attacking.   In none of his eight points did he show himself a truer disciple of Lulli and Rameau than in this.

The reforms advocated in these two documents amount to an assimilation of Italian to French opera in almost everything except *divertissements*, and they point to abuses none of which was marked in France and most of which were absent there.   In other words, Gluck's reform does indeed amount to a reaction to the Lullian type, still represented by the only lately deceased Rameau.   One might add that the giving up of historical subjects for mythological or legendary ones is also a step in line with French practice.

It is relevant to inquire whether Gluck was himself faithful to his precepts.

Alceste and *Paris and Helen*, with *Orfeo* before them, do on the whole practise what he preaches, with the exception of the overture to *Orfeo* and the presence of some purely vocalic *coloratura* in *Paris*. But is this true of the three major operas which he composed for the French capital?   Here, one would expect, the fidelity to Lullian

---

[1] (91), 96.

ideals outlined in 1768 would be as close as, if not closer than, in works written for a court where Italian taste prevailed.

They certainly do show that interspersal of *petits airs* with recitative—Rolland mistakes them for *lieder*[1]—which helps to constitute the coherence of Lullian-Ramellian speech. It is nevertheless remarkable that they are less faithful to the preface to *Alceste* and make more concessions to Italian taste than the three operas composed for Italy and Vienna. In *Armide*, the overture, taken from *Telemacco*, is not in the least a warning or an argument. In all three works the contrast between recitative and melody is well marked, not only by formal breaks and even by *ritornelli*, some of them quite substantial,[2] but also because of the difference in interest, especially in the first *Iphigénie*,[3] where the recitative is often as lifeless as *recitativo secco*. In several of the airs the musical interest outweighs the dramatic and the musician dwells as complacently on them as any composer of *opera seria*. Words are repeated to a quite undramatic extent and the first part of a couplet is resumed after the second, so that the air ends on an incomplete meaning, contrary to the precepts of the preface. At least one air contains more than echoes of the concerto-like *aria* of grand opera, with rumbling basses and vigorous reiterations of the common chord.[4]

People have spoken somewhat rashly of Gluck's being forced to comply with the debased taste of Paris. It is certainly curious that Italianisms of the kind he had condemned as abuses should reappear, however attenuated, in works written for the city where the form of opera had arisen which he was advocating a few years earlier. Was Parisian taste at this time already so perverted with *Italianità* that the unfortunate Gluck was obliged to descend from his high-minded pedestal and write down to his frivolous audience? Or had the pure musician which was in him, as it is in every operatic composer whose work is worth listening to, been repressed long enough and did he insist, perhaps unbeknown to his host, on asserting himself here and there? Whether or not these departures from the pure milk of 1768 are regrettable in the first two of the three Parisian operas, it is certain that if he had abided by his teaching as strictly as in *Alceste*, *Iphigénie en Tauride* would not have been the masterpiece of perfect blending of good drama and splendid music which it is.

---

[1] (219), 225.
[2] E.g., "Je t'implore" (*Iphigénie en Tauride*, IV, 1), another borrowing from *Telemacco*.
[3] Everyone accepts Du Roullet's and Gluck's word that their *Iphigénie en Aulide* is "l'*Iphigénie* même de Racine mise en opéra". One cannot insist too strongly that this is not so and that the libretto is as much a travesty of the tragedy as *Hippolyte et Aricie* is of *Phèdre*.
[4] "Calchas, d'un trait mortel blessé" (*Iphigénie en Aulide*, III).

The answer to these apparent inconsistencies is in the fact that Gluck's final attitude may be summed up by saying that he "continued the French tradition while applying cleverly the little reforms of detail suggested by French critics and particularly by the Encyclopaedists".[1]

D'Alembert's *De la liberté de la musique* (1758) is proof of this. This essay is not a brutal and total onslaught on French music like Rousseau's *Lettre*, but a criticism of both French and Italian operas and a plea for the rejuvenation, not the destruction, of the former by certain transfusions from the latter. Writing six years after the performance of *La Serva padrona* he notes that the infatuation for the Bouffons has not turned away the public from French opera. "The Bouffonists who had announced its desertion have been mistaken in their prophecies."[2] Foreigners do not like our opera; yet the form of Italian opera is more monotonous than ours which is "incomparably more varied and more pleasing".[3] The delight afforded by opera is in the "spectacle for the senses" and cannot lie anywhere else; now, French opera touches more senses than Italian since it combines stage machinery, choruses, song and dance, where Italian has only spectacle and song.[4] It would be wrong, therefore, to substitute Italian opera for French.[5]

The superiority of Italian opera lies in its music.[6] But everything is not good in the music that comes from beyond the Alps. If the French change too little, the Italians run too much after novelty. We have much to learn from them, nevertheless. (In all his criticisms of French music one feels that he is thinking mainly of Lulli. Rameau he expressly excepts and there are many pages of unstinted praise for him; the only other French works and musicians he names are Mouret and "un opéra gascon", no doubt Mondonville's *Daphnis et Alcimadure*.) What we must do is to keep our opera but change our music. Which is precisely what Gluck will do in his Parisian operas.

D'Alembert praises Italian *recitativo accompagnato* (which he calls *obligé*). Now all Gluck's recitatives after *Alceste* are accompanied. Recitative, whether French or Italian, must be rid of trills, held notes, *portamenti* and ornaments; this, too, is true of Gluck. French opera must be made to sing. Why is it afraid to do so? Is it not because "for most French people, the music they call *chantante* is nothing but common music, hackneyed by constant repetition; for them a bad air is one which they cannot hum and a bad opera is one of which they can remember nothing".[7] This stifles novelty and originality in composers.

---

[1] (153), 151.   [2] (29), 399.   [3] (29), 404.
[4] (29), 405.   [5] (29), 411.   [6] (29), 413–414.
[7] (29), 444–445.

Italian music needs to be pruned; it will be improved by deletions; French, by having added to it the life it lacks. "Italian music is defective by what it has in excess. French music by what is not there."[1]

This is what Gluck perceived when, thinking of Italian opera, he called for "a beautiful simplicity". He removed from Italian opera what he deemed to be abusive accretions; he was later to bring to French what d'Alembert and his fellow-critics were demanding.

D'Alembert goes on to remark that perhaps the Italians have not taken full advantage of harmony (echoes of Rameau!).[2] But Gluck, with his simple harmonies as well as his normally lighter and thinner accompaniments, is closer here to Rousseau.

French *symphonies* do not need reforming. "Here the Italians are less rich than we"; and he goes on to lapidate "la quantité prodigieuse de sonates" in the passage already quoted.[3] Italian overtures he also criticizes as being no better than Lulli's. And here comes the expression of what the ideal overture should be. It does not quite tally with Gluck's. The latter will want it to "warn the spectators of the action and be its argument". D'Alembert expressly counters this idea, which was not Gluck's or Calzabigi's own but was current well before 1768. It should not be "the preface and as it were the analysis of the opera, as some modern writers" would have it—possibly Algarotti in his *Saggio sopra l'Opera* (1755). (No more, he adds, than the cadenza of an Italian *aria* should be a recapitulation of the *aria*, as others want it to be.) No; the overture should be simply "the announcement of the first scene, the *ritornello* suitable to the picture about to be presented".[4]

D'Alembert was speaking for a large body of moderate opinion which gathered weight in the years that followed. It had its counterpart in Italy in that represented by Durazzo and Algarotti. This was the opinion which influenced Gluck. It was ready to welcome an art in which the bulk of French traditions should be preserved but where the *chant* should be Italian. It is not a question of "new" or "old" but of Italian and French; Gluck is Italian wine in French bottles. Reversing a remark of Prunières'[5] we may say that Gluck's opera, which owes so much to France, is purely Italian in its music. The spirit of its song is as Italian as the structure of its drama is French. The style of Westminster Abbey has been defined as Early English content in

---

[1] (29), 445. [2] (29), 450.
[3] (29), 455-457.—Quoted on p. 533.
[4] (29), 459.—As in some of Rameau's one-act ballets; e.g. *La Guirlande*. He instances with approval Rameau's programme overtures.
[5] "Lulli's opera which owes everything to Italy is purely French melodically" ((214), 368).

French form; Gluck's three last operas and to a lesser extent the three so-called "reform" ones before them may likewise be characterized as French in form but Italian in content.

One of the difficulties of comparing Rameau and Gluck as musicians lies in the fact that Rameau comes alive on the keyboard much better than Gluck, who needs some flogging to resuscitate on the piano but lives with less trouble on the stage and even in concert performance. The complexity of the paraphernalia which Jean-Philippe requires is one obstacle; another is that his music calls for greater imagination and sensibility from the performers, and a higher degree of technical perfection. Gluck is by far the better known of the two. Many judgments on Rameau are made on very slight acquaintance, often after an ill-rendered performance. Few people, to quote Georges Migot, have lived

> with him, reading his music and his writings as if *they* were near him, exchanging general ideas on music and seeking reciprocally the reasons for *their* intuitive judgments and attempting, by dint of deliberate reiterations, to correct certain false opinions of which it is hard to free oneself.[1]

Rameau and Gluck are alike, and opposed to the Italians, in that they put music at the service of the text, even though Rameau has left no pronouncement as categorical as Gluck's. But Gluck had the advantage of better librettists. He also had a sense of dramatic wholes in which Rameau was deficient. There is in *Alceste* a continuity and a feeling for structure absent from even *Castor et Pollux*, structurally the best of Rameau's operas. There is between them something of the difference between Bach's *Passions* on the one hand and his Mass on the other. A Rameau opera, like the B minor mass, tends to be a collection of pieces of beautiful and often great music, more or less loosely linked together; *Alceste*, like the *Passions*, is a whole, conceived and carried out on a grand scale. Within the scenes, too, there is a continuity greater than is normally found in Rameau, except in descriptive and spectacular sections like *Zoroastre*, V, 4, or the broadly conceived storm in *Les Boréades*, III, 4, to IV, 1. This reflects the development of symphonic music since the middle of the century.

Rameau was "in first" with several things in which priority is attributed to Gluck. The later composer knew his Rameau well and it is not surprising that he should have learnt from his predecessor. His use of the chorus as a *dramatis persona* is anticipated by Rameau. The chorus in *Hippolyte*, IV, 4, is very much a protagonist in the

---

[1] (195), preface, 14.

tragedy of Hippolytus' death[1] and there is similar treatment of the chorus in *Zoroastre*,[2] in *Daphnis et Églé* (Sc. 3) and *Acante et Céphise* (III, 2). Leclair had treated it much like Rameau in *Hippolyte* at the end of *Scylla et Glaucus*. Gluck's innovation consisted in the scale on which he used it, especially in *Alceste*, not in the conception itself.

What I am now going to say is more debatable, because it is based on personal impressions.

When one passes from Lulli to Rameau one is conscious of a great enrichment, both in what is expressed and in the means of expression. On passing from Rameau back to Lulli, one is conscious of a corresponding impoverishment. Now, when one passes onward from Rameau to Gluck a not dissimilar impression is felt, and the word "impoverishment" renders it better than any other. The impoverishment is less serious because Gluck is a genius and Lulli is not and because a great deal of what made up Rameau's richness is retained; but the impression is inescapable. This is part of the general *dépouillement* and unloading of goods which accompanied the formation of the classical style at the exit of the baroque age, before the flowering of the end of the century had compensated for the losses.

But "impoverishment" is not the whole of the impression. From Rameau to Gluck and more particularly to *Alceste*, one passes from greater to less freedom, from flexibility of line, from unconstraint of harmony and general liberty of expression to a measure of rigidity. One enters an art more starched, more *gourmé*. In *Alceste* the French scheme is there as in Rameau, with much greater dramatic coherence, but all is harder, with sharper outlines, stiffer and squarer rhythms. Gluck has indeed learnt from French opera to alternate more flexibly between recitative, chorus and air (though actually Alceste's "Vis pour garder le souvenir" in Act III is the only *petit air* in the work), but the passage from one to the other is more sharply marked off; he is more sectional; there is seldom the insensible melting from one into the other which is so typical of Rameau at his best. It is the hard divisions, as well as the remorselessly regular rhythms, always definitely in four-time or definitely in three-time, never hovering between one and the other, and the angular outlines of much of the melody, which make some of *Alceste* seem—dare one pronounce the word?—almost wooden—"marmorean" is a more flattering conveyance of the same feeling!—compared with Rameau.

The Italian recitative, with its monotonous trick of orchestral outbursts between vocal phrases, its tremolos and heavy closes, also contributes to this impression.[3] Gluck's recitative in *Orfeo*, *Alceste*

---

[1] The scene is similar in structure to *Iphigénie en Aulide*, III: "Puissante Déité".

[2] II, 4; III, 2–4; also III, 8, in the 1756 version.

[3] See the quotation from Decroix on p. 113.

and *Paris and Helen* is more expressive than Lulli's and more musical than *recitativo secco*; it is neither "psalmodie" nor patter; it is none the less monotonous and we sigh for the litheness, subtlety, *souplesse*, for the sensitive line that follows, so to speak, the contour of the sentiment, that we know in Rameau. It gains greatly in the French operas and here, at times, it reaches to great beauty, as in *Iphigénie en Aulide*, II (from "Je n'ai plus qu'un mot à vous dire" to the end)[1] and in most of *Iphigénie en Tauride*. On the other hand, it is seen at its worst in the revelation scene of *Iphigénie en Aulide*, II ("Princesse, pardonnez"), a very poor substitute for the most moving scene in Racine and Euripides.

Turning back from Gluck to Rameau—for the comparison of impressions must be made both ways—one feels how free is the older man from the reiterations of Italian art, except in his less dramatic choruses. Gluck never threw off completely the repetition of words for formal purposes in his larger set numbers. The hand of Italian conventions lay heavy on him to the last.

Dramatically, his world at its purest is tenser and more closely knit than Rameau's; musically and emotionally, Rameau's in his greatest works is the richer and the mellower.

Rameau's music is so much more sensitive. His line quivers, coils, rises, falls, curves and unwinds like a living thing; beside it, Gluck's more sectional progress seems almost lifeless. The sensation of quickened life is intense when one returns from the later to the earlier composer. The difference lies deep. Gluck's conception is one in which emotions are expressed, as it were, in blocks within which the sentiment is a whole, and is lighted equally, without shading. This is, of course, less true of his French operas, but it is a fair generalization. Rameau, thanks to a subtler recitative and a much more delicate and varied scoring, and in spite of poorer instrumental resources, follows the changes of sentiment more closely and, through the merging of recitative and air, renders more faithfully the least gradations of feeling, its half-tints as well as its massive changes.

Though he uses a smaller orchestra he makes more of it than Gluck and obtains a plenitude by which the later man set little store, sharing as he must have done Rousseau's dislike of rich accompaniments. "It stinks with music," he is supposed to have said of his predecessor's work.[2] It is the old complaint of "trop de notes", which the Lullist made to Rameau; of "What a lot of notes!" which Joseph II was to

---

[1] Einstein says approvingly that "a flowing and merging between recitative and *arioso*, between loose and strict forms, is characteristic of this opera", without realizing how thoroughly French, and even Ramellian, is this feature! ((144), 141).

[2] According to Beaumarchais, in the foreword to *Tarare* (second edition).

make to Mozart. Rameau, too, could have answered: "Sire, not one too many."

Dancing was less important in Gluck's scheme, even in his French operas, than in Rameau's, though I am not convinced that he introduced ballets into these latter against his will. His operatic dances,[1] with a very few exceptions, enchant us less, and also suggest less vividly the motions of the body, than do Rameau's. They cannot compare with "the picturesque expressiveness and the prodigious variety of the *airs de ballet*" which Gardel admired in Rameau and which, he said, make him the creator of dancing in France.[2] Gluck's dances are seldom expressive of any sentiment and hardly suggestive of attitude, gesture or motion. Dancing itself by 1765 had no doubt become less abstract and more dramatic, but this is not reflected in his ballet numbers, except in the second act of *Orfeo*. Here again it is loss of life that strikes one in the comparison. The immense superiority of all that pertains to choreography in Rameau still needs emphasizing.

> Rameau was the greatest ballet composer of all times. The genius of his creation rests on one hand on his perfect artistic permeation by folk-dance types, on the other hand on the constant preservation of living contact with the practical requirements of the ballet stage, which prevented an estrangement between the expression of the body from the spirit of absolute music.[3]

Action dancing, programme dancing, often coupled with the word *pantomime* after *Pygmalion* (1749), play a great part in his work. Attempts to make dancing more dramatic go back to the 'thirties when Mlle Sallé tried, in Paris and still more in London, "a reform of ballet and costume which announced that of Noverre".[4] Later, she danced in *Les Indes galantes* and in several other Rameau ballets. Rameau was still alive when Noverre published his *Lettres sur la danse* (1760), in which he paid tribute to the aged musician. "It is to M. Rameau's varied and harmonious writing, to the *traits* and witty conversations that prevailed in his tunes, that dancing owes all its progress."[5] And Gardel, some fifteen years later, at the time when Gluck's operas were being staged in Paris, wrote: "He divined what the dancers themselves did not know. We look upon him rightly as our first master."[6]

It is perhaps unfair to Gluck to pit him against Rameau in this field but, in view of the still widely held opinion that Gluck is superior

---

[1] I am not thinking here of his dramatic ballets *Don Juan* and *Semiramis*.
[2] Quoted in (60), 101. [3] (238), Vorwort, vi–vii.
[4] (190), 379. [5] (90), 123.
[6] (70), 29; in (190), 383.—It is clear that people at this date looked on Rameau as a revolutionary in choreographic writing.

to him in everything relating to drama, I wish to repeat, after others, that

> Rameau's dance music distinguishes itself among all others by its exact and varied adaptation *to the circumstances of the drama*, to the character of the *personae* and the particular miming that arises therefrom.[1]

Though *Orfeo* is Gluck's most played opera and *Alceste* is held up as his masterpiece, it is in his Parisian works, when he had assimilated the genius of French opera, that he came into his own. *Alceste* is unconvincing because he fails to express the characters and their emotions from within. He describes their exterior; we see dignified, impersonal features and attitudes and we behold the description, rather than the utterance, of an emotion. This was so in *Orfeo* as well, but it mattered less there because this opera was conceived as a magnified chamber cantata and we are content in it, as in a Scarlatti cantata, with the utterance in harmonious music of pure emotion, divorced from personal psychology. But *Alceste* is a drama, and such depersonalization is a defect. Its almost constant tension and dignity are external, as if Gluck was trying to act tension rather than achieve it, to act dignified rather than be dignified. Dignity passes too readily into mere weight, as in the overture with the "sawdust" of its "empty fanfares"[2] and its tedious repetitions. It opens with evocative splendour but remains stationary and its power of emotion is dissipated long before the end. Like much of the opera, it is redolent of the "Ut pictura poesis" (or "musica") of descriptivist aesthetics and fails to grip us with the illusion of reality once the spell of the first bars has faded. "Racine does more" than tell us something about the human heart, says Bremond; "*il nous le rend présent*, with a contact so to speak mystical, more intimate and deeper than knowledge".[3] This is what we miss in *Alceste* and *Paris and Helen*.

Standing between *Dardanus* and *Idomeneo*, the last great *tragédie lyrique* and the last great *opera seria*, *Alceste* is unreal and its grief shadowy. Its famous Hellenism is the Hellenism of Winckelmann and David, of the Panthéon and the Madeleine. We cannot be moved, other than musically, by the queen's tears and the chorus's laments, nor rejoice in her deliverance, whereas Ilia's sorrow stirs us to the depths and Electra's fury excites us; and how profoundly poignant is the farewell quartet and Idamante's plaint "Andrò, ramingo e solo"! There indeed do we savour the authentic taste of tragedy, the taste we had found in "Hippolyte n'est plus", in "Lieux funestes" and in the "Frappez! frappez" duet of *Dardanus*. *Alceste* offers us the trappings

---

[1] (190), 384.

[2] Martin Cooper's expressions in (130), 128.

[3] (118 B), 48, 49.

of tragedy, tragic attitudes, but not the real pang. Its music is beautiful with the fairness of pure, not dramatic, music. And its beauty is not unmixed with monotony.[1]

In 1767 Gluck had not yet learnt to enter imaginatively into his characters and their situations; he knew the appropriate means for depicting their *affects* but not for imparting souls to them. *Alceste* is therefore a concert of tragic music, not a tragedy; it is in the same category as the concert *arias* written by one composer for another composer's work, like those by Mozart—admirable music, great evocations of *affects* but not the utterances of individuals,—like the collections of airs from Scarlatti's or Handel's operas which have lost by excision from their context all dramatic significance and come to us as disembodied feeling.

Rameau's characters remain of course simple; they are mono- or, at most, bi-emotional; but the composer has got inside several of them. Iphise's heartrending utterances of misery are her own. There is unmistakable terror in the magicians' threats in *Dardanus*, II ("Songe que sous les fleurs"); we are smitten by the "Frappez!" duet in spite of the conventional tussle of generosity which its words reflect. We are smitten by the end of *Hippolyte*, IV; by Télaïre singing of the "tristes apprêts" around her. This gift for at least momentary identification between composer and character is present even in secondary works like *Les Fêtes de l'Hymen*, where so slight a figure as Memphis comes to life an instant as she sings her desolate F minor air, "Veille, Amour" (II, 3). How Rameau succeeded in thus depicting his characters' emotional life *from within* is his secret, but his richer harmonization and more flexible melodic line made his task easier.

Closer contact with French opera heightened Gluck's dramatic power and awakened in him a gift for the creation of characters. "Gluck's characters", says Abert, "are bearers of definite, clear and intelligible basic ideas."[2] In the *Iphigénies*, fortunately, they have outgrown this awkward age and take their stand beside Thésée, Phèdre, Télaïre, Pollux and Iphise. Here, at last, he has got "under the skin" of his men and women and creates airs expressive of persons and not just of a generalized emotion, as in "Jupiter, lance ta foudre", "Tu décides son sort" and especially "Le calme rentre dans mon cœur", one of the uncanniest utterances in all music.[3] Even "Diane

---

[1] A monotony broken once by the bombast of "Divinités du Styx", a number, in its French version, premonitory of Beethoven at his worst.

[2] (114), I, 682.

[3] "We owe Gluck an invention of genius in music of which we have not made enough use; in pathetic pieces to have the accompaniment express what the heart feels, whilst the words seek to hide it" ((154), II, 217, note). Mme de Genlis is speaking of this solo.

impitoyable",[1] which might so easily have been just another impressive royal supplication like so many before it, combines the intimate misery of the father with the impersonal splendour of the King of kings.   Is it mere chance that the finest of these operas is also the most French, with its overture linked to the first scene, its glorification of French descriptive Nature music, the descendant of so many tempests, floods and earthquakes, and its occasional orchestral illustrations of imaginary phenomena?[2]   The fury chorus in Act II is thoroughly French; it is in the tradition of gruesome, syllabic choruses that goes back to Lulli and is found in *Dardanus* and *Zoroastre*.   The happy ending, at which Einstein mocks triumphantly for its Frenchness,[3] is less French than Italian, however; it was Italian audiences, not French, that would not tolerate tragic endings, as Metastasio found when he tried to conclude *Catone in Utica* (1728) in the historical manner.   Several of Lulli's operas end tragically and Leclair's *Scylla et Glaucus* (1746) concludes with the petrification of the heroine and the desolation of the hero.[4]

In one respect Gluck never became French and, moreover, acted inconsistently with regard to his own profession of faith.   This was in the matter of "interchangeable" airs.   The older he grew, the more numbers he borrowed from earlier compositions; *Armide* is almost a *pasticcio* of them.   This was a common practice with German and Italian composers, but almost unknown to Rameau, except for dances, which circulated from one opera to another.[5]   The music for a chorus of admiring acclamation in *Iphigénie en Aulide*, "Que d'attraits, que de majeste", reappears in *Iphigénie en Tauride* in a chorus of mourning, "Contemplez ces tristes apprêts".   The practice is inconceivable in Rameau, so closely wedded in his music to the words it sets.   If music is the handmaid of poetry, as Gluck declares, something is wrong here. In this matter of artistic integrity the palm does not go to Gluck.

Admiration for a great artist is seldom universal.   Gluck had detractors, some of them not necessarily dishonest or narrow-minded, and not all were French.   Such a one was Forkel.

---

[1] Borrowed, as everyone knows, from *Telemacco*, I.

[2] E.g., the illustration by rushes in the strings of Oreste's "Tonnez, écrasez-moi" in Act II.

[3] (144), 169.   [4] See p. 122.

[5] The only exceptions I know are "L'objet qui règne dans mon âme", *ariette* in *Les Fêtes d'Hébé*, III, 7, from *Le Berger fidèle*, and "Non, une flamme volage" in *Zoroastre*, I, 3 (1756 version), which comes, in part only, from *La Naissance d'Osiris*, Sc. I.   Actually there are four versions of this little piece: in the autograph score of *La Naissance d'Osiris* (Opera library, Paris); in the (not autograph) score of the same in the Bibliothèque Nationale; in the (not autograph) score of *Zoroastre* (1756), in do.; and, autograph, on a loose leaf in the library of the Accademia Filarmonica of Bologna.   I owe the knowledge of this last to the kindness of Dr. Jacobi.   All four show differences.

Thanks to Herr von Gluck, old abuses have been abolished only to be replaced by new ones quite as harmful.. . . Let Herr Gluck and his admirers delight according to their taste in his noble simplicity; we will not envy them their pleasures but we will assuredly pray them not to compel us to take any further part in them; may they leave us to prepare in peace, according to our own liking, the feast of our ears and our hearts.

The overture of *Iphigénie en Aulide* "has not the least character of an overture", neither is it "what is truly called a symphony".   He condemns its many repetitions as well as "the progress of the modulation" in the unison opening which he finds "plump und ungeschickt" and "inwardly poor and outwardly clumsy".   The choruses

are far inferior to French choruses; the magnificent choruses of the French, as well as the qualities of their very characteristic dances, have proved themselves and are acknowledged everywhere.

Much of the music is "gemein und niedrig"; the recitatives are "excessively dry and harsh".   In *Alceste*, too, he finds "many tunes dry and stiff".   The terms "niedrig" and "platt" recur constantly in his pages.[1]

Too much is made of Gluck's virtues as a playwright and too little of the value of his music.   "As musicians," says Einstein, Jommelli, Traetta, Francesco di Maio, Davidde Perez and Wagenseil "perhaps all of them surpass Gluck".[2]   The suggestion is that while they were "mere musicians", Gluck was above all a great and good man.   His belittlement on one score, presented as unimportant, is thus a prelude to his belauding on a much more significant one.   Yet it is not because of the moral excellence of his art nor because of his strength of character that we listen to his music to-day with delight.   After his marriage he was always well-off and did not, like Wagner, have to struggle to impose his ideas, and he made no difficulty whatever about departing from his principles when circumstances made fidelity to them unsuitable, as in *Il Trionfo di Clelia* after *Orfeo,* and *Le Feste d'Apollo* after *Alceste.*   His much-emphasized strength of character has nothing to do with what moves us in his music.   Indeed, if one thing is more remarkable than any other in his art, it is that we do not apprehend a personality behind it.   Behind his life-story of course we do, but not behind his music.   That music has certain formal qualities which persist throughout, but the sense of personality is absent.   Perhaps this helps to make him so distinguished a dramatist; yet this absence is not a prerequisite to dramatic excellence.   To remain within the classical world, Mozart is no less of a dramatic artist and covers a wider domain of expression in his operas; yet his personality is unmistakable in them.   Rameau, too, has a range of expressiveness which embraced a much vaster field and he gave himself to the render-

[1] *Musikalisch-Kritische Bibliothek,* 1778; I, 102, 128–129, 131, 164, 172–173, 198, 199.   [2] (144), 45.

ing of every *affect* with the same descriptive exactness and the same
fidelity to his text; yet, if we take a broad enough view of his work and
give it time, through affectionate familiarity, to work upon us, we
apprehend a definite personality running through it, and not merely
a collection of recurring formal traits.   It is this sense of someone
behind the music, a sense distinct from its artistic unity, that we miss
in Gluck.

Though he is a dramatist, it is his merit as a pure musician that has
preserved him for us.   His dramatic qualities are precious but the
excellence of his music is more so.   In fact, the best beloved of his six
great operas is the least dramatic, the nearest to pure music.   The
enchantment of the fabled second act of *Orfeo* is nothing if not musical,
whether we ask it of the terrifying "Chi mai dell'Erebo" or of the
infinitely soothing "E quest'asilo" and "Che puro ciel".   To those
who will seek them out in the score, the beauties of *Paris and Helen*,
"Le belle imagini" and "Fingere più non so", are as divorced from
dramatic significance as an *aria* by Handel or John Christian Bach.
When we call up the *Iphigénies* in our mind we turn to "Diane impitoyable", to "Par un père cruel", to "O toi qui prolongeas mes jours",
even to "Le calme rentre dans mon cœur", and savour them for their
music, without troubling about the skill with which they are integrated in the drama as a whole.   This is not to deny the highly charged
dramatic quality of the last of these airs but to restore the emphasis
where it, in practice, surely lies—on the musical loveliness, or power
to grip, of each of these highlights.   What we really love in Gluck,
if we honestly seek whence our enjoyment of him comes, is not the
reforming dramatist but the accomplished Italianate musician.

Yet it is largely his historical position that has justified his introduction at the end of a study of his most illustrious predecessor.
"Gluck", said Abert, "is unthinkable without Rameau."[1]   So unthinkable, indeed, that every study of Gluck's "reform-reaction" should
open, not with the "abuses" of *opera seria* nor with Jommelli, Traetta
and di Maio, who should appear later, but with the presentation of the
opera form of Rameau.   It should continue by showing more distinctly than is generally done what the "reform" meant for Italy and
what Gluck's appearance on the Paris stage meant for France.   In
Italy, it was indeed a reform; it was a bringing to a head of those
Gallicizing tendencies which existed, diffused, and which aimed at
bringing Italian opera into line with French; that is why the preface
to *Alceste* is really a manifesto of Ramellian opera under the disguise
of a criticism of "abuses".

For France, of course, it was no such thing.   Here it was Gluck
himself who was important.   As all studies of him point out, there

_____
[1] (114), I, 636.

was no dearth of musical geniuses in Italy; his action there is that of a doctrine, though made efficient through his genius. But in France, where no doctrinal reform was needed, it was a personal role he filled. Since the death of Rameau there had been no musicians of the first order working for the Paris stage. If *tragédie lyrique* was dying in the 'sixties and 'seventies, it was for lack of a great *tragique*, not because the form was exhausted. The best composers who wrote for *opéra-comique*, Frenchmen like Philidor and Monsigny, foreigners like Duni and Grétry, had not the stature for Rameau's succession. Till "le chevalier Klouch" came from Austria with his own genius and the musical riches of *opera seria*, ready to pick up the mantle which had fallen from the shoulders of Jean-Philippe ten years earlier, *tragédie lyrique* languished in the hands of men too weak to handle it. In Vienna Gluck's function had been that of a reformer; in Paris, it was that of a musician.

16. Conclusion

RAMEAU's art is graceful like all eighteenth-century art, but his originality does not lie in his grace. Chabanon praised his gaiety, yet the word is ill-chosen, for though lively he is never gay, except when portraying Folly's antics in *Platée* or in the sailors' chorus in *Les Fêtes d'Hébé*. He has conjured up a number of enchanted worlds: the pastoral world of Églé; that of Hebe's Pleasures disdained by Pollux; the dream world in the fourth act of *Dardanus*; the bittersweet worlds so quickly opened and closed in Acts I and II of *Zoroastre*; the world of Pluto in *Hippolyte*. His major works have each their own and in most of them a strain of longing and disillusion can be felt.

Behind the atmosphere of old-world quaintness, of shadowy futility, of *petits poètes* and *fêtes galantes*, which envelops at first sight the music and painting of eighteenth-century France and which is for many the immediate source of Jean-Philippe's charm, there stands a sharply marked and austere, almost grim, personality, in nowise sentimental, gallant or frivolous. In fact, no greater contrast can be imagined than that between the "melancholy desire of ancient things" that "floats like a faded perfume out of the wires", the "melancholy of ancient death" which "the harpsichord dreams of, sighing in the room", the "pallid lovers" with their "unforgotten desires"—"Only Rameau's music remembers the rest"[1]—and the Rameau into which we enter as we come to know him better—the second so much more stirring than the first. It is necessary to strip him of these unreal visions and see him in all his strength. Such evocations may be in keeping with the lesser pieces of François Couperin, with those of Dandrieu, Daquin, Dagincourt or Duphly; in Rameau's presence they are unseemly.

Let us not labour to seek in his music reflections of his age; these, too, are so much more patent in the works of his lesser contemporaries. His age, indeed, served him ill. It did not supply him with a form ready-made as if for his use, as Racine's and Mozart's gave them classical tragedy and the sonata; it offered him no frame which would enable him to unfold all the breadth and power which so often and so

---

[1] Arthur Symons: *On an air of Rameau*, in *Images of Good and Evil*.

unseasonably break out in him. A cadre like the oratorio might have allowed him to exert his power of sustained dramatic composition; fifty years later he might have been a great symphonist. At another time imitationist aesthetics would not have compelled him to illustrate his text so meticulously and he could have developed that gift for pure music so evident in his dances and *symphonies*.

Born half-way through Louis XIV's reign, he remained a child of the Grand Siècle in that, in a century when the arts were becoming playthings, he cherished a serious conception of his calling. There is a misfit between the severity of his nature and outlook and the frivolous genre to which he gave himself. He was not an entertainer like Campra or an actor and mime like Lulli. He was denied the opportunities that came to Gluck of raising opera to the level of his own nature and artistic philosophy.

In the work of Lulli and Quinault *tragédie lyrique* is the reflection of a society and a way of life. With the intrusion of Rameau's strong personality the balance between society and musician is broken. The unbalance is music's gain, but the form as a whole has suffered. Rameau's relation with the opera is not unlike that of Beethoven and Wagner with the art forms of their times. The difference is that out of the ruins of the old they were able to create new forms. Rameau could not.

For his constructive power the framework of "late baroque" opera and sacred music was too strait, but his force is displayed as from time to time it bursts through: in the first air and the choruses of *In convertendo*, in the great chorus of *Deus noster refugium*, in the Fates' trio and the chorus of welcome in *Hippolyte*, in the volcano scene of *Les Incas*, the second storm of *Platée* and the harrowing by the Winds in *Les Boréades*. Can we conceive his genius at work in other surroundings? A century later, though it is tempting to picture him as a writer of symphonic poems, I think that opera would still have been his favourite form; La Laurencie surely exaggerates when he says that "Rameau is in truth more of a symphonist than of a dramatic composer".[1]

His impressionistic palette seems more suitable for dramatic than for symphonic writing. All his music, as Max Kenyon says of Mozart's, has a "tangible quality ... It seems immediate, tactile"; it has an "immediacy of expression, ... a magic which Bach, with other great composers, does not possess at all".[2] This is why his most direct appeal is through his dances. They are not the whole of his art by a long way but they are what touches us first, in their orchestral colouring nearly as much as in their tune, rhythm and harmony, and it

---

[1] *S.I.M.*, June 15, 1908: review of L. Laloy's *Rameau*.
[2] *Mozart in Salzburg*, 165.

is surprising that no ballet-maker has ever drawn on the almost in-exhaustible store hoarded away in the fourteen volumes[1] of the *Œuvres* so-called *complètes*. Though it is unfair to deny him the gift of melody, he is more of a dance than of a song melodist. Many of his most tuneful vocal pieces turn out to be sung dances and his *symphonies* haunt us more than his songs.

Yet, though there are fewer highlights in his vocal than in his orchestral music, it is only to that extent that we may say he is vocally inferior. His belated champion Decroix spoke of the "joie naïve et franche" which reigns in his songs. They "are so gay and so natural that one hums them easily as one comes away from his operas and that they become so to speak proverbial".[2] They can be both "declama-tory and shapely", as Eric Blom says of Purcell's and Hugo Wolf's, and Rameau could have declared like Wagner: "My declamation is also singing and my singing is also declamation."[3]

His music is not only intensely moving; it is also profoundly human, and its greatness, in the last resort, lies therein. Lulli and his other predecessors had been decorators or entertainers; he is the first French composer to enter with all the force and sympathy of his imagination into the hearts of his characters and the situations he depicts. His power of dramatic imagination is comparable to Racine's. It is enough to place side by side with his the most tragic scenes of Lulli, Campra or Destouches to see the gigantic advance made at one stride. This is one of the chief reasons why, in retrospect, the date of *Hippolyte et Aricie* is one of the most important in the history of dramatic music.

Do we sometimes regret that he never appears to be speaking in his own name, that what he himself felt or thought is never ascertain-able in his music, that he is always describing, or rendering, the feelings of this or that fictitious character, that it is Phèdre's or Pollux's or Iphise's sorrow that is sung, never Rameau's? To a lover of Roman-tic music such impersonality may be distressing. Even in his chamber music he remains the dramatist, invisible behind his work, however emotional it be. We cannot grasp him, even in his most expressive pieces, as we do Beethoven or Brahms or even Bach. We need reminding that he and his contemporaries

> though they believed in *expression* . . . did not . . . believe primarily in *self-expression*. They expressed what they felt about something that was bigger than themselves, whether they called it God or the suffering of Christ or Reason or Nature

or Telaira's bereavement or the Revels of Hebe and Polymnia or the birth of Louis XVI—Osiris.

---

[1] Volumes V to XVIII.   [2] (60), 176–177.
[3] *Gesammelte Schriften*, V, 128.

MS. page of *In Convertendo*

> Belief in self-expression is not necessarily inferior to belief in an Absolute, but neither is it necessarily superior.[1]

Yet we have seen more than once that his person may be sensed in his music if we know when to seek for it. Even though he appeared to experience only by imitation the sentiments he rendered, at many a stage the intensity of the expression exceeds what the words demand and Rameau is caught singing in his own name. In the *symphonies*, particularly in the set dances, there are moments of "un-reserved" music in which no model is being imitated. In his minuets and gavottes we come nearer than almost anywhere else to beholding the unveiled face of Jean-Philippe.

More than once we have dwelt on the irresistible impression of personality that arises from prolonged frequenting of his music and writing. Now and again, this personality bursts upon us with surprising force. I shall never forget the first time that I saw and handled one of his autographs. I am not usually sensitive to hand-writing, yet an immediate impact of a personality sprang at me from the sheet—one highly-strung, spiny, acerb, with claws out, meticulous and loving of detail. The pages, which contained scarcely one straight line, were all covered with tiny curves like fish-hooks which tore at one's eyes, whilst the notes were interspersed with the same spiny, hooked little writing—either the text, or sharp, fussy remarks about the execution. Many passages were crossed out; some were barred with great red X's; others stuck over with blank sheets. The pungent, strained, thorny, methodical character corresponded to the portrait which both books and contemporary reports leave us, but nothing in them equals the speaking immediacy of these pages.

Rameau, like Bach a master of the "late baroque", came at the end of a period; at his death the gates of fashion closed remorselessly upon him and, like Bach, if he survived at all, it was only in trifles. Luckier than he, Bach has risen again and seen as complete a revival as a dead musician can ever know. The future, it seems, was not for Rameau or the form of opera he upheld. If we accept the clamour of the Encyclopaedists, not much in it was worth saving. But little importance should be attached to late eighteenth-century criticisms of him and of *tragédie lyrique*, whether emanating from Jean-Jacques or from Dr. Burney. In 1764 Lullian opera had been in sole possession of the tragic operatic stage in Paris for ninety years. A public very remote from Louis XIV's wanted an art more superficially and more sensuously attractive. To use the current jargon, "Rokokomenschen" were tired of "barock" art. Their criticism of it has a documentary interest of the sort which attaches to post-1918 criticisms of Wagner and

---

[1] Wilfrid Mellers: *Music and Letters*, April 1949; review of D. N. Ferguson, *History of Musical Thought*.

Beethoven by a generation weary of hearing their music and of listening to their praises. We should not go to such criticisms for a judgment of these composers; neither should we hearken to Rousseau, Diderot or Burney for an appraisement of Rameau.

But is it true that the future was not with what Rameau and *tragédie lyrique* represented? An approximation to "continuous melody", an important orchestral part, spacious choruses, dramatic interest, spectacle: all these are present in opera of the nineteenth and twentieth centuries, to the highest degree in Wagner. Of the two forms of serious opera in Rameau's age, it was the French, not the Italian, which had the future with it, even though it was to be rejuvenated by *opera buffa* and *opéra-comique*. We have noted more than once in the course of this work the ways in which Rameau anticipates Wagner. "Rameau seizes every possible occasion to comment upon the events of the drama through the medium of the orchestra, by descriptive *symphonies* or extensive preludes," by the dramatic and symphonic character of his dance themes. His choruses"'contribute to enveloping the drama in a sort of symphonic atmosphere". It was perhaps his trust in this expressive power of instrumental music that led him to neglect the literary quality of his librettos. It is true that he does not quite attain to Wagner's *Sprachmelodie*; his development remains to some extent sectional. But in him as in Wagner "the illustration of the drama by instrumental themes, independently of the declamation of the tragic text", makes his accompaniments often more important for the drama than for the voice part that they underlie. With Gluck, the accompaniment remains less dramatic and more subordinate to the singing; Rameau in this reaches out to Wagner without the intervention of Gluck.[1]

Sixty years ago Houston Stewart Chamberlain, in an article on "Wagner et le génie français",[2] noted "the real kinship that exists between Wagner's dramatic work and French classical opera . . . , that opera which proceeds from Lulli to Spontini and which it would be impossible to confuse with Italian opera." The only addition to make to this just statement is to insert the name of him who was the strongest link of all in the chain: Jean-Philippe Rameau.

It is therefore all the more regrettable that he should have begun to come into his own on a wave of anti-Wagnerian, and more generally of anti-Italo-German, feeling, expressed amusingly in *Monsieur Croche* and the *Lettre au Chevalier Gluck*, and more ponderously in Georges Migot's book, published in 1930. It is important to dissociate him from this reaction and to insist that he is not just a pretext for national sentiment nor an astringent after a surfeit of German

---

[1] (192).

[2] *Revue des Deux Mondes*, 1896; in (192).

Romanticism and Italian grand opera; that the satisfaction he brings is not to be determined by the last thing to which we have been listening.

*　　*　　*　　*　　*

If we ask of music that it should survive, we mean that it should be of use to us. It is not only sheer merit which keeps a work "immortal" but also its powers of adaptability to a constantly changing musical scene.[1]

Who would have thought, a century ago, when the remark quoted on p. 513 (note 6) was casually penned, that the world would still find a "use" for Bach, that his concerti grossi, his fugues, his protracted ensembles would appeal to thousands? Yet who has conquered the present more completely? An artist's posthumous fame is not, it seems, so irremediably linked to the life of the art forms which he adopts.

Until the process of "adaptation" is applied to it, the adaptability of an artist's work, to which Kenyon rightly refers, cannot be gauged. Does Rameau possess this quality? His small output of chamber music is not unknown and is establishing itself; it is of his dramatic and sacred music that I am thinking in what follows.

Though Rameau revivals are possible, they can never be common, except on the air. His operatic music must come before us in a modified form. Out of *Hippolyte*, *Castor*, *Dardanus* and perhaps *Platée*, concert versions can certainly be made and they would be as acceptable in this guise as *Saul*, *Samson* and *Judas Maccabeus*. There is no difficulty in presenting the motets, entire, or with the excision of certain numbers. Endlessly varied chains of dances and *symphonies* can be woven out of his instrumental interludes, and the only recommendation I would make is to repeat that the selector should not limit himself, in each suite, to any one work but should draw freely whence he list. The difficulties are rather in the actual performance, particularly in the orchestra.

It is useful to enter here a warning for the benefit of those accomplished musicians who judge of works mainly or solely from scores. Rameau—and this is even truer of Lulli—is chary of revealing himself to the rapid score-reader. Reichardt discovered this long ago, at the close of Rameau's own century. When he looked at a score of *Castor et Pollux* he judged the choruses "meagre and weak" ("mager und kraftlos").[2] When he heard the opera in Paris he found they gave him "intense delight".[3] As a result, he concluded, "I become every day more suspicious of all mere seeing and reading of scores [*alles Sehen und Lesen der Partituren*], and I am every day more

---

[1] Max Kenyon, *Mozart in Salzburg*, 163.
[2] *Musikalisches Kunstmagazin*, V, 141.
[3] *Vertrauter Briefe über Frankreich* (Berlin, 1792–1793), Brief no. XXVI.

certain that one can only study his" (Rameau's) "true effect by hearing him [*das Studium des Effekts nur durch Hören statt findet*]."[1]

I will support this experience with that of a good musician of our own time who must remain nameless; his remarks will introduce a further point.

> The real reason for my dullness over Rameau ... as for my dullness over Handel at one time lies in the enormous difference between score-reading and hearing good professional performance. No music so badly needs fine performance as that now universally dubbed baroque ... Palestrina even, still more Monteverdi, Purcell, Lulli and then Rameau, Handel (not so much Bach who is impressive just as "paper" music) need almost ideal handpicking. Until now I've never *heard* *Hippolyte*—just banged out a vocal score at the piano. What an experience! [i.e. after hearing one of the recent broadcasts].

The second part of this quotation raises the important question of the quality demanded for a performance of Rameau. His music, says Pierre Lalo, needs

> an extremely precise, and at the same time extremely sensitive interpretation, intelligent, penetrating and felt. .... There are few notes, but each one has a meaning, and it must be given it; each fiddle, each flute, each hautboy needs an execution that follows and adapts itself to every movement of the musical line, which can mould and so to speak sculpt itself on its clear, precise, supple and tight outline, without overlooking any inflexion, accent, or intention, on pain of losing touch with thought and feeling.[2]

I have already noted Marpurg's opinion[3] that Lulli sounds best on large orchestras. All those who know Rameau well say the same of him. Here is Georges Migot insisting on full-sized orchestras, though without the intrusion of any foreign timbres.[4] Here is Masson declaring that his vigour would be better felt if he were played with bigger orchestras and especially with more strings—to which I would add that the woodwind, also, need strengthening; his scores show, for instance, that in certain passages he would double both flute parts. If cuts have to be made, let them never be at the expense of the *symphonies*. In singing, it is better to use grace notes sparingly unless the singer is experienced; too often an attempt to render them faithfully results merely in singing out of tune. The airs should not be hurried. On the other hand, it is fatal to drag the recitative, yet this is the usual mistake, and it was already prevalent with Lulli's operas in the early eighteenth century, according to Du Bos. Of all these

---

[1] (153), 126.   [2] (170), 45–46.
[3] Page 117, note 3.
[4] Which excludes "Busonizing" and "Mottl'ing".

recommendations, the chief is the first, from the observance of which all other virtues will follow: that conductor and instrumentalists should feel and understand the beauty of what they are playing.

Except for the favour of an occasional broadcast, most of us will never come to know Rameau otherwise than from a vocal score and a keyboard. With these, an average player may reach quite soon to the soul of his art. An inspired imagination, seconded by imperfect fingers, provide a more gorgeous spectacle than any but the most consummate playing, acting, dancing and stagecraft can offer. It is thus that we can make him our possession and that he will be "of use" to us. Written for the pomp of the Académie royale de Musique, his *tragédies lyriques* and *opéras-ballets* live again, with a life more intimate and more spiritual, within the four walls of our music rooms; and the works which first saw the day as amusements for a semi-musical public of opinionated amateurs or a gathering of inattentive courtiers will be numbered among the most loved of our household gods.

Bibliography

A. Works by Rameau

(1) Music

(i) Chamber Music[1]

Pièces de Clavecin, 1706.
Pièces de Clavecin avec une méthode, 1724. ⎫ (Œuvres Complètes
Nouvelles Suites de Pièces de Clavecin, c. 1728. ⎬ = O.C., I.)
Pièces de Clavecin en Concerts, 1741.   (O.C., II.)

(ii) Sacred Music

Deus noster refugium, before 1716.   (O.C., V.)
In convertendo, c. 1718.   (O.C., IV.)
Quam dilecta, c. 1720.   (O.C., IV.)
Exultet coelum laudibus, c. 1720 (lost).
Laboravi, before 1722.   (O.C., V.)

(iii) Cantatas, etc.

Duo paysan, 1707.   (In (184).)
Canon: "Avec du vin", 1719. ⎫
Canon: "Ah! loin de rire", before 1722. ⎬ (In (1).)
Aquilon et Orithie, before October 1727; ⎫
  published between 1731 and 1736. ⎮
Thétis, before October 1727. ⎮
Le Berger fidèle, performed 1728; pub- ⎮
  lished between 1731 and 1736. ⎬ (O.C., III.)
Les Amants trahis, before 1721. ⎮
L'Impatience, before 1722. ⎮
Orphée, before 1721. ⎭
Médée, before 1722 (lost).
L'Absence, before 1722 (lost).
La Musette, no date; doubtfully authentic.   (O.C., III.)

(iv) Incidental Music for the Fair Theatres

L'Endriague, comedy by Piron; February 8, 1723 (lost).
L'Enrôlement d'Arlequin, comedy by Piron; 1726 (lost).

---

[1] Edited by Erwin Jacobi (Bärenreiter Verlag, 2 vols., 1958, 1961 and 1967).

La Robe de dissension, comedy by Piron; 1726 (lost).

Les Courses de Tempé, pastorale by Piron; 1734 (vocal line of airs).

Les Jardins de l'Hymen ou la Rose, pastorale by Piron; 1744 (lost).

(v) *Dramatic Works*

Hippolyte et Aricie, tragédie en musique; Paris, October 1, 1733 (Pellegrin). (*O.C.*, VI.)

Les Indes galantes, opéra-ballet; Paris, August 23, 1735 (Fuzelier). (*O.C.*, VII.)

Castor et Pollux, tragédie en musique; Paris, October 24, 1737 (Bernard). (*O.C.*, VIII.)

Les Fêtes d'Hébé (*Les Talents lyriques*), opéra-ballet; Paris, May 21, 1739 (Montdorge). (*O.C.*, IX.)

Dardanus, tragédie en musique; Paris, November 19, 1739 (Le Clerc de la Bruère). (*O.C.*, X, 1; 1739 version. *O.C.*, X, 2: later versions.)

La Princesse de Navarre, comédie-ballet; Versailles, February 23, 1745 (Voltaire). (*O.C.*, XI.)

Platée, comédie lyrique; Versailles, March 31, 1745 (Autreau & Le Valois d'Orville). (*O.C.*, XII.)

Les Fêtes de Polymnie, opéra-ballet; Paris, October 12, 1745 (Cahusac). (*O.C.*, XIII.)

Le Temple de la Gloire, opéra-ballet; Versailles, November 27, 1745 (Voltaire). (*O.C.*, XIV.)

Les Fêtes de l'Hymen et de l'Amour, opéra-ballet; Versailles, March 15, 1747 (Cahusac). (*O.C.*, XV.)

Zaïs, pastorale héroïque; Paris, February 29, 1748 (Cahusac). (*O.C.*, XVI.)

Pygmalion, acte de ballet; Paris, August 27, 1748 (Ballot de Sovot). (*O.C.*, XVII.)

Les Surprises de l'Amour, opéra-ballet; Versailles, November 27, 1748 (Bernard). (*O.C.*, XIV.)

Naïs, pastorale héroïque; Paris, April 22, 1749 (Cahusac). (*O.C.*, XVIII.)

Zoroastre, tragédie en musique; Paris, December 5, 1749 (Cahusac). (1756 version, Paris, O.R.T.F., 1964.)

La Guirlande, acte de ballet; Paris, September 21, 1751 (Marmontel).

Acante et Céphise, pastorale héroïque; Paris, November 9, 1751 (Marmontel).

Daphnis et Églé, pastorale héroïque; Fontainebleau, October 30, 1753 (Collé).

Linus, tragédie en musique (Le Clerc de la Bruère); unperformed and lost.

Lysis et Délie, pastorale (Marmontel); unperformed and lost.

Les Sybarites, acte de ballet; Fontainebleu, November 13, 1753 (Marmontel). (*O.C.*, XVII.)

La Naissance d'Osiris, acte de ballet; Fontainebleau, October 12, 1754 (Cahusac).

Anacréon, acte de ballet; Fontainebleau, October 23, 1754 (Cahusac).

Anacréon, acte de ballet added to *Les Surprises de l'Amour*; Paris, May 31, 1757 (Bernard). (*O.C.*, XVII.)

Les Paladins, comédie lyrique; Paris, February 12, 1760 (Monticourt).

Abaris ou les Boréades, tragédie en musique (probably Cahusac); unperformed (1764).

Nélée et Myrthis, acte de ballet; date unknown; unperformed. (*O.C.*, XI.)

Zéphyre, acte de ballet; date unknown; unperformed. (*O.C.*, XI.)

Io, acte de ballet; date unknown; unperformed.

In addition to the full scores printed in the *O.C.*, a number of works have been published by Durand in vocal scores. These are: *In convertendo*, *Quam dilecta*, *Laboravi* (all transposed down a tone); *Hippolyte et Aricie*, *Les Indes galantes*, *Castor et Pollux*, *Les Fêtes d'Hébé*, *Dardanus* (1739 version only), *Platée*, *Pygmalion*, and the cantatas *Aquilon et Orithie* and *Le Berger fidèle*.

The publication of the *Œuvres Complètes*, which stopped in 1918, shows no signs of being resumed. Of the operas later than *Naïs*, only *Zoroastre* exists in modern editions. One of these, the vocal score published by Michaelis *c.* 1883, reproduces uncritically the 1749 edition, omitting the middle parts. The other is the scholarly edition (full score) of the 1756 version produced by Françoise Gervais (Paris, O. R. T. F., 1964). Some of the dances from *Acante et Céphise*, arranged for wind quintet, have been edited by Roger Desormieres (Lyre Bird Press), and two suites of dances from *Les Paladins*, in their original scoring, have also been published (Lyre Bird Press).

Most of the works in *O.C.* exist also in contemporary editions, which omit, as I have just said, the viola and sometimes the second-violin parts. Both versions of *Dardanus* were printed, one in 1739, the other in 1744. Of the later works, *Zoroastre* (1749 version only), *La Guirlande* and *Acante et Céphise* alone were published in the years of their performance; all the rest lie in manuscript. Most of the autographs have been preserved in the Opéra library or in the Bibliothèque Nationale; some are represented only by copies made for

Decroix.[1] This Rameau lover collected everything he could find of his hero at a time when the great man's music was falling out of favour, and to him we owe the preservation of some of these later compositions as well as of the unpublished cantatas and those lone survivors of the vanished *Linus*, the two first-violin parts. We cannot emphasize too strongly the great debt which musicians owe to him and to his heirs who gave his collection of Rameau manuscripts and copies to the Bibliothèque Nationale.[2] His printed editions have been scattered; his copy of the 1733 edition of *Hippolyte et Aricie*, with his name and the date "1767", has found its way to the Reid Library of Edinburgh University. Unlike the printed editions, the manuscript copies show the complete score.

The introductions to Vols. I–XVI of *O.C.* are by Charles Malherbe; those to Vols. XVII and XVIII are by Maurice Emmanuel and Martial Ténéo.

(2) WRITINGS

(1) *Traité de l'Harmonie réduite à ses principes naturels*, 1722.

(2) *Nouveau Système de musique théorique*, 1726.

(3) *Examen d'une conférence sur la musique*; in *Mercure de France*, October 1729.

(4) *Réponse à la réplique de l'auteur de la conférence*; *Réplique du premier musicien sur l'harmonie*; in *Mercure de France*, June 1730.

(5) *Observations sur la méthode d'accompagnement pour le clavecin qui est en usage, et qu'on appelle échelle ou règle de l'octave*; in *Mercure de France*, February 1730. *Plan abrégé d'une nouvelle méthode d'accompagnement pour le clavecin* (continuation of the prec.); in *Mercure de France*, March 1730.

(6) *Lettre de M. . . . à M. . . . sur la musique et l'explication de la carte générale de la basse fondamentale*; in *Mercure de France*, September 1731.

(7) *Dissertation sur les différentes méthodes d'accompagnement pour le clavecin ou l'orgue*, 1732.

(8) *Lettre au Père Castel*; in *Journal de Trévoux* (*Mémoires pour servir à l'histoire des sciences et des arts*), July 1736.

(9) *Génération harmonique*, 1737.

(10) *Remarques de M. Rameau sur l'extrait qu'on a donné de son livre intitulé Génération harmonique dans le Journal de Trévoux, décembre 1737*; in *Le Pour et Contre*, XIV (74–96 and 141–144).

(11) *Lettre à M. de Sainte-Albine*; in *Mercure de France*, July 1749.

---

[1] J. J. M. Decroix (*c*. 1750–1826), one of the editors of the Kehl edition of Voltaire's works.—The Fitzwilliam Library in Cambridge possesses eighteenth-century manuscript copies of *Les Indes galantes* and *Les Paladins*.

[2] See (176A).

(12) *Démonstration du principe de l'harmonie*, 1750.

(13) *Nouvelles réflexions de M. Rameau sur sa Démonstration du Principe de l'Harmonie*, 1752.

(14) *Lettre de M. Rameau à l'auteur du Mercure*; in *Mercure de France*, May 1752.

(15) *Réflexions sur la manière de former la voix*; in *Mercure de France*, October 1752.[1]

(16) *Extrait d'une réponse de M. Rameau à M. Euler*; in *Mercure de France*, December 1752, 6–31.

(17) *Observations sur notre instinct pour la musique*, 1754.

(18) *Erreurs sur la musique dans l'Encyclopédie*, 1755.

(19) *Suite des erreurs sur la musique dans l'Encyclopédie*, 1756.

(20) *Réponse de M. Rameau à MM. les Éditeurs de l'Encyclopédie*, 1757.

(21) *Code de musique pratique*, 1760.

(22) *Nouvelles réflexions sur le principe sonore*, 1760.[2]

(23) *Lettre à M. d'Alembert sur ses opinions en musique insérées dans les articles Fondamental et Gamme de l'Encyclopédie*, 1760.

(24) *Réponse de M. d'Alembert à M. Rameau et réponse de M. Rameau à la lettre de M. d'Alembert*, 1761.[3]

(24A) *Origine des sciences, suivie d'une controverse sur le même sujet*, 1761.

(25) *Lettre aux Philosophes*; in *Journal de Trévoux*, 1762.

(25A) *Vérités intéressantes* (unfinished ms.); ed. Jean Chantavoine, *Revue de Bourgogne*, 1924, 667–689; Erwin Jacobi, in *Revue de Musicologie*, L (July 1964).

(25B) *Complete theoretical writings* (edited by Erwin R. Jacobi); American Institute of Musicology. Vol. I, containing the *Traité de l'harmonie*, 1967. The edition will be complete in six volumes.

B. Works, by other authors, earlier than 1800

(26) ANONYMOUS. *Essai d'Éloge historique de feu M. Rameau*; in *Mercure de France*, October 1764.

(27) ANONYMOUS. *Mélanges de musique latine, française et italienne*, 1725.

(28) ADDISON, JOSEPH. *The Spectator*, I (1711).

(29) ALEMBERT, JEAN LE ROND D'. *De la liberté de la musique*, 1758; in *Mélanges de litterature, d'histoire et de philosophie* (2nd edition), IV; 1763.

---

[1] Reprinted in *Revue musicale*, numéro spécial 260 (1964), 48–53.

[2] The Bibliothèque Nationale catalogue says 1757 by mistake.

[3] Undated, but Rameau's answer cannot be earlier than 1761 since it contains an allusion to Rousseau's *La Nouvelle Héloïse*, which came out that year, a work "où, s'il s'agit de musique, ce n'est que pour jeter au feu toute la musique française". Also in *Mercure de France*, April 1761.

(30) —*Éléments de musique théorique et pratique suivant les principes de M. Rameau*, 1752.

(30A) — Second edition of (30), preceded by a *Discours préliminaire*, 1762.

(31) — *Réponse de M. d'Alembert à M. Rameau*, 1760.   See (24).

(32) — *Œuvres et correspondances inédites*, Paris, 1887.

(33) AQUIN DE CHÂTEAULYON, D'.   *Siècle littéraire de Louis XV ou lettres sur les hommes célèbres*, Amsterdam, 1753.

(34) ARGENSON, MARQUIS D'.   *Journal et Mémoires*, éd. Rathery, Paris, 1859–1867.

(34A) — *Mémoires et Journal inédit*, publiés et annotés par M. le marquis d'Argenson, éd. P. Jannet, Paris, 1858.

(35) BÉTHIZY.   *Exposition de la théorie et de la pratique de la musique suivant les principes de M. Rameau*, 1754.

(36) — *Théorie et pratique de la musique suivant les nouvelles découvertes*, 1764.   A second edition of (35).

(37) BLAINVILLE, C. H.   *L'Esprit de l'art musical*, Genève, 1754.

(38) BOILEAU, NICOLAS.   *Satires.*

(39) BOLLIOUD-MERMET.   *La Corruption du Goût*, Lyon, 1746.

(40) BRICE, GERMAIN.   *Description de la ville de Paris*, 1713 edition.

(41) BRISEUX, CHARLES-ÉTIENNE.   *Traité du beau essentiel dans les arts, appliqué particulièrement à l'architecture*, 1752.

(42) — *Traité des proportions harmoniques*, 1752.

(43) BURNEY, DR. CHARLES.   *A General History of Music*, 1776–1789; 1935 edit., London.

(44) CAHUSAC, LOUIS DE.   *La danse ancienne et moderne*, 1754.

(45) CALLIÈRES, FRANÇOIS DE.   *Histoire poétique de la guerre récemment survenue entre les Anciens et les Modernes*, 1689.

(46) CARTAUD DE LA VILLATTE.   *Essai historique et philosophique sur le Goût*, 1736.

(47) CASTEL, PÈRE LOUIS-BERTRAND.   *Extrait de la génération harmonique de M. Rameau*; in *Journal de Trévoux*, December 1737.

(48) — *Lettres d'un Académicien de Bordeaux sur le fond de la musique*; in *Journal de Trévoux*, 1754.

(49) — *Nouvelles expériences d'optique et d'acoustique adressées à M. le Président Montesquieu*; in *Journal de Trévoux*, August 1735.

(50) — *Réponse à la lettre de M. Rameau*; in *Journal de Trévoux*, September 1736.

(51) ANONYMOUS.   *Éloge historique du Père Castel*; in *Journal de Trévoux*, April 1757.

(52) CAUX DE CAPPEVAL, N. DE.   *Apologie du goût français relativement à l'opéra, poème, avec un discours apologétique et des adieux aux bouffons, en vers*, 1754.

(53) CHABANON, MICHEL-PAUL-GUI DE.   *Éloge de M. Rameau*, 1764.

(54) CHAULIEU ET LA FARE.   *Poésies*, 1821 edition, Paris.

(55) CLEMENT. *Les cinq années littéraires: 1748–1752*, The Hague, 1754.

(56) COLLÉ. *Journal et mémoires*, Paris, 1868.

(57) CORANCEZ. *Sur Gluck*; in *Journal de Paris*, August 1788.

(58) CORNEILLE, PIERRE. *Andromède*, preface, 1650.

(59) DAGOTY LE FILS, GAUTIER. *Galerie française ou portraits des hommes et des femmes célèbres qui ont paru en France*, Paris, 1770.

(60) DECROIX, J. J. M. *L'Ami des Arts ou Justification de plusieurs grands hommes*, Amsterdam, 1776.

(61) DIDEROT, DENIS. *Les Bijoux indiscrets*, 1748; Assézat edition, IV.

(62) — *Lettre au sujet des Observations du chevalier de Chastellux sur le Traité du Mélodrame*, 1771; Assézat, VIII.

(63) — *Le Neveu de Rameau*, ed. Jean Fabre, Genève, 1952.

(63A) — *Principes généraux de l'acoustique*, 1748; Assézat, IX.

(64) DU BOS, ABBÉ JEAN-BAPTISTE. *Réflexions critiques sur la poésie et la peinture*, 1719.

(65) DUBUISSON. *Lettres au marquis de Caumont*, Paris, 1882.

(66) DUCHARGER. *Réflexions sur divers ouvrages de M. Rameau*, Rennes, 1761.

(67) *Encyclopédie, ou dictionnaire raisonné des sciences, des arts et des métiers*, 1751–1772.

(67A) ESTÈVE, PIERRE. *Nouvelle découverte du principe de l'harmonie*, Paris, 1751.

(68) FONTENELLE, BERNARD LE BOVIER DE. *Discours sur la nature de l'églogue*, 1688.

(69) FRÉRON, ÉLIE. *Lettres sur quelques écrits de ce temps*, 1749–1754.

(69A) — *L'Année littéraire*, 1754–1790.

(70) GARDEL, J. *L'Avènement de Titus à l'empire*, discours préliminaire, 1775.

(70A) GENEST, ABBÉ CHARLES-CLAUDE. *Dissertation sur la poésie pastorale*, 1707.

(71) GRIMM, MELCHIOR. *Correspondance littéraire*, Paris, 1813.

(72) — *Lettre sur Omphale*, 1752.

(73) GRIMAREST. *Traité du récitatif*, 1707.

(74) LA BORDE, JEAN-BENJAMIN DE. *Essai sur la musique ancienne et moderne*, 1780.

(75) — *Recueil de pensées et de maximes*, 2nd edition, 1802; introduction.

(76) ANONYMOUS. *Jean-Benjamin de la Borde*, Nantes, 1849.

(77) LA BRUYÈRE, JEAN DE. *Les Caractères*, 1688.

(78) LA DIXMERIE. *Les deux âges du goût et du génie français*, 1770.

(79) LA FARE, MARQUIS DE. See (54).

(80) LA MOTTE, HOUDAR DE. *Réflexions sur la critique*; in *Œuvres*, III, 1; 1754.

(81) LA PORTE, ABBÉ JOSEPH DE. *Anecdotes dramatiques*, 1775.

(82) L. T., M. DE (LA TOUR?). *Dissertation sur le bon goût et la musique italienne et de la musique française, et sur les opéras*; in *Mercure de France*, November 1713.

(83) LE CERF DE FRÉNEUSE DE LA VIÉVILLE, JEAN-LAURENT. *Comparaison de la musique italienne et de la musique française*, 1704.

(84) MABLY, ABBÉ GABRIEL BONNOT DE. *Lettres à Mme la Marquise de P . . . sur l'opéra*, 1741.

(85) MARET, DR. HUGHES. *Éloge historique de M. Rameau*, Dijon, 1766.

(86) MARMONTEL, JEAN-FRANÇOIS. *Examen des réflexions de M. d'Alembert sur la liberté de la musique*; in *Mercure de France*, July 1759, II.

(87) MAUGARS. *Réponse faite à un curieux sur le sentiment de la musique d'Italie*, 1639; Paris, 1865.

(88) MONTESQUIEU, CHARLES DE SECONDAT DE. *Lettres persanes*, 1721.

(89) MOZART, LEOPOLD and W. A. *The Letters of W. A. Mozart and his Family* (tr. by Emily Anderson), London, 1938.

(90) NOVERRE, JEAN-GEORGES. *Lettres sur la danse*, 1760; Paris, 1952. (My quotations are from the latter edition.)

(91) PALISSOT, CHARLES. *Rameau*; in *Le Nécrologe des hommes célèbres de France, par une société de gens de lettres*, I; 1767.

(92) PIRON, ALEXIS. *Lettres d'Alexis Piron à M. Maret*, Lyon, 1860.

(93) PLUCHE, ABBÉ NOËL-ANTOINE. *Le spectacle de la nature*, 1732.

(94) RAGUENET, ABBÉ FRANÇOIS. *Parallèle des Italiens et des Français en ce qui regarde la musique et les opéras*, 1702.

(95) — *A Comparison between the French and Italian Music*; Engl. tr. attr. to J. E. Galliard, 1709; repr. in *Musical Quarterly*, Vol. 32 (1946).

(96) RAYNAL, ABBÉ GUILLAUME. *Nouvelles littéraires*, 1747–1755.

(97) RÉMOND DE SAINT-MARD. *Réflexions sur l'opéra*; *Œuvres*, V; 1749.

(98) ROCHEMONT. *Réflexions d'un patriote sur l'opéra français et l'opéra italien*, Lausanne, 1754.

(99) ROUSSEAU, JEAN-JACQUES. *Confessions*, ed. Baudouin, 1826.

(100) — *Dictionnaire de la Musique*, 1767.

(101) — *Lettre à M. Grimm au sujet des remarques de la Lettre sur Omphale*, 1752.

(102) — *Lettre sur la musique française*, 1753.

(103) — *La Nouvelle Héloïse*, 1761.

(104) ROY, PIERRE-CHARLES. *Lettre sur l'opéra*; in *Lettres sur quelques écrits de ce temps*, II; 1749.

(105) — *Réflexions sur l'églogue*; *Œuvres diverses*, I; 1727.

(106) SCHEIBE, J. A. *Der critische Musikus*, Hamburg, 1740.

(107) SCHMID, CHRISTIAN-HEINRICH. *Chronologie des deutschen Theaters*, Leipzig, 1755.

(108) SCHÜTZE, J. F. *Hamburgische Theater-Geschichte*, 1794.

586 BIBLIOGRAPHY

(109) Séré de Rieux. *La Musique, poème divisé en quatre chants*, 1714; 2nd edition 1727; 3rd edition in (110). (References are to the 1727 edition.)

(110) — *Les dons des enfants de Latone*, 1734.

(111) Titon du Tillet. *Le Parnasse français*, 1732.

(112) Voltaire, François Arouet de. *Voltaire's Correspondence*, ed. Th. Besterman, Geneva.

(113) *Théâtre*, 2; in *Œuvres* (Beuchot), III.

C. Works since 1800

(114) Abert, Hermann. *W. A. Mozart*, Leipzig, 1919–1921.

(115) Arnold, F. T. *The Art of Accompaniment from a Thoroughbass*, Oxford, 1931.

(116) Berthelot, René. *La sagesse shakespearienne*; in *Revue de métaphysique et morale*, 1926.

(116A) Berthier, Paul. *Réflexions sur l'art et la vie de Rameau*, Paris, 1957.

(117) Bézard, Yvonne. *Une famille bourguignonne au XVIIIme siècle*, Paris, 1930.

(118) Borrel, Eugène. *Un paradoxe musical au XVIIIme siècle*; in *Mélanges . . . offerts à Lionel de la Laurencie*, Paris, 1933.

(118A) — *L'interprétation de la musique française (de Lully à la Révolution)*, Paris, 1934.

(118B) Bremond, Abbé Henri. *Racine et Valéry*, Paris, 1930.

(119) Brenet, Michel (Marie Bobillier). *La jeunesse de Rameau*; in *Rivista musicale italiana*, 1902 (658–693 and 860–887), 1903 (62–85 and 185–206).

(120) — *Les concerts en France sous l'ancien régime*, Paris, 1900.

(121) — *La librairie musicale en France de 1653 à 1790, d'après les Registres de privilèges*; in *Sammelbände der Internationalen Musikgesellschaft*, April and June 1906–1907.

(122) ⎫ Bresson, Abbé. *Histoire de l'église Notre-Dame de Dijon*,
(123) ⎭ Dijon, 1891.

(124) Bricqueville, E. de. *Deux abbés d'opéra au siècle dernier*, Amiens, 1889.

(125) Bukofzer, M. *Music of the Baroque Era*, London, 1948.

(126) Carse, Adam. *The Orchestra in the Eighteenth Century*, Cambridge, 1940.

(126A) Chailley, Jacques. *Rameau et la théorie musicale*; in *Revue musicale*, numéro spécial 260 (1964), 65–96.

(127) Champigneulle, Bernard. *L'âge classique de la musique française*, Paris, 1946.

(127A) Charlier, Henri. *Jean-Philippe Rameau*, Lyon, 1955.

(128) Christ, Yvan. *Églises parisiennes actuelles et disparues*, Paris 1947.

(129) COMBARIEU, JULES. *Histoire de la musique*, Paris, 1913.

(130) COOPER, MARTIN. *Gluck*, London, 1935.

(131) — *French music from the death of Berlioz to the death of Fauré*, London, 1951.

(132) CORNIANI, G. B. Introduction to: Sannazaro, *Arcadia*, Milan, 1806.

(133) CRUSSARD, CLAUDE. *Marc-Antoine Charpentier*, Paris, 1945.

(134) CUCUEL, GEORGES. *La Pouplinière et la musique de chambre au XVIIIe siècle*, Paris, 1913.

(135) DACIER, E. *L'Opéra au XVIIIe siècle: les premières représentations de Dardanus*; in *Revue musicale*, April, 1903.

(136) DALE, KATHLEEN. *The Keyboard Music of Daquin*; in *Monthly Musical Record*, August 1946.

(137) — *The Keyboard Music of Rameau*; in *Monthly Musical Record*, December 1947 and January 1948.

(138) DESNOIRESTERRES, GUSTAVE. *Voltaire et la société au XVIIIe siècle*, 8 vols., Paris, 1871–1876.

(139) DICKINSON, A. E. *A Reconsideration of "The Nibelungs' Ring"*; in *Durham University Journal*, March 1952.

(139A) DOOLITTLE, J. *A wouldbe philosophe, J. P. Rameau*; in *Publications of the Modern Language Association of America*, 1959, 233–248.

(140) DUFOURCQ, NORBERT. *Le clavecin*, Paris, 1949.

(141) — *La musique française*, Paris, 1949.

(141A) DUPARCQ, JEAN-JACQUES. *De la conception du principe de l'harmonie selon Jean-Philippe Rameau et Jean-Sebastian Bach*; in *Revue musicale*, numéro spécial 260 (1964), 123–143.

(142) ÉCORCHEVILLE, JULES. *De Lulli à Rameau: essai d'esthétique musicale*, Paris, 1906.

(143) — Review of: Ernest Closson, *Le manuscrit des Basses Danses de la Bibliothèque de Bourgogne*, in *S.I.M.*, November 1912.

(144) EINSTIEN, ALFRED. *Gluck*, London, 1936.

(145) — Köchel, *Chronologisch-thematisches Verzeichniss der Werke W. A. Mozarts*, 3rd edition by A. Einstein, Leipzig, 1937.

(146) FAURÉ, GABRIEL. *Opinions musicales*, Paris, 1930.

(147) FORQUERAY, LOUIS. *Les Forqueray et leurs descendants*, Paris, 1911.

(148) GARDIEN, JACQUES. *Le procès de Claude Rameau contre Publot*; in *Revue de Musicologie*, May–August 1936.

(149) — *L'orgue et les organistes en Bourgogne*, Paris, 1943.

(150) — *Jean-Philippe Rameau*, Paris, 1949.

(151) GARROS, MADELEINE. *Mme de Maintenon et la musique*; in *Revue de Musicologie*, January 1943.

(152) GAUDEFROY-DEMOMBYNES, J. *Histoire de la musique française*, Paris, 1946.

(153) — *Les jugements allemands sur la musique française au XVIIIme siècle*, Paris, 1941.

(154) GENLIS, MME DE. *Mémoires*, Paris, 1825.

(155) GERHARDT, MIA. *La pastorale*, Assen, 1950.

(155A) GERVAIS, FRANÇOISE. *La musique pure au service du drame lyrique chez Rameau*; in *Revue musicale*, numéro spécial 260 (1964), 21–36.

(155B) GIRDLESTONE, CUTHBERT. *Some thoughts on Rameau*; in *Monthly Musical Record*, February 1942.

(155C) — *Rameau's self-borrowings*; in *Music and Letters*, 1958, I.

(155D) — *A plan for the production of "Dardanus"*; in *Music and Letters*, 1959, I.

(155E) — *Le Cerf de la Viéville's "Comparaison": its non-musical interest*; in *French Studies*, July 1962.

(156) — *Voltaire, Rameau et "Samson"*; in *Recherches sur la musique française classique*, VI (1966), 133–143.

(157) GREG, W. W. *Pastoral Poetry and Pastoral Drama*, London, 1906.

(158) GROS, ÉTIENNE. *Philippe Quinault*, Paris, 1926.

(159) GROUT, DONALD. *Some Forerunners of the Lulli Opera*, in *Music and Letters*, January 1941.

(160) HARASZTI, ÉMILE. *Jean-Benjamin de Laborde*; in *Revue musicale*, June 1935.

(161) INDY, VINCENT D'. Introduction to: Destouches & Lalande, *Les Éléments*, Paris, 1883.

(161A) JACOBI, ERWIN. *Nouvelles lettres inédites de Jean-Philippe Rameau*; in *Recherches sur la musique française classique*, III (1963), 145–158.

(161B) — *"Vérités intéressantes". Le dernier manuscrit de Jean-Philippe Rameau*; in *Revue de Musicologie*, July 1964, 77–109.

(161C) — *Rameau and Padre Martini*; in *Musical Quarterly*, L, 4 (October 1964), 452–475.

(161D) KEANE, SISTER MICHAELA. *The theoretical writings of Jean-Philippe Rameau*, Washington, 1961.

(162) LA LAURENCIE, LIONEL DE. *Les créateurs de l'opéra français*, Paris, 1921.

(163) — *L'école française du violon de Lulli à Viotti*, Paris, 1922–1924.

(164) — *Le goût musical en France*, Paris, 1905.

(165) — *La musique française de Lulli à Gluck*; in A. Lavignac, *Encyclopédie de la musique: Histoire*, III, Paris, 1913.

(166) — *Quelques documents sur Jean-Philippe Rameau et sa famille*; in *S.I.M.*, June 1907.

(167) — *Rameau*, Paris, 1908.

(168) — *Rameau, son gendre et ses descendants*; in *S.I.M.*, December 15, 1911.

(169) LALO, CHARLES. *Esquisse d'une esthétique musicale scientifique*, Paris, 1908.

(170) LALO, PIERRE. *De Rameau à Ravel*, Paris, 1947.

(171) — *Vue d'ensemble sur le théâtre lyrique en France au XIXe siècle*; in *Conférences sur la musique*, Paris, Poste national Radio Paris, XI, 8–9.

(172) LALOY, LOUIS. *Rameau*, Paris, 1908.

(173) LANCASTER, H. CARRINGTON. *A History of French Dramatic Literature in the Seventeenth Century*, Baltimore, 1929–1942.

(174) LANDORMY, PAUL. *Maurice Ravel*; in *Musical Quarterly*, Vol. 33 (1947).

(175) LÁNG, PAUL. *Music in Western Civilization*, London, 1942.

(176) LASSERRE, PIERRE. *L'esprit de la musique française*, Paris, 1917.

(176A) LEBEAU, ELIZABETH. *J. J. M. Decroix*; in *Mélanges ... Masson*, II, Paris, 1955.

(177) LEWIS, ANTHONY. Introduction to: John Blow, *Venus and Adonis*, Monaco, 1949.

(178) LOEWENBERG, A. *Annals of Opera*, Cambridge, 1943.

(179) LOMBARD, A. *L'abbé Du Bos*, Paris, 1913.

(179A) McGOWAN, MARGARET M. *L'art du ballet de cour en France, 1581–1643*, Paris, 1963.

(180) MACHABEY, ARMAND. *Les origines de la chaconne et de la passacaille*; in *Revue de Musicologie*, 1946 (1–2).

(180A) MALIGNON, JEAN. *Rameau*, Paris, 1960.

(181) MARSAN, JULES. *La pastorale dramatique*, Paris, 1905.

(182) MASSON, PAUL-MARIE. *Le ballet héroïque*; in *Revue musicale*, June 1, 1928.

(183) — *Les Brunettes*; in *Sammelbände ...*, 1911.

(184) — *Deux chansons bachiques de Rameau*; in *S.I.M.*, May 15, 1910.

(185) — *"Les Fêtes vénitiennes" de Campra*; in *Revue de Musicologie*, November 1932.

(186) — *La Lettre sur "Omphale"*; in *Revue de Musicologie*, 1945 (1–2).

(187) — *Une lettre de Rameau à l'Abbé François Arnaud*; in *Mélanges ... à Lionel de la Laurencie*, Paris, 1935.

(188) — *Lullistes et ramistes*; in *Année musicale*, 1911.

(189) — *Musique italienne et musique française: la première querelle*; in *Rivista musicale italiana*, 1912.

(190) — *L'Opéra de Rameau*, Paris, 1930.

(191) — *Une polémique musicale de Claude Rameau*; in *Revue de Musicologie*, May–August 1937.

(192) — *Rameau and Wagner*; in *Musical Quarterly*, 25 (1939).

(193) MELLERS, WILFRID. *François Couperin*, London, 1950.

(194) — *Rameau and the opera*; in *The Score*, January 1951.

(195) MIGOT, GEORGES. *Jean-Philippe Rameau et le génie de la musique française*, Paris, 1930.

(195A) MOREAU, MARIE-GERMAINE. *Jean-Philippe Rameau et la péda-gogie*; in *Revue musicale*, numéro spécial 260 (1964), 47–66.

(196) MÜLLER-BLATTAU, JOSEF. *Händel*, Potsdam, 1933.

(197) NAVES, B. *Voltaire*, Paris, 1942.

(198) NEWMAN, WILLIAM S. *Concerning the Accompanied Clavier Sonata*; in *Musical Quarterly*, 33 (1947).

(199) NEWTON, ERIC. *European Painting and Sculpture*, London, 1941.

(199A) PAPPAS, JOHN N. *D'Alembert et la querelle des Bouffons d'après des documents inédits*; in *Revue d'histoire littéraire de la France*, 1965, III.

(200) PARRY, SIR HUBERT. *Oxford History of Music*, III, Oxford, 1902.

(201) PINCHERLE, MARC. Introduction to; Mondonville, *Sonates*, Paris (Société française de Musicologie), 1935.

(202) PIRRO, ANDRÉ. *Les Clavecinistes*, Paris, 1924.

(203) — *Louis Marchand*; in *Sammelbände* ..., 6 (October–December 1904).

(204) — *Louis Marchand*; introduction to: *Archives des Maîtres de l'Orgue*, 3me Année.

(205) — *Louis Marchand*; in *Tribune de St. Gervais*, January 1, 1900.

(205A) PISCHNER, HANS. *Die Harmonielehre Jean-Philippe Rameaus*, Leipzig, 1963.

(205B) POLE, WILLIAM. *The Philosophy of Music*, London, 1877; 6th edition, 1924.

(206) POUGIN, ARTHUR. *Rameau: essai sur sa vie et ses œuvres*, Paris, 1876.

(207) — Introduction to: Rameau, *Zoroastre*, Paris (Michaëlis), c. 1883.

(208) PRODHOMME, J. G. *Écrits de musiciens*, Paris, 1912.

(209) — *Gluck*, Paris, 1948.

(210) — *La musique à Paris de 1753 à 1757*; in *Sammelbände* ..., 6 (pp. 568 ff.).

(211) PRUNIÈRES, HENRI. *Le ballet de cour en France avant Benserade et Lulli*, Paris, 1914.

(212) — *Lecerf de la Viéville et l'esthétique musicale classique au XVIIIme siècle*; in *S.I.M.*, June 15, 1908.

(213) — *Monteverdi*, Paris, 1925 (Engl. trans., London, no date).

(214) — *L'opéra italien en France avant Lulli*, Paris, 1913.

(215) REESER, E. *De Klaviersonate med Vioolbegleiding*, Rotterdam, 1939.

(216) RICHEBOURG, LOUISETTE. *Contribution à l'histoire de la Querelle des Bouffons*, Paris, 1937.

(217) ROBERTSON, J. G. *Lessing's Dramatic Theory*, Cambridge, 1939.

(218) ROCHEGUDE AND DUMOLIN. *Guide pratique à travers le vieux Paris*, Paris, 1923.

(219) ROLLAND, ROMAIN. *Musiciens d'autrefois*, Paris, 1908.

(220) — *Un vaudeville de Rameau*; in *Mercure musical*, May 15, 1905.

(221) — *Voyage musical au pays du passé*, Paris, 1920.

(222) ROWEN, RUTH HALE. *Early Chamber Music*, King's Crown Press, New York and Oxford University Press, London, 1949.

(223) WYZEWA, TEODOR DE, and SAINT-FOIX, GEORGES DE. *W. A. Mozart: sa vie musicale et son œuvre*, 2nd edit., Paris, 1936.

(224) SANDS, MOLLIE. *The Decline and Revival of the Counter-tenor*; in *Monthly Musical Record*, June 1952.

(224A) SCHAEFFNER, ANDRÉ. *L'orgue de Barbarie de Rameau*; in *Mélanges . . . Masson*, II, Paris, 1955.

(225) SCHÉRER, JACQUES. *La dramaturgie classique en France*, Paris, 1950.

(225A) SCHIER, DONALD STEWART. *Louis-Bertrand Castel, anti-Newtonian scientist*, Cedar Rapids (Iowa), 1941.

(226) SCHWARZ, STANLEY. *Jacques Autreau, a forgotten dramatist*; in *Publications of the Modern Language Association of America*, 1931, 498 ff.

(227) SEZNEC, JEAN. *La survivance des dieux antiques*, London, 1940.

(228) STREATFEILD, R. A. C. *The Opera*, London, 1896; 5th edition, 1925.

(229) STRIFFLING, LOUIS. *Esquisse d'une histoire du goût musical en France au XVIIIe siècle*, Paris, 1912.

(229A) SUAUDEAU, RENÉ. *Introduction à l'harmonie de Rameau*, Clermont-Ferrand, 1960.

(230) SYMONDS, J. ADDINGTON. *Renaissance Italy*, 1912 edition.

(231) TESSIER, ANDRÉ. *Gaspard Le Roux*; in *Revue de Musicologie*, December 1922.

(232) — *Gaspard Le Roux*; in *Revue musicale*, March 1, 1924.

(233) — *L'œuvre de clavecin de Nicolas Le Bègue*; in *Revue de Musicologie*, August 1923.

(234) THOINAN, E. *Vie de Jean-François Rameau*; in Diderot, *Le Neveu de Rameau*, ed. Monval, Paris, 1891.

(235) TIERSOT, JULIEN. *Lettres inédites de Rameau*; in *Revue musicale*, January 1935.

(236) — *Lettres de musiciens écrites en français de XVe au XXe siècles*, Paris, 1924.

(236A) VALLAS, LÉON. *Un siècle de théâtre et de musique à Lyon*, Lyon, 1932.

(237) VIOLLIER, RENÉE. *Jean-Joseph Mouret*, Paris, 1950.

(238) WALTERSHAUSEN, H. W. VON. *Tänze aus "Zoroastre"*, Munich, 1922.

(239) WANGERMÉE, ROBERT. *Lecerf de la Viéville, Bonnet-Bourdelot et l' "Essai sur le bon goust en Musique" de Nicolas Grandval*; in *Revue belge de musicologie*, July–December 1951.

(240) WESTRUP, J. A.   *The Originality of Monteverdi*; in *Proceedings of the Musical Association*, 1933–1934.

(241) — *Purcell*, London, 1937.

(242) ZAKONE, CONSTANT.   *Rameau au théâtre*; in *Revue musicale*, July 1, 1903.

Appendix A

ABODES AND CHURCHES

THE writer of the obituary article in the *Mercure* had been told by Rameau that when he first came to Paris he took lodgings opposite the Cordeliers, or Franciscans, in order to be near their church where Louis Marchand played the organ. The church occupied what is now the broad part of the Rue de l'École de Médecine and its entrance was approximately opposite the present No. 4, Rue Antoine Dubois, then Rue de l'Observance, a house which was itself a dependency of the priory. (The present Dupuytren Museum was the Fathers' refectory.) If this information is to be taken literally, Rameau's first abode must have been in or near the Rue Antoine Dubois. Jean-François, his nephew, was to lodge in the neighbouring Rue des Cordeliers nearly fifty years later.

In 1706, when he published his first book of harpsichord pieces, he was living in the Rue Vieille du Temple, as it is called to-day. The frontispiece bears the following homely address: "Chez l'Auteur, Vielle [*sic*] Rue du Temple, vis à vis les Consignations, chez un Perruquier." I do not know where the Consignations were but they must have been south of the Rue des Francs Bourgeois, north of which the Vieille Rue du Temple at that time changed its name to Rue Barbette.

In 1726, when he married, he was living in the parish of St. Eustache, in Rue des Petits-Champs.

By August 3, 1727, when his son Claude was born, he was living Aux Trois Rois, Rue des Deux Boules; this address figures on the undated *Cantates françaises* and the *Nouvelles Suites*. The house cannot be identified. The street, which was never any longer than it is now, runs between the Rues Bertin Poirée and des Lavandières Ste. Opportune, near the Châtelet, and contains several old houses.

By 1731, when the harpsichord pieces of 1724 were republished, he was living in the Rue de Richelieu, "près l'Hôtel de la Paix." Some copies of this same edition bear the address "Rue St. Honoré, proche la Rue de l'Échelle".

By November 15, 1732, date of the christening of his daughter Marie-Louise, he was living in the Rue du Chantre. The site of this small street, which was almost a continuation southward of the Rue des Bons Enfants, is now covered by part of the Magasins du Louvre. This address is also given on the 1733 edition of *Hippolyte et Aricie*.

When *Les Indes galantes* was published, late in 1735 or early in 1736, he had moved to the Hôtel d'Effiat, on the west side of the Rue des Bons Enfants. This house was standing till recent times and bore the number 21; it was pulled down for the opening of the Rue du Colonel Driant.

In 1744, when the second version of *Dardanus* was published, he was living in the Rue St. Thomas du Louvre. This street ran from the Seine to the Rue St. Honoré across what is now part of the later Louvre; it reached the Rue St. Honoré on the site of the present Pavillon de Richelieu. It was in this street that Mme de Rambouillet's hôtel had stood a century earlier.

A deed of October 4, 1745, shows him living in the Rue St. Honoré; various publications give his address as "Vis à vis le Caffé Dupuis" or "proche le Palais Royal". The house must have been nearly opposite the famous Café de la Régence.

A deed of June 15, 1746, shows him living in the Rue de Richelieu; we know he took up his abode with La Pouplinière about this time; he must also have kept the Rue St. Honoré address which figures on the editions of *Les Fêtes de l'Hymen* (1747), *Zaïs, Pygmalion* (1748), *Platée* and *Zoroastre* (1749). But a deed of August 14, 1751, and the editions of *Acante et Céphise* and *La Guirlande* of the same year, give his address as Rue de Richelieu, "vis à vis la Bibliothèque du Roi", which is La Pouplinière's hôtel (site of the present No. 59).

Finally, the second edition of the *Pièces en concert* in 1752 gives his address as Rue des Bons Enfants, where he stayed till his death. Nothing enables us to locate his house in this street, but the inventory of his belongings made after his death shows that it stood on the west side, with its back overlooking the Palais Royal gardens which had not yet been curtailed by the building of the Rue de Valois.

The inventory states that the chief tenant in the house was one Lavoisier. This was the father of the future farmer-general and famous chemist, who was a youth of twenty-one when Rameau died and was still living with his father. The Lavoisiers had moved from a house in the Rue du Four St. Eustache (the present Rue de Vauvilliers) some years earlier. It is unlikely that the aged and solitary Rameau exchanged any but the most frigid salutations with his young neighbour. (Cf. Ed. Grimaux, *Lavoisier*, Paris, 1888.)

Of the churches mentioned in this book, I have already spoken of the Cordeliers. It was pulled down in 1804.

In 1706, Rameau was organist at the Jesuit College in the Rue St. Jacques and at the Pères de la Merci in the Marais. The former, the Collège de Clermont, has become the Lycée Louis-le-Grand. The latter, of the Order of Mercedarians for the ransom of prisoners, had their church and convent in the Rue du Chaume. This street has been superseded by that part of the Rue des Archives which runs between the Rues des Francs-Bourgeois and des Haudriettes. The conventual buildings, rebuilt from

1727 to 1731, still stand (No. 45), opposite the Hôtel de Clisson; the church, which had a portal by Boffrand, was on the site of No. 47.

The site of La Madeleine en Cité was in the present Rue de la Cité, east side, opposite the Rue de Lutèce; it is covered by part of the Hôtel-Dieu. Its last remains disappeared in 1843.

St. Paul—not to be confused with the present St. Paul-St. Louis, which has inherited its name—stood in the Rue St. Antoine; its site is approximately that occupied by the cinema of that name.   It was destroyed in 1799.

The Jesuit Novitiate was in the present Rue Bonaparte (No. 82); it was pulled down in 1806.

Ste. Croix de la Bretonnerie was the church of the Pères Croisiers.[1] Their house stood in the street of that name, occupying the site where now stands the Square Ste. Croix.   It was pulled down in 1790.

St. André des Arts, originally des Arcs—a name with the same meaning as St. Mary le Bow—stood on the west side of the Place of that name.   Abbé Mathieu, the pro-Italian enthusiast, was curé here at the end of the seventeenth century.   It was pulled down from 1800 to 1808; its site has never been built over and is still recognizable at one end of the Rue St. André des Arts.

St. Germain l'Auxerrois, where Rameau was married, and St. Eustache, where he lies buried, are well-known churches still standing.

---

[1] Patres Cruciferi, Crutched Fathers (not the same as the Crutched Friars); an order founded in Hainault in 1211 by Theodore of Celle.   They follow the rule of St. Augustine.   In Rameau's time they had the title of canon.

Appendix B

TITLES

The only title in this book that needs explaining is that of *Vénitienne*. The absence of the article excludes a personal or descriptive intention. There is no dance form of this name but the title is frequent in collections of *airs* and contredanses in the first half of the century. Pieces bearing it are most varied in form and time-signatures—2/2, 3/4 and 6/4; I have found up to five different rhythms; Le Roux even has a courante *La Vénitienne* which is just a French courante of the usual kind. I think that Michel Brenet was right when she connected Rameau's title with La Motte's *comédie-ballet La Vénitienne*, set by Michel de La Barre and performed on May 5, 1705, a date by which he may well have arrived in Paris. This opera contains an *air des barcarolles*, that is, gondoliers, which is not without analogy with Rameau's *Vénitienne* (ex. 313). Brenet suggests that Rameau's tune may have figured in the opera though it is not in the printed score.

Ex. 313
Air des Barcarolles

This piece should be played *moderato*, with a barcarolle lilt, and not like a dapper 3/8; its character stands forth much more clearly than when it is tossed off.[1]

Le Rappel des Oiseaux.—The "rappel" is the bugle call that sounds the "rassemblement" or fall-in; the meaning is therefore the "falling-in" of the birds, not their recall or their homecoming. Once the presence of the bugle effect is recognized the speed will be determined by the tempo at which a bugler could play the opening notes, as well as the pianist the ornaments. —I know of no other piece with this title.

La Villageoise.—A character title used also by Moulinier, Chambonnières, Caix d'Hervelois, Bouin and, later, Fiocco and Bailleux. There is also a contredanse called *La Villageoise cadette.*

---

[1] See p. 20.

Les Tendres Plaintes.—A descriptive title used also by J. B. Dupuits (*airs pour vielle et basse*, opus 5). Dandrieu has a *Les Tendres Reproches* in his second book (1731).

Les Niais de Sologne.—There exist several *airs* and contredanses called *Le* or *Les Niais* or *La Niaise*, but I know of none with Rameau's title. The natives of Sologne, a marshy region south of the Loire between Orléans and Blois, were traditionally reputed to be dolts. I suspect that Rameau's tune is a semi-popular air with words relevant to the title; a search through Ballard's many *recueils d'airs sérieux et à boire* might perhaps reveal it.

Les Soupirs.—A descriptive title. The only contemporary instance I know of its use is in Chèdeville the younger; his *Galanteries amusantes*, opus 8, contain a sonata entitled *La Française*, one movement of which is called *Les Soupirs*. Used later by Dussek, Kalkbrenner and others; also by Jean-Philippe's son Claude in a MS. suite in the Bibliothèque Nationale.

La Joyeuse.—A character title, used also by Daquin (first book, third suite, 1735); several contredanses bear the name.

La Follette.—A descriptive or character title, used also by Dandrieu (third book, 1734), Caix d'Hervelois (piece for German flute and bass, 1726) and many contredanses, one of them *La Follette anglaise*.

L'Entretien des Muses.—An imaginative title of which I know no other example. Chambonnières's *L'Entretien des Dieux* comes nearest to it.

Les Tourbillons.—Descriptive of "les tourbillons de poussière agités par les grands vents", says Rameau in his letter to La Motte. It was used also by Dandrieu in his first book (1724) and by Dornel. *Le Tourbillon* is the title of several contredanses.

Les Cyclopes.—Descriptive. I know of no other piece with this title. Vulcan's cave was familiar in Italian operas of the previous century, and Vulcan's smithy figured in Lulli's *Isis*, IV.

Le Lardon.—"Lardon" or "petit salé", as every cook knows, is a preparation of salted pork. One of its uses consists in inserting little pieces of it into a joint. These pieces stuck into the joint are suggested by the little jabbing quavers in the left hand. *Le Lardon* should be played with mock stateliness, marking well the contrast between the *staccato* and *sostenuto* sections. The impression of "interlarding" will then become apparent.

"Lardon" has also the derived meaning of "quip" and "lampoon", which suits the perky, mocking character of Rameau's piece.

La Boiteuse.—So-called because of its limping rhythm. A character title used also by Luc Marchand.

THIRD RECUEIL

Les Trois Mains.—A piece written in two parts which gives the impression of being written in three. I know of no other piece with this title.

Fanfarinette.—A girl's nickname and character title; it occurs later in Josse Boutmy's first book (1738).

La Triomphante.—A character title. Couperin used it for a quite different piece. Several contredanses bear this name.

Les Tricotets.—"Tricotets" are described in Richelet's dictionary as a "sorte de danse élevée et en rond (elata et in circuitum alta saltatio)". The 1750 edition of Ménage's dictionary says it is "gay, called thus because the movement of the feet is as swift as the hand of a man or a woman knitting stockings" (tricoter). Benserade mentions Louis XIV as dancing "un tricotet poitevin". *Les Tricotets* is the title of Michel Corrette's ninth *concerto comique* for three instruments and bass and it occurs several times in collections of contredanses. Pierre Rameau does not speak of it in his *Le Maître à danser.*

L'Indifférente.—A character title, used also by François Bouin in *Les Muses,* a suite for two *vielles;* by Dandrieu (second book, 1728); and by Caix d'Hervelois (a piece for viol and bass); also by several contredanses.

La Poule.—Rameau's only onomatopoeic piece. I know of no other French musical hen but the descriptive fancies of Kerll and Murschhauser and Bach's fugue *all'imitazione della gallina cucca* are obvious relations.

Les Triolets.—The triolet is a verse form of mediaeval origin which came back into fashion in the second half of the seventeenth century; it was much used for satirical or scurrilous themes. Here is an example of one by Ranchin which is neither.

> Le premier jour du mois de mai
> Fut le plus heureux de ma vie.
> Le beau dessein que je formai,
> Le premier jour du mois de mai,
> Je vous vis et je vous aimai;
> Si ce dessein vous plut, Silvie,
> Le premier jour du mois de mai
> Fut le plus heureux de ma vie.[1]

There existed a traditional *air des triolets,* dating from the first half of the century and used for many poems, including the one just quoted. But other tunes were used; one of them occurs in a collection of contredanses transposed for the *vielle.* Rameau's piece does not follow any fixed pattern but the line of the opening theme returns in various forms throughout, somewhat after the fashion of the first line of the triolet.

Les Sauvages.—This was a dance "characterizing" the performance of two Louisiana natives at one of the Fairs in 1725. That it is a dance should determine its tempo; it is generally played much too fast.

L'Enharmonique.—So called because of the enharmonic change in the twelfth bar after the double bar.

L'Egyptienne.—A character title indicating a gypsy girl dancing.

---

[1] In *La Clef des Chansonniers* (Ballard, 1717), I, 56.

La Dauphine.—"Extemporized in 1747 for the Dauphin's second marriage" (with Maria-Josepha of Saxony), says a note on a copy from the Decroix bequest. It was first printed in 1895. *La Dauphine* is a name often found in collections of airs and contredanses.

Pièces de Clavecin en Concert

Besides a couple of minuets and tambourins the 1741 book contains a few pieces with character titles: *L'Agaçante; La Timide, La Pantomime,* a loure, and *L'Indiscrète.* The connexion between title and piece is natural but not close, and the titles may have been given after the music had been composed. Rameau speaks in his preface of "several persons of taste and skill . . . most of whom have done me the honour of naming some of these pieces" (*d'en nommer quelques-unes*). This suggests that he wrote them and then asked his friends for titles; or it may mean that these said persons consented to "give their names" to some pieces—as it were, to select from among the pieces those they would like to see bear their names. In either case it implies no very close link between title and content.

This is certainly so with *Le Vézinet* (which should be *La Le Vézinet,* since the *Le* is part of the name). This outer suburb of Paris was well in the country in 1740 and may have been a favourite *but de promenade* for Rameau or the abode of some friend. There is nothing evocative about the piece called after it.

La Coulicam, as Michel Brenet first showed, celebrates the hero of Father Jean-Antoine Ducerceau's *Histoire de la dernière révolution de Perse,* first published in 1728 and reissued in 1741 as *Thamas Kouli Khan, nouveau roi de Perse ou histoire de la dernière révolution en Perse arrivée en 1732.* Father Ducerceau probably belonged to a circle of Jesuit acquaintances of Rameau of whom Father Castel had been the chief. By 1741, however, Rameau had quarrelled with Castel and was no longer organist at the Jesuit Novitiate.

The mock bellicosity of the piece is in keeping with the title.

The remaining eight pieces bear people's names. Of these I feel that *La La Poplinière* is a sketch of the financier. It has a waywardness, a lack of poise and of soul, a mingling of whimsicality and dryness, an alternation of original and commonplace bars, which correspond to what we know of the great man. Like him it is here, there and everywhere and never pursues any train of thought for long. Cucuel suggests that it was written for the house-warming of the Rue de Richelieu mansion, which was also the time of christening of the La Pouplinières' godchild, Alexandre Rameau.[1]

The Laborde to whom the piece of that name is dedicated is generally assumed to be the future author of the *Essai sur la Musique,* Jean-Benjamin. He should not be confused with the inventive Jesuit Jean-Baptiste de Laborde who in 1759 built an electric piano, nor with the other J. B. de Laborde,

---

[1] (134), 114.

"inventeur du nouveau clavecin chromatique" whom Riemann-Einstein's *Musiklexikon* confuses with the Jesuit, nor yet with the marquis Jean-Joseph de Laborde, for whose misdeeds he lost his life. He became a farmer-general and was condemned under the Terreur by mistake for his namesake who had broken the currency regulations; he was guillotined in July 1794, five days before Robespierre's fall. According to Maret he had studied harmony and composition with Rameau and, according to Palissot, the harpsichord as well. He was the most universal mind of his age. In addition to his operas and the *Essai* he drew up maps of many parts of the world and left studies of chronology, historical memoirs, travel narratives, society verse and thoughts and maxims. He carried out what Rameau merely threatened to do and forestalled Darius Milhaud by setting to music the *privilège de librairie*,[1] "impelled by a society joke, a challenge of Mondonville's and a desire to show that music's charms make even the most barbarous words pleasing to the ear".[2]

Unfortunately, he was born in 1734 and was therefore only seven when the *Pièces en concert* were published. We know too little about his father to say that it was he whom Rameau intended to honour. On the other hand, Jean-Benjamin was exceedingly precocious; he was to write his first opera, *La Chercheuse d'Oiseau*, before he was fifteen and he may have been in touch with Rameau before he was seven, thus qualifying for a dedication.

La Boucon perpetuates Anne-Jeanne Boucon. Born in 1708, she was "renowned for her musical talents" and especially for her harpsichord playing. Rameau must have known her family by 1729 at the latest if, as I surmise, her father was the "someone whose daughter is an excellent clavecinist" in whose house he and another, possibly Montéclair, met in that year to quarrel over harmonic theory.[3] In 1747 she married Mondonville, who was three years her junior, at which Daquin exclaimed: "Apollon et l'Amour pouvaient-ils mieux faire que d'unir ensemble deux de leurs plus intimes favoris?" Duphly also dedicated a piece to her. She was the niece of Jean-Baptiste Forqueray's first wife (see below).

The touching piece that bears her name may be a portrait; if so, it reflects a very sweet, if melancholy, soul.

Of the Comte de Livry I have spoken at length in Chapter 13.[4] His death in July 1741 and the character of *La Livri* make it clear that this piece is a *tombeau*.

La Forqueray and probably *La Cupis* are also occasional pieces.

The Forquerays were descended from a Scotsman who came to France with Mary Stuart in 1548. This man's great-grandson, born *c.* 1635, was the first known musician in the family. At that time there were two branches; both had sprung from Chaumes, the home of the Couperins, and both had moved to Paris by the end of the seventeenth century. To the

---

[1] See p. 544.
[3] Cf. pp. 485–486.

[2] (75), xxxix.
[4] Cf. p. 477.

elder belonged a couple of organists, uncle and nephew, Nicolas and Michel, who between them held quite a number of Paris organs; one of them was that organist of St. Eustache who gave up his instrument to Rameau on the occasion already mentioned.[1] The younger branch is the better known, thanks to two of its members, Antoine (1672–1745) and Jean-Baptiste-Antoine (1699–1782), composers and viol players of distinction whose reputation rivalled that of Marin Marais. Antoine figures in a picture by Rigaud, now in the National Gallery, with Michel de La Barre, the two Hotteterres, and perhaps his son, but not, as is sometimes asserted, Lulli. He quarrelled repeatedly with his wife and they finally separated after a lawsuit in which each one uttered the vilest calumnies against the other. Jean-Baptiste showed a precocious talent for his father's instrument and, whether from jealousy or because the child took his mother's side, the father became his enemy and obtained an order for his banishment from the kingdom— an order which was rescinded almost as soon as issued. From about 1730 he retired to Mantes where he died, with his reputation as musician undimmed. The son was as fine an executant as the sire. In spite of his treatment, he had the piety to publish in 1747 some of Antoine's pieces arranged for harpsichord, adding a few of his own to make up the requisite number for five suites. It was almost certainly to one of these two that Rameau dedicated his piece. The estrangement between father and son makes it unlikely that the dedication was a joint one. In the fifth suite of those published by Jean-Baptiste is a piece called *La Rameau* which might indicate that Antoine was on friendly terms with our composer. But the appearance of several other titles such as *La Laborde*, *La Boucon* and *La Leclair*, names of persons considerably younger than he, makes one suspect that Jean-Baptiste gave titles of his own choosing to his father's music. What confirms my opinion that the Forqueray of Rameau's trio was Jean-Baptiste is the fact that, a widower, he had married again in March 1741. Surely Rameau's beautiful *fugue*, whose suggestion of swinging and pealing bells has been noted,[2] is a wedding present to a fellow-musician.

Jean-Baptiste's first wife was an aunt of Anne-Jeanne Boucon on her mother's side, and both her father Étienne and she herself were witnesses at his first marriage in 1732. He did not belong to La Pouplinière's group.

The manuscript by Claude Rameau, Jean-Philippe's son, in the Bibliothèque Nationale, contains a movement called *La Forcray*. The name was also spelt Forcroy and Fortcroix.[3]

The Cupis dit Camargo were a large family of musicians, ultimately of Italian origin, who had come to Paris from Brussels about 1725. The two best-known members are Jean-Baptiste (1711–1788) and his sister the dancer. I am inclined, however, to think that Rameau intended this piece for their younger brother François (1719–1786) and that it celebrates the birth of his son, another Jean-Baptiste, who, according to Fétis and Riemann, first saw

---

[1] Cf. p. 476. [2] See p. 48. [3] (147).

the light of day in 1741. If this is so, we recognize easily its *berceuse* character, and the swinging and swaying figure in thirds which concludes each half becomes the rocking of a cradle.

La Marais honours one of the many children of Marin Marais, who had died in 1728, the best-known of whom was Roland. The piece has a festal tone which suggests that it was written for an "occasion" whose nature might be established by further research into the lives of Roland and his brothers.

And *La Rameau*? For whom was it written?

This is not one of the most musical pieces in the collection and at first sight it is unpromising. It comes forward exceptionally four-square and rigidly symmetrical, bearing a pedagogic mien; its prim little imitations between keyboard and strings and queer chirping figures alternating with arpeggios and *trommelbässe* exclude any hint of melody. On further acquaintance it reveals its humour, and its likeness to a lesson shows that it is meant to be a parody of "practising"—a gentle forerunner of the overwhelming scale-pounders in *Le Carnaval des Animaux*. Without forgetting the claims of that shadowy sister, the Demoiselle Catherine Rameau mentioned in Maret's *Éloge*, I think that its patrons are none other than Jean-Philippe and Marie-Louise, that it is a family joke and reflects the keyboard practising that went on in the Rue de Richelieu. Seen in this light, the apparently colourless piece comes to possess a benevolently mocking character all its own.

The *Pièces en concert* have thus a more intimate setting than the solos and an interest beyond their musical appeal. Their grouping shows a certain planning. The first suite frames a lament between a historico-fictitious conqueror with a ridiculous name and an agreeable resort; it is the most violently contrasted of the five. The distinguished amateurs figure in the second and third; if it was ungallant to follow up the piece for Anne-Jeanne with one dubbed *L'Agaçante*, it was seemly to bring into proximity that jack-in-the-box of a La Pouplinière with two of Rameau's most unmelodic and vertiginous tambourins, with the wonderful *Timide* separating them, as *La Livri* had parted the warrior and the suburb in the first suite. The occasional intempestiveness of the household's practising may be hinted at by *La Rameau* rubbing shoulders with *L'Indiscrète*. The last suite, the grandest of the five, is reserved for the professionals, and the imperfect sequence Wedding-Christening . . . might be completed if we could discover what event in the Marais households was commemorated by the last of these pieces.

So we are allowed a glimpse into a corner of Rameau's world of friends which our knowledge of La Pouplinière's circle does not afford us, since neither the generous patron Livry nor the amateur Anne-Jeanne nor the professional Forquerays, Cupis and Marais ever crossed its circumference.

"The major mode in the keys of C, D and A is suitable for cheerfulness and rejoicing; in those of F or B flat it is suitable for storms, furies and suchlike purposes; in those of D, A or E it is suitable equally for tender and happy strains; solemnity and magnificence are also in place in those of D, A and E.

"The minor mode in the keys of D, B and E is suitable for gentleness and tenderness; in those of F or B flat it is suitable for mournful strains. The other keys are not used and their suitability is best learnt by experience." (From *Traité de l'Harmonie*, II, 157.)

FRENCH AND ITALIAN TERMS

Adagio or *Largo*	is equivalent to	*Lent.*
Andante or *Grazioso*	,,	*Moins lent, Tendre, Gracieux.*
Vivace or *Allegro*	,,	*Vif* or *Gai*; *Vite.*
Presto (in two-time)	,,	} *Très vif.*
Prestissimo (in 3/8)	,,	

(From *Traité de l'Harmonie*, II, 23; p. 152.)

Appendix C

Prelude from the Second Book of *Pièces de Clavecin* (1703), by Louis Marchand

Appendix D

(i) *Hippolyte et Aricie*
Prelude to Act III.   Written for the 1742 Revival

en retenant

(ii) *Dardanus*, IV, 1
Version written for the 1944 Revival

Bn.

Vns.

Gravement

Dardanus

Lieux fu - nes -

doux

- tes, où tout res - pi - re La honte et la dou-leur, Du déses-poir

sombre et cruel em — pi - re, L'hor - reur que votre aspect m'in -

-spi - re Est le moindre des maux qui dé chir - ent mon cœur,

L'hor-reur que votre as-pect m'in - spi - re Est le moin - dre des

maux qui dé - chi - rent mon cœur.

fort

doux

Fine

L'ob - jet de tant d'a - mour, la beauté qui m'en-

(iii) *Dardanus*, IV, 4
Version written for the 1944 Revival

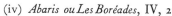

(iv) *Abaris ou Les Boréades*, IV, 2

J'éprouve, hé - las! de - plus cru-els— mal - heurs, J'ai per-

-du pour ja - mais— la beau-té — que j'a - do — re!

à demi   doux
Sans es - poir,   con - su - mé, lan-guis-

-sant — de dou - leur,   mes yeux, de l'une à lautre au-

Index of Names

Index of Subjects

Index of Books and Articles by Rameau

Index of Musical Works by Rameau

Index of Operas, Masses and Oratorios by Composers other than Rameau

A CATALOGUE OF SELECTED DOVER BOOKS
IN ALL FIELDS OF INTEREST

A CATALOGUE OF SELECTED DOVER BOOKS
IN ALL FIELDS OF INTEREST

WHAT IS SCIENCE?, *N. Campbell*
The role of experiment and measurement, the function of mathematics, the nature of scientific laws, the difference between laws and theories, the limitations of science, and many similarly provocative topics are treated clearly and without technicalities by an eminent scientist. "Still an excellent introduction to scientific philosophy," H. Margenau in *Physics Today*. "A first-rate primer . . . deserves a wide audience," *Scientific American*. 192pp. 5⅜ x 8.
S43   Paperbound $1.25

THE NATURE OF LIGHT AND COLOUR IN THE OPEN AIR, *M. Minnaert*
Why are shadows sometimes blue, sometimes green, or other colors depending on the light and surroundings? What causes mirages? Why do multiple suns and moons appear in the sky? Professor Minnaert explains these unusual phenomena and hundreds of others in simple, easy-to-understand terms based on optical laws and the properties of light and color. No mathematics is required but artists, scientists, students, and everyone fascinated by these "tricks" of nature will find thousands of useful and amazing pieces of information. Hundreds of observational experiments are suggested which require no special equipment. 200 illustrations; 42 photos. xvi + 362pp. 5⅜ x 8.
T196   Paperbound $2.00

THE STRANGE STORY OF THE QUANTUM, AN ACCOUNT FOR THE GENERAL READER OF THE GROWTH OF IDEAS UNDERLYING OUR PRESENT ATOMIC KNOWLEDGE, *B. Hoffmann*
Presents lucidly and expertly, with barest amount of mathematics, the problems and theories which led to modern quantum physics. Dr. Hoffmann begins with the closing years of the 19th century, when certain trifling discrepancies were noticed, and with illuminating analogies and examples takes you through the brilliant concepts of Planck, Einstein, Pauli, Broglie, Bohr, Schroedinger, Heisenberg, Dirac, Sommerfeld, Feynman, etc. This edition includes a new, long postscript carrying the story through 1958. "Of the books attempting an account of the history and contents of our modern atomic physics which have come to my attention, this is the best," H. Margenau, Yale University, in *American Journal of Physics*. 32 tables and line illustrations. Index. 275pp. 5⅜ x 8.
T518   Paperbound $2.00

GREAT IDEAS OF MODERN MATHEMATICS: THEIR NATURE AND USE, *Jagjit Singh*
Reader with only high school math will understand main mathematical ideas of modern physics, astronomy, genetics, psychology, evolution, etc. better than many who use them as tools, but comprehend little of their basic structure. Author uses his wide knowledge of non-mathematical fields in brilliant exposition of differential equations, matrices, group theory, logic, statistics, problems of mathematical foundations, imaginary numbers, vectors, etc. Original publication. 2 appendixes. 2 indexes. 65 ills. 322pp. 5⅜ x 8.
T587   Paperbound $2.00

A Short Account of the History of Mathematics,
W. W. Rouse Ball
Last previous edition (1908) hailed by mathematicians and laymen for lucid overview of math as living science, for understandable presentation of individual contributions of great mathematicians. Treats lives, discoveries of every important school and figure from Egypt, Phoenicia to late nineteenth century. Greek schools of Ionia, Cyzicus, Alexandria, Byzantium, Pythagoras; primitive arithmetic; Middle Ages and Renaissance, including European and Asiatic contributions; modern math of Descartes, Pascal, Wallis, Huygens, Newton, Euler, Lambert, Laplace, scores more. More emphasis on historical development, exposition of ideas than other books on subject. Non-technical, readable text can be followed with no more preparation than high-school algebra. Index. 544pp. 5⅜ x 8. Paperbound $2.25

Great Ideas and Theories of Modern Cosmology, *Jagjit Singh*
Companion volume to author's popular "Great Ideas of Modern Mathematics" (Dover, $2.00). The best non-technical survey of post-Einstein attempts to answer perhaps unanswerable questions of origin, age of Universe, possibility of life on other worlds, etc. Fundamental theories of cosmology and cosmogony recounted, explained, evaluated in light of most recent data: Einstein's concepts of relativity, space-time; Milne's a priori world-system; astrophysical theories of Jeans, Eddington; Hoyle's "continuous creation;" contributions of dozens more scientists. A faithful, comprehensive critical summary of complex material presented in an extremely well-written text intended for laymen. Original publication. Index. xii + 276pp. 5⅜ x 8½. Paperbound $2.00

The Restless Universe, *Max Born*
A remarkably lucid account by a Nobel Laureate of recent theories of wave mechanics, behavior of gases, electrons and ions, waves and particles, electronic structure of the atom, nuclear physics, and similar topics. "Much more thorough and deeper than most attempts . . . easy and delightful," *Chemical and Engineering News.* Special feature: 7 animated sequences of 60 figures each showing such phenomena as gas molecules in motion, the scattering of alpha particles, etc. 11 full-page plates of photographs. Total of nearly 600 illustrations. 351pp. 6⅛ x 9¼. Paperbound $2.00

Planets, Stars and Galaxies: Descriptive Astronomy for Beginners,
A. E. Fanning
What causes the progression of the seasons? Phases of the moon? The Aurora Borealis? How much does the sun weigh? What are the chances of life on our sister planets? Absorbing introduction to astronomy, incorporating the latest discoveries and theories: the solar wind, the surface temperature of Venus, the pock-marked face of Mars, quasars, and much more. Places you on the frontiers of one of the most vital sciences of our time. Revised (1966). Introduction by Donald H. Menzel, Harvard University. References. Index. 45 illustrations. 189pp. 5¼ x 8¼. Paperbound $1.50

Great Ideas in Information Theory, Language and Cybernetics,
Jagjit Singh
Non-mathematical, but profound study of information, language, the codes used by men and machines to communicate, the principles of analog and digital computers, work of McCulloch, Pitts, von Neumann, Turing, and Uttley, correspondences between intricate mechanical network of "thinking machines" and more intricate neurophysiological mechanism of human brain. Indexes. 118 figures. 50 tables. ix + 338pp. 5⅜ x 8½. Paperbound $2.00

THE MUSIC OF THE SPHERES: THE MATERIAL UNIVERSE — FROM ATOM TO QUASAR, SIMPLY EXPLAINED, *Guy Murchie*
Vast compendium of fact, modern concept and theory, observed and calculated data, historical background guides intelligent layman through the material universe. Brilliant exposition of earth's construction, explanations for moon's craters, atmospheric components of Venus and Mars (with data from recent fly-by's), sun spots, sequences of star birth and death, neighboring galaxies, contributions of Galileo, Tycho Brahe, Kepler, etc.; and (Vol. 2) construction of the atom (describing newly discovered sigma and xi subatomic particles), theories of sound, color and light, space and time, including relativity theory, quantum theory, wave theory, probability theory, work of Newton, Maxwell, Faraday, Einstein, de Broglie, etc. "Best presentation yet offered to the intelligent general reader," *Saturday Review*. Revised (1967). Index. 319 illustrations by the author. Total of xx + 644pp. 5⅜ x 8½.

Vol. 1 Paperbound $2.00, Vol. 2 Paperbound $2.00,
The set $4.00

FOUR LECTURES ON RELATIVITY AND SPACE, *Charles Proteus Steinmetz*
Lecture series, given by great mathematician and electrical engineer, generally considered one of the best popular-level expositions of special and general relativity theories and related questions. Steinmetz translates complex mathematical reasoning into language accessible to laymen through analogy, example and comparison. Among topics covered are relativity of motion, location, time; of mass; acceleration; 4-dimensional time-space; geometry of the gravitational field; curvature and bending of space; non-Euclidean geometry. Index. 40 illustrations. x + 142pp. 5⅜ x 8½.   Paperbound $1.35

HOW TO KNOW THE WILD FLOWERS, *Mrs. William Starr Dana*
Classic nature book that has introduced thousands to wonders of American wild flowers. Color-season principle of organization is easy to use, even by those with no botanical training, and the genial, refreshing discussions of history, folklore, uses of over 1,000 native and escape flowers, foliage plants are informative as well as fun to read. Over 170 full-page plates, collected from several editions, may be colored in to make permanent records of finds. Revised to conform with 1950 edition of Gray's Manual of Botany. xlii + 438pp. 5⅜ x 8½.   Paperbound $2.00

MANUAL OF THE TREES OF NORTH AMERICA, *Charles Sprague Sargent*
Still unsurpassed as most comprehensive, reliable study of North American tree characteristics, precise locations and distribution. By dean of American dendrologists. Every tree native to U.S., Canada, Alaska; 185 genera, 717 species, described in detail—leaves, flowers, fruit, winterbuds, bark, wood, growth habits, etc. plus discussion of varieties and local variants, immaturity variations. Over 100 keys, including unusual 11-page analytical key to genera, aid in identification. 783 clear illustrations of flowers, fruit, leaves. An unmatched permanent reference work for all nature lovers. Second enlarged (1926) edition. Synopsis of families. Analytical key to genera. Glossary of technical terms. Index. 783 illustrations, 1 map. Total of 982pp. 5⅜ x 8.

Vol. 1 Paperbound $2.25, Vol. 2 Paperbound $2.25,
The set $4.50

IT'S FUN TO MAKE THINGS FROM SCRAP MATERIALS,
Evelyn Glantz Hershoff
What use are empty spools, tin cans, bottle tops? What can be made from rubber bands, clothes pins, paper clips, and buttons? This book provides simply worded instructions and large diagrams showing you how to make cookie cutters, toy trucks, paper turkeys, Halloween masks, telephone sets, aprons, linoleum block- and spatter prints — in all 399 projects! Many are easy enough for young children to figure out for themselves; some challenging enough to entertain adults; all are remarkably ingenious ways to make things from materials that cost pennies or less! Formerly "Scrap Fun for Everyone." Index. 214 illustrations. 373pp. 5⅜ x 8½. Paperbound $1.50

SYMBOLIC LOGIC and THE GAME OF LOGIC, *Lewis Carroll*
"Symbolic Logic" is not concerned with modern symbolic logic, but is instead a collection of over 380 problems posed with charm and imagination, using the syllogism and a fascinating diagrammatic method of drawing conclusions. In "The Game of Logic" Carroll's whimsical imagination devises a logical game played with 2 diagrams and counters (included) to manipulate hundreds of tricky syllogisms. The final section, "Hit or Miss" is a lagniappe of 101 additional puzzles in the delightful Carroll manner. Until this reprint edition, both of these books were rarities costing up to $15 each. Symbolic Logic: Index. xxxi + 199pp. The Game of Logic: 96pp. 2 vols. bound as one. 5⅜ x 8.
Paperbound $2.00

MATHEMATICAL PUZZLES OF SAM LOYD, PART I
selected and edited by M. Gardner
Choice puzzles by the greatest American puzzle creator and innovator. Selected from his famous collection, "Cyclopedia of Puzzles," they retain the unique style and historical flavor of the originals. There are posers based on arithmetic, algebra, probability, game theory, route tracing, topology, counter and sliding block, operations research, geometrical dissection. Includes the famous "14-15" puzzle which was a national craze, and his "Horse of a Different Color" which sold millions of copies. 117 of his most ingenious puzzles in all. 120 line drawings and diagrams. Solutions. Selected references. xx + 167pp. 5⅜ x 8.
Paperbound $1.00

STRING FIGURES AND HOW TO MAKE THEM, *Caroline Furness Jayne*
107 string figures plus variations selected from the best primitive and modern examples developed by Navajo, Apache, pygmies of Africa, Eskimo, in Europe, Australia, China, etc. The most readily understandable, easy-to-follow book in English on perennially popular recreation. Crystal-clear exposition; step-by-step diagrams. Everyone from kindergarten children to adults looking for unusual diversion will be endlessly amused. Index. Bibliography. Introduction by A. C. Haddon. 17 full-page plates, 960 illustrations. xxiii + 401pp. 5⅜ x 8½.
Paperbound $2.00

PAPER FOLDING FOR BEGINNERS, *W. D. Murray and F. J. Rigney*
A delightful introduction to the varied and entertaining Japanese art of origami (paper folding), with a full, crystal-clear text that anticipates every difficulty; over 275 clearly labeled diagrams of all important stages in creation. You get results at each stage, since complex figures are logically developed from simpler ones. 43 different pieces are explained: sailboats, frogs, roosters, etc. 6 photographic plates. 279 diagrams. 95pp. 5⅝ x 8⅜. Paperbound $1.00

PRINCIPLES OF ART HISTORY,
H. Wölfflin

Analyzing such terms as "baroque," "classic," "neoclassic," "primitive," "picturesque," and 164 different works by artists like Botticelli, van Cleve, Dürer, Hobbema, Holbein, Hals, Rembrandt, Titian, Brueghel, Vermeer, and many others, the author establishes the classifications of art history and style on a firm, concrete basis. This classic of art criticism shows what really occurred between the 14th-century primitives and the sophistication of the 18th century in terms of basic attitudes and philosophies. "A remarkable lesson in the art of seeing," *Sat. Rev. of Literature.* Translated from the 7th German edition. 150 illustrations. 254pp. 6⅛ x 9¼.   Paperbound $2.00

PRIMITIVE ART,
Franz Boas

This authoritative and exhaustive work by a great American anthropologist covers the entire gamut of primitive art. Pottery, leatherwork, metal work, stone work, wood, basketry, are treated in detail. Theories of primitive art, historical depth in art history, technical virtuosity, unconscious levels of patterning, symbolism, styles, literature, music, dance, etc. A must book for the interested layman, the anthropologist, artist, handicrafter (hundreds of unusual motifs), and the historian. Over 900 illustrations (50 ceramic vessels, 12 totem poles, etc.). 376pp. 5⅜ x 8.   Paperbound $2.25

THE GENTLEMAN AND CABINET MAKER'S DIRECTOR,
Thomas Chippendale

A reprint of the 1762 catalogue of furniture designs that went on to influence generations of English and Colonial and Early Republic American furniture makers. The 200 plates, most of them full-page sized, show Chippendale's designs for French (Louis XV), Gothic, and Chinese-manner chairs, sofas, canopy and dome beds, cornices, chamber organs, cabinets, shaving tables, commodes, picture frames, frets, candle stands, chimney pieces, decorations, etc. The drawings are all elegant and highly detailed; many include construction diagrams and elevations. A supplement of 24 photographs shows surviving pieces of original and Chippendale-style pieces of furniture. Brief biography of Chippendale by N. I. Bienenstock, editor of *Furniture World.* Reproduced from the 1762 edition. 200 plates, plus 19 photographic plates. vi + 249pp. 9⅛ x 12¼.   Paperbound $3.50

AMERICAN ANTIQUE FURNITURE: A BOOK FOR AMATEURS,
Edgar G. Miller, Jr.

Standard introduction and practical guide to identification of valuable American antique furniture. 2115 illustrations, mostly photographs taken by the author in 148 private homes, are arranged in chronological order in extensive chapters on chairs, sofas, chests, desks, bedsteads, mirrors, tables, clocks, and other articles. Focus is on furniture accessible to the collector, including simpler pieces and a larger than usual coverage of Empire style. Introductory chapters identify structural elements, characteristics of various styles, how to avoid fakes, etc. "We are frequently asked to name some book on American furniture that will meet the requirements of the novice collector, the beginning dealer, and . . . the general public. . . . We believe Mr. Miller's two volumes more completely satisfy this specification than any other work," *Antiques.* Appendix. Index. Total of vi + 1106pp. 7⅞ x 10¾.

Two volume set, paperbound $7.50

THE BAD CHILD'S BOOK OF BEASTS, MORE BEASTS FOR WORSE CHILDREN, and A MORAL ALPHABET, *H. Belloc*

Hardly and anthology of humorous verse has appeared in the last 50 years without at least a couple of these famous nonsense verses. But one must see the entire volumes — with all the delightful original illustrations by Sir Basil Blackwood — to appreciate fully Belloc's charming and witty verses that play so subacidly on the platitudes of life and morals that beset his day — and ours. A great humor classic. Three books in one. Total of 157pp. 5⅜ x 8.

Paperbound $1.00

THE DEVIL'S DICTIONARY, *Ambrose Bierce*

Sardonic and irreverent barbs puncturing the pomposities and absurdities of American politics, business, religion, literature, and arts, by the country's greatest satirist in the classic tradition. Epigrammatic as Shaw, piercing as Swift, American as Mark Twain, Will Rogers, and Fred Allen, Bierce will always remain the favorite of a small coterie of enthusiasts, and of writers and speakers whom he supplies with "some of the most gorgeous witticisms of the English language" (H. L. Mencken). Over 1000 entries in alphabetical order. 144pp. 5⅜ x 8. Paperbound $1.00

THE COMPLETE NONSENSE OF EDWARD LEAR.

This is the only complete edition of this master of gentle madness available at a popular price. *A Book of Nonsense, Nonsense Songs, More Nonsense Songs and Stories* in their entirety with all the old favorites that have delighted children and adults for years. The Dong With A Luminous Nose, The Jumblies, The Owl and the Pussycat, and hundreds of other bits of wonderful nonsense. 214 limericks, 3 sets of Nonsense Botany, 5 Nonsense Alphabets, 546 drawings by Lear himself, and much more. 320pp. 5⅜ x 8. Paperbound $1.00

THE WIT AND HUMOR OF OSCAR WILDE, *ed. by Alvin Redman*

Wilde at his most brilliant, in 1000 epigrams exposing weaknesses and hypocrisies of "civilized" society. Divided into 49 categories—sin, wealth, women, America, etc.—to aid writers, speakers. Includes excerpts from his trials, books, plays, criticism. Formerly "The Epigrams of Oscar Wilde." Introduction by Vyvyan Holland, Wilde's only living son. Introductory essay by editor. 260pp. 5⅜ x 8. Paperbound $1.00

A CHILD'S PRIMER OF NATURAL HISTORY, *Oliver Herford*

Scarcely an anthology of whimsy and humor has appeared in the last 50 years without a contribution from Oliver Herford. Yet the works from which these examples are drawn have been almost impossible to obtain! Here at last are Herford's improbable definitions of a menagerie of familiar and weird animals, each verse illustrated by the author's own drawings. 24 drawings in 2 colors; 24 additional drawings. vii + 95pp. 6½ x 6. Paperbound $1.00

THE BROWNIES: THEIR BOOK, *Palmer Cox*

The book that made the Brownies a household word. Generations of readers have enjoyed the antics, predicaments and adventures of these jovial sprites, who emerge from the forest at night to play or to come to the aid of a deserving human. Delightful illustrations by the author decorate nearly every page. 24 short verse tales with 266 illustrations. 155pp. 6⅝ x 9¼.

Paperbound $1.50

THE PRINCIPLES OF PSYCHOLOGY,
William James
The full long-course, unabridged, of one of the great classics of Western literature and science. Wonderfully lucid descriptions of human mental activity, the stream of thought, consciousness, time perception, memory, imagination, emotions, reason, abnormal phenomena, and similar topics. Original contributions are integrated with the work of such men as Berkeley, Binet, Mills, Darwin, Hume, Kant, Royce, Schopenhauer, Spinoza, Locke, Descartes, Galton, Wundt, Lotze, Herbart, Fechner, and scores of others. All contrasting interpretations of mental phenomena are examined in detail—introspective analysis, philosophical interpretation, and experimental research. "A classic," *Journal of Consulting Psychology.* "The main lines are as valid as ever," *Psychoanalytical Quarterly.* "Standard reading . . . a classic of interpretation," *Psychiatric Quarterly.* 94 illustrations. 1408pp. 5⅜ x 8.
Vol. 1 Paperbound $2.50, Vol. 2 Paperbound $2.50,
The set $5.00

VISUAL ILLUSIONS: THEIR CAUSES, CHARACTERISTICS AND APPLICATIONS,
M. Luckiesh
"Seeing is deceiving," asserts the author of this introduction to virtually every type of optical illusion known. The text both describes and explains the principles involved in color illusions, figure-ground, distance illusions, etc. 100 photographs, drawings and diagrams prove how easy it is to fool the sense: circles that aren't round, parallel lines that seem to bend, stationary figures that seem to move as you stare at them — illustration after illustration strains our credulity at what we see. Fascinating book from many points of view, from applications for artists, in camouflage, etc. to the psychology of vision. New introduction by William Ittleson, Dept. of Psychology, Queens College. Index. Bibliography. xxi + 252pp. 5⅜ x 8½.   Paperbound $1.50

FADS AND FALLACIES IN THE NAME OF SCIENCE,
Martin Gardner
This is the standard account of various cults, quack systems, and delusions which have masqueraded as science: hollow earth fanatics. Reich and orgone sex energy, dianetics, Atlantis, multiple moons, Forteanism, flying saucers, medical fallacies like iridiagnosis, zone therapy, etc. A new chapter has been added on Bridey Murphy, psionics, and other recent manifestations in this field. This is a fair, reasoned appraisal of eccentric theory which provides excellent inoculation against cleverly masked nonsense. "Should be read by everyone, scientist and non-scientist alike," R. T. Birge, Prof. Emeritus of Physics, Univ. of California; Former President, American Physical Society. Index. x + 365pp. 5⅜ x 8.   Paperbound $1.85

ILLUSIONS AND DELUSIONS OF THE SUPERNATURAL AND THE OCCULT,
D. H. Rawcliffe
Holds up to rational examination hundreds of persistent delusions including crystal gazing, automatic writing, table turning, mediumistic trances, mental healing, stigmata, lycanthropy, live burial, the Indian Rope Trick, spiritualism, dowsing, telepathy, clairvoyance, ghosts, ESP, etc. The author explains and exposes the mental and physical deceptions involved, making this not only an exposé of supernatural phenomena, but a valuable exposition of characteristic types of abnormal psychology. Originally titled "The Psychology of the Occult." 14 illustrations. Index. 551pp. 5⅜ x 8.   Paperbound $2.25

FAIRY TALE COLLECTIONS, *edited by Andrew Lang*
Andrew Lang's fairy tale collections make up the richest shelf-full of traditional children's stories anywhere available. Lang supervised the translation of stories from all over the world—familiar European tales collected by Grimm, animal stories from Negro Africa, myths of primitive Australia, stories from Russia, Hungary, Iceland, Japan, and many other countries. Lang's selection of translations are unusually high; many authorities consider that the most familiar tales find their best versions in these volumes. All collections are richly decorated and illustrated by H. J. Ford and other artists.

THE BLUE FAIRY BOOK. 37 stories. 138 illustrations. ix + 390pp. 5⅜ x 8½. Paperbound $1.50

THE GREEN FAIRY BOOK. 42 stories. 100 illustrations. xiii + 366pp. 5⅜ x 8½. Paperbound $1.50

THE BROWN FAIRY BOOK. 32 stories. 50 illustrations, 8 in color. xii + 350pp. 5⅜ x 8½. Paperbound $1.50

THE BEST TALES OF HOFFMANN, *edited by E. F. Bleiler*
10 stories by E. T. A. Hoffmann, one of the greatest of all writers of fantasy. The tales include "The Golden Flower Pot," "Automata," "A New Year's Eve Adventure," "Nutcracker and the King of Mice," "Sand-Man," and others. Vigorous characterizations of highly eccentric personalities, remarkably imaginative situations, and intensely fast pacing has made these tales popular all over the world for 150 years. Editor's introduction. 7 drawings by Hoffmann. xxxiii + 419pp. 5⅜ x 8½. Paperbound $2.00

GHOST AND HORROR STORIES OF AMBROSE BIERCE,
edited by E. F. Bleiler
Morbid, eerie, horrifying tales of possessed poets, shabby aristocrats, revived corpses, and haunted malefactors. Widely acknowledged as the best of their kind between Poe and the moderns, reflecting their author's inner torment and bitter view of life. Includes "Damned Thing," "The Middle Toe of the Right Foot," "The Eyes of the Panther," "Visions of the Night," "Moxon's Master," and over a dozen others. Editor's introduction. xxii + 199pp. 5⅜ x 8½. Paperbound $1.25

THREE GOTHIC NOVELS, *edited by E. F. Bleiler*
Originators of the still popular Gothic novel form, influential in ushering in early 19th-century Romanticism. Horace Walpole's *Castle of Otranto*, William Beckford's *Vathek*, John Polidori's *The Vampyre*, and a *Fragment* by Lord Byron are enjoyable as exciting reading or as documents in the history of English literature. Editor's introduction. xi + 291pp. 5⅜ x 8½. Paperbound $2.00

BEST GHOST STORIES OF LEFANU, *edited by E. F. Bleiler*
Though admired by such critics as V. S. Pritchett, Charles Dickens and Henry James, ghost stories by the Irish novelist Joseph Sheridan LeFanu have never become as widely known as his detective fiction. About half of the 16 stories in this collection have never before been available in America. Collection includes "Carmilla" (perhaps the best vampire story ever written), "The Haunted Baronet," "The Fortunes of Sir Robert Ardagh," and the classic "Green Tea." Editor's introduction. 7 contemporary illustrations. Portrait of LeFanu. xii + 467pp. 5⅜ x 8. Paperbound $2.00

EASY-TO-DO ENTERTAINMENTS AND DIVERSIONS WITH COINS, CARDS, STRING, PAPER AND MATCHES, *R. M. Abraham*
Over 300 tricks, games and puzzles will provide young readers with absorbing fun. Sections on card games; paper-folding; tricks with coins, matches and pieces of string; games for the agile; toy-making from common household objects; mathematical recreations; and 50 miscellaneous pastimes. Anyone in charge of groups of youngsters, including hard-pressed parents, and in need of suggestions on how to keep children sensibly amused and quietly content will find this book indispensable. Clear, simple text, copious number of delightful line drawings and illustrative diagrams. Originally titled "Winter Nights' Entertainments." Introduction by Lord Baden Powell. 329 illustrations. v + 186pp. 5⅜ x 8½. Paperbound $1.00

AN INTRODUCTION TO CHESS MOVES AND TACTICS SIMPLY EXPLAINED, *Leonard Barden*
Beginner's introduction to the royal game. Names, possible moves of the pieces, definitions of essential terms, how games are won, etc. explained in 30-odd pages. With this background you'll be able to sit right down and play. Balance of book teaches strategy — openings, middle game, typical endgame play, and suggestions for improving your game. A sample game is fully analyzed. True middle-level introduction, teaching you all the essentials without oversimplifying or losing you in a maze of detail. 58 figures. 102pp. 5⅜ x 8½. Paperbound $1.00

LASKER'S MANUAL OF CHESS, *Dr. Emanuel Lasker*
Probably the greatest chess player of modern times, Dr. Emanuel Lasker held the world championship 28 years, independent of passing schools or fashions. This unmatched study of the game, chiefly for intermediate to skilled players, analyzes basic methods, combinations, position play, the aesthetics of chess, dozens of different openings, etc., with constant reference to great modern games. Contains a brilliant exposition of Steinitz's important theories. Introduction by Fred Reinfeld. Tables of Lasker's tournament record. 3 indices. 308 diagrams. 1 photograph. xxx + 349pp. 5⅜ x 8. Paperbound $2.25

COMBINATIONS: THE HEART OF CHESS, *Irving Chernev*
Step-by-step from simple combinations to complex, this book, by a well-known chess writer, shows you the intricacies of pins, counter-pins, knight forks, and smothered mates. Other chapters show alternate lines of play to those taken in actual championship games; boomerang combinations; classic examples of brilliant combination play by Nimzovich, Rubinstein, Tarrasch, Botvinnik, Alekhine and Capablanca. Index. 356 diagrams. ix + 245pp. 5⅜ x 8½. Paperbound $1.85

HOW TO SOLVE CHESS PROBLEMS, *K. S. Howard*
Full of practical suggestions for the fan or the beginner — who knows only the moves of the chessmen. Contains preliminary section and 58 two-move, 46 three-move, and 8 four-move problems composed by 27 outstanding American problem creators in the last 30 years. Explanation of all terms and exhaustive index. "Just what is wanted for the student," Brian Harley. 112 problems, solutions. vi + 171pp. 5⅜ x 8. Paperbound $1.35

FABLES OF AESOP,
according to Sir Roger L'Estrange, with 50 drawings by Alexander Calder
Republication of rare 1931 Paris edition (limited to 665 copies) of 200 fables
by Aesop in the 1692 L'Estrange translation. Illustrated with 50 highly
imaginative, witty and occasionally ribald line drawings by the inventor of
"mobiles" and "stabiles." "Fifty wonderfully inventive Alexander Calder
drawings, impertinent as any of the artist's wire sculptures, make a delightful,
modern counterpoint to the thoroughly moral tales," *Saturday Review.* 124pp.
6½ x 9¼. Paperbound $1.25

DRAWINGS OF REMBRANDT
One of the earliest and best collections of Rembrandt drawings—the Lippmann-
Hofstede de Groot facsimiles (1888)—is here reproduced in entirety. Collection
contains 550 faithfully reproduced drawings in inks, chalks, and silverpoint;
some, hasty sketches recorded on a handy scrap of paper; others, studies for
well-known oil paintings. Edited, with scholarly commentary by Seymour
Slive, Harvard University. "In large matters of appearance, size (9 x 12-inch
page), paper color and weight, uniformity of plate texture, typography and
printing, these two volumes could scarcely be improved," *Arts and Architecture.*
"Altogether commendable . . . among the year's best," *New York Times.*
Editor's introduction, notes. 3 indexes, 2 concordances. Total of lxxix +
552pp. 9⅛ x 12¼. Two volume set, paperbound $6.00
Two volume set, clothbound $12.50

THE EARLY WORK OF AUBREY BEARDSLEY
Together with *The Later Work,* the standard source for the most important
Beardsley drawings. Edited by John Lane, *Early Work* contains 157 full-page
plates including Burne-Jones style work, the *Morte d'Arthur* series, cover
designs and illustrations from *The Studio* and other magazines, theatre
posters, "Kiss of Judas," "Seigfried," portraits of himself, Emile Zola, and
Verdi, and illustrations for Wilde's play *Salome.* 2 color plates. Introduction
by H. C. Marillier. xii + 175pp. 8⅛ x 11. Paperbound $2.50
Clothbound $8.50

THE LATER WORK OF AUBREY BEARDSLEY
Edited by John Lane, collection contains 174 full-page plates including
Savoy and *Yellow Book* illustrations, book plates, "The Wagnerites," "La
Dame aux Camellias," selections from *Lysistrata,* illustrations to *Das Rhein-
gold, Venus and Tannhauser,* and the "Rape of the Lock" series. 2 color
plates. xiv + 174pp. 8⅛ x 11. Paperbound $2.50
Clothbound $8.50

Prices subject to change without notice.

Available at your book dealer or write for free catalogue to Dept. Adsci,
Dover Publications, Inc., 180 Varick St., N.Y., N.Y. 10014. Dover publishes more
than 150 books each year on science, elementary and advanced mathematics
biology, music, art, literary history, social sciences and other areas.

Due